"In Old Friendship"

Lewis Mumford

Henry A. Murray

"In Old Friendship"

The Correspondence of Lewis Mumford

and Henry A. Murray, 1928–1981

Edited by Frank G. Novak, Jr.

Syracuse University Press

The paper used in this publication meets the minimum requirements of
American National Standard for Information Sciences—Permanence of
Paper for Printed Library Materials, ANSI Z39.48–1984.∞™

For a listing of books published and distributed by Syracuse University Press,
visit our Web site at SyracuseUniversityPress.syr.edu.

ISBN-13: 978-0-8156-3113-2   ISBN-10: 0-8156-3113-8

Library of Congress Cataloging-in-Publication Data
Mumford, Lewis, 1895–1990.
"In old friendship" : the correspondence of Lewis Mumford and Henry A. Murray,
1928–1981 / edited by Frank G. Novak, Jr.—1st ed.
p. cm.
Includes index.
ISBN-13: 978–0–8156–3113–2 (cloth : alk. paper)
ISBN-10: 0–8156–3113–8 (cloth : alk. paper)
1. Mumford, Lewis, 1895–1990—Correspondence. 2. Murray, Henry Alexander, 1893–1988—
Correspondence. 3. Social reformers—United States—Correspondence. 4. Sociologists—United
States—Correspondence. 5. Psychologists—United States—Correspondence.
6. Authors, American—Correspondence. 7. United States—Intellectual life—20th century.
I. Murray, Henry Alexander, 1893–1988. II. Novak, Frank G., 1949– III. Title.
CT275.M734A4 2007
818'.5209—dc22
[B]
2006100023

Contents

Frank G. Novak, Jr. is professor of English at Pepperdine University where he teaches American literature and courses in the Great Books Colloquium. He is the author of *The Autobiographical Writings of Lewis Mumford: A Study in Literary Audacity* and the editor of *Lewis Mumford and Patrick Geddes: The Correspondence* (1995). He has published articles on Emerson, Melville, Cather, Fowles, and Updike. He served as a Fulbright Scholar at the University of Maribor, Slovenia, in 1994 and recently was a visiting professor at the Pepperdine University International Program in Florence, Italy (2005–6).

Acknowledgments

WORK ON THIS PROJECT was supported by research and publishing subvention grants from Pepperdine University. I am grateful to David Baird, dean of Seaver College, and Lee Kats, assistant dean of Research, for their assistance in providing this support. I owe special thanks to my former division chairperson, Professor Constance Fulmer, for her encouragement and assistance. I am indebted to the following for making the manuscripts of the letters and related materials available to me as well as for their generous assistance and valuable guidance: Harley P. Holden, Patrice Donoghue, and the staff of the Harvard University Archives; Nancy Shawcross and the staff of the Annenberg Rare Book and Manuscript Library at the University of Pennsylvania. Robert Wojtowicz, Vincent DiMattio, and Kenneth Stunkel—my fellow Mumfordians—generously assisted with various aspects of the project. Caroline (Mrs. Henry A.) Murray gave her enthusiastic support to the project from the very beginning; her hospitality during an afternoon visit to her home on Nantucket was a special gift. Lora Adrian Novak contributed significantly through her application of a keen editorial eye and probing questions.

Lewis Mumford

A Chronology

1934   Publishes *Technics and Civilization,* first volume in the Renewal of Life series

1935   Daughter Alison born, 28 April

1936   Settles permanently in the Leedsville community, near Amenia, New York

1938   Publishes *The Culture of Cities,* second volume in the Renewal of Life series

1942   Serves as head of the School of Humanities at Stanford University (resigns in 1944)

1944   Publishes *The Condition of Man,* third volume in the Renewal of Life series; son Geddes killed in combat in Italy

1947   Publishes *Green Memories: The Story of Geddes Mumford*

1951   Publishes *The Conduct of Life,* fourth volume in the Renewal of Life series; serves as visiting professor at the University of Pennsylvania, an appointment that he holds for ten years

1956   Publishes *The Transformations of Man*

1961   Publishes *The City in History: Its Origins, Its Transformations, and Its Prospects*; the book wins the National Book Award

1963   Writes last "Sky Line" column for the *New Yorker*

1967   Publishes *The Myth of the Machine: I. Technics and Human Development*

1970   Publishes *The Myth of the Machine: II. The Pentagon of Power*

1982   Publishes *Sketches from Life,* his autobiography

1990   Dies at his Amenia home on 26 January

Henry A. Murray

A Chronology

1893	Born in New York City, 13 May
1911	Graduates from Groton School
1915	A.B. in history, Harvard College
1916	Marries Josephine Rantoul ("Jo")
1919	M.D., Columbia College of Physicians and Surgeons
1920	M.A. in biology, Columbia University
1921	Daughter Josephine Lee Murray born
1924	Conducts research at the Rockefeller Institute for Medical Research under Alfred E. Cohn; reads *Moby-Dick* for the first time en route to England
1924–25	Conducts research at Cambridge University, England
1925	Visits Carl Jung at Zurich; begins relationship with Christiana Morgan
1926	Appointed research fellow in abnormal and dynamic psychology at the Harvard Psychological Clinic
1927	Ph.D. in biochemistry, Cambridge University
1927	Appointed director of the Harvard Psychological Clinic
1928	First letter to Lewis Mumford (August)
1932–33	Undergoes Freudian analysis with Franz Alexander
1935	Publishes "A Method for Investigating Fantasies: The Thematic Apperception Test" (with Christiana D. Morgan)
1938	Publishes *Explorations in Personality: A Clinical and Experimental Study of Fifty Men of College Age*

1943   Writes "Analysis of the Personality of Adolph Hitler, with Predictions of His Future Behavior and Suggestions for Dealing with Him Now and After Germany's Surrender"

1944–46   Serves as lieutenant colonel, Office of Strategic Services

1945   Publishes *A Clinical Study of Sentiments* (with Christiana D. Morgan)

1948   Publishes *Assessment of Men: Selection of Personnel for the Office of Strategic Services* and *Personality in Nature, Society and Culture* (with Clyde Kluckohn)

1949   Publishes edition of Herman Melville, *Pierre*

1951   Publishes "In Nomine Diaboli"

1962   Wife, Josephine Rantoul Murray, dies; he retires from Harvard; publishes "The Personality and Career of Satan"

1966   Publishes "Bartleby and I"

1967   Christiana Morgan dies

1969   Marries Caroline C. Fish ("Nina")

1988   Dies in Cambridge, Massachusetts

Editor's Note

THE BULK of the Mumford–Murray correspondence is located in the Papers of Henry A. Murray, 1925–1988, Harvard University Archives. A few letters are in the Lewis Mumford Collection at the Annenberg Rare Book and Manuscript Library, Van Pelt–Dietrich Library, University of Pennsylvania (these letters are noted as LMC). In 1979 Mumford returned the letters he had received from Murray and Christiana Morgan to be donated to Harvard (see his letter of 8 June 1979). Most of the Mumford–Murray correspondence at Harvard is in two boxes (HUGFP 97.17); other letters are in the general correspondence file and elsewhere in the Murray Papers. The letters in the Harvard collection are indifferently organized by date; this edition arranges the letters chronologically. Murray frequently neglected to date his letters; Mumford was much more scrupulous in dating his own letters and often noted the dates of his replies on Murray's letters. Most of Mumford's letters are typed; most of Murray's are handwritten. The following transcriptions correct obvious errors in spelling and mechanics. Certain idiosyncratic spellings and usages have been retained (such as Murray's spelling of "narcism" and his random capitalizations for emphasis as well as both men's misspellings of personal names). Both men rarely underlined titles in their letters; the transcriptions reflect this practice. Some of the letters are reformatted by setting salutations and closings on separate lines to achieve consistency of design.

This edition reprints some 500 of the approximately 600 letters (including cards, notes, and telegrams) that Mumford and Murray exchanged. Some of the letters are edited for length; the omissions in the text are indicated by bracketed ellipses: [. . .].

A bibliography of Mumford's publications is conveniently available online: Elmer S. Newman, ed., Robert Wojtowicz, rev. ed, *Lewis Mumford: A Bibliography* (2000), http://www.library.upenn.edu/collections/rbm/mumford/. For a bibliography of Murray's publications, see Edwin S. Shneidman, ed., *Endeavors in Psychology: Selections from the Personology of Henry A. Murray* (New York: Harper and Row, 1981).

"In Old Friendship"

Introduction

THE CORRESPONDENCE of Lewis Mumford and Henry A. Murray documents
the fruitful intersection of two remarkable careers. Between 1928 and 1979 Mumford and Murray exchanged some 600 letters amounting to approximately 1,600
pages in manuscript. The correspondence portrays the intensely active, sometimes
dramatic lives of these important intellectual figures through five decades of devoted friendship: Mumford as a wide-ranging critic of culture and self-described
"professor of things in general"; Murray as a Melville scholar and Harvard psychologist. The letters detail personal concerns having to do with family and lovers,
illness and death, success and disappointment. They trace the evolution of works
in progress, recording the germination and refinement of key ideas though discussion and debate. They demonstrate how each man relied upon and encouraged the
other; they also reveal differences in personality and outlook and the resulting tensions that developed. Depicting the lively engagement of two incandescent minds,
the correspondence provides perspectives on American cultural and intellectual
life throughout much of the twentieth century, discussing issues relating to the arts,
politics, publishing, and academe. In these respects, and others, the letters present
a compelling story of friendship. They disclose deep, complex connections, both intellectual and emotional, between two ambitious and successful men of contrasting
backgrounds and different careers, yet highly dependent upon one another and
sharing many of the same values and interests.

Lewis Mumford (1895–1990) has been variously acclaimed as "America's preeminent twentieth-century public intellectual," as the most "radically innovative"
of recent writers of nonfiction, and as "the last of the great humanists."[1] Undoubtedly, the monumental oeuvre he produced during a literary career spanning sixty

---

1. Preface to *Lewis Mumford: Public Intellectual*, ed. Thomas P. and Agatha C. Hughes (New York:
Oxford Univ. Press, 1990), vii; Leo Marx, "Lewis Mumford: Prophet of Organicism," in Hughes and
Hughes, *Lewis Mumford*, 164; quoted in Donald L. Miller, *Lewis Mumford: A Life* (New York: Weidenfeld
and Nicholson, 1989), xvii.

years represents a signal achievement in modern American letters. Mumford was an extraordinarily prolific, wide-ranging writer whose work is characterized by its audacious originality and comprehensive vision. Most renowned for his writings on architecture and the city, Mumford also wrote literary criticism, art criticism, biography, and histories of science and technology as well as works concerned with politics, philosophy, and ethics. Notable works among the twenty-eight books he authored include *The Story of Utopias* (1922), *The Golden Day* (1926), *Herman Melville* (1929), *Technics and Civilization* (1934), *The Culture of Cities* (1938), *The Condition of Man* (1944), *The Conduct of Life* (1951), *The City in History* (1961), and *The Myth of the Machine* (two volumes 1967, 1970). He also wrote hundreds of essays and reviews, including his well-known *New Yorker* magazine column "The Sky Line," which appeared regularly between 1931 and 1963. He appeared on the cover of *Time* in 1938 after the publication of *The Culture of Cities,* and he won a National Book Award for *The City in History.*

Trained as a physician and scientist (with an M.D. and Ph.D. in biochemistry), Henry A. Murray (1893–1988) was important both as a pioneering Melville scholar and as a major figure in American psychology. He has been hailed as the most "versatile" psychologist since William James and as one whose writing is unequaled in "verve and boldness."[2] He is widely recognized as "one of the few who have really shaped the history and structure of psychology in the United States."[3] Although the early years of his career were devoted to medical research, the coincident events in 1924 of reading *Moby-Dick* while voyaging to England to study at Cambridge and meeting Carl Jung in Zurich a few months later profoundly redirected both his personal life and public career. Consequently, he turned his attention from science to psychology and began a lifelong devotion to the study of Melville. He went on to author several classic, influential essays on Melville, such as "In Nomine Diaboli" (1951) and the lengthy introduction to the edition of *Pierre* he edited (1949). Throughout his life, he collected material on Melville and labored intermittently on a biography that he never completed. Murray helped to establish the Harvard Psychological Clinic, which became an innovative research center, and he served as its director from 1927 until his retirement in 1962. During his tenure at Harvard, he edited and wrote substantial portions of the important psychological texts *Explorations in Personality* (1938) and *Assessment of Men* (1948). As a psychologist, he played a key role in introducing Freud and Jung to the American university; he brought psychoanalytic theory to bear on literary and cultural studies as well as the discipline of psychology. Declaring that "academic psychology has contributed practically nothing to the knowledge of human nature," he sought to expand the discipline, which had emphasized the experimental method and highly specialized

2. Joseph Adelson, "Against Scientism," review of *Endeavors in Psychology: Selections from the Personology of Henry A. Murray* by Edwin S. Shneidman, *New York Times Book Review* (9 August 1981): 10.

3. Hiram Hayden, "Portrait: Henry A. Murray," *American Scholar* 39 (1969): 127.

research, to accept a more broadly based, "humanistic" perspective.[4] Accordingly, he pioneered an interdisciplinary approach that sought to map the "whole" personality, developing an area of psychological study he termed "personology." Working with devoted students and associates at Harvard, who included Donald MacKinnon, Erik Erikson, and Merrill Moore, he was instrumental in establishing psychoanalysis and personality theory as important components of academic psychology in America.

A third person who figures prominently in the correspondence and who played an important role in the lives of both men is Christiana Morgan—the strikingly beautiful, highly creative, and remarkably independent wife of one of Murray's Harvard classmates. Morgan was an analysand and devoted disciple of Jung; she provided the material for his famous Visions Seminars.[5] She was an associate at the Harvard Clinic and collaborated with Murray to develop the widely used Thematic Apperception Test (TAT). From 1925 until her death in 1967, Murray and Morgan maintained an extramarital relationship, known only to their closest friends. They conceived their relationship as a bold experiment in love that sought to realize the Jungian "dyad" uniting "anima" and "animus." They jointly authored a private document entitled "The Proposition," the "testament of love" describing the history and principles of their relationship; here and in other private documents they sought to show how their religion of love might serve as an example for others seeking erotic and spiritual fulfillment in a post-Christian age.[6] Morgan became Mumford's friend and confidante during the early 1940s, and they corresponded regularly until Morgan's death in 1967, exchanging approximately 100 letters. Murray also read many of the letters Mumford addressed to Morgan, and he occasionally responded to them.

Both natives of New York City, Mumford and Murray grew up in very different social and economic circumstances. Attending Groton and Harvard, "Harry" Murray was the wealthy, patrician son of Edith Wharton's "Old New York." At Harvard, he was a prominent clubman and captain of the varsity crew; compiling a mediocre academic record as a history major, he quipped that "he majored in the three Rs—Rum, Rowing, and Romanticism."[7] He went on to Columbia College of Physicians and Surgeons, where he graduated at the top of his class; while affiliated with the Rockefeller Institute for Medical Research in New York, he completed a

4. Henry A. Murray, "Psychology and the University," reprinted in *Endeavors in Psychology: Selections from the Personology of Henry A. Murray,* ed. Edwin S. Shneidman (New York: Harper and Row, 1981), 339. This convenient anthology includes a variety of Murray's important writings.

5. Claire Douglas, *Translate This Darkness: The Life of Christiana Morgan* (New York: Simon and Schuster, 1993), 156–74; Claire Douglas, ed., *Visions: Notes of the Seminars Given in 1930–1934 by C. G. Jung* (Princeton: Princeton Univ. Press, 1997).

6. Forrest G. Robinson, *Love's Story Told: A Life of Henry A. Murray* (Cambridge: Harvard Univ. Press, 1992), 324–30.

7. Ibid., 27.

doctorate in biochemistry from Cambridge University. He inherited (and married) substantial wealth; he often traveled abroad and owned residences in fashionable Beacon Hill and later in Cambridge; he enjoyed vacationing at the family farm on the St. Lawrence in Upstate New York as well as the farm he purchased at Topsfield, outside of Boston. He married Josephine Rantoul in 1916; she died in 1961; they had one child, Josephine, born in 1921. In 1969 he married Caroline C. Fish, known as Nina.

In contrast to the affluent and privileged background of Murray, Mumford was the illegitimate child of a woman who worked as a housekeeper. He attended public schools and roamed the streets of Manhattan from his earliest years. He attended the evening session of the City College of New York but never completed a degree there. As a young man, he was profoundly influenced by Patrick Geddes—the versatile Scots biologist, city planner, sociologist, and educator—who served as Mumford's mentor and teacher. During the 1920s Mumford began to establish himself on the New York literary scene, writing and reviewing for such journals as *Freeman, New Republic, Nation,* and *Saturday Review of Literature*; in 1931 he began a long association with Harold Ross's *New Yorker*, writing both "The Art Galleries" review column during the 1930s and "The Sky Line" through 1983. He and his wife Sophia Wittenberg, whom he married in 1921, moved from the city to a rustic old farmhouse near Amenia, in Dutchess County, New York, in 1936. They had two children: Geddes, born in 1926, was killed in action in Italy in 1944; a daughter Alison was born in 1935. Leading a frugal, austere writer's existence, Mumford apparently never accepted any of the several cash gifts and loans Murray offered him. Murray was very much the public man, a leader, an organizer, a bon vivant with a large circle of colleagues and friends. Mumford preferred a private, strictly disciplined writer's routine; however, primarily for financial reasons, he held several visiting professorial appointments at Stanford (where he served as head of the School of Humanities during the early 1940s), Dartmouth, the University of Pennsylvania, Massachusetts Institute of Technology, Brandeis, and Harvard.

His correspondence with Murray amplifies and extends the story of the life begun in Mumford's autobiography *Sketches from Life*, which ends at 1940, more or less the midpoint of his career.[8] As a sequel to the Mumford–Patrick Geddes correspondence (1918–1932), which documents the education and literary apprenticeship of the young Mumford, Mumford's letters to Murray detail the unfolding of the mature writer's career as he produced his major works, which include the four-volume Renewal of Life series, *The City in History*, and *The Myth of the Machine*. His friendships with Geddes and Murray were arguably the most important of his life in their influence on his intellectual development and literary career. Both relationships were initiated, sustained, and defined through correspondence. Although

---

8. Lewis Mumford, *Sketches from Life: The Autobiography of Lewis Mumford—The Early Years* (New York: Dial, 1982).

Murray and Mumford occasionally met in New York, Cambridge, and Amenia, correspondence was their primary means of contact and dialogue. Mumford considered his letters to be an important facet of his literary achievement; he claimed that they "tell as much about my literary as about my intellectual and personal development."[9] He wrote, "I have always said that my letters were better than any formal work I had written: my correspondents drew out something that an anonymous audience never received."[10] Indeed, he saw his correspondence as possessing enduring qualities his published works lacked: "When the social challenges I have responded to, when the intellectual issues I have raised, when the diagnoses I have made of our civilization have been superseded by other situations and other, more adequate responses, my collected letters may still have value as a human testimonial of our times, and as an uncensored sidelight upon personal relationships, at a certain moment, in a certain setting."[11] His letters to Murray supplement other published editions of Mumford's prolific correspondence, including that with Geddes, Van Wyck Brooks, Frederic Osborn, and Frank Lloyd Wright.[12]

The correspondence is also important for what it discloses about Murray. Although there are several editions of Mumford's letters, none of Murray's correspondence has been published. Although Murray produced notable publications on Melville and in the field of psychology, he was not nearly as prolific as Mumford. Constantly struggling to complete his writing projects, Murray was burdened by heavy administrative obligations at Harvard and by military service during World War II. He left several projects unfinished at his death, including the Melville manuscript he had worked on for so many years. Therefore, his letters to Mumford more fully reflect the range and depth of his knowledge concerning Melville and psychology as well as other topics, and they reveal his impressive learning, his wide range of interests, his "zest" (a favorite word) for the intellectual life, his deeply humane and sensitive spirit, and an eloquent prose style. He discussed various aspects of Melville's life and writings; he offered medical advice and consolation when Mumford's lover, Alice Decker, was involved in a nearly fatal automobile accident; he criticized what he saw as Mumford's "oracular," Ezekiel-

9. Undated note, UP f. 7969 (Lewis Mumford Collection, Annenberg Rare Book and Manuscript Library, Univ. of Pennsylvania).

10. Note, 31 July 1946, UP f. 7963 (Lewis Mumford Collection, Annenberg Rare Book and Manuscript Library, Univ. of Pennsylvania).

11. Lewis Mumford, introduction to *Lewis Mumford: A Bibliography, 1914–1970,* by Elmer S. Newman (New York: Harcourt Brace Jovanovich, 1971), xx.

12. Frank G. Novak Jr., ed., *Lewis Mumford and Patrick Geddes: The Correspondence* (London: Routledge, 1995); Robert E. Spiller, ed., *The Van Wyck Brooks–Lewis Mumford Letters: The Record of a Literary Friendship, 1921–1963* (New York: E. P. Dutton, 1970); Michael Hughes, ed., *The Letters of Lewis Mumford and Frederic J. Osborn: A Transatlantic Dialogue, 1938–70* (New York: Praeger, 1971); Bruce Brooks Pfeiffer and Robert Wojtowicz, eds., *Frank Lloyd Wright and Lewis Mumford: Thirty Years of Correspondence* (New York: Princeton Architectural Press, 2001).

like tone; he wrote moving tributes to his friend's achievement in books such as *The Transformations of Man* and *The City in History.* Murray discussed his work at Harvard and as a military officer in the Office of Strategic Services during World War II; he lamented his inability to complete the long-languishing Melville biography as well as several other books he had outlined. His letters to Mumford substantially enrich the published record, disclosing much about the life and mind of Murray's complex, powerful personality.

Melville was a frequent topic of their letters, and in addition both men were especially concerned with the "organic" connections existing between the individual and society, between personality and culture, between past and present. Mumford shared Murray's interest in personality, the nature of the "self" in its complexity and totality; in fact, the letters reveal how each realized his intellectual role as what Murray termed a "philosophical psychologist" (HAM 12 February 1940).[13] They discussed many topics: Murray explained Freudian theory and terminology, providing material that Mumford used in his books; he helped Mumford clarify his understanding of myth, the meaning of ritual, and the purposes of human sacrifice. They analyzed American education, values, and culture—particularly in the context of the U.S. soldier's contact with foreign cultures during World War II. They conducted an extensive debate concerning the roles of chance and purpose in human evolution. On personal matters, they discuss the health of mutual acquaintances such as Van Wyck Brooks and Eva Goldbeck, and Mumford frequently reveals a preoccupation with his own medical and dental issues. Upon publication of *The Condition of Man* (a series of biographical portraits that trace the connections among personality, myth, history, and culture), Mumford wrote, "Your friendship, dear Harry, is an essential part of The Condition of Man" (LM 2 September 1943). In his letters to Murray, Mumford explored key ideas and arguments incorporated into that book and other books; indeed, the letters indicate the significant extent to which Mumford was influenced by Murray's critical responses in the give-and-take of epistolary debate, borrowed ideas from him, and was sustained by his praise. The letters show that Murray read substantial portions of Mumford's forthcoming books in draft or proof form and that Mumford relied on his criticism and suggestions.

"The Vesuvian Explosion"

Murray had been collecting Melville material for several years when Mumford—who was researching a biography of Melville he had been commissioned to write by Doubleday, Doran—first contacted him in August 1928. In their initial letters,

---

13. All citations to the correspondence are noted parenthetically by initials of the author and date (where provided). Mumford notes a received or response date ("ans") on some of Murray's undated letters.

they discussed access to Melville documents in the New York Public Library, which were jealously guarded by Victor Hugo Paltsits, and they reassured each other that they were not rivals in their research and writing. In fall 1928, they met in New York to discuss their work. When Mumford's critical biography was published in 1929, Murray hailed it with effusive praise: "Your book is a work of art—because you yourself have found yourself & have at your disposal a superior literary talent. . . . The chief point is that you have found your way into the beating heart of a complex myth-creating man and by a supreme alchemy you have recreated him. I know of no biography—ancient or contemporary where there is to be found so much writing of the very first order—so tempered by poetic apprehension & wisdom.—Wisdom—the book teems with it. You have the sanity of one who knows the shadows of the self" (HAM March 1929).

What had begun as a professional association based on their mutual interest in Melville quickly developed into fervent friendship. By this time Mumford's relationship with Patrick Geddes, the intellectual hero and "master" of his youth, had cooled as far as any influence and productive association were concerned. Geddes, at age sixty-five, was growing senile and making impossible demands of his disciple, begging Mumford to become his amanuensis and to join him at the Collège des Éccosais, a grandiose and impractical project he had founded in Montpellier, France. Mumford's personal meetings with Geddes (in New York in 1923 and in Edinburgh in 1925) had been profoundly disillusioning, destroying his youthful dreams of becoming Geddes's associate and collaborator. Mumford sensed that in Murray he might find the intellectual companionship that he craved but had never been realized in his relationship with the much older, importunate, and impatient Geddes: "I feel that I have much to get out of you, perhaps a little to give; and the great regret I had in Edinburgh in 1925, that Geddes and I had not been contemporaries back in the eighties, is somewhat counterbalanced by discovering you" (LM 21 April 1929). Murray concurred that they could realize an ideal friendship and responded with fraternal effusion: "It is inevitable—We shall make up for all the promising friendships in the world that came to nought—we shall redeem those that became sluggish & ran to desert sands & those that were disrupted when integrity compromised with envy & malice; & all others that for unnamable reasons were blasted to dust" (HAM May 1929). Just as he was seeking to recreate love with Christiana Morgan, Murray envisioned nothing less than a restoration of an Aristotelian ideal of friendship in his relationship with Mumford. Mumford responded in kind, reiterating that in Murray he had discovered "another Geddes," but as a peer whom he might approach on equal terms rather than an inflexible, tyrannical "master": "Falling in friendship is a rarer thing, I think, than falling in love; and while I have a handful of partial friendships, I have yet to experience a friendship that is complete, that involves all one's attitudes and interests—with no disguises or only profile views. Heaven knows such friendships are rare; probably more so than a complete marriage; but the two who achieved it would constitute an army!"

(LM 16 May 1929). Thus began a vital intellectual and emotional relationship between these two important figures, each on the threshold of his mature achievement, each destined for a position of authority and eminence.

Both Murray and Mumford responded to Melville's work, particularly *Moby-Dick* and *Pierre,* in ways that were personal and dramatic. The encounter each man had with Melville at a decisive moment in his life profoundly transformed his thought, writing, career, and even his love relationships. Mumford wrote that in 1928 his "discovery" of Melville concurrently with certain "crucial events" in his personal life catalyzed a "profound inner change" that was "to reconstitute and energize all my later work."[14] Mumford encountered Melville as he was confronting a harrowing personal crisis: he was experiencing unsettling doubts about his marriage, he was struggling to determine the direction of his future work, and he was questioning his fundamental values and beliefs. Mumford's biographer Donald L. Miller describes this stage in Mumford's life as "A Period in Purgatorio": his wife, son, and then Mumford himself each experienced severe physical illness between fall 1928 and summer 1929; in July 1929 he made an ill-timed, disappointing, and prematurely aborted visit to Geneva to lecture (cancelling a scheduled meeting with Patrick Geddes); and in 1930 he began an extramarital affair with Catherine Bauer. Reading Melville helped him to understand and to resolve the conflicts of his personal, philosophical, and spiritual struggle. He claimed that Melville forced him to engage "the more basic religious and cosmic questions, for until I had wrestled with Melville I had never formulated my reasoned beliefs or even been sufficiently conscious of my oversights and evasions."[15] His encounter with Melville prompted Mumford to undertake an introspective analysis of his own values and purposes, to confront unacknowledged forces within his own personality. He wrote, "Melville's tragic exploration of his depths would in time unbare parts of my own life which I had never been ready to face."[16] He was stirred by the example of Melville's unsparing honesty and audacity: here was a writer who boldly confronted both the problems in his immediate world and the metaphysical terrors beyond. One can read the chapter on *Moby-Dick* in *Herman Melville* as an intensely personal statement in which Mumford's inner quest parallels that of Melville. Challenged by Melville to realize his literary potential by undertaking an epic project, Mumford states that "as a writer, until I wrote my study of Herman Melville, I had never pushed myself to my limits."[17] In fact, *Herman Melville* marks the point of transition from the early phase of Mumford's career, in which his books are concerned almost exclusively with American art and culture, to the dramatic expan-

---

14. Lewis Mumford, *My Works and Days: A Personal Chronicle* (New York: Harcourt Brace Jovanovich, 1979), 299, 273.

15. Mumford, *Sketches from Life,* 441.

16. Ibid., 445.

17. Ibid., 459.

sion of the next phase. This major phase of his work produced the unprecedented, wide-ranging Renewal of Life series—four massive volumes that surpass his earlier works as much in depth as in breadth and provide a comprehensive interpretation of the Western cultural and intellectual tradition.

Some five years earlier, Murray had also been inspired and redirected by his encounter with Melville, first by reading *Moby-Dick* and then *Pierre*. Murray identified Melville and Carl Jung as the most important of those writers and artists who gave him "something wholly novel and astonishing, never dreamt of in his philosophy, with a dimension of depth and elevation" as he turned from scientific research to the study of psychology in the early 1920s.[18] A profound transformation occurred in Murray's life with the coincident, related events of reading *Moby-Dick*, meeting Jung, and beginning his extramarital affair with Christiana Morgan. Murray's biographer, Forrest G. Robinson, writes that the novel "not only sealed him in his decision to take up psychology, but it helped to define the specific direction that his new interest would take"; this path followed the explorations of Freud and Jung into the realms of the unconscious and the meaning of archetypes and myths. A fellow disciple of Jung who was quite knowledgeable about his work, Christiana Morgan was also inextricably linked with the reorientation in Murray's life and interests. Robinson writes that after *Moby-Dick*, *Pierre* "confirmed Harry in his initial shock of recognition." Murray saw his own life and relationships prefigured in Pierre Glendinning's situation, with Isabel as a version of Morgan, irresistibly beckoning him to a new and unconventional life; the "entangled souls" of Pierre and Isabel "were in some nearly literal sense the parents to Harry's encounter with Christiana." Consequently, the psychoanalytic interpretation of *Pierre*, written some twenty-five years after his first encounter with the novel, reads the text as a fictionalized autobiography of Melville that possesses uncanny similarities to Murray's own experience. Soon after his discovery of Melville, Murray spent three weeks with Carl Jung at Küsnacht, near Zurich, observed Jung's "shift" in interests "from types to the anima," and learned of his extramarital relationship with Antonia Wolff. This meeting with Jung encouraged and confirmed Murray's own inclinations, intellectual and personal. Consequently, Robinson writes, "Jung had joined Melville on the template of Harry's destiny." Influenced first by Melville's writings and then by his discussions with Jung, Murray turned from medical and scientific research to the study of "depth psychology"; during the same period, he began his relationship with Christiana Morgan.[19]

Murray discloses some of this transformative experience in his early letters to Mumford: "I, myself, was ensnared within the Ambiguities of Pierre six years ago when I first discovered Melville, & that perhaps was the element of personal identification which caused the Vesuvian Explosion in me. . . . For I was almost insane

18. Henry A. Murray, "The Case of Murr," in Shneidman, *Endeavors in Psychology,* 58.
19. Robinson, *Love's Story Told,* 112–22.

then, & guessed Pierre before reading it, i.e. after Moby Dick & Mardi—for Pierre is merely a restatement in more concrete terms of the same soul turmoil. . . . The only decent thing I have done in my life was to follow all the riddles that this situation presents & for myself at least solve them to the ecstatic limit & give them some assimilative form" (HAM, LM ans 2 May 1930). Murray recognized in Mumford's experience a similar eruption of unconscious desire and creative energy, with Melville as the catalyst: "But to become still more personal & private, your affairs are close to mine. Aside from several temporarily agitating upheavals of the heart, I was not really unhorsed until 1925 (age 32 years). Since then I have voyaged heatedly & subterraneously with love & have managed somehow a dual relationship" (HAM, LM 12 August 1930). This "dual relationship," of course, refers to his lover Christiana Morgan and wife Josephine, who was cognizant of her husband's affair from the beginning. As Murray was redirected by his "astonishing" encounter with Melville and his conversations with Carl Jung soon afterward, Mumford's synchronous immersion in Melville and contact with Murray in 1928 had a decisive impact on his outlook and writing—particularly as these two influences alerted him to certain psychological tensions, philosophical questions, and ecstatic possibilities of human experience. To paraphrase Robinson, one might say that Murray joined Melville on the template of Mumford's destiny; both ignited a "Vesuvian explosion" in Mumford's life and creativity. Emboldened by both Melville's fearless explorations of the spirit and the example of Murray's unconventional relationship with Christiana Morgan, Mumford began an extramarital affair with Catherine Bauer that lasted for five years, 1930 to 1934. Theirs was an intensely passionate relationship, both physically and intellectually, and was conducted with Sophia Mumford's knowledge, another "dual relationship" (the phrase Mumford echoes to describe his own situation, LM 12 May 1931).

The degree of Melville's impact on both Murray and Mumford reveals much about the character and responsiveness of their minds. Melville profoundly influenced their thought and priorities and affected their careers in practical ways. Melville challenged Mumford to look within, to "formulate" his own deepest beliefs, values, and goals and to act on them. He wrote Van Wyck Brooks that his "wrestling" with Melville, "my efforts to plumb his own tragic sense of life, were the best preparations I could have had for facing our present world."[20] Murray similarly recalled that in reading *Moby-Dick*, "I was swept by Melville's gale and shaken by his appalling sea dragon"; he asserts that "this book changed me," leaving "a stupendous imprint, too vivid to be dimmed by the long series of relentless analytical operations to which I subsequently subjected it."[21] Moreover, Mumford's *Herman Melville*, particularly the chapter on *Moby-Dick*, and Murray's introduction to *Pierre* and "In Nomine Diaboli" (his essay on *Moby-Dick*) not only provide interpretations

20. Spiller, *The Van Wyck Brooks–Lewis Mumford Letters*, 254.
21. Henry A. Murray, "In Nomine Diaboli," in Shneidman, *Endeavors in Psychology*, 83–84.

of the texts but also represent profoundly personal statements, reflecting their deepest values and viewing the novels as allegories of their own life experiences. Their interpretations of Melville's works reveal striking similarities. For example, both liken *Moby-Dick* to a Beethoven symphony in its epic scale, complexity, and artistic power. Both offer powerful, challenging interpretations of Ahab's pursuit of the white whale. In the first of his two interpretations, Mumford states that the "white whale stands for the brute energies of existence, blind, fatal, overpowering"; Ahab represents "the spirit of man," doomed, but heroically confronting "that persistent force of destruction" the whale symbolizes. In the second, Mumford writes that "the whale stands for the practical life," for monetary gain, comfort, and security; and in opposing this, Ahab "stands for human purpose in its highest expression" transcending complacency and conformity.[22] Murray similarly sees the whale as the embodiment of the "Freudian Superego" and, more specifically, "the Old Testament Calvinistic conception of an affrighting Deity and his strict commandments" as appropriated and defined by "the upper-middle-class culture of the time." In opposition stands Ahab, a figure both heroic and satanic, "captain of the culturally repressed dispositions of human nature . . . the 'Id.'"[23] Mumford writes that in *Pierre* Melville "sought . . . to arrive at the same sort of psychological truth that he had achieved, in metaphysics, in *Moby-Dick*. His subject was, not the universe, but the ego . . . those implicated and related layers of self which reach from the outer appearances of physique and carriage down to the recesses of the unconscious personality."[24] Along the same lines, Murray sees the novel as "the biography of Eros" in which Melville journeyed within to discover "the Darkest Africa of the mind, the mythological unconscious."[25]

The Evolution of a Writer

Mumford's letters to Murray chart the evolution of his thought and works-in-progress as he formulated ideas and essayed theories that subsequently appeared in his published writings. An early letter recorded the germination of the Renewal of Life series: "In the meanwhile, I write a philosophy of the *environment*: machines, buildings, cities, regions!" (LM 9 August 1931). This projected "philosophy of the environment" would eventually find expression in four lengthy volumes written during the next twenty years that would deal with technics, the city, the personality, and moral values.

While working on *Technics and Civilization*, the first volume of the series, Mumford announced what became an important, recurring theme in his writing: how

22. Lewis Mumford, *Herman Melville* (New York: Harcourt, Brace, 1929), 184–89.
23. Murray, "In Nomine Diaboli," 88.
24. Mumford, *Herman Melville*, 211.
25. Henry A. Murray, "Introduction to *Pierre*," in Shneidman, *Endeavors in Psychology*, 420, 423.

civilization's apparent technological and scientific advances on one side are ironically accompanied by barbaric recidivism on the other. He wrote, "On a casual reading of history, it seems to me that the final stages of civilization look a little more ferocious than the earlier stages: that the natural and to some extent rational savagery of the earlier battle with nature and other men finally becomes, when the battle is no longer necessary, the source of a deeper sadism which increases in proportion to the pressure exerted by civilization—or mechanization" (LM 28 October 1933). As early as 1938, alarmed by the brutal tactics and crude ideology of Nazism, Mumford called for economic sanctions and, if those failed, military action against Hitler's Germany.[26] Mumford explained his compulsion to confront what he viewed as growing militarism and "barbarism" in the West, abetted by technological advances in weaponry: "Perhaps for the first time since 1914, I feel that the odds are finally stacked too heavily against the decencies and sanities: if we escape the paralysis of world-barbarism now it will be, not just by our efforts, but by some accident or miracle, like a severe influenza epidemic in the fascist countries! In one sense, the situation is a real test of my philosophy: if I can write a book that rings true in the present world, my beliefs ought to hold water for any conceivable society or any moment of the individual's life: not fair weather philosophy for these days" (LM 8 October 1938). The Renewal of Life series thus became not only an epic historical survey of Western technological and urban development but also an assertion of human values and an impassioned call for political reorientation and moral renewal, radically expanding and redirecting the compact "philosophy of environment" Mumford had initially contemplated. Commenting on *The Condition of Man,* Mumford confessed, "I have curious reservations about the book: it is not one I planned to write, but one which, as it were, interposed itself, in order to answer certain more immediate questions that are asked by the period in which we live. It is a disappointment to me, if I think of it as Volume III of the big series; on the other hand, taking it out of that context, it is a pretty satisfactory, sometimes even original, account of the role played by the ideas that have guided or misled Western man during the last two thousand years" (LM 24 July 1942).

A 1947 letter discloses the origins of both *The Transformations of Man* (1956) and *The Myth of the Machine* (1967, 1970): "I discovered that my ample notes [from the early 1940s] . . . suggest another book, a prolegomenon to the whole [Renewal of Life] series, on The Nature of Man. What I have discovered on that subject, and what I have added by way of systematic thought the last month, gives me much that I want to discuss with you at length when we get together; for I find myself wanting to go further on the trail Bergson opened up in Creative Evolution, rein-

---

26. See, for example, "Call to Arms," *New Republic,* 18 May 1938, 39–42; or Mumford's famous and controversial essay "The Corruption of Liberalism," *New Republic,* 29 April 1940, 568–73; both are included in Mumford's *Values for Survival: Essays, Addresses, and Letters on Politics and Education* (New York: Harcourt, Brace, 1946).

stating—and radically redefining of course—the idea of finalism" (LM 12 August 1947). Stimulated by epistolary discussions with Murray, Mumford began to envision the next stage of his life's work, following the Renewal of Life series, a direction suggested more by the upsurge of "unconscious" and hoarded thought than by the force of external events: "The book I'm working on (The Transformations of Man) has come without effort: a gift from the unconscious, re-assembling in a fresh pattern all I've been thinking for the last twenty years, and stimulating me to fresh explorations: so that I face it, each morning, with an expectant quizzical smile, as a wise man might have consulted the Delphic oracle" (LM 4 May 1955). He projected this book as "an attempt to give a sort of mythical picture . . . of the successive stages that transformed man from an inarticulate animal into his present historic self. In a sense the book is an attempt to do in a single, compact volume what Toynbee did not succeed in doing in a dozen long ones" (LM 5 September 1955).

Engaged with *The Transformations of Man*, Mumford posed a question that he would fully explore in *Technics and Human Development* a decade later. He began to doubt conventional assumptions that "primitive man's creativeness" was "oriented almost entirely to survival" and "that technical inventions resulted in more drastic transformations of human behavior than any other kind of variation"; he queries, "What tool or weapon or machine transformed man as much as language?" (LM 17 March 1956). Seven years later, Mumford described "the little book I am now beginning to write on the origins and the present day outcome of technological development. I began this book very confident, a month ago"; however, he continued, "before I knew it I was floundering around in a speculative swamp, trying to put together a plausible picture of the development of language and ritual, and then finally trying to carry further a thought you implanted in my mind twenty years ago, on the function of repetition in the human psyche" (LM 4 August 1963). Yet he confidently predicted to Murray, "I think I can at least remove one obstacle to sound thinking; and this is the exaggerated notion people have acquired of the making of tools as the prime attribute that defines the human species. Language was already a highly articulated machine at a time when tools were little more than roughly formed stones" (LM 4 August 1963). This theory would become the beginning point and informing thesis of *The Myth of the Machine* (1967, 1970).

The letters provide considerable detail about the conception and growth of *The City in History* (1961), the book widely considered to be Mumford's masterpiece. Mumford had initially intended to undertake some relatively minor, straightforward revisions and updating of the historical sections in *The Culture of Cities* (1938), but the revising quickly expanded into a much larger and more original project. Rather than beginning with the medieval town as he had done in *The Culture of Cities*, he sought the origins of communal and urban life in "pre-history": "I've had a lot of fun tracing the history of the city back into its buried past, where I find myself confronted with the débris of ancient religions and the divinity of kings; since the city first took shape, as it now seems to me, as the home of a god—at the very moment when the matriarchate was turning into a patriarchate & the gods of the soil were giving way to the gods of the sky. My city planning colleagues won't like this delving: for *their* city is an amorphous mass, neuter, with neither male nor female imprint upon it" (LM 14 January 1958). Mumford described his excitement in the unexpected efflorescence of the work: "During the last twenty years my interest in cities had grown sluggish; I could barely keep it alive enough to give even a mediocre course on the subject. . . . But suddenly, almost as soon as I began to write, the subject opened up anew and spread out before me in the most fascinating way, drawing on all that I had absorbed in these last twenty years, and pushing me onto a dozen new trails . . . What I am doing seems to me to throw a light, not just on cities, but on the whole course of human development" (LM 7 April 1958). He initially intended to entitle the book "Power & Form" (LM 19 September 1959). Upon publication of *The City in History,* Mumford, typically a severe critic of his own work, was pleased with the outcome: "It is by all odds my solidest work, I am sure, and at the same time my most original. . . . In that sheer nakedness of spirit that is possible only between old friends, who have outlived their reserves, I can say that I know only three other American books I would put on the same shelf with it, for its combination of scholarly exactitude and human richness: James' Psychology, Adams' Mt Saint Michel, and Marsh's Man and Nature" (LM 3 December 1960).

Mutual Encouragement and Praise

Mutual encouragement and praise constitute an important dimension of the correspondence, serving as both impetus to creativity and confirmation of achievement. They read and responded to each other's work in draft and in published form. As the far more prolific writer, Mumford often benefitted from Murray's evaluation and approval of his work; in fact, Murray read and commented on each of the books and many of the essays and reviews Mumford wrote during their association. Early in their correspondence, for example, Murray wrote, "Your two reviews gave me that gift which only the fusion of vitality & style can impart; aroused in me that ordered, nervous Insurgence which creates a new prospect for living—a feeling of insistency that life can never be banal again—that every step of it will be suffused with its allegory—You always do that to me; & hence I have come to feel that I cannot be complete without you—your writing is necessary to me" (HAM, LM ans 2 May 1930). Here Murray identified what became vital elements in the Renewal of Life series, the four-volume work Mumford was just beginning to plan: the theme of "insurgence" and the ways in which the forms of human expression are "suffused with . . . allegory."

As he read *The Culture of Cities,* Murray confirmed Mumford's intention to create cultural criticism combining historical analysis with philosophical, moral, and prophetic purposes: "I have moved on in your book to page 300. This has taken me through some of the grandest writing that I have encountered for many a day. Not till I arrived at the Megalopolis did I realize that you were Elijah, Ezekiel, Jeremiah and Isaiah. I prefer Isaiah because I can see from the peeps that I have taken into the last section of the book that you are ending with a new world, rather than lamenting like Jeremiah over the horrors and sins of the old. Now that I have the larger vision of your plan, it appears increasingly true and important" (HAM 5 May 1938). Murray would continue to comment on Mumford's prophetic persona, in both its positive and negative aspects, throughout their relationship.

As he was reading drafts of *The Condition of Man* in 1944, Murray's praise must have reassured Mumford that he had succeeded in his efforts to write a book that could reclaim human values and help renew a devastated civilization: "It is thick with wonderful visions into the nature of men & society & with marvelous germs for creating a fresh future. I need the book as a man with myocarditis needs digitalis, because I am in the state of being appalled at the blight that is Americanization when it takes place in foreign lands imposing itself—almost always in a detrimental manner—on the native culture" (HAM 28 April 1944). Shortly after *The Condition of Man* was published, he wrote, "We [Murray and Christiana Morgan] have started your book and are thrilled by its vast scale and scope, its freshness and vivid eloquence, its smooth & confident pace. You are at your best, sir, abounding in vigor, stored experience & wisdom, & having got hold of the most important topic on earth, you are certain to render up a revelation. . . . A man like yourself is creating the *form* for a new superego" (HAM 31 August 1943). The unstinted praise continues in a subsequent letter: "You are a hound for usable Truth, as Melville called it, & we bless you for it. The Condition of Man contains more usable Truth for our generation than any book that has been written. It is our Bible or rather the Prolegomenon of a Bible to be written" (HAM June 1944). Murray provides a similar endorsement of *The Conduct of Life,* the final volume in the Renewal of Life series and Mumford's most rigorously philosophical work, a treatise presenting his views on art, society, and human values: "In its special way, it is the top creation of your own great powers of interpretation and communication. First it is full of unappreciated truth—rejuvenated truth, lost in the last 50 years, and reshaped into something New. This truth is an encouragement & ground for fresh faith. Then, second, you have compacted your conceptions into so firm a structure that it stands like Gibraltar in the midst of today's confused flux of thoughts about man's nature. You submerge entirely the mechanical analogy, & restore man to his proper heritage as transformer (I would say). Finally your language—your words & style—is stirring—powerfully exciting—without any of the weakness of texture that so often characterizes enthusiasm in speech" (HAM 3 January 1951). Thus, for Murray, this book contained "truth," a formidable system of thought conveyed in consummate literary style. Mumford could not have wished for a more encouraging or more understanding reader.

Mumford considered *The Transformations of Man* (1956) to be one of his most original and important books, although its critical reception and sales were disappointing. Here he set forth the original theory of human development that informed the much longer works that followed, *The City in History* and *The Myth of the Machine*. Exhibiting sympathetic insight and offering invigorating praise, Murray recognized the depth and originality of Mumford's accomplishment in *The Transformations of Man*: "You can rest on this; your whole future in the minds of men can rest on this, since here you have compacted and set forth in animating prose the essence of Lewis Mumford. All your vast stores of knowledge, brooded over & ordered into new shapes, weighed in the scales of your sensitive spirit, tested and retested, are herein crystallized into the absolutely needed truth for our time. It is a beautiful symphony of ideas and judgments, not a superfluous or wasted sentence, not a single inert thought, nothing irrelevant, nothing trite, all fiery and vital. This is the Elan Vital in words, creative evolution from the anthropoid to modern man with his two options—to keep going as he is now going or to change realizing that the old ways are obsolete. Harpers should send this book to every member of the Federal Government. It should be required reading for every Freshman & and then a second time for every Senior" (HAM July 1956).

Mumford received such praise with deep gratitude. He frankly acknowledged the immense value of Murray's intellectual influence and discerning approval. Responding to Murray's comments on drafts of *The Condition of Man*, Mumford wrote, "As usual, you have given me exactly the right criticism, and it comes at exactly the right moment, sanctioning my bold excisions, re-enforcing my confidence in places where I was still a prey to doubt, giving me the energy I need for the last touches" (LM 23 November 1943). In fact, Mumford acknowledged the extent to which Murray functioned as a muse if not co-creator of that work: "no one recognizes better than I do how much you . . . contributed to The Condition of Man, and how much of what you found there had been implanted there by you at a much earlier period—coming back to you, perhaps, with the appearance of something fresh or more thoroughly clarified only because it had been strained through another mind. My final volume [in the Renewal of Life series] would be terrifying to contemplate, to say nothing of writing, if I did not have the sense of having both your positive work and your personal experience as a constant support for whatever I shall be able to contribute" (LM 29 July 1944).

In turn, Mumford provided generous and thoughtful appreciation of his friend's writings, especially his Melville studies. He extolled the lengthy psychoanalytic, biographical essay that serves as the introduction to the edition of Melville's *Pierre* that Murray edited: "It is the most colossally compact and compactly colossal summation of scholarship and human understanding anyone has brought forth in our generation. . . . What I admire most, I suppose, in the whole performance is the staggering thoroughness of your execution combined with an utter freedom from pedantry and ostentatious learning. . . . Your thought has dimensions that are lacking, so far, in any other American biography I've seen" (LM 29 June 1949). Mumford was similarly enthusiastic in praising Murray's celebrated essay "In Nomine Diaboli" while deftly touching on his friend's inability to complete his long-languishing book on Melville: "Even the prospect of seeing you this coming weekend cannot keep me from saluting your marvellous essay on Melville, written In Nomine Dei, which I read with unbounding admiration and delight last night. It is not merely the very best thing you have written, in its clarity, its penetration, its subtlety, its charity, its depth; but it is the very best thing anyone has written on Melville: volumes have been written without saying half as much. Even after your masterly introduction to Pierre I had been a little worried over the fact that your long researches on Melville hadn't yet come to full fruit in a whole book; but after this essay, which not merely complements and completes what you say in Pierre, but carries the whole interpretation to a final point, I feel no misgivings whatever. Rest easy! It is not by the quantitative results that good thinking and feeling shall be judged. No one can do better than the best" (LM 25 February 1952).

One can only speculate how such a friendship might have affected the literary career of Herman Melville himself, isolated and embittered by criticism of his greatest works. How might his life have been different, what else might he have written, if he had such an encouraging friend and understanding reader as Mumford had in Murray and Murray in Mumford? As leaders of the Melville revival during the twenties and thirties, both were acutely aware that they possessed in friendship what Melville lacked with Hawthorne or anyone else. Mumford comments that Melville was defeated by the "the absence of such visible proofs of friendship and love" that Murray had given him (LM 4 May 1944); he describes "the feeling of quiet security" Murray's support gives him, "so different from the bitterness Melville must so often have felt in his many hours of need" (LM 12 August 1947).

Criticism and Controversy

Although the correspondence contains much mutual encouragement and praise, it also shows that Mumford and Murray engaged in considerable debate and, occasionally, criticism of one another. They had brief exchanges debating issues such as the reputation of Thomas Wolfe and the quality of *Wolf Solent* by John Cooper Powys, one of Murray's favorite novels. Murray's essay "Unprecedented Evolutions" challenged Mumford to resume an argument, broached years earlier, concerning the operation of chance and purpose in evolution that dominated their correspondence throughout 1963. Mumford wrote that the essay made him aware of "our fundamental difference about the roles of chance and purpose in the transformations of life." He continued, "I find it impossible to accept chance as the key to the whole progressive sequence. . . . But purposiveness, in my interpretation, must exist on the lowest level, long before there is any detectable appearance of consciousness" (LM 7 June 1963). Murray's response attempted to clarify his position:

"I mentioned a number of factors, of which Chance is surely one, but my emphasis was on *Creativity* in nature (& finally in human nature) . . . You were arguing with Darwin, *not* with Murray, because I made a *special* point *against* accident or chance as a sufficient explanation. . . . It is only man's narcism which leads him to believe that the *purpose* of 2 billion years of evolution was to produce *Him*" (HAM n.d.). Seizing on Murray's notion of "creativity," Mumford rejoined, "Then is your 'creativeness' sufficient to cover what I mean by 'purpose'? Unfortunately not: for creativeness (spontaneity, exuberance) though an essential part of the process, does not embrace the peculiar attributes of purpose, as I see it. . . . But of one thing, dear Harry, I feel pretty sure: that the phobia of rigorous men of science before the very word 'purpose' is a suspicious symptom. . . . When purpose is ruled out of the universe by definition, the only purpose left is that of science itself, which is then at liberty to deal freely with all phenomena, by substituting the question-begging term mechanism (as if machines were not the very paragon of purposeful contrivances) for that of purpose. . . . Without purpose, creativity would not have a chance, and chance would not so often turn out to be a marvellous instrument of creativity!" (LM 4 August 1963). Mumford had similarly questioned Murray's scientific bias some twenty years earlier; he identified their occasional "misunderstanding" to involve what he viewed as Murray's recurring "conflict": "At times you take the accepted scientific view, that science alone will be as immediately effective in social life as in machine technology, and at other times you see, more truly I think, that the process is not so simple in the case of social facts, since subjective manifestations must be included and utilized in society, though they can be dismissed as 'secondary qualities' or aberrations in the physical sciences" (LM 24 January 1941).

Murray's most persistent and direct criticism of Mumford involves his prose style and tone of moral superiority, or, as he bluntly states, "a too pronounced moral contempt for your audience" (HAM, LM 16 March 1948). Commenting on *Men Must Act* (1939), Murray wrote, "I am in hearty accord with your main points & was much moved by the driving energy of it & the mountain-air aphoristic Emersonian rhetoric & countless clever hits & husky solar plexus blows & sock-in-the-jaws. In the course of it you called many people some pretty vile names for thinking or doing a great variety of things (about 2 dozen of which apply to myself by the way). You set up a rather high standard & open yourself to the query: 'how long, how hard & how sincerely has this guy been living up to all those commandments himself.' . . . Your procedure, however, is autocratic. . . . I cannot help feeling that you are encouraged by an underlying assumption that you can forcefully impel people by machine gun-phrases to agree with you" (HAM 1939). Commenting on a draft of Mumford's argument against the development and deployment of atomic weapons, Murray again objected to his "autocratic, Mount Sinai mode of dictating policy. In other words I don't think you will succeed in your main objective, if you so arbitrarily assert that *your* way is the only effective way of attaining it. . . . I am strongly in favor of your proposals & hence regret that you have yielded to a spirit which will precipitate their defeat" (HAM, LM 28 February 1948). Mumford objectively considered the criticism as that coming from a concerned friend, and responded in good will: "If I were indeed in an 'autocratic, Mount Sinai' mood I should, I think, be a little more upset over your calling my attention to it; but on the other hand, I can't altogether dismiss the possibility that you have laid your finger on something in my personal development which may, by reason of its very unconsciousness, be obstructive. When a man's best friend and his most voluble enemies unite in pinning the same vice on him, there must be *something* there to produce that unanimity!" (LM 28 February 1948). Shortly after the publication of *The Conduct of Life* (1951), a work Murray otherwise praised as "the book of our generation & decidedly your Everest" (HAM 6 October 1951), he reiterated, "My *only* petty but persisting quarrel with you, if it could be given such a malodorous term, is your dogmatic way of saying what you have to say. We have discussed this several times and I feel that you are talking in the tradition of Emerson, Thoreau, etcetera, etcetera, back to Ezekiel, if you will, and do not realize well enough that the mental climate has been so changed by science—for better or for worse—that minds with even an average amount of training and discipline begin to bristle the moment one man speaks like an oracle" (HAM 31 January 1952). Mumford replied that he is not inclined to modify his style and tone, for they represent an authentic and necessary voice: "On the matter of my written style, . . .I have no defensive reaction against what you say, unless an explanation can be counted as such. I was brought up in exactly the tradition you beg me to go back to; and some of my earlier work was so hedged about with qualifications and so tentative that it required a little probing to find out what I meant. When I started in on the big series, however, I decided that the time had come to speak in a firmer voice, with less beating around the bush . . . to be forthright and deliberately challenging." Mumford suspected that it was the "ideas themselves," not his "literary style," that "account for the failure of my books and essays to find a wider audience" (LM 5 February 1952).

Murray several times lamented that more frequent, unstinting, mutual criticism was the one vital element lacking in their relationship. Ironically, however, Murray confessed that he was reluctant to be the object of just the sort of criticism he was handing Mumford about his prose style: "Looking into myself I find what I have missed more than anything is constructive criticism from friends who understood what I was about, or, to be more concrete, tough but good-natured discussions as to the truth of this or that conception engendered in the mind of any one of us. . . . When it comes to literary form, however, I am much more sensitive, because I am not at all confident that I can improve it, & if it is flat that is the end of it. Thus, I might have to conclude that I want criticism for my ideas (because I can do better next time as a result of it), but appreciation of the form (because I can't improve on it)" (HAM 8 January 1947). They did in fact conduct "tough but good-natured discussions" on such topics as Melville and purpose in evolution, and Mumford never appeared to flinch at such engagements or to let disagreement compromise their friendship, whether their differences concerned matters of style or substance. However, he was particularly sensitive to criticism by Murray, and others, of his literary tone and style.[27]

For his part, Mumford did not view the infrequency of mutual criticism as a barrier to friendship; indeed, he saw his own reluctance to criticize as a measure of his respect for Murray: "I've mulled over your reproach about our never getting close enough to look into the differences you feel exist between us and need to be reconciled in some fashion; and I am still troubled by it. Partly, it's a defect of my own character, no doubt, which time and habit and a rather solitary life have etched in ever deeper. . . . This weakness is mixed with something that, if not pushed too far, is a virtue: a tendency, when I am with a person, to identify myself with my companion, and 'try on' his ideas, as if they were clothes, to see if they fitted my native form: so that . . . for the moment I seem to be in greater accord than I actually am. And when the person concerned is someone I have learned so much from as I have from you, and respect so much that, when I am conscious of a difference, I first suspect my own views rather than yours, the identification is even greater" (LM 12 February 1958). Their differences over the criticism issue appear to reside more in differences of temperament and working style than in any personal animosity. Murray attempted to explain his attitude toward criticism: "What you call my 'reproach' stems from my own nature. I love to discuss questions, face to face, and thrive on good criticism, which is more helpful to me than anything. Praise merely confirms me in my entrenched errors. Criticism tells me that I have not clarified my ideas, that I have omitted something, that I have made a mistake which requires correction—or that the other fellow has a temperament, set of values, or expertness which is so far from mine that a synthesis is not possible for some time to come. Any one of these outcomes advantages me" (HAM 6 March 1958).

However, when Mumford disclosed his plan to write a biography of his son Geddes, killed in action in 1944, Murray responded with criticism and discouragement that Mumford never forgot and, apparently, found difficult to forgive. Mumford envisioned the work both as a memorial to his son and as a consolation to other bereaved parents and surviving soldiers who had lost comrades; moreover, as he admitted, the project offered a means for him to express his love with a candor that had been withheld during Geddes's life and to assuage his grief. After reading some twenty pages in manuscript, Murray discouraged the project: "I have been thinking a lot about the Life & Death of a Son, & I can't escape from the conclusion that it is a spiritual impossibility as planned. It might be done on an idealized

27. For example, see Mumford's spirited response to criticism of his writing style in the Renewal of Life series by his friend Van Wyck Brooks: Mumford describes his style in the series as one "in which the imaginative and subjective part is counter-balanced by an equal interest in the objective, the external, the scientifically apprehended" (letter of 22 January 1952 in Spiller, *The Van Wyck Brooks–Lewis Mumford Letters*, 367–73).

level—simple & true, but yet omitting all the private, detailed psychological factors. The reader, knowing from the start that you, the Father, are the author, will feel uncomfortable, & embarrassed by some of the personal & intimate facts. . . . He will not believe that a parent—at this point—could be truly honest & impartial & even if he could, he shouldn't be. The impression will be gained that you have imposed a kind of crucifixion on yourself as an atonement for something—some hurtful action or failure to act—which overshadows & bears down upon your spirit. To some extent every parent must pass through a period of ruthless self-criticism after being struck so hard by Fate, but a public confession—a reader will inevitably see it in this light—does not seem proper, since the world can learn nothing from it. . . . I feel that this is the first thing you have ever written which did not come self-assuredly from your creative center. And from this I surmise that some member of your Congress of personalities is forcing you to do it, to do the impossible" (HAM 17 October 1946). Murray subtly alludes here to Mumford's guilt for neglecting his son who never did well at school, who had difficulty fitting in socially, and who was much different temperamentally from his intellectual, strictly disciplined father so often preoccupied with his writing.[28]

In a detailed, scrupulously tempered response, Mumford sought to justify the project: "But in choosing the material and the method of dealing with it I have not sought merely to satisfy Sophy and myself; I have rather asked myself, what would this mean to some other human being, even one who has not lost his child? Incidents and passages that lacked this universal quality I have tried to leave out. But, because of Geddes's nature and ours this book could not, without repudiating his very essence, be a pious and decorative account of his life: its value, it seems to me, lies in a certain kind of honesty in facing mischance and evil and sin and death, while keeping one's eye mainly on the facts of life and growth and joy. . . . Whatever the imperfections it reveals in me, whatever the limitations, it will show that my theoretic knowledge and ideal insights have been duly paid for in the process of living" (LM 19 October 1946). Moreover, he claimed that Murray's criticism only confirmed their friendship: "I shall even show you the finished manuscript as a whole when it is done. Even then we may be at odds; and even then I may stubbornly go my own way, but it will not be without gratitude, deep gratitude, that in this matter you spoke up, plainly and sternly, as becomes a friend. Believe me, that will only deepen a friendship that needs no deepening" (LM 19 October 1946). Upon the publication of *Green Memories*, Mumford honestly and graciously admit-

---

28. In an unpublished "Random Note" dated 21 December 1945, Mumford writes: "I feel that I was but half a father to him: I did not make up by love & sympathetic understanding what life deprived him of. . . . I never changed my own plans & purposes so as to embrace his more fully. There lies the weakness of my life: the weakness & the tragedy. When he needed me in 40 and 41 I was not there. By 1942 I was not able to repair the neglect." UP f. 8238 (Lewis Mumford Collection, Annenberg Rare Book and Manuscript Library, Univ. of Pennsylvania).

ted that Murray's reservations actually improved the completed work: "Your own share in the writing of that manuscript was not, dear Harry, a little one; for the warning you gave me became a challenge, and in meeting that challenge the book . . . has gained enormously in strength; and I feel grateful for that quality in our friendship which made it possible for you to say *what* you did, and for me to take it *as* I did, without further harm or grievance to either of us" (LM 22 June 1947). Despite this profession, Mumford had been stung, albeit challenged, by Murray's initial response to the project. Unlike Murray, Christiana Morgan enthusiastically supported the project from the beginning and said what Mumford wanted to hear about the manuscript that eventually became *Green Memories*: "It's wonderful— truly wonderful! What a sturdy living picture is emerging. The pattern you are weaving of child-background is so rich and makes so vivid that elemental aspect of Geddes' nature—indigenous as a vigorous plant. Your plan is so organically *right* and it is written with such great tenderness—but withal humorous and vigorous. My God, Lewis, you do have courage. I have read it with the greatest possible care from the point of view of your request to indicate any passages that seem dull or superfluous. Quite honestly I find not one thing to omit or to abbreviate. Again I say your 'touch' is perfect."[29]

There is a note by Mumford in the Harvard file, before the letter in which Murray discourages him from undertaking the project (HAM 17 October 1946): "These letters by H.A.M. & Christiana account for the growing alienation that continued, until, on my initiative, a few years ago we clasped hands again. LM Amenia 7 June 1979." Forrest Robinson states that after Murray's criticism of *Green Memories*, "Real intimacy between the two old friends was now a thing of the past."[30] However, the letters themselves provide scant evidence of "growing alienation" or cooling of "intimacy" between them. Whatever withdrawal and injury there may have been on Mumford's part were unspoken. Indeed, prolific exchanges of letters occurred in subsequent years—especially, for example, in 1959 and 1963. They continued to debate, to encourage, and to commiserate; Mumford sought Murray's response to his theories and asked Murray to read his manuscripts. They continued to praise each other's published work and reaffirmed the depth of their feelings for each other on the occasion of Christiana Morgan's death in 1967.

"In Old Friendship"

Occasional differences never compromised the foundation of their friendship. Beginning with his letter of 26 January 1947 and in a dozen others written during the next twenty years, Mumford adopted the habit of closing with the phrase "in old friendship." Indeed, their friendship endured over a half century, encompassing a

29. Morgan letter to Mumford, 22 November 1946.
30. Robinson, *Love's Story Told*, 304.

variety of concerns and phases: love and death; literary success and frustration; intellectual inquiry and debate; criticism and encouragement; intimacy, separation, and reconciliation.

While Mumford and Murray communicated and maintained the friendship primarily through their correspondence, they sometimes met in New York and Cambridge; Murray several times visited Mumford at Amenia and Hanover (when Mumford was teaching at Dartmouth). Some of these meetings are recorded in the letters and a few in Mumford's personal, unpublished "Random Notes" (sometimes designated as "RN" in the manuscripts). Their meetings described in these Random Notes are characterized by brotherly warmth and intense, serious conversation. A note of 1930, for example, describes "a few hours of talk with H. Murray at the Harvard Club." Murray explained his exploration of "the almost unreachable elements of the unconscious" in artists. They also discussed religion; Mumford wrote, "His ideas of modern religion almost exactly parallel mine: no one man, no one institution, no one scripture hold it, but it is coalescing nevertheless: and the poets who have explored the depths & fringes of our consciousness have each brought back precious samples. The supernatural has not been wiped out: it is now in the unconscious." They agreed that " 'Humanism' mistakenly attempts to eliminate" the "Christian paradox" of defeat and triumph, pain and joy; however, "true humanism seeks to resolve & compose," not to "do away" with these elements (RN 3 April 1930, f. 8235). A 1935 note records a conversation in New York in which Mumford explained to Murray that his "thinking on Technics" led him "to use two broad categories, order and insurgence, both necessary activities and expressions of life. My views got closer to Bergson's: but did not deny that mechanism itself might be an instrument of life." Murray described "the three categories he [had] come to: sameness →creativity ←change in Hegelian rhythm. They seemed to me close to my order & insurgence, especially when one added the organic as the middle term=creativity—that expresses their dynamic relationship in life" (RN 21 June 1935, f. 8235). A 1937 entry recounts a visit to Murray's farm at Topsfield, outside of Boston, and to the "Tower" Murray and Christiana Morgan had constructed on her nearby property at Rowley, Massachusetts. Mumford described the tower as "a cloister for work and love" and explained its various levels and perspectives. He continued, "We talked incessantly when we got back to Topsfield and drank rum & ginger-ale and talked again. Harry criticized modern architecture as 'porous' and emphasized the need for a place of complete retirement or 'claustrum' for lovers. . . . In the morning we talked much about love, and I told him about Helen [Ascher] & Sophy, something of my experience with Catherine. . . . He gave me hints of some of his ultimate moments with Christiana: their making a chalice of each other's blood & drinking it ritualistically, with pledges & ceremonies. It was a day of full rich revelations—and stimuli" (RN 17 October 1937).

The war years, 1942 to 1945, represent one of the most prolific periods of their correspondence. During this time of turmoil and uncertainty, the two men drew upon their friendship as a source of strength and consolation. Confronting what both viewed as a crisis for world civilization, they shared their concerns and analyses of the situation; they also discussed their roles and responsibilities during the war and its aftermath. For example, Mumford encouraged Murray to stick with his intellectual and academic work rather that to accept a military assignment: "I am still a little troubled, dear Harry, by your own decision to give up the important work you are doing for the routine tasks of war. It shows a great self-discipline and a great humility; but as things are shaping up at present, the more disengaged minds we have, capable of a continued exercize of thought, experiment, and criticism, the more likelihood will there be that the war will be fought to some purpose: whereas if the military tasks absorb everybody, the soldiers who have fought it will find that all the regressive and purposeless forces that dominated our life in the past have become mightier in their absence and the serious business of making the planet fit to live on has been indefinitely postponed" (LM 23 October 43).

Military encounters with cultures in the East and the West prompted both men to assess American life and values. Although they believed the United States to be engaged in a moral struggle against evil, they agreed that the experience of war exposed the superficiality and materialism of American life.

In 1942 Murray lamented the absence of a "strong moral system," intractable problems of racial inequity, pervasive materialism and greed, the debasement of the arts by "Hollywood, Broadway, & all the rest," and "the tolerance we have acquired for everything and anything"; in his view, "These are some of the horrors that the War has brought glaringly to the forefront" (HAM August 1942). Murray believed that his country could effectively combat the enemy beyond its shores but not the insidious dangers within: "Because Fascism has reared its Brutal head we can attack it, & in attacking it gain strength, but Advertisitis slips in the ears & eyes & runs down the nerves & eats the vitals out of the ganglia without our knowing it" (HAM, LM 23 October 1943). As a military officer responsible for the psychological testing of soldiers to be assigned especially dangerous combat duties, Murray was impressed by the energy and bravery of his young compatriots; however, he was alarmed by their superficiality, their lack of cultural and moral values: "I have been wrestling with the immense spiritual dilemma created by a craving to identify with the American Ethos as a whole and yet being outraged repeatedly by its prevailing trends—the profit motive that spoils everything it touches, its revolting voice as heard in advertising, the vulgar distortion of life it creates in the movies, the values that are engendered by it, etc., etc., endlessly & then the superficiality, the quick smiling pithless contacts, the attention to surfaces & the neglect of depths, the deodorized exteriors" (HAM, LM 26 September 1945). He retrospectively summarizes how the war affected his outlook and his work at Harvard during the postwar years: "As soon as Fascism began to get arrogant I saw that basic philosophic values were at stake & this conflict compelled my attention & thought. During the war, perhaps for the first time wholly & consciously I felt identified with my countrymen & their destiny. More recently, however, I have become more appalled by their commitment to cynical ruthless materialism and by the general degradation of cultural values—by their lack of appreciation of the ways & beliefs & profounder accomplishments of other societies—by their bantering superficiality, irreverence, & adolescent self-assertion, etc." (HAM 17 April 1948).

Mumford echoed such concerns both in his letters and in his books, *Faith for Living* (1940) and *Values for Survival* (1946). Like Murray, he saw how the soldiers' responses to combat exposed flaws in American education and, especially, "the purposelessness of the university": "But our system of education . . . has tried to eschew, or rather extirpate, all but the more seemly or the more trivial emotions: we have ignored the necessary role of hate and fear, and thus have kept them from being focussed on appropriate objects. I have little doubt that this anesthesia has been responsible for not a few war neuroses, for who can face the terrible ordeals of battle without the mobilized support of his emotions. . . . Our teaching at all its levels, has been attempting to eviscerate and de-emotionalize the human personality, as the pedagogic alternative to bringing all its areas under discipline and purposive direction" (LM 4 April 1945). By the end of the war, Mumford had became so disenchanted with American culture that he actually considered the possibility of settling in England, where his books sold well and his name was one of recognized authority: "I still love all that is permanently lovable in the American ethos, and that is much; but for the first time in my life, it is conceivable to me that I might spend the rest of my life in some other country, preferring to share the constricted lot of England, say, than to enjoy the odious ease and the fat advantage of my own country: purchased by hardening the heart, closing the ears, and concentrating upon 'full production'—for ourselves" (LM 26 September 1945). During the postwar years, Mumford and Murray became concerned about the development and deployment of nuclear weapons, and their correspondence of the late 1940s and early 1950s often discusses the issue and the several articles Mumford published on the subject.

The correspondence contains intimate exchanges concerning their states of mind, their successes and failures, their experiences of both love and suffering. They confided in one another about their several love affairs; Mumford, for example, wrote, "Being domestically in love with Sophia, romantically in love with Alice, and intellectually in love with Catherine, I ought to count myself thrice blessed: but the fact is that each of them in her heart of hearts wants to exist in all three relations: so that what is complete and perfect for me is fragmentary & imperfect for them" (LM 8 July 1935). Throughout 1936 they corresponded extensively about Alice Decker's medical condition after she suffered a serious concussion in an automobile accident in Louisiana; during this period, Murray provided both medical advice for Alice and solace for his traumatized friend. Murray was also generous in providing sympathy and encouragement after the death in combat of Mumford's son Geddes in September 1944. When Mumford reported the following spring that he had experienced a transformation, a rebirth of hope and purpose, Murray replied with warmth and insight: "I rejoice at your renewal. . . . There is no key to the renewal as such. It just happens as a gift of Nature, evidence of the abundant fertility of the universe, the quenchless spirit of man. Such key as there is resides in the depth and sincerity and sympathy and solitary single-mindedness with which, in your grief, you relive the life and feelings, extract and absorb the virtues, and experience the difficulties and frustrations of the one for whose physical presence you will never cease to crave. Out of this comes the tragic sense of life, knowledge of the basic human situation, and without this, how can anyone say anything that is profoundly true?" (HAM 22 May 1945). In turn, Mumford offered concern and encouragement when Murray experienced occasions of loss and suffering—the death of his brother (LM 8 July 1935), the painful back surgery Christiana endured (1943), the death of his wife Josephine (1962), and the death by drowning of Christiana while vacationing with Harry in the Caribbean (1967). As soon as Mumford received the shocking news of the last event, he wrote, "Your letter came this morning beloved and bereft friend. . . . My first concern is for you: the incredible shock: the effort at resuscitation: the emptiness and desolation of the days that followed and of the days that are still to come. . . . You will need all your immense vitality, all your well-earned knowledge, to offset this blow; and when you find this lacking, come to us, draw upon us, even though we share your grief and know that our own energies are fading, too. Just yesterday, going through an ancient file of letters, about Alice, I came upon a magnificent letter from you in which you made just such an offer to me. And I can only say, in the same spirit, 'If you need me, I am your man' " (LM 21 March 1967).

The correspondence repeatedly documents the deep, abiding friendship that was so vital and necessary to both men. Attempting to explain his dubiety about "inflicting" himself upon Mumford at a time when his own work was not going well, Murray wrote, "I think I am imagining that you are expecting a great deal from one—energy, a fund of ideas, wisdom, etc., or I want you to like me & feel that I will disappoint you. In any case I find myself avoiding those whom I respect the most—for fear they will say: how are your books getting along?" (HAM February 1933). Again invoking the marriage analogy, Mumford encouraged the visit: "What on earth is friendship for if it is not to endure, at a pinch, the dull and soggy moments of life as well as the electric ones: it is, like marriage, the ultimate life-boat relation, in which the saving element is that both people are afloat together under the same conditions, ready to face all kinds of weather together. Other relationships don't, in general, survive bad weather: one gets bored, one gets irritated, one yawns, one walks away!" (LM 12 February 1933). Indeed, Murray suggested that, alongside his relationship with Christiana Morgan, his friendship with Mumford was one of the most important in his life: "My *work* has been a long series of abortive failures for six years—during which time you have steadily increased in depth and power. This is partly because with me Love & Life has come first—This has succeeded beyond my last dream but everything else has failed. I have en-cysted myself from everyone. I have lost all my friends—unless perhaps your gen-erosity still included me—but you are the only one" (LM 24 March 1935). It was typical of Murray to address Mumford as "my best & most loyal friend" (HAM n.d., 1935). Mumford and his writings were often in Murray's thoughts: "Indeed you have become a permanent inhabitant of my brain—someone with whom I can sustain an almost perpetual conversation" (HAM 23 December 1941). Similarly, as he was grieving over the death of his son Geddes, Mumford wrote, "my truest of friends . . . You stand closer to us, Harry, than anyone else in the world; and that will sustain us, if any human aid can, in the long dark pilgrimage which will, I trust, eventually lead us out into the world again, fortified, ready to do for those who re-turn . . . what we can never do for our own son" (LM 20 October 1944). Recalling the inception of their association some thirty years earlier, he avowed, "My friend-ship with you, dear Harry, is the best reward I got for writing my study of H.M." (LM 12 August 1947). Expressing gratitude for a copy of a Festschrift published for Murray at age seventy, Mumford wrote, "Thank you and bless you: for I would have to write a whole book of my own to record my gratitude for all that your work and our friendship has brought me" (LM 11 June 1963).

Their relationship had its periods of silence and distance, even as both were liv-ing in Cambridge when Mumford held visiting appointments at Massachusetts In-stitute of Technology, Brandeis, and Harvard. Well into the fourth decade of the friendship, their exchanges having become less frequent than in earlier years, Mumford concluded a letter by stating, "May the dry branch of our friendship again bear flowers, as of old!" (LM 29 December 1966). In response to Murray's question about the meaning of this statement, Mumford replied, "As to our friend-ship, I don't think we'll hasten its fresh blossoming by pulling it up to see if a worm has been gnawing at the roots. Love has its seasons, and friendship, though stead-ier and more equable, may know winter & summer too" (LM 5 June 1967). One can speculate about the reasons for their drifting apart after 1960, at least as measured by the less frequent exchange of letters. Both men had passed age sixty-five and were still engaged in challenging work. After the death of Josephine Murray in 1962, perhaps Mumford disapproved of Murray's not marrying Christiana Morgan despite his stated intentions of doing so. Mumford did not attend the memorial service Murray arranged for Morgan because of plans he had made before her death to travel to Italy; nonetheless, Murray was obviously disappointed that Mumford, as a close friend of both and one of the few who had known about their relationship, was not present.

In his early seventies, Mumford recalled the value of their friendship to both his thought and personal happiness, a friendship that began with a common, schol-arly interest in Melville but quickly developed into a deeper, intimate relationship: "Our friendship began, dear Harry, with your generous sharing of your knowledge of the Gansevoort papers & was sealed by your over-generous response to my

Melville study. Going through my notes of the last forty years—notes never included in my published work—I am repeatedly reminded of your intellectual companionship and personal understanding, with stimulating ideas and helpful admonitions at the right moments, and repeatedly" (LM 4 April 1967). A few years later, Mumford wrote that reading a recently published collection of essays on *Moby-Dick* "put me so immediately in your presence that I felt bound to resume the long conversation we began in 1928 & will never be finished this side of eternity. . . . I never showed you the poem I addressed to Melville, shortly after I met you: but I came upon it the other day and decided to keep it in my autobiographic chapter . . . where I deal with the great shaking up of my life in 1930 when I recognized how different the inner man was from the outer one. Both Melville & you had a part in that awakening" (LM 9 September 1973).

As aging but still active octogenarians, Mumford and Murray reaffirmed their friendship as they engaged in a tender adagio of reconciliation. In 1976 Murray described the hallway of his Cambridge house containing "photographs of the archangels to whom I am most indebted for benefits received over the years," one panel displaying "the triangle of Mumford, Freud, and Jung." Murray wrote that he was "aided . . . by sight of your thoughtful visage as I go to and from my desk, say seven times a day." And he continued, "The thought that maybe you were reliving a portion of your life—in connection with the autobiography—led me to think below the surface about our friendship, its vicissitudes, its recent lag. . . . I have several times broached this topic in a mild way; but with increasing degrees of failure. Is there any enlightened way you can suggest of my dealing with my present nearly hopeless state of mind?" (HAM 1 June 1976). After noting how difficult it would be "to disentangle the intellectual and emotional reasons for our drifting," Mumford answered, "How monstrous it would be if either of us were to die without gratefully recognizing how much our friendship has meant to each of us & how deep a mark it has left on our lives! More than once during these later years I have found myself repeating Melville's Monody over Hawthorne: all the more aptly because my way of avoiding *oral* discussion of our differences . . . corresponds to Hawthorne's silences with Melville. 'And then to be estranged in life, / And neither in the wrong.' . . . Your *action* here has done more to re-unite us than the lengthiest inquest into our lives, or different temperaments, or deepest convictions, could do. This at least is solid ground: we have re-affirmed the reality of our friendship. No matter how far we have been blown apart—or may be driven again!— here is our unmistakable landing field!" (LM 6 June 1976). Reaffirming the depth and significance of their friendship, even in the twilight of their lives and despite some unresolved differences, Murray responded, "In Aristotle's judgment wasn't Magnanimity the topmost virtue? If he did not express himself in just those words, my faltering memory tells me that they are consonant with his central plexus of values. Anyhow, regardless of Aristotle and his wisdom—*there* at the top of the pyramid you stoutly stand, proved for the nth time by the last letter just received here.

Beautiful! was Nina's immediate declaration—beyond the compass of what even the best of this age is capable, was my thought" (HAM 9 June 1976). More precisely, of course, in the *Nicomachean Ethics,* Aristotle describes friendship as the "topmost virtue," as a relationship permitting the highest, most complete expression of virtue.

Mumford was a prolific correspondent, and his correspondence with Murray was longer in duration and more voluminous than with any other person. In 1942 he wrote, "I have been going through the files of my correspondence, and have had a delightful sense of what a rich, varied, exciting, amorous, eager, intellectual, imaginative life I have been leading all these years. . . . The oblique reflection of my own life in the words of my correspondents has given me a sense of its many dimensions and its amplitude. . . . And your letters, dear Harry: at the moment of our first exuberant recognition of our friendship and our capacity for understanding each other and revealing ourselves to each other: I only hope my letters were half as good, or a quarter as generous in their expressions" (LM 24 July 1942). Murray reciprocated, emphasizing the stimulation and inspiration he found in Mumford's letters: "You speak of our early letters of discovery, but in my case the discovery has been greater & more exciting each time I have seen or heard from you since those first days. Because you have grown steadily & by leaps, without regressions, & I never know where I am going to find you, though it always proves to be before some new vista which modifies the complexion of things & gives a fresh impetus to action. I have not said a quarter of what I feel—the delight, the wonder, sympathy, exhilaration, pride in fellow feeling" (HAM August 1942). Indeed, Mumford recognized the importance of their letters both as a record of his personal life and literary career and as the monument of a great friendship. Reviewing their correspondence for selections to be included in his biographical "miscellany," *Findings and Keepings,* Mumford wrote, "Someday, perhaps, my collected correspondence, if intelligently selected, will give a more adequate account of our friendship & all that it has meant to me" (LM 11 May 1977). This volume is an effort to provide such an account.

1928–1932

A Friendship Established

ALTHOUGH THE CORRESPONDENCE between Lewis Mumford and Henry A. Murray began because of their mutual interest in Herman Melville, the friendship quickly developed because of their intense interest in each other. Each man recognized in the other a stimulating mind as well as a kindred spirit who held similar beliefs and values. Mumford anticipated that the Melville biographies they were writing would be complementary works: "To be right and left eyes . . . both will be necessary, like bi-focal vision, for perspective and depth" (LM 26 August 1928). A few months later, Murray hailed Mumford's *Herman Melville* (1929) as a magnificent, masterly achievement that "speaks to me of a new order" (HAM March 1929). Both men effusively depicted their nascent friendship and its potential in idealized terms. They commenced candid and intimate discussions of their work, their aspirations, and their love lives. Mumford revealed his affair with Catherine Bauer and described the challenges it presented for his marriage as well as for his work. Murray compared Mumford's situation to his own extramarital relationship with Christiana Morgan. Another prominent subject of discussion in the letters of these years was the condition of Mumford's friend, Van Wyck Brooks, who had suffered a mental breakdown in 1926. Mumford sought Murray's advice as a physician, and Murray became actively involved in the case—recommending that Brooks undergo therapy with Carl Jung.

[typed]
Amenia, New York
14 August 1928

My dear Dr. Murray:

I had a talk with Mrs. Metcalf last week which made me feel that I should in all kindness have written you at an earlier date, and allayed any fears you might have about our books overlapping or competing with each other.[1]

When I undertook more than a year ago to do a short critical biography of Melville for Doran-Doubleday's Murray Hill series, I conceived of writing primarily a literary criticism of Melville's work, assuming that the biographic part had already been done by Mr. Weaver.[2] After talking to Mr. Weaver last fall, hearing of your own work, and examining for the first time Mr. Weaver's book in relation to Melville's complete works, I saw that the surface had only been scratched by him. He told me that you had a great deal of firsthand data about Melville's life which you would not divulge to anyone, as you intended to do a psychological study of him. With this fact in mind, I planned my own book so that the two would presumably make a whole: I have made my analysis of Melville solely on the basis of his writings, their point of view, their style and internal development, and so forth: and I have used only such external data about Melville's life as was necessary for a skeleton. This task had never been done before: and when the first draft of my manuscript was half done, I saw that I had a full length biography on my hands which no longer would fit into the original box. My chief concern with Melville is a literary and philosophic one: to such an extent does this dominate my plan, that in the case of Moby Dick I have dispensed entirely with it as a biographic document. In short, my book is focussed upon that part of Melville that is accessible to anyone who will take the pains to read his complete work.

The first time that I was aware of a possible conflict in our interests was when, the other day, I sought to consult the Gansevoort Lansing letters. My approach to these documents, like my approach to Mrs. Metcalf, came at the end rather than at the beginning of my studies for an obvious reason: for me, they are of interest solely because they are objective data against which I should like to test my independent conclusions, drawn from a study of Melville's literary work. I am quite willing to risk my own judgments without this objective verification: but naturally, I should be greatly the gainer, certainly in the smaller details, if the Gansevoort Lansing letters were as open as the Duyckinck letters are. Mr. Paltsits feels that you have a prior right to this information.[3] You have; and I honor it. For this reason I made no effort, in talking to Mr. Paltsits, to minimize the amount of conflict between our works: rather I overemphasized it, and I said that you might very well feel, after all your labor in other departments, that it would be unfair for me to reap the advantages, by a last moment entry, of your researches. He then very properly said that without written permission from you, he did not feel able to give me

---

1. Eleanor Melville Metcalf (1882–1964), Herman Melville's granddaughter, author of *Herman Melville: Cycle and Epicycle* (1953).

2. Raymond M. Weaver, author of *Herman Melville: Mariner and Mystic* (1921).

3. Victor Hugo Paltsits, New York Public Library librarian, compiled *Family Correspondence of Herman Melville, 1830–1904, in the Gansevoort-Lansing Collection* (1929).

access to the collection before he himself published its contents. Have no fear of any corpses floating in the Charles River: the key to the situation is in your hands!

In dealing with you, however, I can be a little more free and forthright than in dealing with Mr. Paltsits. My own study of Melville is primarily a literary one: yours, I take it, is chiefly psychological. If there is one point where we inevitably overlap, it is, I fancy, on the subject of what happened in the years that included Pierre and The Confidence-Man. On these years my own analysis must necessarily be sketchy and diffident: I may commit myself to a skepticism or dubiety where you, as a psychiatrist, must have a more definite and authoritative point of view. Pierre means one thing according to Freud, another according to Jung, and a third according to one who would view that novel as a parallel to the Manfreds and Werthers of the Romantic movement. I am not committed to any of these views: I must give them all for what they are worth. If your book existed, it would contain a good deal of material, interesting in its own right, which would be utterly foreign to my purpose; and the opposite of this doubtless holds, too, although you must trespass on my ground far more often than I need trespass on yours. After weighing the matter for more than a week, I still frankly think that I could make use of the Gansevoort Lansing collection without injuring your interests. As for the fact that more than one book on Melville is coming out (there is still at least one other to my knowledge) do not be alarmed by this in the least: one book tends to sell another or pave the way for it: in the long run, the good book comes to the top, no matter how many competitors it may have. You are probably doing a job that won't have to be done over again; I am seeking to do the same thing, for my generation, in another department: priority is of no concern whatever to me, and my book is scheduled for next spring only because, as a writer, I am dependent upon my books for the income and must publish them when the wolf barks at my door, whether they are complete or incomplete, infirm or final.

If this explanation should make you feel that I might consult the Gansevoort Lansing letters without injuring your rights, I should be very happy; but if you are still embarrassed, I shall understand it, and bear it cheerfully!

Faithfully yours,
Lewis Mumford

[handwritten]
Mid-River Farm
Clayton Post Office, N.Y.
[LM] Ans. 26 Aug. 28?

Dear Mr. Mumford,

I am somewhat disappointed with myself at the idea of causing you inconvenience & delay.

I left on my vacation the day that your letter was mailed & it was not until last night that it reached me here in midstream on the St. Lawrence. I believe that you are overgenerous in your considerations of me.

Kindly tell Mr. Paltsits that I consider it very decent of him to have my interests on his mind—but as regards the N.Y. Public Library literary material I claim *no* priority whatsoever. I hope that you will enjoy the same privileges and benefits that have been mine during the past two years.

Due to certain obligations in Cambridge I am unable to make more than occasional periodic visits to New York, & so it happens that I have not yet finished gathering in the harvest.

I expect to spend 10 days in the Manuscript Division between Sept. 9th–19th & if you are in N.Y. at that time I shall be glad to see you. My address will be 105 E 67. Rhin 1906.

As far as my own labors are concerned I have been engaged at intervals upon a full length biography of Melville without any special considerations of his work as Art, i.e. its place in history, its relation to recoiling Romanticism, its derivations, its general form, etc., etc. Schematically I might divide my interests into: (1) Factual biography—from Weaver, Mrs. Metcalf, N.Y. Public Library & a few odd bits here & there unearthed. (2) Psychological analysis of principal trends, major conflicts, impasses & regressions. (3) The esoteric Melville—subjectively, poetically & metaphysically apprehended.

For 2 & 3 his works are sufficient. The recorded facts of his overt life are relatively meaningless except in a negative sense; so that all real knowledge of the man must come to the permeable through sap rising from the written page—In other words I think that each of us will commence in the same wild forest with no handicaps or benefits except our own intuitions.

I believe that we will overlap from the beginning to the end—but what of it? You may have pictured me concocting one of those stale little treatises in which heavy thought is given to proving that superiority, Oedipus, Castration, or Birth Trauma was at the Bottom of his Nature. I am more interested in his attempts to break the Gates of Paradise & in his 'teasing the world for grace.'

I have talked at some length with Grant Watson who is confining himself to (3)—we agree in all fundamentals. He was planning to bring out his book this winter (1928–29)—Weaver is publishing a short memoir this fall with suggestions as to (2).[4]

If there is anything left for me to write I might finish within 18 months—but only by a prodigious display of energy.

4. E. L. Grant Watson, "Melville's *Pierre*," *New England Quarterly* 3 (1930): 195–224.

I hope we can meet in N.Y. at the Public Library & then talk. I must thank you for your letter & ask you to excuse the unnecessary delay in answering.

Yrs.

Henry A. Murray

I leave this address on Sept. 1st.

[typed]

Amenia, New York

26 August 1928

Dear Dr. Murray:

This was almost as hard a letter to write as my first one was, although it is gratitude over your generosity and friendliness, and not foreboding that makes it so. Forgive me for doing you the injustice of thinking that you would merely professionally botanize over Melville's grave: I should have known better from Mrs. Metcalf's description of you; but if you were making merely a clinical picture of Melville of the kind that you dismiss in your letter, it would be easier for me to accept your generosity, and so my own wish kept me from thinking clearly. My own book is practically written; and in anticipation of your own work, I shall resist easily the temptation to fill in the details. I am going down to New York at the end of this week, if I get Mr. Paltsits' permission, to make a preliminary survey of the material, if that is possible; so that I may know whether to stop work on my manuscript immediately and pitch it, or defer that—as I hope I shall be able to—till you are also in the city. I look forward keenly to meeting you; and your attitude has given me a feeling just the opposite of Melville's Timonism; indeed, I trust only that in one way or another I may give some practical and positive evidence of my appreciation and thanks. I trust that our biographies will turn out—since they are not as dissimilar as I first hoped—to be right and left eyes, and that both will be necessary, like bi-focal vision, for perspective and depth.

Faithfully yours,

Lewis Mumford

[typed]

19 Beaver St.

Cambridge, Mass.

Sept. 21, 1928

[LM] Ans 22 Sept

Dear Mumford:

It was good meeting you in New York and I only regret that our conversation was so abruptly terminated. If you have any more questions, fire them at me. Of course I may not answer every one of them because we all have our pet little vanities, of which we are not entirely purged.

I did not have a chance to examine the Melville letters on this visit because Old Paltsits was expending his industry upon them.

Did you see Weaver's article?

Let me know when the time comes to write to Dr. Jung. I am anxious to do whatever I can for such a noble fellow as Van Wyck Brooks.[5]

Sincerely yours,
Henry A. Murray, Jr.
HAM:H

[typed]
After 5 Oct. my address will be
4002 Locust Street
Long Island City, N.Y.
Amenia, New York
22 September 1928

Dear Murray:

I am sorry that Paltsits' activity burked you in New York: all the more so because I fear that my inquiry stirred him to self-righteous effort—which he might not have dreamed of doing for another ten years otherwise. If he doesn't omit or cut anything, on the other hand, he may save you a lot of tedious work; so I trust my butting in will not turn out altogether to be a debacle. You have been more than generous, as I shall acknowledge in the proper place; and I don't know any questions I could legitimately ask you further, until my book is published and my own cards are on the table. The one critical point for the later interpretation of Melville's life is the mood of his late adolescence, just before the impulse that sent him off to sea. If you succeed in digging up anything on this, you will fill in the one place where I don't trust Weaver's intuition, and can't be sure of my own—and everything else in the picture will alter accordingly. Your note that he was in good health in 1867 made me a little uneasy about the early date I had so plausibly assigned to Clarel, and I have now established beyond doubt, I think, that he wrote Clarel *after* the Battle-Pieces. There is an allusion to the Civil War in the fourth part of Clarel that had hitherto, for some occult reason, escaped me. Also, this corresponds to Frances Melville's memory—which I had hitherto dismissed, thinking she had remembered the fuss about publication, not the date of writing.[6] I have now only to do my last chapter and write an Epilogue; and for me, the end doesn't come too soon, since I begin to feel the wear and tear and jar and can't, like Mortmain, annul completely the effect of it with "coffee and cigar." I have not seen Weaver's article.

---

5. Van Wyck Brooks (1886–1963), prolific American literary critic; as editor of the *Freeman,* he helped Mumford launch his literary career in New York; Brooks experienced a mental breakdown in 1926.

6. Frances Melville Thomas (1855–1938), Herman Melville's daughter.

Where was it, and has it anything fresh? Have you, by the way, noticed Melville's identification of himself with Christ and Rama in Clarel? I haven't made anything of it; it seemed a little off my track, and I did not have anything interesting to say; but I may have to touch it in the final chapter, because Billy Budd is the story of the stern father and the scapegoat, too.

As for Brooks, the situation has grown much more alarming since I saw you. I shall speak frankly and of course privately: but this need not forbid your communicating the gist of this to Mr. Zinsser. Brooks returned from a posture and breathing cure at Monhegan Island, Maine, in worse condition than ever. One of the reasons for this was that his mother was up there with him: he has had a relapse each time she has paid a visit to him or he to her. His depression is now acute: and it has taken various delusional forms, of which Eleanor told me only one which I break to you as physician, so you can form an intelligent opinion: namely, his belief that he must be buried alive in order to save her or his family. "Buried alive" is, I need scarcely suggest, the equivalent of the asylum. This however is not the worst of the situation: ten days ago Eleanor paid us a brief visit, alone, and she went over with me the whole ground she had covered before. The signs of strain in her were very obvious; and she herself is losing her grip, and covers it over, desperately, with a continuous patter of conversation and frantic attempts at sociability. Going to Jung is now apparently entirely out of the question; and as for his treatment here, Brooks is in the hands of his relatives: Eleanor herself has a set against analysts, and comes forward with elaborate rationalizations to avoid taking any steps toward consulting one. The thing that she is struggling with is self-reproach: because she took on herself the responsibility for keeping Van Wyck out of a sanitarium last year, and in the meanwhile, under home treatment, he has grown worse. Plainly, something must be done, and somebody must make the decision. She is now incapable of doing this. I therefore suggested to her that she appeal to Dr. White of St. Elizabeth's as consultant, to suggest what further should be done, who should do it, and where the treatment should take place. As I suspected, she said she had no faith in analysts; and I answered that White was an all-round practitioner with no single method. Probably you could have suggested some one as good or better; but on the moment, this was the best that I could do. She promised to write him. I do not think she will. The whole family has suffered from what Shaw's dustman, Mr. Doolittle, called Middle clawss merellity, and middle clawss respectability. They are fussy about money: although I have pledged Eleanor that a dozen of Van Wyck's friends would be happy to step into the breach; that anything he received, he would receive as a writer and a public character; and I reminded her that when Huxley needed a long rest Darwin and a group of his friends got together a purse and presented it to him—and he gracefully and decently accepted. No use: they had rather kill Van Wyck through his family than rescue him through his friends. Their physician, Dr. Lambert, chucked the case some time ago because of family interference. Lambert, I learned from Eleanor, is one of the school—who is the leader of it now—Salmon?—who looks for the source of the disorder in a physical lesion of some kind, and who has nothing whatever to say or suggest or do on the psychological side. As far as I can see Brooks might as well be in the hands of a veterinary. The immediate treatment may of course be chiefly physical: but to put on flesh and to keep a man from committing suicide is a long distance, it seems to me, from getting to the bottom of Brooks' trouble; and sooner or later Brooks must be in some other hands. Have you any suggestions to make—supposing that Eleanor does not call in Dr. White. I repeat: I doubt if she will. Have the Zinsser's any weight with Eleanor? The worst of it is: she will soon be in need of treatment herself. This is the first time I've felt really desperate about the whole matter; so forgive this lengthy eruption.

Faithfully,
Lewis Mumford

[typed, Penn f. 3455]
Harvard University
19 Beaver Street
Cambridge, Mass.
September 25, 1928

Dear Mumford:

I am dreadfully concerned about Brooks. The point of view of the family is perhaps justified in view of unfortunate experiences in the past, but as you, of course, realize it is disastrous for the health of the very person they wish most to benefit. It is a peculiar thing that the nearest and dearest, who in one sense know the most about the inside history, should be the very ones least able to manage such a situation. Everybody will make mistakes, and because one mechanic puts sand in the carburetor it does not imply that one should never again intrust one's motor to a machine shop.

It seems from your description that it is inevitable that the poor fellow will find himself in a sanitarium. On the whole this is not as bad as it seems. In the better institutions there are more advantages than disadvantages. I believe that I know one man who could handle this situation as intelligently as it is possible to do so, namely Dr. Donald J. MacPherson, 270 Commonwealth Ave., Boston Mass. He is not an analyst by any strict interpretation of that term, but is an all around man, experienced, tactful and intelligent. I should advise the Brookses to come to Boston. There is no question that Van Wyck can be helped and it is criminal not to allow him this benefit. If there is anything that I can do I wish you would let me know.

As regards the question of Clarel, I have a definite reference somewhere that Melville was rewriting the poem during the year before it was published. I think that you are right about Melville's attempt to seek consolation in his isolation through an identification with Christ.

I will speak to Zinsser as soon as possible, as I believe he has considerable influence.

Sincerely,
Harry Murray
HAM: H

[typed, Penn f. 3455]
Harvard University
Psychological Clinic
19 Beaver Street
Cambridge, Mass.
October 27, 1928

Dear Mumford:

I have been kept posted in regard to Brooks' history. Of course my direct knowledge is meager but yet it is sufficient to convince me that the whole situation is really obvious enough in its essential features. I cannot agree with Dr. White's judgment in sending Van Wyck back to the Westport sepulcher, but it would be meddlesome and most presumptuous on my part to interfere.

I read your Herman Melville article with enthusiasm.[7] It is evident that we view the matter from the same Pisgahish outlook. It may be that I shall have nothing important to say after I have read your book. I should be disappointed if it developed that the difference between us was minute; because it would be like cutting off an arm to stop at this point.

Of course you understand that I am withholding a certain amount of information, none of which is of great importance, which I might give you to fill in a few insignificant crevices in your writing. This miserliness seems to me at the present time to be perfectly good cricket. It may be the only reason that I will have for continuing with my own work. If your book, on the other hand, fulfills the glorious promise of your New Republic article, I will be disgusted with myself for not having rendered up the final molecule. There is no one else to whose labors I should more gladly contribute. I hope that some day we may endlessly discourse of such matters.

There were a number of specially fine things you said which made the blood sizzle. Good luck to you with the finish of it. Have you decided on a title?

If you come up this way do not fail to notify me. I am here at 158 Mt. Vernon Street, Boston Mass.

Yours,
Henry A. Murray, Jr.
HAM: H

---

7. "The Significance of Herman Melville," *New Republic* (10 October 1928): 212–14.

[telegram, Western Union]

CAMBRIDGE MASS FEB 28

DEAR LEWIS MUMFORD HOSANNAS TO YOU THE BOOK IS MAGNIFICENT AND YOU ARE A MASTER YOU HAVE CONQUERED THE WHITE WHALE WITH GOOD FAITH AND WITHOUT MALICE THE WHOLE PROBLEM SEEMS TO HAVE BEEN SETTLED BY THE POET IN YOU HARRY MURRAY

[handwritten]
4002 Locust St.
Long Island City, N.Y.
1 March 1929

Dear Murray:

Your words make me proud and happy: I am dancing on air, for you are the only person competent to judge in entirety what I have done. And your generosity moves me to something nearer tears than exultation.

Gratefully
Lewis Mumford

[handwritten]
[LM] Ans 17 March 1929?
158 Mt. Vernon Street

Dear Lewis,

For the new title—blame the book which precipitated me into intimacy with you.

To begin with, you overdid yourself on me in the foreward.[8] I shriveled to microscopic dimensions before my own critical gaze. You see, my dear fellow, I should have given you All. Did I not write you that I was not giving you All? Because this will be the guilt that I will take into the grave.

Morison wanted me to review the book for the Quarterly, so that he lent me his copy for three hours on Friday night.[9] I was enormously impressed. It cast a spell over me & all idea of my own writing passed serenely & painlessly away into the ether. It was under the still-suffusing magical influence that I sent my telegram.

Today I received my copy,—which I will treasure coming from you—and now

8. In the preface to *Herman Melville,* Mumford expresses gratitude to Murray, "who shared with me his knowledge of certain Melville letters otherwise inaccessible—an act of pure chivalry, since Dr. Murray is himself at work on a biography of Herman Melville. Such deeds sweeten one's notions of human conduct: they give one not so much a feeling of gratitude as a renewed sense of human dignity, and I warmly place them on record" (vi).

9. Samuel Eliot Morison (1887–1976), distinguished American historian; founder and editor of the *New England Quarterly.* Murray's review appeared in *New England Quarterly* 2 (1929): 523–26.

I can set about reading & brooding over it at leisure. I have three months for the Quarterly review.

I wish it were some other journal. The idea of writing an article to join company with the domesticated effort of those pew-holders does not heat my blood. If you find it a bit chaste you will know that I wasn't able to banish the image of the Editors encrusted in their small gentlemanly & scholarly conceits. I did not feel I could refuse my neighbor Morison—whom I had never met before this evening.

I hardly feel like commenting on the Book after such a hurried acquaintance—but I will say a few things on second reading.

It is a whole. The background is dexterously sketched out—America in the 20s, 40s and 60s—the general climate of sentiment & level of culture.

A great business you make of the bourgeois—you efface him without Menckenesque rantings & thus prove yourself a free spirit. Your disposal of parents is likewise superb. I believe that you are a master of this kind of material i.e.—cultural ideas & and their interpretations. (It occurs to me that you are the one person in the world to do the Life of Charles Pierce—America's greatest philosopher—but more of this when we meet again.)

Your whole treatment of Melville is so similar to my own notions that I am really too prejudiced in your favor to give any objective criticism.

I thought your management of the sexual factors was so skillful that it seemed like the dawn of a new Age—another Freedom—freedom from an obsessional morbidity—either of abnegation or abandon.

I agreed with you almost word for word in your estimate of the adventure books, Mardi, Moby Dick & Pierre. You made the right—in my eyes—references to Blake, Dostoievsky, Beethoven & Wagner, etc.

I do not know yet whether I shall write—since Saturday a few bits of the previously evaporated material have returned, which may be seeds to recommence another centripetal movement about this great Man.

I believe that you did not quite bridge the gap between the concrete & the abstract—that in your treatment of Moby Dick & Pierre—you tended to flow off a bit into generalities which were not living realities—that you did not quite explain the growth of the whale—you rather stated him as an abstraction—almost a philosophic concept. However, I may change when I read again. Your book is a work of art—because you yourself have found yourself & have at your disposal a superior literary talent. I have mentioned hurriedly a few of the general topics which formed parts of the complete whole. This bit of fragmentation on my part is more or less irrelevant. The chief point is that you have found your way into the beating heart of a complex myth-creating man and by a supreme alchemy you have recreated him. I know of no biography—ancient or contemporary where there is to be found so much writing of the very first order—so tempered by poetic apprehension & wisdom. Wisdom—the book teems with it. You have the sanity of one who knows the shadows of the self.

I liked *particularly* what you said about the fusion of the pungent concrete with the spiritually creative in Moby Dick. That is the *core* of the modern freedom. No longer a divorce—no longer a compartmentalization of an exotic dream on the one hand & a materialistic substantiality on the other. And then again what you said about Moby Dick as a modern myth—that was another treasure I was nurturing.

What seems to remain are a few more facts—the product of some industrious snooping on my part; an infiltration into a deeper layer to feel the furnace when the elements were being commingled for Ahab; a more precise & intricately woven psychological analysis & synthesis to explain the breakdown & the family relations, etc.

This seems paltry when I range it along side your monument.

I honor you for writing such a book—It speaks to me of a new order

& so my salutations

Harry Murray

[typed]
4002 Locust Street
Long Island City, N.Y.
16 March 1929

Dear Harry:

Your telegram and your letter have done one fatal thing: they have robbed any other person's praise of my Melville of any interest or meaning: indeed, all other criticism must seem tepid and diffident alongside the things you have been generous enough to say. I know some of the book's weaknesses; and I realize that you will be able to detect weaknesses, other than matters of fact, which by some opacity of mine are still closed to me: so I take your praise with due humility. You are quite right about my failure to explain the genesis of the White Whale; I discovered this blank, to my horror, last November, when it was too late to rectify; and I comforted myself with the reflection that the last word was still far from being said, and such a lapse as this would perhaps serve to encourage you to keep right on with your plan. Had I not been deluded as to your character and purpose, before I met you, I should never have attempted such a comprehensive treatment of Melville; and I have such a guilty feeling about having gone on with it when I found out what you were up to that your own regrets about not giving me any more facts is nothing in comparison: so let us cancel out our reproaches and start from scratch again! I am delighted that you are going to review the book: had there not been a natural delicacy about suggesting this, I could easily have arranged for a criticism in some more public place than the New England Quarterly. Weaver did a very handsome review in the New York Post, without a trace of cattiness; and in general, I have been very lucky indeed; so much so, that I cast an anxious look occasionally up at the sky to see what new thunderbolts are about to fall; for the winter has been one long terror of illnesses, culminating in my little boy's almost too-late operation for a double mastoid; and I have come to look upon heaven's sudden kindnesses and largesse with a very dubious eye. Your suggestion about Charles Pierce shows that we have another bond, too: I could kick myself for my negative treatment of his generation in The Golden Day, for I should have dwelt upon Pierce and Emily Dickinson, and permitted the people with larger reputations to shrivel down naturally, by contrast, to their proper dimensions.[10] But is any life of Pierce possible: that is, are there documents, memories? I agree with you in our estimate of Pierce; and ever since reading his essays I have resented William James's attitude of charming condescension toward him. . . . By the way, I wonder if your assiduous researches have tempted you to look up the ship's log of the United States? The other day I received a long letter from an "admirer" of Melville in Washington, Mr. Nelson Gaskill, who had done this; and I will send it on to you as soon as I get round to answering him; but the main point that he makes is that there is no record at all in the ship's log of his having been called to the mast for punishment, or, what is more important, of his having fallen onto the sea. In other words, the best passage in White-Jacket is a feat of imagination. I was of course aware of Melville's invention at other points; but I confess I had not suspected the fall—and this vindicates him as an imaginative writer, even if it casts further factual doubts on Redburn. Hurrah!

I have not seen Brooks since the time I saw you last November; but from Eleanor's reports, he is marking time, and I judge from the quality and quantity of his work that he is no worse. At my instance, Eleanor has made arrangement with Dutton's to publish the Emerson if he will consent; and she has put this matter up to Dr. White, to broach to him. Has Mrs. Metcalf told you of the sweet punishment I have contrived for Paltsits? I have suggested she give the Melville mss. to the New York Public Library, on the condition that the library persuade the custodians of all other collections of Melville documents that are in the library to open them to public inspection! Paltsits, I understand from Yarmolinsky of the Russian department, has been stirred by my Melville to further activity on the letters: but the good Pole has a torpid liver, I am afraid, and it remains for us to see whether this will do you any good.[11] I am eager to see you, and am looking forward to your visit to New York. There is half a chance that I may run up to Boston early in April, to attend a New England planning conference: so one way or the other we will, I hope, meet.

Lewis

---

10. Lewis Mumford, *The Golden Day: A Study in American Experience and Culture* (1926).

11. Avrahm Yarmolinsky (1890–1975), head of the Slavonic Language Department at the New York Public Library; husband of the poet Babette Deutsch, also a friend of Mumford.

[typed]
4002 Locust Street
Long Island City, N.Y.
21 April 1929

Dear Harry:

Does the universe, in the long run, even things up, as Pierce and the laws of chance say: so that our friendship shall redeem the emptiness of Hawthorne's and Melville's, and my Sophie's delight in meeting you shall make up for the other Sophie's jealously of H.M.?[12] A rhetorical question, of course: but I feel that I have much to get out of you, perhaps a little to give; and the great regret I had in Edinburgh in 1925, that Geddes and I had not been contemporaries back in the eighties, is somewhat counterbalanced by discovering you.[13] He will be seventy-five next October, and has just sent me a touching plea to spend a few weeks with *him before it is too late*; and I find myself wishing that you could know him, too. . . . I've just had a letter from Frank Jewett Mather, with an item in it that I had never come across before; doubtless you have; but if you haven't it would be worth while taking note of.[14] I quote: "A reminiscence to close. When first I saw Elizabeth Melville, a transparent figure with lace covering her hands, I stupidly offer her mine. She hesitated and I held a hand which had never had fingers. It was a lesson in deportment which I have never forgotten. I tell this because it is one more landmark in Melville's domestic Calvary." I need not underline the dreadful questions that come to mind. But if her hand had been always without fingers, it could explain her ineptitude in housekeeping; and if it came by accident, a great many things might be cleared up by finding out when and how. Is this the unforgivable sin Mrs. Thomas darkly keeps to herself? Did Melville have any part in that accident? A ghastly thought, whether accident or frenzy was responsible . . . I have been thinking over the Pierce biography; but I can't fit it in with other tasks that more intimately link up with my present thinking, and so I defer it. I suspect that you yourself are the one to write it; and that you are merely gallantly attempting to avert a second rivalry, by withdrawing before it begins?

Lewis

[handwritten]
Ans 16 May 1929

Dear Lewis,

It is inevitable—

We shall make up for all the promising friendships in the world that came to

---

12. Sophia Hawthorne was "the other Sophie."

13. Patrick Geddes (1854–1932), Scots biologist, educator, and city planner in Edinburgh and India; corresponded with Mumford 1917–1932.

14. Frank Jewett Mather (1868–1953), Princeton art historian.

nought—we shall redeem those that became sluggish & ran to desert sands & those that were disrupted when integrity compromised with envy & malice; & all others that for unnamable reasons were blasted to dust.

Instantaneously, Mrs. Mumford was to me a Reality. She has the Thing. It makes no difference what she thinks of me, or of modern psychology—to me she is heroic, true and magnificent.

I told Felix Frankfurter about you both, & he told Justice Holmes about you both—It came about in this way:—The Judge was enormously thrilled by your book & sent Felix an S.O.S. for information—Perhaps you heard yourself—because he wanted the pleasure of meeting you.[15]

I know that you are Real. I don't care what you do or what you say—either Sophie or yourself—You can do no wrong—Impersonally & personally I have recognized you & no fitful fate can budge me.

I have discovered some far, far experiences in love—the farthest mysteries—the unspeakable—but in friendship—there are still walls. Aiken has no walls—but I have when I am with him.[16]

I tried not to be influenced by my affection for you when I scribbled off the two reviews—for instance—I tried to be critical—but perhaps I did not really succeed—I am more interested in your friendship than I am in the New England Society for the Preservation of the Wayside Inn (especially since they refused to buy Arrowhead 2 years ago when I offered it to them for $20,000)—but I am still more interested in a friendship that will stand the strain of printed criticism—honest criticism.[17]

(1) I didn't know about the Hands. She suffered from very painful arthritis. Her daughter's fingers were knotted into a clutch—My first guess would be—amputation to save pain.

(2) Pierce is not on my horizon—the next man against the sky is a myth & there is a woman with him & nobody else & they don't correspond to anyone that has died.

(3) If I could only know Geddes! I might consider 1930. Are you going? You had better. I have the money to give you for the trip. I have just sold a house & if you have six months of doctor's bills—Why not?

My regards to your wife. Don't forget Topsfield.

Harry

---

15. Felix Frankfurter (1882–1965) and Oliver Wendell Holmes Jr. (1841–1935) were distinguished jurists.

16. Conrad Aiken (1889–1973), poet and friend of Murray.

17. The other review of *Herman Melville* was "Timon of America," *Hound and Horn* 2 (1929): 430–32. The Wayside was Hawthorne's home, 1852–1853 and 1860–1864, near Concord, Massachusetts. Arrowhead was Melville's home, 1850–1863, near Pittsfield, Massachusetts.

[handwritten]
[LM] Ans 16 May (1929) probably
158 Mt. Vernon St.
Boston

Dear Lewis,

Since writing to you about Mather's note—it has occurred to me that he is speaking of the daughter—Elizabeth Melville—which makes it more probable that the fingers were amputated for arthritis.

I read MacLeish in the Bookman & thought him absurd & told him so Friday Night.[18]

MacL. has separated himself from his own entrails, he believes a work of Art—a pure thing untainted and uncontaminated by the human mind—In fact he is not at all interested in the human soul—

He does not bear looking at (But he is a fine fellow & brilliant & has skill of a high order) Don't you agree?

Harry

[typed]
4002 Locust Street
Long Island City, N.Y.
16 May 1929

Dear Harry:

Your first letter reached me in Chicago: a heady cordial at the end of a fine dinner—for the week I spent at Meiklejohn's Experimental College, though arduous, was refreshing: for the first time all winter I felt completely alive.[19] He has started something in Wisconsin: the germs of a genuine education. He begins by completely disrupting the students: they are not used to freedom and at first it knocks many of them to pieces, but those who recover, and they are the majority, are more capable of independent work at 18 than most Ph.D.'s are ten years later. I talked on the development of American culture and gave one lecture on Melville and the Tragic Sense of Life: and everything went very well. It was good to be back in an atmosphere of ideas, instead of among the bored journalists and tired-businessmen-of-culture who hide in the rat-holes of New York. Not that I see very much of them, but the sense that they are there is depressing. I now see more clearly, incidentally, what my own task is, and what further preparation I need before I can get fully under way: and before I start on another book I must patch up all the weak places in my education. Did I ever tell you of my experience in Geddes's old apartment in Edinburgh, when I came upon a portrait of him at thirty or thirty-five, a man eager,

18. Archibald MacLeish, review of *Herman Melville, Bookman* 69 (April 1929): 183.

19. Alexander Meiklejohn (1872–1965), president of Amherst College (1912–1923); founded an experimental college at Wisconsin (1926–1932).

active, intense, plastic, not yet limited by his thought-cage, and felt that if only I had known him then, instead of thirty years later, we might have reinforced each other, complementing each other's weaknesses, and have given something great to the world. This feeling renewed itself in me after I'd talked with you in Boston: I had found another Geddes! And I have been quietly chuckling to myself ever since at the thought of it; all the more, no doubt, because I feel so helpless, tongue-tied, mute, and ineffectual when I am in the presence of the "other" Geddes; for there is no possibility of give and take with him any more, and the main question that governs my relation to him is how much of the living spirit of Geddes I can salvage. Falling in friendship is a rarer thing, I think, than falling in love; and while I have a handful of partial friendships, I have yet to experience a friendship that is complete, that involves all one's attitudes and interests—with no disguises or only profile views. Heaven knows such friendships are rare; probably more so than a complete marriage; but the two who achieved it would constitute an army! Don't fret about any criticisms you have made or may make: my marriage, in its early and very stormy days, survived Sophy's doubts about my work and disparagement of my literary aims: where there is an underlying sympathy one can stand doses of criticism which would be poisonous if administered by a hostile personality. As for my going abroad, your generosity made me dance: but fortunately there is not the slightest need for it: the Melville has removed all financial difficulties for at least the next two years, and my reluctance to travel is due chiefly to the disappointment of not being able to go with Sophy—which we had planned to do last January.[20] All that happened this spring with little Geddes has undermined our not-too-blithe willingness to leave him behind in the first place: although he is now in good health and almost finally healed, we can't quite face it; and if we took him with us, the free and footloose joy of the trip would be gone. I have at last decided to go by myself for six weeks, through August probably: but it is a sense of duty, rather than the inner man, who has made this decision. I know it will help me assemble my thoughts and that I will probably come back refreshed: but the going itself still leaves an ashy taste in my mouth.

MacLeish has an acute mind: but he is in the same sterile predicament as T. S. Eliot, and he is bound to feel inimical to any work which does not accept that predicament. The only thing I disliked about his review was his assumption that I was not aware of what I was doing—namely, spoiling the formal perfection of a single theme, stated, elaborated, rounded-off, in order to achieve a complete presentation of Melville's work. The result is a certain intermittent dullness, and at times—I regret this—apparent lack of perspective on Melville's lesser works: but I made the choice deliberately when I realized that no one had ever read all of Melville's books and reported on what was in them: my loss was Melville's gain, and it seemed to

---

20. The Literary Guild published an edition of Mumford's *Herman Melville,* earning him $6700. Donald L. Miller, *Lewis Mumford: A Life* (New York: Weidenfeld and Nicholson, 1989), 283.

me a precious small sacrifice to make, particularly since I had showed in the Golden Day that I could, if I pleased, write a tight, formally complete work. Of course, I can't philosophically, accept MacLeish's isolation of the intellect: it's the same weak and essentially brutal piece of surgery that Krutch makes in The Modern Temper; whereas all good science and metaphysics established a multiple, reciprocal, and organic relationship, which, in the interests of truth, would ultimately connect the kind of blacking Melville used on his boots with his notion of blackness and whiteness in the human soul—but if only we had a name for this truth and relationship![21] Wholeness: synthesis: organism: these all indicate something, but are pretty useless as handles. This manner of looking at the world slows up all immediate, practical results; and paradoxically, the isolators of the intellect are looking for such results as ardently as the financier who wants to turn the results of the laboratory into a commodity in as short a time as possible. MacLeish and Eliot, at bottom, want to be saved; or, what comes to the same thing with them, absolved from effort.

But more of this later. Sophy and I will probably make up a jaunt to Boston the weekend of the 25th—I have to speak to a New England planning Conference the following Tuesday—and we hope you and Mrs. Murray will be in town then.

Lewis

[typed]
4002 Locust Street
Long Island City
1 June 1929

Dear Harry:

Our Topsfield visit was a great delight to both of us: and the impression of it is still simmering pleasantly in our bosoms.[22] I am sending you a copy of MacKaye's The New Exploration, not in the hope that you would will read it cover to cover, but just so that you may have a sense of other people rallying to the things you have been carrying around privately in your trips through the countryside.[23] I sweated much and accomplished little in my regional planning speech: heat and lack of sleep took the edge off my talk: but it was very touching to see how pleased the New England planners were at the notion of three New Yorkers making the trip to Boston and joining in the conference without having an ax to grind! A little disinterestedness goes a long ways. Your symbolic house is embedded in my mind: that is the value of symbols—they stick better than abstract ideas.[24] I am glad you are

21. Joseph Wood Krutch, The Modern Temper: A Study and a Confession (1929).

22. Murray had purchased a farm in Topsfield, Massachusetts, in 1927.

23. Benton MacKaye, The New Exploration: A Philosophy of Regional Planning (1928).

24. Mumford describes Murray's "symbolic house" in a letter (1 June 1929) to Patrick Geddes: "You should see the consulting chambers he is equipping for himself in his country home—doing a great part

treating Moby-Dick in relation to Melville's life: I shied away from that, but doubt-less would have read much more deeply into the book itself if I hadn't. The Satur-day Review has just given me Pierre to review; and I have been mulling over your notion that there was an actual basis for the incest theme. Of which more later. Please note down any more books you may think of that I should now be reading, particularly in the sciences. A few years ago I did a select bibliography of 3000 titles for a symmetrical library, a sort of key library to all departments of knowledge and experience, and was appalled at the number of important works I had never even glanced at.[25] Even I, alas! am a specialist, much though I try to avoid it. Perhaps the solution is to be symbolically acquainted, or at least oriented to, all branches of thought, though actually the most erudite can only half-master a few. The round-ness exists in life, not in multiplying the radii of knowledge.

Lewis

[handwritten]
Topsfield
Massachusetts
[LM] Ans 7 July 1929

Dear Lewis

Some correspondent, ain't I?

Ungrateful too—after basking in the high ozone of your company for 2 days & then the book, the letter & and the magazine. The haggish Trio played me a little joke in the beginning by hiding your billish looking envelope amongst my other June 1st bills—which I never pay for 3 weeks—hence you remained unopened for that time.

—I am ready to dig bulwarks & plant trees & amaranthus across the streams of metropolitan traffic—anything to ameliorate, muffle, screen, beautify, perfume or sweeten that ever streaming stream. MacKaye is a theosophic prophet of the real

---

of the painting and carving himself. One enters a dark, seventeenth century room, with chains, hand-cuffs, and instruments of torture hanging on the wall: the room of repressions, the burdens of past evils. Under treatment, the patient rebels against this past and climbs a flight of stairs to leave it behind him. His next consultations take place in a beautiful flame colored room, black, red, orange, yellow—the stage of his individual Götterdämmerung, where all his old idols are consumed. He is now ready to work out his problem more concretely, and he passes over to a great atelier and workshop, where he may paint, carve, carpenter, sculpt, working out his fantasies in maturer form. That over, he goes down stairs to a modern room, from which he either goes out into the world, to the same society he left, or works out his salvation in more withdrawn fashion, by passing through one further tunnel of trials, with a skeleton barring his way at the end of it until he climbs a tower stairs, and emerges with a new view of the world." Frank G. Novak Jr., ed., *Lewis Mumford and Patrick Geddes: The Correspondence* (London: Rout-ledge, 1995), 287–88.

25. In 1927 Mumford selected titles for the Manhattan office library of the J. Walter Thompson ad-vertising agency.

Scot stamp—a bit obsessive, but apostolic in the name of normal grace.—Thanks awfully—here at last is a Cause in Politics—I will write every candidate to find out whether he's read MacKaye & and will vote for Leaves.

I haven't read Geddes yet; as for the present I am immersed in other cogitations & web-spinnings—but I thank you for it. Some afternoon I'll purr with it in my lap & drink a Julep to you & yours—thinking of you listening to the Pewees pewing in your country sequestration—

An idea—it seemed to me brilliant—Ralph Eaton—whom you met down here—as you know is Prof of Phil. at Harvard & Whitehead's lieutenant,—he was approaching a crisis when you saw him—of the Van Wyck B's type.[26] Three weeks ago he & his wife parted. He is still in confusion, needs a change & he wants to get away from all kinds of rehashing of his problem. He has been trying to finish his book on Logic without success—My thought—I wonder whether Lewis has a companion for the steamer to Scotland: You spoke of readings in Physics & Philosophy & Science—& I immediately thought how much you would have to exchange 'entre vous'—reciprocities of a complimentary & fertilising kind. How does it strike you? What are your plans? Are you alone? Out of choice?

I have so much to say to you. I am dropsical with it—Do you mind returning the enclosed—I wince at one or two phrases in the H&H article—a friend of mine in New Bedford wants to know where you got the Melville wharf incident. He knows something of Ryder—in case you ever write of him—I saw Weaver for a moment. He is on a new phase—the rotund sophisticate—Gidesque—he has dropped H.M. Best regards to Sophie. Will you tell me of the latest about Geddes' progeny.

Harry

[typed]
Amenia, New York
7 July 1929

Dear Harry:

I am sorry that my plebian airs kept us apart for a few weeks but no matter: your letter and your reviews made ample amends. Your praise is generous and your rod is gentle; in fact, if I was disappointed at all in your comments upon my failures in the Melville, it was the fact that you had not sailed into them more heavily. I didn't get to the bottom of Melville's unconscious, and I am inclined to think that the reason is that I have never opened the trap door to my own, or done more than take a hasty peak at the cellar: never, that is, since, after going through the war

---

26. Eaton was unstable; he fell in love with Christiana Morgan; underwent analysis with Jung in Zurich; committed suicide in 1932 after disappearing from an institution near Topsfield where Murray had placed him. See Forrest G. Robinson, *Love's Story Told: A Life of Henry A. Murray* (Cambridge: Harvard Univ. Press, 1992), 209; Claire Douglas, *Translate This Darkness: The Life of Christiana Morgan* (New York: Simon and Schuster, 1993), 209–10.

I turned aside from dramatic writing, because of some inward block, and applied myself to political and philosophic criticism. I knew of course that the whole key to his life was there: I even set apart the chapter, Azzageddi, for dealing with it; and then, when the time came, I muffed the business completely: and the result is that my rational picture of Melville has the same relation to the real portraiture as the Arrowhead portrait by the itinerant painter has to one of Rembrant's heads. It is amusing to look back and see how, despite my awareness of what ought to be done, I tricked myself into this; how in part it was due to my animus against Weaver's melodramatics, an attempt to take the same facts and explain them by the hypothesis of normality instead of "insanity," and how in part it was due to the fact that I appropriated Moby-Dick to serve as a vehicle for my own philosophy, and so, though conscious of the turmoil, kept it limited and in hand—like a fireman with a hose, cooly spraying the flames of Mt. Etna. I resented Krutch's criticism of my weakness here: but I could have taken a much harder drubbing from you without wincing.[27] I remember, some time last December, when all that I had done was irrevocable, suddenly becoming aware that the real title for the book should have been: The Unreturning One, and that I should have emphasized that aspect in all the later bafflements. I say none of these things by way of apology: for I wrote the book under the most favorable mental and physical conditions possible and I said to myself at the time that if I failed to make the thing live heroically I could not, for once, blame the state of my digestion or my marital relations or my finances. But although I am used to guarding against the effect of anger, irritation, or ill-health when I make my judgements, I did not count upon the bias of euphoria: to the extent that my eyes were so wide open that they proved for all practical purposes, to be closed! . . . I have had a bleak week or two trying to make up my mind finally about the European trip, for the plans that were originally made for Sophie and Geddes during this period have come to naught, and I dislike the prospect of leaving Sophie in boredom and lonesomeness whilst I, very half-heartedly, follow the call of duty and vanity in Europe. I stewed so long over all the possible alternatives that, though the conflicts were all conscious ones, the effect was almost as bad as if they were all secret and repressive: and I looked at myself wryly, and wondered whether I was deliberately working myself up into a breakdown so as to escape making a rational choice. I went down to New York the other day to arrange about my passage, still stewing and fretting, and spent a gruesome night in that inferno, listening to my own thoughts and the periodic choking of a child with whooping cough: and after the misery of the night I awoke the next morning with my mind suddenly composed and settled, prepared during the next fortnight to face any eventuality, even the departure. This letdown in my morale is partly due to the fact that, with the winter at last behind me, I am for the first time relaxed and off guard: the events of January and February are claiming their emotional tribute! Hence my

---

27. Joseph Wood Krutch's review in *Nation* 128 (8 May 1929): 561.

failure to respond generously to your suggestion about Eaton; for I need the quiet and silence of the voyage to recuperate a little more firmly: and I fear we should be bad medicine for each other, at least on the voyage out. I sail the nineteenth for Cherbourg, whence I shall go via Paris to Geneva; and I will return from Southampton on the Majestic, 4 September, if my present plans hold. If Eaton goes to Europe, please let me know where he is and I shall look him up. My address will be in care of the Bankers Trust Co, Place Vendome, Paris, till 10 August; after that, in care of the Sociological Society, 65 Belgrave Road, London, S.W. 1. . . . As for the incident at the New Bedford Wharf: it happened to John Gilbert, the American composer, better known I suppose in Paris than here. As a young man, he had fallen asleep drunk one night on the wharf, and awoke the next morning to see H.M. quietly sitting there. Gilbert, on falling into conversation, observed that H.M. knew all the nautical terms, and he asked H.M. if he knew his favorite author, Herman Melville. H.M. then revealed his identity. I got the story from Gilbert's brother-in-law, Gilbert himself being now dead. . . . My latest reading has been Müller-Freienfels' Mysteries of the Soul: in parts very acute, and in other parts curiously superficial; but worth getting hold of.[28] How promptly you put your fingers on MacKaye's weakness, his obsessive narrowness, which is in turn, too, the secret of his strength. His style is as relentless as a trip hammer; and though I tried to edit it a little and introduce a little variety MacKaye inexorably predominates. But in real life, he is very lovable and has a prime colloquial sense of humor: so all his friends welcome him, even whilst they smother a yawn. The last three weeks up here have ironed many of the wrinkles out of both Sophie and Geddes; almost all the strain and tension has gone; and, meanwhile, we are getting tough and brown. I trust your little girl escaped the measles?[29] I should have inquired about this in my note. Sophie joins me in warm greetings.

Lewis

[typed]
Amenia
New York
26 July 1929

Dear Harry:

Your flattery would have fallen on heedless ears, were it not for the fact that I postponed my sailing a week: I now leave on the Ile de France Friday. The postponement has enabled me to go away with a good heart: for at the last moment, when it was almost too late, the simple, the inevitable solution occurred to me: namely to take charge of Geddes myself, and pack Sophie off to Martha's Vineyard for a vacation from both of us. She was a little dazed by the notion: it is the first time

28. Richard Müller-Freienfels, *Mysteries of the Soul* (1929).
29. Murray's daughter, Josephine, was born in 1921.

she has left me, though I have left her, alas! often: but cottoned to it readily: and from vague, ejaculatory letters I gather that she has enjoyed herself. It is at least a brief psychic vacation: and she really has no need of a physical one: and by cutting a week of my stay abroad it will ease things all round. The only thing I regret now is that I should have been sunk so completely in sloth and torpor as not to think of it at least a week before. But better late than never. I am ordering Wolf Solent for Sophie, and you shall have her verdict: I am reserving the Magic Mountain for the steamer.[30] My sociology lectures have at last shaped themselves: Magic and Science in Modern Society: and I have suddenly discovered, in the act of thinking them out, that I know far too little about magic, and that, for my purposes, no one else knows quite enough either. What I should like to know is if secular magic has always existed side by side with religious magic, or if it has gradually issued out of it? The secular kind seems externalized, like Newtonian science: hence it is not as subjectively effective and replenishing as religious magic: hence, too, perhaps it must try to get down to business and achieve external results. If historians were ethnologists, or if ethnologists would only work a little more on the institutions of the Kulturfölker we'd be much forwarder with this sort of problem. Despite my ignorance, the lectures look good now: at least they seem to point to something: and I shall step on the boat with an easier mind as well as a lighter heart. I trust your work is prospering, and if you are now deeply in the midst of it, don't bother to write even a line: correspondence, like all the rest of one's vital debts, including birth and upbringing and marriage, can never really be squared off: and I'll write again anyway, if the spirit moves. My address will be a roving one: so if you should have any occasion to write, send the letter up here.

Lewis

[handwritten]
Topsfield
Massachusetts
[LM] Ans 10 Sept 29

Dear Lewis,

You must tell me whether to read 'The Magic Mt.' I have always held it in reserve,—for an illness perhaps. I have read Freienfels as far as The Americanization of the Soul—which looks rather good and found it either banal or utter piffle. He has picked up the vocabulary of the Intuitional School of philosophical psychology (descendants of the Transcendentalists & Fichte, Hegelians, etc.), mixed it with a little Adler,—'style of life' & Jung & a spatter of Austrian pepper & called it a book. I am terribly sorry I cannot agree about it; it is to me first words, words, words—of course, *that* is German—which I like when good as in Spengler, let us say—but dislike it in this style,—pretentious, as if the author was saying 'I'll let you into a se-

---

30. John Cowper Powys, *Wolf Solent* (1929); Thomas Mann, *The Magic Mountain* (1927).

cret,' 'I'll show you the 'essence'—& then we find windy phrases. The essence is feeling—if one wants to grasp it intellectually, one must refer it to the apperceptive subject. The essence of a work of art consists in what was being felt by the man who created it & how it makes other persons feel—persons of different nerve delicacies—in different straits, strata, lands, times—etc. If you want to grasp it with feeling then you write poetry—The first is empirical psychology & the second art. Freienfels thinks that he is writing about generalizations derived from facts, but he is in truth trying to put his own boundless feelings & desires for life into philosophical terms. This is projection writing—animating the world with your own fervorous expansions—I am addicted to this—hence the Rise. You never told me about your Sociology lectures & I do not quite understand now—

What is magic? Well, magic may be good magic—Poetry; or bad magic—Freienfels—Psychology, theosophy, psychoanalysis & all cults are mostly magic & of course Religion is magic. But what do you mean by secular magic? Magic, I should say, was the Art-science of getting things done without the effort of applying yourself to a study of the natural laws governing the object itself. In the past if you wanted the Gods, or Nature or the Earth to work in your behalf you touched things, carried things around your neck, anointed yourself with fluids, prayed, sang, danced, embraced, copulated & so forth—a good deal of physical effort, but not psychological effort—it's Tom Sawyer and the Fences again. Work is what you have to do (Necessity & applied Science & physical force) & Play is what you want to do—(in other words magic—creative fancy, Emotion).

Nowadays, I should think that these words could be made to apply to (1) Exerting power over physical objects & men's bodies (Science) & (2) Exerting power over psychological objects—minds (Magic).

Magic also has the connotation of something Bogus—You might let me divide Magic then into (Good) & (Bad)—Everything that avowedly & truly & directly speaks to man's feeling (cf. Poetry, Literature & psychology at its best in private conferences—parts of the New Testament, etc.)—should be considered Good Magic—but everything that tries to subtly misinterpret nature; that holds out hopes to man for his body—for things—that is Bad Magic.

Religion is only good for the intellectually paralysed or dishonest members of the community. There are deeper roots, that no present Religion taps—

But I haven't found it yet—secular magic? Is it a waterfall in Central Park, the Dolly Sisters, the Prohibition amendment, Y.M.C.A.s, a Kiwanis Jubilee, or the Skull & Bones? The Cross=religious magic Fratpin=secular magic

May you prosper in abundance
Harry

[typed]
Amenia, New York
10 September 1929

Dear Harry:

I have just come back from an afternoon's reverie in the apple-orchard; and I am afraid that the letter I wrote you there may evaporate before I can put it on paper. There is nothing like half a dozen apples, a warm day, the slight discomfort of the stubble and the scent of wild carrot to stir up one's thoughts: old Geddes says that the apple is the most thought-stimulating of fruits: hence our ancestral fall by way of it! Whisky for courage, wine for conversation, liqueurs for love: but cider for thought; at all events, the juice of the apple is in me and this letter is the result. Your letter just caught up with me. It followed me to England, where I did not go; for my trip was a brief one, consisting of a week's seminar at Zimmern's School of International Studies, a few amiable dinners and drinks, and nothing more.[31] I've been back three weeks. When I got there I found that Europe was not in me, and that I was regurgitating the thought of it violently. Many causes: swollen tonsils on the steamer, one last day of bad weather topt by a night of sleeplessness and a harried day of travel: and no time whatever to rest up before I plunged into my lectures. Until I reached Geneva I went through five days of black depression—if only I'd known what they were like before last summer! They must have been something akin to what Melville felt when he walked along the strand of Joppa. Geneva cleared everything up: companionship and intellectual stir, but I was in no mood to go on alone, with the prospect of returning to a highly disordered household: so I came back immediately. I am glad I did. We've all had time to rest up, and little Geddes has to face a tonsillectomy before the fall closes in. We are still a little jumpy with the effects of last winter: it wears off more slowly than our outer health indicates: and I have resolved to abstain from writing any more masterpieces until another year, at least, passes: what will happen in the meanwhile will be only valetudinarian busy work. I have forgotten what I said in praise of Müller-Freienfels: I daresay I wrote you while I was still in the passive mood of absorbing him and attempting to identify myself with his point of view, and had not reached the stage of criticism; indeed, the only thing that lingers is his account of his boyhood but I am glad that you sailed into him and demolished him: for it makes me feel a little easier about Wolf Solent! I read the first book faithfully, and skipped through the second, eking out the blank places by questioning Sophie; I read and read until I found myself too irritated to go on. Parts of it were very good; more than once I said to myself: Yes, this is the real thing; but I was shocked by his way of skipping the difficult parts—like actually getting Wolf married to Gerda—and vexed by all the fake mystery, wickedness, sinisterness, and the macabre touches

---

31. The International Summer School in Geneva (1925–1929), founded and directed by the British political scientist Alfred Zimmern (1879–1957); Mumford had lectured there in 1925.

which mean villainy no more than a coal heaver's complexion means sin. Something genuine is undoubtedly there: a real inner experience of Pan and his many earth-moods; and the women are all well-felt and well-understood, particularly Gerda: but the hero's overstressed reactions to every aspect of his new environment gives an air of falsehood—for me—to the whole book. He isn't wicked: the people around him aren't wicked either; and his way of clinging to that illusion recalls Huckleberry Finn much more than it does an approximately adult person. The theatrical pretense spoiled even the good parts of it for me—and I do not deny the good parts. Again and again I felt like shaking Powys; for he had within his hands the making of a great book, and fumbled it. I was not consciously biased by a slight personal acquaintance with the Powys family; but on looking back upon my reaction, I see that it squares up with my knowledge of them particularly of Llewellyn and John. Some childish love of pantomime, of exhibiting himself and shocking people has tempted John to sacrifice a great career as a writer to a shadowy triumph as a lecturer; the faults in the book run through the grain of his life. Perhaps I am wrong, of course; and have automatically closed my mind to a reality you approach and embrace readily; if it's my limitations I'm exposing in the criticism, well, that's that! As for The Magic Mountain, it proved the worst book in the world for me to read on the steamer: but it is a grand, a ponderously magnificent work, and now that I review it in health I see that certain parts of it have already woven into my consciousness like certain fragments of The Brothers Karamazov or War and Peace, as parts of my life, not merely as something read. By all means read it: but don't reserve it for an illness. I daresay your medical preparation will be some protection against the revolting physical details: but the atmosphere itself has an insidious invalidism in it, which the keen intellectual discussions of some of the characters doesn't remove. But the people—Hofrat Behrens, Settembrini, the classic idealist, Naphta, the profound Catholic reactionary, Mynheer Pepperkorn, even the still young German hero—"life's delicate child" make a marvelous gallery; and Mann makes none of the obvious possible missteps in carrying out his fable. It is a picture of life, but life on the down-curve, life reversed, with reality, our time and our space, become a phantom, and disease become a value. . . . I have been helpless before Eddington's The Nature of the Physical World; and it would take more than a course in advanced physics to make me able to cope with it; but I have read Haldane's Organism and Environment with profound admiration, and I am looking forward to his newest philosophic work, which is announced, I see, for the fall. You of course know his Mechanism, Life, Personality?[32]

We are in the exciting act of buying a house up here, with all the incidental calculations and plannings: I need not dilate. How has your work gone this summer?

---

32. Arthur Stanley Eddington, *The Nature of the Physical World* (1928); John Scott Haldane, *Organism and Environment as Illustrated by the Psychology of Breathing* (1917), *Mechanism, Life, and Personality: An Examination of the Mechanistic Theory of Life and Mind* (1914).

You of course got Paltsits' publication; but did you run across Mr. Gleim's theory of Moby Dick—Swedenborgian influences—in The New England Quarterly?[33] Evening is falling and the paper is coming to an end: so I pause.

Lewis

[handwritten]
Topsfield
Massachusetts
[LM] To ans in pers 14 Oct '29

Dear Lewis,

[. . .] The Ethan Brand item is of the deepest mysteries—Melville never saw the 1849 Ethan Brand in the Boston Museum, but did see the 1850 Ethan B. in the Dollar Magazine (January). The two printings are identical. Hence he read the great invective against the Stars & the unrelenting destinies at almost the time that he was writing his own. He had also Tamburlaine of Marlowe with him. I think Hawthorne was a kind of untouchable separate one who held a mirror before Melville, that he might see Ahab glaring out of his own bloodshot eyes. Hawthorne's very passivity might have forced Melville to crystallize his forces. Hawthorne's role was like an analyst's—or like some analysts' & the transference phenomena was not dissimilar—But yet that does not explain Ethan Brand—

Harry

[handwritten]
[LM] Ans 10 Feb 30

Dear Lewis,

Terribly sorry to miss you in N.Y.—Hope you & Sophie & Geddes are well—I was busy at all other times in N.Y.—had tickets for the Gotterdamerung & and had to reprise Gladys B's, etc.

I have missed seeing your recent writings. Let me announce for all time that I am not 'au courant' in literary matters & hence may easily be unaware that you have just written something startlingly good. For instance has your Process & Reality article been published? I want to see it—Whitehead thinks a lot of the Golden Day & of You. I should like to feel that I could count on reading everything that you wrote—It renews me with new wonder for life. You spoke once of sending me a series of 4 articles that appeared in the Tribune Supplement???—Sometime will you refer me to about a dozen of the recent things that please you the most—I will find them in the Library.[34] Without them I go back to your Melville to recapture your

---

33. William S. Gleim, "A Theory of Moby-Dick," *New England Quarterly* 2 (1929): 402–19.

34. The series appeared in *New York Herald Tribune Books*: "Prelude to the Present," 11 January 1931, 1; "The Mood of a Decade," 18 January 1931, 1; "Predicament of Emptiness," 25 January 1931, 1; "Autopsy Upon an Immortal," 8 February 1931, 1.

heroic flavor again. Do you, by the way, know Mr. Jack Chapman? If not read his Life of Wm. Lloyd Garrison. It is short & has some of your mettle in it.[35]

As companion pieces to your 'Mysteries of the Soul' I have recently been interested in Middleton Murry's 'God' & Fausset's 'The Proving of Psyche.'[36] I think the former is Lost, but he's in possession of a certain instinct for the right trails,—Dostoeivski, Keats, Shakespeare, Melville, etc. Fausset—intrigues me—I wonder how much he knows, i.e. has proved at the hand of his own Ecstasy. I am very much occupied by that problem at present—the stubborn actuality of exaltation & misery & its relation to the eroticism of the mind—the rhythms of the two—knowing it solar plexuswise & writing metaphysical phantasies of it. I am for a very tough Romanticism that is somehow an allegorical elaboration of the Actual & that never projects itself into hallucinations—except to return again very certainly; to contend step by step against the brutish world. This sounds trite enough—I suppose everybody believes that; but I am interested in that fuzz-edged, fogfumed zone where we begin to make up high toned phrases & grandiose images to anaesthetize our realization that we have not concretely formed that for which we were starving. Personally I am terribly happy despite the fact that I have become so utterly lost in certain psychological problems that the larger expanse & Melville have temporarily dissolved—

We are planning to go abroad on a cheap cabin steamer May 25—Jo & Josephine to stay all summer, whereas I am returning about July 1—England—Lakes, Yorkshire, London, Paris, Provence, Zurich & Home. I walked up Bald Mt. today & thought of you & Sophie & lying on that cedar-studded slope, talking our drifting imagery. I am dying to talk to you but don't bother to answer this.

Harry

P.S. I took the liberty to talk to Pres. Lowell. I wanted him to make you a Prof. of English & put you at the head of one of these New Houses (Colleges).[37] I thought you would actually have more time for your writing & also $6,000 besides. You'll probably hear nothing from it & won't want it if you do.

35. John Jay Chapman, *William Lloyd Garrison* (1913).

36. John Middleton Murry, *God: Being an Introduction to the Science of Metabiology* (1929); Hugh l'Anson Fausset, *The Proving of Psyche* (1929).

37. Abbott Lawrence Lowell, president of Harvard, 1909–1933.

[typed]
Lewis Mumford
4002 Locust Street
Long Island City, N.Y.
10 February 1930

Dear Harry:

Your letter made me realize how much I'd missed you this winter. It was good to get it: for though it is hard to restore shaken confidence, once one's energies have knit together again, an additional fillip sets one bountifully and impetuously in motion: and your letter was that fillip. A queer summer was that I left behind: and this is a queer winter, too, but for just the opposite reason, for my old strength and pugnacity have all come back again; and despite little interruptions, like Sophie's illness through the greater part of December, I have been riding on the top of a long steady wave that still hasn't reached its crest. What have I to show for it? Precious little except my good health and poise: it is only during the last week that I have begun to write again on the level I left off at a year and a half ago: and all my desultory reviewing and essay writing contains nothing that I'd care to bring to your notice, my "review" of Whitehead being little better than a notice that the book was published, since I haven't thoroughly grappled with Process and Reality yet.[38] Still: something has happened: out of last summer's disintegration something firmer and better seems to be coming through again in me. I have left behind one or two adolescent fears and inhibitions; and, out of the new release, have begun to write poetry again: if indeed the feeble verses I used to write ten years ago, or the slack compromise of the Little Testament can be dignified with such a title.[39] It is queer, and it may not last, this sense of rejuvenation; for it is partly based on the fact that I have temporarily, for the first time, inhibited my usual impulse to turn my back resolutely on any other girl than Sophie that there was the faintest possibility of my falling in love with: and though I haven't fallen, in any full and final sense of the word, the mere recognition of the fact that cowardice had acted quite as much as loyalty as the restraining element has given me a firmer bottom all round—and particularly in my relations with Sophie, which is something that can be easily put alongside the Ambiguities that tormented poor Pierre.[40] Meanwhile, I gave my Dartmouth lectures, with a certain satisfaction, and I have been plowing slowly through the literature of Aesthetics, in preparation for a little book on the arts I in-

---

38. Alfred North Whitehead, *Process and Reality: An Essay in Cosmology* (1929); Mumford's review in *New Republic* 61 (18 December 1929): 117–18.

39. "The Little Testament of Bernard Martin Aet. 30," in *The Second American Caravan: A Yearbook of American Literature,* ed. Alfred Kreymborg, Lewis Mumford, and Paul Rosenfeld (1928); autobiographical fiction.

40. Mumford is referring to his developing relationship with Catherine Bauer (1905–1964), who wrote on housing and urban planning; their love affair lasted through 1934.

tend to do this spring: and, like a thousand other exasperated critics, I have just written a long essay demolishing the New Humanism and—but that is quite enough; and I need scarcely add that I have been editing the American Caravan, too.[41] Have you read Haldane's philosophy and the Sciences yet?[42] It is an elaboration of his earlier little book on mechanism and vitalism, and very good. Robert Graves's Good by to All That is the best of the numerous war autobiographies I have read: it apparently took him and Aldington ten years to effect a Catharsis: and perhaps it would be worth while to set one of your students to timing the interval of recovery and seeing if there was any rhythm in it: there was a great crop of Civil War memories in this country to serve as control.[43] Outside these books, my reading has been of a narrow kind; and when one has been wading through literally hundreds of manuscripts, as I have been doing, every added work, no matter how pleasurable at any other time, becomes a horrid duty. Your postscript about your suggestion to Lowell warmed me: I was able to be all the more grateful because of the extreme unlikelihood of anything coming out of it. It is the sort of job that I would probably do to Queen's taste after I am forty-five; but at present all the method and regularity I can muster is needed for my work, and I am afraid I would not stand the harness well. Did you ever read Mann's Death in Venice? Is an extraordinarily interesting psychological study, and I recommend it; but I mention it now because he draws a portrait of an author, probably himself, who by tremendous concentration and moral effort brings his talents, which are something short of genius, to the highest state of cultivation they will stand. I am that sort of a writer, making up by conscious acquisition, in so far as it can be made up, for the weak places in my original gifts. I have no specific literary talent: my earliest essays showed no more than a mastery of grammar, and my first verse was the feeblest doggerel: there was none of the promise that makes one recognize a Hilda Conkling at sight, nor has there been that sudden growth which turned Melville into a colossal manipulator of words within a few short years.[44] Some arcane eruption inside of me might possibly unleash the demons that I need: there was a hint of that in the fact that I began writing the Little Testament, with a furious vitality, after a single night's departure from the usual routine of impeccable domesticity and sobriety: but one cannot turn on such eruptions as one would light a firecracker, and failing that, I must go along expanding on my present base. Hence the virtues of regularity and certainty and decorum, which would be so helpful if I needed a bal-

41. "Towards an Organic Humanism," in *The Critique of Humanism*, ed. C. Hartley Grattan (1928). Mumford served as an editor of *The American Caravan: A Yearbook of American Literature* (title varies) 1927–1929, 1931, 1936.

42. J. S. Haldane, *The Sciences and Philosophy* (1929); Mumford's review in *New Republic* 62 (7 May 1930): 331–32.

43. Robert Graves, *Good-bye to All That: An Autobiography* (1929); Richard Aldington, *Death of a Hero* (1929).

44. Hilda Conkling at age ten published *Poems by a Little Girl* (1920).

ance wheel, and which would make the Cambridge post ideal, would probably now reinforce that part of me which least needs reinforcement. Another ten years, and I may cry a different tune: meanwhile, I can only thank you for such friendly thoughts—and the gods for your friendship. . . . I am still itching to complete my last year's trip abroad, which I terminated in such a panic: so I shall follow your trip through Europe with almost morbid interest. But the itch is a very light one, though it recurs often: for I must finish my book, and I must help put our new country house in order; and there would be no fun in going abroad again unless Sophie went, too: so I put that temptation behind me for another year or two. Geddes will probably still be in Montpellier early in June; but you should meet Branford, too, if you have the time while you're in London: there is a fine touch of the Elizabethan pirate in him which doesn't come out in his writings, overloaded though they are with turgid, euphuistic metaphor . . . Let's meet if you come down here again this spring.[45] There is little chance of my getting up to Boston.

Lewis

[handwritten]
158 Mt. Vernon Street
[LM] Ans 2 May

Dear Lewis,

Your two reviews gave me that gift which only the fusion of vitality & style can impart; aroused in me that ordered, nervous Insurgence which creates a new prospect for living[46]—a feeling of insistency that life can never be banal again—that every step of it will be suffused with its allegory—You always do that to me; & hence I have come to feel that I cannot be complete without you—your writing is necessary to me, so please do not shut me off from it by modesty—I am not following the literary world or any other world at present—I have my serpentine coils around a few mysteries of the psyche at present & am insulated from all else. I do not even hear people when they speak to me. So help me.

I, myself, was ensnared within the Ambiguities of Pierre six years ago when I first discovered Melville, & that perhaps was the element of personal identification which caused the Vesuvian Explosion in me.[47] It was the same, to such a mysterious degree—even to the mother, the color of the hair, the dreams, the stating of the

45. Victor V. Branford (1864–1930), devoted colleague of Patrick Geddes and editor of the *Sociological Review* (1912–1930).

46. "A Modern Synthesis," *Saturday Review of Literature* 6 (12 April 1930): 920–21; 6 (10 May 1930): 1028–29. Revised as "Towards an Organic Humanism," Mumford's response to Irving Babbitt and the "new humanism," in C. Hartley Grattan, ed., *The Critique of Humanism* (1930).

47. A reference to the beginning of Murray's relationship with Christiana Morgan, whom he identified with Isabel in Melville's *Pierre*.

problem, etc., that I attribute much of my Insane Delight with Melville to a Narcissistic feeling of feeling rather than to a detached & yet interpenetrating one. For I was almost insane then, & guessed Pierre before reading it, i.e. after Moby Dick & Mardi—for Pierre is merely a restatement in more concrete terms of the same soul turmoil. So that I dismissed my immediate & spontaneous lava, until I had solved the problem within & without. Melville's heroic attempt—though vain—made it possible. The only decent thing I have done in my life was to follow all the riddles that this situation presents & for myself at least solve them to the ecstatic limit & give them some assimilative form. Now that I have passed on to other knots it seems harder to return to Melville. Somehow one can gather oneself to the white heat & pitch in behalf of an attitude for which one is reaching, better than for one which has become a part of the tissue of personality. Nevertheless I have begun to think of Melville again & I may return to him this summer, but I have a hunch I may never be able to write it.

I have not read Haldane. I had the pleasure of talking to him about the book several years ago when he was commencing to compose it. Perhaps I will have at look at it—I suspect it a bit—have a faint fear that in some concealed fashion Hegel will intrude between the observations on respiration, reproduction, and the quantum.

Neither have I read Graves. I had read some trivial flippant essays & some flimsy verse that he wrote a number of years ago & the remembrance infringed upon me when I considered buying his latest.

Of course this Humanism business is the hugest Joke. Babbitt is a Witch-Hunter—Jean Jacques being he who has made the compact with the Devil.[48] It is a bloody farce, an emasculate rationalization of banal & arid prejudices. I hope you slaughtered them—will you send me the article?

But, don't you approve of the *word Humanism*? I was going to refer to humanistic psychology as the psychology which dealt with the problem of human values as subjectively experienced—the conflicts that anteceded these emergent attitudes & the technique of consciousness in respect to them—preparation, assimilation, etc.

I would call Blake a humanist, wouldn't you? It seems to me that Superhumanism has been absorbed by humanism, i.e. it has been discovered in the unconscious of the human & hence is really a part of him & should be within Humanism.

I enjoyed your comments upon the Harvard job, Mann's 'Death in Venice' etc. I heartily agree. It was a bit of selfishness on my part—I am always thinking that Harvard may be changed—that you & Aiken & Spence & a few others & myself could center around a book shop–coffee house within touch of Whitehead & keep our fertilizations alive & warm—

Tell me about Geddes—would he see me? It would be worth a trip to Montpel-

---

48. Irving Babbitt, *Rousseau and Romanticism* (1919).

lier—& please, again, give me a list of his writings—I have temporarily lost a note I made last spring after talking with you. Aside from the Biological Volume in the Home Library, I cannot recall the title of any book; & what is his full name?[49] My memory seems to have failed me here also. We are sailing to Glasgow & will go immediately to Edinburgh—but if he is South it would not be out of the question to seek him out—unless such a visit would sadly interrupt his contemplation.

Your letter was gorgeous—in this respect at least I will never be able to reciprocate—but my salutations to Sophie & yourself are, nevertheless, without humanistic restraint, decorum & measure.

Yrs.

H.

[typed]
4002 Locust Street
Long Island City
2 May 1930

Dear Harry:

Your introduction to Dr. Cohn has come just at the wrong time for me to take advantage of it: between the persistent infection of my damnable tooth and Geddes's tonsil operation—which he passed through nicely—and our preparations for getting up to the country and my desperate need to begin working again and on top of all this the most stunning and amusing and instructive emotional crisis I have been through in ten years: with all this, I say, I have been in no mood to meet Confucius: but I should not like him or you to think that it was churlishness that has kept me away.[50] . . . The Saturday Review people butchered my essay as if it were a round worm and each part could live entirely without the other: the next section will be out next week I believe: so don't judge the first too harshly till you see the second. A word of warning about your visit to Geddes. Things at Montpellier have gone badly, I learn; partly because the mad pile of buildings is just a mad pile of buildings, and partly because Geddes, pathetically needing aid and understanding, accepts the help of mean little second rate people who only betray his purposes when he can't rely upon anyone else.[51] Don't let yourself be driven by sympathy or admiration for him, if either come into existence, into promising any financial support for these schemes; the whole project isn't sound; and were Geddes not dominated by a bull-like will he would have acknowledged this long ago. Like Carlyle, he has never had power adequate to his ambitions, even when he was planning cities for the Maharajahs in India; and his plans have become more

49. Patrick Geddes and J. A. Thomson, *Biology* (1924).

50. Murray had worked under the eminent cardiologist Alfred Einstein Cohn (1879–1977) at the Rockefeller Institute for Medical Research.

51. Geddes founded the Collège des Écossais at Montpellier, France, in 1924.

grandiose as his means have become more limited. There is something in himself that he has always fled from by means of these practical enterprises; I don't quite know what it is, but it is what kept him from being a major influence in his heyday between 40 and 60. Visit him by all means; but guard your pocketbook! Somehow this makes me feel a little like Judas in relation to Geddes; but I am concerned for the Geddes whose sun is rising, as well as for him whose sun is only by an optical illusion above the horizon.

Lewis

[typed]
Hanover Inn
At Dartmouth College
Hanover, New Hampshire
12 May 1931

Dear Harry:

Ironic that our first decent opportunity to see each other should have come when it did. I had spent the previous five weeks, driving myself through my book on The Brown Decades, at a furious rate: by last week it was finished, and I was momentarily finished, too, so much so that I cancelled the engagement I had to lecture at Ann Arbor last Thursday and Friday.[52] Fortunately, I recover quickly: so I am now in decent shape again; but Sophie and I both want to get up to the country quickly, so I spent the weekend packing books and getting ready for our removal next Friday or so. Had I just had a little more energy, I would have postponed our trip to Amenia a few days and would have joined you, alone if not with Sophie. I am sorry there was any mixup about telegrams. There may have been a Freudian significance to my substituting 152 for 158: on the other hand, 152 was the number of the old Dial, and the ruts of association are very deep: so take your choice.[53] I have given up my plans for going to Europe, probably till next spring. Old Geddes' letters grow more and more urgent; for he is afflicted with diabetes and sees his time limited: but his mind keeps on spinning in its old grooves and I fear his grandiose plans and projects are more a sign of senile dementia than of his real greatness: the old devil has wantonly poured about $90,000 into his collection of more or less empty buildings at Montpellier, because, dreaming of a new college, with himself as planner and educator, he found it easier to gather the stones than the students. The whole business makes one profoundly sad: it shows the flaw of willfulness, a stubborn refusal to face any other reality than his own, which is doubtless in part the secret of his genius: but it also explains his failure, too. If I went to him, I could only wring my hands and shake my head despairingly: and it

52. Lewis Mumford, *The Brown Decades: A Study of the Arts in America, 1865–1895* (1931).

53. Mumford briefly served as associate editor of *The Dial* magazine, under the editorship of Robert Morss Lovett, in 1919.

is safer, cheaper, easier, kinder, to do this at a distance. So I shall stay in America this summer; and in June will put together all my architectural papers, to be published as a book next spring; in July, will attend a conference on Regionalism at the University of Virginia; and in August and September will try to do a little free and spontaneous writing, a spell that is long overdue, since my last bout at it was four years ago, and if I am ever to vindicate the talented young man who started out to be a dramatist—I re-read some of the things he wrote at twenty or twenty-two with both admiration and respect!—I must manage to do something about it during the next five years or at least so I tell myself, despite the fact that Cervantes wrote Don Quixote when he was past fifty! Sophie and I have both had a good winter in health and spirits, perhaps the best that we have had in four or five years, despite the fact that the last year has been for us a period of intense and painful spiritual house-cleaning—during which we have opened all the dusty closets of our marriage, emptied out drawers that were kept under lock and key, and run the vacuum cleaner over apparently immaculate surfaces, only to find them covered with dust and bacteria. We have been married ten years; she is now 31 and I am 35; and I have observed that this is a critical period in the lives of a great many friends and acquaintances. What happens so often is that the woman begins to hunger again for romance, and the man, while not altogether past romance, begins to look around for spiritual companionship, particularly, I should say, intellectual companionship; and all the deep ties that have been formed become shaken, sometimes momentarily, sometimes permanently. We are in the midst of that now, alas! In a superficial sense, I have of course potentially been in love more than once before; but have always withdrawn hastily when there was the faintest show of the relationship becoming deep enough to disturb our marriage, or even momentarily to draw me out of its orbit. But the last year has been different! The relation deepened into the sort of thing marriage becomes, almost before we knew it, although I was aware from the beginning that there lurked a greater possibility of permanence than there had in any previous interest; and Sophie and I and the other girl have been struggling for the better part of a year to face the whole business honestly and to see what could be made of it. More than once I have remembered with a bitter smile Jung's example, but it is of no use to me.[54] The intellectual partner is just 26 years old: sooner or later she will want to be a mother and will resent giving up part of me as much as Sophie does—perhaps with less grace and sweetness than Sophie has shown. So, though a dual relationship has lasted the winter, it cannot last much longer without a great renunciation. One way or another, there must be a renunciation: and it is not an easy moral decision—particularly since there is always the chance of confusing cowardice with rationality and loyalty. To make matters more

---

54. Carl Jung maintained an extramarital relationship with his associate Antonia Wolff with the full knowledge of his wife Emma.

confusing: my relations with Sophie are far from being torn to bits or played out: our marriage is perhaps a greater reality today than it has ever been and the situation is not a sudden rivalry between passion and routine. But there: I have said quite enough! I don't want to embarrass you by a confession: good heavens, you get enough of these in the line of duty without having a friendship embarrassed by one, too: but there would be something shallow and superficial in what I wrote you if I did not give a hint of what has been boiling under the surface during the past year: and please don't think that I expect any reply.

Is there any chance that you can drop in on us during the summer? What are your plans? I am here only until Wednesday evening, and I expect to leave Long Island City for Amenia on Friday. The lilacs should just about be in full bloom, and I am eager to dig my toes into the earth again. When you find yourself at leisure, I shall look forward to either a letter or a visit.

> Ever yours
> Lewis

[handwritten]
[LM] Ans 12 August 30–32?

Dear Lewis,

I let your letter rest a week or so on my desk, thinking that its business like typewritten envelope was enclosing some skimmed milk from a real estate agent or some such unwelcome correspondent, instead of the grade A cream which I found finally to my mortification.

I am sorry we did not meet, because we had much to say to each other. I was loaded with queries & extravagant speculations & your letter tells me that you were not without your high thoughts & dilemmas—

All that you write me about your work is thrilling to me,—that you should be so continuously productive. I look forward with anticipation to your publishings. I reread your reviews of the recent decade & liked them. Some of the works you put forward for special mention I had never read—so that you lead me to some new literature—I like so much of what you said, agreed I think with all of it—particularly as I recall Jeffers & Santayana—You did not mention Tom Wolfe—I am of the opinion that, although as yet undeveloped, he is the greatest genius in our midst. The only novelist that impresses me on the large scale.

I believe that you are more feverishly working for the constructive moral than I am—or sometimes I think you take more stock in vague generalities—but then I read the magnificent shatterings that you bestow upon Keyserling & I am set at ease, in my usual state of admiration of you.[55] Perhaps I am too much impressed by

---

55. Lewis Mumford, review of *The Book of Marriage*, ed. Herman Keyserling, *New Republic*, 9 February 1927, 334–35.

a certain sensuous virtuosity—being deficient in that respect myself—& hence embrace Wolf Solent with passion—or wake up in the night murmuring Tom Wolfe's "O lost & by the wind grieved, ghost come back again," etc.—I have never understood your not liking these books—[56]

But to become still more personal & private, your affairs are close to mine. Aside from several temporarily agitating upheavals of the heart, I was not really unhorsed until 1925 (age 32 years). Since then I have voyaged heatedly & subterraneously with love & have managed somehow a dual relationship—This has partly accounted for my lack of free energies for writing—I have regarded this way of life, due to its unmitigated intensity & integrity, as permanent—Then suddenly this winter something entirely new—a new genius—& in consequence I find myself in a vortex of complexities—So you see we should be in closer contact—but letters are hardly suitable for conveying the subtleties that make such matters mighty dilemmas rather than mere problems of so-called adjustment. I will not therefore attempt to comment upon your affairs, despite the numerous intuitions which surge up. But will hope that some circumstance brings us together. It is needless to add that due to my peculiar (& what you might call official position) you will be favoring me if you do not communicate the fragment of autobiography which I have so egocentrically given. My hopes and solicitations are with you.

Harry

[typed]
Amenia, New York
9 August 1931

Dear Harry:

This letter is so long overdue that it can scarcely be considered an answer to yours, although, heaven knows, I have written many long and loquacious answers to it in my own mind. But in summer I am the ant rather than the grasshopper: a solitary ant, if the entomology would not offend Wheeler: and so having finished my small and quite unimportant book on the Brown Decades, down to the reading of the last galley of proof and having delivered a lecture on Regionalism at Charlottesville early in July, I have spent most of the time since working on my philosophy of environment, the book that I began last year and doubtless have more than once told you something about, although it is only now beginning to emerge into clarity for myself.[57] My Charlottesville experience, by the bye, was a nice psychological footnote to James's essay on the Energies of Men.[58] By now it has happened so often to me that I could almost rely upon it. It was terribly hot down there: I had

---

56. From the epigraph to part one of Thomas Wolfe, *Look Homeward, Angel* (1929).

57. William M. Wheeler (1865–1937), Harvard entomologist; author of *Foibles of Insects and Men* (1928).

58. William James, "The Energies of Men" (1907).

been sleepless: I had eaten scarcely anything: I was passing through a minor emotional crisis: in short, on the morning I was to give the lecture I was so completely done in that I was almost desperate enough to leave town without making the speech. Up to the moment I stood on my feet my mind was a complete blank—and during the next hour and a half I delivered probably the best talk I have ever delivered in my life. Of course it doesn't do to be tired in a half-hearted way: one must be quite dead before one can get the rebound; and unfortunately there is no way of planning beforehand to be in a state of collapse; whilst anything short of this, alas! is a misfortune and a certain guarantee of a bad performance. So here I am working away and beginning, after two or three weeks of fumbling to get my old stride, a stride I have not really recovered completely since doing the Melville. Sophie and Geddes have both been happy up here: we have worked mightily on our ramshackle house and our weedy garden, with the result that the first, at least, is not falling about our heads any more, and one or two spots are even livable, while the latter is, if not a perfumed Eden, at least the scene of a decent spinsterly orderliness. At times the tension of Sophie-and-Catherine becomes unbearable, when one or the other attempts to claim the whole relationship; and at times, when one is the perfect mother and the other the perfect hetaira—you will note that I have been reading Jung!—the question of "either-or" disappears and life is very full and complete. But what living personality is content to remain a psychological type: is a type, indeed, anything but a fixation, and thus to some extent an aberration? There are times when Sophie wants to recover her complete original hold, or, alternatively, have another relation herself which would balance off my own outer interests: while Catherine, too, wants something other than the crumbs from the table of domesticity, and is not so completely wedded to her work but that she can also dream of a home in the country and a baby and all that would complete what is at present only a fragment of life. As for me: I am still the patient medieval ass, equi-distant between two haystacks: a problem in free will that would baffle all the schoolmen. It is not fundamentally a social or legal or even a moral question: even if I had complete freedom from economic and legal difficulties, the question would still be a baffling one, the scales being so nicely balanced that nothing but a decisive thump from some irrational impulse, or some equally irrational circumstance, would make them register decisively in one direction or the other. This has never happened to me before; and I confess I am a little puzzled by it: it even seems psychologically anomalous. I have been greatly amused and cheered and comforted by reading the student's transcript of Jung's 1925 seminar, which Mrs. Spingarn lent to me: it is an exhilarating piece of self-exposure, and even at second hand some of Jung's energy and candor and robustness comes through the lines.[59] His dreams, from the examples he gave there, are extraordinary works of art: they differ from ordinary works in that they are mystery stories without the key and the final unravelment being supplied

59. Amy Spingarn, Mumford's Leedsville neighbor and wife of his friend Joel Spingarn.

in the fantasy itself. But how shallow, how unexplored, I feel after reading him. In sheer envy, I began to will to dream before going to bed, and found that my unconscious played the practical joke on me of offering the stalest banalities. I am still awaiting the event or the insight that will redeem this imaginative shallowness, and will unlock and permit the full development of the two plays that I have written, and the three or four other works that I have planned, but that are still unwritten.[60] But I am patient; and in the meanwhile, I write a philosophy of the *environment*: machines, buildings, cities, regions! John Gould Fletcher was here for a weekend recently: I wish you could have met him before his return to England: he has a fine mind, and I found myself warmed and stimulated by him, perhaps because we discovered beneath the surface underlying identities of interest we had not suspected.[61] If you are in this neighborhood, please drop in, for as long as you can stay. I work in the mornings, from seven-thirty on, and after noon have a clear, free mind: if you weary of it, there is a lake to swim in and—but you are probably engrossed and all my wiles and temptations go for nothing anyway. Forgive my tardiness in sending back this essay of Jung's. Tell me if you have ready anything good. I am going through Cohen's Reason and Experience, which is keen, but not particularly deep; and I am tussling with Geddes and Thomson's confused and irritating, but somehow masterly summary of their life-experience and philosophy: do have a look at the philosophic chapters: there is Geddes himself, with all his limitations and all his power.[62] Sophie sends warm greetings.

Lewis

[handwritten]
[LM] Ans 30 Nov 31

Dear Lewis,

I rejoiced at your letter. We had better be good company to each other, because we shall not so easily lose our direction, become aggrieved, morose or mad. We are out on the same Cape, although our quicksands may be of different texture. How we could discourse, given the proper time & place!? Internally I am out of my dislocations—that is, grown clearly out of a most intense high-frenzied love of the last six years with C & passed on to an equally consuming focussing of a different nature with E.[63] C revealed to me the underworld—the maddened hollowed-out woe

---

60. Mumford's plays: *Asters and Goldenrod: An American Idyll* (unpublished) and *The Builders of the Bridge*, eventually published in *Findings and Keepings* (1975).

61. John Gould Fletcher (1886–1950), American poet.

62. Morris Raphael Cohen, *Reason and Nature: An Essay on the Meaning of the Scientific Method* (1931). Patrick Geddes and J. A. Thomson, *Life: Outlines of General Biology*, 2 vols. (1931); Mumford's review in *New Republic* 58 (16 September 1931): 130–31.

63. "C" refers to Christiana Morgan; "E" to Eleanor Clement Jones, a writer who worked at the clinic, 1930–1933 (see Robinson, *Love's Story Told*, 197–202).

of the whole world since Adam—Melville's world, Dante's Inferno—the world of witchery, hate, Krakens & claws. The ugliest in both of us was burned up by an utter unrelenting compassionate hospitable love that welcomed ALL. E on the other hand is a poet & a genius who leads me back to the sun. My God! How inadequate these meager inkmarks to convey my meanings—I put the matter in this somewhat general way because I believe that it is important in such circumstances to see what particular meaning each person may have for the other spiritually—exactly what are—as far as you can understand them—the reciprocations. It is as if we went for our opposites—what was at that moment of our growth our opposites & then loved it & assimilated it—a cyclic, interesculating, mutual, reciprocal process. So that each person incorporates the other. I have had four or five minor flurries which I recognize in a short while had no integrity to them—they were too uneven or too heterogeneous—or merely represented a superficial interest or compatibility, etc. My difficulty at present is the external situation with C—how not to leave her broken. I feel like a devourer—Jo is the ever-loyal—disapproving, of course, but yet maintaining with me all the original ground structure of life—the earthy constancy & continuity. You will see a story by Eleanor in the October Harper's—write me what you think of it. It's named 'The Basket.' I've been doing a fair amount of work—on psychology as well as on Melville. Several minor discoveries recently about the latter—South Sea experiences, a love affair before marriage, & some Pittsfield data. I have just finished one chapter devoted to the Hawthorne–Melville relation. I am writing four psychological articles—one on Hawthorne as Master Analyst & a story (long short story). When shall I finish any of these things? I am always beginning. I am thrilled by the idea of the 'Psychology of Environment.'

Yrs.
Harry

[handwritten]
[LM] Ans 30 Nov 31

Dear Lewis,

Well, you did the trick again—another high score for you. I liked The Brown Decades a lot, not as much as the others because I am less interested in office buildings & in the work of Richardson—but I learned many things & I enjoyed as usual your fine tall style—your certain erect march through the welter of detail. Of course you had to stretch yourself a bit to fit all these events into the Brown Decades as defined, but everything is connected with everything else in this world & there are no beginnings & no endings—so why not?

The aesthetic surroundings—city & countryside—are more important than any other single factor for the generation of a true marrow & sinew culture it seems to me. It is basic & mostly unconscious—but it ferments Love & from this comes all good things.

What are you about now?

Are you to have a caravan this year?

I hope you received a letter from me sometime back—I'm in no letter writing mood tonight—but I did want to mention my gratitude for your book—for your having enlightened me once more—

Yrs
Harry Murray

[typed]
Lewis Mumford
4002 Locust Street
Long Island City, New York
30 November 1931

Dear Harry:

I have answered you September letter, in my mind, a hundred times: but what avails it, since I haven't written, and since your note on The Brown Decades, far more generous than it deserves, had come on its heels. I had, as I think I wrote you, a good summer: but I had planned to have two free weeks at the end of it, with not a single "must" or "now" in them: and the freedom didn't materialize; for I was low in funds, and had to accept a hasty call to Dartmouth just as I was bringing the second draft of my new book to a close, and from that time on I have been travelling and talking and writing in a long and unrelieved round. Every three weeks I go up to Dartmouth and spend five days there: when I come back my calendar is doubly crowded. This will last through the middle of January: so will my lectures on The Machine Age at Columbia, and after that I hope to have a little surcease. The beat of too many engagements is as cruel a form of torture, almost, as the Chinese method of dropping water on a prisoner's head: add to this the fact that Sophie and Geddes have both been ill with colds and that I returned, tired, from a trip to Dartmouth only to spend the next week nursing them and—well, that's that, and here I am. But at least you know why I haven't written. Among other things, I waited to see the story by E in October Harper's: but I could not find it either there or in the November number: was it postponed? Every time I go up to Dartmouth I wonder if it wouldn't be possible to slip over to Boston during the weekend to see you, but each time a series of engagements has been cooked up for me, and it turns out to be impossible. My lectures at Columbia and Dartmouth are both driving me to do more rigorous and complete thinking about the subject of Form: and by now I am on the verge of suggesting to the publisher that he issue it as a series of small books, under a general title: with just a little more effort, I think I may be able to say something definitive for my generation on the subject of Form and Civilization—and at all events, the effort will be amusing in itself. The Brown Decades is a tired book: it really isn't good enough, and I am now a little at odds with myself for having published it, for at no point in the process did I have any illusions about it. Perhaps the one use of making such a mistake is that it serves as warning and bids me roll up my sleeves and be more ruthless and unsparing of myself in my work on Form: so much for compensation! [. . .] Incidentally, I am giving two lectures at Union College, one on Whitman and one on Melville during the next month, and for *the first time in three years* I have begun to read Melville again. Nothing has diminished. Moby Dick is still great poetry. But perhaps I am more conscious of the enigma of Melville than before: more ready to face it. Going to Whitman from Melville is like putting one's feet on solid ground again, after having crossed the ocean in the midst of storm, fog, pestilence, and mutiny: the trio will live forever in one's memory but one is glad to feel the earth again! Have you, incidentally, come upon anything which would reveal Melville's feeling about Leaves of Grass: he discussed the poem with young Stedman, but Stedman, you will remember, forgot to record what Melville said.

Are you coming down to New York during the holidays? We hope to see you.

Warmly
Lewis

[typed]
4002 Locust Street
Long Island City
10 January 1932

Dear Harry:

I know how one's pleasure may be spoiled by the pressure of impossible engagements, even when one would like to make them and keep them: so, after my third effort to get in touch with you during the Christmas holidays, I desisted, realizing that you had probably got into a jam. Let me begin the New Year properly by answering your question about the Caravan: we shall not publish one in 1932, and we are still discussing the literary and commercial possibilities of getting one out in the late spring of 1933. We shall not make a general call for manuscripts in any event: but if you, or E, have anything for us, we would be glad to see it: so I will let you know if and when we decide to launch a Fifth Caravan. . . . I just came down last night from Schenectady, where I gave a lecture at Union College on Melville. The following morning, they held a colloquium in my honor on Melville's early life at Albany. Nothing very revealing about H.M. developed out of the little excursion into the history and social life and morals of the eighteen thirties except the extraordinary prosperity of upper class, shopkeeping Albany in those days, as thousands of wagons plied their way through the streets, starting over the Mohawk trail: a prosperity that left in its wake however two hundred paupers and the necessity for soup kitchens, insufficiently supported by the rich. William James, the grandfather of William and Henry was a great power in the town then, and, incidentally the Gansevoorts were in 1832 building for themselves a grand house: no wonder they grudged the widow help! In my lecture, I did better by Melville than I did by Whitman: but your own remarks about Whitman, in your last letter, stirred me into a defense of the old devil, and if I were not still in a perfect whirl of work, with four books definitely planned and demanding all my preparatory efforts, and with all sorts of interruptions, lectures, personal encounters, decisions, and so forth, pressing for attention too, I would sit right down and write a biography of Whitman that would compel you to eat at least half your words: the other half I would have to swallow too. As for Melville's picture of the Confidence Man: I don't think he meant Whitman but Emerson—the optimistic and bland and self-reliant Emerson whom he had actually seen and listened to, was the image that infuriated him: it was the leader of Transcendentalism that was the terrible fraud. Was there perhaps some resentment here connected with his failure to get a hearing at Concord? Have you discovered whom he stayed with when he visited Concord? Have you the faintest notion if Hawthorne ever talked about him to Thoreau or any of the others; and if he didn't, why he didn't? If Hawthorne really was impressed with Moby Dick how could he have possibly kept this under his belt? It is very mysterious. Did I incidentally ever tell you that the copy of the Confidence Man which Melville sent Uncle Peter, and which now reposes in the rare books room of the New York Public Library never had its pages cut until I cut them? I wonder if the same was true with Pierre: old Mrs. Melville's copy was perhaps equally uncut. . . . This strained, rushed, distracted last three months, with the mindless round of lectures, lectures on architecture, city planning, the machine age, and literature, lectures that demanded fresh materials and revised judgments have left me little time for anything but strictly professional reading: so I can make no return for the little budget of books you've given me, and alas! I myself have read none of them, except Savage Messiah. You probably long ago read Geoffrey Scott's fascinating portrait of Zelide; and I don't suppose De Sanctis's History of Italian Literature swings into your orbit, penetrating, rich, and harmonious though it is—a sort of Golden Day of Italian literature in extenso—to speak immodestly.[64] . . . I am glad your Melville makes progress, and as for the countering delays, I understand some of them only too well. If you don't come down here during the Easter vacation I shall probably make a trip to Boston in April, one way or the other, we must meet.

> As always, my warmest wishes for
> the new year—
> Lewis

---

64. H. S. Ede, *Savage Messiah* (1931); Geoffrey Scott, *The Portrait of Zélide* (1927); Francesco De Sanctis, *History of Italian Literature* (1930).

[handwritten]
4002 Locust St
Long Island City, N.Y.
2 April 1932

Dear Harry:

Alas! That it's been so long since we met. I am sailing on the twentieth and expect to be gone til about the middle of August. A Guggenheim fellowship will carry me at least part of the way. I expect to be in Zurich a few days. Is Jung accessible? Or would I merely be adding to the burden of an overburdened man? I don't want to do that: but of course it would be a treat to talk with him. How goes it with you?

Warmly
Lewis

[handwritten]
[LM] Ans 26 June 1932

Lewis—

My glorious fellow—why haven't we met! I have so much to propose to you—so many queries, doubts, hypotheses, affirmations & negations—You must teach me something about Architecture & Art—Large order?

Do not take my deficiencies in letter-writing & friendly visiting as indifference or divergence or any form of separateness whatsoever.

I have not had the uninterrupted winter that I bargained & laid my defenses for—quite the reverse—a poor unquiet friction full winter it has been—As a result I became irresponsible about civilities & avoided the heartening pot roast humanities which though rare enough, may be occasionally sniffed out and enjoyed.

Whenever I get a sizeable chunk of the Psychological book & of the Melville behind me—then I shall be in a mood to relax in good temper & discuss Heroics, to spawn a million speculations about the destruction & recreation of one world.

I am delighted about the good sense of the Guggenheimer Committee. Where are you going? Geddes? Of course visit Jung—Write him now, giving him, if possible, the time of your arrival. I do not think it will do harm to mention my name although I understand that he is not very pleased with me since he heard that I was being analysed by Dr. Alexander, a Freudian, for professional purposes.[65] In the last few years he has lost contact more & more with the concrete problems—particularly of American life & he has been surrounded by riff raff of middle aged spinsterhood who gave him a pretense of understanding—something strange happened this Fall & no one in this country, as far as I know, has heard from him for four months. Two years ago I found him still the Grand Old Peasant Wiseman of

---

65. As part of his psychoanalytic training, Murray underwent Freudian analysis with Dr. Franz Alexander in Boston and Chicago, 1932–1933.

the world & I should hate to have you miss him—When you write him mention Melville—the two have points in common.

I shall look forward to a Whitman–Melville discussion sometime. I love them both, but prefer the latter, because he had more mind & was more representative— much of my opinion depends upon the interpretation, which I perhaps project into him. To me the thing which chilled the century was the repressive God-Father-Methodist-Puritan-Hellfire *Conscience* (Ishmael) held in place, fortified & reconstructed by the Religious-Orthodox-Social-educational structure (External). Consequently for me the *Whale* is Conscience—originally the Punishing Parent, backed by Organized Society, the *Jehovah.* Hence Ahab vs. Whale is the Son against Parent (Mother & Father in HM's case) Man vs. Man, the Primitive Individual vs. the wolfish institutionalized world, Satan vs. God & so 'Paradise Lost.' Now this was *true* for New England and most of America & for Melville. But Whitman escaped it, & hence left it out & so, much of his sentiment is indiscriminate unreal Euphoria—which is music to us now—the Whale is Slain—Pardon the trite phraseology of this condensed formula.

P.S. Give my best regards to Sophia—& write me from the steamer telling me your opinion of Van Wyck Brooks & his new work which I haven't had time to read, & why you do not think Thos. Wolfe the only first rate novel writer in America & have you a spare photograph of yourself to refresh me & how is young Geddes, etc. etc.

—Harry

[handwritten]
American Express Co.
London
26 June 1932

Dear Harry:

You know what H.M. says about travel—it takes the money out of one's purse & the ink out of one's pen. The first difficulty hasn't so far troubled me: but the latter alone accounts for my long silence. Throwing myself into new scenes, feeling my way through a strange idiom, wrestling with other people's minds & meanings, I have had no world of my own to retire into, and therefore nothing to come forth with. England unlocks me: for the first time I pause and look around me! The whole trip has been a magnificent procession of days, far beyond any expectation of mine: I never studied to such purpose or lived quite so intensely before. And I had such luck in meeting people, & getting inside their houses, if not their heads—an old burgher-patrician family in Lübeck, a government official in Berlin, a banker in Frankfurt, Thomas Mann in München, Le Corbusier in Paris, to say nothing of dozens of accidental rubbings and touchings of "common people" all the way: I couldn't have planned a better itinerary step by step than what actually befell me. I have a month more of travel before me—Sophy joins me here on 6 July—and then

I shall return to Amenia eagerly to count over my loot—including fifty books whose existence I had not even suspected! The trip has finally brought to something of a head my personal dilemma of the last two years. For I spent three weeks of it in Catherine's company—we had a common problem in a housing & city planning series of articles for 'Fortune' we were doing together—and I emerged from that with the quite definite feeling that two such intense & acute & sensitive egos as ours could only exhaust themselves completely by constant companionship.[66] The incubation of an idea demands a certain apartness, a certain womblike *secrecy*: one must not give it birth at too early a stage, as one is constantly tempted to when one's lover has similar interests & responses. I found myself anticipating Sophy's obtuseness as a great relief, and the intervals when I was alone were always periods of exhilaration & renewed wholeness. The situation is a little paradoxical, for it arises really out of our extraordinary sympathy, compatibility, likeness—re-enforced by a sexual life that is complete and satisfactory for both of us to the point of perfection. One of the root difficulties of my relation with Sophy is that we are not physiologically matched. When we were first married I used to think that this was solely because I was an inexperienced duffer at sex: but this is no longer true, and Sophy's extreme slowness in reaching an orgasm is either barely physiological or the indication of the need for another kind of partner. Yet, in spite of this, the need for Sophy, and the deepening confidence in our relationship, has grown steadily during these last two months. Catherine, to have me, would willingly say good-bye to her literary & intellectual career: but what would this mean? Thus she would become another Sophy, incapable of sharing all my interests, instead of remaining the unstable but tremendously stimulating Catherine who, under the limitations of our occasional meetings, has been such a powerful influence on me these last two years! The possibility of marrying Catherine, imminent and recurring all through our intercourse, has now been sealed by a deep inner No. *I go back to work.* The difficult rhythm of sex and work, so completely broken in favor of sex during this last period, begins again, because perhaps after all my desire for a book is deeper than that of Catherine for a baby! . . .

As you doubtless know, I started out for Old Geddes too late: he died a few days before I sailed, peacefully & suddenly, without illness or struggle. I missed seeing Jung in Zürich, because I was momentarily under the weather: this is the one major regret I have about my trip so far. We must arrange to have a long chat together before Autumn sets in, in Topsfield or Amenia. At the moment I am so weary of transporting my body that I am afraid it will have to be Amenia or nowhere: but maybe by the first of September this will have worn off.

You ask about Van Wyck's book. It is a portrait, almost a self-portrait of Emer-

66. Catherine Bauer and Lewis Mumford, "England's Two Million Houses, New," *Fortune* 6 (November 1932): 32–37; "Machines for Living," *Fortune* 7 (February 1933): 78–80; "Taxes into Houses," *Fortune* 7 (May 1933): 48–49.

son, in the manner of Virginia Woolf: to me it seems a rich & juicy book.[67] He wrote it during a period of tremendous exhilaration and euphoria that preceded his breakdown in 1926: it lacks intellectual completeness, such reference to ideas as one might expect in the self-portrait of an intellectual man: but as a picture of Emerson in his daily environment it seems to me altogether brilliant. But it gives no indication of the present man, whose steady toughening & strengthening, since I saw him a year ago, has been a great joy. He talks easily about his illness & seems completely at ease & re-integrated. Thomas Mann, incidentally, reminded me oddly of Brooks: the same probity, but with all the Puritan devils hitched & bridled and actually helping to pull the chariot! A man completely fluent and "unreserved"—in the sense that a host is unreserved when he has so much wine on the table that he knows there will be no call to unlock the double-bolted door to the cellar.

An organ is piously braying in the street—my hotel is just a block from the British Museum—and the pennies clink when they fall to the pavement: I fear this peaceful soliloquy, dear Harry, is over. I am eager to hear from you. Eager above all to see you & feel you in the flesh: but if time elapses before this happens I shall understand. I trust your work in the meanwhile has prospered.

Warmly,
Lewis

[typed]
Amenia, New York: 14 August 1932

Dear Harry:

Your letter was a flower on a dunghill of bills, bank statements, political platforms, advertisements, pleas for money, economic panaceas, and urgent telegrams whose urgency, at a distance of two months, left one with a feeling of ironic amusement. The prospect of your coming here delights us: we have plenty of room and trust you will stay much longer than the promised few hours: the domestic environment is spartan, but the beds have broken no backs and there is always milk and honey. The slip of my typewriter just now, which turned the h of honey into an m, was sheer raw wish-fulfillment: I have already begun to work like a bear to turn it into a fact, and have been so completely stimulated and exercized and satisfied and rested by my excursion to Europe that it is almost a lark to realize that I am, in company with most of my countrymen, skating on thinner ice this year than I have been since 1926. What cheers me, in addition to all the inner cheer provided by the last four months, of which you shall hear more than enough when you come, is that 1926 is, on retrospect, probably the best and fullest year of my life to date: at least in realization. That, too, came after a trip to Europe in 1925: so all the auguries are good for 1933. Sophie joined me at the beginning of July, and we had four good weeks together, in England, Holland, and Germany. The old watchman of the skies,

---

67. Van Wyck Brooks, *The Life of Emerson* (1932).

not wishing me to lurch and reel in drunken ecstasy, brought me to my senses with a slap on the face and a dash of vinegar five minutes after The Bremen docked: little Geddes, three weeks before, had had an abscessed ear, had spent a few days in the hospital, and had only the day before been discharged by the doctor. We would have been miserably helpless for a fortnight had we known: so it all turned out for the best, thanks to the doctor who kept our relatives from cabling: but the first hour in New York was a nightmare. A whiff of the earth the next day wiped it all away however: and our lad makes us very proud, for he never for a moment whimpered for us, and when he went on the operating table he kept on telling riddles to the anesthetician and joking until he fell asleep. So much for the tough gritty reality of life. Now as to getting here. We will be here the week you say, and if you'll send us word in advance, as to the day, we'll be in or around the house. Should you come by any chance unexpectedly and should we not be at home, look for us in our other haunt: Troutbeck Lake, on Spingarn's place: any villager will direct you there. Since you'll be coming from the north or west, the last village before you reach ours which is Leedsville, will be either Amenia or Sharon. Here is a map of the final stage. Our house is a gray one with buff trim and blue doors, facing a green house on the other side of the road.

Godspeed and thrice welcome!

Lewis

P.S. What American books published this year have most interested you? The Atlantic has asked me to do an article on them, and I want to check up on my own judgements & partialities.[68]

[handwritten]
Topsfield
Massachusetts
[LM] Ans 10 Dec 32

Dear Sophie & Lewis,

It is as clear as if it was yesterday—being with you in the mosquitoless garden, talking over coffee & into the dark hours—stealing your precious sleep. Was any work accomplished the morning after I left?

When I arrived in Cambridge I found myself swept into an iron-bound routine. There seemed to be a concentration of Personages—Dr. Sachs from Berlin on psychoanalysis, L.J. Henderson on Pareto & a few other odd ones such as T.S. Eliot; and without knowing what I was in for—all my hours were accounted for & only now have I pushed an hour ahead of my schedule—to write letters.[69]

---

68. Lewis Mumford, "What Has 1932 Done for Literature?" *Atlantic Monthly* 150 (December 1932): 761–67.

69. Hanns Sachs (1881–1947), psychoanalyst and member of Freud's inner circle; emigrated from Berlin to the United States in 1932 and became affiliated with the Harvard Medical School; founded the

A number of unexpected events postponed this—for instance one patient commenced a series of preposterous dreams in which I seemed to figure as the Mad Hatter, March Hare, etc., & so I had to take an evening rereading Alice in Wonderland.

Well—seeing you just made me feel how empty my life had been without you in it—more permanently or more frequently.

In the webs & tangles of thought you are always there—but if you could only be bodily just around the corner that would be like Rhine wine—without which a dinner is not really a dinner.

It was a *splurge* seeing you—despite the little creeping guilt which was with me to the effect that I was adding nothing to your lives. No feeling is such as despair. To be dry & to nourish no one & not to feel the dancing feet of thought discovering pastures new.

Well—I am going to Chicago for 4–6 weeks after Xmas. Will you recommend me what & who to see? I want to know the answer to a million questions. When are we going to meet next? I'll be in N.Y. just before Xmas—I had a beautiful time at Amenia & you were both good to me

—Harry

[typed]
4002 Locust Street
Long Island City
10 December 1932

Dear Harry:

This is not so much an answer to your October letter as a prelude to your arrival in New York. I too have been busy all autumn: making notes on my book, amplifying my single term course on the Machine Age at Columbia into a two-term course, dashing up to Dartmouth for my conferences, and getting into a most frightful and disgusting jam on a series of bad articles. Except for the last, I could have borne up under the rush quite decently: but hack work leaves me with a very bad taste in my mouth, and the articles I did for the Atlantic and the Forum and Fortune were, alas! the worst sort of hack work, even worse than my weekly stint in the New Yorker which is, on the whole, fairly amusing, even though it is as superficial as the rest.[70] Against this bad taste, I know of no sort of available purgative or emetic or antiseptic: it leaves me full of black misery and self-reproach, all the more deadly because, now that I see my position more clearly, I am spared the privilege

---

journal *The American Imago*. L. J. Henderson (1878–1942), Harvard biochemist and physiologist; author of *The Fitness of the Environment* (1913); after completing his medical degree, Murray served as Henderson's research assistant in 1920; influenced by Vilfredo Pareto, Italian economist and sociologist, Henderson became interested in applying scientific theories to society and human relations.

70. Lewis Mumford, "In Our Stars: The World Fifty Years from Now," *Forum* 88 (December 1932): 338–42.

of rationalizing about it and softening it with justifications. At bottom, it all goes back to the fact that last April I was still a very divided man: I wanted to go to Europe about my own work: I wanted to go there with Catherine: and I didn't want to do anything that would upset the increasing stability of my relations with Sophy. It was just by a miracle that I managed the summer so that I did actually get a part of my own work done, a large enough part to offset all the other disappointments that attended the trip: but the aftermath of that divided mind was all the extra work I took upon my shoulders to make Catherine's work in Europe and Sophy's trip possible—aggravated as it all was by Geddes's illness. I am a united man once more. I have my work cut out for me and feel it growing steadily within: Catherine is no longer a compensation for a scanty youth and a dubious marriage, to say nothing of a ravishing intellectual intoxicant; and Sophy, being better poised herself, has more to give—a tremendous change in five years. Once the last hack article I have contracted to produce is done, I shall probably be greatly the gainer for all that has happened: but in the meanwhile, I chafe, and there are black hours. At present, with respect to the mere tactics of existence, I shall have deliberately to go back to the lean years of 1925 and 1926 or go in for a regular academic position. I am inclined to favor the first: if it weren't for the miserable school at Amenia, I'd live up there all year, and concentrate for the next half a dozen years upon two or three things that need a long uninterrupted space of thinking and writing for their completion. But why do I plague you with these matters? This is stuff for my notebooks, rather than for a letter. Well, in friendship, as in marriage, one mustn't let too much get buried: and if I say all these things now, we'll have that much more time free for philosophy and literature and heaven knows what else when we actually meet. There is much for you to see, too, in New York. You must, for one thing, see the new Benton room in the Whitney Museum—much finer in every way than his New School paintings—and if you haven't seen John Howard Lawson's play you must see that.[71] Had Mädchen in Uniform been in Boston? It is one of the good movies of the last few years. We'll discuss Chicago when you come: I know precious few people there; but the few I do know are rather nice. But fortify your soul against the bite and blare of Chicago: it is a raw, energetic city, a super-Berlin, and both the body and spirit ought to be toughened to face it. I exaggerate; but the fact is there, too. Do try to squeeze in a little time for us here; but if you don't succeed—and I know how hard it is on a visit—I'll follow you with a letter to Chicago, if you give me your address there.

Lewis

---

71. Probably *Success Story* (1932), Lawson's longest running play.

1933–1936

Literary Labor and Love's Entanglements

WORK AND LOVE are the dominant themes in this period of the correspondence, four years of emotional turmoil for both men. Mumford completed *Technics and Civilization* (1934), the first volume in the Renewal of Life series. Murray read drafts and galley proofs of much of the work, and Mumford made substantial changes in the introduction as a result of Murray's suggestions. Murray was much engaged in research projects at the Harvard Psychological Clinic. However, he sometimes found such work and the necessity to publish it inconsistent with natural rhythms of thought and creativity: "We all seem to be diseased by this fracturing tempo. It is infectious—to produce, produce, produce. Can the human brain gestate under such forced conditions?" (HAM 20 January 1933). Mumford encouraged his friend when he felt depressed and uncommunicative because his writing was not proceeding apace, and he offered consolation when Murray's beloved brother Ike died in July 1935. Murray reciprocated the encouragement when Mumford confronted what he termed "a bitter period," conflicted between his love for his wife Sophia and his regret at ending his relationship with Catherine Bauer (LM 20 July 1934). Nevertheless, in late 1934 Mumford embarked upon another intensely passionate relationship with Alice Decker, an affair that was in progress when the Mumfords' daughter Alison was born in April 1935. Alice's nearly fatal automobile accident in Louisiana in December 1935 traumatized Mumford, and he became frantic with desperation during his subsequent separation from her. Throughout this ordeal, Murray proved to be a steadfast friend who provided medical advice for Alice and psychological counseling for Mumford. Mumford acknowledged the generous assistance that Murray had offered Alice as well as his friend Eva Goldbeck, who was suffering from anorexia nervosa, saying that "year by year" his indebtedness to Murray has grown heavier (LM 11 December 1936). Murray replied that Mumford should never thank him again because, as he wrote, "We are linked always & you must use me as you would use your own arms and legs" (HAM 15 December 1936).

[handwritten]
Friday Jan 20
[LM] Feb 12, 33

Dear Lewis—

I had an exceedingly hurried visit to N.Y. I would have called you if I could have found your telephone number or known how to reach you in New York. Besides, I have not attained to enough serenity or poise to inflict myself upon my friends—particularly upon you. Why? I think I am imagining that you are expecting a great deal from one—energy, a fund of ideas, wisdom, etc., or I want you to like me & feel that I will disappoint you. In any case I find myself avoiding those whom I respect the most—for fear they will say: how are your books getting along? And they are doing very badly & the fault seems to be with me—with my native ineptitudes—which I cannot overcome. Is this enough to explain why I didn't do just what I wanted to do—rush down & see my Lewis & Sophie—who are the salt of my earth?

I read your Atlantic article & thought it was very decent—as usual I agreed with what you said & that is always pleasant & as I remember, you said a good word for Wolfe! I forgot what you said about Hemingway & Faulkner, but I am a bit impatient of this Sound & Fury—Men without Women—Be-a-Brute-Man at all cost literature. Somehow it seems a bit forced—this fear of sentiment. 'Horizon Fever' by Robert Dunn is worth reading. I haven't seen it mentioned by any reviewers. Dunn is another plain-spoken, self-reliance-with-a-vengeance man, who knocks people down as a prelude to his friendships & puts women away from him by rough & tumble tactics—sets them off against mountain peaks & finds them wanting. He has altitude phobia & yet climbs & climbs, & forces himself to go in aeroplanes. Choosing always what he fears—

I must subscribe to the New Yorker if you write for it. I did not know that you had a weekly stint there.

It was a delight to hear of your state of inner welfare & unity—despite the pressing hackwork. We all seem to be diseased by this fracturing tempo. It is infectious—to produce, produce, produce. Can the human brain gestate under such forced conditions? Is a new type being evolved which includes men who can write Faust in a fortnight on a Guggenheimer? I know that horticulturists force plants to a certain extent, but are they as strong & do they enjoy it?—the plants I mean. What do you think of Harvard's new Society of Scholars? Three to six years of complete irresponsibility.

I have been here in Chicago for 10 days—The Whitehall, 10 East Delaware Place—finishing up my analysis with Alexander, reading papers at the Psychoanalytic Institute & at University of Chicago, visiting laboratories & doing a bit of writing. I am going to Madison over the week-end—hope to see Meiklejohn, etc.—meeting Hutchens next week & learning what I can about their new system—Chicago is taking the last 2 years of High School with the 1st two years of College into one unit & then later for the best scholars—two years of intensive work in one of four divisions: Physical Sciences, Social Science, Biological Science & Humanities. I will be here for a week longer—to Jan 28.

I don't like Chicago as a whole—particularly the general run of humanity. It is just a big blaring blasting show & utterly heartless. Of course, there are a few things here and there—a good bookstore, good restaurants & shops—the Palmolive Bldg at night, the beach on the lakefront—I spent last Sunday in Cleveland—which I liked—I am in the middle of Magic Mt. It is having its cumulative influence on me. My best to Sophie & Geddes.

Yrs
Harry

[typed]
4002 Locust Street
Long Island City
12 February 1933

Dear Harry:

It is Sunday morning: the sky is blue and the snow still hangs in clumps to the roofs: and hours of freedom stretch before me, the first I have had to sit down quietly in for months and months. They are yours: but I warn you, slavery is a poor preparation for freedom, and my many little chores and drudgeries, though sometimes amusing enough in themselves, and even at times in the line of public duty, are bad introduction to the nobler art of letter writing. The winter has been slipping by one, two, three; and I find that while I have done the work I had set out to do last fall, I have not somehow managed the long open spaces for reflection I had also planned, even though for the last six weeks or more I have put a ban on all evening engagements and have been living a strict and regular and ruthless life. The city swallows one, fend though one will against it; or rather, it does *not* swallow one, for one could run away from any such formidable attack: it nibbles at one, taking here a mouthful of time and there another until one's day is gone, and one is full of empty holes, like a piece of cheese left too long exposed to the scurrying mice. But meanwhile, despite all these diversions, my book is becoming immense: the first chapter, on the origins and developments and possibilities of the Machine, has expanded already into a whole book by itself. No one, it turned out, had done exactly the job that needed to be done: the nearest approach, from the limited standpoint of Capitalism, had been that of the German economist, Werner Sombart, who exemplifies German Scholarship and understanding of Life at its best: so instead of sketchily summing up my already acquired views of the machine, I have had to deepen and expand them, which means pushing farther back in every direction, into history, into the development of science, into technology itself, and into the psychological and social milieu in which the machine developed.[1] I am working out, more fully than anyone else has done, the part that war played in stimulating the machine: but back of that, of course, there are the racial myths having to do with the conquest of nature—the seven leagued boots, Dedalus's wings, the flying carpet, the invisible hat, and so forth. These were present more or less in all cultures, were they not? But why did they suddenly become externalized and find a path for themselves into the outer world from the tenth century onward? Why did all the scattered inventions of other cultures somehow get knit together into a system between the tenth and seventeenth centuries: a system that is, to a certain extent, self-sustaining and self-justifying. I think I have a clue to the social conditions that made this happen: but the psychological processes are still somewhat obscure; and if you have any clues here I shall seize upon them avidly. The point is that the whole change of mind, which made possible the developments of the last two hundred years, was already pretty well accomplished by the end of the seventeenth century. So much for my present quest. By working diligently, I may be able to get the Machine book written by the end of the summer; and I am afraid it will have to be published by itself, as Volume 1 of a larger work. . . . Next time you come down to New York, dear Harry, please leave all of your Boston inhibitions behind. What on earth is friendship for if it is not to endure, at a pinch, the dull and soggy moments of life as well as the electric ones: it is, like marriage, the ultimate life-boat relation, in which the saving element is that both people are afloat together under the same conditions, ready to face all kinds of weather together. Other relationships don't, in general, survive bad weather: one gets bored, one gets irritated, one yawns, one walks away! Since you have been undergoing an analysis, and a Freudian one at that, I don't wonder at your not being able to get any work done: I can't imagine any situation more unfavorable to productivity: a department store might as well complain at its loss of business if it tried to keep open while the front was being torn down and the whole store remodelled. Even if the work is no more than cleaning and stock-taking one can't very well take care of customers at the same time! But apart from this the thing that thwarts us all is the inability to acquire time for consecutive thought. A month of uninterrupted brooding and thinking and writing is for most people infinitely more fruitful than a whole year in which part of every day is broken into or cribbed by other interests. But our present day life is in fact founded on interruptions: the schedule of our days is a succession of them, and against the few interruptions we can manage to pack away in our spinal column there are a dozen which require our notice and effort before we can dispose of them. It is the ability to avoid them that accounts, I think, for the extraordinary superiority in productivity of Europeans over Americans. I find that I have economized an enormous amount of energy this winter by refusing to answer the

1. Werner Sombart, *Der Moderne Kapitalismus,* 6 vols. (1902).

telephone and insisting that anyone who wants to have anything to do with me shall leave a message or write a letter. We still respect, all of us, the claims of the outer world too much, forgetful that these claims, from the standpoint of our own work and development, are half the time as deeply irrelevant as the vaguest wish thinking is in the inner world. The outer world is, in fact, full of King Charles's heads that other people thrust upon us. . . . I am running up to Dartmouth for a few days this week; but alas! my Tuesday lecture at Columbia keeps me from dropping in Boston for a chat with you on my way back. I am eager to hear verbally or literally, about your adventures in the raw and ravenous environment of Chicago.

Lewis

[handwritten]
[LM] Ans 23 Apr 33

Dear Lewis:

I realize that it will be three years before my hibernation will be terminated, & I will be able once more to greet my friends with all the rotund & enveloping cheer which is now stamped down with the sediment of my heart. I have been sick for 15 months & I have only just realized that a fair proportion of my illness can be attributed to the untamed streaming of the subterranean regions which were steamed up by the analysis but never found expression. I went through the experience without mentioning it to anyone & never holding the analyst in high enough esteem to bother to explain the problems which really absorbed me, & always having my scientific reservations in respect to the Freudian doctrine. It was not simply the usual resistance, because we had that all out. It was that when the real problems came up—spiritual & intellectual—I was not met by the wisdom which in certain respects I had found in Jung. I am, nevertheless, an authentic Psychoanalyst—certified & trade-marked. One thing I might mention which developed during the last week was that I was a sort of Patricide (the old familiar) who had been surreptitiously seeking the Perfect Father but critically & skeptically & maliciously; that I had been drawn to one master after another, proved them wanting, discredited them & then passed on to the next victim. & now I had got to a position where I could do no work because I was playing each of them off against the other—the chief figures being L.J. Henderson (science) Pareto & Jung & Melville (political & religious & literary) Freud (psychology). Any one of these attitudes was attacked by the other two & more or less annulled. This ambivalence from the start is of course as old as the hills, but somehow I seemed to see it differently. It illuminated the fact that just when H.M. was writing Hawthorne affectionate letters, he was writing the Duyckincks that there was something wrong with N.H. He needed rare beef.

Which reminds me that a fellow in Duke University is publishing a memoir on H.M. in the South Seas—based on the log of the 'United States' which I copied out 2 years ago after your generous suggestion & then one Larrabee from Union College is coming out with a treatise on Melville's Albany years based on local news-papers.[2] You know this man I think. I have about persuaded the Morgan Library to buy Mrs. Metcalf's collection of letters, etc. She was planning to present them to the N.Y. Public library. As you know I start one new thing after another, cannibalisti-cally—but without digesting it pass on to the next. I have just done it again for *the last time.* The Clinic fund is going to be so low next year that we will have to close down on everything, & so before the crowd disbanded I set in motion a giant scheme for the spring—Fifteen experimenters performing about 30 tests on each of 30 or 40 subjects (unemployed) & then coordinating & correlating our results on the basis of a notion of Determination by a Pattern of Multiple Variables. The idea of causation, or one cause at least, disappears, etc., etc. We are planning each to write several chapters & make up a swan song before the summer, 'An Expose Approach to Personality.' This will postpone other books, articles & works, but I think it's just as well. I want to overcome the publishing inhibition.

[. . .]

Your letter was most heartening to me—your treatise on the perpetual nibbles of the city gave me words to satisfy my own impulsion towards the expression of the gradual wasting away that I have felt when one person after another took their little bite at the precious hours. Your book on the Machine excited me—even me—I would be the last; because in Henry Adams' system of priorities, I stand with the Virgin, & look leagues away towards the Dynamo. Of course intellectually I am with you & if you can make the machine *affectively* palatable to me you will swing me entirely on your side.

How did the machine originate?

A short examination of Kohler's 'Mentality of Apes' will show how under the stress of a Need (Food Hunger in this case) a Monkey will by trial & error & sudden *insights* discover the utility of objects, which then become agencies or tools, for achieving their purpose.[3] Needs are fundamental (i.e. necessity), an environment of heterogeneous objects, play, trial & error, sudden insights (the perception of means-end gestalten), etc. After the tenth century there was the sudden concatena-tion of two things: a new attitude (objective interest) & the earliest devices (brought by the Arabs?) Emergence does not take place until there are many separately de-veloped nuclei (the compass & other minor inventions) ready at hand to be com-bined or to infect the popular mind with the idea of other possible inventions. The chief question seems to be: Why the new attitude? *Why* the prepared mind—ready to leap at nature to use it?

An analyst named Sachs asked himself: Why did not the Romans use machines for industry? He proved to his own satisfaction that in the latter century of the Em-

---

2. Charles Roberts Anderson, *Melville in the South Seas* (1939); Harold A. Larrabee, "Herman Melvile's Early Years in Albany," *New York History* 15 (1934): 144–59.

3. Wolfgang Köhler, *The Mentality of Apes* (1925).

pire there were relatively *few* slaves—many had become freemen & *hence* it was *not* because there was no necessity for machines. Also he showed that they had a rudimentary steam engine & slot machine, but that these were used for *amusement*, at festivals, etc. His answer was this: Body Narcism. The Romans had not emerged from the primitive state of body-worship, & they could not bear to see an inorganic contrivance serving the function of a human body. The projections of certain schizophrenic patients who feel that they are attacked by machine monsters (Frankensteins) give some credence to this theory. According to Sachs the Middle Ages was directed *against* the body—it was vile, unclean, evil, etc. Thus an inhibition or deep repression of body narcism (love of one's own body) took place, which allowed the next generation to create bodies (machines) outside themselves i.e. bodies which were ugly.

I think that Sachs's ideas (unpublished) are extremely vague & I can not explain them, but there seem to be germs of some kind there. In other works this may be one variable which was operative, one variable among the many which characterize Primitive temperaments. I have nothing better to offer, but here are a few free-associations.

(1) I differentiate subjective & objective emphasis in functioning. The subjective emphasis is characteristic of children, primitives, women, hedonists, artists & all truly creative men. The subjective emphasis has in it more egocentricity, narcism & emotional intensity & eroticism. It gives rise to phantasy, play, activity merely to 'let off steam,' pleasure-seeking, visions, mythological constructions & cosmic schemes. All these people, all these activities are Anti-Machine. No inventor was ever a great lover. And hence, assuming that these things are more primitive, they must be subdued or repressed in the personality before a person can obliterate his own soul (i.e. dismiss his narcism) sufficiently to work upon soulless substance. A man who loves to look at himself in a mirror could never invent a machine. The objective emphasis involves a concentration upon the Means-End relationship. And of course the ultimate end is food & preservation—(not hedonistic pleasure, eroticism & poetry) & hence when there is great necessity men are forced into *objectivity* etc.

(2) Northern climates—more struggle at first, later adolescence, less emotion, more means-end emphasis. Hence there were more inventions, more industrial develop'ts in the north of Europe. You could not imagine a Machine in Polynesia.

As I go on expanding the Notion of Narcism or Subjectivism I begin to see more in it—not quite as Sachs described it, but more in terms of Piaget (4 easy books on Child Mentality). Subjectivism is an emphasis on one's own free functioning, bodily or mentally. Later developments bring about rationality with a special emphasis upon internal coherence & structure—*not* upon *correspondence* with external reality. Hence Medieval Philosophy represents the highest develop't of subjective thinking (later examples: Idealistic Philosophies: Fichte, Hegel & now Spengler). The Reformation brought about an extreme reaction back to the concrete, the irrational. Inductive scientific thinking belongs to the objective attitude. Pareto (who will be published in English this spring) is an example.[4] What I have described as subjective, Jung treats in part as Introversion. (cf. Section on Extravert & Introvert thinking) The arch subjectivists are Jews & Russians: very few of either have invented machines or painted good pictures. Music is the medium of the subjectivists (children may compose music but not paint pictures)—Well these are all random shots & if I don't stop now I'll never stop.

My best love to Sophie.

> Yrs
> Harry

P.S. Ahab smashing sextant is subjectivist in meglomanic episode. Ship's carpenter (extraordinary chapter) is epitome of objectivist.

> [typed]
> 4002 Locust Street
> Long Island City
> 23 April 1933

Dear Harry:

Your tremendously stimulating letter of early March came to me just as I was in the midst of writing my difficult chapter on the origins of the Machine: and I was torn between a desire to write you and an even greater compulsion to translate all the suggestions and confirmations of your thought into my own statement of the problem. The latter won out: and it is only now, with about seven-ninths of the first draft written, that, in a state of temporary exhaustion I put my book aside to talk to you. It really will be a good book: my confidence in it grows with the difficulties it presents, for the harder my problems get now, the more resolutely and toughly I attack them—a good sign. This is the first book I have yet written which, apparently, draws freely and demandingly upon all my power: a fine confession for a man to make at the age of 37, with five books behind him! Last fall I thought the book would be in the printer's hands by the end of June: but I will be lucky now if it is done by the end of November. The trouble is partly due to the fact that I must do a lot of elementary spade-work as well as synthesis and critical revaluation: in addition, there are weak parts of my own equipment that must be patched up before I can go further with some of the problems: but underneath it all—which makes it exciting—is the fact that I have something fresh to say, perhaps even something fresh to contribute by way of method. Even the problems that I must leave untouched are, heaven knows, fascinating: the disproportionate number of monks and clergymen who were inventors, for example! It is partly accounted for by the theory you yourself broached, which I was working around to in my own way; but perhaps there is even more to be dug up here, if one only knew where to look. You

---

4. Vilifredo Pareto, *The Mind and Society: A Treatise on General Sociology* (1935).

mistake my attitude if you think I am on the side of the Dynamo: in a sense, the whole book is an effort to get beyond the dichotomy of Dynamo and Virgin, utilitarian and Romantic: but I have taken the route *through* the machine, instead of slipping away from it, as the Romantics sought to do. I have in fact one whole chapter on Reactions from the Machine, which shows how justified the attitudes were, even though the objectives were so remote and unapproachable. But the only sufficient inkling as to what I have been doing will be the second draft of my manuscript; and I only dearly pray that your mind will be temporarily disengaged when that moment comes . . . say around the middle of next August. If however you are deep in either your own work or the remarkable collective research you outlined, don't let it prey on your conscience and good nature—though I count upon you as one of the few people who will be able to see what I am doing in this book. I am doubly sanguine, I suppose, because this is the first time I have ever been able to work at high tension for six weeks steadily in the city: not only in the city but through what would ordinarily be a disabling cold and, along with that, a serious emotional crisis. Somehow these things were as unimportant as a rainstorm when one is travelling in a railroad train: my speed and direction were not lost for a second. The emotional strain was due to the fact that the work that I was doing with Catherine, which had kept us artificially together for a whole year, had just terminated: and we had to face, for a bitter fortnight, the altered state of our relations, which we had kept buried in silence, despite the fact that each was secretly and overwhelmingly aware of if from the time we parted in Europe. The symptoms were simple enough: Catherine had begun a series of restless flirtations: and I was far too preoccupied with my book to attempt to recapture my lost ground, and meanwhile, she had acquired a guilty conscience to such a degree that she had tried to hide what was happening from herself. The airing and sunning of this mess would ordinarily have thrown me off my balance for a month or two: but I went on writing the book steadily and we even patched up a sort of new relationship on top of it. (But underneath this is the now-acknowledged fact: each of us has given up the hope of permanently capturing, of marrying the other! And how profoundly this alters a relationship: it is the possibility of permanence, the attitude that goes with it, that makes the critical difference.) . . . [. . .]

We go up to the country the first week in June. Do try to drop in on us there, dear Harry. Your all too brief visit is one of the bright recollections of last summer. Meanwhile, all power to your work!

> Sophie joins me in warmest
> greetings.
> Lewis

[typed]
4002 Locust Street
Long Island City
28 October 1933

Dear Harry:

The devilment of returning to town and finishing my further preparations for the book and getting my lectures running smoothly—interrupted as it was by equally hectic weekends tidying up the house in Leedsville and worshipping at the fires of autumn—all this has kept me silent since your note came; and I did not want to be silent. [. . .] So I have begun work again: I have already done the first two chapters of my third draft; and they are so much firmer, solider and compacter than the second draft, which I was going to show you, that I am ashamed to let the earlier version, with all its vagueness and verbosity, reach your eyes. Will you wait for the final version? I can send it either chapter by chapter, or all at once, around the middle of January: in either case I should still be able to profit by your criticisms and suggestions. But if in turn you are preoccupied, don't take this on out of friendship: be hard. Friends and lovers must be hard with each other: politeness is a virtue only for the remaining part of the race! All the vigorous manual work I did in September, plus the six weeks of mental relaxations, stood me in good stead: and while I am not completely rested, and while my Columbia lectures and my New Yorker piece are both being scandalously done, on a shamefully low level, because I begrudge them the energy I need for my book, I think I shall pull through nicely if I have any sort of luck. I feel a little like an aviator during the first few hours of his transatlantic flight: buoyed up by the adventure itself, but conscious that he has just enough gasoline to keep him up three or four hours beyond his destination: so that if he encounters headwinds or storms he may be forced down before reaching the coast. On the other hand, the motor is humming smoothly now and the weather reports are good: so my eyes are glued on the dials, and I am ready to take my chances. The book *is* good; and the fact that my publishers, least moveable and most skeptical of men, even felt that way about the second draft, which seems to me so poor, gives me extra confidence in doing the third. There is one point that I should like to discuss with you in relation to one of the later chapters in my book, on the Reaction to the Machine. To what extent do you think that the mechanization and regularization of all our habits and impulses has been compensated for by a more primitive—i.e. more brutal—unconscious. On a casual reading of history, it seems to me that the final stages of civilization look a little more ferocious than the earlier stages: that the natural and to some extent rational savagery of the earlier battle with nature and other men finally becomes, when the battle is no longer necessary, the source of a deeper sadism which increases in proportion to the pressure exerted by civilization—or mechanization. Hence the baiting of the Christians in

Rome: baiting of the Jews by Hitler—and so on. Have you any observations here; or has anyone else made any?

Are you coming down here this fall? It would be fun to see you.

Lewis

[handwritten]
4002 Locust St.
Long Island City, N.Y.
29 January 1934

Dear Harry:

It was impossible to show you the ms. with all its filthy corrections: but I am sending you now the first ten galleys, hoping that they'll tempt you to ask for the rest. But if you are overwhelmed with work, don't bother—though I should dearly value your critical eye & judgment. It has been a long pull and I still have to do a hundred things on the ms.

Catherine Bauer is now in Boston and I've told her she should introduce herself to you. As you've suspected she is Sophy's absolute antithesis. I hope she gets hold of you, and I leave you to discover her special wit & intelligence for yourself—altho, having desperately finished a book of her own, she is a little frayed at the moment.

I shall drop in some time this spring. Possibly in March. Have been working with desperate concentration.

Warmly
Lewis

[typed]
Hanover New Hampshire
19 February 1934

Dear Harry:

Your letter and you comments came at exactly the right moment. I am up here on one of my brief visits and I spent all of yesterday going through my galleys, and your comments were an effective stimulus at just the point I needed them most. That introductory section never satisfied me, although almost every other part of the book is in excellent shape: and though I am too exhausted by now to make it positively better, I have drastically cut it down and thus shorn it of some of its weaknesses, thanks to your aid. Forgive me for even bothering you with the galleys: nevertheless I am glad that they came under your eye. I have been working like a donkey on the final revision of the ms. ever since last October and am full of surprise everyday to find that my strength isn't even more spent than it is, for, physically speaking, my life has been a mean and unhealthy one. It argues well for the internal harmony and underlying contentment, despite the irritated and over-sensitive surface. The book is good: perhaps the first thing I have written that shows more than a faint sign of originality combined with tough, stubborn effort. It is scheduled to come out in the middle of April. Before that, or soon after that, I hope to drop in at Boston on my way to or from Dartmouth to have a chat with you. But eventually you must make a pilgrimage up here: for the Orozco murals are a profound and exciting work.[5] I have been doubly stimulated by them because three of his panels are independently symbolic condensations of my own interpretation of the machine.

Drop in on us if you are down in the city.

Warmly and gratefully
Lewis

[typed]
Mumford
Leedsville
Amenia, New York
19 June 1934

Dear Harry:

[. . .] Sophy and I are both settling down for a long rest, after the pressure and tension of the last few years, and with everything in the garden growing lushly, we look forward to the otherwise abstemious life we'll be spending the rest of the summer, till my regular work begins again in October. Don't count reading Technics an obligation of friendship: I would rather you waited till you were fully in the mood for it, by which time, if that doesn't occur till another few years are over, I will have the two later volumes ready, and my whole outlook and philosophy will be more plain.[6] Even generous and intelligent and well intentioned friends, like Fletcher and Frank, have hastily jumped at conclusions that are not warranted by the book, because they took the statements in Technics as final, instead of as preliminary, to be qualified, in turn, by what I write about the group and the personality.[7] From this experience I begin bitterly to think that the old adage about not showing fools and children unfinished work should be extended: although, at the beginning and at the end, I emphasized that this volume, though it could stand on its own legs, was part of a larger survey. Enough of these wails and imprecations. The image of one-self that one finds in one's friend's mind drives one into a state of ultimate loneliness . . . But this is the usual physiological Timonism, with an undercurrent of smoldering rage and exacerbated vanity, which led me to break with Catherine and quarrel with my publisher and feel generally alienated and bitter all in one short month. Incidentally—perhaps I noted this in my last letter—I began Technics the

5. Mumford used panels from the mural by José Clemente Orozco in the Baker Library at Dartmouth as illustrations in *Technics and Human Development*.

6. *Technics and Civilization* (1934), first volume of the Renewal of Life series.

7. Waldo Frank, novelist and critic (1889–1967).

spring I fell in love with Catherine, and our drawing apart was, apart from her having an affair with her present colleague in Philadelphia, finally symbolized by the fact that the book fell from the press without drawing forth a response from her, although it had been in a sense the leit-motif of our whole intellectual and sexual adventure together. Further fact: I did not really throw my whole energies into the writing of Technics until after our trip together in Europe, when it became plain to both of us that we could not collaborate on our work together and that a closer union would merely reduce Catherine to the status of Sophy: so that the publication of the book and the actual breach merely completed and solemnized the state that had begun to come into existence two years ago. We probably would have parted sooner, for Catherine had a flurry about her present lover in the spring of 1933, just as I was beginning the actual writing of Technics, were it not for the fact that our physical relations were almost unimaginably perfect for both of us, and our bodies refused to recognize the state of our intellect and our affections, until the full weight of circumstance declared itself. So much for my personal life.

I am eager to hear all you have been doing and thinking; even a fragment of it will probably keep me chewing actively at the cud for weeks at a time. So come soon, dear Harry.

Lewis

[handwritten]
[LM] 20 July

Dear Lewis,

What a generous, forgiving & forbearing fellow you are! I am not worthy to have such a friend.

In brief, I have been no kind of a human being except perhaps to three persons, Christiana, my wife & my daughter. I laid out a big program at the Clinic three years ago & I have been slaving to achieve it ever since. Last week I was finally brought to the humiliating knowledge that my brain had struck—simply sat down on its haunches & refused to take another step.

You told me all this last fall, but I couldn't act on it. Now I have to. In 2 days Josephine & my daughter, & I are starting on a six day walking trip down the Long Trail in Vermont. That will be a change—

Now, I must see you. I can stop for a night around Aug. 7th on my way to the St. Lawrence River, but that is too little. Could you by any chance take a few days with me in September? I have a log cabin on a lake in Vermont. We could walk, swim & endlessly converse. *Please.*

Have you heard from John Parke?[8]

I have just started your book & am thrilled by it.

What livens & pleases me so is the freshness & vitality of it—the enormous

8. John Parke, essayist and editor, long-time friend of Murray.

wealth of novel & appealing comparisons, associations, relationships—linking up the monasteries with mechanism, business with science, technics with warfare, etc. In this connection I have always been puzzled by the widespread & spontaneous appearance of regular repetitive acts—touching things a certain number of times; counting steps, repeating words, etc.—in children, usually boys. In adults it appears as a symptom associated with an unconscious sense of guilt. It is related to magic & religious ritual but is more fundamental than any of them. You find it in the infant who wants a story repeated with exactly the same words—it is the most elementary form of mechanization & in contrast to the whimsies of impulse. Well, we can talk about that & lots more when we meet. You are at your best in this book. It is exciting reading because it is knowledgeable & intellectually lively! I cannot wait to get on with it.

I enclose a small check—the Clinic eats up all my spare cash.

> Yrs
> Harry

My best regards to Sophie

[typed]
Mumford
Leedsville
Amenia, New York
20 July 1934

Dear Harry:

Thanks for your generous check. I am now entangled, at the moment, in the red tape of college bureaucracy, and the money that was promised Behrendt has for the moment been snatched out of reach again, though his invitation still holds: so perhaps your bread will come back to you eventually, untouched but laden with virtue.[9]

We shall probably be here from the 24 of July on, since our journey up to Dartmouth now seems dubious; but at all events we'll be here from the fifth of August on and you will be heartily welcome from that time on. We'll expect you on the 7th unless we hear otherwise. I wish I could say yes to your suggestion for September: but so many things might prevent it that I had better say No now and hope that I may reverse the answer later.

I've not had a word from John Parke since I last walked with him around the hills of Vermont. He said he was more pleased with that walk than on any previous one; so since he is a hard young man to suit, I was pleased, too, and fully expected to hear from him before this.

9. Walter Kurt Behrendt (1884–1945), German architect; Mumford helped him come to the United States to escape Nazi Germany and solicited contributions to support a professorship for him at Dartmouth.

What you say in relation to my book about repetitive acts is very exciting and suggestive. It brings up a point I have often thought when looking at Negro textiles from Africa, as indeed, when thinking over the part played by fixed tradition in the social life of savages: namely, that mechanism may be a relatively primitive fact: the simplest way out of chaos. Only after long years of frustration and torture are we forced, perhaps, to conceive more complicated patterns of order, more kind to our natural spontaneity and variety.

Can we conceive of the machine as a projection of the primitive which enables us to get hold of our old stultifying regularities, and by externalizing to—in part— escape them? I throw this out at random of course; it is probably all nonsense.

For the moment—did I tell you this before—I am going through a bitter period. It comes with the realization that the happiness that Sophy and I have experienced together these last four years has been bound up with the continued presence of Catherine, as a balancing factor in my intellectual and sexual life; and with Catherine gone, the deep physiological weakness of our marriage, despite our extreme fondness for each other, is exposed again, as nakedly as it was during the five years that separated Sophy's giving birth to Geddes and my finding Catherine. To make matters worse, we came up here both looking forward to the possibility of Sophy's having another baby: the specialist down in New York having told her to go ahead.

Life! Life! Life!

Don't be afraid to drop in here if you feel tired and irritable. We both rebound quickly, and after a few days of salt bathing we'll probably wonder about what was tearing at our bosoms these last ten days. If the worst comes to the worse, there is rum and brandy and white wine and port in the cellar!

Warmly,
Lewis

[handwritten]

Dear Lewis:

I hope you will find it convenient to have me next Sunday, Aug 5th—night—I will arrive late in the P.M. & then we may talk—that evening & the next morning if you can afford the time. Poor Lewis—your last letter distressed me, but we'll see about it when we meet. Christiana has finished your book & she's as excited about it as when she read Faust Part II for the first time. It has already changed our lives through her. I myself have not had my eye on it since I wrote you but I hope to read a good deal of it before I see you. C thought it was rich, exuberant and original—the way you made the inorganic come to life & relate itself to the pulse of our present life—the fertility of reference & associations, the vision of man in respect to this, your development of the themes of subjective & objective times, your emphasis on the erotic—creative rhythms & lots of other things which I shall tell you when I see you next Sunday.

Yrs
Harry

[handwritten]
[LM] 2 Feb 35

Dear Lewis

The sight of your hand gave me a delicious spring. I was about to write you myself.

How delighted I am to hear about Sophy![10] I saw you last when a near-catastrophe was impending, but I heard nothing of later troubles. Were they of the same nature? As usual Fate falls in upon you and you slay him—for me Fate is masculine when it is Evil, despite the fact that most of my miseries have come from women. The solid virtue of my Jo, and the unpoisoned inexpressible delights which Christiana showers upon me have wiped out the evil that women do. Embrace Sophy for me & tell her how happy I am.

I have a vague recollection of your telling me that you would send me an outline of your book—the chief topics to be considered. I had in mind a scheme of the major social forces & wanted to test it against your analysis. I am glad to hear that the bubbles are rising in your mind again.

I heard that you made an eloquent, passionate & beautifully tactful address at the Pittsfield dinner. Olson told me.[11] He said that he himself blurted out a few discourtesies.

My fall has been full of my life with Christiana and our work at the Clinic. The first is an unending rhythm and advance into new kinds of synergy—each with its own special grace. The only outward experience has been the posing for Gaston Lachaise.[12] The thing started as a bust and grew under Lachaise's mounting passion into an exceedingly vigorous—almost startlingly natural—statue. It is positively the most living figure I have ever seen in any material—raw, impressionistic, electric—at once serene & violent. We are immensely pleased with it. The posing for it & the business of settling for it, however, has been at times disagreeable as Lachaise's infantilisms were brought to the foreward. He worked in the fury of some kind of phantasy which pictured me as a forbidding, depriving rival male. It was all too absurd, but it became tense when he proposed having other casts made & selling them to Museums which had already begun to bid on it. I shall tell you the story sometime. By the way, can you give me information on one point? I contracted for the bust & later for the statue—paying him in full. I told him in the be-

---

10. Sophia Mumford was pregnant.
11. Charles Olson (1910–1970), poet, author of *Call Me Ishmael* (1947).
12. Gaston Lachaise (1882–1935), sculptor, notorious for conflicts with his clients.

ginning it was for myself. Question: Am I entitled to the plaster cast, or must he destroy it, or can he later at his own discretion have reproductions made of it? I hope you will go to Lachaise's Exhibition in about 2 weeks time and write me what you think of it. He expects to have it cast in bronze before that date, at this time there is some question about it.

The work at the Clinic has progressed marvelously well. We are studying 15 more graduate students throughout this year. Most of the material will be collected and written up by June, but I expect it will take the summer to put it into final shape.

John Parke spent 2 days with me, and I was impressed by the progress he had made. He was moody, was hurt by some casual remarks I made & then became a Timon, & went off to Vermont to gather his forces on a farm.

I am finishing 'Men of Good Will' but I haven't reached the later novels—The Proud and the Meek, etc.[13] I like the former immensely, but there are some tiresome passages. It is all too long. Again my prejudice is in favor of the world seen from one Consciousness. The contrast of H.G. Wells & J.C. Powys in the Autobiographies is exciting. Let me know when you're coming up. At the last minute I had to give up calling you in N.Y. I was so disappointed.

> Yrs
> Harry

> [typed]
> Mumford
> 4002 Forty-Fourth Street
> Long Island City, New York
> 2 February 1935

Dear Harry:

There are so many things to write you about that I hardly know where to begin. As to an outline of my book it must have been only my immediate desire to please you that made me promise to send you it: when I am ready to begin writing, I do have such an outline, chapter by chapter, but I am much more likely to discover what I have been writing about when I reach the third draft than I am before I begin. Logical analysis for me is the derivative rather than the scaffolding upon which I hang ideas; and though I could give you my own scheme of the major social forces, for I have not been a student of Geddes for nought, it would have nothing directly to do with my book, and probably would not be as useful as what I shall be able to give you when the work is done. (You have incidentally anticipated my so far secret plan to follow the three books I am writing with a short book in which I will finally *state* my philosophy.) Your letter recalls all sorts of ancient memories:

---

13. Jules Romains, *The Proud and the Meek,* vol. 3 of *Men of Good Will* (1933–1946).

some pleasant, some painful. The Pittsfield jaunt was disjointed but amusing: and Olson's fault, incidentally, was not discourtesy but a failure to appreciate the difference between an academic audience and a gathering of townspeople. I suppose that by contrast I did have tact; although when I finally proposed the toast at the end, drunk in very bad sherry, I did remind them of the fact that Mr. Mansfield and Mr. Duyckinck had supplied the earlier literati with Champagne.[14] Your happiness with Christiana put a final dagger, by way of contrast, into my feelings about Catherine: by now, I think, the corpse of Catherine-and-Lewis is buried, although a letter from her, now intimate as if nothing had happened, or now casual, as if we had been introduced for the first time the day before, can fill me for days with a black resentment. What does Chaucer say? There is noughte so dead as a deadde love. . . . And by contrast this brings me to Lachaise's exhibition. At his best, there is really no one in America now to top him; his whole series of standing women seems to me fine, and the big one with the uplifted arm, his archetypal and perfect figure, topnotch. Most of his pure abstractions seem to me empty. As for the portrait, I looked at it so hard for the character I was trying to fathom, and for the part of you I was trying to know more intimately that I doubt if I have anything like a pure esthetic response: it did seem to me to have a vitality that none of the other male heads, fine that they were, touched, the only rival to it being the small head of a girl that was next to it. The passion and intelligence of that head make me think that Lachaise did a good job; I even accepted, though I do not altogether understand, the blurred mouth. . . . As for the ethics and law of the purchase, I haven't the faintest notion about it; except that it seems to me than an order puts the piece solely in the possession of the one who has ordered, being different from a piece done by the sculptor for chance sale.

Did I tell you that the Carnegie Corporation has granted me $1500 towards travel for my next book? Unfortunately I cannot do it this year, any more than I can say yes to your own generous proposal for vacation in June; for it is then that I shall probably be needed most in the household. . . . in addition to which is the fact that I lost the first two months of Geddes's young life by going to Europe and want to fill up this gap in my experience. At the moment, I am tired and want to go away for a short trip; but all places that tempt me are too far away: so if the weather remains cold I'll probably break the routine by ice-skating in Central Park! Fortunately, I am not in a hurry to begin the first draft of my book; in fact, I have no intention of tackling it till next summer at earliest, perhaps not till next fall. Sophy is big and at peace; so at least the hub of our world here is in place. As for me my fatigue is prob-

14. Evert Duyckinck attended the famous literary picnic in the Berkshires at which Melville met Hawthorne (August 5, 1950); Oliver Wendell Holmes actually provided the champagne for the occasion. On August 8, Melville visited Hawthorne and was served champagne that Lewis W. Mansfield had given to Hawthorne.

ably due to a cycle of things, half-neurotic in origin, beginning with an ultra-abstemious sexual life, in marked contrast to the last ten years, and in colossal contrast to the last four of them: then comes over-pressure in other departments and that leads to tenseness and that ends up eventually with indigestion. "Well does the drowning man know his danger; willingly would he avoid it; and yet the unfortunate wretch will drown." I have not read that passage of Melville's for years, but the sense has stayed by me. And speaking of sense, have you ever run across the writings of Lady Victoria Welby? She was one of that galaxy of late Victorian ladies who include Vernon Lee and Jane Harrison, and she wrote a series of papers and books on the meaning of meaning that anticipated much of Ogden and Richards.[15] (They mention her in passing, I believe; but I don't think they appreciated her distinction between sense, meaning, and significance, or they would have given a better account of meaning than they did. Their definition is really a tautology.) I think you will like Lady Victoria. I picked up a book of hers at second hand the other day and am reading her for the first time, although Geddes had told me of her long ago. And did you ever run across Mary Boole, the wife of the mathematical logician?[16] There was another mind. You must surely have heard legends about Boole at Cambridge. They still, I understand, withhold publication of his mss. because they do not know if he was insane or a genius.

So much for tonight, dear Harry. And—this is true of all I write, or at least is true too often—I haven't begun to say anything yet. Your being an analyst slightly inhibits me; not because I am afraid to disclose all that I am feeling and thinking, but because I don't want to appear to be adding a patient to a friend.

Lewis

[handwritten]
[LM] Ans 24 March 35

Lewis, my poor fellow,

I should like to take you quietly away some place where you could rest in peace for a time & mend. You were a brick to write me about the statue. I haven't seen it since it was done in clay. I will be disappointed if the bronze is less than that. The blurred mouth was what Lachaise saw—a conflict between passion and restraint—expression & reticence. Excuse me for asking about your conceptual scheme—I was under the impression that you had mentioned something of the sort—a scaf-

---

15. Lady Victoria Welby (1837–1912), correspondent of Charles Pierce and author of *What Is Meaning? Studies in the Development of Significance* (1903). Vernon Lee, pseudonym of Violet Paget (1856–1935), prolific author of essays, fiction, and drama. Jane Harrison (1850–1928), Cambridge classical scholar, authored *Prolegomena to the Study of Greek Religion* (1903). C. K. Ogden and I. A. Richards, *The Meaning of Meaning: A Study of the Influence of Language Upon Thought and the Science of Symbolism* (1923).

16. Mary Everest Boole (1832–1916), wife of logician George Boole, published works on mathematical learning and psychology.

folding which you intended to follow. It seems to me much more right for you not to traffic in such things. With me it is otherwise. I build, tear down, build, tear down. . . . ad infinitum & never come to anything. And, then, in a kind of desperation write anything that happens to be in my head. My difficulty is that there is no preliminary classification or set of fundamental concepts to go ahead on—there are too many empty spaces which need to be filled in before any adequate map is possible, and altho' there is a lot of work going on here we can not possibly get more than a bird's eye view of each region. Nevertheless we are pushing ahead & I hope, if all goes well, to have 'Explorations in Personality' finished by the fall. I am mortified to think that my mention of Christiana should have stabbed you so unmercifully. My *work* has been a long series of abortive failures for six years—during which time you have steadily increased in depth and power. This is partly because with me Love & Life has come first—This has succeeded beyond my last dream but everything else has failed. I have encysted myself from everyone. I have lost all my friends—unless perhaps your generosity still included me—but you are the only one. I don't have anything to do with students or faculty. I have read practically nothing, have worked like a slave—doing an enormous amount of routine work for which there is nothing to show—But I am happy & now my head is clearing. At the moment, however, I am undone by a fearful stroke of fate which I can hardly bear.[17] I am going to N.Y. to be there from Thurs, March 6-Sat M 16. Will you call me at my mother's 105 East 67, Rhin 4-1906.

Yrs
H

[typed]
4002 44 Street
Long Island City
3 May 1935

Dear Harry:

I am afraid I have only breath for a short letter, not because my days have been too crowded, but because they have been disjointed and interrupted. But there have been, nevertheless, Events: or rather, an Event, for Sophy gave birth to a girl, last Sunday morning, as the light was breaking over the rooftops of the dark tenements in back of the Doctors Hospital on the East River and as a warm wind was surging through the window. The pains were hard but the duration short: the obstetrician turned out to be a fine fellow, and the young lady herself, Alison—pulled by the neck out of Chaucer—has a shapely head and an alert eye and a well-formed body: so that, all in all, Sophy and I have had a feeling of rich beatitude and fulfillment, and even young Geddes, though he despises the sex he will presently adore, thinks that Alison is a pretty good example of the species and is on the whole rather

---

17. Murray's brother, Cecil ("Ike"), was fatally ill with Hodgkin's disease.

proud and, apparently, not in the least upset by her arrival—although the tension just before the end reduced him to a slightly infantile state in school. Sophy, as always in the difficult moments, has been magnificent: and as I walked out on East River park in the early morning, feeling as fresh within as the air that was blowing the smell of salt and earth in my face, life had never seemed more complete. I was at one with Sophy and with the universe and—at the other pole—with Alice: indeed, part of the reality of those five hours of Sophy's travail was that, in cold clarity, the image of Alice shared the vigil with the image and the reality of Sophy.[18] We had parted a fortnight before; and just the night before Sophy's delivery Alice had been able to stand it no longer and appeared suddenly at a meeting where I was expected to be; and instead of attending it, we both wandered about in Central Park, feeling tragic and desperate and ecstatic. But it was part of her character, for her passion for motherhood is as deep as Sophy's, to take Sophy's baby gladly, despite the fact that having one herself is her deepest wish and need. So here I am, dear Harry, with the bounty of life running over me, feeding as it were on the pain and blood of two women, with nothing lacking for my own completion except the sober even rhythm of work. I shall be going up to the country toward the end of the month: but I have a commencement address to give at Oberlin, and a week's course at Syracuse early in July, before I will be free to wander and ponder and wonder and write. . . . Meanwhile, what of you? Forgive these egoistic vaporings. I merely meant to write: Sophy has given birth to a girl and we are all very happy. That would be true, too.

Lewis

[handwritten]
64 Plympton St.
Cambridge

Dear Lewis,

I have a head full of ideas to discuss with you. Your life, my life & destiny. Is there any chance that you might come to Mexico City with Christiana & myself by boat on July 11th or later? We would stay in a delightful spot—a little inn next door to Rivera's studio for a week or so.[19] I have a double cabin both ways with an extra bunk so that your steamship passage would cost you nothing. I don't think that the R.R. fare would be very expensive. You would be, of course, entirely free & we

---

18. Alice Decker, a sculptor married to Duncan Ferguson; Mumford's love affair with her lasted from late 1934 through 1937. See Donald L. Miller, *Lewis Mumford: A Life* (New York: Weidenfeld and Nicholson, 1989), 344–53.

19. Diego Rivera (1886–1956), Mexican mural painter.

would not encroach on your time. We would just be there—in case you wanted to talk

July 11th–July 30th or July 11th–August 6th. Wouldn't it be a good thing? It would be extremely exciting for us if you came.

> Yrs
> Harry

[handwritten]
Amenia, New York
23 June 1935

Dear Harry:

Your letter, which was waiting here for me, reminded me how inadequately—since I was conscious chiefly of the sad impossibility of the plan—I thanked you for your generous invitation, so deeply in the pattern on which our friendship was first formed. Believe me, Harry: there is not another man to whom I feel anything like the same tie . . . though our meetings are always so scattered and incomplete.

The tension between Alice & Sophy had been mounting steadily these last six weeks: because before that Sophy, in self-protection, to ensure a serene childbirth, would not let herself face what was happening. It was brooding like a storm over the landscape when I went down to New York: it came between Alice-and-me, caused a new tension there as the decision stretched me to the breaking point, and, after a bad afternoon we had together Thursday, flung me into a black mire of jealousy over Alice's arrangement to leave me & have dinner with an otherwise unthreatening male friend—to conceal our afternoon from Duncan. Wracked by that I came back to Amenia in blackest misery to find my whole domicile here in ruins: the storm had finally broken during my absence—leaving Sophy with defeat in her heart, regrets over having born the baby, and suicidal thoughts of seeking a "solution" by drowning, since Alice, as a permanent, perhaps a growing, feature of the landscape—or a succession of Alice's—left her with a sense of complete unfulfillment & emptiness.

In the midst of this double wreck I am now tossing around: miles from shore: no bearings till daylight comes: and two drowning women, both dear to me, unable to keep afloat without my help—whilst my own strength, partly spent in the necessities of my work, will scarcely suffice to drag one alone safe to shore.

May the strength of Hercules & the wily skill of Old Odysseus keep this battered swimmer afloat!

(What a strange letter to be prompted by my original desire to grasp your hand & say thanks again. You offered to make me a steamer-companion & I reciprocate by throwing myself overboard & playing the drowning man!)

> Lewis

[handwritten]

Dear, dear Lewis

After seeing you I went to Cambridge, but almost immediately returned to New York & here a few days later I received your troublous letter. I immediately thought of what you said about the Government—people are apt to forget that it takes time to create & establish a new thing. My heart warmed to you & I longed for the time to go to you. Again I thought this might be the proper moment for Mexico. But no—there in Amenia you'll settle down & remain quiet & everything will fall into place in Time. Our marriage customs are firmly fixed in the minds of us all and it's hard to dislodge them—particularly if you try to force them out too violently. But even drops of water can bore through a stone in Time. You'll probably have to stop any action or a further advance of action until everyone concerned has become acclimatized to the new state of things. Keep stout heart Lewis & cement your loyalties, but don't give up anything. Retract not & the others will probably move into the scheme you are creating. You are helping to form a new mode of living & you must give it a universal meaning.[20] It is much more than being in love with two women. Poor Lewis—miserable on the verge of Paradise. You see I am determined that you find your paradise—

As for me, my best & most loyal friend, I have lost my long-cherished gallant brother. After a long heroic struggle against some relentless & baffling organic foe the poor lad finally succumbed as the sun rose on Independence Day. This cut in & made a scar that will never heal, but it may make me even more aware of the preciousness of every hour of health and the nearness of the Eternal Victor. My next address will be c/o Wells Fargo & Co, Mexico City. I expect to be back about August 1st & will call on you—Harry

[handwritten]
Syracuse, New York
8 July 1935

Dear Harry:

Here is my hand, which is all I can offer to console you for your loss: "take comfort in what remains behind." What you say about my own dilemma gives me renewed courage: during the last three weeks all my natural juices curdled and became poisonous and your words have been a brave antidote. The tension & conflict would have been bearable but for the fact that both parts of the relationship went to pieces at once. My union with Alice had been so complete and so unbroken over the six months in which it had developed that we each had the illusion that we knew each other completely: the last episode, trivial in all its external manifestations but deeply disturbing in the supercharge of affects it developed in both of us, showed us that there was a darker side to each of our planets we had not explored.

---

20. Mumford's note: "His own object! LM 1970."

It's perhaps well that this discovery came now—and over a trivial series of mistakes—than later, over a more important issue: but the psychological reactions could not have been more painful no matter how grave the issue.

Enough of this: life goes on! I trust that your days in Mexico with C. will be healing days. Please remember me to her: having said no to the possibility of meeting her now, I almost feel as if I *had* met her: internally, my attitude was all prepared.

Incidentally, the one thing that's at all appeased the torment of the last three weeks was a fine letter from Catherine, from whom I parted a year ago. In three sentences she at last honestly faced what she had done at our parting, and so opened the way to a resumption of our intellectual friendship. Being domestically in love with Sophia, romantically in love with Alice, and intellectually in love with Catherine, I ought to count myself thrice blessed: but the fact is that each of them in her heart of hearts wants to exist in all three relations: so that what is complete and perfect for me is fragmentary & imperfect for them. Of the three, Sophia is the most generous, because she has had the greatest fulfillment: Catherine has not accepted and Alice has not been able to have a child. When things are in equilibrium they are all three very friendly, too: so, when Sophia was in the Hospital Alice & Catherine sent her a bunch of flowers & invited her to be a co-member of their newly invented "League Against War, Fascism, & Lewis Mumford"! Sophy answered in kind & accepted charter membership and said in a postscript "He's a nice man anyway."

But you have better things to do in Mexico than to decipher this scrawl.

Affectionately
Lewis

[handwritten]
Mid-River Farm
Clayton, N.Y.

What a blessing, dear Lewis, to receive your letter in Mexico. It was the only word I received, since none but you knew I was there, and it came to add the final touch and to be inseparably fused with my delight. Everything I saw was new, interesting, amusing or exciting—tropical vegetation, agriculture, pulque raising & production, the Asiatic Indian with a lust for revolution, the Aztec & Toltec remains & the problems which they raise, the countryside & snow-mantled Popocatepetl, the Franciscan convents & monasteries, Carmelite churches & native fiestas—the strange primitive-partially Christianized dances, the temper of the people—bullfights, red light district, foods, market, habits, the hospitals & insane asylum—all these were wonder to us particularly as followed by six relaxed days at sea & closed by an airplane flight from Mexico to New York in 27 hours—Night-flying—the wonder of it. It was so pleasant that I couldn't escape from a slight feeling of corruption.

When I returned I did 15 days work in 9 days then stopped & came up here.

Now I am off to New Mexico to see something of the Navajos—the dances & a short pack trip with my two miraculous Josephines into the canyons & cliff-dwelling districts. So you see I have really ceased working this summer—have even temporarily lost the thread of the book. My mind has been still as regards psychological concepts. As far as love goes—and with me it goes *all* the way—I keep forgetting that Christiana had a very hard time making a go of it with me, & I was continually disturbed, elated, depressed, frantic & disheartened during the first year or two, & then it was only 4 years ago that another woman came into the picture for 6 mos, and so the now-just-ten years of our love has not been without turmoil & it took 7 years to reach a to-the-end-of-life utter inward understanding & even now we are discovering further darker points every season. So, take heart Lewis—it will come out. I wish Alice could talk to Christiana. I hope you have found some peace this month. I shall be looking forward to some word from you in Sept (after the 15th when I return).

> Yrs
> Harry

> [typed]
> Amenia, New York
> 12 September 1935

Dear Harry:

Your letter which brought joy, in that it had so much of the joy and tingle of your own life and your recent experience, found me beginning the first draft of my book: since then I have been working steadily, picking my way through the treacherous first chapter in the way that a man leaps from hummock to hummock in a sticky swamp, not cutting a very direct line, not sure at what point he is going to come out, and with none of the exhilaration that comes from a dash downhill in the open. The pace and the attitude both come from the fact that my jumping off place is really unfamiliar ground, and that I am trying to cover it in a way different from that of the conventional anthropologist and sociologist, different from even my old Geddes himself: I am too conscious of the dangers, at the moment, to get the pleasure of the view: but I have a notion that this chapter may turn out to be better, in the end, than the material I know too well and have explored perhaps too often. The summer? A quiet one: a domestic one. The worst part of it, and that was very bad indeed, was over by the middle of July. I saw Alice on my way back from Syracuse and had a half dozen very exhilarating hours with her. Before another day was over her husband announced to her that he had discovered that she had resumed relations with me—after promising, under duress, that all was over in April. This time it was plain that he wanted her back: in April he had pretended to be indifferent and she had run to cover quickly, partly out of fear, partly because everything else seemed a blind alley. She had two or three stormy weeks trying to make a decision; then she went back with him to Maine to gather up their household goods. They had spent the first three years or so of their marriage in Maine, at Cape Neddick; those had been good years for both of them; and the return to the old scene, the finding of somebody's diapers in the living room and a neglected bed in the garden brought them together and made them friends. She decided to remain with him and go down to Louisiana; hoping to write me and receive letters from me secretly, if it could be arranged. But the deceit was as hateful to her as it was to me: and when I pointed out that it would make a bitter wreck of their parting, if the discovery of it became the reason for Duncan's insisting on separation, she argued it out with him and received a sort of half-permission to continue our correspondence. So there we are. She has been gone three weeks. I have received a postcard: our love is embalmed for the nonce in a platonic heaven, since any letters we exchange are, as it were, subject to postal inspection and the censor. As for my own feelings? I must confess that I dreaded equally either decision: her staying because it would have wrecked the happiest period of domesticity I've yet experienced: her going because it equally wrecks the deepest union, in a spiritual sense, I have yet had with anyone. Fortunately, my work canalizes all my waking hours; and as for my dreams, when I dream of her at night my damned realism prevents them from having even a tinge of symbolism to say nothing of satisfaction: they are the all too factual dreams of wanting to make love and knowing that her husband is in the same hotel, or is in the next room, and may break in upon us. What price Freud? (Speaking of whom, I've recently read an English criticism of Freud's theory of hate, by Ian Suttie, an English analyst, which seemed to me very sound indeed.[21] It was also a criticism of the scientific "taboo on tenderness." Do you know him?). . . . [. . .]

Warmly,
Lewis

[typed]
4002—44 Street
Long Island City
9 November 1935

Dear Harry:

The reprints of your articles came yesterday, and I read them last night before going to bed, delighted as I always am, to get even some fragment of your thought as you take it in stride. I am sure that your surgical dissection of the weakness of your various colleagues, considered collectively, must have awakened, and will continue to awaken, a great deal of resentment: the reaction is bound to be hot because your case is unanswerable, and the attack that you advocate is bound sooner or later to unite that scattered army which—so like that other religion, the communists—wastes its energies bickering and fighting with rivals within the camp, while the enemy outside is safe and unchallenged. You have stated the whole situation

---

21. Ian D. Suttie, *The Origins of Love and Hate* (1935).

from the standpoint of psychology precisely the way in which I should like to state it from that of sociology. Fortunately a growing body of people are of our way of thinking: the special reception that Technics has received, both here and in England, gives me extra personal conviction as to that. The fact of the matter is that the essence of both sociology and psychology is better *perceived* in literature than it is in science: the problem in both disciplines is how to achieve order and calculable results without displacing the veritable subject matter that is to be treated. The novelist, the dramatist, the poet at least know where the subject matter lies and have some inkling as to the hierarchy of values to be observed. In both our sciences, however, the tendency is to make the dominant abstractions into fields of investigation, instead of realizing that they are merely instruments for exploring quite different fields, namely, the personality itself, the community itself. During the last few months I have been trying, as a foundation chapter of my book on cities, to revise current sociological notions as to the way in which groups function, and I think I have got the beginnings of order in my own department—results that please me because they check up with the work of some of the better sociologists, arrived at by quite different means. When I get it re-written next spring I want to submit this chapter to you for criticism: this chapter specially, more particularly the part on the role of signs (language), symbols (arts), patterns (manners, morals, and laws) and form (architecture and environmental transformations) in expressing and embodying community.

My winter schedule seems to be working out well: never have I been less burdened with either work or financial anxieties; and if I am able to keep up my present schedule the first draft of my book ought to be done by the end of January, and I shall be ready to leave for Europe at the end of April. Alison is still sweet and lovely and very adorable; and I have no difficulty at all in understanding all the latent incestuous impulses that exist between a father and a daughter! She has a way of lying—I suppose all girl babies must do it—with her legs spread apart as if waiting for her lover, which is very fetching indeed. . . . As for my personal life, it was pretty badly disrupted for a while by Alice's leaving for Baton Rouge in September; and it was thrown into a perfect tumult of indecision and cross desires by her quite accidental return northward in the middle of October, to act as a judge of sculpture for the P.W.A. in Washington. We had corresponded together, under Duncan's eye, since the end of September: but the first letter of mine that he read, which was chiefly about the weather, had such an effect on him that he wouldn't speak to Alice for two days. (Which proves, of course, that one can't really disguise an honest feeling: it likewise proves the futility of formal censorship.) Alice had reached the conclusion, before this sudden summons to Washington came, that we'd have to give up writing to each other; so that she could give her marriage with Duncan one last fair trial. Seeing each other was a terrible mistake; it made her going back almost impossible for both of us, and when she actually did go it left me with all sorts of self-hate for having been an acquiescent coward. Fortunately, I got one last illicit note from her, as she speeded southward, to say that everything between us was still fair and fine; at least she didn't hate me as much as I had been hating myself. So now we face a year of silence: the crazy romanticism of which is in the very mood of the whole interrupted life of perpetual partings and stormy reunions that we have so far had. Meanwhile, Sophy and I have sailed into calm water again: the depth and peace of which made me fear Alice's return almost as much as I welcomed it. Never indeed had I been the victim before of such a powerful ambivalence!

You will have to come down to see the Van Gogh show, dear Harry, even though the people are already being packed into the Museum daily as if it were a Bronx subway train at the rush hour. That will be before I shall be able to visit Boston; but if you don't come, I will stop off in early February at latest, if all my present plans keep straight. What have you been reading?

Warmly,
Lewis

[typed]
4002—44 Street
Long Island City
10 January 1936

Dear Harry:

I've been meaning to write you; but I've been fathoms deep in my book, and since the first of November managed to block most of the first draft, about 135,000 words, which is a great deal. And at the moment, instead of gossiping freely, I come to you with my troubles, and even a professional problem.

Last Saturday I got word through Catherine that Alice and her husband, Duncan, had been in an auto accident that took place on 27 December. Duncan was only slightly hurt: Alice was knocked against the side of the car and suffered a severe concussion. This happened near Lake Charles, La., and they had been taken to the St. Patrick's Sanitarium at Lake Charles.

I needn't describe my own frantic and helpless reactions: the only saving element has been that Catherine has relayed to me all the information that has come through from Alice's parents, who were summoned down there on New Year's day.

The concussion was followed by a hemorrhage: when that took place I do not know. Apart from this she apparently sustained no physical injuries. She was unconscious for two days and when she came to was in delirium: at times became very violent and had to be held down by three people. This has gradually abated; the violence comes less frequently; and at the end of last week she recognized her parents for the first time, and has patches of almost rational conversation: but does not know what has happened or where she is. Pulse and temperature apparently normal; appetite good.

I phoned Dr. Israel Wechsler of the Neurological Institute about Alice: he was friendly when she was a social service worker there and she trusted him. He gave me the name of two New Orleans men, Holbrook and May, which names Catherine forwarded to the parents suggesting the advisability of a consultation.

As far as concerns Alice, Duncan has been behaving very fine: constant attention, fierce devotion, been with her day and night, and is naturally worn to pieces. Unfortunately, he was sent into a paroxysm of jealousy by the bouquet of flowers that I in my helplessness and anxiety lest Alice should die without even having the consolation of a symbol from me, sent down: and out of this hate and weariness he sent me a little letter warning me to "keep out of it." (He little knows how near he came to seeing me there in person!)

I tell you all these weary details in order to lead up to what I am asking about. Duncan probably suspects every move of Catherine's as a move of mine: with some reason, since Catherine would naturally consult me even if I didn't prompt her. The last telegram from Alice's parents says that the doctor on the case knows Dr. May but does not feel that a consultation is necessary, and that Alice within a week will probably be taken up to Baton Rouge in an ambulance with a nurse.

Could you say, with this third-hand information, and at this distance, whether a consultation with a neurologist is indicated? It happens that Wechsler is going down to Memphis next month, and I think he might be interested enough in Alice to travel the extra distance to Baton Rouge. Or do you know of any one in Baton Rouge? Or would you suggest calling in a New Orleans man? Or is it—as it may well be—just a matter of more or less indefinite and undecipherable time before the condition will be cleared up by nature, without the benefit of further therapeutics?

There is just a possibility that the whole thing has been complicated by the mental strain Alice has been going through: for against her solemn word of honor to Duncan she smuggled through a note and a keepsake at Christmas. Very fortunately, she has not mentioned me during her delirium: this has been a great comfort to Duncan, and the fact that she might mention me or want me has been one of the greatest torments and fears I have suffered: so in the very act of taunting me with this fact, Duncan, poor fellow, really reassured me. Still, in part the psyche may have taken the accident as an excuse for escaping from the unbearable strain: may it not? I suppose that possibility and the proper approach to it need only be faced after nature has been given due time for the natural processes of healing.

As usual, Sophy has behaved magnificently all this last week; and when I am honest with myself, I pray for Duncan's reunion with Alice, not because I love her less, but because I know no way of managing a life attached to two loves of such equal valence. It was her own perception of this that made Alice decide to stick to Duncan, or at least make one last try this winter. A new Duncan, a Duncan who had become a man and had outgrown his narcissism, a tender Duncan, a devoted Duncan, emerging from this horrible tragedy, may be able to give Alice something she had never known till she met me. (Only I am afraid the burden of the past will cripple him; and he will, in order to consolidate his position, make me real again to her by trying to persuade her to share his hatred of me. And unfortunately neither I nor anyone else can warn him against this very probable folly.)

But I started, dear Harry, not to pour out my heart, but to ask a simple question. Namely, does it seem that anything can be done except by care and rest and time? There is fortunately a rich aunt up here whom Catherine can approach if a consultant is needed; and I don't think Duncan will be suspicious of my hand in relation to *her*.

Warmly

Lewis

P.S. Harcourt's are looking forward eagerly to your Clinic book: so am I.

[handwritten]

Dear Blessed Miserable Lewis,

I have just opened your letter. It was addressed to me in New York. It must have arrived here two days ago companioned by a lot of riff raff, but only today did my eye light upon it. What a plight! I should say that A. had already passed the critical period & that, for the immediate future, it was a matter of quiet and immobility—a slow convalescence. Concussion is any blow on the head followed by unconsciousness. It may be of no significance whatsoever. With hemorrhage it is more serious—because of the longer recovery & the possibility of pressure at some particular point which may later give rise to a little trouble. The immediately (at the time of the accident) important point to determine is whether or not there is a fracture of the skull. This is recognized by X-Ray, eye symptoms, bleeding from nose, etc. A fracture may cause no impairment. Aside from a few technical procedures—such as spinal puncture which any doctor can do—the medical profession are quite helpless in such cases. The only treatment is rest. Therefore, I should say that the time for a specialist had passed or perhaps was coming, but that now nothing was to be gained by consulting. It is hard to tell at this distance, and, of course, one is apt to call a specialist just to make sure that nothing has been neglected. Since the doctor has said it was not necessary & since Duncan would call one if he was worried & since the promotion of any such measure by you might cause disturbance, I believe that I should pray. It looks as if everything was coming out alright. She should be allowed a long rest.

It is all too unfortunate—particularly the coercion of Duncan's narcism upon A. This seems to me to be an ignominious & shameful bondage. There should never be a barrier put between you & A at such a time. But these are matters for the future.

I do not know any neurologist in Louisiana nor does a neurologist friend of mine here just consulted. If Dr. Wechsler could see her it would be a great relief & I should think he might be persuaded to make the trip. I am dreadfully sorry. It makes me sick to think of your frantic helplessness. I feel sure it will come out alright—but now it is hell. My heart to you.

[typed]
4002—44 Street
Long Island City
5 March 1936

. . . I would have written you weeks ago, dear Harry: but there was both too much and too little to write. Nothing had happened, and everything had happened. The week after I wrote you last, after Duncan had gone back South, Alice had a relapse: her suicidal impulses were so violent that Wechsler ordered a watch on her night and day. I interpreted this as due to the fact the absence of Duncan had placed the burden of censorship over her relations upon Alice, and that the strain, in the state of her health then, was unbearable, because her original conflicts were now doubly keen and exacerbated. Since I knew that Duncan did not know enough to tell Wechsler about Alice's state when the accident had occurred and that Alice herself probably did not remember enough, I wrote Wechsler a long letter explaining, as objectively as possible, her state before the accident had happened, giving him also a picture of the reasons for the breakdown of her marriage before I arrived on the scene. He apparently did not care to discuss it any further with me; although he thanked me, when I met him at an evening party a few days later, for supplying him with the missing links for his understanding of the case. I had imagined that he would attempt to lift the censorship for Alice: instead, he clamped down on it more heavily: told her to forget the past, to live in the present and the future, and—presumably—to forget me and to concentrate upon resuming her relations with Duncan. As to the latter, her conscious self needed no inducements: he had become during her illness, as I had predicted originally, the sort of man she had all the time wanted but never possessed: not merely was she in a state of psychological dependence upon him, but she felt that only he could understand her present state completely, since he too had been the victim once of manic-depressive impulses that led to his attempted suicide. In short, they were now in complete rapport; and, so far from making any effort even under cover of illness to get in touch with me, she did not even send a message through Catherine: rather, I became the obstacle that was in the way of her complete re-union with Duncan: the memory of me increased her sense of guilt toward him. I became, in a sense, the enemy of her marriage: to be conquered and fought down. Wechsler had told her that the burden of her recovery must rest on her; and she accepted this—although a fortnight ago she had reached a state of self-awareness in which she told Catherine that she realized that her desperate desire to go to New York was a desire to be near me, and that even her insistence upon Wechsler's aid was an attempt to be linked up with me—for the tenuous reason that I had once met Wechsler and said that I liked him.

Resurrection

I will go on, you will go on,
We two will go on together.
The grave is dug, you the earth, you the digger,
There I will lie, asphyxiate, while you heap
The dust, the rubble, the torn sod.
Quick random weeds will almost close the gash,
No slab will stand, no flowers droop
In dull remembrance:
And there will be no mound.
I will be deep below: the surface will not tell
Your feet when you lead his feet across,
Your double heels upon my face,
Unfleshed,
The chalk eyes unwincing,
Alone the teeth remembering to smile.
I will remain inviolate, unvisited,
Within the grave you dug,
You tamped in haste
Lest my expired breath should ruffle chaos
On your brow.
I know, you know
That such a savage grave
(You the digger, you the dark earth)
Belongs
Not to the dead
Nor the forgotten.

LM

[handwritten]
158 Mt. Vernon Street
[LM] 1936

Dear Lewis,

I was distressed not to see you in New York. I went straight through to Washington on the night train & on my way home planned to have a day in New York to see you. I received a night call in Williamsburg from Marc Blitzstein, however, who wanted to see me on an emergency. So I came up a day early, saw Eva's doctor & spent about five hours with them. Unfortunately it was very unsatisfactory & nothing was accomplished.[22] Her trouble is so deep-seated that nothing short of an en-

---

22. Mumford had referred his friend Eva Goldbeck, a writer and wife of the composer Marc Blitzstein, to Murray for treatment. She was suffering from anorexia nervosa and died in May 1936.

tirely satisfactory Love or a year's analysis can be counted upon to help. I am ashamed that I have accomplished so little—I was a bit out of mood the 1st time I saw her—well, the result was I missed you. (By the way if you insert your telephone no. in your next letter it would help matters.) I wept over your poem & so did Christiana & I have thought about you constantly since then. I am so grateful to you for writing me at length & so clearly that I can get a really intelligible picture of your desperate situation. It is possible that somehow according to primitive ways of thought A's mind took the accident as a divine punishment & that now she is in a temporary phase of atonement or self-incrimination. The fact that Duncan was there to nurse her, & that your marriage & your creative work naturally made you somewhat ambivalent about your relationship may have furthered this disposition. For the present, since nothing utterly satisfactory can be done—it must be better not to disturb her by bringing the conflict into consciousness. Poor fellow. Have you been able to do any writing?

Affectionately

H

[typed]

4001—44 Street

Long Island City

18 April 1936

Dear Harry:

I am overwhelmed at your generosity toward Eva Goldbeck, and at the same time am full of remorse for the fact that I am responsible for originally putting this burden on your shoulders. At the time I had no notion at all of what I was letting you in for. The chief reason that I haven't written you before about her is that I was so damnably preoccupied by my own affairs that I had no time or thought really to give to Eva: in addition to which, at such brief meetings as she and I had this winter, she was very reticent about her whole dilemma, and it wasn't till two months ago that I really grasped how grave it was. You have probably gotten out of her all the essential data: her hatred of her beautiful self-absorbed mother, her resentment against the failure to pay attention to her during her childhood, plus her envy of her mother's beauty, her introduction into the *subject* of sex by a homosexual boy, the fact that her first marriage, though apparently quite normal, was to a cousin who lacked very strong male attributes particularly in relation to his career and working life, etc., etc. The one thing that is possibly missing from the picture you could not deduce from Eva's present appearance: namely, that up to about seven years ago Eva was a deeply feminine girl in every way, with apparently an excellent, probably varied, sex life, full breasts, buttocks, and curves, and plenty of sexual charm. Even her face, which in the abstract was "ugly," was often beautiful. It was not until she met Mark that she cropped her hair and deliberately de-sexed herself. She took over from her father her Prussian sense of duty, which has probably been responsible for the fact that she has ground out her soul doing hack work when she should have been developing her real creative talents: there is a chapter in her last novel in which she expressed her sense of frustration at the possibility of not getting a chance to express herself till it is too late. She has sacrificed herself to her lovers as her father apparently did toward her mother. She has never been ruthless enough in her work to cast the economic burden of her support on anyone else, as at some point the artist usually has to do in our society if he is to go on in his development.

Yesterday I had a long talk with her, and saw how difficult she was to deal with. She *wanted* me to tell her that she should *not* let Mark know that she was in New York; but when I found that she had a notion of living on in New York and commuting up to Boston to see you, I suggested that she let Mark take her up to Boston and settle her there, since she had been badly battered by the trip down and was obviously in no condition to undertake another trip alone. I finally persuaded her to postpone her break with Mark until it could be clear and continuous; that is, until she could be settled in a new place, either in Cambridge or in New York. Her return to New York last Thursday was entirely irrational, because it was based on the assumption that she did not have enough money to cover her Boston expenses; whereas the fact was that I had placed a hundred dollars at her disposal—originally saved against Alice's possible return to New York—and there was nothing whatever except her own self-assertive pride to keep her from staying up in Cambridge.

Eva said, incidentally, that she gets most out of you when you treat her most harshly; for otherwise she suspects you are covering up some difficulty with "kindness." I have been tempted to tell her myself that she was making a nuisance of herself, and that she was claiming your time without adopting the helpful acquiescent mood that a patient must take if she is going to profit from a doctor's advice and treatment: for I detected in the course of our interview yesterday how unwilling she was to take a lead, no matter how weak her condition and how incapable she was of making an intelligent decision about it. But I hesitated to be drastic in her present condition, with important decisions as to where she should live and how still lying ahead. If you advise me to administer this medicine to her, I will.

As for my own work, I have been so deep in research on my book and so busy with my Board of Higher Education duties that I have not had time to examine the state of my soul—except to realize that Sophy and I have found each other once more with a new delight.[23] (Although Eva's plight comes as an unfortunate interruption, because of its overtones of Alice—despite my long remoteness from Eva and the fact that, though we were fond of each other, and sexually responsive, we were never lovers.) But otherwise things go well; and I hope to be up in the country permanently before another month is out.

Warmly yours
Lewis

23. Mumford served on the New York City Board of Higher Education, 1936–1937.

[handwritten]
[LM] (23? May) 1936

Dear Lewis,

I might have been able to do something for Eva if the conditions of my life were different. We started on the wrong tack in September when she came *not* as a patient but as a friend of a friend. The main difficulty has been that she has consulted me to be treated in her own way.

I arranged to see her in Cambridge 3–4 times during a four weeks period (about once a week). She had such extraordinary insight, however, & we made such rapid progress in the beginning, that I was encouraged to see her 3–4 times a week & allow each session to stretch out for 2 hours; despite the fact that it upset whatever order there was to my life & wore down the last shred of healthy nerve. She came & made extravagant demands—notes, telephone messages in the middle of the night, etc.—& she resisted every step of the way—blaming, complaining, rationalizing. I knew from a psychological point of view that it was either (1) a love affair with a man who was willing to give All or (2) a 3 years psychoanalytic job. I thought, however, since there was no prospect of these two—it would be worth working for a combination of psychology & medicine *in a hospital* (insulin injections & perhaps tube feeding). What has to be done medically cannot be done outside a hospital. Therefore, I moved towards the hospital idea, & four days ago moved her into a private room on the best division (Mass Gen Hosp) in Boston. That used up all her desire or ability to cooperate. She went on strike & raised the roof—damned everything & everybody, refused to eat, complained about every step of the procedure. Her condition is now considerably worse, but her will to refuse is indomitable. As far as the health of her body is concerned the safest thing to do would be to remove her to a Psychopathic Hospital & tube feed her. But in her present state this would drive her into a final mental fury & life would be a torment for her. Better to die. We are taking her out of the hospital tomorrow to an apartment, where another doctor (Michael Murray) & myself & Marc are going to try to regain the ground we lost when she went to the hospital. She is so resentful, however, that I have no great hopes, & feel that in a few weeks she will either be in a mental hospital (not insane, of course, but there because it is the only place where tube feeding can be properly and regularly carried on) or dead. What is dominating her now is suicide from *spite*. She feels she isn't loved enough &, therefore, will impose the blame & guilt on others by dying.

With more freedom & more resilience I might have done something—because I secretly admire these self-willed Narcists when they are hypersensitive & proud, & in her case, know every important contributing factor—but I was already overloaded to capacity, so much so that I haven't been able to write a word of my book for 4 months, & will probably lose my job in consequence, etc. I was glad to take her, but it was the kind of mistake that I have never feared not to make—to take on more than I can handle & botch everything. I am ashamed to have to write you such a miserable report. It is very distressing.

Around June 3rd, I expect to leave her for a few days as I am bordering on homicide. Will you be in New York or Amenia? I think I shall motor in that direction—walk around the country & return to make a final effort with Eva.

How are your circumstances? I hope time is ministering to the pain of the winter.

> Yrs
> Harry

[handwritten]
[LM] 1936
"Mid-River Farm"
Clayton Post Office
New York

Dear Lewis,

It is long since I have written you but during this interlude I have frequently recalled the open-armed lifting welcome that you and Sophy gave us in Amenia. It was generous of you to talk so freely about your thoughts & I hope we didn't temporarily deplete you. I hope the geyser did not fail you on the following morning. I feel that we are once more very close as to subject matter, although probably quite far apart as to method of approach or treatment. Fundamentally, we're the same in that we wish to heighten the zest for life & expand the range of it. We have as it were, a love or lust for more abundance & at points a doctrine or vague notion of the way to get it. Thus, we are together against those who would diminish it & those who regard tangible objects and power as the Summum Bonum (DeVoto & Pareto, etc.). However, I do not feel that you are so intent about communicable or verifiable truth. Are you? Or is it that we disagree about the method of discovering it? I think I am more Paretian than you. You, like Lucretius or Erasmus Darwin, would put the theory of Evolution in a poem, whereas I, in the manner of Charles Darwin, would think it worthwhile to spend a lifetime establishing it. Not that I could or would, but relative to you I would.

Somehow, I got started on a long subject. What I wanted to say was that you & Sophy were lovely to us, that I hoped you were well & progressing, that I was well and coming along slowly & that if you would like it, I should very much enjoy having a meal or spending a night with you (August 20) on the way back here—

Please answer: 64 Plympton St, Cambridge, Mass where I am going now—tomorrow.

> H.A.M.

[typed, LMC]
Amenia, New York
14 August 1936

. . . Your letter, dear Harry, came in answer to several unwritten ones to you that rose naturally to mind this week after I had brought to an end the draft I started on the first of June—about 175,000 words in all. I finished with plenty of wind to spare; but never the less the relaxing of the tension is grateful; and I am going to complete it by running over to Cape Cod, in Geddes's company, next Tuesday. Alas! that this will deprive me of my chance of seeing you; but all arrangements have been made, at various houses at the other end: so only Sophy will be here to greet you if you pass by. As for our several works and ways of life and thought, I have a feeling that we start from similar intuitions, each screened through a radically different temperament and life-experience, and that we will probably meet at some ultimate destination: in the meanwhile, we seem farther apart than we actually are because we have different jobs to do. The difference arises, not because I assign a different value to objective truth—communicable and verifiable—than you do, but because my material is mainly drawn from the arts, and because my method, as sociologist and philosopher, is that of the artist: using objective truths as building blocks toward the construction of a fresh edifice. As far as possible, I use only blocks whose size and weight and tensile and compression strength have been ascertained; but, as there was architecture before there was scientific engineering, so I should go ahead and build anyway—as I must still in spots—even if the qualities and performances of my materials had not yet been satisfactorily tested. Whereas you, being in the tradition of science, are engaged more in shaping and testing the separate blocks themselves; and though as a man you care deeply, no doubt, that they should be put to good use, your honor is even more concerned with the testable validity of the separate parts: that is the point where the creative challenge rises for you, and that is why, perhaps, you distrust the synthetic act, the artist's act, even when the temptation to perform it arises in your own bosom. I don't however agree with your notion that a Pareto is either scientific or objective: on the contrary, if I didn't believe that the materials I was using would stand up to a test far better than those in which Pareto puts his faith, I'd regard myself as a duffer or a charlatan. Perhaps I could make my own position a little clearer if I set down the logical schema in which I do my thinking. It has three parts: the objective: the subjective: and a realm which contains elements from both sides, which one might call the "empirical" or "practical." The objective is the fact conditioned side: the brute reality of things is disclosed, so far, by the compared and verified reports of the senses, abstracted, systematized and enlarged as science. The subjective is the wish-conditioned side: life and experience as influenced by organic necessities and urges: the ideal and the ego-centric as opposed to the factual and geo-centric: all of which is systematically put together in religion and philosophy, and may some day be further formulated in an esthetics. Each of these realms is canalized into life through the arts; and he who thinks about the arts, seeking therein to create fresh structures and fresh destinations for life, must be prepared to utilize both the objective and the subjective departments of thought, although, in the nature of things, it is only a rare bird who will be able, at the same time, to make direct contributions to verifiable truth along any specialized line of research. Indeed the artist who seeks for this truth, as Leonardo did, must pay for his effort by leaving behind half-finished structures. On the other hand, it had become plain ever since Kant that our most objective truths are conditioned by the nature of the knower: not purely his metaphysical nature or bias, but the nature of his social instruments, like language; and the very direction of his search may be dictated not by a pure love of truth alone, but by class biases or preferences. Hence there is a mythical element in all objective thought, in the sense that it is life conditioned: and one must allow for it in every judgement, as the navigator allows for the drift of the gulf stream or the marksman for the wind. Charles Darwin was certainly a more competent naturalist than Erasmus: he contributed infinitely more to the fund of biological observation: but what was the mainspring of his great theoretical researches but a myth which he and Wallace had independently drawn from the same source, namely Malthus: "the struggle for existence," innocently framed as a universal law of nature, but historically a subjective reflex of the class war which had been going on actively for a few centuries and had reached a keen pitch of oppression during the wars and economic crises that ended the eighteenth century. And probably the difference between a first rate mind in science and the plodders who attend to the detail is that the first are capable of utilizing, as stimuli, the subjective and socially conditioned impulses—while the ideologue, on the other hand, like Erasmus Darwin, is too easily content with his subjective formulation, and never submits to the duty of independent verification. As far as possible, those whose work lies in art, who seek to change the form and color of the environment or the conduct of men, must be at home in both realms; but their method and end is essentially different, because their work is incomplete until they establish direct connections with life. The reason I distrust thinkers like Pareto is that they, too, are plainly not merely socially conditioned; but they are eager to exert a direct influence on life: yet all the while they conceal from themselves the wish-elements in their thinking and flatter themselves on their "science" or "objectivity." Shall I just, for the fun of it, set down my schema: asking your pardon if I've done so before. If I'm not mistaken I think you have the picture of my work as being mainly a-logical and intuitive; which shows, perhaps, that I have done a good job in concealing the bare bones; but doesn't prove they are non-existent. Here goes:

Objective	Practical		Subjective
Fact-conditioned Sciences	*Life-conditioned Arts*		*Wish-conditioned Ideologies and Myths*
Social Sciences	Town plan Industry, etc.	Ethics Politics	Religion Literature
Biological Sc.	Medicine Hygiene	Education Gymnastic	Philosophy
Physical Sciences	Engineer Painting, etc.	Architecture	Esthetics
Mathematical Sce.	Statistics	Language	Logic[24]

Although the great advance in thought during the last couple of centuries has been due to the building up of the knowledge and practice on the left hand side of this diagram, the right hand side not merely remains important in its own right, but continues to infiltrate toward the left: this is no less clear than the contrary movement from left to right, which in the form of positivism proposed to abolish metaphysics, in the form of mechanistic materialism sought to abolish religion, and in the form of scientific ethics proposed to abolish a normative ethics. While my own work consists in synthesizing the wish-conditioned with the fact-conditioned by focussing them on the life-conditioned sphere of the arts, it is true, I think, that I am more at home on the right side of the diagram than on the left: and perhaps that is what you mean when you suggested that I was not so intent about "communicable truth" . . . meaning, rather the preliminary discovery of fact-conditioned truth, preliminary, that is to say, with respect to application in life. But if I were an ideologue I would write my book on the Culture of Cities by an entirely different method: instead of immersing myself in the plans and historic documents and actual institutions of cities, I would use such chance suggestions as came to me out of the air and my own untutored consciousness to conjure up a lovely picture of "the" ideal city; and I would go to my grave wondering why no such city ever would come into existence or could function in actual life. Whereas not merely do I devote two-thirds of the book to an analysis of the actual forms and institutions of historic cities, since the tenth century; but there is not a single suggestion for the future which does not have a bottom in some actual structure or institution or force that now exists, and is visible to other people beside myself. Indeed, when I come to my final draft, I intend to let myself go at one or two points beyond these well-marked paths, lest the suggestions all remain too closely

24. Mumford's later annotations on the manuscript: "8 June 1979 These boxes falsify the ideas, as in Geddes's graphs. They partition & compartmentalize the dynamic interaction. 1 July 80 In my first exposition of the above—essentially Geddes's original window in the Outlook Tower—in my first Stanford lecture I added the dynamic element, by showing that, as in chess, the interaction could take a place in any direction, and with the knight's move even jump."

on the pedestrian level, without the capacity to fire the imagination or further the impulse to creative change. What a letter! Your words somehow made me conscious and articulate about a process that I am usually no more conscious of than the beating of my heart—for my enlightenment if not for yours, dear Harry!

> All good luck to you
> Lewis

[handwritten]

Lewis, hero, write to me every day, every hour. Ask me to come to New York, ask me anything. I will say No if I can't possibly do it. Until Dec 1st I am grinding out words like a sausage machine & therefore condensed & cold to the outside world. But you're inside forever. *Now* there is one fine wise *woman*—I hope women are not *out*—in New York. She is originally a Swedish doctor, now a psychoanalyst—a sensible one, the *only* sensible one perhaps in N.Y. & sensitive. Her name is Karen Horney & her office is near Madison Ave & 76 St. (?).[25] Find her in the telephone book. As far as I know there are no neurologists or psychiatrists who are wonder workers of the human heart. They are competent men in dealing with textbook cases—particularly if it is a matter of physical injury, but they are less competent than a normally sensitive man or woman when it comes to following the complex tender fluctuations of the spirit. Give them all a wide berth except when it is necessary to obtain a diagnosis on skull, optic nerve, etc. The analysts have the knowledge of the emotions but most of them are lob-sided & a bit cracked. Dr. Horney, however, is a striking exception. There are a few little rumors circulating about her but pay no attention to them. She is warm, understanding, knowledgeable & experienced. I think it's time that a Woman made her special wisdom felt. A. has been torn between *men*. I can completely recommend Dr. Horney as the right person. My own impression is that Rest and Peace is needed for some time more—preferably in the country & not in Baton Rouge. Couldn't that be arranged? Couldn't A. stay with a friend in Virginia? I suggest Savannah, Georgia, or Jamaica in the Caribbean. Is that out? But before you do anything go to see Dr. Horney. If A. has no faith in woman doctors (even when one is better than the men) I should advise Dr. Jack Millet, because he's a fine, sensible man who has a farm house sanatorium in Connecticut. He's also a psychoanalyst with an office in N.Y. He has long experience with Dr. Riggs in Stockbridge, is quite sane & has a good heart. He isn't as intelligent or deep-seeing as Dr. Horney, but is competent & reliable. His wife is a Hindoo—a dancer whom you may have seen on the stage.

Please Lewis if you have any trust in Man or Woman go to see Dr. H.

> Yrs
> H

---

25. Karen Horney (1885–1952), actually a German-born psychoanalyst who rejected several of Freud's basic theories and emphasized environmental influences on personality.

[handwritten]
158 Mt. Vernon Street
[LM] 2 Dec 36

Dear Lewis,

I have written Alice that I shall be in New York on Friday Dec. 11th—From 9 am–5 pm. If she wants to see me her wishes are mine & my time is hers. Perhaps I could see you also—I shall probably eat breakfast with my mother—105 E 67 (Rhin 1906)—If you could see me Thursday I might even get off for two days. Drop me a line. Unhappily I do not know any of the doctors you mentioned. Quite a few younger analysts must have grown up since I was in touch with the situation. Having seen a number of second note psychiatrists I am naturally not inclined to be optimistic about anyone that I have not seen. Alice may not like Frances Wickes & the Freudians, of course, would be against her.[26] She touches the pain with healing words almost unfailingly & I should feel comfortable if Alice were in her hands. It is well to mention charges for consultation as Frances has no sense about money. She does prodigious things for nothing & then suddenly sends some unsuspecting person a big bill. O I wish I were with you now—

Harry

[typed]
Mumford
Amenia, New York
11 December 1936

. . . I have been waiting all week, my dear Harry, for this moment to write to you: to embrace you in gratitude, because you are such a marvellous friend, and to embrace you a second time, in admiration, because you are such an excellent physician—a true physician who knows how to use the healing touch and the magic word. The change that Alice's single interview with you brought about passes all expectation: I couldn't dare believe that so much of the load she had borne could be lifted at a single thrust, by even the wisest of men. When I met her on Monday, she was again a healthy looking girl, the bleak look of pain had gone from her face, and even her breathless laughter was a sign of true release and had nothing hysterical in it; though at first her sense of relief was so great she couldn't talk. She was a little startled at it herself; was afraid it would have to be paid for by a depression; but every succeeding day has only made her better: her weeping stopped entirely after seeing you and her aunt, who had no clue to it all, since Alice did not tell about her consultation with you, said: What has come over you Alice? You are a changed girl. I only hope that it's your sculpture that has done it! Alice has gone back to her work

---

26. Frances G. Wickes (1875–1967), Jungian therapist in New York.

with renewed energy; working gaily and confidently for the first time, really, in over a year; and she has gone back to her friends, too, has met them easily and talked easily with them, plunging into a normal social life again, with a growing sense of self-confidence at taking so easily, with a mere lift of the reins, what used to be an impossible fence, leading to humiliating balks. Alice was delighted over you as well as deeply grateful: you said all the right things, and said them in a way that made them, for the first time, seem real to her: when I met her Monday she was still apologetic over the fact that she had talked so much to you and listened, relatively so little: but I told her that you had probably brought just that reaction about, knowing that it would be the best thing for her. Her old self has come back again; and though all the obstacles haven't been cleared away—for Duncan is still on her conscience, all the more because a "kind friend" in Baton Rouge wrote her to say what a bad time he was having—though this is true, the energy to deal with the obstacles has returned: it flows so freely again that there are no gaps or painful hiatuses in her conversation, and scarcely any visible sore places. I tried to find out from her what you had said, specifically, about her relations with me: but she is a great tease, and led me on such a merry chase here that I don't know what you did say—although I gathered, as I was deeply happy over this—that, seeing her, you saw what I had found in her, and made her feel that I needed her quite as well as she needed me. Last Monday she arranged to take an apartment with Catherine Bauer. When this matter was broached a few weeks ago I was a little doubtful: it seemed like Alice's instinctive way of establishing a censorship over our relations; and I felt that no matter how our intimacy developed, it should at all events not have any external shadows or compulsions hanging over it. But living alone would be too great a burden for her, even though her recovery is well begun; and so the other night we three had dinner together, Alice wisely insisting on it, just to see how the three chemicals would work in the same test-tube; and we were all, even Catherine, quite natural and unconstrained and our wisecracks weren't of the wounding kind: so maybe it will work all right. Alice tells me that you are coming to the city for the Holidays; and since I must come in every week, usually from Monday to late Wednesday afternoon, I dearly hope you and I will be able to meet. Gratitude, as you know dear Harry, is the hardest thing in the world either to express or to repay the debt for: a harder burden in the case of our friendship, at least as far as I am concerned, because our original coming together was in response to an act of great generosity on your part, and year by year the burden has grown heavier. I pray for an occasion to reciprocate it; and if it does not occur, I can only hope that I will be equally good and equally selfless in doing a similar turn to some one else. (As in the Jewish story of the three little birds that were being rescued by their mother. One said it would give his mother all the money it had when it grew up, if only his mother would save it. The other said that it would love her and always do everything to please her. But the third said: Mother I will never be able to repay you; but when I grow up and have children, I will do for them what you have done for me.

So the mother rescued the third little bird and told the other two they were little liars.)

> My warmest greetings to you—and
> all blessings.
> Lewis

[handwritten, LMC]
[LM] From Henry A. Murray—my
Melville friend
15 Dec. 36

Lewis, my bountiful God, I did nothing. Alice is a love—an enchanted reflection of the soul—and you mustn't thank me for delighting my nature by seeking her out. Alice will take the vehement, compassionate, laughing Daemon, namely yourself, or no one. I felt very close to her elusive despairs & inner mirth. She seemed torn between dissolution & a willfully creative sustaining man.

I have a few *suggestions.* No analysis, at least for the present. I think that a gradual recuperative healing will take place this winter if Alice could see you once a week, find some regular employment (preferably sculpture) & occasionally talk with Frances Wickes. I think your life's routine should remain undisturbed this winter. Keep your relationship with wonderful Sophy *solid* & give Alice an oasis in her week. You'll have to shoulder most of the guilt if you can manage it because Alice is swamped with it. Let her weep in your arms, but keep your aplomb & don't modify the shape of your life. You're the only man in America who can save her from drowning. She'll save you next. She doesn't know that she's a mystic who has been almost defeated by Americanization. She'll deny her value with tears & laughter.

Your letter was the warmest blood stream of goodwill I have felt in my life. I was utterly moved to find that anyone could open himself so generously. But never thank me again. We are linked always & you must use me as you would use your own arms & legs—Don't they feel well when exercised? I could write on & on, but the sun is already over Holland & it will catch me awake if I don't stop. You and Alice are at the germinal centre of things where everything is precarious & anything is possible & the will is necessary.

HAM

[typed]
Mumford
Amenia, New York
28 December 1936

. . . I was quite overpowered by your magnificent gift to Geddes, dear Harry, as he was: and that is saying a great deal. It had an exalted and comet-like effect upon his Christmas, making the whole sky shine with its radiance: he has been using it steadily and very seriously, keeping a written record of what he sees on the slides, making new ones, and so forth. I shall have great fun with it too; and if it leads Geddes further into science, where most of his heart seems to lie, I for one will feel the exquisite rightness of it: for if I had never looked into a microscope I might never have run across the name of old Geddes himself; and that would have changed so much of my life that it might even have wiped out, in the long chain of consequences, his living namesake! We were all touched by your imagination and your memory, no less than by your generosity, dear Harry. And in short: it was a very good and merry Christmas all round: full of mild warmth and occasional ecstatic bursts of sunshine, like the day itself up here.

[. . .] Never before have things been more real between me and Alice: and never—even if this seems to contradict what I have just been saying—less anxious. Our coming together again has released a block in my own work; and this last month I have been making all sorts of important decisions about myself and my work: one of them being to throw off the yoke of the New Yorker articles, along with its security, and to devote more of my time to the only part of my writing that counts.

Sophy and I are going down to New York Thursday for a New Year's party and while she returns home on Friday, I will remain down over the weekend. If you are in town, please let me know, either before Thursday up here, or after that by letting Alice know: I want to grasp that strong hand of yours for a moment before I plunge into the New Year. All good luck and blessings to you at all events.

Yours forever
Lewis

1937–1941

Renown and the Looming Threat

DURING THIS PERIOD of the correspondence, Mumford achieved literary celebrity with the publication of *The Culture of Cities* (1938), the second volume in the Renewal of Life series. Critical praise of the book, along with the appearance of his photograph on the cover of *Time* magazine, established Mumford's position as an eminent urban historian and critic of architecture. Murray was unstinting in praise of his friend's achievement in *The Culture of Cities*: "Your book is teeming with living values, chock to the brim with important facts and ideas. . . . It is beautifully written and continuously startling with its exciting analogies and parallelisms" (HAM 12 April 1938). In the same year, Murray and his colleagues published the influential psychological text, *Explorations in Personality,* a work that Murray edited and to which he contributed several chapters. However, their enjoyment of literary achievement was tempered by troubling developments overseas. What Mumford wrote Murray about his idyllic visit to Hawaii in June 1938 ironically forecast coming events in the larger world: "This trip, dear Harry, has left me breathless: it has been so flawless, so rich, so exciting that I am almost superstitious about my good fortune, and am waiting for the harsh breath of the dragon to rouse me from this flowery dream" (LM 26 June 1938). Personally, "the harsh breath of the dragon" poisoned his return visit to Hawaii with his family two months later when Sophia contracted a serious infection. Shortly afterward, in the grand theater of world events, the dragon's breath swept across Europe and on 7 December 1941 from Japan to Hawaii itself, awakening the United States from its "flowery dream" of isolationism. During the late 1930s, Mumford became one of the most outspoken of liberal intellectuals to attack America's isolationist position and to denounce Hitler and totalitarianism, yet his prescient call for decisive economic and military action against Nazi Germany went unheeded. Mumford and Murray both criticized their nation's pusillanimous position and lack of preparation in confronting threats from Germany and Japan. Murray described political leadership in the

United States as "morally enfeebled" and wrote, "To combat ruthless totalitarian-ism we must ourselves become somewhat totalitarian & ruthless. . . . To go back to one of our classic examples—The dictator nations are like Ahab & his crew, & the U.S. is like Starbuck" (HAM 1940). Shortly after the Japanese attack on Pearl Harbor, Mumford bemoaned his nation's short-sightedness and the ineptitude of military command: "It looks as if our entire country, from our generals and admirals down, has been suffering from schizophrenia: was there ever such a gigantic mal-adaption to reality in the world before, except perhaps among the old Roman diehards just before the City of Rome finally fell?" (LM 10 December 1941).

[typed]
Harvard University
Psychological Clinic
64 Plympton Street
Cambridge, Mass.
February 8, 1937

Dear Lewis:

Just a word to say that I have been away for two weeks on a cruise to Guade-loupe, Granada and other islands of the lesser Antilles. I returned to find your all-too-generous letter. When are you going to stop thanking me for nothing? I shall feel we understand each other perfectly when you take the small things that I can do for granted. I have a million things to say to you but I do not suppose there is any chance of you coming to Cambridge in the near future. I hope you will start plot-ting now to lay aside a few days in June before I start on my travels.

I hope Geddes has the necessary books now so that he can go on with his stud-ies of animal life. There won't be much for him to do until spring, but I hope the books will prepare him for a comprehensive investigation of the neighboring flora and fauna. By the way, I took The Flowering of New England with me and was de-lighted by it.[1] I think Van Wyck gave a vivid and closely present picture of the New England setting and was most successful in positively representing each of the characters. The literary and ideological background was all so well done. Love as a factor was conspicuously absent, and there was very little about the creative process itself and the works that resulted from it. Furthermore, there was no struc-ture of underlying concepts except for a rather hesitating reference to Spengler.

---

1. Van Wyck Brooks, *The Flowering of New England, 1815–1865* (1936).

However, it was not meant to be that kind of a book and I think that he completely achieved what he evidently set out to achieve.

Yours,
Harry
Mr. Lewis Mumford
Amenia, New York
HAM: MI

[handwritten]

Dear Lewis:

Everything you write from pot-boiling to high philosophy comes like the sun from behind a cloud lighting up ambiguous shades & giving definition to conditions seen uncertainly and confusedly. I am always surprised & excitedly pleased. Your article on Surrealism was no exception—your division into the irrational, the comic and the unconscious for example.[2] Here, there is an interesting course of speculation which explores the possibility that the unconscious (being, in a sense, our common racial or human inheritance) is more public than the objective world common to any one space-time culture. New York City and the Jungles of Bali are very different as objective environments but the dreams of a pursuing demon are very similar (to a child in a Park Ave. apartment and to a child in Bali). Thus it may be that artists—like the Surrealists—are approaching something that is more common (or public) than what our senses reveal to us. However, I did not mean to write about this. Thanks for your article.

I haven't yet found an open space in time for writing & at this distance I cannot follow the delicate thread of your thought or eddying currents of your feeling. Obviously, what you embarked upon is enough to preoccupy the entire creative attention of an exceedingly solid man. Only a firm core in Alice could make the venture successful. It is hardly possible to be a rock on the one hand & a sensitive receptor of impressions on the other—Alice wrote me, but I have delayed answering until I had a breathing spell. As regards her work as artist I am sure you are right—but then it would be easier if she had a common-place husband that was no artist. Two artists together! What hope? Particularly with a concussion to complicate everything. If you do not succeed in ordering & calming the course of anxious & piteous emotion, don't blame yourself. King Canute could not hold back the sea. Be Orientally still & apathetic for a while & see what happens. When the storm comes fold your wings, close your eyes & ride the waves like a seagull.

Yrs
HAM

2. Lewis Mumford, "The Art Galleries: Surrealism and Civilization," *New Yorker,* 19 December 1936, 72–79.

[typed]
Mumford
Amenia, New York
27 September 1937

Dear Harry:

Your postals have been coming so teasingly; and I have wanted to at least hal-loo an answer at a distance with a promise of more to come: but ever since the mid-dle of last June I have been bound up in my book, and not till yesterday did I finally make the last corrections on the final draft. The summer has passed like a dream, because most of it has been lived with my own thoughts: despite all my long work of preparation, I did not feel myself inside the book—both inside it and above it—until I had this last period of submersion, undistracted by any other jobs and tasks: so completely absorbed that for four months—except for a week's interlude at Martha's Vineyard—I scarcely moved more than a mile away from this house in any direction. The main part of the work is now over: but I have a good stiff month left on my bibliography and the preparation of illustrations; and meanwhile I shall be devilling around with lectures. I do hope that we can meet this fall: that's one of the reasons I am writing this in advance of your homecoming. But although I shall be within hailing distance on the fifteenth, giving a founder's day lecture at Wheaton College, I must return here directly: so I'll have to hope that you'll be coming down in this direction. Sophy has stood by patiently during my absorption, and on the whole we have had a good, though meagre, summer: Geddes has sud-denly passed into adolescence, and Alison has become a full-fledged person: so much for the family constellation. Alice had a stormy summer, most of it by herself, about which she is more competent to tell you than I am; but I think she is emerging on the other side again, with some good solid work behind her.

There are a thousand things I want to mull over with you: so let's try to come together one place or another. The early part of November I shall be in Princeton, giving a short course of lectures at the Architectural School; but from the seven-teenth of October to the twenty-seventh I shall be here. Here's to our early reunion.

Warmly
Lewis

[handwritten]
Mumford
Amenia, New York

Dear Harry:

Last week I spent a night in Westport with Van Wyck Brooks; and he told me something about his brother-in-law, J. Frank Stimson, that may interest you. Stim-son is a great authority on Polynesian folklore—he abandoned architecture for this after reading Typee, I believe—and he happened to pick up a copy of Mardi, which he had never read, on his last visit to the Brookses. Van Wyck said that a great many of the things Stimson glanced at immediately had meaning for him in terms of Polynesian myths: and Brooks suggested that if you sent Stimson a copy of Mardi and explained your interest Stimson might write back a commentary on its many allusions.

His address is:

J. Frank Stimson

Papeete

Tahiti

At the moment I'm still buried in proofs: half-way through. The book is tougher and solider than anything I wrote before: massive: with an occasional touch of brilliance in the early chapters! More later. A warm embrace.

> In friendship
>
> Lewis

P.S. I'm meditating on your comments upon "porous" architecture: it will lead to a modification of one of my statements on architecture. I *have* a good section on preserving the wilderness as *claustrum*.

> [typed]
> Mumford
> Amenia, New York
> 27 November 1937

. . . . This is just a hasty answer, dear Harry to your telegram, which just came. My nose is still so deeply buried in my book—I have ten thousand words of captions to write for my photographs and the revised galleys still to correct, to say nothing of making dozens of verifications!—that your suggestion didn't even cause the wince of regret that would have existed if there had been any possibility of my taking advantage of it. As things look now, I won't be released and footloose until the middle of January, at earliest. But meanwhile, I trust, you got the letter I wrote the other day, forwarded from Cambridge, and that I will either see you with Alice, on Tuesday evening, or that we will be able to spend a few hours together—and that will be even better, because I will be rested a little!—on Wednesday morning. If there's any possibility of your coming up here that would be fine; for you know that, even under my most rigorous and spartan regime, I never work after noon. The book, now that I begin to see it in its final outlines, is better than I had any reason to hope it would be when I so ploddingly laid out its first draft; and my lectures in Princeton a few weeks ago were so successful that they not merely earned an invitation again for next year, but were the occasion of a very significant student editorial I shall show you: proving that the Princeton boys recognize the need for a roving professor when they see one!

> Ever yours
>
> Lewis

[typed]
Mumford
Amenia, New York
8 February 1938

. . . At the moment, dear Harry, I am in an absurd little jam, and I am writing you on just the off-chance that an opportunity may present itself which will enable you to help. My friend Spingarn, who knows that I would welcome at the moment a temporary professorship, began to speak about me the other night to Neilson (of Smith); and for some reason, which I can't quite fathom, suggested to Neilson that some university should give me an honorary degree. He was modest enough to suggest an honorary M.A.; and Neilsen said he would talk to Conant about it, so that it might come from Harvard.[3] Now the point is that I haven't the faintest use for any honorary degree, and would have to turn it down if it were offered to me: so if any one ever mentions the subject in your presence, or if it comes up at a Faculty meeting, please scotch the idea. The only terms on which it would be possible for me to accept such a degree would be if I were getting a professorship and if the university wanted me to have the degree in order to save its academic face by doing away with the awful bald spot behind my name.

Don't bother to *do* anything about this, unless the matter thrusts itself at you.

This week I am putting my O.K. on the final proofs of the very last item in the book, the Index: so the moment for celebration has come, and if I weren't so sweetly tired I'd celebrate. I will be sending you a nice fresh copy of the book in a few weeks, I trust. Here's to our reunion!

Lewis

[handwritten]
Peter Brigham Hospital
—But Address: 64 Plympton
Cambridge as usual

Lewis my great companion in arms.

I am revelling now in thoughts of your long labor & final achievement & the peace that must be yours on this score. I just missed you Monday at Harcourt Brace: but saw Pierce who said that your book was their proudest accomplishment.[4] I am waiting expectantly. You should have heard more from me, but we have had our

3. Joel E. Spingarn (1875–1939), professor of comparative literature at Columbia University and later senior editor at Harcourt, Brace and Company; Mumford's home adjoined Spingarn's estate at Leedsville near Amenia, New York. William Allan Neilson (1869–1946), president of Smith College, 1917–1949. James Bryant Conant (1893–1978), president of Harvard University, 1933–1950.

4. "Pierce": Probably a reference to Charles A. "Cap" Pearce, Mumford's editor at Harcourt, Brace. Murray was apparently confused about the name; see his letter of 2 April and Mumford's response of 17 April 1938.

troubles lately. Christiana has been sick with pain & it was discovered that she had a stone in her right kidney & last Tuesday Dr. Quimbly operated & after a nervous fifteen minutes dexterously found & extracted it. (Surgery is the most unequivocal gift of the scientific era: its justification. Anesthesia, the aseptic technique & a hundred detailed operations—for example they took an X-Ray of the kidney as it lay in the surgeon's hand out of the body—two exploratory needles having been inserted previously—& in 4 minutes the developed picture showed exactly where the little offender was located—and then *Morphine*). Christiana had 3 bad days with renal colic—about the worst pain on record but controllable with juice of poppy. Now today we are jubilant to say that the pain is most gone & everything seems different. This will modify my plan of spending a month or so in N.Y. I went down for one day Monday to see the Oxford press about paper, type, binding, etc. There was so much to do in a short time that I did not notify you ahead, but I will next time. I have at least a month's research to do in New York before going on with Melville: N.Y. Historical Society, sermons that were preached during his boyhood, pictures of things referred to in his books, references to Melville in the correspondence of contemporaries, etc.

I have been reading a little in Thomas More, Byron & Spenser & have found illustrations of almost all the forms taken by romantic feeling during the Rococo period of morals (1830–1850). This was extravagantly elaborated by the Annuals, Godey's magazine, Grahams, N.Y. Mirror, etc. It seems that this was enough to twist any man of lusty appetites—granted he had a sensitive conscience—into a troubled & partly self-deceived moralistic mystic. These words are insufficient; but the sexual side of Melville is the root or near the root of his misery. How Whitman escaped it all, & dared to speak plainly is a problem of major psychological importance. He was not brought up to be a Respectable & had no strong ties to any fixed socio-religious pattern & he was homosexual & he came (as an author) a little later. He dodged Conscience, had unchecked confidence & was influenced in some way. His mother doted on him which gave him a chance to become exhibitionistic—but it's still a mystery. He & Melville are similar in many ways & yet exact opposites, & hence complementary. I cannot wait for the new Whitman book which explains his inspiration.[5] Pierce is going to send me a copy to review. Have you run across any new Melville leads? I am reading Sunderman's monograph: a conscientious Teutonically systematic arrangement of Melville's opinions on Life, God, immortality, Christianity, good & evil, etc. No new flashes of insight. I have found Melville's words, phrases & sentiments in some other writers: Edward Young, Grey, Plutarch, Carlyle, Browne, etc.—have discovered the derivation of some names: Yillah, Hautia, Maramma, Alma, Fedallah, Ahab, etc. But none of this is of much importance. What was the exact nature of the wish or wishes that were frustrated—why did he pretty much make up his mind to be annihilated? Perhaps you are no longer inter-

5. Esther Shephard, *Walt Whitman's Pose* (1938).

ested in Whitman & Melville. I want to see you as soon as possible—I hope you & Alice after the distancing effect of a few months can come to terms as friends because we have become so fond of her. When I have some time I am going to see A. DeWolf Howe & others & see what I can do to push.[6] It would make life worth living if you came here. I have been vaguely thinking of leaving Harvard myself, but if you were here the place would be different.

Harry

P.S. Can I lend you some money? I have some to spare. Please give me a chance

[typed]
Mumford
Amenia, New York
7 March 1938

. . . . The main part of your letter that came this morning, dear Harry, was very distressing: but your tone as well as your words were reassuring; and the great consolation about physical pain, as opposed to even minor anxieties of a psychic origin, is that it leaves so few scars. I can well imagine what your feelings were: even their very shadow, in my own sympathetic reaction, was sharp enough. You have our most fervent congratulations on the happy outcome of it.

For the last couple of days I have been in bed, nursing a cold, dreading the thought that it might, in my present state of depression, sink into pneumonia—I conveniently remembered the observation of some famous British diagnostician that a depression paved the way for more cases of pneumonia in his experience than any other cause—but by today my boredom was sufficiently high, and my temperature sufficiently normal, to enable me to get up and face the world. Your letter, with its warm undercurrent of life stirring, and friendship working, and love feeling, partly prompted my resurrection: the other major contribution was the appearance of the first copy of my book.[7] The words in it are by now so tedious, and seem so unbearably clumsy, that I cannot bear to read the text again: but the appearance of the book is like the arrival of a baby: it is a miracle even if it is ugly and weak. Physically, it is exactly what I designed it to be; and I think it has turned out very handsome. That it exists, that it was produced during the last three years of distraction, frustration, and misery, is quite incredible. It might be much poorer, and I would still, objectively speaking, have to take off my hat to the spirit that made it possible. In a sense, another person wrote the book: my main office was to deplete his energies, to put barbed wire in his way, to frustrate him and handicap him at every turn; and yet somehow, though his arms are cut and his clothing is

6. Mark Antony De Wolfe Howe (1864–1960), Boston editor and prolific author of biography and history.

7. Lewis Mumford, *The Culture of Cities* (1938), second volume of the Renewal of Life series.

torn, he got past all these barriers and came through with something. You will get a copy soon, dear Harry.

Which brings me to another thought: that I expect to be in Cambridge on the sixteenth, staying with Gropius, your new German professor of architecture, and having dinner that night at his house with the Conants.[8] It almost looks as if this were a polite roundabout way of looking me over without committing anyone; it is on those terms, indeed, that Sophy and I will be going up. If you happen to be free the next day for lunch, or at any other time, it would be fine to see you, of course; but I can well imagine that your body and your thoughts will both be far away from Cambridge. But at all events, you can drop me a note in care of Gropius, and if I haven't sent you a copy of The Culture of Cities by then I will leave it at the clinic for you. You are very thoughtful and generous, dear Harry, to mention the matter of a loan; but financially, I am still quite tight and sound, and unless my book goes very poorly, I can always, in a pinch, borrow from my publishers on my next book. I have a hunch that some deep change in my life is imminent: one symbol of release is that I will be going out to *Honolulu* in June to attend an educational conference. I can imagine a lot of better reasons for going to Honolulu, but when one's fairy godmother grants one's wishes, one mustn't pout over her wry interpretation of them.

Alison has been going through a very distressing, and psychologically very interesting neurosis, springing out of a complex of fears: Sophia and I have made long notes about it and would like some day, when you have put your book behind you and have a free mind, to discuss them with you. Fortunately, the worst symptoms seem to have died down; but we will need advice about the sequelae, and about handling her generally; and if there happens to be any child psychologist in New York whom you have great confidence in, please give us his name. Do you happen to know a man named Langford at the Baby Hospital? He seemed very intelligent about my sister-in-law's child, who was a frightfully difficult case.

More later, or when we meet—for I had thoughts about Whitman and Melville when I read your letter this morning, and in the gathering mental fog of the afternoon, that by-product of coryza, they have disappeared.

Warmly,

Lewis

P.S. I forget whether someone opened your Cambridge letters or whether they are inviolate. My uncertainty accounts for the brevity and cryptic quality of the first paragraph. I leave your friendly eyes to read more.

N.B. Alice has now set up a studio at 41 Washington Square, S. Dr. Millet sent her first patient for sculpture therapeutics last week; and she had a promise of two more. My ruthlessness of last December is bearing good fruit. The last two months have been marked for her by an unbearable burden of family difficulties—a para-

---

8. Walter Gropius (1883–1969), Bauhaus architect who became head of the Department of Architecture at Harvard.

lyzed mother and father—and she has risen to the task heroically, almost unfailingly. She *looked* well, too, when I saw her a week ago.

[typed]
Harvard University
Psychological Clinic
64 Plympton Street
Cambridge, Mass.
April 12, 1938

Dear Lewis:

Just returned to find your letter.

Everything smooth and happy; but matters to settle with the publisher, the arrival of proof and the sudden death of my aunt changed my plans. I did not motor to New York and was there so busily for such a short time that I didn't telegraph you. I pictured you stretched out in Amenia, taking short walks, recuperating from your two years' work, and cursing the publishers for postponing the date of publication.

Your book is teeming with living values, chock to the brim with important facts and ideas. One paragraph sets me thinking at such a rate that I make no progress. There should be an injunction at the beginning of the book that no one should read more than ten pages a day. It is beautifully written and continuously startling with its exciting analogies and parallelisms. You put the reader's imagination to the furthest stretch. I am not half-way through it, but it is nonetheless a magnificent book to me no matter what is coming. I had planned to get right along with it the moment you left but immediacies and expediencies came crashing in on my leisure. Much against my inclination, I had to put it off. I am entertaining myself, among other things, by working out the hidden conceptual schemes. I am a little troubled by the parallelisms between the Baroque period and Rome as well as Egypt. (Many of your Baroque traits are also traits of Emperialistic Rome, etc.) I seem to get the impression from your book that the characteristics of the Baroque epoch as you name them are considered to be something new. I have a thousand questions, and I shall go on with this letter at the next available moment. This morning I am faced by a hundred and seven letters which are too dampening to allow a springtime expansion.

Yours,
Harry
Mr. Lewis Mumford
Amenia, New York

P.S. I am very disappointed that I wasn't free to take off 2 weeks immediately to read & discuss your book. It deserves it & I am appreciating it prodigiously even though I have been proceeding by jerks & starts. I shall start from the beginning again at the first breath. Now my proofs are curling about the brain. I hope you will pardon my jumping at you on the great question of Fact and Sentiment. I was just trying to involve you in my chief problem of the winter.

Could you let me know the name of your Harcourt Brace friend? He sent me Walt Whitman's Pose asking for comments. I skipped hurriedly; was interested in the ill-digested mass of detail & convinced that W.W. had read George Sand; but the difference between the two is yet as wide as the Atlantic (which remains to be explained). I thought the author, Mrs. Sh., was enjoying the prosecution of a man who never gave his heart to a woman & proving that his Masculine Exhibition was conceived by a woman. I should like to see Mrs. Sh's husband.

Let me know how you are—more fully when you have a moment. I felt like taking you to the country for a month when you were in Cambridge: away from publishers & public. The book will be out in 10 days?

Of course I am concerned about Alison: not that she won't of her own accord grow out of this; but I should enjoy seeing you work her through the overcoming of the Beast (Crow, Whale) that she 'seeks & shuns.' When I visit you I hope to see her 'playing crow'—pecking at you. (Every man becomes a beast while he writes a book.)

I see the end of the sheet warning me that my time is up—Affectionately to Sophy and yourself

>[typed]
>Mumford
>Amenia, New York
>17 April 1938

. . . Your letter, dear Harry, was an especially welcome one: for, though I had not exactly feared the worst, I was troubled by the thought of what might be happening; and I am glad that all my forebodings were only ghosts. It has been a troublous spring for all of us; but I know, from experience, that another's woes and ills are much harder to bear than one's own: so you have my fullest and most constant sympathy. In all outward ways I am by now fully recovered: from the end of March onward the sunny days in the open—tramping the ills (sic!), spading the earth, planting bushes—did their healing work: toughness came back to my muscles again, and I became so bored with my vacant mind that, occasions pressing, I started work again. Among other things I did a devastating review of Mrs. Shephard's book: a pretentious piece of "scholarship" by someone who seems to me alas! a psychological and literary illiterate, who treats as peculiar aberrations of Whitman, all the normal accompaniments of the literary life: certainly the normal accompaniments of the nineteenth century.[9] Whitman's narcissism is of course an acute representation of that trait: but his work is its justification, as Rembrandt's

---

9. Review of Esther Shepard, *Walt Whitman's Pose, New Republic,* 11 May 1938, 23–24.

work is his, particularly in his self-portraits, where the trait is nakedest. Also, I was stirred by the international situation to write a sharp critical analysis and a sharper emotional call for the New Republic, which they are now reluctantly going to print: reluctant because it is an attack upon their position.[10] My own attitude toward the fascist barbarism that is now making head so rapidly through the world is both historically and psychologically a different one from that which Jung so benignly put forward in his obliquely straightforward essay on Wotan; and my position is different, as concerns the duties of the United States, from either the interventionists or the isolationists.[11] It is one of the few times in my life, indeed I can honestly say the only time, on which I have wanted to speak on a nationwide radio hookup!

. . . Meanwhile last week my book came out, and my face is now being plastered over the literary pages, stern or grinning, sooth or sardonic, beyond the reach however of the accompanying text, since I am following, even more rigorously than with Technics, my new practice of not reading reviews till six months is over. By then one no longer is sensitive to misunderstanding or neglect; and if there is anything to learn—once in a while there is!—one is at last in a mood to learn it. The fact that my picture is now on the cover of Time seems to me almost the funniest thing in the world: the only thing funnier being that a man with a face like a Hollywood low comedian could become the ruler of German and Europe.[12] If that keeps up, my well preserved privacy will soon be at an end; and I should rather like another ten years of my present modest obscurity, so that I may have all my energy for my work. What you say of the book is a prelude to a day's talk. But as for the historic parallelisms and repetitions, I was of course aware of them; but I felt that nothing was gained in the present context by their emphasis, because, though I accept in the main the Spengler-Toynbee scheme of culture-development, I do so with my own set of interpretations and limitations; and to have explained my position at length would have been too distant an excursus from the main topic.

[. . .]

My own personal life had a curious kink in it lately: due to the fact that I found myself the embarrassed recipient of an abundant and overwhelming and obsessive love, offered me by a poet, now 29 and married, whom I admire, and who stimulated me imaginatively beyond reckoning, but for whom a brotherly tenderness, like Shelley's desire of the mouth (sic too!), is all that I can offer, or have been able to offer these last ten years, whilst unknown to me her whole emotional life was centered in me.[13] I must tell you more about it: one of life's insoluble problems—and

10. Lewis Mumford, "Call to Arms," *New Republic*, 18 May 1938, 39–42.

11. Carl Jung's essay "Wotan" (1936) relates the psychological forces in the German mind symbolized by Wotan to the National Socialist Movement.

12. Mumford is pictured on the cover of *Time*, 18 April 1938.

13. Josephine Strongin; see Donald L. Miller, *Lewis Mumford: A Life* (New York: Weidenfeld and Nicholson, 1989), 383–88.

flagrant cruelties! In six or seven weeks I leave for Honolulu, as I think I told you: so let's meet soon, here if possible.

Lewis

P.S. The two Harcourt Brace friends, either of whom might have written you, are Samuel Sloan and Charles A. Pearce.

N.B. I kept the two *sics* for your delectation!

[typed]
Harvard University
Psychological Clinic
64 Plympton Street
Cambridge, Mass.
May 5, 1938

Dear Lewis:

Despite the arrival of another great batch of proof and a sojourn in the hospital with an inflamed hip, I have moved on in your book to page 300. This has taken me through some of the grandest writing that I have encountered for many a day. Not till I arrived at the Megalopolis did I realize that you were Elijah, Ezekiel, Jeremiah and Isaiah. I prefer Isaiah because I can see from the peeps that I have taken into the last section of the book that you are ending with a new world, rather than lamenting like Jeremiah over the horrors and sins of the old. Now that I have the larger vision of your plan, it appears increasingly true and important. I think your three great divisions of the Mediaeval Town, the Court's Capitol and the Insensate Industrial town, are very useful. For example, I have found it helpful to think of poor Allan Melville as caught up in the transition between the ideology of a Christian courtier and the requirements of new business methods. I have quite automatically labeled various parts of my environment Paleotechnic, Neotechnic and Biotechnic. The best proof of a good theory is when it begins to work, as it were, by instinct; when the appropriate words just pop to mind without any reflection. I reveled in each and every one of your descriptions of the horrors of city and urban sights, sounds and smells. I can't tell you how many thousands of such evil impressions I have received and how they destroy my digestion and my nervous system and my good-will towards mankind. I would be an entirely different personality, unrecognizable by Mrs. Ingalls who is now writing this letter, if by some master stroke of legislation all the hot-dog stands and gas stations and sign-boards and bungalows and other frights were removed from the Newburyport Turnpike. I would rather see a solid line of old-time backhouses than the sprightly, glittering, semi-citified ugly blotches of construction that my eye cannot escape. I bless you a thousand times for giving a billion minor rages a final and consummate catharsis. Everything that I have read so far is finely conceived and magnificently expressed. I could hug you with delight.

I know that this is not a satisfactory way for you to hear from me about your book. An author should be able to decide, as a musician does, that his work be read in one, two, or three sittings, as the case might be. However, the only other possibility for me would be to put the book aside until June 15th when I expect to get through with proof reading, and my appetite is much too great to stand the deprivation. I hope you will excuse me.

Let me know whether you will be at Amenia between May 13th and May 27th.

> Yours,
> Harry
> Mr. Lewis Mumford
> Amenia, New York
> HAM:MI

[typed]
Mumford
Amenia, New York
8 May 1938

. . . . You are a more generous man than I am, dear Harry: for in the last stages of finishing up my book I resolutely refused to look at any one else's work, no matter how strong my curiosity: and I can well imagine how preoccupied you have been with your proofs, and how distracted you have been with your inflamed hip. (I had a wrenched sacro-iliac last summer, to bear you company as it were, in the midst of my final re-writing: there are a few bad pages of prose, still embedded in the last chapters, that I charitably attribute entirely to this!) But slow intermittent reading is an honor to any book, if it persists long enough; and all you say is as the nectar of spring flowers to one who is recuperating his energies, getting ready for a new start. My book has been badly handicapped, from the standpoint of circulation, by the complete falling off of sales throughout the booktrade; but otherwise, Sophy tells me, I have no cause for complaint. I have much to talk over with you; and we both beseech you to come, singly or doubly, any time between the evening of the thirteenth, when I'll be returning from my last visit to New York before going off to Honolulu, and the twenty-seventh. The Harvard professorship, by the way, looks much nearer, and from what I gathered from Hudnut the other day my trip to Cambridge in March, which seemed so miserable and disastrous, did not kill my chance with Conant: on the contrary, I'll have the chance to give a sort of trial series of lectures next year under the auspices of the English and the Architectural departments.[14] More of this and many other things when I see you. Come soon!

> Warmly
> Lewis

---

14. Joseph Hudnut, dean of the Harvard Graduate School of Design.

[typed]
Halekulani and Bungalows on the
Beach at Waikiki
Honolulu, Hawaii
Mid Pacific: En route Los Angeles
26 June 1938

. . . . This trip, dear Harry, has left me breathless: it has been so flawless, so rich, so exciting that I am almost superstitious about my good fortune, and am waiting for the harsh breath of the dragon to rouse me from this flowery dream. My nine days in Honolulu have so far been the crown of it: everything else must be a sort of anticlimax. I worked hard: toured the island: visited slum areas and plantations: prepared two lectures: sat in at conferences: there was this undercurrent of the reality principle, so to say, even in the midst of those enchanting islands. But the overwhelming impression was of something quite different, of the exciting contrast between the stark jagged outlines of the old volcanoes with their almost perpendicular slopes and the lush tropical vegetation of the foreground, great vines writhing over tree trunks, vast banyan tress, seeming less to be rooted in the earth than to be capturing it, the scarlet blossoms of the royal ponciana tree peppering the roadways beneath, the great bell-like and staminate flowers of a dozen other kinds of plant swaying back and forth under the elm trees like lovers who had divested themselves of all but their sexual organs. I never read travel books: so I don't know how many other people have shared this intense visual excitement; probably thousands have; but even if one didn't add that to all the extraordinary beauty of these mixed oriental and Polynesian types, it would be quite overpowering. The hula itself is something quite other than one I had pictured, when it is danced under the palm trees, not by a bored wench paid by a cabaret, but by someone capable of making love and expressing every gesture of love in the liquid perfection of her flowing hands and arms: to which the strong hip movement serves as a sort of basic earthy counterpoint. Melville, I suspect, with an eye to his genteel realities and his cowardly public, tuned his own emotions down when writing about the scene in Typee and Omoo: there is more of the real Polynesia in Mardi, though he felt the need to supplant it or to modify it by sober political satire about the state of the world. You doubtless know what this tropical air is like, dear Harry: the fragrance that follows one down to the very water's edge; and so you are better prepared to deal with this part of Melville's experience, and to reckon the hold it had on him than I was when I wrote about it. Coming to a young man, who had been none too kindly treated, either by the Albany climate, his relatives, or the system under which he worked, the beauty and kindliness of this life, the equal beauty and kindliness of its people, must have made what came before and what followed seem like preparation for death and like death itself. . . .

Well, I gave two lectures, and since I had to speak in a large hall was forced to write them out: one was on the development of the modern power complex—militarism, mammonism, mechanization, mis-education—and the other was on the Culture of life: the earth, the body, work, personality, and society. On the subject of the body I disparaged negative sex education and spoke, with more than a lecturer's frankness, about the current practice of love. Hawaii was a good place to say such things in: the native population haven't forgotten the meaning of sex and even the haole teachers, though they are timid themselves, were more openminded than I expected they would be. The result was a genuine success: far beyond what I had dared to hope. And so much have I been taken in by Honolulu, even by the families who run the place, that I have been invited back for a month to give them advice about park development and slum clearance. If Sophy can join me, I will go.

So much then for the first part of my Odyssey. During the next month I will be in Stanford to give more lectures, and then in the Pacific Northwest, Oregon and Washington, at the request of their regional planning commission to give them whatever help I can in setting about their work. It is a little like Plato's invitation to Syracuse, this last; but unless I am mistaken the auspices are more favorable. If you are prompted to write me, as I hope you may be, send the letter in care of Sophy and she will know where to forward it. I took White Jacket with me, and believe more than ever that it is one of H.M.'s best; it gave him a clue as to what to do, what material to use and how to reshape it, which led directly to Moby Dick; but the book I shall reread with a new interest when I get back is Mardi.

I hope we'll have another long talk together in September; though I am afraid you'll have to clamp my tongue beforehand if you want to get in a word.

Affectionately
Lewis

When will your book be out?

[handwritten]
Mid-River Farm, Clayton,
New York
Until about Sept 6
[LM] Ans 28 Aug 38

Dear Lewis:

It was cheering to hear that Hawaii had so stirred you, that you felt the pulse of the tropics & the lithe vitality of the Noble Savage. I felt the stir of your experience in my blood. It encouraged my own tentative plan to go to the Islands in the Fall or Winter. Is there a season to be especially avoided? I revelled in the thought of your speeches, or talks rather, contrasting the A extraceptive-material-possessive-aggressive ideology with the B intraceptive-organic-expressive-creative scheme of living. Unless the State provides a full opportunity for B, then the real individuals ('B's') will remain alienated. One can't give oneself to institutions which are entirely dedicated to A: big profits, navies, empire. The difficulty is that a Nation that goes for B is eventually conquered by a Nation that Concentrates on A. A is needed to protect B. A, a strong A, is necessary to make a country safe for B, real living. It is difficult to keep A (which is built on greed, fear & hate) in first rate condition, if it is only to be used for *Defense.* (An offensive Nation, like Germany, has an advantage in this respect.) Also, the moment one turns one's attention to B, A is apt to suffer; & thus B (which relies on A for its continued existence) is jeopardized. But there is no true life outside of B. Well, I must stop. You pressed a bell and I am pouring out free-associations. It suggests the question that bothered Melville: What is a man of good-will (a man of Christ, let us say) to do with his endowment of aggressive in-stinct (or the pent-up aggression that society fosters)? Repress it?, sublimate it?, turn it against animals, inferiors, heretics, scape-goats, kings, captains of industry, God, Devil, woman, witches or animals? I hope the Northwest has not shaken you violently out of your flower scented Polynesian dream. I agree that a few nights with Fayaway & many days in the beatitude of that tropical loveliness would be enough to make Eliz. Shaw & money-grubbing an eternal desperation.

Melville is raising seventy times seven problems & I agree that White Jacket is of the stuff that made Moby Dick so amazingly substantial, that it leads to Moby Dick through Melville's consciousness. But Mardi is the unconscious portal. It shows the insubstantial poppy dream of Yillah, the frustration, the crippling of Eros, which led to the revengeful Hero-Monster thema of Moby Dick. This is foreshadowed, of course, by the Sailor-Captain battle-to-death thema in White Jacket (even the ampu-tation of the leg preparing the way for Ahab's ivory limb), but here it is on a realistic conscious level, & does not show the role of the Captain in Melville's soul life.

I am still in the early period—having digressed widely though profitably on the subject of the exciting, though corrupting, stimulation of the early Romantics. Much of Mardi is not Polynesia at all, but Persia & the Vale of Cashmere after trick-ling through the Englishmen. Yillah is anglicized Hinduism from one point of view (the Anima from another, the path of the Spirit from another). I have found many names coming from the Orient (Yillah from Zillah, Mohammedan name for Abel's (the good son's) wife; and Taji for Taj, sun-worshipping follower of Zoroaster). This leads to Fedallah in Moby Dick. Naturally, I am not particularly concerned over these derivations: only in so far as they stand for something operating in Melville's mind. C has just read *Clarel* & picked out certain passages which bring certain psy-chological problems to clear issue: Why did early Christianity (as all other reli-gions) draw men together (away from women)? Is the desire for complete communion of spirit not to be satisfied (indeed frustrated) by women? Is it that lust aroused by woman corrupts the spiritual understanding, or is it that woman's spir-itual understanding is not on a par with man's? All such questions relate to the state of things in 1850–70, of course, but they also have a universal application. Unfortu-nately (or perhaps fortunately because it is a perpetual thorn: eg. Christ, Plato, Shakespeare, Michel Angelo, Whitman, etc.) I shall have to consider in some detail the role of homosexuality & its operations in religious experience. Did you ever think that Christianity offers no myth or allegory of a man-woman type (husband-wife) to enoble Eros or marriage? Christianity is fundamentally anti-marriage, though the Church has tried to join them, concealing the discrepancy—

Afly

Harry

P.S. I did not mean to let forth such a blast: a far cry from Oregon & not very closely related to the Culture of Cities which I shall now leave until we meet in September. It is a *Monument*.

[typed]
Ame—
(That homesick unconscious
beginning gives the best clue
to the rest of the letter!)
2997 Kalakua Avenue
Honolulu, Hawaii
28 August 1938

. . . . Moby Dick, dear Harry, still haunts these waters; for, by a flick of his tail, he turned this whole trip from a tropical idyll into a nightmare of anxieties, which began a fortnight ago when Sophy was stricken with a cold that became pneumonitis, and sent her into the hospital for treatment within a couple of days of its outbreak. The first eight days gave us much anxiety; for Sophy had been run down all summer; her resistance was low; her temperature chart was extremely jumpy; and she created an internal lesion from coughing that for the whole day had the doctor worried about appendicitis, since the pain appeared in almost exactly the same region. During the last six days, Sophy has been slowly turning upward for the better; and a couple of days ago her temperature became normal. But instead of gaining a new health, a new refreshment here, she is wasted and weak; and we will be lucky indeed if she is even able to start for home on the ninth of September, a week later than we planned. . . . I had indeed, looked forward to this part of my tour with something like foreboding: everything had been so perfect up to the last day or two I had spent in the Northwest that I kept on saying to myself: Life just can't be as perfect and as triumphant as this for so long: it is all a deception; something terrible will happen. But when I met Sophy and the children at San Francisco my fears were eased: for the terrible thing had already happened: Sophy had risen from a sickbed (with a bad septic sore throat) in order to make the journey; and though I secretly cursed the country doctor for letting her start out in this wan condition, I felt that at least we had made proper sacrifice to the gods, and their jealously would abate. I couldn't guess that much worse was in store: indeed by now I scan the sky every morning wondering if some new mischief be not brewing. I have undoubtedly transferred a little of my own feelings to the landscape; but by now I think I can understand why people have attributed a sort of malignity to the tropics: it is because along with its lush sense of life, its overpowering perfumes, which one encounters with the great ginger plant a-bloom in the jungle as much as in a garden, its radiant invitations to the senses, it also has a way of sapping the vitality and disorganizing the normal rhythms of the body. Women apparently menstruate with great irregularity here, at least the white women. Colds, once acquired, hang on forever, or in the very face of the sunshine become worse: then a spell of humid "Kona" weather sets in, with the wind blowing from the south, and the sick die off like flies, or at least sink into deeper misery. Along with this great ease of living, goes danger. Even the absence of snakes here is something of a deception: the even deadlier black widow spider lurks under the rocks. Unless one has hacked one's way through the sprawling tangled branches of the jungle, as Geddes and I did yesterday in the company of Sophy's doctor, one can scarcely realize what a perpetual struggle must go on in order to capture a little quiet space for man's life. For the first time I realize what a thoroughly good job O'Neill did psychologically in The Emperor Jones. . . . Incidentally, speaking of the weather and your possible trip, the bad times here are the span of months between September and October, which are very hot, through January, February, and sometimes even March, which are muggy and rainy. From April to September the temperature rarely climbs above 82 and the humidity is generally low. . . . Sophy has taken this blow with her usual heroism and fortitude; and if nothing happens to the children before we get back they at least will have benefited by it: Geddes has at last found an environment that equals or surpasses his own exorbitant expectations; and that is saying quite a lot. Hawaii is near enough in race and scenery to the Marquesas to make me look forward to re-reading, with a new eye, all that H.M. wrote about these parts; those who have been to the southern islands have pointed out to me various regions here that resemble them closely topographically; but of course the old life has been so far torn to shreds here, because of the over-influx of modern civilization, that as far as human beings go what I have achieved here is not a sense of the Polynesian past, but of the oriental cultures.

Your letter, as usual, was full of stimulating thoughts; and your resolution of both the Christ and the homosexual problems—even your statement of them—will bear not a little on my next book and color it from one end to another. You have given me something to think of on the long journey home—unless I am too preoccupied with nursing—and the trip has given me much, too. My chief desire at the moment, after months of observation, externality, superficial adjustment, politeness, social intercourse, banality, emptiness, over-stimulation is to settle down for a long quiet round in the country, and to make a reckoning with what I have been through. Next thing to being home in Amenia, a visit from you is what I look forward to. In the meanwhile, affectionate greetings from us all.

Ever yours,

Lewis

[handwritten]
[LM] 8 Oct 38

Dear Lewis.

I led your letter a hectic chase & it did not catch me for ten days or more, I passed Amenia just before your return & then spent a week with my sister, whose husband Bob Bacon died very suddenly in the flush of his career. Then battling my way through the N.E. havoc to the Tower & then Topsfield & here Boston.[15] What a fearful hurricane swept through your thriving life! Give my love to Sophy & embrace her especially hard for us all. What a misery! Your letters depicting the heights & depths of tropical possibilities was an epic of Romantic rise & fall—the Melvillian thema or one of them. I only hope the Greek balance of your conjoined lives has been now restored. Only Geddes perhaps still harbors the aromatic dream of Happy Isles. He bears watching, & may need a warning before he dedicates his life to it. I trust that the damage at your hermitage is not extensive. The Tower & Topsfield were rather slightly disrupted: a few trees, a few pigeons & all the technics dependent upon electric juices.

I have not your letter at hand & have forgotten whether you asked me any specific questions. C rather expected a visit from Sophy in the summer, was much disturbed to hear of her illness. We were called upon by Alice & her new husband: an agreeable fellow who hangs on her whims & words & seems to give her some comfort & balance, though she appeared inclined to apologize for him. I have written about 400 typewritten pages but have only got Herman as far as Tahiti. I am spending a disproportionate amount of time on youthful influences & am cutting down the last 40 years of spiritual—though not aesthetic as you pointed out—anticlimax to a bare 3 or 4 chapters. What are your plans for the next few months? We must meet soon. I am closing as I have a stack of letters ahead of me. But love to all. Send me a word.

Harry

[typed]
8 October 1938

. . . . Your letter, dear Harry, reminded me of the long drought of not-seeing you that has accompanied all my travels, triumphs, disappointments, and subsequent desolateness; and I was tempted to answer it by my sudden appearance in Boston, had a dozen and one domestic duties, real and imaginary, not prevented me. We escaped the ravages of the storm here, though many of our neighbors suffered grievously; but hard upon it Sophy came down again with a bad cold—in reaction against a cold inoculation—and the depression that hung over our household was not a little

---

15. "The Tower" was the retreat on property (adjoining the Parker River near Rowley, Massachusetts) owned by Morgan, which Morgan and Murray designed and decorated.

deepened by the treacherous black state of the world. Perhaps for the first time since 1914, I feel that the odds are finally stacked too heavily against the decencies and sanities: if we escape the paralysis of world-barbarism now it will be, not just by our efforts, but by some accident or miracle, like a severe influenza epidemic in the fascist countries! In one sense, the situation is a real test of my philosophy: if I can write a book that rings true in the present world, my beliefs ought to hold water for any conceivable society or any moment of the individual's life: not fair weather philosophy for these days. But the pit of Timonism yawns invitingly: it is easier to sink into it than to keep struggling in the opposite direction, where one's utmost effort merely keeps one's head about the swamp. How far all these black thoughts are touched by the debacle of my personal life this last year I have hardly dared to ask: more, perhaps, than I should willingly admit. The cure, probably, is to plunge into work again; and by now my study is almost tidy enough again to permit it. . . .

We want to see you both. Will you come down for a weekend: or are you coming to New York: or shall I have to manage a Boston trip later in the fall? (The last week in October—have to go down to Washington.) In the meanwhile, my—our— most affectionate greetings.

Lewis

[handwritten]

Valuator & Creator of New Life—dear Lewis.

I am now in the middle of the Insensate Industrial City—strongly with you. You are opening my eyes to things I dreamed of perhaps—but never saw or knew. I prophesy that you will change, in fundamental respects, the ideology of the generation. It is a masterful exposition. You came off very well with Dominant, Recessive, etc. I am going to take these conceptions immediately into Psychology—from your suggestions. . . . I am going slowly with it as I am deep in my own labors— more later.

I *must* see you before you go. If everything else fails Christiana & I will motor down within 3 weeks. Thanks for Pearce's name. I wrote him a short note in regard to Walt Whitman's Pose & the Culture of Cities. I was up till 2 A.M. discussing the menace of Fascism vs. Communism with Felix Frankfurter & my brain is an ashtray of cigar butts. I shall end for the moment.

I hope you speak vs. Fascism. Let us know

HAM

Mumford
Amenia, New York
4 December 1938

Dear Harry:

Are you back yet? I am running up to Boston on Thursday, chiefly to speak about the state of the World to the Harvard students on Friday. If you are free either

Thursday evening or on Saturday please leave word for me at the Bellevue: I expect to get there sometime between six and eight in the evening on the eighth. If you are away or busy I'll write at length later. I have learnt much from your Explorations of Personality and will learn more when I have more fully mastered it: it is an immensely valuable piece of work.[16] There is a further stage in the evolution of "need" that I would like to put to you if I only had it clear in my own mind: when it is projected into a social situation it seems to me to transform itself into what I should call a "claim": thus n Succorance become cl food: n Sex becomes cl intercourse. When such an outlet presents itself the very character of n seems to me to be altered: n becomes more conscious, more exacerbating, if the social situation denies cl or if it does not itself create cl. And thus the direction of need, outward toward the social situation or inward forward fantasy or self-satisfaction, seems to me to alter the quality and intensity of n: the claim often diminishes the active impact of the need, as with well-nourished people, fed regularly and amply, who never experience the need for food because the claim is so well satisfied. Probably this is all nonsense, or you have said this better yourself and some n cog plus n aut has led me astray!

Lewis

[typed]
Mumford
Amenia, New York
4 January 193[9][17]

Dear Harry:

I've been working so hard, putting the finishing touches on Men Must Act, that I haven't had a breath in which even to thank you for your very welcome Christmas gift of the Virginia Quarterly.[18] This breath has now come: my thanks with it, for try as one will in the country I find myself losing contact with just those things which the Quarterly recalls one to. As for my little book, it is in the classic tradition of pamphlets: over-incisive and over-simplified, of course, but perhaps not without a momentary merit. (It can claim no more!) Events have been moving so fast that proposals that were novel and outrageous for most people last spring may now seem commonplace. I shall be in New York around the seventeenth and will stay there till the twentieth. Shall you by any chance be there? Or are you likely to be in Cambridge just before or just after this? I am thinking of running up to look over the Cambridge School,* to see if its teachers impress me as well as its prospectus and its general reputation. Geddes might profit by a year away from his family; and though I don't like being as much as five hours away from him, this school presents

16. Henry A. Murray, ed., *Explorations in Personality: A Clinical and Experimental Study of Fifty Men of College Age* (1938).

17. Mumford misdates the letter as 1938.

18. Lewis Mumford, *Men Must Act* (1939).

itself as one of the possibilities for him next year. . . . I am at last settling down to the preparation of my book, with nothing to interrupt me for a whole year except the preparation of the Harvard lectures for next fall. Unfortunately, they are so far off the present track of my thinking that I view their approach with reluctance, almost distaste: if it weren't that so much more may hang on them I'd chuck them altogether. American history and American architecture are, at the moment, as far away as the moon from me. I'll send you an early copy of Men Must Act. In the meantime our affectionate greetings and blessings for the New Year.

Lewis

    *Do you know any other boarding school to recommend in New England? Not of course in the Groton-Andover tradition.

[LM] 1939

Lewis, you are the breath of the Lord. My last dictated letter contained none of the thoughts which I had been entertaining about you & *Men Must Act*—I meant to follow it with another letter, suggesting that at some point you be concrete: tell what *individuals* might do in the way of boycotting German goods, steamship lines, etc. But you have written on a different level, no doubt. I am waiting excitedly for the volume to appear. I want a channel for my own indignation to express itself. Frankfurter, by the way, was much impressed by your New Republic article. I wonder whether you have touched on the Jewish question, or have discussed your own passion as similar to Hitler's, but in a different cause. The question of Ahab coming to resemble the whale. How about that? Is it the problem of not becoming embittered or blinded—but never has there been more provocation. C & I will be in New York from Jan 19 to Feb 10—a note to the Harvard Club will reach me in 2 days. We shall be wanting most particularly to see you. Dine with us on the 19th, meeting in the lobby of the New Weston at 6 P.M. (We shall not be staying there however.) The Cambridge School is as good as any—very good from all reports—but there is a softness about all these progressive schools which leaves its graduates with vague flabby minds—but yet this is better than rigidities about outworn principles. My best to Sophy.

Hurriedly
H.A.M

[typed]
Mumford
Amenia, New York
10 January 1939

Dear Harry:

    You will probably be as pleased and surprised as I was to find that Men Must Act incorporates most of your suggestions: at the very end indeed it raises the problem of Ahab becoming like the whale—I quote A.E.'s great sentence, A man becomes the image of the thing he hates—and suggests the answer to it.[19] The psychological diagnosis in the early part of the book is a little rough-and-ready, as must happen in such an elementary exposition; but the book has a weight now that even the longer unpublished version did not have last spring. The enclosed clipping should amuse you both: send it back at your convenience. The result will be that probably three times the number of people will read the report as would do so ordinarily; and I expect that twenty years hence it may turn out that I have won; because I have the ancient gods of the island on my side. Sophy will probably be down with me on the nineteenth; but on that night I have to speak at a Menorah Journal anniversary dinner: the only time when we'll be free is the next day for lunch. But if you are going to be busy then, let's all four meet during the next fortnight when Sophy and I dash into the city again. Her cold inoculations have worked out badly, largely I suspect through the lack of diagnostic tact on the part of our local doctor and for the moment she is in bed with another severe cold; but she'll probably be up and around next week. We are both eager to see you both. If you want to reach me after next Tuesday drop a note to me at Harcourt's in care of Charles Pearce marked Hold.

> Warmly
> Lewis

[handwritten]
[LM] Ans 9 Oct. 1939

Here I am, noble Lewis, lying full out on a hot beach near a cabin where I am keeping myself hearty company, and up on the bank are several cows—from a race that hasn't committed murder for centuries—& it is the hardest thing in the world to picture how vile Man can be when he gets whipped up to it. Goethe's Faust said 'In the beginning, was the Act,' but his Nation has proved that 'In the beginning was the Word'—the Logos of Goebbels propaganda & Hitler shrieks. Deprive these men of tongue & everyone would go back to his farm, open a bottle of wine & embrace his wife.

We have been separated this summer by a butterfly. I promised Alison I would bring her a nice one when next I came & though I spent several hours in the fields, could only get the commonest varieties. And so, though I passed Amenia twice I was too ashamed to turn in. Would she be permitted a canary in N.Y.? I am sure her whole soul life is going to grow by way of birds. She will be an ornithologist, write more Odes to the Nightingale, manage an aviary, or be a bird herself—dance like Pavlova or marry a Lindberg. At 11 yrs her favorite poem will be The Raven.

---

19. Æ was the pen name for George William Russell (1867–1935), Irish poet; Mumford was influenced by Russell's efforts to improve Irish regional and rural life.

Your letter told me nothing. How is your drama of Eros in verse? What are the dates of your lectures? Can you stay for a while in Boston, Topsfield, Tower on the Marsh? And wonderful Sophy?

Melville is coming very slowly—but I am finding a few more interesting things—I have only just reached Moby-Dick. I agree on White Jacket. You yourself are very much like W.J., but 10x as good.

I hope you are pleased with your new place, near where H.M. & Thomas Paine lived—Let me hear by Oct 9 (when I shall return to 64 Plympton).

Yrs
Harry

[typed]
Lewis Mumford
393 Bleecker Street
New York, N.Y.
9 October 1939

. . . It was good to get your letter, dear Harry, with the full hot sun upon it, and the full hot sun of yourself adding its own beams. It found me in the shattered state that usually attends moving, and that is doubly formidable when one is going not just from one house to another, but from a peaceful, simple rural environment to the hard, exciting, sometimes ecstatic pressures of New York. Except for fatigue, we have all withstood the change better than I had counted on: Alison is delighted with her school and the abundance of other children, for lack of whom she was badly starved, I am afraid; and though Geddes grumbles about his new school, and though he hates the city just as a city, with its stale smells and its crowded streets and its lack of openness and green and all the keen scents of the forest, he nevertheless has been plainly stimulated by the new interests and new fields that the school has opened out to him. Our apartment is really charming: Sophy is already happy in it; and the abundance of neighbors we know gives the place the informality of a village. In fact, for the moment, everything in the outward environment has been going so well that I am prepared for some jealous blast from the skies at almost any moment, and go around with my fingers crossed. I haven't settled down to a productive routine of work, yet; and I am so far behind in my schedule of preparation for the Harvard lectures that I shall probably have to re-write my lectures the very week before I am giving them, right up to the last week. I expect to give my first lecture on the seventh, the second on Thursday the ninth of November; after that, on Tuesdays and Fridays until the twenty-fourth. The first weekend I shall have to be down in Washington; but after that I hope to stay on in Cambridge fairly steadily, if that should work out: this depends partly upon whether Sophy can join me for a couple of days and partly upon whether any special engagements call me down to New York. I have just prepared a new preface for Men Must Act, which brings my program of last February up to date, and tonight I am having a debate with Norman Thomas on the whole matter of neutrality versus participation.[20] Shall you be down in New York before November? The only weekend I expect to be away is that of the twentieth. Our telephone number is Chelsea 3-7441. We are very eager to see you: the earlier the better. I want to hear all that you have done on your book: Christiana mentioned that you were doing some chapters you thought she wouldn't like, but I am as incredulous about that as I fancy she was. Pray for my Harvard lectures: for some reason or other I am still a little apathetic about them, and if I don't come to life soon may make a horrible mess of the whole business and bring discredit upon all the earnest souls who have been trying to stir up the universities with new blood from the non-academic outside.

In friendship
Lewis

[handwritten]
[LM] 1939

Dear Lewis:

I read your splendid Call to Faith & Arms last week & despatched a letter to Harcourt Brace, which summed up my general impression. I trust you see these notes & also that we shall have an opportunity for some long talks about it later, so I shall not say much now except that I am in hearty accord with your main points & was much moved by the driving energy of it & the mountain-air aphoristic Emersonian rhetoric & countless clever hits & husky solar plexus blows & sock-in-the-jaws. In the course of it you called many people some pretty vile names for thinking or doing a great variety of things (about 2 dozen of which apply to myself by the way). You set up a rather high standard & open yourself to the query: 'how long, how hard & how sincerely has this guy been living up to all those commandments himself.' I liked particularly re-reading your discussion of emotion: the Liberal's fear of it & its utility in apperception & judgment. You bring out the neutrality & sterility of scientific objectivity *per se*, but you dodge the issue of *agreement*—the purpose of it all. Science is hard discipline, painfully worked out, to reach agreement. It is a truly Democratic procedure. Your procedure, however, is autocratic. If everyone stood up & spoke as you do, there would be no community, no comradeship, no love, no sacrifice—except among the members of each of the hundred sects that would arise. Science is entirely non-sectarian & so should a proper Democracy be. I cannot help feeling that you are encouraged by a underlying assumption that you can forcefully impel people by machine gun-phrases to agree with you. Unless we have all sunk as low as the Germans, at least some people—the class who read your book—will demand more reality-sense & more justice. I suspect an uncon-

---

20. Norman Thomas (1884–1968), socialist; in 1938, he founded the Keep America Out of War Committee.

scious identification with a negative sign between you and Hitler. But of course I agree—having murder in my heart for everything Fascistic & believe in you implicitly & share your sentiments & will go along with you & Sophy world without end—how well the Melville quotations fitted it!

Affly

Harry

P.S. At last I have found a fine birdcage for Alison. Now there is only the bird. What delayed reaction I have had toward Geddes & Alison! Drop me a line up here (Mid-River Farm, Clayton, N.Y.) where I shall be for 10 days, working on Pierre & Melville's frustrated need for sacrifice. I expect to reach the Tower about Oct. & why not come & stay with us?

[typed]

393 Bleecker Street

New York, N.Y.

19 December 1939

Dear Harry:

I have thought of you often since coming back here; but I had been hoping that you would, by some happy miracle, drop in here; and so with a great pile of work and many engagements waiting for me—and another infection in my mouth to slow down all my motions and to make my mind foggy—I have been silent. Looking back on November, our various meetings and talks stand out as the only very real and vivid part of the whole experience. From the moment I put my nose in Cambridge I detected that the atmosphere had subtly changed and that my being there, in the light of all the old proposals and suggestions, was almost an embarrassment; and nothing that Hudnut said or did while I was there, or in the letter he wrote afterwards, changed this feeling of mine. If he were a little more frank I should know what had happened, not as a result of my lectures, but before I got there: but then, if he had told me early enough, I might never have come. In all, I count the time wasted and feel a little cheated; or rather, I feel that I was a little gullible and over-pleased a few years ago, when the only sensible thing to do was to stand pat and make no move whatever. Fortunately, the experience has only made me more eager to plunge deeper into my book; and although there have been constant breaks and interruptions, I have at last got started on at least the preliminary stages of reading; that process of holding converse with the great minds of the world and by purely accidental associations, discovering one's own thoughts. For the present my reading is omnivorous and unsystematic; for the bibliography of my "subject" won't be in existence until I have mastered it! I already however begin to have the sense that one has, when one has spent too much time on the lowlands, and, with a high mountain to climb, begins to get a feeling of being in a loftier site after progressing a few hundred feet, even though one knows that the real work has only begun, and that the great view will not be visible till one is quite tired, perhaps exhausted, with the strain of the effort. Coming back to all the deeper experiences of philosophy, religion, and personal behavior has for me a sort of rejuvenating effect; perhaps because my earliest love was philosophy. The other week I gave a lecture before the philosophical society of N.Y.U. on the logical scheme within which I think: an elaboration of some of Geddes's diagrams, and I think I have pushed certain things here farther than I have carried them before, for they face me with new problems. Perhaps we'll get a chance to discuss some of these things when we meet. Incidentally, I have at last found the simple psychological equivalent for Geddes's organism: function: environment diagram in terms of personality: need-response: situation. This requires further discussion, too, because it brings with it a psychological concept that perhaps is a commonplace to you, but only lately struck me with any force, and that is that all psychological function (more or less) may be in either a passive or active mode, depending upon whether the organism plays an aggressive or seeking role or a patient and receptive or suffering role.

I have been wading, with great exhilaration, through the Lincoln: a truly cyclopean book, which is on the borderline between biography and history, and which carries the objective method of writing biography to its extreme limit—so that he nearly, though not quite, gives one an illumination on the subjective reference of events.[21] But it is all from the outside—as if Sandburg distrusted the processes of empathy and identification, and resolved to overcompensate against them. Everything is there. Even Melville makes his quiet entry among the horde of clamorous office seekers, shakes hands, and departs without the coveted job. The interesting part about the whole business is that, in the first volume, Lincoln is Chamberlain and the Confederates are the Nazis—all over again.

We are staying in New York for the holidays; so we eagerly look forward to a visit from you if you are down here then. All luck and good fortune for the New Year, to you and the book!

Affectionately
Lewis

[handwritten]
Harvard Club
27 West 44th Street
[LM] Ans 31 Dec 39

Dear Lewis:

I can well sympathize with your feeling of being cheated by the Harvard Dep't. After expending yourself as you did. Everyone I have seen who attended your lectures was impressed, & I can say I have never heard anyone with a greater gift for communication—just the right balance between fact, theory, value & enthusiasm. I

---

21. Carl Sandburg, *Abraham Lincoln: The War Years* (1939).

have no gossip about the internal policies and rivalries in the Architectural Dept, & cannot explain their present silence—except the general trend, emanating from above, of dismissing rather than acquiring men on the faculty. Harvard is now talking poor & no one can believe this is justified, having become accustomed to the Expansion period.

I expected to be in New York for several days & have a good long talk with you; but as it has turned out I have to leave tonight, after 24 hours here, for Urbana, Illinois, where there is a meeting. After that, Iowa City, Kansas City, Lawrence, Topeka, Denver, Minneapolis, Madison, Galena, Chicago, Ann Arbor, Detroit, Buffalo, Rochester. If there is anything in the way of very good or very bad housing along this route—or anything else you think I should see—drop me a line (Jan 4: Hotel Jayhawk, Topeka, Kansas, or Jan 8: Hotel Cosmopolitan, Denver, Colorado). I shall be at the universities most of the time, but a few excursions into the Steel Industry, Art & Music & Architecture would give me a more balanced picture of culture in the Prairies.

My autumn has been almost a total loss—not a page on H.M. I spent three weeks on an article about psychoanalysis which I can see, now that it is off my hands, will antagonize and alienate both the analysts & the academics. I am somewhat surprised at how critical I become when I get going—despite the fact that I am basically joyous. I seem to detect the same tendency in you—to disparage & attack before embarking on your positive ideas & hopes. Your Havelock Ellis review I thought was good, but informed by too high a standard of human capacity.[22] A man is not responsible for his glandular endowment. Ellis did the most with what he had—he might, for example, have been an anti-erotic intellectual.

Well, I am hungry for more talk with you & January appears in the guise of a barrier—February, however, shall see me in N.Y.

> Affly
> Harry

[typed]
Lewis Mumford
393 Bleecker Street
New York City
31 December 1939

Dear Harry:

An embrace for the *new* year, and my hope that it will be a new year for all of us: to add *happy* to it is almost a redundancy. I said good-bye to the year with that elegy on time which appeared in the New Yorker this week: I trust, in some bored mo-

---

22. Lewis Mumford, review of *My Life: Autobiography of Havelock Ellis, New Republic,* 20 December 1939, 265–66.

ment of your travel, you happened upon it.[23] Whether it has any real vitality by it-self I do not know: its real function was to release the brakes and get me started on my novel a year ago; and in all likelihood, it will not even appear in the finished novel, because I don't know what on earth it has to do with it. The New Yorker ed-itors, curiously, are asking me for more verse; and I am working over another sec-tion of the novel that I think you will like even if the editors don't: on the taste of New England.[24] It will be fun if, in maturity, I pick up the thread of imaginative writing again, which I dropped when I became an editor of the Dial and assumed responsibility for my own economic support. My imaginative talents are not by themselves high: but skill and the ability to draw fully on one's experience may partly atone for this; and I look forward with a smile to my own kind of second blooming. At the moment smiles are rare; for I have been going through a devastat-ing depression which I, with my materialistic bias, am more inclined to attribute to an infected tooth, which is real, than to any remoter kind of frustration. The Har-vard business is quite washed out of my system; and I have been working so in-dustriously on my book that the last month, apart from my infection, has sped past with that speed which only sleep and intellectual absorption give. You are going through parts of the country that I scarcely know. But Minneapolis is a place with character, and if you meet Malcolm Willey there, who is dean or assistant to the President, you should also make acquaintance with the Frank Lloyd Wright house he had built for himself. You will find Willey good company. You probably won't have time to dash out to Frank Lloyd Wright when you are in Madison; and he may be down in Arizona at the moment, or off somewhere else; but he is the essence of the corn-fed Middle West, the same order of man as Sherwood Anderson, but with a more positive and dominating ego than most of his fellow-countrymen. I am sure he would be worth seeing on his native heath; though I have never had that experi-ence. In Chicago you should give yourself the experience, at least for one night, of getting a room for yourself in the Auditorium Hotel, on the seventh or eighth floor, facing the lake. It was one of Louis Sullivan's great works; and since it was done be-fore the days of steel frames and light curtain walls, it should satisfy your need for solidity, as well as for spaciousness. I think I've told you about my own experience of going there, in an exacerbated state, in January 1938 and being healed by the light and space and beauty of the sky. If you are free in Buffalo, please call on my friends, Walter Curt Behrendt and his wife Lydia, 700 Auburn Avenue. He was, in Germany, an architect and administrative official; she was and is a talented concert

23. Lewis Mumford, "Fantasia on Time," *New Yorker,* 9 September 1939, 16; from Mumford's unfin-ished verse novel, *Victor*; reprinted in *Lewis Mumford, My Works and Days: A Personal Chronicle* (New York: Harcourt Brace Jovanovich, 1979), 434–35.

24. Lewis Mumford, "The Taste of New England," *New Yorker,* 27 February 1943, 20; reprinted in Lewis Mumford, *My Works and Days*, 296–97.

pianist, with a marvellous command of everyone from Bach to Hindemith. You will find in both of them a rich sense of life, a fineness of perception and a depth of feeling that is rare even among "good" people. Don't be put off even for five minutes by their surfaces: she is no German Hausfrau but a passionate woman, with a fine demon of humor, and he, who is her temperamental opposite, is an organic philosopher capable of following your thought to its utmost boundaries.

When you come back we'll compare notes.

With affectionate greetings
Lewis

[handwritten]
Monday, Feb 12
[LM] 40

Lewis, my high-reaching comrade-in-arms, it has been almost 2 months since I have written you, & before me are 3 letters: Dec 19 & 31 & Jan 10 to Christiana. I shall start methodically with the first: I trust that the infection in your mouth has been conquered by the battalions of good leucocytes in your better-than-human blood. I feel a fine fresh wind coming from you, as you take flight from your reading. You don't mention the books you have found but I can imagine. Let me know occasionally. I should agree that for Geddes's 'organism' (which is merely pointing to an entity) one might more specifically substitute 'need' (or 'drive' as a better word for the need in operation—it may be a response or an initiation (*seeking* a stimulus to which to respond)); & for environment I should more specifically substitute *press*. Press can be used alone, to represent the kind of force to which the organism is momentarily responding; or you can speak of 'field of press' to represent the total situation at the moment [p Cold (a draught coming from the windows) p Heat (a fire in the grate), p Affiliation (a friendly visitor, like myself, sitting in a chair), p ideo-Cognizance (a question as to your ideas emanating from the friend), p Duty (a job you should do before supper), etc.]—or the 'field of press' to represent the temporal series of a day or a season. According to my language some needs are active (or are fused with general need for activity) others are passive (or are fused with a general need for passivity). Need for succorance (sustenance, aid, sympathy, protection, support) & need for abasement (suffering, injury, belittlement, frustration, coercion) are typical examples (also need for sentience, receiving sensuous impressions) of functioning in the passive mode. The 'reception vector' concept covers this sort of behaviors.

As to need, I have attempted to make the general tendency specific by adding the concept of cathected object (the particular thing needed) & the concept of cathected mode (action or sub-need, by which the thing is obtained). Together they make a complex pattern or integrate: the need to eat certain kinds of food at certain times & places, the need to approach & converse with a certain person in a certain way, etc. The cathexes of a person (likes and dislikes) are as important as his needs. In morals, for example, some people lay emphasis on the latter ('war (aggression) is wrong'), others on the former ('Aggression for a good cause (your country) is noble')—I missed the elegy in the 'New Yorker'—I couldn't get it in the West by the time I got your letter. If you send me a clipping of it I shall return it immediately.

I enjoyed my month in the Middle West immensely. The level of good will is higher there than any place I have been to—They meet your train, take you to the hotel, have you for meals, arrange a program so that you can see everything you want to see within the allotted time. I had a few speeches sprung on me; but otherwise I was in an irresponsible mood, except at Chicago where there were 3 consecutive days of talk at Dan Prescott's American Council of Education. I heard that you were scheduled to hold forth in February. When I got home I heard from the Rockefeller that they would be unable to supply the grant they promised for the Clinic—which means that unless I get the money elsewhere or from them in 1941, the Clinic & I will part company. C & I expect to go to New York in 10 days for a month & we are plotting to see you & Sophy as much as possible.

I haven't touched Melville since September & am far behind my schedule—just working up to the battle with the whale. Now that you have become a philosophical psychologist we are as close as can be in our interests & I am hungry for communication—

> Affectionately
>
> H

> [handwritten, undated]

Dear Lewis my valiant:

I appreciated your hand—My personal loss is all taken up by the world loss & has become a part of the general misery—Paris, for example, has been my mother's Mecca for fifty years & she knew every stone in the city & was acquainted with its history, its people and its immeasurable beauty. Looking through her things I find photographs of buildings & scenes that may be non-existent in a week.[25]

I am glad to hear you are engaged in another book, because most of your prophecies have come true, as far as Europe is concerned, and you are one of the few leaders of thought—strong virtuous thought—in this country. The difficulties in my mind are these:

(1) To combat ruthless totalitarianism we must ourselves become somewhat totalitarian & ruthless. Whatever we do in this direction must be done with a clear consciousness that we have been compelled to adopt a philosophy & executive scheme of which we disapprove under ordinary conditions. How much free speech & quarrelling & dissension among themselves a people can tolerate when opposed by a unified fanatical nation is questionable. To go back to one of our classic exam-

---

25. Reference to the death of Murray's mother, Fannie Morris Babcock Murray.

ples—The dictator nations are like Ahab & his crew, & the U.S. is like Starbuck—Remember 'morally enfeebled, also, by the incompetence of mere unaided virtue or rightmindedness in Starbuck' (your 19th Century Liberal). In other words there is no question but that Might makes Right when life is brought down to the lowest & simplest level, that is to say, the ultimate principle is Force & Force establishes the laws—The Nietzschean philosophy *works—but only for a time*—It spends itself, & other forces (the desire for ease & affection & beauty) come in to take its place. Thus the Chinese minister with his ageless philosophy thinks that in 2 or 3 years the dictators will be in disrepute with their own people. A hundred years ago the Germans were the most peace-loving people in Europe. It was Napoleonic France & Imperialistic England that were disrupting peace & spreading havoc. Well, it seems to me we are facing a situation in which there will be three gangster nations—Germany, Russia & Japan—and ourselves in the world; and we shall have to function as a Nation of G-men. How many of our liberties we can preserve during this period is a question, but I think those who govern should do what has to be done deliberately & with full consciousness of adopting the program of Might & dictator-like centralization as a necessary & *temporary* expedient. The more excited we get for War the more like our enemies *in every respect* we shall become, unless we keep reason & our own principles enthroned.

(2) What is most disheartening to me is the widespread prevailing selfishness of the businessman. We cannot act morally if we are thinking of dollars & cents. The continuation of our aid to Japan & through Italy to Germany stands as a huge blot which all our talk of liberty cannot efface. Liberty for what? For more & more materialism? We go in for Economic warfare & slavery & call it by fine names. Our leaders are good bargainers, full of moral cant & complacency. I find much more to admire in a soldier than in a businessman. What I am saying here is that I should like to fight *for* something, rather than merely *against* something, and the business philosophy & practices of America is not something that one can fight for. Thus I want a positive program for America. To me it is a disheartening fact that men never get aroused to full cooperation except for war. Therefore I am for—

(3) Universal National Service for youngsters & women to work for National Art, Science & Social relations & as much military training thrown in as the times call for. America is corrupt because it has used its liberty for materialism & created more unspeakable ugliness in the world than any Nation that has ever existed. How contemptuous the Germans might have the right to be if after winning this war they turned all their geist & spirit of sacrifice & reverence & thoroughness to peaceful enterprises—to the science & music & learning & philosophy & happy ways that made Germany the spiritual home of so many Americans in the 19th Century. Let us clean house & make America a refuge & a breeding-ground for those who can live & create the good life.

(4) Of course I believe in the greatest possible aid to the allies, preparedness & everything. It is too easy to see that that is necessary; & I think Wilkey can do this

for us a little better than Roosevelt. No other men stand out. But let us at the same time start something *Positive* in this country. I meant to write one page & then overflowed—but this is just an opening wedge for further discussion when I pass your way in early or late July.

Love to Sophy—

> Yrs
> Harry

May you have your best energies for your book.

> [typed]
> Lewis Mumford
> Amenia New York
> 11 November 1940

Dear Harry:

I chortled with pleasure and heaved a sigh of relief at the same time when your pamphlet on Psychoanalysis came last week: it wiped away the tiny ugly doubt that I might ever have laid eyes on it before—because, knowing the strain and distraction of my days last spring, that still remained a possibility.[26] It is a beautiful clarification of the whole problem; and it is written with an ease and a freshness that recalls William James, who will always remain my ideal of the one thinker since Plato who has managed to carry through a formal argument in an informal style: something I aspire to do but have never achieved. Your doubts strike right to the heart of the matter, and your questions, particularly those addressed to the Freudians, are extremely acute; even though, as in your paper on Freud, you manage to do substantial justice to everything about them except their vanity and pride, to which only Satan perhaps could pay the proper meed of tribute. Thanks heartily for letting me have this. On going through my notes for my new book—a colossal heap it has taken me a week to assort in even rough style—I find with pleasure how often I have been compelled to use your terminology in Explorations or to take over some insight of yours, expressed there or elsewhere. Yesterday I started work on the first draft, lest further delay should simply pile up difficulties: in following the trail back from our difficulties and dilemmas today, I am already back in seventh century Judea and sixth century Athens; and if I don't call a halt to that I will find myself presently sunk in the mire of the Nile, with a pyramid looming above me to mark the spot where I was last seen. I find the early Ionian philosophers fascinating; and the course of Greek philosophy makes me wonder whether your own development, from surgeon to analyst, does not in fact repeat the historic pattern—

---

26. Henry A. Murray, "What Should Psychologists Do about Psychoanalysis?" *Journal of Abnormal and Social Psychology* 35 (1940): 150–75; reprinted in Edwin S. Shneidman, ed., *Endeavors in Psychology: Selections from the Personology of Henry A. Murray* (New York: Harper and Row, 1981), 291–311.

the discovery of the self after a long roundabout excursion through external nature: from cosmology to personology. The election relieves me only a little; for I still believe that the next four months, particularly our reaction to an open rapprochement between Stalin and Hitler, will probably be decisive in this war, possibly in the history of the next five centuries. But I confess I like the way in which our countrymen went to the polls, under a formidable barrage of threats from the opposition, and, contrary to their own normal habits, brought back into office the one man they had some reason to place their confidence in—Wilkie being the obvious dud that he is. It gave me the feeling that our democracy is still far sounder, far closer to the realities of life, than any of the European countries before the war. Have you by any chance read Jules Romains' incredibly naive self-exposures in the Saturday Evening Post: with fatuous pride, he proves himself to be a political innocent, or what is worse, an outright jackass—always under the impression that he was playing an important and effective role.[27] He actually puts a gardenia in his button hole, at a moment that requires sackcloth and ashes. The English don't know when they are beaten; but the French apparently don't know when they are betrayed. . . . The grey clouds and the reddish grass on the upland pastures are very fine; the cold gloomy mornings make it easy to face the typewriter. Are you back at your book too?

Lewis

[handwritten]
105 East 67
[LM] Dec 21? 1940

Dear Lewis:

I have been on the verge of writing you these many weeks. Your comments on my Psychoanalytic article were sparkling Moselle to me, but I felt a touch of guilt—having almost forced the thing on you. It was friendly of you to read it in the midst of your simmering creativeness. I was much impressed by the *City of Man,* particularly the appendix.[28] There is much for us to discuss. During the last two weeks, with many interruptions, I have been in a brew over the scheme I mentioned to you—of a Social Science Dep't at Washington. It would fit in with or provide an agency for some of the measures you have advocated. Not knowing exactly how you are at the moment (steamed up or quiescent) I am sending you a first draft, (in a couple of weeks) with the understanding that you will not look at it unless it falls

27. Jules Romains, "Seven Mysteries of Europe," series of seven articles in the *Saturday Evening Post* (21–23 November 1940).

28. Committee of Fifteen (including Mumford, G. A. Borgese, Herbert Agar, Reinhold Niebuhr), *City of Man: A Declaration on World Democracy* (1940); a denunciation of fascism and call for war on Nazi Germany.

right in with your present state. I am sending it to 5 or 6 friends for rigorous criticism before making the final copy, as I want to make it as invulnerable as possible.
I do not consider it a personal contribution, but something that should be pushed—
as I think—by all who approve of the scheme. The City of Man I have only first
seen, & I want to refer to it in the second draft, as it is a fine testament. I heard Dr.
Cohn say he thought it was one of the two inspiring works that had been excited by
the crisis. (The other being Laski's *Where Do We Go from Here?*—but he hasn't read
Faith for Living yet . . . I find Brentano's exhibits the latter on its shelf of Religious
books!) I am going to a few meetings in Philadelphia & elsewhere; then Cambridge,
then New York about Jan 10.[29] I hope we can meet as soon after that date as possible
as there are personal & impersonal things for us to dive into. There must be something very wrong about my way of writing or talking that makes you suspect animus in me, because on all levels & in all compartments of my self there is nothing
but admiration, sympathy & love for you. There are certain differences but you
don't require undeviating similarity, do you? NO.

> Affectionately
> Harry

> [handwritten]
> Lewis Mumford
> Amenia New York
> 26 December 1940

Dear Harry:

Your letter came as a Christmas greeting; and I answered it amid the distraction
and malaise of the holiday—made tense by all the little things that upset a household, like our maid's coming down with influenza, or like Geddes's very unfavorable scholastic report from school. (Apart from his compete inattention to studies
he is fine: handsome: better-balanced: affectionate!) At the moment I am rather at
sixes & sevens in my own work; for after working most of November on my book I
found that I was over-prepared on the earlier sections—I know far too much about
the origins of Christianity and the sins of Rome!—and that I had scarcely bitten into
the immense literature that awaits me after the sixteenth century. Unthinkingly last
winter, in a long spate of work, I let myself be trapped into the preoccupations of
the professional! As a result I have almost more notes on the medieval period alone
than I had on all of Technics & Civilization. So I have dropt writing & have gone
back to books again, a little ruefully, a little distractedly, because of the pressure of
all these political events in the world beyond—which I am so keenly aware of and
from which my continued residence here keeps me so aloof. Once I was in my book

---

29. Harold J. Laski, *Where Do We Go From Here?* (1940); Mumford, *Faith for Living* (1940).

the world could go hang: but now I am keenly aware of the claims of the citizen & one ear is always listening for an approaching footstep. I must stay up here till the middle of January: then a series of lecture & dental engagements, chiefly the latter, will take me to New York. . . . I am mighty interested indeed in your reactions to the City of Man—and Cohn's. Borgese had a very hard job in writing that memorandum; and considering the difficulties I think he did well, though each one of us has reservations about various particulars. That we had enough self-abnegation to sign it—to express our unity in the face of our temptation to heresy & dissent!—was perhaps as important as anything the book said. For this was no perfunctory signing. We wrestled over every word. I am glad you think there is something in it: particularly in our further plans; for the declaration of faith, if it stopped there, would have been purely a subjective gratification.

As for our misunderstanding over my own Faith for Living, I feel like repeating the story about Samuel Butler's man Alfred, to whom Butler had learnedly explained the phases of the moon. "Do you understand now?" asked Butler. "I think so, sir: but please to never mention the subject in my presence again!" The fact that old friends can misunderstand one another at critical moments makes one patient with the apparent obtuseness or malice of the rest of the world; and it chastens one's contempt for one's opponents. Every man & woman on the planet, with any pretense to sensibility, is now probably on edge and in no little degree distraught— if only because of all the humane impulses that are frustrated from day to day by the devilish uncertainties that hang over us & all we hold dear: there is sand in all our rice, as Melville would have said. No wonder our teeth are so easily set on edge.

I look forward to your report & shall read it & react to it promptly.

> Affectionate greetings & all good
> hopes for the new year
> Lewis

> [typed]
> Lewis Mumford
> Amenia New York
> 24 January 1941

Dear Harry:

This is a splendid presentation of the need for science in the guidance of public affairs: the best since Bacon's, and it carries the argument beyond the confident reaches of physical science and mechanical invention.[30] It prompts a dozen relevant ideas; but none of them, in the present urgent moment, could be anything but an embarrassment; though I will discuss them with you when we meet; eg. the need

---

30. Murray wrote to President Franklin D. Roosevelt proposing a government department of social science; see Forrest G. Robinson, *Love's Story Told: A Life of Henry A. Murray* (Cambridge: Harvard Univ. Press, 1992), 267.

for placing the whole effort, from the beginning, within an international frame-work, for one of the things that must be overcome, by a Department of Social Science, is the obsessive parochialism that developed, first with nineteenth century nationalism, and second with the relapse into autarchy that followed the world war. Also there is a conflict on the level of systematic thought, between your belief that science and reason are the necessary implements of change (with which I agree) and that the rejected artist may subvert the order we seek to create; and this conflict, I think, is basic to the misunderstanding that occasionally crops up between us, because at times you take the accepted scientific view, that science alone will be as immediately effective in social life as in machine technology, and at other times you see, more truly I think, that the process is not so simple in the case of social facts, since subjective manifestations must be included and utilized in society, though they can be dismissed as "secondary qualities" or aberrations in the physical sciences. But I mention these things now only by way of memoranda. Given the form of presentation you have chosen, I see nothing that could be well left out. If you have time, however, I should advise writing a simple three page summary to precede this, perhaps with page references to the document as a whole. It will have a much better chance of meeting the President's eye in that form than if you merely indicate the passages that should especially command his attention. From what I know about executives they read nothing; at best they pick at headlines, and so you must supply the headlines.

I have not been out the house since coming back here; but I am getting back into shape rapidly. At the moment, a fine soft snow is falling, and the landscape has become a delicate silverpoint etching.

Warmly,
Lewis

[typed]
Lewis Mumford
Amenia New York
21 March 1941

Dear Harry:

In spite of the fact that the weather has remained so wintry in externals, there has been a touch of spring up here this last fortnight, associated with my own returned health, that has kept me working so incessantly that it is hard to realize how many weeks have passed since I last laid eyes on you, at breakfast. I owe you an extra debt of gratitude for bringing Alfred Cohn and me together; although I have spent more than one unhappy hour since summoning up my fortitude and purpose, to resist his altogether rational and worthy proposals for me to hold forth at Campo Bello. We had a couple of first-rate hours together, in which we explored each other and the universe whilst ostensibly canvassing our immediate problem; and it is a long time since I have met a more rewarding mind. I had to say No to participating in the work next summer, because if I didn't I'd never get started at my book; and if I don't get started soon, I shall never finish it: as it is, I am like a waiter with his tray piled so high with dishes that he fears he will never be able to get to the table or unload even the first platter! At the moment I am swinging through the seventeenth century: a little horrified because I find myself so close and sympathetic to the Jesuits. About the only thing of importance I have read is Reinhold Neibuhr's Nature and Destiny of Man; the first volume of his Gifford lectures.[31] I confess a little disappointment about them: partly because I find his fully developed Lutheranism a little obsessive in its concern to spot sin everywhere—as if life weren't largely neutral patches, flecked with sunlight and shadow—and partly because his dialectical method mistranslated verbal distinctions into hardcut differences of experience, and gives the appearance of actuality to myth. But he has helped me to sharpen my own point of view; and he has given me a sort of reassurance about the method of my next book, which will be in every way so different— and as I hope, so much richer, because of the very naturalism which he open-eyedly rejects.

What of your own work and plans? I expect to be up here, till I start down for Alabama around the 14 or 15 April.[32] If you are in the neighborhood, do drop in for a night if you can manage it. There is an unholy smell of fresh paint around the house; but by now the mess in which we have been living for the last couple of months is beginning to be cleared up and we will be ready for company in another week when Geddes, the first of our new guests, will return for the Easter vacation.

Warm greetings
Lewis

[typed]
Lewis Mumford
Amenia New York
10 December 1941

Dear Harry:

It looks as if our entire country, from our generals and admirals down, has been suffering from schizophrenia*: was there ever such a gigantic maladaption to reality in the world before, except perhaps among the old Roman diehards just before the City of Rome finally fell?[33] I am afraid it will take a few more huge shocks, which probably are coming, to awaken us; and by the time the shocks take effect the patient may be dead.

But it is not to sing a Jeremiad over the state of the country that I am writing

---

31. Reinhold Niebuhr, *The Nature and Destiny of Man: A Christian Interpretation* (1941).

32. Mumford delivered the Dancy Lectures at Alabama College, published as *The South in Architecture* (1941).

33. Japan attacked Pearl Harbor on 7 December 1941.

you. I expect to go to Cambridge to attend a student's conference on the twenty-seventh, possibly going with Geddes, possibly alone; and I wonder if we can get together for an hour's chat, perhaps, on the morning of the twenty-eighth. If you are overwhelmed with work then and can't I shall understand, and more than understand. We are moving down to the city the first of January; so please note our new address: 56 East 87. Near enough to you to run in for breakfast when you are in town, or for us to connive at walks in the park.

Warmly

Lewis

*Or is there a better name for this radical dissociation?

[handwritten]

Dec 23, 41

Dear Lewis:

Although I haven't written to you since receiving the copy of your fine vigorous exciting address to the Californians, hardly a day has passed that I haven't had you—your zest, your high aims, your prophecies—in mind.[34] Often have C & I talked of you & Sophy in one connection or another. Indeed you have become a permanent inhabitant of my brain—someone with whom I can sustain an almost perpetual conversation. My silence—my extreme reluctance to settle down to a letter these days—is nothing but a serious frailty of the will, an inability to push unessentials aside & express myself on paper.

I haven't been able to write a readable word on Melville since the invasion of France, & I have not tried to persist when the spirit was so unwilling, or at least distracted. Consequently I had to return to Harvard humiliated by the lack of closure. I had vowed to myself that I would get clear of him before taking up the new work. Now he is packed away in a file while I rush ahead on a hundred and one other things. I have been acting as moderator of an International Seminar, composed of emigres, & we have spent out time discussing German social structure—what elements are open to what appeals? etc., etc. & then I have been giving a Seminar on Morale for graduate students, & another seminar on Personality & Culture with Mowrer (in Education) & Kluckhohn (in Anthropology); & now the College has been put on a war footing; that is, courses will run continuously through the summer. Men will be graduated in $2\frac{1}{2}$ to 3 years, & many courses have been modified to include topics pertinent to the crisis—preparatory to combat sources. Our researches have centered around the problems of testing for leadership & for latent neurotic tendencies. It is very difficult to predict: some normal men break down under the strain of army life & some more or less neurotic men suddenly get well when lifted out of their own juices by the collective spirit of a fighting unit. All my

34. "California's Possibilities; Aims for the Post-War World, The City of the Future; Planning in a Democracy," *Agenda for Western Housing and Planning* 1 (July 1941), 3.

work is connected in some more or less tenuous fashion with Army psychology or Naval intelligence, or Donovan's office—but I still feel too far removed from the marines on Wake Island.[35] Academic life is too sedentary & I am beginning to get into physical training.

I was enormously relieved by Japan's attack on us, because I knew it would anger & so solidify the country. The Navy's 'not alertness' is symbolic of the state of the American people, & losing a dozen ships was necessary to wake us out of a hapless lethargy. Now I think we can go ahead united & determined. New England is very active—Harvard most of all, & you will find a receptive audience, though only a small fragment of it will be from this college. I hope the result of it will be the consolidation of all student organizations into one of National scale & scope. It will be successful just so long as the now-masked Communists do not forward their grievances & hopes to the detriment of the common aim.

Let me know when you are arriving & when I can see you. I should like to have you spend as many nights as you can afford in Boston or in Topsfield; *or* you can be by yourself in my room in Cambridge. Dr. Cohn may come up to hear you, as he is interested in pushing the I.S.S. at Harvard.

I have lots to discuss with you—particularly in connection with 3 addresses which lie ahead of me this winter—I am not experienced in this sort of thing & I need your advice.

I hope we can arrange to see as much of each other as possible during these troublous months & years—because we are working with different tools along very much the same line, & we should have much to exchange. Merry Morale for the season & Love to lovely Sophie & looking forward to seeing you.

> Yrs
> Harry

---

35. William Joseph "Wild Bill" Donovan (1883–1959) headed the Office of Strategic Services (OSS) during the war.

1942–1947

War, Death, and Remembrance

DURING THE WAR YEARS, Mumford and Murray carried on a prolific correspondence despite their demanding commitments of work and writing. As an army officer, Murray was engaged in psychological assessment for the Office of Special Services. In October 1943 he wrote a lengthy report entitled "Analysis of the Personality of Adolph Hitler, with Predictions of His Future Behavior and Suggestions for Dealing with Him Now and After Germany's Surrender." He was also involved in evaluating the fitness of soldiers for hazardous duty and researching propaganda methods. In 1942 Mumford moved to Stanford University to head the School of Humanities; explaining his purpose in accepting the position, he wrote Murray that he hoped to "have a hand in forming leaders who will have a better reality sense than the products of the last generation of schooling and living" (LM 12 July 1942). In addition to his teaching responsibilities at Stanford, Mumford worked to complete the third volume in the Renewal of Life series, *The Condition of Man* (1944). Murray read draft sections of *The Condition of Man* and wrote lengthy explanations correcting Mumford's representation of Freudian theory. The Mumfords experienced a harrowing tragedy in October 1944 when they received confirmation that their nineteen-year-old son Geddes had been killed in combat in Italy. As in other periods of emotional crisis that Mumford had faced, Murray provided sensitive consolation and sound advice. However, Murray attempted to dissuade Mumford from undertaking *Green Memories* (1947), a biography of Geddes. Murray argued that writing such a work would violate the intimacy of the father-son relationship and would be traumatic for Mumford himself. Although Murray's reservations about the project certainly hurt Mumford's feelings, he conceded that Murray's honest criticism strengthened both the book and their friendship. Upon reading the completed work, Murray generously wrote, "You have finished the hardest possible job, so hard that I did not think it could be done in the way you planned to do it.

But I understand that you *have* done it, as it has never been done before, & so given Geddes his triumphant immortality" (HAM 8 January 1947).

[typed]
Lewis Mumford
Amenia New York
24 July 1942

Dear Harry:

It must be April since I last laid eyes on you or heard from you; and I am very eager to know what has been happening to you. My own annals have been simple: in the middle of May I got my three year appointment to Stanford and in the same week was called down to Washington, by a Hawaiian friend who was one of Donovan's assistants, to see if I had anything to contribute to a job that was in hand in the C.O.I.[1] It would have been a tough decision to have made if the work had in fact been up my alley; but unfortunately—or as it turned out, most fortunately—the job was concerned, not with the formulation of ideas but their visual presentation, and I turned it over, therefore, to a far better man in that department, Lee Simonson.[2] In another fortnight, as you know, the C.O.I. vanished: and of the visual presentation scheme there was not even a trace left. So we came up here and I spent the next six weeks devilling night and day at the second draft of my book. That is now finished; and though it is not actually ready to go to the printer, a month's work would probably make it ready. I have curious reservations about the book: it is not one I planned to write, but one which, as it were, interposed itself, in order to answer certain more immediate questions that are asked by the period in which we live. It is a disappointment to me, if I think of it as Volume III of the big series; on the other hand, taking it out of that context, it is a pretty satisfactory, sometimes even original, account of the role played by the ideas that have guided or misled Western man during the last two thousand years. Since the book will probably have to be printed on dingy paper, with small type, and all the other marks of wartime economy, I am inclined to publish it by itself, and go back to my original plans for volume three when I have had a chance to work out its leading ideas a little further at Stanford. My hard, driving bout of work left me with the usual sense of blackness and desolation that follow the writing of a book: I felt bitter, deserted by the world, frustrated—until I recalled all the good advice I had given other writers about the pregnancy and after-care of authors, and, instead of going onto the preparation of my Stanford lectures, I relaxed and slept in the sun and swam: all of which I am still in the act of doing: even writing this letter at nine in the morning, a time usually sa-

1. Stanford offered Mumford a position as professor and head of the new School of Humanities. Donovan directed the Office of Coordinator of Information (COI) which became the Office of Strategic Services (OSS).
2. Lee Simonson (1889–1967), theater director and critic.

cred to work, is a relaxation, almost an act of moral defiance! The other thing that has helped is that, in search of some letters by H.L. Mencken—of all people!—for a collection that someone in Princeton is gathering, I have been going through the files of my correspondence, and have had a delightful sense of what a rich, varied, exciting, amorous, eager, intellectual, imaginative life I have been leading all these years. This visit to past scenes and people, so far from being nostalgic in its results, has had an energizing effect: given me a great boost forward: just the oblique reflection of my own life in the words of my correspondents has given me a sense of its many dimensions and its amplitude. And the praise! At the moment I needed praise and understanding, and was amazed to find it unexpectedly in letters whose very reception I had forgotten, as in the one from Walter Lippmann, just returned from Rome in 1929, who said that Santayana still felt that I was the one person in America for him who redeemed it from barbarism. (Praise that would choke a horse and even upset the stomach of a public relations counsel: but tonic to me in the mood of black alienation that had been creeping over me.) And your letters, dear Harry: at the moment of our first exuberant recognition of our friendship and our capacity for understanding each other and revealing ourselves to each other: I only hope my letters were half as good, or a quarter as generous in their expressions. The middle thirties are, when all is said, the great moment of life, though Thomas Aquinas, writing when the expectations of life were perhaps curter, placed the perfect age at Thirty, which as you know is the age everyone enjoys in Heaven! I can remember the altogether lordly feelings of those middle thirties, when life was extremely good, evil was not even lurking in the bushes, and nothing seemed impossible, when love came freely, Helen, Josephine, Catherine, and when embryonic loves, waiting for maturation, seemed to lie in reserve, like the partly formed eggs in a hen's oviduct![3] There is a letter of yours, dear Harry, in which you say that evil did not exist for you any more: I can well imagine the fine, yea-saying, abandoned moment in which we both made that discovery. Now, whether in active or in passive mood, one is aware of the negation of that heaven: grim tasks occupy one's imagination if not one's practical activities.

During these last six months I have been silent, as far as political writing goes, though again and again I have been tempted to speak out. The lack of political and moral grip in Washington is still appalling: despite all the loud cackles about progress in our war effort one has only to note the disposition of the U.S. forces on a map to understand that the army and navy are both still fighting a defensive war, with scattered defensive outposts spread across the whole planet, waiting for a German success in Russia and a Japanese success in Siberia before they all crumple like so much tissue paper. No one has yet had the guts to concentrate our forces and

3. Mumford had an affair with Helen Ascher in 1929 (Donald L. Miller, *Lewis Mumford: A Life* [New York: Weidenfeld and Nicholson, 1989)], 287–88); he also had relationships with Josephine Strongin and Catherine Bauer.

fling them into action, even if this temporarily means abandoning the Australians or abandoning the Mediterranean area to their fate: there is no sign whatever that any such will and resolution is forming, as far as I can see: instead, pathetic speeches, like Hull's last, show that our leaders are still trying to convince themselves that the folly of defense, which led to the debacle at Pearl Harbor and the Philippines, was actually justified.[4] No one in Washington has repented: they are all following the same line that has led to disaster, and Churchill with them. This indecision, this paralysis, makes our present situation worse than it was in 1940, because at that time we at least had the excuse of actual weakness to cover our inner weakness: whereas these qualities now are indications of an organic failure which will require years of heroic struggle to counterbalance and make up for. Look at Stephen Vincent Benet's radio play in this week's Life, with its soft banalities and empty boasts, if you would have an index of our plight: injections of morphine are mistaken for strychnine! As soon as I finished my book, I took advantage of a note from MacLeish to say these things to him; but I will wait long, I am sure, before getting a reply. The fibre of our countrymen generally still seems to me sound; this is true of the common people in England too. But the governing classes, including the vast armies of anonymity that prevail in the bureaucracy and the military arms, are not tough enough either to think this war through or to act it out. Our good neighbor Admiral Hart confessed at a public meeting that it was hard to give orders that would send so many fine young men to their death. If that is the sort of thought that governs an admiral who is faced with battle, it is no wonder that all our dispositions are defensive, and all our acts are but half-formed because they are inwardly inhibited.

I say these things to you in private, dear Harry, because I see no way of saying them helpfully in public; and I begin to justify my presence at Stanford in the hope that, within that small compass, I may have a hand in forming leaders who will have a better reality sense than the products of the last generation of schooling and living. You are probably busy with momentous tasks and undoubtedly have a better perspective as well as a closer knowledge than I can have: so correct me if I am wrong in my diagnosis. The great mischief, as I see it, is that those who oppose the weaknesses of the administration do so, like the isolationists, because their own position is even weaker and because their own moral sense is even flabbier: whereas the administration, from Roosevelt down, needs to be stiffened by criticism from those who want a harder, stronger, more fearless, more realistic leadership. If I knew how to frame this criticism without giving aid and comfort to enemies both within and without the country, I should do so.

Are you ever in New York? Is there a chance of your dropping up here for even a day? I'd come down to the city expressly for a talk with you if you will let me know in advance. We expect to leave for California around the first week in Sep-

---

4. Cordell Hull served as Secretary of State under President Franklin D. Roosevelt, 1933–1944.

tember. Geddes is now on a sheep ranch in Washington. Sophy is restless to have her teeth in a war job. Alison has become a young woman, self-possessed and autonomous, who makes friends like a born extravert! With a warm embrace I am

Ever yours

Lewis

P.S. Who is Susanne Langer? Her book, Philosophy in a New Key, is an extremely able piece of work: the best re-statement of the problem of meaning I have come upon: in places, brilliant and original—or, at least, (perhaps there is some bias in the adjectives) closely along the lines I have been developing myself![5]

[handwritten]

64 Plympton St.

Cambridge Aug. 42

Beloved Lewis:

What a letter you have written me—us! I have been waiting for a breathing space in which to answer it. Now I have captured one, up here at the Tower, elbowing a lot of work aside to make room for it. You speak of our early letters of discovery, but in my case the discovery has been greater & more exciting each time I have seen or heard from you since those first days. Because you have grown steadily & by leaps, without regressions, I never know where I am going to find you, though it always proves to be before some new vista which modifies the complexion of things & gives a fresh impetus to action. I have not said a quarter of what I feel—the delight, the wonder, sympathy, exhilaration, pride in fellow feeling. Indeed it seems now that I have reserved my letters for criticism, such as the cutting words that were ignobly set down after 'Faith for Living,' which, as a matter of fact, stirred me very much. We have never talked this out, talked out the whole matter of mutual criticism, which I believe belongs to the refinement of solid hearty friendship—good for the sinews & for the whole soul. I could profit by more of it from you.

Just now, in this confusion of ideas, sentiments, intentions, greeds, compulsions, ambitions & hostilities, you stand out as a perpetual re-discovery that is invariably on the right track—indeed I don't know anyone like you in America or in the world for that matter, so that my warmth & sustained exuberance about you & your work & your Sophy—& Sophy on her own account—& Geddes & Alison & Amenia & everything that interests you, is higher & more constant than it ever was—but, of course, there is one great blot, my inveterate scriptophobia, or what have you, which makes me the poorest correspondent in the world.

Well now, what am I doing & thinking? I am working about 15 hours a day, which goes well enough with my constitution, though there are times when the quality of the performance is on the deadest level. We have been trying to find what

5. Susanne Langer, *Philosophy in a New Key: A Study in the Symbolism of Reason, Rite and Art* (1942).

psychologists can contribute to a giant enterprise of this sort, & have been pretty well frustrated at every turn. We have worked at 1.) tests for leadership qualities, particularly for combat officers (trying to eliminate those who might break down under strain); 2.) psychology of interrogation (of German prisoners), methods of cracking the shell of taciturnity & evasion; 3.) attitudes of college students toward the war, avowed & unavowed; 4.) propaganda to Germany, leaflets to be dropped on German soil; 5.) the present state of sentiment in various social classes & groups in France; 6.) the morale-lowering or -raising features in 8 New England newspapers; 7.) the psychology of cartoons, & so forth. We get out our findings in the form of mimeographed, greatly summarized brochures which are immediately sent off to every conceivable government agency—but I have no assurances that any of them are ever used. I have seen no signs of an aggressive, confident, thought-out policy put onto execution by COI, Facts & Figures, Military Intelligence or any other office dealing with morale or psychological warfare. What I have seen at Washington along this line is done with good will and conscientiousness, but is exasperatingly hesitant, inexpert, cautious. In the last 20 years everyone in the country has been utterly *deconditioned* to war, taught that wrathful aggression was the greatest sin, & that everything that we now find must be done to defeat our dastardly enemies was thoroughly *evil.* Thus all of us are suffering from a *bad conscience,* at every turn inhibited by a hundred and one finicky scruples and compunctions. Men of pure hearts & goodwill are absolutely counting on our winning this war, but none of them want to dirty their own hands with blood. Our leaders daily illustrate the harm that good men are capable of doing—so much so that I must choose to be on the side of the good that evil men can do—for the duration. I don't remember the context of my insipid remark about evil not existing for me anymore—but I may have meant that my own evil was no longer a serious problem. Anyhow I am planning to get my hands dirty with a clear conscience & a good vengeance, for I think I have found a job that I can perform—Combat intelligence officer on an aircraft carrier, the chief duties being to report the observations & to take care of the morale, health, spirit, fighting edge & zest of the aviators, many of whom get terribly shaken nervously when operating from such uncertain ground, particularly in a fog when they cannot find their mother. This should get me to the Pacific as a member of one or another task force. Before I do this however, I must fulfill certain obligations & commitments here. You may have heard that they have put psychologists on the deferred list, with doctors, etc., & as a result we have instituted a series of courses on military psychology which require my teaching time until December or thereabouts. I think it can be worked alright. The point is that I cannot say what I have to say if I do not practice it myself—and this fact has muffled me from the beginning.

But all this is fairly peripheral—since even in some battle of the Marshall Islands I expect I shall be brooding over the great problems that concern me most. The question of whether a moral system can be taught & enforced without the aid of supernatural figures. Pragmatism guided by moral intuition & sensibility is good enough for me & others of a sort; but for those who are not seeking happiness in a community, what deterrent can be set up equivalent to Hell-fire & the Gestapo? I am for socialism & a classless society, but then I have a horror of the politicians (able to hold office without any training qualifications). I am for the almost limitless extension of democracy, but then I can see the image of a Negro Republic in the Southern States & the possibility of another Civil War. (Paul Robeson has just been with us.)[6] I am still strong for Social Science in the Federal Government. I am not sure that Socialism would take care of compulsive greed—which is the root of all evil in America—but there is a good chance that it would check it sufficiently. And then there is the lack or debasement of the Aesthetic Element—the complete debauchery & vulgarization of our tastes & emotions by Hollywood, Broadway & all the rest, which seems to be a natural concomitant of an affluent Democracy—What are we going to do about that? We are suffering from what our professional entertainers have been doing to us as much as from anything else. The tolerance—oh the tolerance we have acquired for everything & anything. Well, these are some of the horrors that the War has brought glaringly to the forefront & I am not the one to find the remedies. My office is with the individual & his development & his discovery of value—but unfortunately this has come to a dead-end, since the individual can't enjoy much value now, & can only thrive by putting it in the common pot & dedicating it all to the extermination of Satan.

My own life & work is running along more vigorously than ever before—except for the complete renunciation of certain major problems & intentions, such as Melville. Christiana is greater than ever, & helping us to discover things at the Clinic. We've got enough for another book, new methods, new correlations, new concepts—& occasionally we get off together up here for a swim, a sunning & an unbroken sleep. I am going into training, have started rowing on the river in a scull & toughening up generally.

We are just finishing the best year of the Clinic's history—paradoxically enough—with a staff of the ablest, most loyal and industrious live-wirers I have ever worked with. It is the best kind of communism with good will all round—& a fine mixture of men & women, Jews & Gentiles—but only one Black, & no Catholics (It would be hard to get along with a Catholic today). We have a psychiatrist from Budapest, a philosopher from Vienna, a psychologist from California & one from Zurich & one from Alabama, & a medical man from Toronto, & a host of students from all over the world—tremendous interest, but all of them to the core inoculated with pacifism. It is largely because of this that I must leave—cutting everything off in the middle.

---

6. Paul Robeson (1898–1976), singer, actor, and political activist, had been a friend since 1920, when Murray treated him for a football injury in New York (Forrest G. Robinson, *Love's Story Told: A Life of Henry A. Murray* [Cambridge: Harvard Univ. Press, 1992], 90).

Jo is a Red Cross Nurse working in the hospital & Josephine is getting A's & B's at Radcliffe preparatory to training as an Army Nurse. Both are well & Happy. We have remained in town all summer with some Sundays in the country—by train mostly.

Christiana has spent a little time at the Tower, where Ken Diven has been doing a magnificent mahogany door, carving out a great design of Byzantine derivation, a pattern of fawns, birds & leaves,—the place is richer than ever with Mana & reminiscences of unnamable delights—I could go on & on, but I must stop here or you will sicken.[7] I must see you before I go on, before you leave. How about next Sunday or Monday? I could take a train to Amenia Sunday P.M. if you think you can manage to have me (train from N.Y.) *or* meet you in N.Y. on Monday. We both send all love to you both,

Harry

[typed]
Stanford University
30 November 1942

. . . . I have long been wanting to write you, dear Harry, if only to thank you, as I fear I did not at the time, for the magnificent letter of recommendation you sent for Geddes. He has been having a troubled time, poor boy, plagued academically by the inadequate grounding he received in the fundamentals and by general inattention to duties the last few years, plagued even more by the fact that his beloved is in St Louis and the rather constrained dull life he lives here is enough to drive him moping melancholy mad. He has not yet learned to be tough with himself, in preparation for a distant objective, though I must say he has wrestled with his school work more manfully than ever before. But I was kept from writing you, not simply by the incessant round of committee meetings here in the university or by my own need to spend time on my lectures, refreshening my knowledge in various fields long neglected: what really was responsible for my silence was the sad state we were all in, compounded of real illness of the physical kind, plus downright homesickness and fish-out-of-wateriness! Sophy is just on the point of entering her menopause and has a growth in her womb which contributes to making her periods pretty ghastly, leaving her wan and anemic: this coincided with our arrival here and has given a touch of strain and anxiety to all the subsequent days. I might have borne the pressure cheerfully but for the fact that I recorded it in my own typical way by an infection in my teeth, which undermined my health and poisoned my normal outlook on life. Now that the infection has been conquered I have recovered my equilibrium; but there were days and weeks when this whole venture seemed, not a splendid enterprise, but one of the worst mistakes of my life. All this is noth-

---

7. Kenneth Diven, a research student at the Clinic who executed wood carvings at the Tower.

ing to talk about in days like this; to have personal misfortunes now is to be ridiculously out of tune with circumstances: hence my correspondence file has grown to mountainous dimensions as a result of my silence, and I shall have presently to confess my bankruptcy! I could not write you and keep silent about all this even now when I am well again: and if I had written you before I am afraid that the dreary note would have been worse. . . . What about my work here? On the whole my lectures have gone well, and the challenge of preparing them has been a welcome one. We have a hundred students in the course; and there are usually ten or a dozen colleagues from various departments listening in: so I have been keyed up to do my best, and sometimes have succeeded. My book, when I come to re-write it, will be the richer for this additional thinking; and I wish I could discuss with you some of the by-paths into which my lectures have wandered. In one of them I found myself using Freud's concept of the id, the ego, and the super-ego to analyse the nature of culture itself: but here I paralleled Rank, somewhat unconsciously at the time, in placing the super-ego itself within the personality, instead of representing the social demands made on it from the outside.[8] This seems to me to put the inhibitory functions in their true natural setting: namely, as a necessary development that enabled man to live in a much more complex environment, made additionally complex through his capacity for symbolization, without being overwhelmed by it: discrimination, selection, and therefore inhibition became the basis of an integrated response. Freud has always had an ambivalent attitude toward both the super-ego and the censor, as though they existed outside of nature and were somehow arbitrary and anti-vital in their operation; whereas from my standpoint they become the key to that intensified vitality which is made possible with civilization itself. There is one thing that needs clarification, dear Harry, in relation to the doctrine of needs; and this is whether they are on an equal footing, or whether there exists a hierarchy of values here which give some needs a definite precedence over others when choice has to be made. In discussing the higher developments of culture I finally was driven to emphasize the following needs: order, continuity, intelligibility, expression, and integration. These needs seem to me to thread through all the manifestations of the arts and sciences: when they are unfilled, life becomes chaotic and meaningless, no matter how well our material needs may from moment to moment be satisfied. . . . All this is just to indicate faintly the path of my own ideas, as they have worked out in the course: it would need a whole day of discussion with you to set them forth with any clearer amplitude. The students have, on the whole, taken well to the lectures, though they have been a little puzzled by the method, which has been broad and philosophical, rather than narrow, detailed, and safe: but at least for a few of them the process of inter-relating their previously acquired knowledge has begun to take place. Indeed, the students have done better here than my staff; for the fact is that two of my three younger colleagues are, for my

8. Otto Rank (1884–1939), disciple of Sigmund Freud.

purposes, a disappointment; and I have begun to think that my two great mistakes in taking on this course were, first, engaging to come here in September instead of in January; and second, permitting the people out here to gather the staff without consulting me. They should have made a longer and closer canvass of possible candidates before they selected these three; and I should have had the final decision. One of them, a young philosopher named Jeffrey Smith, is all that I could have desired; the other two do not really believe in what we are doing and are not equipped to do it; though they are nice fellows, and if I should succeed in changing their minds, there might be some hope for conquering the rest of the university! As for our days there, they are naturally circumscribed; our life is bounded by the campus, which means that it is bounded by the environment and atmosphere of suburbia, with all its inert and elegant middle-classness and remoteness from reality. I find myself walking by preference along the back-alleys to escape the trim gardens and tidy lawns of the streets themselves; and by the same token I almost welcome the slatternly streets and drunken roustabouts on encounters in San Francisco as one leaves the railroad station. This easy gentility is foreign to all of us: by now we are all too country bred to like it; and Alison, in particular, has been disconsolate for Amenia. Our return East may not be so far away as it seemed when we moved our furniture here in September. Under war conditions, there is precious little space left for a school of humanities, and I am beginning to meditate the possibility of asking for a leave of absence for the duration of the war, or at least for the next year or two, by which time, if the present successes continue, Nazism at least will be liquidated. I have hardly given the job a fair try; but when Alison says: Hello Mister Professor and laughs loud I find myself in entire sympathy. The life and position do not belong to me: it is not so much distasteful as unreal: and I feel pretty sure already that my early estimate of myself, that I was not a teacher, whatever else I may be, was a correct one.

What of your own work and plans, dear Harry? Are you still of a mind to go into the Navy? If there is any debate left, let me put my word in favor of your staying out of this war. The push into the armed service now has reached a point that will be dangerous to the very continuity of our civilization; and since there seems small prospect of saving the seed-corn of the younger generation as long as the present policy prevails, I think we must try to hold together a saving remnant in other age-groups. We still show a tendency as a people to attempt to win the war by a purely quantitative effort: to atone by numbers for our lack of confidence in strategy and free manoeuvre, although the latter already show in Africa what big dividends they can pay with relatively small expenditures of energy and man-power. Two years ago I felt that we had to show our bodies to the enemy, if nothing more, as the only alternative to ignominious defeat. But now the situation has changed; and, if this war is to be fought through to good purpose, there must be a sufficient number of highly charged and active intelligences, in every department of life, ready to contribute their researches and their plans to the rebuilding, not merely of the physical world, but of the whole structure of cooperative thought. Drop me a line if you are too busy for more: we all join in affectionate greetings. Give me news of you both.

Lewis

[handwritten]
[LM] Ans Mar 43
Dec 20, 42

Dear Lewis,

It's a peculiarity of mine to believe that I have hurt someone who has received but not answered a letter of mine for a long time, & yet never imagine that he could possibly suppose there was anything wrong, if I leave a letter of his waiting for an answer. I was sure this time that you thought my letter about Geddes was thoroughly inadequate & so it was; but I had very few facts to go on, & I have discovered that over-enthusiastic letters are regarded with suspicion by deans & other officials. However, I was mightily relieved to get your letter & discover that *you* thought it was O.K. You did not say whether Geddes was a freshman at Stanford, or was at some other school. I wish I could see a little of him, & you could see a little of Josephine. They are both possessed by the same devil; & a parent is at a great disadvantage in trying to deal with it.

What a train of tribulations you have had! But you & Sophy have been valiant in facing them, & I feel like a 'softy' here with nothing but weather of ten below to battle with, everything else running as smoothly as possible under the circumstances of my being turned down on account of age for combat intelligence. Now I am committed to Harvard & the Rockefeller Foundation until July 1, when I hope to get into the psychiatric division of the Medical Corps to care for war neuroses at the front if possible. From now till then I am going to drive through as much work as possible, get it published, make a will & say goodbye to it for the duration. My chief difficulty is that I have too many irons in the fire or rather too many omelets on the stove & several of them are sure to spoil. The English & Canadians are using our tests for officer selection, but not the Americans. It is an odd experience to hear that an *old* thing of ours is being applied in Edinburgh, but that a much better new thing has not yet been accepted by the ROTC at Cambridge, Mass. C & I are working on some articles: student attitudes toward War, Sex, Own Family & Religion & I am brooding on the problem of pride, a fascinating psychological puzzle—its emergence with individuality, its holding out against the collective spirit, its revolt from totalitarianism (Catholic Church), its creation of the exact opposite doctrine (opposite to its own insistence upon free will) of predestination, its final winning through to democracy, but then going on too far into individualism, leading to a state of atomistic chaos without social responsibility, etc., etc. Pride transferred from the ego to the leader & the group as it is in Germany today & a hundred & one other relationships. All through these evolutions you have conflict between the ego (the individual will, conscious rationality) & the superego (which, as you said, is an endopsychic institution). Sometimes one speaks *loosely* of an *external superego,* such as the Catholic Church headed by the Pope (Father-figure) in the Middle Ages. The Reformation was an act of the ego (aided by the id in Luther's case) which necessitated the creation of a much stronger superego (under the tutelage of Calvin) to make up for the loss of external priestly support & discipline (the old Superego plus the Church to bolster it). Hitler is the end result of Luther, the final throwing off of the burdensome (inner) categorical (moral) imperative. This happens whenever the authorities, or powers-that-be, become corrupt, & their morality is seen as hypocrisy (Catholic Church in 1500, George III in 1776, Capitalism in our time). Now is the time to fashion a new superego in harmony with the ego & the id. I believe the superego can be arrived at step by step through clear-headed individual & social experimentation, although it is probably time that the vicious & the ignorant & the morally diseased must be held in check by the best restraints that are now available while the experimentation is going on—led by creators like yourself & checked & verified by social scientists like myself. I agree about Freud. He hated the Superego. But the Superego is in truth the eternal values to which everyone should be loyal. When the leaders, however, do not represent these values, & attempt to impose damaging prohibitions, then there is some reason to hate your superego (built up through childhood on the basis of these prohibitions). According to my interpretation Moby Dick is the Superego (a viciously severe Calvinistic conscience) & Ahab is the ego in conspiracy with the Id (Fedallah—the devil Allah). Whitman, Thoreau, Emerson were all on the side of the Ego (in one way or another) against the Superego *of their time.*

I should say that there was a hierarchy of needs among individuals & among societies; but that it would be hard to say on the basis of past experience which hierarchy was absolutely the best.

More important than the hierarchy of needs as such seems to be the hierarchy of values (goals, objectives) toward which the needs are directed.

For example *n Construction* may be manifested by making mud pies or writing a philosophical treatise

n Dominance by captaining a ball team or governing the Roman Catholic Church

n Continuity by holding to a bad habit or perpetuating the Supreme Court.

Your list of needs interests me very much: I think I might be inclined to speak a good word for:

1. Clarity of purpose (aim, goal, or complex of major objectives)

2. Affectiveness (power to move, to evoke & involve emotional participation, exaltation, breeding, etc.)

3. Comprehensiveness (inclusion of the essential element; through condensation a single symbol (like the cross) might include much)

4. The proper ratio of Continuity/Change or Sameness/Novelty (there must be new elements continually being added)

I wish I could sit down at your feet & have you lecture on the great sweep of ideologies & personalities through history. We have found in our work that it is very important to keep the conscious ideology (assertion of assumptions & sentiments) distinct from the pattern of actual behavior. There is a strong *negative* correlation on many variables between what an individual thinks should be done (how others should behave) & how he acts himself. For example the Calvinist preached abject humility to a despotic god, but in his life was spiritually proud & haughty, intolerant of other sects, etc., & our experiments show the same for graduate students.

I feel sure that as you get into things a little further you will come to like your present occupation more than you do now. There are ways of minimizing committee meetings, & shaking free from the middle class consciousness of faculties & their *wives*—it's largely the *women* that professors marry! They do a lot to dull the atmosphere—this is a sociological problem which needs investigation. But I haven't seen Stanford since 1916 & I am too uncertain of your exact situation to prophesy. Have you met a psychologist named Stone? I don't know him, but they say he is good, at least in his special field (psychology of sex in animals).

Embraces to you both & a good Christmas to you all, Geddes & Alison. Send me pamphlets or anything you have.

Yrs
Harry

[typed]
694 Alvarado Row
Stanford University
7 March 1943

. . . . This is a springlike morning, dear Harry, and the fragrance from the beds of violets and the nearby hyacinths makes up for the temporary overclouding of the sky, though it was the sun itself that tempted me from pottering around the garden to writing this long-postponed letter to you, for I write this in the open, on a brick terrace at the side of the house, as I might have done almost any Sunday morning during the last month. [. . .] My own plans for the future are still in a state of suspense, and no definite decision will be possible till around the first of April. Stanford will possibly get one or another of the new schools of military government that is being set up; and in going over the proposed curriculum I suggested a course on the unification of the world from the 13th century on, as a means of giving rational insight into the present world crisis and the duties that it imposes upon us: from one-sided missionary zeal and imperialistic conquest to world cooperation. Strange to say, admirable to relate, the army seemed impressed by the notion; and if it goes through the higher ups I shall stay on here and work the course out. Since the active teaching in this course will not begin till the close of next September, I even have hopes of being able to finish my book in the summer vacation: whether I succeed in doing this will depend, partly, on how well I succeed in recovering my old energies by next June. I know now what I want to write; but though a doctor's examination doesn't disclose any easily real weakness, I find myself blocked in my plans by having only a portion of my normal energy available. It may be that I need nothing more than a couple of weeks complete rest, in order to get rid of all the inner snarls that the anxieties and defeats of the last year have created: it may be that some deeper emotional conflict is robbing me of vitality, for I am conscious of giving my lectures under too great a pressure and of being thoroughly exhausted after each one. Not that my work hasn't been rewarding, in its way: though I have not had the time to saturate myself in my material—just the contrary, in fact, I have been like Eliza skipping over the ice floes, one leap ahead of the hounds—I nevertheless have been conscious of contributing a fresh interpretation to various neglected parts of Greek civilization—an interpretation which makes it particularly rewarding when considering our own fate. (My best lecture, so far, was one on Demosthenes: for those frustrations I felt a most brotherly kinship.) My class however dropped to less than half for the winter quarter; and there are only a handful of students who really have the faintest sense of what I am talking about: their immaturity, their apathy, their polite dullness are all, I think, a little worse than they would be in a similar group in the east, just because they have lived an even more sheltered and meaningless life. I might doubt my own objectivity about this; but one of my good students, who has lived in Alaska and been deeply shaken by its grand primitive qualities, feels the same way about it. Whatever wisdom I possess is of little use, I am afraid, for undergraduates: they don't understand, because I challenge all their bourgeois genteel prejudices: it is only with a handful of post-graduates, all already married, that I manage to get to first base. This of course will have an effect on any eventual decision I may make about staying on here. But I don't think it is premature to say that I am not, at least here, a professor, and I would never want to look upon teaching as a full time job: indeed, my perpetual absence from the typewriter this last six months may well be the major cause of my depleted energies.

As for your own plans, dear Harry, I am so glad to see that you are keeping so much of your work going, and I trust that the deadline of July will force you to bring to a head your major projects. There is a touch of Leonardo's great vice in you, more than a touch: the desire for perfection. Nothing ever gets finished unless one is resigned to its falling short of what one wants it to be. Imperfection is the very price of birth.

I speak from experience on this, heaven knows: for the book that I have been working at is the victim of over-preparation, and by wanting to make it too complete, too sound and waterproof in its scholarship, I have merely succeeded in complicating my job and in dodging the responsibilities of creative thought—whereas my most original book, Technics, though much poorer in all the factual apparatus of demonstration, has in all its imperfections a vitality I must now try painfully to recapture for my present work. If Stanford did nothing else for me this year, it gave me the freedom to stand aside from my manuscript for a whole year and survey its defects; and that, I trust, will prove a great boon, more significant than the fact that my salary, thank heaven, will cover my medical and dental bills!

When we invaded Africa last November I had hopes that the European phase of the fighting would be over by the middle of the summer; but the weakness of our political leadership seems to have been augmented by a military weakness—if indeed the latter is not the result of the first—and I am not so sanguine now, unless Russia's power and effectiveness continues to mount and turns the scales all by itself. The appeasement of the Fascists in France and Spain means to me only one thing: Roosevelt's policy will be to uphold Catholic fascism in Europe as a counterbalance to Russia; and if this does not lead to further conflicts and to the undermining of all that we have been fighting for, it will only be because it awakens, in time, a sufficiently strong counter-protest. I have been biding my time for the right moment to launch this. The difficulty is, apart from the cowardice and supineness of the press, that the Republicans who should be a political counterweight against Roosevelt's weakness are now, as before Pearl Harbor, even more outrageously on the side of appeasement and compromise, so that they represent something worse than the administration policy, and except for Wilkie and his followers, nothing that promises better. We will pay heavily for our opportunism; and I shall not be surprised if we pay in Spain and Africa first of all: even now Franco's army, at Eisenhower's back, is worth several divisions to Hitler.

I am eager for news of you both. (Alison has found an ideal playmate and is at last happy and reconciled to her new home. Geddes failed to enter Stanford, for the Struldbrugs in the Registrar's office took refuge in their peacetime forms; so he will try to get into San Jose College and will stay there for a term until he is called by the Army. He wants to get into the Marines; but I think it would be a mistake to do so on the basis of a four year enlistment.) Sophy joins me in affectionate greetings to you.

Lewis

P.S. Did you see my New England poem in The New Yorker—27 Feb?[9] I wrote it as part of a novel 4 years ago; but everyone here suspected a more recent nostalgia.

---

9. "The Taste of New England," *New Yorker,* 27 February 1943, 20.

[handwritten]
[LM] June 1943

Dear Lewis,

What a preposterous ingrate I have been, carrying your letter round in my pocket day in and day out for weeks, intending every day to answer, but postponing until I could have a long stretch to give all our news & problems. Those hours of leisure have not arrived, & so I shall see what can be done at midnight before rolling in. Two or three times a week C & I talk about you in some connection or another, & have several times agreed that you are the only man alive who gives us complete & utter satisfaction, whom we trust all over, & admire at all times, & accept in every phase, bright or dark. We both doted on your New England poem, one of your best things, better than Frost. It did sound nostalgic, so full of realized, appreciated, colors, shapes & meanings—only a New England lover could have written it. This suggests a recent book "On Native Grounds" by Kazin which we have relished as the most knowledgeable, erudite, and literary-wise volume of criticism we have ever read covering America 1920–40.[10] Kazin has a broad moral outlook without having any point of view of his own that is clearly discernible. It is entirely sympathetic criticism, not creative except by implication. I won't go on because I think you must know it; but in case you have missed it on the Pacific, don't fail to get hold of a copy. I enjoyed your public remarks printed in the New York papers on Liberal Education & the importance of Plato on Guadacanal.[11] All the news I get is to the effect that no vision or no hunger for a vision has yet appeared on any of our fronts, although it has definitely emerged among the British of the Eighth Army. Our boys are still wondering what they are going to get out of it, & writing home that they are fighting for blueberry pie as Ma used to cook it at home. On the whole, however, I am pleased with the progress of affairs, & do not feel indignant as I did a year ago at the bungling & apparent lack of dedication. In fact I am full of boundless pride as I read about our Air Force—the aviators have acquired a special type of skilled virtue which sets them apart. After six months training I have seen striking transformations of character which are heartening to admirers of worth. My friends in Africa write that they expect to be in France by September, but the stolen German films picturing the fortifications around Europe plainly show what a costly enterprise that will be at best. The war neuroses, I understand, are worse than in World War I & I am anxious to get to the front to see what can be done. I have a few ideas. But I am still plugging away here, finishing up a couple of mono-

---

10. Alfred Kazin, *On Native Grounds: An Interpretation of Modern American Prose Literature* (1942).

11. Mumford's 8 May speech at the Conference on Humanities at Stanford University was reported in the *New York Times*, 9 May 1943, 8; the article quotes Mumford: "The valid reason for urging a more intense dedication to the humanities during the war is not merely so that we can live better after the war but so that we can fight better now." Mumford published the speech, "The Making of Men," in *Values for Survival: Essays, Addresses, and Letters on Politics and Education* (New York: Harcourt, Brace, 1946), 218–39.

graphs, so as to rescue some of our 2 years work from oblivion. It has all been postponed, in fact, by a sudden request 3 days ago to write a book on Hitler for the government (in one month) as a guide to measures now & after a victory.[12] My aim is to devise a method for preventing the immortality of another 'hero myth,' another Napoleonic legend which will excite adolescents in future centuries. I am afraid he will arrange a martyr's death for himself before we can get our hands on him, but if we do capture him, I have hit upon the perfect de-bunking scheme. This job will take me about 3 weeks. Then C & I have to finish our monograph on the Sentiments of College students, 7 months after Pearl Harbor. It amounts to an indictment of the education our generation have been giving young people in the period between wars.[13] I don't believe I will be finished until September 1, which will amount to just two years of the Rockefeller Grant Project. Considering the circumstances, the tension, the other duties, the loss of our best men, quite a bulk of research has been finished—to be published in a series of separate papers after I leave. On July 1 Harvard becomes a Military Academy—mostly Naval, with a few hundred civilian students under 18, & 4Fs, etc. Now what I want to know—Is there a chance of seeing you? Alfred Cohn seemed to think you were coming East, was even hopeful you would take the editorship of the magazine he was planning. When you last wrote you were discouraged with the situation at Stanford. I met a girl who had been to Reed, Stanford & California & she explained that the Dating, Necking & Rating Racket at Stanford took all the girls' energies & they only gave half an ear and a blasé one at that to anything the lecturer said. She had heard from a friend that you were a great success as a lecturer, but she guessed that you would have a spirit-breaking wall of inertia and adolescent pre-occupation to break through before you could stir their imaginations & set them on a course of disciplined effort. It sounded pretty hopeless. Radcliffe is easy in the field of psychology—in fact the response is much more than I can handle, & when I let the lectures run down & get dull like this tired letter I have fewer girls hanging round & asking for appointments, & so more time to get my real work done. But I am not satisfied with psychology now, not until I have linked it up with living values & spiritual experiences will I be keen to give any more courses. I need months of rest & as that is impossible in war time, I am glad to be getting months of complete change, even though I must go back 20 years & learn how to write prescriptions.

---

12. Murray wrote "Analysis of the Personality of Adolph Hitler, with Predictions of His Future Behavior and Suggestions for Dealing with Him Now and After Germany's Surrender" (October 1943, 227 pages), for the Office of Strategic Services. The Cornell Law Library has recently made this report available online at http://www.lawschool.cornell.edu/library/donovan/hitler/. Walter C. Langer included much of Murray's material, without attribution, in *The Mind of Adolf Hitler: The Secret Wartime Report* (1972); see Robinson, *Love's Story Told*, 276–78.

13. Christiana Morgan and Henry A. Murray, *A Clinical Study of Sentiments, Genetic Psychology Monographs* 32 (1945).

We are all well. Josephine is in Rawah, New Mexico, for one month living in a hogan with some Navahos who can't speak English, 40 miles from the railroad. She is taking notes on the rearing of children, etc. She graduates from Radcliffe in September & then will go to Presbyterian Hospital for nurse's training. Jo has been working right along as a Nurse's Aid at the City Hospital. Christiana is wonderful as usual. We are consulting with lawyers & putting the final touches on our plan to make the *Tower on the Marsh* a permanently endowed retreat for creative writers, one a year appointed by you & 4 others. We have linked it up with Governor Dumner Academy on the adjoining property. They are going to supervise the upkeep, etc. We have been mainly concerned, of course, with the great social & moral dilemmas of our time & it is this which we must discuss—the New World & the Education required to be equal to it.

Now we are hankering for news from you. Have you found any congenial spirits among the faculty? How is Sophy after all her hellish unluckiness in the Fall? Has she become an ardent Californian? And Geddes? I was distressed that my letter was futile, & that he missed college by a small technicality. I do hope he is finding a right way. Will you have a chance to finish your book this summer? Is there any chance of our meeting?

> Pax Vobiscum
> Harry

> [typed]
> Harvard University
> Psychological Clinic
> 64 Plympton Street
> Cambridge, Mass.
> July 19, 1943

Dear Sophie and Lewis:

A little late for a bread and butter letter, but I must say you were very generously quick to take in a visitor so soon after your arrival. Needless to say, I had a gorgeous time. Although we never have time to get through everything we have to say to each other, I left with the feeling that we had covered a good deal of ground with mutual exchanges, although I have noticed that most people who have a sense of great satisfaction after such meetings have been doing all the talking. If that was true in this case you may not have recovered for two or three days after I left. I trust in any event that you are revived now and Lewis is well launched again on his last voyage with the finale of the trilogy. You will probably be too busy to write for a while but when you do, be sure and tell me about Geddes as I am much interested in his anticipated career with the Marines.

Having pinned down Corporal Schicklgruber and outlined a policy for treating paranoid individuals, and from this drawn certain conclusions as to the treatment of Germany (aided by your suggestions on the subject), I am now putting the finishing touches on the Thematic Apperception Test which the Harvard University Press is going to publish, and bringing out a new test to be used by the Army in the selection of officer candidates.[14]

I am planning to be in New York during the week of August and if there will be any chance of seeing you for a moment then it would be a great joy for me.

> Yours,
> Harry
> HAM:MI

[typed]
Amenia, New York: 20 July 1943

Dear Harry:

Your coming gave my book the final warming up it needed before I opened the throttle and started down the runway: since then I have been steadily gathering altitude, and I hope soon to level off in order to have more energy for the hardest stretch of all, the final chapters, when I come in sight of the real target: modern man, his state, his dilemmas, his future. (You will understand the heavy effect of the raid on Rome on my prose!) Your contribution to the problem of the mystery religions, and why they flourished just at the moment that reason seemed about to prevail, is already incorporated in the first chapter: so, in the hope that I shall, like an aphis, stroke some more of this precious juice out of you—shades of Wheeler! It's you who is the aphis, isn't it—I herewith invite you up to Leedsville during your week in New York, if it isn't too great a burden, or, failing that, I will come down to New York. I shall have other business in New York around then and perhaps will come down anyway. Let me know where and when to reach you: the Harvard Club?

Lord, how I wish you were free enough to read even a part of my book. I don't dare ask you to; but if you'll have enough spare time even to taste a chapter I'll bring it along! I think that I have at last given a rational account of Christianity which does justice to both its benefits and its perversions: perversions that are almost inevitable once one understand the society in which it had its origin.

> Warmly
> Lewis

P.S. Geddes left for Albany yesterday in high hopes that he would be taken for the Marines; but their quota was filled, he phoned us, and he now is in Camp Upton, being screened out. Once he was on his way to the army, all his malaise disappeared: the last week was a family idyll, and our ride over with him to Rhinecliff yesterday in the cool of a radiant summer morning was for all three of us, touching shoulders in deepest intimacy, a poignant consummation of eighteen years: he, good-humored, happy, deeply satisfied over his homecoming and his acceptance,

---

14. Schicklgruber: the name applied to Hitler by some of his political opponents; *Thematic Apperception Test* (1945).

even by the old men of the region, as one of them: full of love for the countryside and full of satisfaction over his memories of times past, renewed at the trout hole and up in the pastures with his gun. The night before leaving he had killed a woodchuck with an incredibly lucky shot, against all odds, with the sun in his eyes; and he counted that a good omen. (We did too!)

> [handwritten]
> 64 Plympton Street
> Cambridge
> Written 2 or 3 weeks ago—
> This should be read first
> if you have a stomach for it

Dear Lewis,

This is merely to say that it was a great treat to see you in New York & I only hope that I did not throw you out of gear by introducing too many irrelevant & discordant ideas. A man writing is vulnerable to bombardments of confused thought & I was too little aware of this last Monday.

We have started your book and are thrilled by its vast scale and scope, its freshness and vivid eloquence, its smooth & confident pace. You are at your best, sir, abounding in vigor, stored experience & wisdom, & having got hold of the most important topic on earth, you are certain to render up a revelation. We have only had a taste of it so far, but the sweep and tempo of it is clearly indicated.

In respect to one point: you are not justified in using *superego* as you do in the Introduction. There are certain essentials: 1. it is an institution *in the mind of individuals* (you might, however, speak of the nature of the superego shared by the majority of the members of a certain society—the Hellenic superego, the Renascence superego, the Puritan Superego, etc.; or you might speak of works of art or church rituals as *reflections, expression, incorporations* or *objectifications of the superego*); 2. the superego always refers back to sentiments & opinions (*moral especially,* but also aesthetic, religious or merely conventional) shared by the authoritative & respectable members of a society. It is the system of Do's & Don'ts that operates in your community, internalized in the mind. At the lowest level it is something that tells you that if you do *this* (or *fail* to do *this*) you will be punished (criticized, blamed, rejected, imprisoned), & if you do *that* you will be commended. On the highest level the superego is placed in God or in some ideal society of the future, so that even though you incur the moral or aesthetic hostility of your contemporaries, you will be rewarded by God or by future generations if you do this or that. To be influenced by the superego is to be loyal to your parents, to your community, to the present world, to the future world or to God. Thus, although the superego is conscience, & therefore an internal private affair, it is something that looks at you (approvingly or disapprovingly) as an ideal judge would look at you, a judge who represented humanity.

A man like yourself is creating the *form* for a new superego, & if this is accepted in the future, & children are brought up (rewarded & punished) according to your values, then your form will become the superego of later generations. But nothing can be called a superego that is not *operating in somebody's mind,* giving him a sense of rightness & grace when he acts one way & a sense of guilt when he acts another. The *superego is the representation of the total organism in the mind of the cellular individual.* When he thinks of what is good for himself only he is operating without a superego, when he *acts in terms of the totality his superego is dominant.*

The word that describes the summit of a man's ambition as he sees it in his mind is *Ego Ideal* (or, as I write it now, *idealego*). This may be immoral (& therefore in conflict with the superego) i.e. the ambition of being a Master Criminal—or it may be moral (& so in accord with the superego) i.e. the ambition of being a great benefactor. In describing individuals typical of a culture's ambitions you are setting forth ideal ego figures—cf. the Renascence gentleman—hundreds of people took him as a model. He was a collective idealego. Other examples: Rousseau, Napoleon, Byron, Daniel Boone, Andrew Jackson, Theodore Roosevelt, Clark Gable.

Now comes the problem of whether ideal ego can be extended to include the works of an ideal ego. The artist might think not so much that he wants to be with Shakespeare (cf Keats) but that he wants to write another Hamlet. He thinks of the ideal work, not the ideal self composing it. Such a conception of his work would operate very much as does an ideal ego—he would be discouraged if he fell short of the standard & encouraged if he approximated it. Perhaps ideal goals would be more suitable & ideal works after they had been achieved.

Probably it is better to keep idealego for the *human figure in the mind.* If they are reproduced in art one might speak of *reflections, expression replicas, externalizations* of the ideal ego. It is a complex topic, & if I have not been clear come back at me— Love to Sophy

Best energies to you!
H

[handwritten]
64 Plympton Street Cambridge
Tuesday Aug 31

Dear Lewis:

I wrote the enclosed a few days after seeing you but didn't mail it as I had the impression that my account of the superego was more darkening than lightening. I expected to find time in a day or two to send you a revised definition as it is generally used & as it might be used without doing extreme violence to its essential nature. However that moment of freedom has not yet arrived. I am still hemmed in with work & for a week have been mentally paralyzed by the grippe.

Let me add a few brief statements to fill out the picture a little more—superego again.

1. The superego is *always* an institution in the mind that operates to control behavior: it coerces, makes a person do what he is disinclined to do; it restrains; it commands & reprimands, & so engenders a feeling of grace or a feeling of guilt.

2. The superego is a system of principles—moral, aesthetic, intellectual, conventional—which dictate what an individual should do if he is to contribute fully to the whole of which he is a part. The superego is the ambassador of the whole at the seat of government of the part.

3. Each whole of which an individual is a part may be said to have a set of principles governing the relationship necessary to its best health, & so we might speak of a family superego, a community superego, a rational superego, a world superego (what that little bitch calls 'globaloney').[15] This necessarily results in conflicts within the individual: allegiance to parents vs. allegiance to nation; allegiance to nation vs. allegiance to church. There are conflicts between superegos of different degrees of inclusiveness. The isolationist, like the fascist, has a circumscribed superego, national or trivial, but not universal. The communist has a class superego—it is permissible to tar & feather a businessman but a working man is sacred. There are also important differences along the concrete-general continuum. Some people who claim to have a universal superego, who speak for humanity or God, as Christ did, are incapable of a single concrete relationship with anyone. They are loyal to an idea, but incapable of realizing it & exemplifying it in practice. I would respect Christ a great deal more if he had been willing to give himself—to lose & find himself—in a single relationship. His aloofness, his union with the image of God, is the essence of pride (from a humanistic point of view), & he was only saved by spending his life in the service of the afflicted. 'Blessed are the meek' can be understood in part as an injunction to himself, a reaction formation to an inner inflation, an incipient paranoia. But this is a digression—the point is that Christ introduced a new superego, new content & great breadth. After him the superego embraced everybody—barbarians, prostitutes, criminals, children & later animals & nature (Wordsworth extended it to daffodils).

4. Beside the space dimensions (running from the family unit to humanity at large) there is the time dimension (running from the existing contemporary set of principles to some ideal set of principles which might govern a perfect society in the distant future). This again creates conflicts within the individual: allegiance to the mores of your world vs. allegiance to some hypothetical principles of the future. Loyalty to traditional values vs. loyalty to ideal values which may not be values when put into practice & tested by experience.

5. Finally there are several other variables, e.g.—parts of the superego which were inculcated in childhood & operate unconsciously vs. the parts which are con-

15. Claire Boothe Luce coined the term "globaloney" in her maiden speech on the floor of the House of Representatives (9 February 1943) to deride the postwar, "global thinking" proposals of Vice President Henry Wallace.

scious & verbalized; parts of the superego that are objectified in behavior & parts which are merely preached (not practiced).

6. A distinction is often made between the superego proper (conscience, an internal institution) & an externalized superego (an improper use of the term but nevertheless useful) meaning the representations of moral authority in the community—the police, popular opinion, etc. A man is said to have no superego when the control of his behavior is entirely in the hands of external authorities, as in a dictatorship, so that when he is given freedom he runs amuck. The only test of a superego is how a man will behave when all external checks are removed. A man who feels guilty when others do not blame him *has* a superego; a man who is honest among grafters has a superego; a man who works for perfection in art, science or fellowship at a time when no one notices the difference between good & bad work *has* a superego; The American superego, or rather the superego of the average American, is at a low point in many respects—but there are hopes of development along certain lines, an extension of the superego, for example, to include all nations & creeds—

I find it helpful to remember that the superego always refers to principles governing a relationship—whatever improves the relationship, enlarges it, deepens it, solidifies it, sustains it, is good, & is approved of by the superego; whatever disrupts it, weakens it, shakes it, trivializes it, is bad. There are 2 chief sorts of relationship: personal & group, & each of these has an internal & external phase.

i intrapersonal (relationship between parts of the personality i.e. ego & superego for instance) & ii interpersonal (between 2 lovers or friends)

&

i in-group (relationship among members) & ii out-group (relationship with other groups)

As I see it, superegos govern each of these.

O Lewis, please excuse this flow of talk. I was prompted to start because you have used the concept & I think it will serve your aims, but you did not use it always in the right way & I thought I could clarify it. Actually, like all other psychological concepts, it is extremely complicated when you come to examine it & possibly I have done more harm than good in trying to elucidate it, perhaps I have merely pointed out the difficulties without supplying solutions, possibly—& this would make me guilty—I have thrown a monkey wrench into your smooth running machinery.

I am half way through *The Condition of Man* (a wonderful title) & like it *immensely*. It is altogether fresh & vivid & spirited & appealing & enlightening. I have made a few comments along the margin—occasionally when the metaphors were a little fuzzy, occasionally when I thought I detected a logical contradiction. I do not know enough about the ancient world to detect errors of fact, if there are any. Perhaps later, after the Reformation I will begin to feel more at home. It will be a week or more, however, before I can return to the Mss & finish this section of the book. It is very exciting—I like your plan & of course your style is as always exhilarating. More power to you

Harry

[typed]
Amenia, New York
2 September 1943

Dear Harry:

Your two generous letters came only an hour or so ago; and I am sitting down at once to tell you how grateful I am for your exposition and how helpful, how clarifying, every word of it has been. I cannot wait to see the criticisms you have made on the margins; but I want to make sure, here and now, that you send the mss. back here—if you can't bring it in person!—in order that I may go through it carefully and take advantage of it before I hand in my final copy to the printer. My work has been going well, better since the break of meeting you in New York than before, because that taught me the value of a weekly rest, and by taking full advantage of one and even two days of untrammeled outward idleness every week I have increased my productivity, and in particular, my fertility: the sabbath more than justifies itself as a hygienic measure! If all goes well I hope to finish this draft by the third week in September; so if you are deterred by your own work from finishing that part of the mss. in your possession, please send me back what you have so far read so that it reaches me around the twentieth and if on the other hand, by some miracle, you should find yourself ahead of the game and willing to read what remains—the most important part and the part that would benefit most by your incomparable criticism—I will send it on to you; though I dare not ask you to do it even out of love.

Your analysis of the superego completes that of Freud, because you are aware of the social implications which he resolutely avoids: therefore I shall revise every passage where I use it in terms of your explanation. I should explain that my previous draft did not use this concept: I was aware of its existence, but had not been deeply impressed by it, and had not read Freud's New Introductory Lectures. Then last fall, in preparing my sociological analysis of personality, I came upon Freud's exposition and was struck by its correspondence with the social categories I had been more loosely using: in class I found the analysis particularly useful; and I found myself wanting to extend it to parallel functions in the community. I never had the time to work this out; and when, in doing this draft, I decided to utilize the super-ego terminology, I sought, not without misgivings, to cover a wider territory by broadening the concept instead of using a paraphrase or inventing a new term. Someday I may be driven to invent the necessary sociological terms that go with the super-ego; but the Condition of Man is not the place for this, and I have had no good thoughts in the matter; so what I must do now is to shave the super-ego down to its original figure, when I have stepped outside the bounds, and use descriptive phrases for its objective, social manifestations. Thank heaven you have made this clear; and thank heaven this has happened in time!

Incidentally, your sharp criticism of Jesus clears up something that I had never adequately expressed, or even begun to formulate, though I skirted it more closely in dealing with St Francis. Unless you want to keep the thought for some fresh exposition of your own I am going to carve a place for it in the Jesus chapter!

Today I finished up a pretty damaging criticism of Marx, as a false incarnation of socialism, who projected his self-hatred—for he himself was a parasite on Engels—upon all who stood in his way; and thereby created a heritage of hate for the whole movement he represented. Some of the more original parts of the book are in these later sections, where I deal with familiar material.

Your friendship, dear Harry, is an essential part of The Condition of Man. Don't let me prey on your time too heavily; but for the sake of whoever reads the book, don't spare a minute that you might give! There's an ambivalent plea for you!

Affectionately
Lewis

[typed]
Amenia, New York
16 September 1943

Dear Harry:

Your cheering note came this morning, just when I could make good use of it. Our little niece Erica is in bed with a cold, Sophy ditto, I myself have been warding one off; and all the while, day by day, almost hour by hour, I keep grinding away at the book, cursing the heavens, and wondering why on earth I dedicated a good five years of my life to such a task. You have read the less original part of the book, where I was treading over well-established ground; but though the second two-thirds are probably better I feel again the secret sense of disappointment I had when I let the first draft grow cold. The present manuscript is all very well; quite the best I can do by a sheer effort of will; but nothing has happened in the course of writing this manuscript which would turn effort into inspiration; and now I must wait and hope for last moment flashes, when the book is in proof, to give the whole thesis what I still feel it lacks.

Meanwhile, the book I originally planned still remains to be written, and perhaps it will come in its own good time: the material in the present book was originally gathered merely by way of serving as a brief historical introduction, and it finally swamped every other intention and diverted me, or rather dragged me away from, my original goal. I am glad that you noticed the absence of pictures of types: for it is implied in all my material, and yet only here and there, in the later portions, have I managed to translate it into something solid. It is the most ticklish of jobs, for it is the most subtle sort of synthesis, and mere effort never effects the right result. I am now one and a half chapters from writing finis, and though the odds at the moment are slightly against it, I still hope to turn in my ms. on October first. Long experience has taught me how unsafe one's most rational judgments are when one is tired from a prolonged effort; and it is the better part of safety for me to turn in my manuscript with all its present imperfections, than risk the suicidal impulses, or rather *infanticidal* impulses that sometimes overtake an author at the last critical moment. Your proposed visit to New York is well timed, as far as I am concerned; and by that time I trust I shall be fully recovered from the present doldrums: the hint that you may be willing to look at some of the remaining chapters, if not all, greatly comforts me; because I have recently added a few sections on Freud and Ellis and Geddes about which I am naturally full of misgiving; and I need your sane eye and your wise judgement precisely at that point. Incidentally, after pondering the need for a more extensive terminology to fit my need than the proper definition of super-ego permitted, I belatedly remembered that when I wrote the Story of Utopias I had re-coined the right word—idolum—to indicate the objective content of one's ideal self; and though I was forced to drop the word then because it didn't take on there is no reason why I shouldn't revive it more successfully twenty years later: and all the better because it shows the organic connection between my earliest and my latest books.

Since I will have to be running down to New York to gather illustrations and check my bibliography all through October, phone Harcourt's if you come in unexpectedly to see if I am there—unless we've had time to make arrangements beforehand. I trust your own work has gone forward well—and many thanks in anticipation for all that you have done on the ms. to clarify and stimulate my own.

Affectionately

Lewis

[handwritten]
158 Mt. Vernon Street
[LM] 23 Oct 43

Dear Lewis,

I hope that recuperation is bringing you back to form—I want to say that while I was reading the first $2/_3$ of the slice you lent me I was going on the assumption that you had until Jan 1—I remember your saying that you were granted 6 mos. Therefore I put down a lot of comments that could have been nothing but sand in the machinery of someone who was hurrying with his corrections.

I pictured you ruminating & rewriting for the next 3 mos. I was shocked to hear that you had no more than a week—

I am making very slow though steady progress with my two monographs— very impatient to get off.

At the moment I am trying to get "Arrowhead" bought & endowed as hallowed ground against the forward march of advertisitis which is corrupting, or has corrupted, the Emotional Integration of the whole Nation.[16] Because Fascism has reared its Brutal head we can attack it, & in attacking it gain strength, but Advertisitis slips in the ears & eyes & runs down the nerves & eats the vitals out of the ganglia without our knowing it.

Best luck to you
Harry

[typed]
Amenia, New York
23 October 1943

Dear Harry:

I have been wondering from day to day whether you'd soon put in an appearance at New York; and since I had to spend all this week revising my last chapter, which was still ragged and inconclusive—till I discovered I'd really written the conclusion in the middle of the first section!—I was afraid you might turn up at a moment when I could not come down to New York or even ask you up here. That moment is past. I am now free; and the sooner you make your appearance the happier I'll be; for I still have a final favor to ask you and that is, even if you can't read the last half of my book, to give your severest criticism to the section I've written on Freud. I won't show it to you until it is in galleys and so easy to read: but I scarcely dare publish it till you have looked at it. I hope to heaven these galleys come through before you hie off.

At the moment I am still sunk in fatigue, but no longer anxious or disheartened about the book itself, as I was during the closing days in September, when the whole thesis seemed to me a changling; and I felt like Jacob, awaking to find the handmaiden in his bed, instead of his wife. I think I wrote Christiana about all those inner misgivings. Now I think the book is good of its kind, and that it is even in certain ways, a fresh kind: even though large parts of it have been anticipated in a very fine book that the Austrian scholar, Erich Kahler, is just about to publish: Man the Measure.[17] (I recommend it: an astonishingly good job in its main outlines.)

Please erase from your mind the slightest feeling of guilt about your criticisms of the ms.: they were all pure gold to me, and so far from impeding my own thought, they gave it a stimulus that I only wish had been more constantly present during the revision of my earlier drafts. My haste to get the book finished was due to my knowledge that it would be impossible to put a book like this through the press without being constantly on hand to supervise it: if I had turned it in as late as November the process of production would have been a mess, for everything is de-

---

16. Arrowhead: the name of Herman Melville's home near Pittsfield, Massachusetts, where he lived from 1850 to 1863.

17. Erich Kahler, *Man the Measure* (1943).

layed, and one is forced to juggle even the length of the book, in such things as bibliographies and indexes, in order to meet the paper shortage. This requires all my time and attention; and I simply could not have managed it along with my Stanford work.

The other day I had a good talk with Alfred Cohn before he went to the hospital for his operation; and it even seems possible now that I might take over the editorship of his review of higher education, if he can get the backing for it: it would be a way of filling in the remaining war-years, before I am needed on a full schedule at Stanford. This of course remains only a possibility. The probability at the moment is that Sophy and Alison and I will return to Stanford in January and stay there till June: then come back here and remain here till the end of the war. They want me at Stanford, not to take part in the military courses any more—my part has become insignificant under a revised program—and not necessarily to teach in the humanities, since the number of students hardly justifies the presence of three of us: but the new president wants me to help re-plan the curriculum of the university; and I think I can probably be of some real use at that job.[18] That is my main justification for going back, instead of prolonging my leave of absence.

I am still a little troubled, dear Harry, by your own decision to give up the important work you are doing for the routine tasks of war. It shows a great self-discipline and a great humility; but as things are shaping up at present, the more disengaged minds we have, capable of a continued exercize of thought, experiment, and criticism, the more likelihood will there be that the war will be fought to some purpose: whereas if the military tasks absorb everybody, the soldiers who have fought it will find that all the regressive and purposeless forces that dominated our life in the past have become mightier in their absence and the serious business of making the planet fit to live on has been indefinitely postponed. Three years ago I should gladly have thrown Einstein and Freud into the front line of battle, for then the question was not so much one of success in our venture, but bare survival against the barbarian. Now, it seems to me, our survival is assured; but our success may be indefinitely postponed by the cowardice and the shoddy thinking of our statesman—combined with an absence of thought in those places where it normally exists. This is reopening a closed question with you, probably, Harry: maybe it is almost as brash as my proposing to tell Waldo Frank what I thought of his proposed marriage. But I think that the soldiers need you more at this moment in your capacity as thinker, than they could possibly do in your capacity as physician.

My pleas to you may seem like a rationalization of my own position, transferred for convenience to you; but I think there is much objectivity to be said for them, whether my own ego is involved or not.

I am eager to see your monographs; and not less to behold you and talk to you. Come up here for a couple of days if you can: the November landscape is one of my

18. Donald Tresidder, president of Stanford University, 1943–1948.

favorite ones, and even if I have proofs to correct at the moment I am not so seriously rushed but that I can throw them aside for a day or two for real refreshment.

Affectionately

Lewis

P.S. Bravo to your efforts to save Arrowhead! Can I help in any way? Thinking of your plans for the Tower, could it perhaps be saved as a writer's home, instead of as a museum?

[typed]
Amenia, New York
28 October 1943

Dear Harry:

Yesterday was a particularly good day: in rummaging through a lot of old papers and pamphlets I came upon your two essays on Freud and on psychoanalysis; and the re-reading of them gave me a much deeper insight into what you were talking about—and into what I have tried to talk about in parts of my book—than I had had before. It was a great satisfaction to come upon them again precisely at this moment; and on top of that, the first proofs of my book came through. That was a great relief: I feel much better about what I have written now: print has given it a certain clarity and solidity I was not quite sure about before. Herewith I am baiting you and tempting you and teasing you with the new introduction I have written (These are duplicate proofs. Write on them freely if you are tempted to.): one which I put together hastily when I was quite tired, and which I am now far from satisfied with, though it is nearer to my purpose than the original introduction was. I am going to keep it by me till I finish correcting the proofs: this will take up another three weeks. If you should have any time during this period to read what I have written and to note what I have said badly, what seems downright wrong, and what I have omitted but should have put in I will be deeply grateful; but if you are still preoccupied with your own work or just feel tired and want to be let alone, don't feel any obligation whatever; just stick it in an envelope and send it back. No one will understand better than I!

Warmly

Lewis

[handwritten]

Dear L.

The 2nd operation is over & after 2 transfusions & continuous feeding by vein for 2 days, most of the perils are past—possible collapse of the lung, post-operative pneumonia, etc.[19] I might say *only* the pain, or *nothing* but the pain remains, except

19. Christiana Morgan underwent a radical sympathectomy to curtail high blood pressure; this was an excruciatingly painful, two-stage operation severing nerves on each side of the spine (see Claire

that pain can fill the whole world. However pain when you have a full beckoning future is different from pain when you have merely the old rut to anticipate.

So now a great weight has lifted, and with thanksgiving for your letters, I am free to turn to your Introduction, hoping that I am not too late to be in some slight measure useful.[20] Well, right off, I think this *Introd.* Is a most *excellent survey* of the broad outlines of the Human Situation. It is *perfect* as it stands with due weight given to everything form atoms to dreams, physics to mysticism. My odd notes are unimportant. I like the way you take off from the fact of death in the 2nd paragraph—That gives me, as reader, a feeling I can trust you not to deceive me with eyewash later. (The recognition of death is something that the modern American avoids at all cost.) It is exciting reading & yet balanced & informed. It is sound & yet inspired. I have indicated the passages which startled me by their presenting some new aspect of the truth or some old aspect in new words. Congratulations. The Introduction certainly whets one's appetite—Love to Sophy. What news from Geddes?

> Yrs
> Harry

> [handwritten]
> 64 Plympton Street
> Cambridge

I sent off your Mss early this morning, dear Lewis, & they assure me it would reach you tomorrow (Tuesday) morning. I am sorry that it will arrive a day later than you anticipated.

You will find very few notations in the end sections; that is *because* I was reading faster as I went on, having brooded a good many hours on the earlier parts & then having found that the deadline (today) was approaching, & *because* there is nothing but perfection in the later chapters & I found no errors.

You are writing a great book. I am excited by all of it & agree with all of it. I see the plan & I like it, & I admire the execution beyond words. It is all you—a gust of fresh wind blowing down the centuries. You did a marvelous job on Thomas Aquinas, Machiavelli, Luther, & Calvin. The only part I didn't have time to read were the last few pages on the Protestant Character. I wanted especially to read this as it is one of my specialties, the only one you have reached. However, I will have another chance. Your judgment on the capitalists tickled me to pieces.

I think it is important to make clear in each case whether you are talking about

---

Douglas, *Translate This Darkness: The Life of Christiana Morgan* [New York: Simon and Schuster, 1993)], 235–37). Mumford began writing Morgan regularly at this time, November 1943; their correspondence continued until her death in 1967.

20. Murray encloses a list of suggestions for the introduction to *The Condition of Man.*

a very general common type, a typical artist (or merchant or scholar) or whether you are talking about an ideal (e.g. Machiavelli or Machiavelli's *Prince,* Nietzsche or *Zarathustra,* Milton or *Satan,* etc.)

Christiana, by the way, is as enthusiastic as I am—More power to you

Affly

H

[typed]
Amenia, New York
23 November 1943

Dear Harry:

Despite all the miseries and uncertainties and torments that remain, you letter could not help bringing great relief: I pray that C. has passed the worst dangers, and that you have passed the most harrowing moments. I have a pretty good notion of what you have been through, and have followed my own experience in keeping silent, remembering moments of anguish in my own life when even the friendliest touch was almost unbearable. There is no cure for these stony moments except the flooding back of life itself in the one loves; and there is almost no better moment than when the flood tide masters the ebb. May that moment come soon.

I could almost weep at the thought that you have turned your attention to my poor introduction in such a period; though that impulse is coupled with admiration over the mastery of yourself which your comments, even your hand-writing, showed. As usual, you have given me exactly the right criticism, and it comes at exactly the right moment, sanctioning my bold excisions, re-enforcing my confidence in places where I was still a prey to doubt, giving me the energy I need for the last touches. During the last fortnight my cumulative exhaustion finally registered: the changes that I had hoped would come by inspiration did not do so: I had to use my utmost of craftsmanlike skill as substitute. Since it is by deletions rather than additions that I have, at last, made a few necessary improvements.

[. . .]

I won't go into your comments seriatim: you shall see when the book comes out how well I have profited by them. In the meanwhile, my thoughts and my affection continue to hover around you.

Lewis

P.S. We got an enigmatic telegram from Geddes, saying that his basic was over on the 27th and asking for $50, which may mean that he has hopes of a furlough before he goes off to his next training ground: we are dearly hoping to see him and sent him a telegram, mentioning Alison, which may help him to get leave, if they are granting any. I have much to tell you about him and us, of a merely gossipy nature—future plans, etc.—but I spare you till another letter gives even firmer proof of C.'s upturn.

[handwritten]
158 Mt. Vernon St.
Boston

Dear Lewis,

You have had 6 mos of prodigious labor—but from what I have seen of the results of it you have reason to be well satisfied. Perhaps you are too exhausted to know just how you do feel about it. When will it be published?

I have given 4 copies of the *set*, Technics & Cities, to our four most socially conscious "subjects" (subjects studied at the Clinic) with the word that these were the best instruments I could give them to understand & participate in the making of a new world. They were greatly pleased.

[. . .]

I think you must be responsible for the latest job that was offered me—I think this because you are the only distinguished writer who gives me a boost in public—Last week the 2 heads of British psychiatry visited me at the end of a 5 weeks tour of the U.S. & asked me whether I would take the job of Psychological Consultant to the War Ministry (a big hole for a small peg-brigadier!). They left for England with the warning that they expected considerable opposition to appointing an American over the heads of their own men, so that it is not probable that their scheme will be accepted. I expect to hear in a week or so. If the answer is 'Yes' I will go to England around Jan 7—go through 3 weeks basic training with a medical unit & then 3 weeks with a tank unit, & then take up quarters in London, with a great deal of traveling to report on work of all branches—in other words, will be in position for the greatest invasion in the history of the world. Simultaneously I was offered the job of running a testing or assessment centre at a country estate (900 acres) in Virginia, specially designed to pick spies & underground agents who will operate behind enemy lines. This would be an interesting problem in character-structure—i.e. selecting "trustworthy law-breakers" or "honorable crooks." Most of those who volunteer are foreign born engineers with revenge in their hearts, but there are numerous other types. (This is all *secret* of course—& my part in it has been that of devising a 2 day program full of day & night life-like situations demanding the qualities that are necessary for such work—I had to refuse the job of permanent head).

What I really expect to do is to go into the Medical Corps, & trust to continuous "go-getting" (all the kinds of behavior I most dislike) to push my way up through the great impersonal machine & eventually get overseas. My reason for doing this is purely mystical. The only rational point I can think of is that the 6,000,000 men who return after the war will not be in a mood to trust anyone—or to learn from anyone—who has not experienced what they have experienced. This is not what makes me go, because I think I know it all—or almost all—in my feelings & imagination—but it may, of course, be even worse than I think it is.

My writing has gone very badly—what with Christiana's illness, 2 or 3 government jobs to be done, plans changing every week, settling a lot of petty businesses, & general exhaustion—*A Clinical Study of Sentiments* (300 page monograph) is a fairly mediocre performance. I thought you might be interested in the Thematic Apperception test, & so I asked the Harvard Press to send you a copy. I must see you before you go. When exactly are you leaving? I am planning to be in Washington (c/o Mrs. R.L. Bacon, 1801 F Street, Wash.) during most of the week of Dec 27. Best Xmas Solicitations to you all.

> Yrs
> Harry

[typed]
694 Alvarado Row
Stanford University
6 March 1944

. . . I have thought of you often these last three months, dear Harry: more than once I have wished for your counsel and sometimes for the mere comfort of your friendship: but I kept putting off writing you, because I had nothing good to report; and I knew that you had been through a gruelling enough experience last fall to have earned some respite from other people's woes, no matter how much you loved them!

The quickest way to tell about the beginning is to announce the end: and that is, that we are going back to Amenia toward the end of April. I came out here with the most serious inner misgivings; every fibre of me was tense and tired from the savage pace at which I had finished the book: a pace occasioned by the very fact that I was slated to come back here in January. I knew that I wanted only one thing: at least three months vacation: I groaned at the thought of putting another burden on myself, even the smallest. But during the fall, funds had sunk low and doctors' bills had piled up; and I flogged myself into coming out here on the pretext that, though it would be a strain, the climate and the even round of work away from my desk would be relaxing rather than otherwise.

Never before have I committed such folly with such wide open eyes; for my heart had been pounding far too hard and too swiftly for two months before leaving. Ten days ago, just as I fancied I was beginning to pick up energy, I got a slight spasm: just a tremor: but enough to send me to bed and to give me the energy to correct my mistake. The doctor can find nothing organically wrong with the heart itself; after a week in bed even the blood pressure was normal; only skipped beats remain. So the trouble is one that really involves the whole organism; and the only answer to it is rest and ease. I am taking an indefinite leave of absence from Stanford; and I have given up all hope or plan of making myself into a professor. The last resolve is a great relief: when I finally made it understood here I began automatically to feel better. This excursion into academic life might have worked had I been in normal health in 1942 when I first came out; but I had then exhausted myself trying to finish up too hurriedly the earlier draft of my book; so the odds were against my success, even if I had developed the necessary patience to handle the routine of university living.

Enough of these doldrums. There are plenty of difficulties ahead for me; but there is at least some brightness, too; not least, the hope of seeing you if you are on this side of the Atlantic. As you can guess, I have had to postpone my English trip, too, for however rapidly I recover the absence of any income next summer from the university would make it impossible for me to spend two months away. That is perhaps the keenest part of my disappointment: for I have really achieved a place in English thought, if not here; in the matter of planning and building after the war I have a fresh point of view to bring, that of an outsider who has lived intimately in England; and my hosts had planned a marvelous itinerary in every part of Britain, which would have brought me face to face with their university and municipal leaders. They have already renewed the invitation for next year; and I hang on that hope.

We won't leave here before the middle of April; so do drop me a line and tell me what your plans are and where you will be in May, if you know. I wrote Christiana a little while ago, in one of my good moments: but I won't tell her about my present state till I am well out of if. The news of her own progress last January was cheering; and I hope it has kept up.

Affectionately

Lewis

[handwritten]
[LM] 4 May 44
Box 2605 Washington, D.C.
April 28 44

Dear Old Lewis:

Returning recently from England I found your letter waiting for me, and although I do not have it with me out here, its unhappy message is written on my brain and I can answer it without present reference. You, like other creative men, have always worked on subjective time, and you can rely on your own physiology to warn you when you digress very far from your proper rhythm. Your heart is probably a very sensitive index of appropriate pace, and so it seems to me that your leaving Stanford at this moment is just right. Everything depends on your continued exuberant vitality—there are hosts of Americans whose thoughts & sentiments are largely guided by what you write, & you cannot let them down by permitting yourself to get checked and frustrated by monotonous routine, committee meetings and academic red-tape. Besides this is no time to be lecturing at a university— In your audience there will be only a few really capable students—the rest will be left-overs whose low morale will permeate the climate. Also, as I told you, the girls at Stanford are almost exclusively interested in dating & necking, and classes are merely places in which to ruminate about past & future evenings. Therefore, I am not sorry, despite my regret that all this could not have been foreseen. I forget that date you gave in your letter, but my memory tells me that you are just about now arriving home. I hope, in any event, that this letter will reach you before long and that I will have an answer to reassure me as to your present state of body and soul.

I am now in the Army & have no use at all for some of the money that we once lived on, & so I am sending a check, so that I can have the pleasure of sharing the existing surplus with our best friend. I am thinking of doctors' bills, etc.[21] I believe entirely in the communism of wealth & therefore you must not disappoint me by taking this as a loan.

I had a most successful 5 weeks in England. I went over from Washington to London (via Maine & Scotland) in 36 hours & back (via Iceland & Greenland) in 2 days. In London I became involved in several different enterprises: plans for dealing with the casualties of the invasion, assessment boards in the country for selecting officers, the interrogation of German prisoners, propaganda & psychological warfare of all sorts & then the special mission which took me to England in the first place. I went over with but one specific purpose in mind and was surprised & embarrassed to find that all the young Turks of modern psychology & psychiatry in England had read Explorations & spoke of it as their Bible & expected me to make speeches & deliver wise judgments on a hundred issues. I decided that there were more disadvantages in being over-estimated than in being under estimated.

The British have changed very much as a result of their very strong desire to win the friendship of Americans. They feel that their whole future rests upon Anglo-American cooperation & unity, & they are willing to put aside many of their stuffy old habits & attitudes to achieve this goal. They are exceedingly cordial nowadays, & have taken on numerous American fashions of behavior & speech. They call you by your first name, to pick one example, after knowing you for a few days. Their war morale is exemplary & their attitude towards the future is much more advanced than ours. Everyone I talked to was a socialist of one sort or another, whose reflections were oriented by a determination to build healthy communities with solidarity of spirit. They spoke of a community as being the patient with whom the psychiatrist must deal & as you know, they are greatly interested in improving education & in housing. Architects are handing in plans for the reconstruction of London & other cities & towns, just as Christopher Wren did after the fire of London. All this is of immense interest to you & it is disheartening to hear that you will not have the opportunity to go abroad this spring.

I have just returned from Cambridge where I went for a few days after reporting in Washington & there I found what I had been hoping to find—*The Condition of*

---

21. An uncashed check for $1000, dated April 28, Guaranty Trust Company of New York, is in the manuscripts of the correspondence.

Man.[22] Certainly the format & the illustrations are very appealing, particularly fine when you consider that this was published a few weeks before the great invasion when there's a shortage of paper & manpower. I am palpitating with prospective excitement & am planning to begin this weekend, but will probably not finish for two or three weeks as I have only a few hours of Saturday at my disposal each week.

I believe that the publication of this book should be a great source of strength & satisfaction to you. I have read enough, for example, to know that it is thick with wonderful visions into the nature of men & society & with marvelous germs for creating a fresh future. I need the book as a man with myocarditis needs digitalis, because I am in the state of being appalled at the blight that is Americanization when it takes place in foreign lands imposing itself—almost always in a detrimental manner—on the native culture. (At this moment I have Iceland in mind.)

Well, we have much to discuss. Let me hear from you soon & tell me particularly about Geddes & of course all about Sophy & yourself.

Yrs

Harry

By the way I am now a Major!

[typed]
Amenia, New York
4 May 1944

. . . Your quite overwhelming letter, dear Harry, was written the day before we left New York, where we lingered a couple of days en route; and it found me in a state of inner serenity that not even the long weary journey across the continent and the even longer and wearier unpacking could ruffle. And first, I don't know whether to be remorseful and self-rebuking at not having followed up my original letter to you, written when I had reached the very nadir of the winter, with one which would have told you of my recovering health and spirits: or to rejoice because that omission left the way open to such an act of imaginative generosity as only you would be capable of. You are the only friend, dear Harry, from whom I would dare to take such a gift, without fearing that it would bring about the end of our friendship: about that I am entirely at ease. And you are right in thinking that, if I should have a run of ill fortune during the next six months, such a sum might very well tide me through a period of depression and so save my life, or bring about an earlier recovery. Was it not indeed the absence of such visible proofs of friendship and love that, at a critical moment, brought Melville down? The mere reassurance that money is there, ready, to pick me up if I stumble, so to say, is in itself enough to make me surefooted: that aid, dear Harry, is beyond all thanks, and I accept it fully

---

22. *The Condition of Man* (1944), volume three in the Renewal of Life series.

in the spirit in which it is given. But actually, I am in no present need: we sold part of our extra furniture in leaving Palo Alto at quite handsome prices, and that has defrayed the costs of moving: I even managed my hegira so that it would coincide with the final meeting of the Commission on Teacher Education in Chicago, and that paid my expenses across the continent. So what I propose to do, dear Harry, is to keep the cheque in my safe, uncashed, as insurance against the future: if at any time during the next six or seven months I should need it, I will cash it and unhesitatingly use it: more than that, I will not, so long as I need rest, push myself prematurely into earning my living when by doing so I would delay my own recovery. If by some miracle my book should do well, I may not need the money at all and at the end of the year I will give the cheque back, just as deeply grateful as I will be if I should actually use it. Meanwhile the very thought of your friendship mingles with the gay bird calls that blend with my sleep in the morning: part of that spring's awakening that I already feel within me, now that the exhausting efforts of the last year and the hard decision I made in February are behind me. You are right in your diagnosis of my symptoms: that is why my doctor's bills have been next to nothing; for all the tests and cardiographs show no impairment in any organ whatever, and all the doctor could tell me was what I already had told myself—that I must be lazy for a while and avoid emotional pressures, taking life at my own pace. You have made this an easy prescription to follow, dear Harry: though the Condition of Man may be my Moby-Dick I need not write that "dollars damn me." Even the postponement of my trip to England I have at length been able to reconcile myself to, because I doubt whether the extensive itinerary that had been planned for me, from Cornwall to Aberdeen, will prove as feasible in July as seemed possible last February—even if—which is doubtful—I could have stood the tension and strain of such steady consultation and lecturing at this early date. But how I envy you your opportunity to see for yourself what is going on there, and to have a responsible part in the effort itself. It was the lack of such an opportunity that probably, as I look back on it, made me make the spurious "sacrifice" of going to Stanford before my book was really finished: otherwise that step was a denial of every insight and intuition I have had about this war and its necessary results.

All that you tell me about your trip makes me eager to hear even more: is it not one of the good omens of friendship that we both should stand higher in England than in America, so that I now even begin to get inquiries and solicitous letters from people who had never bothered about my contributions to planning during the last dozen years, inquiries, it turns out, that were prompted by the enthusiasm of some visiting Englishmen, like the Archbishop of York. One would be inclined to attribute this blindness to our inveterate colonialism; but it was not always so: Emerson did not need Carlyle's credentials to be accepted in America. And it may be that original thought of any kind finds a less willing acceptance in its home environment: old Geddes is being read and quoted in England now, not by direct influence, but because my own writings have brought him to their attention. Your observations of the British change in attitude re-enforces my own second judgements: but what I fear is that, with no corresponding change going on, to all appearances, in the mind and heart of civilian America, the gap between us may be as great as that which separates us from Russia, precisely because of our blindness and emotional immaturity and irresponsibility. If the change necessary for our renewal is to take place, it must take place in the armed forces; and I wonder whether you find any there? Our last word from Geddes must have been written the beginning of April, just before sailing: we have not yet heard whether he reached the other side safely, though he said the War Department would inform us. Part of his division, we have heard, has reached Ireland. He is an infantryman, attached to a headquarters company, and though he is a little impatient for promotion—he is only a Pfc—he reckons he will earn it in action, if not before. I know how well-filled your days must be, dear Harry: but I would run down to New York even to see you for an hour, if you should be passing through. When I am down there, your can reach me at either Harcourt's or my brother-in-law's: Orchard 4 2807.

In the meanwhile, our love to you—and our gratitude

Lewis

P.S. I'll write again presently when I am more fully rested: the household is still in the muddle of unpacking.

[handwritten]
Tuesday 2 AM
[LM] 6 June 1944

Dear Lewis:

Besides carrying a back-bending burden of work over the last month I have been involved in an unsought but unavoidable conflict with an individual who has shared with me the guidance of the unit in the OSS to which I have belonged since December. It was a conflict of conceptions which led to a situation in which many people became engaged & when this other fellow—who happens to be named (James) Alexander Hamilton—was transferred to another branch, I, for a while, became the target of his many friends' wrath & had to pass through a fire of criticism & suspicion which stimulated me to perfect & validate the principles for which I had taken up arms. Now everything has become suddenly serene & we have a band of workers whose cohesiveness is based on complete trust & goodwill.—All this has stood as a barrier between me and The Condition of Man which has constituted, with the Oxford Dictionary, my entire library for the past four weeks. Christiana's visit to Washington, as you might imagine, was the stimulus which drew me out of the maelstrom of urgent and importunate action onto the verdant land of long range creative thoughts & so, (after a hundred devastating postponements) into the heart of your book. I shall be writing you about your great work for the next year or more—certainly a single letter can do no more than serve as a slight prelude to a series of exchanges which might be fruitfully continued for a long time to come.

Christiana & I found that it was not a book to be read at the usual rate. At the end of almost every paragraph we were impelled to stop and comment—the majority of comments being prompted by some bewildering leap of your imagination by which you showed the affinity of two superficially unrelated events or people. This, we say, is one highly developed aspect of your genius—the perception of similarity amid diversity. Another feature which we both revel in is your insistence on measuring everything on the human pulse. Nothing is judged by itself in vacuo, but rather as facilitating or hindering the good community or the development of the individual. The third, and probably most exciting virtue is the way you have of examining all of history from the point of view of Modern Man struggling to evolve a new synthesis for himself & others. You are a hound for usable Truth, as Melville called it, & we bless you for it. The Condition of Man contains more usable Truth for our generation than any book that has been written. It is our Bible or rather the Prolegomenon of a Bible to be written. Although in my absence Christiana could not resist reading ahead into "Uprising of the Libido," we did not get further than "Capitalism, Absolutism, Protestantism" & so I am going to leave detailed comments until later—until I have had the opportunity to read to the last page and see your achievement as a whole. This book more than justifies the clear-headed stand you have taken in regard to active participation in the war. Certainly you are one individual—and Christiana is another—who should stand somewhat apart during this hectic & confused period and view events with the whole range of past events and future possibilities in the background of your mind. I certainly would have done the same thing if it had not been for my faith in Christiana. She, as you, with your unfailing intuition, have long realized, is the creative nucleus of our unity, the one who had the vision of our potentialities and shaped our relationship from the beginning. I have taken everything from her. And so now when I become centrifugal she can become centripetal & maintain the proper balance. Thus I am not much depressed when I discover that the staleness which has developed from overwork holds my mind in habitual & ungenerative grooves. Christiana, engaged in a single-minded pilgrimage into her own depths, is going in the opposite direction.

From the beginning we have recognized that we can only work as one person, which accounts for the fact that Christiana, often with some reluctance, has devoted the greater part of her time to helping me at the Clinic & with Melville. By a sort of tacit agreement of long standing, however, it was understood that the time might come when she would feel compelled to write, out of a lower layer than that from which my ideas appear to flow, and when that season arrived I would devote my energies to her work just as she had spent herself to assist me. Recently a change has been taking place in her—accelerated no doubt by our situation & her freedom from the yoke of science—& it is possible that when the war is over she will want me to give the larger share, if not all, my energies to collecting material as background for the things which she feels that she must say before we die. If this occurs it will mean leaving the Clinic & a new orientation which will carry us all the way in your direction. This is a possibility—still vague—which may appeal to you—perhaps you will wonder why this step was not taken sooner. Is it because Science is God, or has been until The Condition of Man? I am speaking secrets—

Affectionately,

Harry

[typed]
Amenia, New York
24 June 1944

. . . The last two months, dear Harry, have glided by so swiftly that I can hardly believe that your last letter, received June 5, which has been so near to me all this time, remains unanswered. It should have been answered long ago, if my hand were as prompt in response as my spirit. I badly needed these effortless days; and I have etherized my puritanical conscience sufficiently to enjoy them; though I have only to put my state alongside your urgent and effortful existence to feel completely ashamed of myself. For it was not any choice or decision of mine that caused me to "stand apart" while this war was going on: little did I think, between 1938 and 1941, that I would have so small a part in the actual living out of the war: the terrible but fundamental experience of my generation. If I could have found a niche that would have even half used me, I should have welcomed it: perhaps sacrificing a higher duty to a lower one for the sake of the inner peace that the lower would have given. But outside the OWI there is no place, as you know, for my unspecialized talents: the veriest tyro who has achieved a decent mediocrity in one single field has a hundred times more opportunity to get connected than one who has tried to bring a number of fields into focus: so I remain outside because I am fundamentally unemployable under present conditions: which is cold consolation.[23] The only thing I have actually stood out from is the OWI: not that they made any attempt to enlist my services. But I knew, from what promptly happened to the people I had confidence in there, that it was no place for me. This will always be a tender spot; but I am resigned to it by now as I finally resigned myself to writing The Condition of Man in the form it actually took, instead of in that form I had contemplated and outlined in 1938: there are moments when, no matter how one struggles, one's decisions are made for one; and one meets only further frustration if one does not accept that fact meekly.

Meanwhile I have good news: and since I was so prompt to tell you of my misfortunes last February I hasten to tell you how favorably the tide has turned in my

---

23. OWI: Office of War Information, U.S. government propaganda agency, 1942–1943.

direction. Not only has my health been restored: that was to be expected. But in spite of the extremely spotty reception that The Condition of Man received in the press, compared with all my other books, it has actually sold better than The Culture of Cities: indeed, it will probably have reached the 7000 mark by the first of July, which is better than the other book did in eight months. This not merely wipes out my debt but ensures an ample income till next January, even if not a single other copy were sold. I am pleased—and immensely relieved; for I can now, once I am fully rested, settle down to blocking out the final volume, without being under any undue pressure to earn my living by other courses. Incidentally, dear Harry, I no longer have to take advantage of your generosity: your impulse will remain as dear as ever, for in my heart I accepted your gift and was vitalized by it. I would send it back to you herewith but for the fact that I should like to keep it, in a sufficiently mutilated and uncashable state, among my papers: as a silent testimonial to posterity, should anyone ever look over my papers. At all events, cancel it from your cheque book: *that* account is now payable in heaven!

In all the bliss of this relaxation, my life has been a far more superficial one than Christiana's: indeed, I need a month or two more of gardening and swimming before I shall be ready to tunnel inward, as she is doing. But of course I understand her impulse: all the better because of my firsthand experience with the university, whose inner reconstitution I had thought more easy than it actually is: indeed, I now think that the university will probably be the last institution to respond to the crisis adequately or prepare to meet the needs of the days to come: its very perfection of routine makes the resistance greater, and there are only a handful in the university who realize that their own weaknesses are in any way bound up with the state of the world outside. So long as we could hope that our institutions were sound in their main design, though perhaps weak in this or that detail, it was natural that we should feel hopeful about them, and think of our own tasks in the light of *their* main concerns, following the patterns they had collectively worked out. Under such circumstances a modest, cooperative part was all that it became us to demand: continuity demanded precisely this allegiance. But now we can see that the mere refinement of method and the extension of positive knowledge, without life-wisdom, is fatal even to the quality of our thought: it loses sight of the very conditions that are essential to its own continuity and self-preservation.

The change that must now take place in the whole design of our intellectual life is one that is reserved for people like yourself and Christiana to make: it can have authority only when it comes from those who have submitted fully to the rationale of objective science before they begin to burrow, as fully, as confidently, into the subjective world and to lay the foundations for its discipline: one that will eventually permit two worlds to be as unified in thought as they actually are in every germinal and significant experience. . . . I was just about to go on to say that this is probably for your life and hers, not a matter of reversing the leadership, but of finding new ground in which her qualities will become dominant in your work; and that this change could hardly come about by any mere act of will on your part, especially at this moment, when you are naturally carried on by the momentum of your common past, and cannot detach yourself sufficiently from the large pressure of your military responsibilities even to imagine what your new role and your new province would be. And at that moment there came a note from Christiana, supplementing another little letter she wrote the same time you did early in June, saying that you had already found your way and yourselves: which only shows how little my prudent counsels were needed. But of course that is only the first step: the process of living out and working out the idea remains before you. If I am not mistaken, only those who are capable of this change will really live through this crisis: the rest will only go through the motions and not know that they have thereby cut themselves off from the future.

When I began my book in 1940, with the picture of Fourth Century Rome uppermost in my mind, as the true parallel to our own day, however much better we might picture our plight, I did not realize how many people silently shared this intuition. Rebecca West for instance. Have you read her Black Lamb and Grey Falcon? (First pub. In 1940.)[24] If the whole book is anything like the first hundred pages, it is a great work, and a unique one: better than anyone who knew only her extremely clever but somewhat brittle early work could have believed she would be capable of writing. Throw out The Condition of Man and read Black Lamb. . . . !

What you said, dear Harry, about my book's containing Usable Truth pleased me immensely; for at that moment I came upon an old note I had made reading Coleridge, where he observed that Leibnitz's own doctrines had not produced the effect that Leibnitz himself described as the criterion of philosophy; namely, "that it would at once explain and collect fragments of truth scattered through systems apparently the most incongruous." Not intentionally was this my object; but perhaps it has been the practical outcome of the method I used—and perhaps this explains why the public has taken to it, despite the miscomprehension and hostility of the reviewers. Alfred Cohn, whom I saw the other day in New York, said something to the same effect.

Don't let this letter lie on your conscience: I can imagine how crowded your days are even though their contents, to an outsider, must remain undecipherable. I will write again presently, whether I hear from you or not; for writing letters is one of the joys of this period of irresponsibility; and by the time next September comes I may have my head buried again in my next book. Before I do that, however, I have it in mind to write another pamphlet like Men Must Act, under some such title as Antidote to Disillusion; for it seems to me that because of the moral infirmity and political paralysis of our leaders we have already generated a cynicism and a disillusion which may, unless we muster up positive forces to combat them, rob hu-

---

24. Rebecca West, *Black Lamb and Grey Falcon: A Journey Through Yugoslavia* (1941).

manity of the real promise this war held for them. I shall write the pamphlet primarily I suppose to fortify myself; in the hope that if I succeed there I may also hope to touch a few other souls who feel the same way.

Affectionately & gratefully
Lewis

[typed]
Amenia, New York
21 July 1944

. . . . A week ago, dear Harry, I hung around Harcourt's office far longer than I had any real reason to: but still my instincts weren't strong enough to make me hang around the extra five minutes that would have given me a chance to grasp your hands and look into your eyes. What a misfortune that was! I was probably drinking a beer at Child's when you dashed by, unknown to me; or I had just gone over to the Mercantile Library in 47 Street, to become a member. Alice said you were looking splendid; and the girl at Harcourt's, who was greatly impressed by you, either knew or guessed that you were off on new missions: so it may be long before you will get this note.

The current news about Germany seems like a turning point: when the rats begin to turn upon each other we may count upon a large and beneficial campaign of mutual extermination; fortunately, they are all "killer" rats that have already tasted the blood of their own species and have become deadly.[25] It would be an ironic but not unexpected turn of history, if our too-long delayed second front proved abortive and if the real collapse of Germany were engineered mainly from within, through an internecine war. Something or other, incidentally, made me think once more on your own suggestions for decontaminating the leaders of Nazi Germany; and I wonder if it would not be a better method to avoid both trial and imprisonment of any kind, by giving orders that at least a hundred of the best known criminals, beginning of course with Hitler, should be shot on sight, by whomever has the first chance to do so. That is the most ignominious ending possible: precisely the kind that would be meted out to any other notorious and desperate criminal who had too long evaded the law.

A trial would give these people a chance to strut upon the stage once more and even elicit the sympathies of the perverse and the morbid; even sequestration in an asylum would lend itself to the same sort of legendary halo as hangs over

25. A reference to the unsuccessful attempt to kill Hitler on 20 July 1944 with a bomb hidden in a briefcase; the plot was led by Colonel Claus von Stauffenberg and other senior German military officials.

Napoleon at St Helena. A quick exit, without discussion, is what is needed, it seems to me; even the swift formalities of a courtmartial would be too tedious as well as too respectful of the self-condemned criminals.

Geddes's letters have become infrequent and completely lacking in any local color: so I fancy he has been moved up nearer the battle zone. Otherwise, we have only tranquil news to report, of the same nature as I told you of in my last letter, only more so: the book has gone so well that Harcourt's have increased their estimate from 10,000 to 15,000 for the first year, though it has so far sold only about 7500 copies. Did I say only? That is enough and plenty as far as I am concerned: so lucky indeed that I hold my breath and look around superstitiously wondering at what point in our family anatomy the gods are going to hit!

My affectionate thoughts follow after you, dear Harry, wherever you are: don't feel the slightest sense of inequality at not being able to answer these notes of mine: I will continue them regularly, leaving you to fill in the vacant responses when we meet.

Lewis

[typed]
Amenia, New York
29 July 1944

Dear Harry:

The gal at Harcourt's had told me that you were to go immediately overseas; but I am glad that my dawdling over a letter didn't cause it to miss you, since you had stayed here longer than I had counted on. I feel the same urgency for closeness, over and above all our natural, long-founded closeness, that you do: no one recognizes better than I do how much you both contributed to The Condition of Man, and how much of what you found there had been implanted there by you at a much earlier period—coming back to you, perhaps, with the appearance of something fresh or more thoroughly clarified only because it had been strained through another mind. My final volume would be terrifying to contemplate, to say nothing of writing, if I did not have the sense of having both your positive work and your personal experience as a constant support for whatever I shall be able to contribute. One of my Stanford colleagues has suggested that the final volume should be a collaboration of specialists who would work together under my general guidance; but the only way I can envisage such a collaboration is among a society of well-tried friends; and the nearest I can hope to come to it is through our triple friendship, both quickening and steadying me as I venture forth, barehanded and badly shod, on very thin ice! Your letter today came in the same mail as one from Geddes, the first to reach us since he has been in battle. He is now in Italy and writes: "I celebrated my birthday (5 July) by coming as close to getting killed as I want to be. I felt the machine gun bullets passing my shoulder; two of my buddies were hit . . . It's a great life if you like excitement. At the first I had six hours sleep for as many days and exerting myself physically to boot. I got a little tired toward the end . . . I just had my first bath and hot meal since we started to play for keeps." Just in case you should be anywhere near his unit I will give you his address: Pfc Geddes Mumford, Co. L, 363 Inf.; A.P.O 91; P.M. New York. With you so far away, I feel as if I must get back into harness again and begin some serious work; my much needed vacation has done its good work, and I am ready to carry on again. I am glad that you are scheduled to return in September, and come hell or high water, we must somehow arrange to meet. It is always a safe bet to call up Harcourt if you are in New York; as they will know my whereabouts when I am in town. Affectionate good wishes and all good luck.

> Ever yours
> Lewis

> [handwritten]
> Amenia, New York
> 12 October 1944

Dear Harry:

The happy news of your safe return last Monday was followed the next day by another kind of announcement: Geddes has been reported missing since September 13. Knowing him, we have only the slimmest hopes that he may still be alive. You, dear Harry, are almost the only person we could now bear to see: but if you *can* come you will be thrice welcome. I didn't want you to come here unprepared for the blow that has fallen on us.

> Affectionately
> Lewis

> [handwritten]
> Amenia, New York
> 18 October 1944

Dear Harry:

Our uncertainty is over: Geddes was killed in action on 13 September, in Italy.

> Lewis

> [typed]
> Amenia, New York
> 20 October 1944

Dearest Harry, dearest and most loving of friends:

Your letter yesterday was the only one that brought us any sort of consolation, not because it erased our grief, but because it truly participated in it and even deepened it, if that were possible.[26] What you saw in Geddes is what we saw; what you

---

26. Murray's letter of condolence cannot be located in either the Papers of Henry A. Murray or the Lewis Mumford Collection.

had no opportunity to see was something that made his death even more terrible: the inner mastery the last year had brought him, which we noted in his bearing and in his eyes when he came to us at Stanford last January, and which came forth once more in the letters he wrote us both before and after he went into combat. The Ishmael and the Ahab in him, that had once seemed to promise only ultimate defeat, if not doom, had been mastered by an angel of light: approaching life from the dark end, from the moment of his birth when he refused food, he at last had come to the end of the tunnel and had found sunlight, too; he was at the end equal to anything that life or death could offer, mature and whole as few of us are ever mature and whole. Two years ago he asked our permission to join the Marines and we had refused; he had asked out of despair, out of self-distrust, because his life, in spite of himself, had become snarled; and if he had gone into battle then he would have been driven toward a goal he desired: death. But the series of choices that brought him so quickly into combat this year were of a different nature: what he sought was a post that could use his utmost skill and mastery, his highest intensity of life. He had no intention of dying; he was closer to it than he wanted to be on his birthday; and in response to my plea he wrote a description of his first six days of combat which, in its spartan brevity of detail, brought the pain and the horror, the daily pain, the daily horror of the soldier's life closer than any more labored accounts I have read. He was eager for life, gravely eager for all that it would still hold for him; but that did not swerve him from the fullest use of his present hour: in August, he got himself transferred from his post in Headquarters Company to that of the first scout in a line company. That satisfied him: "the transfer," he wrote us, "seems to have changed my luck"; the work was something for which all his young life had trained him, going alone, ahead of his squad, ahead of his company, the foremost feeler in the advance movement, to spot out danger and perhaps draw the enemy's fire. There was neither insensibility nor bravado in that choice; he had found his place in the army as he had found himself even before this. Nor was it lack of ambition that kept him from attempting an officership; he had decided for himself, he told us, that he would get out of the army in a higher rank than private first class; but since those that got advancement easiest on this side were those who curried favor with their officers and made themselves conspicuous in little ways, he had decided to master every part of his art so that, in battle, he would demonstrate his skill and eventually have a post of responsibility thrust on him. There was no uncertainty or drifting in his course: he had faced the chances of death before he left these shores and had put it out of his mind. On this matter, he was more manful than we dared to be; a few weeks before leaving Oregon he wrote us: ". . . Anyhow, this looks to me like the real thing. Those knives and short bayonets aren't for training. I however wish you (especially you mother) would stop worrying about it all. My training as a soldier is plentifully sufficient for me. It might have stood some city bred lad a little short but I'm sure I know at least as much, if not more, than most of the riflemen here. . . . You would do better to be happy that you, I, and all of us are alive than to be worried about the day when one of us is dead. To me death is a thing to be left alone. It comes when it is least expected and there are no ifs and buts about it. Once it has happened, nothing could have stopped it." He was deeply moved by the death and mutilation of his comrades; touched to the quick by the death of his boyhood friend John, who was killed in an air crash just three weeks before he was; they had fished and hunted together since they were five and had known each other since Geddes was but a year old. He knew what fear was too; he acknowledged it; and he mastered it: "I can still laugh," he assured us, "ten minutes after a barrage."

Knowing Geddes, neither of us had any other thought at the moment he was reported missing than that he had met his death: the thought of his being taken a prisoner never entered our mind any more than I am sure it entered his. That is why, my truest of friends, we took such deep comfort in your letter: for you did not seek to utter a word of hope until you had fully faced the essential fact about Geddes that made such hope improbable. For a day or two last week we outwardly responded to the solicitude and the advice of our friends; we sought aid in Washington for a quicker routing of a report on his whereabouts, we asked the Red Cross to search out if he were a prisoner; we did this out of a loyalty to him, not to comfort ourselves; it was for his sake, should he still stand in need our help, that we found out how to send food packages to prisoners of war. But in our hearts we knew what you knew: he was dead, though those same hearts betrayed us in fantasy by conjuring miracles and putting words of welcome and rejoicing on the tongues that were otherwise silent. We have a long passage of grief to live with before we can summon up in ourselves the same love and devotion by which he finally lived. Our grief is not grief at separation; we had weaned ourselves from him so that he might stand firmly on his own, as Sophy had once weaned him from the breast. To fulfill himself that separation was necessary. What is intolerable is the thought that the vitality, the intensity of life that was his, should not have continued to grow and to flower: that he is never to give the girl he would have loved his strength and his tenderness; that no children have issued from his loins; that the pulp of our own diminishing lives remains, while the fruit of his young life has been plucked before it had fully ripened. What you said about Josephine, Harry, echoed a thought in my own mind: after the war, the difference in their ages would have been reversed; our secret hopes might then have flowered into reality.

There are letters of Geddes's here that we want you to read and that you will want to read; though they are scarcely necessary to deepen your insight into him: they will only confirm it. You stand closer to us, Harry, than anyone else in the world; and that will sustain us, if any human aid can, in the long dark pilgrimage which will, I trust, eventually lead us out into the world again, fortified, ready to do for those who return, for the sons and daughters the dead have left behind, what we can never do for our own son.

> In deepest affection
> Sophia & Lewis

[handwritten]
Amenia, New York
22 October 1944

Dear, dear Harry:

Two letters are waiting for you in Washington. The first was a note written Tuesday to tell you that our waiting is ended: our dear son was killed in action on 13 September. The second was a longer letter to tell you that you—you alone, dearest Harry, found the only words close enough to our heart to be worthy of the precious spirit, the daring and resolute youth, who was lost, not just to ourselves, but to the world he gravely loved. We are lonely, not just for his presence, but for the lack of those who could understand his presence or could sufficiently respect the valor that thousands like him have shown. That is why we turn, with ever deeper gratitude, to you. If you can spare us a day or even a night and only part of a day, we would by that fact feel closer to Geddes again, through your ability to share & embrace our love in our grief. [. . .]

Phone or wire in advance: we will meet you at the station.

Affectionately

Lewis

[handwritten]
Harvard University
Psychological Clinic
64 Plympton Street
Cambridge, Mass. [crossed out]
[LM] Ans 29 Oct 44

Dear Lewis:

I am *so* disappointed. I thought my plans were bullet-proof, but I hadn't counted on the necessary military formalities of reporting to the N.Y. Headquarters & giving an account of my activities. I have been on a recruiting trip & according to the rules I must hand in a record on each man approached—I shall try again.

I have been thinking of having a bust made of Geddes's head. What do you think of the possibility of Alice's doing it from photographs and memories. Is there anyone else capable of it?

Just in case you might be interested we are looking for someone who would interview men from overseas who have executed particularly hazardous missions (more or less single-handed). The aims being: (1) To show them that we are interested in and appreciative of what they have done; (2) To record their experiences & psychological reactions for the history of the OSS that is being written (the question of publication is still unsettled) & (3) To decide whether they are fit for other assignments in the Far East. We might do this together under unusually favorable circumstances for several months & thus get an intimate knowledge of a sample of American youth—the effect of war upon their views and aspirations, etc.

I assume that you have other undertakings—more important ones—in mind, & so I will not urge you. Besides, our own plans are still tentative.

Alfred Cohn, whom I saw yesterday, was much saddened by hearing of your misfortune—

Personally I am so proud to have known Geddes—and now my brave beloved Sophy & Lewis, we must so live & speak as never to break faith with the spirit which he exemplified.

Affectionately
Harry

[handwritten]
Sunday, Oct 29

Dear Lewis,

I did not receive your immediate open-hearted generous answer to my letter until I returned to Washington & by a peculiar accident—reminiscent of the letter slipped under the carpet in Tess of the D'Ubervilles—I did not find your letter to the Hotel Westbury until I looked into a nondescript brown envelope in my brief-case on the train to Philadelphia. (The hotel, it seems, makes a practice of putting their guests' mail in brown envelopes which are placed without a word on the bureaus.) I had paid no attention to it thinking it was something of Jo's & later, packing in a great hurry after she had left, I threw it with a mass of papers into my bag. If I had received it earlier & known that my visit would have been as welcome to you as it seemed necessary to me I might have telephoned to Washington & received permission to extend my absence beyond the allotted time. As I wrote you I was on a recruiting trip—with instructions to persuade half a dozen psychiatrists & psychologists that they were needed in Washington—& as I hadn't seen my family or Christiana for almost 3 months I had to squeeze in several short visits along the way but I was confident that nothing would interfere with my day in Amenia—

I appreciate tremendously your writing me of Geddes in some detail, including those telling extracts from his letters. They will stay with me for a long time—perhaps you can tell me more when we meet so that the image of him, and all that he embodied, will be still clearer, and so stand as a needed symbol of American promise. After you and Sophy have considered the possibility of a head in bronze, let me know what you decide.

I wish to tell you more about the job in Washington if you are interested. Your part in it might be postponed until January, & you might take it as a half-time assignment. Plans are as yet indefinite, but it seems important to give these returning young men a sense of the significance of what they have done, and to record their state of mind at this crucial point in our history—

My best love to you three
Yrs Harry

[typed]
Amenia, New York
29 October 1944

Dear Harry:

Your telephone call came on a day when we had reached one of the lowest depths of the many deeps we have been exploring these last three weeks: I am sorry we could not muster a better answer or put on a braver front. But on that day the first bundle of undelivered letters to Geddes had come back, with a postmark dated October sixth by which time, on the other side, his death had been checked; and somehow these letters put an end to all those little wayward fantasies of hope that kept trying to find a crevice to lodge in, at some point where the solid wall of rational conviction was weak. Two or three times before I have faced the imminent possibility of the death of one's beloved, the first time when Geddes himself was just a little over three: you can easily recollect the terrible forebodings of those moments, from your own experience last fall, dear Harry: but the reality is infinitely worse than the imagination lets one picture.

Yes: those letters put an end to hope; but hope, which is only life refusing to admit the fact that it is vanquished, cannot be altogether quenched even by demonstrable finality: in unguarded moments I find myself welcoming Geddes back, conjuring up the necessary series of miracles that would lead to his return. Yet when I look back over his letters, I know that he was infinitely better prepared to face death than most of us are: little though he relished the thought, he had made his peace with it before he left for the other side; and he had no more intention of dying than of being taken prisoner. Yet every move that he made hastened this final event: he refused the three weeks of grace offered inductees and demanded to be taken in the current batch; he alone of his company at Camp Roberts was sent to the 91 Division, at his special request, because it had been on the point of going overseas for almost a year; and finally, when he was transferred from a communications company to a line company, and took on the lonely job of first scout, he felt that his luck was at last *with* him, albeit he knew that part of his job, in every advance, was to draw enemy fire.

Certainly he wanted to go on living; for the army had helped him to master himself, and he had achieved a quiet self-confidence that went with his inner discipline: the Ahab in him had submitted to a benigner master; so that the fears I originally had had for a tragic ending to such a turbulent spirit had been replaced by a confidence that thenceforward he would be victor, not victim. But above all, he put all his life into every moment of the present: in that sense, every part of his life had been lived unconditionally; and that is what makes him and the thousands like him a pattern for those of us who are left behind.

It is a dear and generous thought of yours, dear Harry, to think of having Geddes's head done in sculpture; but I don't think it can be done. Good work of that kind, of which the Lachaise torso of Christiana is a supreme example, is the product of a living contact. Study and memory could do something, love could do even more, to recapture the spirit behind that face; but unless the impulse came spontaneously from Alice, without the faintest prompting from the outside, the result would be worthless; and I fear her own attitude is too tangled here to let her generous instincts have free play. She has never been able to accept Sophy in the sense that Sophy has, with utmost generosity, accepted her; even with the adoption of her own two children, she never spontaneously has asked after Alison or Geddes; though we have been in correspondence more frequently this last year than at any time since 1937, and though she has reached a certain kind of tranquility and stability, both in her family and in the civic work she is doing. As for anyone else being able to do a head, I think it is out of the question: it might be very good sculpture, but it would still be a mockery. Before the winter is over I shall try a different kind of portrait in the medium of words, for our family record, if not for publication; and I only pray that I can make it as lean as severe and soldierlike as his own prose.

As for the possibility of work together, dear Harry, you don't know what conflicts that thought aroused in my bosom. To share your work and gather strength from your strength would be a great event in my life, and would add much to the debt I already owe you. But mature consideration makes me realize that you need another kind of person to help you with those interviews, some one both more passive and more extroverted, who would be able to put down the results swiftly and limpidly. That is not my forte: there are many people otherwise possessed of much less literary and psychological talent than I have who would be far more useful in such a job: people like those who have done reportorial jobs for the New Yorker. My own limitations here, deepened by a lifetime of solitary work, done at my own pace, are too deeply bitten to be overcome by any voluntary effort. But again I thank you for the thought itself.

At the moment, my teeth are infected and I shall probably have to have the entire upper set removed. That thought makes me patient with the fact that we probably won't meet for yet a while: toothlessness even without depression is nothing to thrust on one's friends, if only because it makes conversation but a painful mumble. Sophy's sorrow and her courage have both been magnificent: it was from her that Geddes got his dauntless spirit and his unqualified integrity.

> Affectionately
> Lewis

[handwritten]
Sunday
[LM] 26 November 44

Dear Lewis:

Our last two letters crossed in the mail but I have assumed that you would take it for granted that I understood why it was impossible for you to come down here this winter to do a piece of work for the government with me.

Since writing I have been out of town most of the time, involved in a hundred and one administrative details. Now I am just beginning the actual work. The men from Italy have not come home yet—all those I have seen so far are from France or Africa. They—those from France—belonged to a very successful unit of paratroopers & have retained throughout a rather high *esprit de corps*. The one universal attitude is that of diminishing the significance of their own achievements (a mixture of self-debunking and British understatement) & yet displaying a good deal of self-assurance, if not cockiness. The creative impulse takes the form of wit, jokes and vivid slang. They have been doing deeds of heroism without the words that might give meaning to such deeds. In the past one often encountered glowing words without commensurate deeds. This is the reverse. I am inclined to believe that the idealism is repressed—the conscious pose being that action speaks for itself, & only the primary motives—to eat & fornicate—are real and manly. Group solidarity is a tremendously important factor. I am inclined to think that one of the reasons why *Freedom*—the word—did not excite this generation is that they had more of it than they could digest comfortably. They had been brought up as free atoms, & what they lacked was social cohesion. They felt powerless as individuals. Perhaps the forces today are pressure-groups of one sort or another. The separate individual can be disregarded. Not an agreeable notion to me.

You and Sophy are forever in my thoughts. There is a faint possibility that I can get to New York for a day within the next three weeks when Josephine leaves for overseas. Will let you know.

Affectionately
Harry

[typed]
Amenia, New York
30 November 1944

Dear Harry:

I could have written you again even before your letter of Sunday came; but we were living—and still live—through a period of Melvillian grief and gloom whose contents were as painful to describe as they were to experience, or almost so. This is my first experience of a deep and irreparable grief brought on by death; and no matter how active one's imagination has been, one is unprepared for it; for the reality cuts much deeper than any preliminary anxiety. Geddes's death has brought a sort of Day of Judgment into our own lives; and it has made us review our past lives as well to discuss their future in new terms. Though I share my own sense of incapacity and guilt with my whole generation, that does not make the burden any easier: what we have demanded of the young, in the way of courage and devotion, may eventually regenerate our society; but that necessity would not have been so terrible and its results would have not been so chancy had we, collectively, brought into our lives a moiety of the discipline and the selfless effort that the situation has finally demanded of them. Your description of the paratroopers tallies with all I learned, first from Geddes, and since then from a half a dozen soldiers scattered as widely across the map as New Guinea. Even the most sensitive and intelligent of them, like Leonard Eaton, a Williams lad who wrote a very able thesis about my own work a couple of years ago, do not understand their part in war in terms of any rational purpose; pushed for a reason, they fall back on something the generation in the thirties seemed to lack, a deep faith in "home and country," a very solid reason indeed in a mere war of survival, but one which of course does not differ from that of our enemies, who are also defending "blood and soil." In one sense, however, they are justified, these young soldiers; spiritually, their generation had no acceptable symbols and no realizable purposes, so they found themselves at rock-bottom and have had to create anew the very soil before they could proceed to cultivate it. The purposes they cannot make real for themselves as part of an international attempt to put down evil and establish justice, they can and do realize through the very loyalties that fighting together establishes: "I have never met a front-line soldier," Geddes wrote, "who would not share his last cigarettes or his last dollar with another man." The war has made them discover the realities of our social existence, namely, that there is no possibility of any individual development without participation in a social group: every attempt to make the personal life a thing in itself is by nature parasitic, and as is the case with a fungus, parasitic upon decay. So these young men have found in the army something that their civilian existence has lacked: the ability to share unconditionally in the life of their fellow men as the very condition of their own survival. This in turn has already given rise to a loyalty far above any mere trivial requirements: think of the number of instances that have been reported of men sticking by a trapped buddy in a plane and refusing to use their own parachutes to seek safety at the cost of deserting him. Already these soldiers have established, or rather re-established, the two ultimate poles in human existence: the sheer will to live which characterizes what Bergson calls a closed society, a will whose very existence was denied in the Thirties by the fatuous "Oxford oath"; and at the other extreme, a will-to-transcend the animal necessities of existence which enables them to do their duty, and sometimes a thousandfold more than their duty, as only the saints and martyrs of the world have ever tried to do it.[27] The difficulty for these men, when they return to civilian life, will be to fill in the middle region of conduct by works and interests that will not betray or corrode all that they have learned at the extremes of life. The other difficulty will be to keep alive, without the pressure of immediate necessity, the capacity for disciplined co-operation they have formed, and apply this to the task of creating a society alert to combat evil and injustice before they have become too monstrous to be avoided.

Before Geddes was killed I had planned this fall to write a little book addressed

---

27. Oxford Oath: the 1933 resolution by the students of the Oxford Union *not* to fight for king and country.

to the returning soldier: to give him a sense of what had happened to make his own effort necessary and what still remained to be done, if that effort was not, like that which had been made in the last war, to be frittered away. Geddes felt that this was one of my main jobs; and now that he is dead, his words have become, in a special sense, a trust to be fulfilled. My energies are too fully drained away at the moment to enable me to do the job at once; but the misfortunes and miscalculations that are prolonging the war in Europe make it sure that even if I don't write the book till next spring, it will be out in good time; and that is my first task, before I go on to outline Volume IV.

. . . . Most of my infected teeth have now been removed; and I trust that they will be replaced in time for our meeting, dear Harry, so that if it takes place conversation need not be too one sided; though maybe half a jaw will be better than none. What is this about Josephine going overseas? We hadn't known she had prepared for that task. Tell us more about it if you can spare a moment. Meanwhile, in harmony with my Melvillian mood, I have been reading Sedgwick's critical analysis of Melville: a work that seems deeply sympathetic toward him and what he was and stood for, deeply appreciative of his religious sense, and yet somehow it gives me an impression of his being at one remove from Melville as even the best of academic minds is always at one remove or more from the creative minds.[28] He has tried hard to establish difference between my treatment of Melville's literary work and his own; yet, when all is said and done, his own exposition only pushes farther, in his own particular philosophic dialect, along the main line I laid down. Sedgwick has wisely evaded all the acute biographical problems; but then, so must everyone, dear Harry, till your release from the war gives you the opportunity to bring your own work on H.M. to completion. I hope that comes early in your postwar calendar.

> With warmest greetings from us both
> Lewis
>
> [handwritten]
> Box 2605
> Washington D.C.

Dear Lewis:

   At last, at last, I have a chance to talk to you. Your letter, the only one of the fifty that I really wanted to answer, has been put on the side, time & time again, because "that letter requires 2 or 3 hours and I have only 40 minutes at my disposal," etc., etc. You and Sophy have been constantly in my thoughts in many guises—best friends, creators of the future, brave sufferers—but my own life, consisting of more

---

28. William E. Sedgwick, *Herman Melville: The Tragedy of Mind* (1944).

duties than I could accomplish in the time allotted, has run along on the surface with only occasional opportunities to dive below.

As you know I have been interviewing returnees from all parts of the world—enlisted men, officers and civilians—trying to understand the situation in this & that distant place, sizing up each man's character & what the war has done to him, & ending with a recommendation as to his further usefulness. I have put together a little memo based on these interviews & on my observations in England & France, & what I have read in "Yank" & in "Stars & Stripes," etc. I have called it the G.I. Mind. I shall draw a picture of it on the other side on this sheet. It is not a very inviting picture, but I think desirable changes will take place after the war provided the returning veterans are appreciatively received and find jobs open to them & their great heroism is commemorated.

The GI's have a culture all their own—the Joe culture—opposed to that of the officers who represent the official army. The virtues of the Joe culture on the positive side are goodwill, loyalty to the unit (sticking by each other) humor & courage, and on the negative side are numerous exhibitions of individuality and dissatisfaction with regimentation & army life in general—attempts to beat the system, in any case to gripe about everything. Time perspective & space perspective are greatly shortened. They are not interested in the future (except getting a job when they get home) & not interested in anything that goes on outside their sector. They hate every country they visit and criticize the inhabitant, especially on a material basis—absence of plumbing & a variety of other comforts, & yet despite all this they show endless fortitude. They won't realize until afterwards the full magnitude of their accomplishments. They have been the best cared for army in the history of the world—the best paid, best clothed, best equipped, best armed, best supplied, best housed, best protected and treated medically, best entertained & possibly, on the whole, the best led—certainly the best trained. For the first time, almost, there is no just criticism that can be levelled at the higher-ups—Roosevelt, Marshall, Stimson, Patterson, Somerwell, Eisenhower—have all been superbly intelligent it seems to me—particularly when you consider their problem—building a force of 11,000,000 out of young citizens who didn't feel like fighting. Personally I find these GIs least appealing on 2 points (a) they are completely irreverent—respect nothing or nobody in any country they visit, and (b) they have a great aversion to ideas and ideologies, they avoid discussions, they distrust words. All this goes for a kind of decerebrate sincerity—behavior without principles or without passions, but in the right direction, & unpretentious & on the whole generous. What they have found in the army—the force that keeps them going & by which they live—is unit affiliation & brotherhood. It is worth much more to them than individuality & freedom. It seems to me at present that before the war the youngsters had more freedom than they could handle & so the slogan "War for Freedom" did not strike home. They had never experienced tyranny. In any event the course of the war is in many ways & by many months better for us than I had dared to expect.

Now the problem is, can we keep going and fight for an effective world organization and a good society in this country after hostilities cease.

Josephine has been in London for several months—she wrote that "the V-1s & V-2s improve one's philosophy"—and is now in Stockholm—the greatest center of intrigue in the world at the moment. Jo is working in New York finding quarters for soldiers on leave, but will soon return to the Boston City Hospital for several months of clinic work. Whereas I am about to leave for China via Egypt & India, to stay for about 3 months. I expect to be back in September. Everyone tells me that it is very disheartening to work in China, since the Chinese have become very apathetic about fighting the war and even go to great lengths to hem you in when you try to fight it for them. Every warlord is afraid (as the French capitalists were) that some rival will come out on top, or that the People will come out on top, and these fears are more pressing than their dread of and aversion to their common enemy. If we would only confine our operations to the communist areas we would accomplish more. But I shall know more about this when I return.

I have resigned—or am officially about to resign—from Harvard, but I am exerting what influence I can to have the Social Sciences put on a new and more enlightened and effective basis. Psychology and Sociology must develop together in unison and together be competent to size up and deal with complex social situations, suggest remedies, etc. I have learn't a lot this last year about the techniques of collaboration between men of thought and men of action; and instead of getting abysmally indignant and angry as I used to, I adopt tactics that have proved successful in many instances. But this is possible here because the OSS has an aim, whereas our universities have none. That is, the OSS are eager to try anything that seems likely to be of use in attaining their goal; whereas the universities having no goal—going no place slowly—do not see any reason for disquieting the entrenched disciplines.

Christiana has just returned from a day of tests at the hospital and she was pronounced Normal in all respects—blood pressure down, hemorrhages in eyes cleared up, etc.—so that we have much to be thankful for. She is studying the Hindoos & the teachings of Budda, whereas I am reading Confucius. We shall see what comes of this when it has to struggle for breath in a tidal wave of Hollywood trash, and advertising syrup & hapless gaiety. If I get an opportunity before I leave (in 2 weeks) I shall write you from a less superficial layer of my mind. This is all I am capable of in the midst of official tasks. I feel like a Zombie with a dead brain. But still I know what kind of winter you and Sophy have had.

Love to both

H

[typed]
46 College Street
Hanover, New Hampshire
4 April 1945

Dear Harry:

I came home here last night after spending a fortnight in New York, Amenia, and points between; and the sight of your letter revived me after the last weary lap of the journey; so that I am writing you this morning even before I have had a chance to assimilate all the important things you managed to say in it. Despite the fact that we spent a miserable ten days in Amenia, cold, rainy, with Sophy in bed most of the time because of bronchitis, I am now a renewed and revived man: and if I only knew the secret I would communicate it to the world, or would, at the very least, employ it as the chief key and open sesame when I finally sit down to write my book on Renewal. The nearest approach to such a description comes, of course, in James's Varieties of Religious Experience; only in my case the crisis and the conversion was an invisible one, and I cannot find a single promoting cause that would account for it—except perhaps that some green shoot within my soul was all this winter struggling toward the light and one morning, when the frost had melted and the sun shone, the shoot finally pushed upward into the light. It happened on the railroad train, going down to New York: and the change took the form of the quiet inner conviction that it was *there* and I was back in the world again. Up to that moment I had looked forward to a lecture I was to give at Cooper Union with dread: it was the first public lecture in two years, and up to a fortnight before I had been on the point of cancelling it, for a dozen good reasons, the chief of which was the erratic and violent manifestations of my heart. That psychosomatic symptom disappeared; and it has not recurred: when I was in Amenia I did as much spading in a single day as I would have done in three any time during the last five years. As I told Christiana, I shouldn't have dreamed that such a complete inner transformation could have been brought about by anything except the return of young Geddes. But there you are. The change has taken place. And though nothing has gone right this last fortnight, except the two lectures I gave and the garden I planted, in my inner life nothing has gone wrong: I am poised and ready for whatever life has to offer. If I had decided not to go to England this summer a month ago the decision would have been the result of sheer cowardice, an inability to take it; now I could go, if the call seemed urgent, or stay, and in either case it would have been the result of sheer cowardice, an inability to take it; now I could go, if the call seemed urgent, or stay, and in either case it would be a free decision; and as a matter of fact, I have decided to stay, for I cannot afford to spend two summers in Europe, and if I go in 1946 I may have a chance to go to Sweden, too, where The Condition of Man is going to be published, in addition to the first two books in the series. Now that I am well I look back with chagrin to all the silly excuses I gave you for the last six months; nevertheless, though my reasons were bad, my instincts were right: to have postponed the experience of the last eight months would have been perilous, far more so than going through to the bitter end of it; and I would have broken down completely on the task, probably before a week or two were past; for I needed every ounce of energy for sheer self-preservation. Your reports about the fighting men who passed before your eyes check with my own observations of students, in the main; though I wonder how much the distance these men feel between themselves and the countries they have been quartered in is due to the fact that they are aviators, and are perhaps a little remoter, a little more in the position of an aristocratic spectator, than the infantrymen are? Also these people come more largely from the comfortable middle class, do they not, with suburban backgrounds and country club expectations; whereas the infantrymen are a more representative cross section of the country; and many of them come from farms and villages where the sanitary facilities, for example, are as inadequate as they are in England, or even Yugoslavia.

As for the disbelief in the word, is that not the nemesis of our dishonorable use of the word in advertising and publicity, on the radio and in the newspapers: people whose whole lives are deluged with words must become impervious to them perhaps, if they are not to be overcrowded, to use Sheldon's term, with unusable stimuli. That is one part of the picture. The other is that our civilization itself, particularly our pragmatic educators, have dishonored the word: the semantic debunking that Stuart Chase has been the popular exponent of, has gone far in our schools, and the role of the word, as the expresser of feeling, emotion, wish and purpose, has been steadily constricted, with a corresponding apathy toward the fields of interest from which they issue.[29] This, in turn, is part of the dissociation of emotion from rational thought that has been regarded as the very criterion of good thinking, not merely by logical positivists, but by the entire teaching profession, with few exceptions. One of my many soldier correspondents is a young Williams graduate, Leonard Eaton, who is now in Italy; I got to know him originally because he wrote a very discerning and able paper on my work, as his graduation thesis. In spite of the fact that he had read me closely and apparently with sympathy, he wrote me from Italy that it was only after he had been under fire, particularly of mortar shells, that he actually found himself hating the enemy; he was a little worried about this, and felt that he was in the way of sin! My answer, of course, was that the least reasonable moment to hate our enemy was when he was standing up and fighting on even terms: that the time to have hated him with all one's heart was when we had learned about the savage treatment of political prisoners of the extermination camps and that the failure to hate evil at that moment was his real sin. Plato has a fine passage on this in The Laws, which I quoted. But our system of education—and this lad is an exceptionally fine example of it at its best—has tried to

29. Stuart Chase, one of the founding members, along with Mumford, of the Regional Planning Association of America; author of *The Tyranny of Words* (1938).

eschew, or rather extirpate, all but the more seemly or the more trivial emotions: we have ignored the necessary role of hate and fear, and thus have kept them from being focussed on appropriate objects. I have little doubt that this anesthesia has been responsible for not a few war neuroses, for who can face the terrible ordeals of battle without the mobilized support of his emotions. One of the few comforts I have about Geddes's death is that he knew what he was fighting for and went out of his way to get close to the enemy and kill him; he loved and hated heartily, and probably was unpopular with his teachers for the same underlying reason: for our teaching at all its levels, has been attempting to eviscerate and de-emotionalize the human personality, as the pedagogic alternative to bringing all its areas under discipline and purposive direction. How right you are, dear Harry, about the purposelessness of the university! The blind professors who resist the notion of any unified objectives in teaching are, of course, preparing the way for the "terrible simplifiers," and those who will reintroduce purpose in archaic patterns, like Hutchins and the St John's crew.[30] Tresidder, the president of Stanford, sees our present weakness in the universities, in all of them, much clearer than anyone else I knew; but he is at loss to find professors who are capable of teaching in any other fashion; and he understands completely why, for lack of sympathetic colleagues, I will not easily be drawn back into university life. . . . One more point that you mention: the need for unit affiliation and brotherhood, as opposed to individuality and freedom. As long as the soldier remains in the war situation is this not a salutary response as well as an inevitable adaptation: for whatever margin of individuality and freedom may remain must be of a private nature, jealously guarded and hidden, as I am sure it is in those who had any of this to start with. Moreover, in a society burdened by the anonymity and impersonality as ours is, in which respect the military machine is only of the same order as the factory or business regime, it seems to me that the need for brotherhood is a paramount one: this is precisely what it means, I believe, in a religious sense, to be "saved." In our world, as in the classic world, to be saved means to be rescued from an inhuman slavery and an impersonal organization and restored to brotherhood in a group small enough to be known and extensive enough to make one at home wherever one travels if one wears the uniform. I remember what Geddes, that most resolute of individualists, said about the value of the army: you could line up four million soldiers on one side, and four million soldiers on the other, and the men who faced each other, no matter where they had come from, would still have something to say to each other and would understand each other, which would be unthinkable if they were civilians—unless by accident. It is the same kind of ritual and discipline out of which the missionary religions, Mithraism, Christianity, Mohammedanism, are made; and the best reason for Uni-

---

30. As president of the University of Chicago, Robert M. Hutchins, assisted by Mortimer Adler, established an undergraduate curriculum emphasizing the "great books" during the early 1930s; St. John's College adopted a similar curriculum in 1937.

versal service, apart from its military aspects, would be that it would create such an improvised church as a first, step, perhaps, to a more spiritual bond.

When I have combed through your letter a few times more, dear Harry, I'll doubtless have other thoughts; but enough for this morning. Your new adventure to China fills me with awe, and perhaps with a sense of guilt, too; for I will never be reconciled to the fact that I, who was so completely immersed in the anxious preliminaries to this war, have had absolutely nothing to do with its actual development: I accept reluctantly it as one of the ironic dispensations of fate; and the only thing that keeps me from having an utter feeling of sterility and remoteness is Geddes's death. Incidentally, I finally finished the long series of verses—I cannot call it a poem—I was working on last winter; and it will be published presently in Twice a Year.[31]

You have been very close to me all these months, dear Harry; and the further you fly away, so to say, the closer you will be. I am delighted about the good news of your Josephine. Sophy and I both embrace you.

Lewis

[handwritten]
New York, May 22
[LM] 17 June 45

Dear Lewis:

I find that I have one day to myself between closing up my transactions with one hemisphere and taking to the air for another. Writing to you seems the most natural thing to do on a free day. You would never guess it; I have had so few of them. All the other transients are griping about the fact that "there's nothing to do round this goddam post," but when there is nothing to do, then is the time I become most active—in a rewarding way the shows that pass before my inner eye are much more engaging than those in the movie houses. I seem to be the only man in the AUS who not only can accommodate himself readily to delays in passage but finds them positively inviting.[32]

I rejoice at your renewal—foresaw it for this spring, having experienced it several times myself—once when the whole cycle occurred within twenty-four hours at and after the death of a lovely young Irish maid we had, whom I took to the hospital and cared for night & day during the influenza epidemic of 1918–19.[33] I became her during her illness, a death rattle developed in my throat, I was in the

31. Lewis Mumford, "Admonition to Those Bereaved in War," *Twice a Year* 12–13 (Spring–Summer, Fall–Winter 1945): 353–56.

32. AUS: Army of the United States.

33. This was Alice Henry, interestingly bearing the same name as a hospitalized prostitute Murray observed while in medical school and for whom he also experienced a "strange attraction" (see Robinson, *Love's Story Told*, 63–66, 77–78).

valley of death for a night, & then suddenly the next day I was possessed by an immense exaltation. It was as if I had experienced all the possible pains, discomforts, anxieties & neglects that patients—that is, the sick—have had to suffer since the beginning of time, and knowing all this inwardly, I could now be like a great rock in a weary land, a tireless source of strength & consolation to every patient that came to me in the future. The great thema is that of Death & Resurrection—the death of a beloved being, or a profound melancholy, or extreme pain as a necessary overpowering first phase which may last months or even years, & then the reaction, creative power & exuberance coming out of grief. Pregnancy—the inward turning & withdrawal, the labor & the pain—& then the birth, a new life, hive of potentialities. Sheer contrast is one fundamental element: no man thrills gratefully with health who has never been sick. I had an intense, though limited, experience of affectionately, thankfully and understandingly embracing the whole world after morphine had relieved the pain of passing a kidney stone. Everybody appeared lovely to my sight—stranger, acquaintances to whom I had previously felt neutral, nurses & doctors—I talked like a God. When it involves the death of a dearly respected person then the true resurrection does not occur until the virtue of the departed one has been incorporated into your own being—so that you in your heart represent the best of what has been lost. The totem feast—at which members of the tribe partook of the body & blood of the dead God—is the symbol—is it not?—first mourning (Good Friday), then eating (Saturday), then rejoicing (Easter Sunday). And Xmas is similar. It is exuberance at the discovery that the light of heaven is not going out forever—the days have stopped getting shorter (blacker), they are getting longer. As new year, new sun, new God (Christ-child), new life has been born—Delight in it, even though it will not warm & fertilize you until spring, so that you can bear fruit in the fall. Read Strachey's mean & cynical treatment of this experience as it occurred at the grave of Cardinal Manning's wife. Perhaps you remember it in *Eminent Victorians.* There is no key to the renewal as such. It just happens as a gift of Nature, evidence of the abundant fertility of the universe, the quenchless spirit of man. Such key as there is resides in the depth and sincerity and sympathy and solitary singlemindedness with which, in your grief, you relive the life and feelings, extract & absorb the virtues, and experience the difficulties and frustrations of the one for whose physical presence you will never cease to crave. Out of this comes the tragic sense of life, knowledge of the basic human situation, and without this, how can anyone say anything that is profoundly true? The future hangs to a large extent on your creativeness—I mean our American future for this and succeeding generations. What is going to become of this country? When I return in the Fall I shall want to talk at length with you about many things—among others the mind of G.I. Joe. I might say that aviators formed a very small part of the sample I examined—also, you misunderstood me in supposing that I was depreciating unit-loyalty & solidarity & fellowship. Why man, that's the force that is winning the war, the force that we civilians are trying to get along without! It's the best thing about the Army. You and Sophy have my whole trust, reverence & love.

Farewell—
Harry

[handwritten]
May 23
[LM] 17 June 45

Dear Lewis:

I did not comment on the bulk of your marvelous letter & I find that I have a little more time at my disposal.

1. It would have been a great mistake for you to have found me in Washington. I offered it as an opportunity for us to work together, for you to get to know a great variety of returned servicemen, etc., etc. What you did was wiser.

2. I am delighted to hear that Sweden is going to have the trilogy. Josephine writes glowing reports of Stockholm. It sounds like an Utopian city—no vulgar displays of riches, no extreme poverty—everyone on bicycles riding out into the outlying country to ski or sunbathe—reindeer meat for dinner, concerts. Josephine will be moving on to Norway soon. On the night of F.D.R.'s death it was as if a pall had fallen over the city. A Norwegian friend said to J: "Roosevelt was *our* President," their king was not much respected.

3. In regard to the distance between the American soldier & the notions of the countries they have lived in or fought over, I have found very few exceptions to the common attitude of distaste—least towards the French & most towards the Orientals—Arabs, Hindoos & Chinese. I may be working with a high standard, because, in my own case, I have never felt distance between me & natives in foreign countries (except in the case of Spanish-Americans), & I am a little intolerant of those who do feel superior & base this feeling on the materialistic advantages of the United States. Altogether I have heard about 10 times as much condemnation as I have heard appreciation, particularly among enlisted men. The charge of "filthiness" is very common at all levels.

4. I think you are entirely correct in your analysis of the determinants of the word-depreciation from which we are now suffering. Advertisers, politicians, sentimentalists & pseudo-scientists have been using words, for their own selfish purposes, with cynical insincerity, to Win Friends & Influence People, etc. Now, the temper of the people says: Act first & talk afterwards, or give us the facts first & generalize afterwards. In certain ways it is very healthy because it does force one to a solid base of realism. But in the meantime, Passion & the imagination are seriously impaired. There is no room for faith. Your answer to Leonard Eaton was masterful. Personally I cannot rely on the judgment of anyone who did not hate the Germans at least 4 years ago. It is odd that a generation or two after the Devil dropped out of our American philosophy, his incarnation should appear on earth,

& become powerful enough to be the cause of a 100 times more suffering than any one man has ever been responsible for. I agree to the bottom of my outraged heart that education has been busy extirpating passion & and building intellects bathed in trivial, seemly emotions. I must start packing—Your letter was full of invigorating truth. I shall read it again & again.

[handwritten]
[LM] Ans 26 Sept (1945?)

O Lewis:

What a joy it was to receive your letter soon after I reached home! It was the one thing I required to fill me to the brim with thanksgiving. On August 10 my work in China was completed & I was about to start on the long 3-week voyage home as I had come (via Calcutta, Karachi, Abidjan, Cairo, Casablanca) when General Donovan arrived & invited me to go home with him in his private plane via Manila, Guam, Kwajalein, Johnstone, Honolulu, San Francisco. So at long last I saw the Pacific & was home in 4 days (or rather 3 days since we dropped a day en route). Three hours after landing in Washington the President officially announced the truth of the rumors we had been hearing at every airport. Christiana was thriving—having been mightily sustained by your letters—and I discovered that I could get out of the Army any day (being an MD over 50). It seemed that a new era was struggling to be born. The General asked me to accompany him to Germany as a kind of psychological consultant on the question of how to present the material brought out in the trial of German War Criminals & publish it, so that it would influence German attitudes in the right direction. He is to be a prosecutor. The idea of seeing Josephine in Stockholm & Jung in Zurich & then watching the reactions of Beelzebub Goering & Co during the trials & obtaining week by week reports of German opinion obtained by systematic interviews—all this was very appealing. Is it possible for a nation as a whole to feel guilty and penitent & a need to redeem itself? Probably not. But then what happens when a people have expressed in violent action all the evil in them? Are they not ready to yield to the more humane tendencies that have been overrun or suppressed? They may be too proud to do so, while their conquerors are judging them. What can they do without losing the last residue of self-respect? Of course like Satan they can go underground and satisfy themselves spiritually with fantasies of revenge. But this time, will they? That is the question.

This problem of a whole people suffering a hangover after 10 years of Satanic possession invited my curiosity, but I refused the opportunity to examine it first hand because, for one reason, I had another job to which I was more intimately committed—writing a book about the methods used and results obtained assessing several thousand men & women over the last 20 months. For this I have lots of help—10 hard-working associates who are now grinding out statistical correlations by the hundreds. We were to be given 4 months to finish the book, but yesterday Pres. Truman suddenly announced the OSS would cease as of Oct 1. Our section is to be taken over by the Army & it remains to be seen whether the Army will see fit to retain our unit merely for the purpose of writing up our results. It is possible that I shall be out of the army shortly instead of quitting in January as I had planned. In any event I shall work to complete this job & then take several months of complete rest—thinking, reading & working on my body. Where? Mexico? New Mexico? The West Indies? My last act before taking the plane to China was to resign from Harvard—the only reason I gave being the shameful retardation of the social sciences in Cambridge. They won't accept it, they say, until I explain myself—which I am planning to do sometime next month. In the meantime, if there is any inspiration left in me, I may write a little piece on the Promise of Psychology, instigated by their skimmed-milk & porridge piece entitled General Education in a Free Society—a overly well-balanced elevatedly democratic document which might have been written in 1900 when we thought that evil was a rare thing & reason was sovereign. This book may be the best thing one has a right to expect from a committee of sequestered scholars untouched by grief or sights that freeze the marrow.

What I shall do next—after my long brood—I can not predict. I am hungry for the feelings & thoughts of our beloved Lewis & of other men standing on the brow of the potential world & of men who grappled with the problem of the universe two or three thousand years ago. I got the feel of India & of China, an identification with the climate & the people without much knowledge of the complexity of details. When I read the old books, however, a familiar atmosphere is engendered which allows me to understand the content in relation to a social structure which has persisted for centuries. Thus Indian philosophy & religion appears to me to be a system that was developed chiefly 1) to avoid inevitable frustration (there being no possibility of satisfying 80 per cent of one's natural desires) by dissociating consciousness (through concentration) from animal & worldly drives, & 2) to avoid the intolerable fact of death by starving the impulses until there is nothing but a mere semblance of life in them & the little step to death is barely perceptible & hence tolerable (to you & to others) and also by leaving family and Friends & taking to the hills, with the result that they, knowing that you are still alive & acting freely, will not break with sorrow, and when you actually do die they have become accustomed to your absence. Absorption in the All is the ultimate end which the imagination magnifies as more than a substitute for identification with the ethos of one's society. It is a withdrawal which approximates the serenity of womb-life—

I have been wrestling with the immense spiritual dilemma created by a craving to identify with the American Ethos as a whole and yet being outraged repeatedly by its prevailing trends—the profit motive that spoils everything it touches, its revolting voice as heard in advertising, the vulgar distortion of life it creates in the movies, the values that are engendered by it, etc., etc., endlessly & then the superficiality, the quick smiling pithless contacts, the attention to surfaces & the neglect of depths, the deodorized exteriors—I found hundreds of confirmations in North Africa, India & China (greatly increased) of what I observed in England & France, namely the opinion expressed by enlisted men as much as by officers that the people are *dirty* (*filthy* in the Far East). Sometimes this comes down to the fact that the women smell, but it includes living quarters, tap water, food, toilets, etc. As you suspected not many of the men come from farms (most farmers were not drafted) but from small towns all over the country. Unanimously they hate every country that they pass through or live in &, judging it solely on materialistic standards, are scornful of its ways & its achievements. I listened in on an argument in which 4 out of 5 of the men asserted that the flushed toilet was a greater contribution to civilization than all the writings of Confucius, etc., etc. But the remarkable thing is that 9,000,000 men who didn't feel like fighting have coolly and systematically gone about the business of winning the war with extraordinary fortitude. They deserve a better society than they are finding on their return. I was not disturbed by the atomic bomb. It is the logical & predictable result of the course we have been madly pursuing for a hundred years. It may help to arouse people to the desperate need for the reformation of man & of society. The world is calling for you, with me helping to bring up the materials you require. It is after midnight, I should stop. I embrace you both with bottomless affection—

Harry

[typed]
46 College Street
Hanover, New Hampshire
26 September 1945

. . . You don't know how glad your letter made me, beloved Harry. You once told me that you yourself always begin to feel a little guilty when someone doesn't answer a letter of yours: maybe it's a give away of my own monstrous egoism that first I begin to worry whether the person I've written to has been terribly ill or has undergone an accident; then after further time passes, I wonder what I have done to alienate us. When Christiana told me, in response to a note, that you were alive and extremely busy and in grand fettle, and had responded to the call of a sick friend in the Adirondacks I was immensely relieved. Her letter came yesterday morning; yours in the afternoon on top of it. And here we are in friendship's embrace once more, with nothing to spoil it or weaken it except, perhaps, my own unutterable depth of envy over the experiences you have been through.

I couldn't have followed you anywhere in the last few years, dear Harry, because I was a sick man, as I now fully realize; whatever energy I had was devoted to overcoming the effect of the illness, so as to achieve at least the appearance of a normal working routine; and the marvel, as I look back on it, is that my work didn't suffer more than it did. But adventure on any plane was out of the question. As I have told you, a deep change, psychorganic in nature, took place last spring; and the only mischief I suffer from now is that the danger signals, of a pounding heart

and unbearable fatigue, are now absent so that during the last week at Amenia—
Sophia drove me up here on Sunday—I did more work than a man who is almost
fifty should have done. Even so, though my heart has been behaving queerly again,
specially at night, I don't feel ill: I don't recognize illness as part of my being, as I
had to recognize it, or succumb completely, all during the last half dozen years.
Looking back on those years I realize they had one compensation: they gave me an
anticipatory experience of old age, the slowing down of movement, the withdraw-
ness, the prudent tapering down of experience, the resignation to death; so that,
when I finally get to writing Vol. IV, it will be with the experience of the whole life-
span as part of my consciousness.

Your own life these last few years, following on your intense inner experience
with Christiana, has probably made you too full for words, until you give yourself
time to let all your experiences settle into place by themselves. It is you, dear Harry,
who have quarried the experiences for a new world; I am at best the mere hewer of
stones, who can trim the rough surfaces and put them together; and I only wish that
half that was in you were written, or talked out, (but for the world's sake, better
written) before I begin work on Volume Four. Among my many friendly envies is
that for your firsthand contact with China and India; for I know what even six weeks
in Hawaii did for me in revealing the essence of the Polynesian consciousness of life;
and though I have pored much over the Hindu and Chinese texts this last year, in
order to come closer to their world view and the values that derive from it, I will not
feel confident of a single judgment or interpretation until I have breathed their air,
gone through the cycle of one of their days, and observed the things that no one can
ever write about. Somewhere in my book, which must look prophetically forward
to a united world—for it is either that or suicide and grim chaos—I must try to sum
up what the great civilizations have stood for in the creation of the human personality, before I try to anticipate the next emergents. That is why, perhaps, I still find myself reluctant even to begin the first draft; though I had planned to begin on it in July;
for it may be that in a year or two I will get an invitation from some Indian or Chinese University which would enable me to follow in your footsteps.

Your analysis of the basis of the Hindu religion and psychology is the most perceptive I have found anywhere. Their objective was sterile and self-defeating; but
their method was massively ingenious: which is perhaps the verdict that will finally be passed upon the polar counterpart of that effort, diminishing the self by
magnifying the outside world, that man has devoted himself to since Galileo. The
thing that I find disconcerting is to discover that some of the most intelligent minds
among us, not the best, but still quite good, are entirely unaware of the limitations
of our own culture; they regard our creation as an absolute, though their own philosophy rejects all absolutes and finalities. This lack of perspective on the highest
level finally filters down through the educational system to the soldiers you have
come to understand so well: the flush toilet has become to them, not a means but an
end, not an end but a fetich. I fear we are surrounded by fetiches we do not recog-

nize as such. There is no part of human culture that a free mind should not be able to renounce and sacrifice, in order to ensure life's own continuity. But just as we have seen starving men crave a cigarette even more than food, so our contemporaries are so enamored of their own creations that they may be willing to dethrone civilization itself, rather than give up any part of the mechanistic ritual they themselves have created.

As in your dilemma over your identification with the spirit of America, the kind of America we have produced during the last seventy-five years, dear Harry, I find myself confronted with the same feelings and the same misgivings. The America I had taken for granted till I was twenty-five and went to England, I returned to in 1920, as I returned to Sophia: they were both objects of spontaneous and freshly conscious love. No small part of my life for the next dozen years was devoted to interpreting America's past, in literature, in architecture, in painting, to show how good and lovable America had actually been; and as I got to know more of the country my love deepened, so that, even before I got to know the far West, I had come to love even the disruptive episode of pioneering, and had seen more fully into the values that had grown out of that phase. Nothing marred this consciousness; though by the time I began Technics and Civilization I realized that it was time to redress the balance; that all the others who had consciously rallied to America were making that allegiance too narrow a one. So my big series was addressed to the "world"—at least to the Western World.

The first shock to this tissue of affections and loyalties came when I published the Call to Arms and found out that the American beliefs I there took for granted, as the foundation stones of policy, were looked upon as old-fashioned and nonoperative. After that came a series of similar shocks, when I slowly came to realize that I was not in communication with my countrymen; the words I addressed to them did not reach them, first, because the radio networks and the magazines would not willingly publish them, and second, because when they managed to make themselves heard, they were not listened to and met with little response. Deep though my anxiety had been from 1938 on, the lowest moment for me came in 1942, when I confronted the profound inertia of our country then, for it was not till 1943 that we really were in the war with something like our full masculine force, and to the end, a large part of the middle classes, and a disproportionate part of the female population, were never in the war at all, either in act or spirit. Roosevelt himself incarnated all that frustrated me; he had some of the greatest qualities of our past and showed I was not wrong in my estimate of our American potentialities; but he was also slack-willed at critical moments, self-defensive and self-indulgent; so that if America did not respond promptly to Pearl Harbor, his own soothing words, his own failure to exert immediate full pressure, were partly to blame.

Now the immediate revulsion against the responsibilities the war piled on our shoulders, symbolized by Truman's brutally abrupt ending of the Lend-Lease supplies for food and our own quick return to a "fat Kitchen"—what I've just called the isolationism of the belly in a recent review—have deepened my alienation. I still love all that is permanently lovable in the American ethos, and that is much; but for the first time in my life, it is conceivable to me that I might spend the rest of my life in some other country, preferring to share the constricted lot of England, say, than to enjoy the odious ease and the fat advantage of my own country: purchased by hardening the heart, closing the ears, and concentrating upon "full production"—for ourselves.

Even the audience for my books has been changing. Judged by sales, I am not yet, like Waldo Frank, a more popular author outside my country than inside it; but my work gets more appreciation in England and Sweden than it does here, and now that the war is over Dutch, Swiss, and French publishers have been demanding the right to translate the big series, most eagerly. I am glad of that: naturally. If we are to build a common world the more books we have in common, to bind us together, the better; so I am proud to be taken in. But I don't like the difference in the quality of appreciation here and abroad. (That, however, may be a permanent experience: the proverbial prophet not without honor save. . . .)

I had hoped that the war would have a transforming effect on our fellow countrymen. In a minority, this has doubtless taken effect; but on the whole, our civilian population not merely continues to worship our old idola but believes in them more than ever; and it remains to be seen what portion of our soldiers have been deeply transformed. On that, I am eager to hear your own fullest report; though as you outline them there they seem discouraging.

There are a thousand things to discuss with you, dearest Harry; so I hail the thought that you may soon be out of the Army and be coming up here: we will count the days, all of us, whether they are weeks or months. I shall be in New York between the 20 and 26 Oct. Otherwise, our arms will be open for you at any day and at any hour.

> Affectionately
> Lewis
>
> [handwritten]
> [LM] 2 Dec 45
> Nov 15, 45

Dear Lewis:

You did not spend yourself in vain in your last letter. Every word was a gratification of one sort or another. I would have answered sooner if I had not been waiting to tell you just when I would arrive in Hanover, but at the last minute I decided not to drive up to Topsfield in my car but to wait until I could take all my belongings up with me in December. And so I took the train instead and spent a few full days in that vicinity. Among other things it turned out that resigning from Harvard was a good move. It evoked curiosity as to why anyone could willfully quit so venerable an institution & thus gave me an opportunity to say my say—that Harvard was like a dinosaur who hoped to avoid slow extinction by bathing in the lake & ridding its skin of accumulated desert dust. Of course the new Provost (Paul Buck) who is taking over a good deal of the management of the university was not given this exact image to suffer, but I put the situation in his own words & some progressive actions have already been taken. I am planning to follow it up with a little book (The Promise of Psychology) in March which will contain suggestions based on your great Trilogy. Until March 1 I shall be busy with the Assessment of Personality—for which MacMillan, Houghton Mifflin & Farrar & Rinehart are now bidding.[34] Have you strong convictions which would help us decide which of these publishers would do most for a book that should sell about 2000 copies, mostly in colleges? Farrar & Rinehart are more enthusiastic than the others, & believe that as a small firm they would push it with more vigor than would a large concern like MacMillan's for whom ours would be merely one among 150 other books on their fall list. Sooner or later you should get a copy of A Clinical Study of Sentiments by Christiana & myself.[35] Christiana is having the 2 parts bound in one volume for you & a few other friends. The first 3 Chapters are boring & pedantic, but you might enjoy the case histories & the final summing up. I finally turned down an inviting proposal from Justice Jackson & Crime Commission to go to Nuremburg to make personality studies of the 24 Super Crooks—23 since the suicide of Ley who was believed to be faking insanity.[36] (It would have afforded an opportunity to work with Russian psychiatrists.) In the meanwhile I have become all steamed up in an attempt to get the Government & the Foundations to invite a dozen Russian social scientists & a dozen British social scientists to come over here & tackle the problem of what social forces in each of these countries are standing in the way of a supernational world organization & what can be done to convert these forces. Social scientists are accustomed to international meetings at which problems are discussed objectively without rancor & they should be able to make headway, instead of blundering into one impasse after another as Truman & the pols have been doing. At the moment, however, our relations with Russia have deteriorated to the point that their Academy of Sciences is not permitted to accept any invitations for its members to visit this country, & so temporarily things are at a standstill. Of course I agree with you: It is One World or No World.

So much for recent extraversions.

You never definitely told us, beloved Lewis, how much your body had identified itself with the world anarchy, but we should have been more astute, & readier more often to share, through all these years of anxiety & trial, the burdens of your keen perceptions. More sensitive than the rest of us and more involved in the clash

---

34. Henry A. Murray, *Assessment of Men* (1948).

35. With Christiana Morgan, *A Clinical Study of Sentiments* (1945).

36. Robert H. Jackson (1892–1954), chief U.S. prosecutor at the International Military Tribunal at Nuremberg.

of social forces, you were quick to anticipate the course of events, and were more alive to the deterioration that man was undergoing. Therefore you *felt* more & thought more imaginatively & more truly & had more to suffer on your nerves than we did. Would that we had been closer to you as you made your brave way through that valley of tribulation. On the one hand we were more withdrawn in our claustery & on the other were protected by the whole systematic discipline of our quasi science which puts one somewhat on the sidelines. Even at that Christiana's blood pressure began its upward course as soon as she foresaw that the war would eventually take me off. From now on I hope we can distribute the trials as they come so that no one person will have to bear it all. You did this for me at the time of Christiana's operation & ever since—I am delighted to hear that the Big Series is being translated into several European tongues. It will go to persuade people overseas that more & more production is not the aim of all Americans & that we have a prophet here with a message for the whole earth. More power to you. I am looking forward to many long confabs in the spring & between now and then at least 2 or 3 meetings—My love to the three of you.

Yrs
Harry

[handwritten]
46 College Street
Hanover, N.H.
2 December 1945

Dear Harry:

I've been up to my neck in work these last two weeks—with my time broken by four days in N.Y. searching for new illustrations for the Dutch & French editions of The Culture of Cities: hence my tardiness in answering you. First: let me thank you for the Study of Sentiments, which came only yesterday: it's up my alley now in every way, and I am eager to get at it. As for the Assessment of Personality, I would advise you against Macmillan, for all that house's reputation: They are not merely impersonal but grasping, according to all reports. Of the three, I should prefer Farrar & Rinehart: though I wish that Harcourt or Henry Holt were also in on the bidding. You should choose a publisher whom you will want to stay with for all your books, including the Melville: it is a great loss to have one's books scattered, for that means that the publisher, if he loses on a particular book at first, loses interest entirely, and never seeks to promote your works as a whole. You might do well to put your mss in the hands of an agent If you have no time to appraise the publishers personally. I know none of them unfortunately; but would suggest Brandt and Brandt, Maxim Lieber, or young Russell, the son of A.E. I'll write again soon when I can catch my breath.

Warmly
Lewis

[typed]
Box 2601, Washington, D.C.
12 December 1945
Mr. Lewis Mumford
46 College Street
Hanover, New Hampshire

Dear Lewis:

I am going to sink into the abyss of melancholia if I do not see you before long. The months have dragged on now, and one promise of a meeting after another has met with defeat. What can we do about it? If I had known that you were going to be in New York, I might have met you there. Hanover, of course, was the target of my inclination, but I only had a short free period and the various affairs that had to be concluded in Cambridge did not give me any leeway. As it stands now I will probably not be free until the first of February, except for a few days around Christmas when I shall be in Boston. Hanover must be beautiful in the winter, and a couple of days of snow-shoeing (I am pretty shaky on skis) with you would be a great blessing; and I am hungry for the sight of Sophy, and therefore should prefer Hanover if this is possible.

I have just received a letter from Ames at the Dartmouth Eye Clinic who has been writing me off and on for three years, to announce that he has made discoveries which necessitate an entirely new orientation toward world problems.[37] I have never met him, but I understand that he was a very popular sporting fellow in college days and then suddenly turned to serious pursuits, first to painting and then to the psychology of perception. Having been used to a large measure of acclaim as a good fellow and sport (I think it was polo), he has been under-nourished as a scientist and for the last few years has been calling for acknowledgement on all sides. Lack of recognition seems to have given him a touch of paranoia, which is legitimate if you have really discovered the secret of the universe. I am very curious, therefore, to see what it is all about and discover whether he has the germ of a new philosophy or not. You never told me that you had written a new book, and that it was full of condensed richness.[38] I ran across it two weeks ago but have not yet had a chance to read it, even though it is a neat volume with contents that should be graspable in a few days reading.

Probably I will not get around to it until after February 1st when I hope to engage in a completed re-reading of Lewis Mumford, particularly the Great Series, because I am intending to make this the basis of some remarks I have to make about education when I get around to the next little volume.

Your advice as to a publisher for this present book on *Appraisal of Men* came too

---

37. Adelbert Ames Jr. (1880–1955), conducted research in physiological optics at Dartmouth; see Mumford's letter of 14 December 1945.

38. Lewis Mumford, *City Development: Studies in Disintegration and Renewal* (1945), a collection of previously published essays.

late for me to act on it, but what you said about Macmillan exactly corresponded with my own experience. I found them a Big Impersonal Institution, and was not invited by them despite their apparent desire for this book. We finally decided on Houghton Mifflin, which might be described as the Harcourt Brace of Boston. I met a very cordial fellow there named Spaulding, whose son, a paratrooper with OSS, had gone through our appraisal procedures, & who had already heard favorable news about it and so was keen to do his best with the book.

This is just a hurried note to acquaint you with the surface situation with me.

Yours,
Harry
HAM: MI

[typed]
46 College Street
Hanover, New Hampshire
14 December 1945

[. . .]

This week I began an experiment, at the initiative of the college: I have been devoting three afternoons a week to consulting with undergraduates, about whatever is uppermost in their minds, and once a week we meet for general discussions. It is a first move on my part to get nearer the younger generation: if it worked, it might pave the way to something more permanent. Even if it doesn't work, it gives me the chance to get close to some of the returning veterans, and thus to make up, in a small way, what I lost by not being able to accept your offer of collaboration. The ones I have talked to are an extraordinarily fine lot; even when their minds are not brilliant, even when four or five years of reduced intellectual vitality has actually dulled their response, or slowed them up, they have a moral sensitiveness and an internal equilibrium that more than makes up for it. They are already setting the tone in many of the classes; and perhaps the slack, country club tradition will get its first paralyzing jolt from the inside. Except on the purely intellectual level, I have little to teach them: at most I can point to the words and the expressions that will help them to greater articulateness and self-consciousness. Meanwhile, they have much to teach me.

I have known Adelbert Ames since 1930 or so; and I see him from time to time. He is, I think, a man of genius, if that description means anything: certainly, an original mind and a very fruitful experimental scientist. His polo playing days lie in the distant past; but he suffers from a double solitude, first a solitude due to the original turn his thoughts took, when he first came up here as a solitary investigator after studying optics at Clark, second, to the self-imposed solitude of a system, which has never received sufficient criticism from the outside, and which, in his loneliness, has now crystallized beyond the possibility of anyone's making a significant change in it. (Fundamentally, though not superficially, he bears many resemblances to old Geddes: in him I feel the same impenetrability, the same demand to be taken over as a whole, and the same pathos of self-frustration.)

I will not describe his researches to you; he is more than capable of demonstrating them to you; and you probably know that he discovered a radical defect in vision that the medical men had never even diagnosed before: aniseikonia—the basis of the Dartmouth Eye Clinic's special fame. What he has done is to establish experimental evidence for the interpretation of "external reality" offered by the subjective idealists, from Berkeley through Kant and on to Mach and Karl Pearson. His system is really a radical empiricism, and to that extent it gives a more refined account of experience than James himself was able to give: at many points he is close to Whitehead, too. He has, I think, undermined the notion that sense-data are in any sense ultimate or neutral: he demonstrates the way in which the "purest" sensation is interpreted by the organism in terms of its own needs. On these levels his work seems to me brilliant and effective.

The difficulty is that he uses two fundamental terms, "purpose" and "value" in a special way of his own. I think he shows that purpose and value both have their origins far below their conscious levels of formulation and action: ultimately, he ties together the original nature of the organism, as being purposeful and valueful, with the ultimate goals of the personality: a splendid piece of unification, if validated. But his use of these terms is ambiguous; and he finally tends to make the reality of all experience a mere function of human purpose and value. I am doing him an injustice in attempting too briefly to point out its weaknesses. Part of what he says is extremely important, and his experimental findings may well prove outstanding in the annals of experimental psychology. But he has gone over the same ground so often, and has so indelibly established his own categories, that it is hard to get him to deal with one's objections or qualifications.

As for his belief that these discoveries necessitate a reorientation to world problems, that seems to me only the monomania of the specialist: like Korzybski's making semantics into a complete clue to human aberrations.[39] Ames's views are a valuable contribution to clear thinking: one of many. My own relations with him sadden me a little: I think he kept on hoping that I would "take" up his experiments and announce them to the world. He believes his difficulty in getting understood is due to a mere failure of communication on his part. I never let him think that I would do this, but the fact that I showed any spontaneous interest raised his hopes. He is too good a scientist to be called a crank, too much a good humored human being to be called a paranoiac; but he is absorbed in his visions, and at 65 begins to be panicky over not being able to share them.

My little book on City Development came out while you were away; so, though I sent a copy to Christiana, I omitted at the time to send one to you. It is all old work;

39. Alfred Korzybski, *Science and Sanity: An Introduction to Non-Aristotelian Systems and General Semantics* (1933).

and, by one of those ironies that fortunately amuse as much as they hurt, the book was given the respectful reception that should have been granted to The Condition of Man. (Some of the academic reviews of the latter, incidentally, have been incredibly supercilious and arrogant: one of them, in the American Historical Review, as I remember, suggested that sometime I should write the book over again, this time decently, from the reviewer's point of view!)[40]

I have spent all my time this last three months correcting proofs on Values for Survival—now in page—and going carefully through The Culture of Cities, to make minor corrections for the Dutch and French editions.[41] I should have liked to re-write the last three chapters of the latter book; for they seem to me horribly diffuse and ill-focussed, indeed soft in texture, too; but that would take at least two months, so I didn't dare begin. Now again, I suspect, the historical portions will seem solid, and the rest of the text a little spongy. That is partly the price one pays for leaving the safe territory of the past and for venturing beyond one's depth. Re-reading these books is a good preparation for doing Vol. IV but I shall not be at ease until I am actually embarked on that work. So far I but mark time.

All things considered, I think you made a good choice with Houghton, Mifflin, in view of their interest: that is everything in publishing.

Sophia joins me in affectionate greetings for the Christmas season and the year to come.

Lewis

P.S. I note, with proper awe, your rise in rank. . . .

[typed with handwritten
addendum, LMC]
Box 2601, Washington, D.C.
March 8, 1946
Mr. Lewis Mumford
46 College Street
Hanover, New Hampshire

Dear Lewis:

It was outrageous of me not to answer your letter immediately. I was full of things to say after what you call our tongue-tied meeting, but I have been more or less dead to the world for the last six weeks and not fit to write anything worth reading. I am afraid I shall not be finished with the tremendous chore of this book of ours for another month.

As things now stand I expect to be in Washington on Wednesday, the 27th, and

---

40. Rushton Coulburn, review of *The Condition of Man*, *American Historical Review* 50 (October 1944): 91–93.

41. Lewis Mumford, *Values for Survival: Essays, Addresses, and Letters on Politics and Education* (1946).

will attend your lecture if it is possible for me to get a ticket. Please leave time for me at any hour that fits your schedule. I can arrange my time accordingly.

> Yours,
> Harry
> HAM: MI

It is preposterous to write you a letter like this. I think of you *every* day without exception & I feel very close, *but* I am nailed down here on a book that is long over-due & my headpiece has stopped running, stopped walking—it can only crawl a few feet a day & so every kind of writing is an enormous burden. I wrote you a let-ter after our luncheon but I think I tore it up. The vision of Geddes was there with us, because we hadn't seen each other since his death, & we couldn't go on until we talked about him, & it seemed a sacrilege to talk about him in that busy restaurant at high noon.

I am signing your petition despite the fact that I don't agree *fully*.[42] I am in favor of declaring now that we will do all these things the moment the others agree to do the same, but not *do* anything until they agree to *do*. Russians I have talked to have convinced me that the men now in control (Stalin, etc.) admire force more than any-thing & that, at this stage, scrupulous honest & outspokenness & *firmness* is the best route to a good relationship with them. I believe in doing a great number of positive acts of creative friendship, embracing them & building up good will in every way—& *not rattling the sword*, but having them know it is there to be used in de-fense of international law if absolutely necessary. We must accept, for the time being, the necessity of linking Power with Fellowship. Instead of throwing away Power, I would advocate increasing Fellowship & understanding. Russia is a young adolescent delinquent in the World Order & she will turn criminal if she is not spanked & and yet embraced at the same time. The first aim, I think, is to open up Communications, to insist on reciprocity of information.

> [handwritten]
> 46 College Street
> Hanover, N.H.
> 12 March 1946

Dear Harry:

I'll have the Forum send you an invitation to the meeting. I hope to convince you that our present policy—based on a threatened war of extermination—is suici-dal as well as monstrous. But don't think I've become an absolute pacifist: I'd keep our army to a much higher level than is now contemplated. The possession of the Atomic Bomb has already corrupted our judgment as well as our morals. I reckon

---

42. In 1946, Mumford circulated "A Petition to the President and the Congress of the United States of America" calling for the dismantling of nuclear bombs and a halt to the testing of atomic weapons (see Miller, *Lewis Mumford*, 431–32).

we have from one to three years in which to call off the race to extermination. After that we will be in jeopardy far more than the Russians. Until you wholly agree I'll withhold your signature!

Affectionately
Lewis

[handwritten]
[LM] 10 May 1946

Dear Lewis:

Your poem is intensely moving—The finely hammered steel of woe. I have read it several times in the last 24 hours. Twice a Year—thanks so much—was here when I returned from Boston a week ago, but I was so entangled in the badly knotted yarns of my own thought, that I could not free myself to read it until yesterday. You wrote of an experience which all poets, except the greatest, should be dissuaded from trying to communicate, and you succeeded as only a few have succeeded. It is the perfect embodiment of the dignity of a grief that has been fully-experienced, encompassed, and converted into an inhering element of a refashioned character. I am more sensitive to poetic prose than I am to poetry, but I was deeply touched by the truth, the firm fortitude, passionate restraint, & concluding resolution of this condensed utterance of yours. I am so grateful to you for sending me this copy.

I am very low at the moment because of discovering that a large portion of the MSS that was supposed to be finished 2 months ago by others is still in a miserable state of confusion, charts unfinished, figures unreliable, and the writing intolerable. It has all been plunked on my desk by the authors who have left for other parts of the country, & at the moment it looks like the most indigestible mass I have ever faced. As things stand now I am planning to motor to Hanover with Jo, arriving Saturday June 1, & leaving June 4, Tuesday—provided you can get a double room at the Hanover Inn for those 3 nights. Jo is spending the day Sunday at Cornish & leaving for Boston early Monday A.M.

Therefore, I suggest that we take a long walk on Sunday June 2 if you are in the mood for it, & that I reserve Monday morning or afternoon for Adelbert Ames with an evening of talk later if he is up to it. By the time you get this letter I shall be at the Tower, so that if you will write me—enclosed in an envelope addressed to Christiana.

Newburyport Turnpike
Rowley R.F.D.
Mass—

whether 1. You are free one of these days, 2. you can engage a room at the Inn & 3. Dr. Ames can see me, I shall be very grateful. I am of, of course, very eager to see you before you leave, & feast my eyes on beautiful Sophy, & exchange fantasies with Alison, & generally devour all that I can absorb of the three of you. If another time would be more convenient, let me know—

Yrs
Harry

The writing of that wonderful poem must have consolidated your feelings into a nucleus of strength.

[typed]
Institute of Sociology
Malvern, Worcs.
1 July 1946

Dear Harry:

I've wanted to write you often; but except for a week at Malvern when I had to rewrite lectures and pick up all the broken threads of my knowledge about England, I have been on the go, rather intensively, ever since being here. Hence my silence. The trip has been a very fruitful one; though I think that with ten days more I could get all I wanted from England. Instead, I will be here for another five or six weeks, depending somewhat upon when the Queen Mary sails. The English have treated me as you predicted they would; and I find my self more intensively, and I think even more comprehendingly read, than I am by equivalent people in America. I have the ear of the students, even those who used to be communists; and that gives me great hope, as well as pleasure. I have learned that my books and pamphlets—two about planning in England—have had an impact upon the cabinet ministers of the present government and have helped to modify their planning and housing policies, in what I should naturally think of as the right direction. They have received me as well as I ever hope to be received anywhere; and on one or two occasions, with a very un-English depth of visible emotion on their own part. They have taken me in so completely that I find myself, against my volition, meeting them half way on little things like manners and pronunciation—even occasionally, to my horror, accent—just to narrow the gap that is already so small. But live here permanently? Never. The thought never entered my mind before coming here; and if it had, it would have vanished on almost the first day. I am a foreigner to this society; and much though I admire parts of it and love other parts of it, I could never identify myself with it: at least, not more than I could with France, Poland, China, or any other foreign country whose citizens made me feel at home. What you thought was my dream was really one of Sophia's who would have been immensely at home here during England's heroic age—the Blitz. She would enjoy it as much as I do now; but she would no longer be at home. I have already gently disillusioned her. I shall have a thousand things to talk over with you, including much that piled up since we met in Washington; so even if you drop in on Sophia before I come back, save another few days for me early in September. Affectionate greetings

Lewis

[handwritten]
Cunard White Star
R.M.S. "Queen Mary"
11 August 1946

. . . Here I am, dear Harry, chafing at the bit over every delay that separates me further from Sophy & Alison; and meanwhile, just off Halifax, where our ship is bound in order to disgorge over two thousand Canadian wives & children, a fog has settled down, so heavy that the Pilot Boat can't even find us. In this pass, I turn to you: for my last letter was only a snatch. Delay or not, this trip has proved a very fruitful one: more one-sided in its preoccupation with City Planning than I should have liked it to be; but I managed, despite that commitment, to encounter a larger segment of England than I ever knew before: at the end, when I was free in London for six days, it even included a dinner symposium at Brown's with Mannheim, Bernal, Read, Waddington, Henry Moore (the sculptor) and an enlightened industrialist named Dickson, who, by the way, has enlisted the aid of the Tavistock Clinic to go further into the matter of bettering his relations with his workers.[43] Yes: and at the very end I had lunch and a talk at the clinic, at the invitation of Bowlby; though Rees & Sutherland alas! were away, and I myself, that afternoon, was in the last throes of fatigue.[44] They all sent their warm greetings to you: particularly one handsome young fellow, whose voice sounded American, but whose name slipt my memory five minutes after I heard it. I visited many parts of England I had never seen, Worcestershire, Shropshire, the Black Country, Lancashire—where they toast the King as both King & Duke of Lancaster!—and saw with a fresh eye many more familiar landscapes; noting for the first time the number of exotic trees, such as the Redwood & the Cedar of Lebanon, and stumbling over a mighty lime tree that reminded me of a banyan, with its low branches rooting into the earth, by a natural process of "layering." My visits to cities had almost an official character: I would usually be met by the mayor's car & find myself having lunch or dinner with him and a group of councilors at the Town Hall: occasions that sometimes called for speeches on my part, which I used as an excuse for telling the English what they needed to hear: namely, that their physical state was more on a par with that of the ordinary American than they imagined, and that morally, mentally, & politically they were, with regard to their internal affairs, much better off. Since February they have rebounded from the fatigue & depression & "nerves" with which they ended the war: an exacerbated state that our sudden & brutal withdrawal of lend-lease made worse; for at that moment they needed badly to relax—there has been a general slow-down in work—the only way

43. Karl Mannheim, sociologist; Desmond Bernal, physicist; Herbert Spencer Read, art critic; Conrad Hall Waddington, geneticist and embryologist.

44. John Mostyn Bowlby, John Rawlings Rees, and J. D. Sutherland were psychiatrists affiliated with the Tavistock Clinic.

that the working classes can get a vacation—if not quite a satisfactory one—under the circumstances; but at least until winter comes they are safe; and even then, the new arrangements for Danish butter and bacon will help. Their present diet is constrained; but except for those doing extra work, or those under strain, it is quite adequate—better than it was for all but the upper tenth in 1920. One no longer sees the pinched anemic faces that one saw then: and war or no war the general standard of well-being has risen—which partly of course, as in our country, accounts for the food shortage.—But I have got off the trail. Officially and unofficially I was treated, as you indeed predicted, dear Harry, in a fashion that may permanently impair my usefulness in the United States! The young gave me a tremendous ovation at my lecture at the Royal Institute of British Architects, on a World Center for the United Nations. Almost a thousand people were there; and I have never had a more receptive, a more eager audience. My influence is far deeper & wider in England than I dared to imagine; and though a larger part of the younger generation has accepted the blinkers of Marxism than would now be so with us, a certain number of one-time Marxists are now drifting over to—Mumford! All in all, it's been a heady experience; and it has given me just the fillip I needed to return to my work with renewed confidence. In forcing myself to go just when & as I did, at a moment when I had become absorbed in something I wanted very much to finish, I achieved a certain kind of inner freedom, including a freedom from fears and anxieties that have haunted me and handicapped me from 1940 onward. Sophy's instinct was right. I had to meet this challenge, whether it was opportune or not, in order to recover my manhood: if I had let myself shrink from this task I might have kept on shrinking. I return to some difficult problems—including that of my mother, who at 82 shows signs of senile decay, after holding together magnificently, in sturdy independence & health, up to now: but there is nothing, in or out of my personal life, that I am not prepared to face.

I shall spend the rest of the month in solitude at Amenia, with Sophy & Alison: at least that's what I'm hoping for: and after that we'll all go back to Hanover for one more winter—though I hope to have another week at Amenia early in October.

How are you, dear Harry and where are you—and what prospects are there of my seeing you? Drop me at least a line soon—and forgive this scrawl. (Now you know why I usually use the typewriter!)

> Affectionately
> Lewis

• • •

[note in Harvard file, before HAM 17 October 1946]
These letters by H.A.M. & Christiana account for the growing alienation that continued, until, on my initiative, a few years ago we clasped hands again.

> LM
> Amenia
> 7 June 1979

[handwritten]
125 East 72
N.Y.C.
17 Oct 46
[LM] Ans Oct

Dear Lewis,

I felt that we parted in Amenia with an unbridged distance between us & so I have been anxious to find the soonest opportunity to regain understanding. Thus I am unhappy at finding that I arrived in New York the day you left. [. . .]

I have been thinking a lot about The Life & Death of a Son, & I can't escape from the conclusion that it is a spiritual impossibility as planned. It might be done on an idealized level—simple & true, but yet omitting all the private, detailed psychological factors. The reader, knowing from the start that you, the Father, are the author, will feel uncomfortable, & embarrassed by some of the personal & intimate facts—facts which are not usually made public, or might be interpreted as depreciation of the boy or his parents. He will not believe that a parent—at this point—could be truly honest & impartial & even if he could, he shouldn't be. The impression will be gained that you have imposed a kind of crucifixion on yourself as an atonement for something—some hurtful action or failure to act—which overshadows & bears down upon your spirit. To some extent every parent must pass through a period of ruthless self-criticism after being struck so hard by Fate, but a public confession—a reader will inevitably see it in this light—does not seem proper, since the world can learn nothing from it. It is a matter between you and your Conscience.

You can see that I cannot express myself clearly anymore than I could in Amenia, but I feel that this is the first thing you have ever written which did not come self-assuredly from your creative center. And from this I surmise that some member of your Congress of personalities is forcing you to do it, to do the impossible. Probably you are too close to the event to write the book in the way you have planned, but, in any event, you can put it aside in its present form & come back to it in a year or two. Geddes will find his immortality in your next book which will be directed toward the future which he sacrificed his life to provide ground for.

I feel like an irresponsible blunderer in writing this letter, an intruder & a meddler, but somehow feel compelled to stumble & fumble on in hopes of finding a clue to my lack of whole-hearted response at Amenia. I have never felt anything but great enthusiasm (with a little sprinkling of minor disagreements) for what you have written & it grieves me to be unable to go all out for this latest labor of love and homage toward a true & courageous son. Forgive these inept attempts to bridge the gap—which may operate in fact to increase rather than decrease the width of it.

My best love to the incomparable Sophy.

Affectionately
Harry

[typed]
46 College Street
Hanover, New Hampshire
19 October 1946

. . . Your letter, dear Harry, spoke the true speech of friendship; and I am sorry only that you had any misgivings about uttering this admonition. You said nothing in your letter that I did not already know about your feelings with respect to the manuscript: if I seemed put off a little by your intuitions at the time, it was only because I was still in the midst of writing, and because at such moments even the most warm and intimate breath of criticism is as a cold wind blowing from the north. I wrote the last pages more than a fortnight ago; and that cold wind is now the native air which blows about the pages, as I set myself in judgment upon the work, so your words, which I could only close the door on swiftly while you were at Amenia, I can now welcome at my ease. The part of the manuscript I gave you to read were sections about which I had my own doubts: indeed, the opening pages were re-written I know not how many times, and will have to be re-written further before I shall be satisfied with them. Your reactions to them were sound. As for the mood of crucifixion, you are right again, in certain parts of the book: partly it sprang out of self-reproach, partly out of a sense of the brevity of Geddes's life and the irretrievability of what was now gone forever. But although my first, and even my second expression of this might seem exaggerated, and even neurotic, that is only the result of the initial shock; for I never had such misgivings until we were on the point of separation. Much more difficult to deal with than my own sense of guilt was the special feeling that a doom hung over him, and that he had received more than the normal number of blows and buffets in his short life: a true enough feeling, perhaps, but one to be counterbalanced by the thought that he also had more than the normal number of vivid and happy days, or at least lived them with more passionate intensity than many of his more sober and fortunate companions did. But you have read less than thirty pages in three hundred; and the book as a whole would not, I think, give you the same morbid impression in its present state, and will do so even less when I have finished my revisions. The question still remains whether any document as intimate as this, which involves unintended—if not unconscious—revelations of both Geddes's father and his mother, should be published, at least in my lifetime. To that the answer is not so easy. I am not in the least anxious to publish this book on my own account; in one sense the writing of it sufficed. But in choosing the material and the method of dealing with it I have not sought merely to satisfy Sophy and myself; I have rather asked myself, what would this mean to some other human being, even one who has not lost his child? Incidents and passages that lacked this universal quality I have tried to leave out. But, because of Geddes's nature and ours this book could not, without repudiating his very essence, be a pious and decorative account of his life: its value, it seems to me, lies in a certain kind of honesty in facing mischance and evil and sin and death, while keeping one's eye mainly on the facts of life and growth and joy. So the book bears the same relation to the final volume of my big series as Men Must Act and Faith for Living did to the Condition of Man: whatever the imperfections it reveals in me, whatever the limitations, it will show that my theoretic knowledge and ideal insights have been duly paid for in the process of living. "Behind facades men build up imposing reputations": you remember that passage in Melville, no doubt, though at the moment I can't recall whether it is in Moby-Dick or Pierre. I have no need to beat my breast in public or to tear down the facade ostentatiously; but whatever comes out in the course of doing an honest job about Geddes I am quite willing to have come out, even though I myself may wince in the process. In the end, the only kind of reader whose respect I care for will be reassured, rather than put off, by this revelation. Perhaps I overestimate my own strength and my own soundness. But I feel that we have now reached a point in our civilization, again like that reached in the development of Rome, when the false front has to be taken down, not because one is an exhibitionist and wants to attract attention by a naked presentation in public, but because one's private world and one's public world must be in more intimate relation. That is probably the origin, come to think of it, of the Christian's confession, originally a public act: just the opposite of all the face-saving devices which maintained the illusion of pagan dignity and the fact of complacency. I have learnt much in the act of writing this book; and I believe that other parents will learn much about themselves and their children, too, however different the outward cast of our lives. As a parent, I was no monster like Rousseau; up to Geddes's death I had always thought of myself as considerably better than the average parent in most ways though I knew the penalties of being a child in a writer's family. What I have tried to deal with are the universal facts in the growth of a child; and whatever special and private things attached to our relation with Geddes merely gave a contour or an edge to the universal. The essential lesson of all biography is that the other men are like ourselves; and similarly, that the weaknesses and errors we find in our own lives can also be found in those who on the surface seem happier or more exalted . . . It may be, dear Harry, that in your professional capacity, as a psychoanalyst, you may feel that I have unconsciously told more than you believe the world should know about me at this state—or more about Sophy. You may be acting on the same impulse that would have prompted both of us, I think, to bid Havelock Ellis burn his autobiography. That impulse to suppress the unpalatable part of a life-narrative is natural enough; but surely it is wrong. Surely it is better for the world, though not for Ellis's reputation, that it should allow for the distortions, the physiological distortions, that underlie the apparent harmony and equilibrium in Ellis's thought: those ideas of his about sex were not wholly the products of life-wisdom for which the life alone is a warrant; and I honor both Augustine and Rousseau more because they gave themselves away; and who can say that their influence was less because they disclosed to their enemies so much that they might well have been tempted to conceal even from their friends?

Yet, now that I have given you my reasons, dear Harry, I shall return to my manuscript with a stricter eye than ever; and I promise you I shall do nothing about its disposition in haste. If your mind is free for such excursions, I shall even show you the finished manuscript as a whole when it is done. Even then we may be at odds; and even then I may stubbornly go my own way, but it will not be without gratitude, deep gratitude, that in this matter you spoke up, plainly and sternly, as becomes a friend. Believe me, that will only deepen a friendship that needs no deepening. I hope that some day I may stand you in as good stead.

Lewis

[handwritten]
Topsfield
Massachusetts
25 Nov '46
I shall be at 125 E 72 on Dec 5—
for a while

Dear old Lewis,

I was very much moved by your long letter defining your position on the question of the biography. I wish I had time to answer it now. I agree with everything you said—but still hold a doubt, or hesitation, connected with the idea of a parent (who is privileged to witness the secret life & humiliations of the child, before the child can control or protect itself, & therefore has a sacred duty to keep the world's eyes off those events which only he, or she, (parent) was in a position to observe)— the idea of a parent publishing anything at all that would bring the slightest discredit to the child.

I believe in the Rousseau model—expose yourself—& even, if necessary, in the Pierre model—expose your parents—but not in the Expose Your Child idea. Of course, I only read a few pages & in these found only too or three sentences. Thus all this comes down to a few episodes which may already have been deleted. The bulk of it seems admirable.

I am suffering under a very painful mental, or rather verbal, block at the moment. Recovering from this double header was much slower than I expected.[45]

Hurriedly
Harry

---

45. "Double header": tonsil and hernia operations.

[handwritten]
125 East 72
8/1/47
[LM] 26 Jan 47

Dear Lewis:

When I returned from Cambridge last night your letter shone forth at the summit of a mountain range of letters which had been built up since Dec 23, when we left here for a Xmas in Boston. It is not that it was last to arrive but Jo, recognizing its source and so knowing it to be the one which would mean the most to me, kept it at the top so that, like the dome of Greylock, it would catch the last & first rays of the sun and thereby hearten me. Greetings to the three of you!

You have finished the hardest possible job, so hard that I did not think it could be done in the way you planned to do it. But I understand that you *have* done it, as it has never been done before, & so given Geddes his triumphant immortality.

The process of criticism—from the self and from others—before, during and after a piece of work, is a matter about which I have little wisdom. I know that every vision of a whole or of a part & that every representation of a part or of a whole is, and should be, regarded with the tenderest concern from its inception to its completion, by the author as well as by his friends. The best soil for productivity—sheer creativity—is tenderness, acceptance, embracement & admiration. But there is something else besides sheer productivity—there is the effectiveness of the products, of the created forms, over the years. And so within the creator there is a censor who examines each vision, each representation against his standard of beauty, truth, fellowship & power. The censor obstructs the free flow and so often appears in the guise of an enemy, but if he knows his place, he will obstruct only the false, the commonplace, the meretricious, the inhuman & the ineffective elements, & what comes through & is finally wrought into the completed incarnation of the vision will have lasting power in the world. Each creator seems to have a ratio of free expression/criticism which is proper to his own being. In *Mardi*, for example, Melville's quotient was too high—productivity was enormous, criticism inadequate, so that Hawthorne wrote of it in these terms: "*Mardi* is so good that I can't forgive the author for not making it better." In *Moby Dick,* the balance was just right. But in *Pierre* the self-criticism was predominant & creativity was impaired. But this, obviously, is an over-simplified statement, because there were many other operating forces. For instance, in *Pierre*, Melville had lost all fellow-feeling, was writing to an inanimate object (instead of to Hawthorne), & his creativity was compounded with hate, & his criticism of his work with criticism of himself as a person (guilt & expectations of being hated, etc.). But to return to the free expression/criticism ratio—this depends on the personality of the author, the stage of the creative process in which he finds himself, the importance of this particular work as he appraises it, the type of work it is, etc., etc. To judge all this is difficult for an outsider, a well-intentioned friend, & so perhaps the best general policy is to maintain an environment of warmth, acceptance, and admiration. Holding steadily to his attitude, however, does not seem to me to be the ideal for a friend, because the creator, as I see him, wants to make something that will live in the world and in viewing his work the proper position for him to take is not at his own receptive center (to please himself) nor in the center of the average reader (to please him), but at a point between the two, making for a relationship between (1) what he feels impelled to say and (2) what will affect the world (a special portion of it)—delight it, instruct it, warn it, change it, etc. In reaching this point of relational equilibrium a friend may be very helpful. But perhaps this is asking too much of the creator & of his friend, & the world being what it is, it is better to resign yourself to a resolutely nourishing attitude towards all creative work with which you sympathize &, for the rest, remain apart. All this is part of an explanation of the way I have treated you & others in contrast to the way you have treated your creative friends. Looking into myself I find what I have missed more than anything is constructive criticism from friends who understood what I was about, or, to be more concrete, tough but good-natured discussions as to the truth of this or that conception engendered in the mind of any one of us. This is partly because I feel at home in the realm of ideas, & if something defective is discovered in this area of activity, I feel confident that it can eventually be repaired. When it comes to literary form, however, I am much more sensitive, because I am not at all confident that I can improve it, & if it is flat that is the end of it. Thus, I might have to conclude that I want criticism for my ideas (because I can do better next time as a result of it), but appreciation of the form (because I can't improve on it).

I meant to write a short greeting for the New Year and a deep acknowledgement of my respect for your accomplishment in finishing a most arduous and profoundly self-involving creative task, and instead, I have wondered off on a course of uninhibited self-expression, or confession, to clarify, I hope for both of us a certain tension that has occasionally arisen in our discussions of topics relative to one of your works in progress. I want to learn—because I am completely identified with both the direction and method of your creative efforts, want them to succeed (in the highest sense) and so any hints from you as to how I can best play my part will be greedily accepted.

As you know, I lumber along at a slow pace, climbing hillock after hillock of criticism & what finally emerges is almost dead from strangulation. I have only finished one piece—a 25 page Introduction to a book on Case Histories (written by others) which gives back no glow when I dip into it, here & there. Now I am working on the final parts of the wearisome *Assessment of Men* & an Introduction to a book of Readings in Culture & Personality.[46] I finished editing the text of *Pierre* some time ago, but I still have the footnotes (30 pages of these) & a 30 page Introduction.[47] My latest conception is concerned with the nature of the development of

---

46. Henry A. Murray, introduction to *Clinical Studies in Personality* (1947).
47. Henry A. Murray, ed., Herman Melville, *Pierre, or the Ambiguities* (1949).

the Hawthorne-Melville relationship, & how it broke down, & how each was compelled to write a book *(Blithedale Romance & Pierre)* to clarify his view of the matter &, as far as possible, justify his position & decision. Plinlimmon (Hawthorne) played the role of the passive, insightful observer—the detached analyst—who never gave expression to his philosophy (Plinlimmon never wrote anything) but seemed to disapprove of Pierre's (Melville's) course, since he was not himself pursuing a similar course and since he gave no encouragement to Pierre in the pursuit of *his* course. What was Plinlimmon's (Hawthorne's) philosophy as far as the conduct of life was concerned? Granting he was a Christian, why did he not believe in a Christ-like life, in dedicating oneself to a sacrificial love? The answer is *Chronometricals & Horologicals* (written by one of Plinlimmon's disciples, namely Melville)—a rationalization of Hawthorne's attitude. Thus one of the chief formulas of *Pierre* is the opposition between Pierre's Melville's dedication to one object (the quest for the path of salvation) & Plinlimmon's Hawthorne's conservative rational morality which is made to conform to God's intention by a Jesuitical, intellectual trick—arguing that God's rules for heaven are different from his rules for earth, & he does not expect a man to attempt to live by the former (heavenly time) during his period on earth (where worldly time is appropriate). Thus Plinlimmon makes God say: adjust to your environment. When you are on earth adjust to the world & when you get to heaven adjust to the company of the angels. By a series of symbols, Melville shows that the assimilation of this doctrine (the incorporation of the pamphlet into the lining of his coat) leads to Pierre's repudiation of his own course, his final self-contempt & suicide—i.e. his spiritual death (his acceptance of the annihilation of his soul). In other words, he is blaming Hawthorne (whom he had chosen as an analyst, or substitute Father) for failing to encourage him in his Promethean path (If he is not with him he is against me), etc., etc. This is merely pursuing the trails which you pointed to, years ago. Well, I'd better end here. Good fortune to Sophy, Alison & your great self—

Harry

[typed]
46 College Street
Hanover, New Hampshire
26 Jan 1947

. . . . The haze of spring morning, dear Harry, hangs over the landscape; indeed, the dirty snow and the melting slush make the streets seem as they do usually toward the end of March; and I am pausing for a moment to catch my breath, after three weeks devoted solidly to the blocking out of the three lectures I am going to give at Berkeley in February, on Christianity in a Time of Troubles. When I accepted that invitation I had something very definite, it seemed to me, in mind, though I hadn't written it down; but by now the great idea, whatever it was, has vaporized and I find myself very reluctant to deal either with Christianity or Trouble: though on the whole I am driven to emphasize the latter in order to escape all the misunderstandings and difficulties that would arise if I attempted to discuss, with a group of parsons—for it is a religious conference I'm speaking to—the first subject. Yes; I've got myself in a pickle, and I am still striking out at random in various directions. The only useful thing that the lectures have made me do is to attempt to formulate a "total change" in a culture: only to find that we haven't even the most primitive instruments for making such a formulation. Analytical thinking, by definition, deals with pieces not wholes: it can describe accurately what happens separately, in little pieces, but not what happens simultaneously, in a whole; in fact, it is almost driven to deny the possibility of a wholesale, to say nothing of a wholistic, change; yet that sort of change seems to me to have occurred, at intervals, in the development of a civilization, for example in the passage from Hellenism to Christianity, and no mere summary of changes in separate departments really covers it. It is a sort of parallel, in history, of trying to find words for the total response of an organism to a situation, in an individual life. I do not flatter myself into thinking that I will find an answer before February 11; all that I have so far done for myself is to clarify the problem. I am afraid that my three lectures will be full of Ambiguities, made worse by the fact that although I can penetrate most of the weaknesses of Christianity I have nothing but a philosophy to put in its place; and a philosophy is by nature too abstract and too rational to serve as the common medium of integration, in which low and high, stupid and intelligent, will find their parts.

You mustn't feel that your reaction to my biography of young Geddes needs any apology; for it had the good effect of putting me on guard against dangers I had overlooked; and in particular, against the injustice of speaking freely and frankly about him, in a fashion that is impossible in the case of living persons, including myself. Out of mere justice to him, I find that I must leave out certain episodes which cannot be fully explained without implicating this or that living person—in some case, with a danger of being involved in libel. I will look at the manuscript with fresh eyes when I come back from California, and will make my final decisions then. On the matter of free expression and criticism, self-criticism, I have in the course of time learned to distrust what I have written when it gives me great pleasure and elation in the immediate act of writing: at that moment, it usually proves, I am favoring a weakness and mistaking it for strength. My judgement may, of course, still be wrong when no such effects appear; so the fact that I wrote the book about Geddes straightforwardly, doggedly, with no sense of release, always with a feeling of inadequacy and dissatisfaction may mean nothing. Whatever it is, it will never be the book I want it to be, just as his life, seen in retrospect in relation to mine, will never be the life I wanted it to be and too easily thought that it was. As for the dealing with another's manuscript, I have often regretted as much the times when I have been too lenient to a friend's manuscript as the times when I have been too severe: it is extremely hard to achieve the right balance. That is why the most helpful criticism is often that which comes from mediocre minds who perform only one function—that of helping you understand what "the world" will say in response . . . I had hopes of being able to stop off long enough on my way to California to have a few hours with you; but the ticket office here has functioned so badly that I don't know quite where I am or how much time I will finally have, since none of my reservations has yet come through. But if not in February, then in March.

In old friendship
Lewis

[handwritten]
1 Feb 47
125 East 72
N.Y.C.

Dear Lewis—

Just a word that might possibly help a little *Total Change in a Culture.*

You, yourself, have gone a long ways toward designing the concepts for representing the culture "as a whole" and the change in the "wholeness."

You must differentiate between i the *Actual Culture,* the way people & institutions *actually* behave & ii the *Ideal Culture,* the way they believe they (behave or) *should* behave & are perhaps striving to behave.

Then you should differentiate, I think, Culture on the Social (or institutional) Level (Religion, Government, Art, etc.) & Culture on the Personal Level (Actual & Ideal current types of personality & the valuations of each).

I agree with what you say about analytical thinking; but, as I see it, this is one of the great mistakes that scientists have made. I believe that a psychologist or sociologist must analyze, then reconstruct each event or series of events into a representation, or model of the reality as a dynamic moving whole (as it is in actual fact).

The "wholeness" of an organism during one event is represented by the *vectional* force (need, drive) which is *organizing* (integrating) all the relevant resources of the organism to reach a goal (which may or may not be clearly visualized) which will temporarily still (appease or satisfy) the need. In ordinary language it is *Purpose* which determines the manner & direction of *Integration* (patterning of thoughts, works & acts). Define the purpose (imagined goal) & then show how the parts are *organized* to attain that goal—this gives you a *unified whole.*

In the personality there are many *action* systems (analogous to institutions) which must be temporally & serially organized in order that each need or cluster of needs may be satisfied periodically, without conflicting or interfering with the satisfaction of others, etc.—Personality is the form of government of the action systems.

To deal with Culture on the Social Level take the various differentiated areas (institutions) of activity—Economics (commerce, Business, etc.—the purposes of which are material growth—physical survival & growth, physical comfort & the ownership of instruments of power, etc.), Government (Power i.e. administration

& development of forms of control), Science, Art, Religion, Morality (which may or may not be divorced from Religion), etc., & then estimate the force with which each is moving towards its goals (number of people involved, rate of growth, prestige in society, power in respect to other activities-institutions, etc.).

A Total Change would be one in which (Here you have your dominant, recessive, emergent, etc.) 1. There is a marked change of status among the several institutions *(eg.* In Puritan New England, *religion* was dominant; by 1750 or so *government* had become dominant; by 1870 or so *business* was dominant. Science has been rising steadily; religion declining steadily; art has fluctuated as a dissociated activity—it has never been an integral part of the culture, etc.).

2. There is a marked change in the orientation & patterns of activity within the institution itself (e.g. Change from N.E. Calvinism to humanitarianism of churches in 1800s. Change of technics—machine, electricity, etc., in industry; Rise of social sciences in recent years, etc.).

3. There is a marked change in the relations (integration & differentiation) among the institutions *(eg.* Integration of applied physical science & big business; differentiation of biological science & philosophy from religion; differentiation of art from everything else (Art for Art's sake, etc.); beginning of integration of social sciences with government, etc.).

Hurriedly

Harry

P.S. I shall be in Cambridge & Topsfield—Feb. 7–24. Wish you good fortune in California. This is an opportunity.

[handwritten]

46 College Street

25 March 1947

Dear Harry:

The fates seem against our meeting: but I'm writing now just on the wild chance that your visit to Albany might coincide with my lecture at Troy on 24 March. I'll be at the Hendrick Hudson from the middle of the afternoon till six: then to Springfield next morning. I've just put the finishing touches on "Played for Keeps" the Geddes biography; but I am still overwhelmed with other unfinished work. If you have a chance, please look at Air Affairs for March.[48]

May we meet soon!

Lewis

---

48. Lewis Mumford, "Atom Bomb: Social Effects," *Air Affairs* 1 (March 1947): 370–82.

[handwritten]
125 East 72
6 April 47

Dear Lewis,

Too bad—The Topsfield Postmaster forwarded your last letter to New York so that I did not receive it until I reached home. As it turned out I arrived in Albany in the middle of your Troy lecture—but I might have run over & had breakfast with you.

I have been laboring against a bulk of psychological impediments all winter, but am now within 2 weeks of finishing *Assessment of Men & Personality in Nature, Society & Culture*—the latter is merely a collection of readings mostly on the determinants of personality.[49] But I still have the introduction to *Pierre* to do, although the research à la Road to *Xanadu* is almost complete.[50] I have found the source for almost everything except the man who said *that God does not expect man to* follow the Sermon on the Mount (Heavenly Wisdom) on earth. Horological time is proper for him. If you can think of a possible candidate for this chief statement of Plotinus Plinlimmon's I would appreciate your guess. So far I have a peculiar unconvincing compound of the Parable of the Unjust Steward (The Children of this world are wise, etc. . . .), a little of Paul, a scrap of Luther, a Jesuitical contribution, a bit of casuistry from Jeremy Taylor, & possibly one of the English moralists like Cumberland—

Jo has just brought in your review of Olson's book.[51] He read me parts of it last year & as he read it with passion that huge 6 ft 7 in frame of his seemed to fit the great space he was talking about & somehow it seemed, as you said, the basis for an Olson Saga about Melville. But reading his job now it seems more or less meaningless. I think the basic idea here that Olson almost grasped was that Melville, as a boy, was closely confined (by his own dependent affections & respect) to his parents' *confined & structured* space—the sentiments, valuations, beliefs, etc., of a narrow upper class, surface Christian culture—then came the revolt & flight to *unconfined & unstructured* space—the West, the Pacific, free imagination, the upsurge of the unconscious, the drift of fantasy, etc. He identified God with this indefinite, boundless, infinite flow—But then all the time there was the repressed longing to find again some satisfying resting place—some relationship, truth, love, final faith—that would contain him. He associated Reason with structured space & structure of space with the Culture of American Protestant City-Dwellers—the Marriage of Puritanism, Capitalism, & Upper Middle Class Pretension, & so in cutting himself off from all this he repudiated Reason & yielded to Passion. This was

49. Clyde Kluckhohn and Henry A. Murray, eds., *Personality in Nature, Society, and Culture* (1950).

50. Reference to John Livingston Lowes, *The Road to Xanadu: A Study in the Ways of the Imagination* (1927).

51. Lewis Mumford, review of Charles Olson, *Call Me Ishmael, New York Times Book Review*, 6 April 1947, 4.

all right in the beginning, but later, when the time came to make a new structured space for himself, he had no Reason to help him. So that in Billy Budd he had nothing to do but return to the fold—not on his terms, but on their terms—I did not mean to go on like this. I meant to say simply that that was a hard review to write, & you did as well as anyone could without showing Olson up as a very confused fellow. I like him very much personally & he has made some kind of deep unconscious identification with Melville that he has not been able to define to himself yet.

I am deeply thankful that your book is finished—the title is terrific. It brought tears to my eyes & I felt completely reassured—Benedicte.[52]

I have been asking for Air Affairs at all newsstands, but have not been able to lay my hands on it. For the next ten days I shall be on the road again. Topsfield & Washington (to get book passed by government censor). Love to the magnificent—Sophy, of course—& Alison—

Yours
Harry

[typed]
Amenia, New York
22 June 1947

Dear Harry:

That brief, damp, drizzly, glimpse of you in New York a few months ago was not long enough to be called a meeting; and now that summertime is here—I hope that the idyllic morning I am writing on is prophetic of more of the same fragrant, dewy quality—I trust that your plans for the summer will bring you, sooner or later, and better sooner than later, to Amenia. I have been spending the last fortnight, ever since we got down here in fact, manfully battling the encroaching army of weeds and over-prolific bushes; and in another fortnight, if things go as well intellectually as they have in every other fashion, I hope at last to begin work on Vol. IV. But as you know, I never write after eleven in the morning; and, thanks to Sophy's heroic struggles, the house is now clean and tidy enough to receive visitors: none more welcome than yourself. So, unless you are staying "put" for the summer in the same fashion that I am, don't on any account pass us by when you are going through this neighborhood. As for me, the tides of life are coming in again, after their long ebbing. The final correction of the galleys of Green Memories, a job which haunted me, one way or another, all spring, was perhaps a symbolic turning point; and now that that is behind me, I feel released and ready for new work, as I realized in my bones that I should never be until the book was written. Your own share in the writing of that manuscript was not, dear Harry, a little one; for the warning you gave me became a challenge, and in meeting that challenge the book, though it may still justify your worst fears: as to that I can give no impartial

---

52. Lewis Mumford, *Green Memories: The Story of Geddes Mumford* (1947).

answer—the book has gained enormously in strength; and I feel grateful for that quality in our friendship which made it possible for you to say *what* you did, and for me to take it *as* I did, without further harm or grievance to either of us. Incidentally, the other day I re-read your original New England Quarterly criticism (and appreciation) of my Melville: the occasion being the prospect—say almost the threat—of a French translation. It was both a generous and a just criticism; and the one large flaw you picked out—that my optimistic interpretation glided too easily over the demonic aspects of Melville—is, I see now better than ever, the largest fault in the book; though my failure to deal with Melville's religious inheritance, a failure due to a sort of positivist greenness and innocence on my part, was surely another, and my externalization of Moby-Dick, as being merely the personalization of a hostile or indifferent universe, was a third, for it did justice to neither Melville's inner dilemmas nor to those aspects of the universe which are, in fact, life-furthering. There were still some weak nineteenth century holdovers in my world view, as late as 1928! If the book is actually translated into French I shall have to make at least a minimum of changes by way of excision, and perhaps add a paragraph here and there to fill in the worst chinks; though I shan't, of course, make any of those radical changes of interpretation which could follow only the publication of your own work. Except for my howler on Ethan Brand, I find myself little touched by the spate of academic criticisms that appeared in American Literature.[53] There were the usual quota of little errors; but the very critic who was most vindictive in attacking those errors, spelled Moby-Dick without a hyphen! I have been re-reading the opening chapters of Pierre and find it impossible to agree with the critics who make out its perfervid English to be satire on the sentimental school of novelists. There is nothing whatever to indicate that intention; and the satire is wholly unconscious, like the farcical ending of the book, in the crude kind of melodrama I used to see as a boy in the old American Theater, on 42 Street! But there is still one thought about Ethan Brand that teases me, though it seems to have escaped altogether the eyes of the professors, who have so enjoyed their Schadenfreude over my error that they close their eyes to the significant trail it opened. Just before Melville went down to New York to finish off Moby-Dick, he told Hawthorne he had just been reading The Unpardonable Sin. That probably occurred too late to cause that drastic alteration in the original manuscript which Olson posits: but may it not have caused Melville to accentuate the alienation motif in Ahab, though he himself proclaims himself, in that letter, on the side of feeling? And if there is no possibility of Hawthorne's conception of Brand having influenced Melville's conception of Ahab; then it raises an even more critical problem in

---

53. In the first edition of *Herman Melville,* Mumford states that "Ethan Brand" was "written during the prime year of their friendship" and interprets what Hawthorne says about Brand as a "warning, to Melville himself" (145). "Ethan Brand" was first published in January 1850 as "The Unpardonable Sin"; Hawthorne did not meet Melville until August 1850.

American literature—and that is how two such deeply contrasting temperaments as Melville's and Hawthorne's should have both turned up, within a few years of each other, with the same type of hero: two intellect-begotten Ishmaels. Are not Ahab and Brand both Modern Man; and is not the Atomic Bomb his final progeny—even though in Moby-Dick Melville was optimist enough to provide a "happy ending," namely someone left to tell the tale.

Enough of that. You can see that I am in the slow grass growing mood and am ready to sprout at almost any spot in the landscape! Tell me about your own plans and thoughts, dear Harry.

Ever yours
Lewis

[handwritten, LMC]
Topsfield
30 June 47

Dear Lewis—

Your letter reached me two days ago as I was building up a pint of steam to blow off in your direction. What you said, though extravagantly overgenerous, made me feel a little better about the damaging & disheartening role I played in your last long season of creative tribulation. An old friend of mine, fellow intern at Presbyterian Hospital, lost his only child, a navy veteran, just 21—last week. He was merely crossing the street & instantly killed by a speeding motorist. I thought of your book immediately as a source of deep consolation to him—& of course to thousands of other stricken parents. Needless to say I am awaiting its publication with keenest appetite. Your article was very fine.[54] You are one of a small number today who are saying things that we Americans disregard at our peril. In fact, I can't think of anyone besides you, although I suppose there must be some others. Again you have dared to go way out on a very shaky limb in boosting me. This is much more magnanimous than Melville's eulogy of Hawthorne, because that "face apart" of "non-benevolence" was a genius & already acknowledged as such. My time will come when I get round—as I will if your Moby-Dick will let me—to what I have to say in the next few years, outside of Melville. I think your Melville is the best there is, & contains some fine insights & stirring eloquence—but yet there is something more to say. Where I think you have really carved out the great outlines of a new philosophy is in the trilogy, supplemented by your shorter, interpolated books, and someday I hope to follow your course taken in Vol. III. I have just reread your *Pierre* chapter & did not find, as I expected, any mention of Hawthorne as Plinlimmon. We discussed this so long ago that I thought the idea was included in your book. Of course, it does not affect the literary merit of the work, but it is of some biographical interest. I found on rereading that chapter that I agreed with all

54. Probably "Atom Bomb: Social Effects."

your aesthetic judgments—down to the details—that is, the outstanding blemishes & other points—but that I had found more to interest & nourish me than you had. I expect to have my footnotes finished & typed in 2 weeks & the introduction in 3 weeks. If you like I shall send you a copy—in case you can use any of it for your French translation.

The opening chapters of Pierre are certainly not satire. As no other major writer, Melville was soaked, during adolescence, in the current literature, including the annuals, gift books, sentimental novels, etc.—particularly (among the better ones) Scott, Cooper, *Disraeli,* & Byron & Tom Moore. The sea had not changed perceptibly the language of his erotic sentiments—what was added was Romeo & Juliet & Plato & Anatomy of Melancholy (on Love). Melville's paean on Love is lifted, mostly out of Agathon's speech in the Symposium, etc. But he was washed out & in no mood for it while he was composing these sections & so besides the artificiality there is insincerity & hollowness—at least as I read it.

I believe that *Ethan Brand* got itself worked into the end of *Moby-Dick.* There are similarities between Brand's last speech to the universe & some of Ahab's orations—to the Candles, for instance. But there is also a sharp distinction in that Brand's sin is *lack of feeling* (i.e. emotional attachment, isolation, dearth—what we call the "feeling of unreality") which is the state in which Hawthorne actually finished his life ➔ depression with a sense that neither he nor others were really alive. In contrast to Brand, Ahab's sin was hate (grief-hate, revenge out of insulted pride) which is passionate & therefore far from indifference. When Melville stood by the heart, he stood by passion—love, if possible, but if not love then grief, & even grief-hate—thus the damage that Ahab did was active, whereas Brand's was passive—he could not feel anything, one way or the other. (The connection between Ethan Brand & Moby-Dick, I believe, was deeper than this, but it would take some time to explain it; when we meet & discuss it you shall see that you were closer to the truth than the critics, strange as this may seem.) Your last paragraph provokes the suggestion that Brand is more like a Physicist (before the Atomic Bomb) who does not care what happens to the world—detached intellectual (Goebbels, say)—& Ahab is more like Nietzsche's Superman & Hitler. But both are Satanic characters coming out of Pride—which was the Catholic's cardinal *sin,* but the Protestant's (unavowed, secret) cardinal *virtue.* It was pride that was the stronghold of his protest against the Pope.

As you say, enough of this.

Sometime this summer—but not for 5 weeks at least—after I have finished with Pierre & had a rest—I shall be on the road & if your invitation holds good for August I shall take advantage of it, as I am in great need of communion with you.

Embrace your beautiful Sophy, the magnificent, and give Alison a warm squeeze for her vivid inner world, from me.

Yours
Harry

[typed]
Lewis Mumford
Amenia
New York
28 July 1947

. . . Your rich nourishing letter has stayed by me the last four weeks, dear Harry, and I've returned to it more than once; though I've been so preoccupied in getting Vol. IV started that I haven't looked up one or two things I wanted to say about Melville before answering it. The shallowness of my Melville interpretation had two sources: the main source was lack of tragic experience on my own part, so that it was only after the book had been published and our son was close to death and all the weak bricks in my own internal structure had fallen about me, so to say, that I had an insight into Melville's dismay, his exacerbation, his despair, his insight into evil, and all that went with it. Five years later I could have written a better book without reading an extra word of Melville. The other source of my weakness could have been summed up at the time in H.M.'s own phrase: Dollars damn me. My first ten books were all written in a hurry because I never had quite enough spare cash, or what is the same spare time, to stand by them and revise them adequately. That is a poor excuse and I would not offer it to the Angel Gabriel: it merely points to another kind of weakness. In fact, it won't do as an excuse at all, for during the last three years I haven't had even a twinge of financial anxiety, and yet I have been stumpt by obstacles in myself even worse than I was in the old days by external ones. That applies especially to Vol. IV. I came to the subject cold this June, for the last serious reading or thinking I had done in preparation really goes back to 1945; and I was determined to begin work the first week in July, come what may. Usually, when I am as well loaded as I am for Vol. IV I have no difficulty whatever; the mere act of writing sets the internal stream flowing, and before I know it I am immersed in it, and have become part of the current I have set in motion. No such luck this time. I have struggled and sweated all this month without turning out a single usable page, though I've written at least fifty; and the more I strain the more costive I become. I realize now that there is probably more than one reason for my being in this state; for to begin with I didn't give myself enough time to re-saturate myself in my material, and so, lacking a fresh grip on the book, all I could pump up was, so to say, the residue of the Condition of Man. But this must be a different kind of book, in tone and temper: and the astringent words I uttered during the war, to combat our pathological optimism, must now give way to words of solace and encouragement, for, our present situation being much more dangerous, I must guard my tongue, as I see it, against any thoroughly realistic canvass of our situation, as a wise man would guard it on a life raft: not putting the danger entirely out of his mind, but conjuring up every life-giving image that would make his companions renew their hope and tighten their grip a little longer, on the promise that the unexpected and the incalculable might indeed save them. I have the health and internal balance to write such a book now; but I have almost become the victim of my habit of "seeing things as they are," or as I interpret them to be without regard to my feelings and desires, and this is now something of a handicap. At all events, I find myself the victim of an internal conflict as to how I shall handle the opening portions of the book, what mood and what purpose shall be uppermost. Perhaps one of my troubles, now that I am vocally making a canvass of them, is that I am so well-balanced at the moment that I can't budge myself from dead center, whereas with almost all my other books, I was just sufficiently in disequilibrium either sexually or emotionally to make the book serve dynamically to restore my balance. As a result of this wasted month and this internal jam, I have abandoned all work in my garden, have turned away everyone who wanted to see me, and have turned myself completely inward, to see if I can recapture by intense concentration the formula by which all my earlier books have been—and so exuberantly for the most part—written. I feel like an ocean steamer that has cut loose from the pier and feels the tugs chugging and chuffing about her, without any perceptive motion: not even half way into the Hudson, and still further from the moment when she will be under way on her own steam. Worst of all at the moment, Alison's need to go back to school in early Sept. will break up my summer before it's really begun; and my only consolation there is that this is our last winter in Hanover; for next year, we'll either go to New York with Alison, or stay right up here, the first preferably if we can find an apartment.

I feel this letter is one long yammer. Don't take it more seriously than I do. Life might become a little monotonous, if all my books tumbled out effortlessly.

Affectionate greetings

Lewis

[handwritten]
Mid-River Farm
Clayton, New York
12 Aug 47

Dear Lewis,

The deadness that you describe is very similar to my own present state except that yours is coming at the beginning & mine at the end of an undertaking. For 4 months I have thought that I had 3 weeks work ahead of me & no more, & even though I was stale beyond words I could beat the horses across the finish line & then a long much needed rest. But the harder I flogged them the slower they went & the words that came out were a mere pile of rusted nails, of no use at all. Probably your last year's labor made deeper inroads into your resources than you calculated & you require a longer period of restful incubation & recuperation than you have allowed for. If money is a factor remember that what I said once holds good continually: you can have any amount you want any time. I should enjoy nothing more than sharing with you something that I did not earn & hence don't deserve. Instead of forcing yourself deeper, why not knock off & wait for the deeps to rise within your reach? At this distance it is, of course, impossible to prescribe for a fellow sufferer even though his account of his state is detailed & precise. But, anyhow, don't you ever apologize for the best book that has been written on Melville. It was a superb job which you did in your stride before all the facts now available had been discovered. This does not count as a letter—it is just a report of dreary weather conditions similar to those you described. Better fortune to you—

> Harry

> [typed]
> Lewis Mumford
> Amenia
> New York
> 12 August 1947

. . . Well, dear Harry, we can at least hold hands in our misery, with a wry smile on our faces, and a deck of worthy rationalizations up our sleeves. I have made false starts before in my life, though never usually on a big book; but apart from all the deeper things that may be plaguing me at the moment, I discovered that my ample notes, which did so adequately for my Stanford lectures, were, at least three-quarters of them, addressed to another problem than that I now have in mind, and no matter how good they were once, they don't fit the present situation—though they suggest another book, a prolegomenon to the whole series, on The Nature of Man. What I have discovered on that subject, and what I have added by way of systematic thought the last month, gives me much that I want to discuss with you at length when we get together; for I find myself wanting to go further on the trail Bergson opened up in Creative Evolution, reinstating—and radically redefining of course—the idea of finalism.[55] All organic activity seems to me purposive in that it cannot be defined simply in terms of past causes, sequences, or motives; and man's activity has a special kind of purposiveness, in that it aims more at development than at survival. Bergson saw correctly that finalism has no fixed and preformed end in the organic world; that the notion of such an end is just a restatement of mechanical determinism, which leaves no place for freedom and creativity; but he went a little too far, I believe, in making the end a too nebulous *elan vitae* and in not giving a more positive role, I would almost say a more formative role, to the shadow that the tendency of an organism casts before it. All this has been implicit in my thought for many years, almost since I can remember: but Bergson's vagueness and Adelbert Ames's inability to define either purpose or value, have made me now want to give a more precise meaning to finalism which will cast off its orig-

---

55. Henri Bergson, *Creative Evolution* (1911).

inal limitations. Science, as its methods were defined by contact with the non-organic world, has been content with purely causal explanations of organic and human phenomena; but it seems to me such a system covers only one half of organic behavior, that related to the past, and does not reveal tendency, direction, and end, which work back from the future to the present, as causes work forward deterministically from the past to the present. I don't renounce a single causal explanation; but by now I am sure that unless we understand the role of "plan," too, we understand only a fragment of human behavior. Unfortunately, the phenomenon I have been trying to define—the relation of an anticipated event acting on a present one—is hard to describe without making that action seem to bring in some force or entity outside the organism, different in origin or texture from it, and that is precisely the mistake of earlier finalism which must be avoided. Purposive action *seems* to be action in terms of a definite, already envisaged goal; but as a matter of fact the goal need not be concrete or envisagable at all, or rather, it may become so, at the end, almost as a surprise. Human goals, which are in fact related as emergents to merely organic ends, have a large degree of visibility; and perhaps the dream got instated into the organism as a means of achieving that result, or at least was speedily diverted into that channel. This is, I realize, not a very lucid account of my endeavor; but it is one of a whole series of topics I'd like to talk over with you. Another is value. None of the current philosophic definitions of value seem to me to get very far; and by now I distinguish in value a whole constellation of things: a need, an interest, a feeling or emotion, a purpose and a consummation. Thus eating has value in human life one does not find purely at the animal level: it is composed of a need for food, an interest in cooking and the preparatory processes, including a setting for the serving of food; pleasant gustatory reactions from the smell, odor, and sight of food; and finally, the purpose of nourishment. The value in this process is not attached to eating or to the purely nutritive aspects of food; the esthetic and social by products are equally essential. The fundamental values work out rather straight forwardly according to this pattern; the derivative values are a little more devious, perhaps, but only because they are at one or two removes from biological or psychological need, as you have described it.

As for the genesis of my present blockage, you may well be right: Green Memories may have taken more out of me than I had supposed. But I thought that January and February marked the lowest point in my reaction; and by April I felt that I had safely rounded that particular Cape Horn. Outwardly, I have never had more energy at my command: there is no visible trace of fatigue about me anywhere—except in relation to the writing of volume IV. By now I am resigned to that fact that, in terms of written pages, my summer has been wasted; but I am also pretty sure that I would have had to spend these extra months of preparation no matter which high plane I had reached beforehand: so I am now prepared to relax. There is no use pushing the inner man. Usually, when I am in normal health, I have only to sit down to my typewriter in the morning to have the first sentence flow from my pen in a few minutes, as easily as in writing this letter; and I have learned by now that when this does not happen, something is wrong. There is no use giving gas to the motor when the brakes are on: so I keep telling myself; and your good advice is welcome re-enforcement to my own common sense on this matter—even though I still occasionally curse my luck for having to let these rich empty hours slip through my hands. As for financial difficulties, at the moment I was never more free from them. But that doesn't lessen my gratitude for your offer of help, nor the feeling of quiet security it gives me, so different from the bitterness Melville must so often have felt in his many hours of need. My friendship with you, dear Harry, is the best reward I got for writing my study of H.M. In an eternal world that now looks as black and ashen as Melville's own interior in his worst years, that fact is a rainbow. (How much your fatigue and my frustrations may be due to general causes, not specific ones in our own present situation, remains to be seen: perhaps these blocks in us are just more rational versions of flying saucers!) How long my present good luck will keep up I do not know; but since the Condition of Man came out, the income from royalties alone has equalled that I would have received as a full professor at Stanford; so I have never been, financially, in better shape. With every new foreign translation—I have just received a copy of Technics from Czechoslovakia!—a little extra comes in, enough to offset the lowering of sales in the United States. At the present moment my English publisher has 5000 copies of The Culture of Cities on the press, which he expects will be sold out in a few weeks from publication; and the plates are so worn out I shall have to spend part of next winter revising it for a new edition. All this is very lucky for me; as my earning capacity through articles, and my will to work that way, have both dropped to almost zero. The New Yorker is the only magazine that wants my work: actively wants it.

Just one question before I stop. (As soon as I do, I shall remember that this is an infernally hot night.) In going through my Melville for the French edition, making little minor stylistic changes, I am of course taking the opportunity to get rid of my awful howler on Ethan Brand, and I am curious about one point in connection with the Hawthorne-Melville relationship on which I have come upon no further evidence. Did they ever see each other or correspond, as far as you know, after their last meeting in Liverpool? If the poem, "to have known him, to have loved him," is to Hawthorne, when and how did the "estrangement" take place? I shall not of course use your answer, except to expunge "they never saw each other again" if they did actually meet in America later. I did not, I find, mention the Hawthorne-Plinlimmon portrait in Pierre; but I did, in speaking of Hawthorne and Melville bring it in indirectly, by asking if Hawthorne said to H.M. what Plinlimmon said to Pierre.

I have talked and talked and have said nothing, beyond making a gesture of consolation, about your condition, dear Harry. Rest and absence of pressure, however, seem to me indicated in your case, too. If both of us are not better in six months we'd better see a doctor—but I suspect that any doctor we'd trust would also be in a similar plight!

Lewis

P.S. Did I mention in my last letter the sequel to my Atomic War Article, over which I am still chuckling and chortling—that the National War College has asked me to give a lecture in a special series on the strategy of the bomb, to a special group of officers, none lower than a lieutenant colonel or a navy captain? It is a tough assignment, for the class will have already read and digested my paper, as required reading for the course!

[handwritten]
Mid River Farm
Clayton, N.Y.
19 Aug

Dear Lewis,

This is a tardy answer to your question & an unsatisfactory one, because I have not found any evidence of a meeting between Melville & Hawthorne after Liverpool. I believe that the "estrangement" took place in the fall of 1851 or a few months later when Melville realized that the estrangement had existed from the beginning. He came to the conclusion that no further *progress* of intimacy was possible, that his own thirst for mutuality of frank confession was thwarted by Hawthorne's wall of reserve, his encystment, his introverted reticence, his immobility of feeling, his detached coolness, his non-benevolence. Hawthorne's face was a thing apart, not included in the human universe. Melville gave freely, encouraged by an illusion of a growing companionship of Spirit, but there was no return. He came to believe that Hawthorne had a secret which he would not confess, that he was imprisoned by some inscrutable inhibition. The whole story is told in *Clarel*. If you read the passages about Vine very carefully you will see that the estrangement was no more than the realization that Hawthorne was a blind alley. There was no quarrel, no definite break. One basic difference was that Hawthorne was a detached, observing artist who could smile elfishly in the Garden of Gethsemane, whereas Melville was passionately involved in a purposeful quest, felt crucified, and wanted the kind of sympathy that his pride could accept. Melville was looking for a lost father, a guide, philosopher, & friend, a psychoanalyst, who would help him on, but he found a silent observer who had no desire to reach beyond the present, whose formula, like, that of most analysts, was "adapt to your world." Plinlimmon proves that the "estrangement," such as it was, took place *before* the spring of 1852. This is confirmed by the *Blithedale Romance* which is Hawthorne's version of the relationship. From the latter it appears that Melville wanted Hawthorne to collaborate with him in some spiritual enterprise & Hawthorne's indifference to it was the occasion for estrangement, or parting of their ways. The great question: what did Melville want Hawthorne to do with him? I hope we can discuss this when we meet next. I have an exciting theory which cannot be spelled out in less than 3 pages, so I shall hold it. Of course, it is *not* that of Melville's repressed homosexuality (which cannot be omitted as a force determining the affair but yet is no explanation for the sublimated form it took). As for 1856, why not say, "We have no record of their ever seeing each other again." Or, is this too scientifically prudent?

As for Finalism:

I would say that you must have a concept for (1) a *present state of tension,* which may be either (a) a surplus of energy, abundance, plenitude,—the "brimful heart—sparkling & running over" as Melville says, which results in the *enjoyment of function per se*—aesthetic perception, fantasy, random imaginings, singing, dancing, wandering, etc., without end in view, or (b) a need which may be one of 2 kinds, either (i) an achievement, to accomplish something—to use one of the above-mentioned functions to bring about some result, merely for the subjective satisfaction of overcoming obstacles and mastering a situation—this is the *will to power* in the broadest sense—power over things, over people, over images, over ideas, over words—it is the manipulative & creative function or (ii) one of a variety of other needs, or a combination of them, which requires, for its fulfillment, some effect in the environment, or in one's relationship with the environment—water, oxygen, food, shelter; protection, affection, prestige, etc. (These I have briefly discussed in *Explorations* under *function, pleasure, achievement pleasure,* & *end pleasure* & in a new book *Men and Their Environment* coming out in the winter; which is a collection of Readings made by Kluckhohn & myself to which I have contributed merely a short essay on Personality.)

So much for the concept of a *present state of tension.* Next you need a concept for (2) *the image of the goal.* In most cases you make a correct diagnosis as to the kind of tension you feel &, on the basis of past experience, create the proper image—that is, one which actually will, if attained, satisfy the need. But, in other cases, you do not recognize the precise nature of the tension, and your imagination throws up a *variety of goal images,* each of which is an hypothesis. To be exact you might say that every goal-image is an *hypothesis,* since you can never be sure that the situation which satisfied you once will satisfy you again. Conservative (epimethean) people are satisfied with the customary tested goals (values). Promethean (creative) people are looking for better goals (values). The concept of *level of aspiration* is useful in characterizing the difficulty of the goals to which a man commits himself. Perhaps the concept of *level of expectation* is even more useful, because it plays such a part in determining contentment & happiness. The ratio, level of achievement/level of expectation as James pointed out, is closely related to happiness. The feelings that adhere to the goal images, which define the quality of expectations, are important, ranging from the zero of hopelessness—up through degrees of hope and faith to complete confidence. One must take account of unconscious expectations also. (I am considering the positive side only. The negative side must also be included: expectations of defeat, disaster as well as expectations of occurrences beyond one's control, some positive, some negative ⟶ Atomic Warfare!)

Now, all this refers to a *present* event. But one of the *chief* determinants of this present event are *present expectations*, i.e. images with a *future reference*. If you are *down* but expect to *rise* shortly you may feel very well; if you are *up* but expect to *fall* shortly, you may feel very badly.

Finalism is a statement of an experiential fact, namely that organisms tend to move from a temporary state of tension, disequilibrium, or need to a temporary state of composure, equilibrium, or fulfillment. If you were omniscient you could look inside the organism & recognize the nature of the tension, & say what finalistic state would relieve it or temporally appease it, but, as things stand, such a prognosis is more or less hypothetical. It is important to recognize that, in most cases, it is not the tensionless state which brings the greatest satisfaction, but the process of reducing tension. Therefore, our happiness depends on the anabolic process of energy-&-tension-*raising*, which occurs mostly during sleep. However, if the chances of reducing the tension (as in India) are small, then your Buddhistic wish may be to abolish all tension, all need.

I agree that it is important to stress Creativity—the generation of new goal images, new solutions, new means of arriving at the goals, etc., particularly during the period of development, but we must remember that most writers are creators & hence stress creativity, but that the vast majority are conservers—after the age of 30, pretty well satisfied to cling to the means & ends which have proven relatively satisfactory in the past. I find it important to distinguish:

i. Generators (creators, prometheans), who find new means, or new goals, or new combinations or new ways of life as overall philosophies.

ii. Conservers, who repeat, champion or defend institutional values.

iii. Destroyers, who attack existing values simply out of hate & despair (nihilism) or with the expectations of replacing them by better ones—Dance of Sera.

iv. Degenerators, who waste their heritage, let everything go to seed are irresponsible—frivolous pleasure seekers, etc.

In treating Finalism I have always been confounded by the semantic problem—the absence of intelligible words to describe the *different kinds of tension* & the aversion of everybody to the introduction of neologisms & new vocabulary. So far it has seemed easier to name needs according to the finalistic state which will appease them, e.g. *need for order*, instead of dissatisfaction with disorder, etc. In some cases we have good words like hunger, but in others we have nothing that seems acceptable. We require a word for each kind of tension—the *general* purpose is to reduce this tension. Then we have the concept of goal, which is the *specific* purpose (factor) which orients the action. For example: Excessive bodily heat arouses need for coolness, say, (this is *general purpose*) but no action will be effective until some specific goal image is generated—letting in a draft of air by opening a window, or taking a bath, or drinking ice tonic. Strictly speaking these goals are really means to the goal of coolness, but the latter is given by naming the need & one must have some concept to describe the specific end toward which the action is directed. This is all a preposterous simplification, because what you are dealing with is a great plexus of interrelated needs, the realization of one is the means of realizing another & vice versa. These are *proximal* goals & *distal* goals, *subordinate* goals & *superordinate* goals, & so the final goal of personality is to create a philosophy of life & become the incarnation of it.

Science must analyze & *reconstruct*—in order to make a *model*, or conceptual representation of the given event. It is not only interested in explanation but more particularly in *prediction*. In psychology & sociology one must know the total situation—inside & outside the person or group—in order to predict, & in order to make a diagnosis of the total situation you ordinarily have to know a good deal about the course of development up to that point.

This is all very confused, no doubt, & fragmentary but I am sure it is possible to define everything without referring to the non-existent future. It is all in the present, the expectations, plans, goals, hopes, confidences, etc., are *all in the mind*—all *hypotheses,* some easily verifiable (like eating) others much more uncertain (like the vision of a book you want to write). I could go on *ad infinitum* but it is lunch time— Adieu, excuse the disorder

> Best luck
> Harry

> [typed]
> 46 College Street
> Hanover, New Hampshire
> 27 September 1947

. . . Your letter from Clayton, back in August, dear Harry, has long been waiting for an answer: it was a very rich and significant discussion, which I have been digesting, and shall put with the rest of my notes for the book. But I see that I have not yet found the right words for the thoughts that I have been thinking about the importance of anticipatory reactions, and about the active effect of imagined futures, or even futures that are being prepared for without being explicitly imagined, in the immediate behavior of the organism. What I am doing is to continue and carry further a description which Lloyd Morgan began some thirty years ago in his discussion of "prospective reference," and, less from obscurity inherent in the subject than in the language of daily life, he never got very far either.[56] Bergson had glimmers of what I am trying to say, too; but before I get done I think I will go further than either of them. The whole field has to be related to the organism's "plan of life" in the dimension of time, without introducing any conceptual ghosts, like ent-

---

56. C. Lloyd Morgan, *Life, Mind, and Spirit* (1926).

elechies, to account for the visible phenomena. More of this when I myself have gone further.

The summer, on looking back on it, was a very fruitful one for me; even when I found myself blocked in my work, I was not dismayed: I only kicked myself on not having consciously taken the time out for further reflection and self-analysis before I prematurely plunged into Vol. IV. I have achieved a better insight into what I have been doing and how I have been living than I ever had before in my life; not that I have discovered anything that I had not known in some fashion before, but because I see everything with greater clarity and courage. At the end of this self-inquisition I was greatly stimulated, as I have told Christiana in detail, by participating in a Rorschach test; and she promised to talk over the results of that with you when your own mind is free from the preoccupations of your Melville; so I won't go into that now. But I have now a sense of great solidity and composure and even happiness, without the pains and stresses that have dogged me the last ten years of my life.

Two weeks ago I went down to Washington and lectured at the National War College on the Social Implications of the atomic bomb and other forms of genocide (total extermination and destruction). On the whole it was a good show; and I discovered that my Air Affairs article had really struck home; in that it was, apparently, the first time the military people were brought to question themselves, and their preparations for atomic war, and to ask themselves whether they had, temporarily, the perfect weapon they believed they had. I followed through that argument; though the topic I dealt with was the possibility of decentralization. The point I made was that any preparation that threw our civilization even more out of balance than it was would turn out to be disastrous; and that every preparation, like decentralizing population and industry, and building up balanced regions, which brought us in balance would not merely be good as military defense, in case we were the victims of a genocide attack, but would be good even if peace and harmony were immediately established. No one in my audience was below the rank of a Lieutenant Colonel or a navy Captain; and after the lecture and discussion were over I retired to have another hour's discussion with a group consisting mainly of generals and admirals and a few State Department experts; and they turned out to be an extremely attentive and respectful lot. Quite different from a university faculty of the same rank and economic class: none of the cattishness and attempt to establish their personal or professional superiority that one would have found in a university group! Some of the participants were very keen; but even the dull ones gave me a very satisfactory sense of integrity and the manly virtues, and I felt a little more at home with them than Ruskin must have felt when he addressed the students at Woolwich!

We came back here at the beginning of September; and I shall spend the first part of the winter revising The Culture of Cities for a new English edition and giving two lectures in the Great Issues course here, while I spend part of my afternoons as consultant for students in the Library. By taking on this much college work I both repair the inroad from the high cost of living and lessen my sense of guilt at occupying a house some other professor has a better claim to! From January first on I hope to be busy with my book. This, we plan, is our last year here; for Alison will be graduated from elementary school, and we hope—though we don't yet quite know how we shall swing it—to spend the winters hereafter in New York, and keep our house in Amenia open most of the year, so that I can work consecutively on my book, amid my books and my notes, without these disconcerting pilgrimages between Hanover and Amenia, a distance of more than two hundred miles, which spoils the possibility of weekends or casual visits.

Don't bother to answer this, dear Harry, till you are well out of the woods. I plan to visit Boston more frequently this winter, both with Alison and with Sophia; and if you are still in Boston then, of if not, then in New York, we should have the opportunity for a real talk.

Warmly
Lewis

[typed]
46 College Street
Hanover
New Hampshire
16 November 1947

. . . . Your letter, dear Harry, gave me deep satisfaction.[57] Not that I was in the least worried about not having heard from you; for I knew you were deep in Pierre and did not expect a word till you emerged from it. Jo's touching letter, meanwhile, had come, and that assured me that the book had arrived. Still: it was good to hear from you and to have from your own lips confirmation of what I hoped would be your response to the book. You mustn't, however, feel the slightest quiver of guilt over your original misgivings: they contributed to the strength of the book, as I told you before, more than you could guess; for if a writer or his thoughts have any inherent strength, they will be stronger and tougher for having been challenged, even though the immediate effects of that challenge may be distressing. Your opposition was nothing compared to Sophy's; for in the act of reading the book matters that had been "settled" and buried for years rose again to the surface of our lives, and the deep temperamental differences between us, too, became acutely separatistic. Yet I don't know which contributed more to the book: her direct aid, which was of course immense, or her opposition. Certainly the book is a far better one than I could have produced without the dialectic struggle that ensued with you and with

---

57. Murray's letter about *Green Memories* cannot be located in either the Papers of Henry A. Murray or the Lewis Mumford Collection.

Sophy: if I transcended some of my own weaknesses in the act of writing it, it was because of that struggle. So if you are pleased with the result, you may give yourself some of the credit, too: as you unsuspectingly did when you asked who said of Geddes that he had "an all-or-nothing quality." Who but you? The book, as I probably told you before, will be forever incomplete for me; I keep on adding notes, and filling out places where, though I sometimes had the material to use, I omitted some decisive touch. I admit that it does not get to the very depth and bottom of his life; but I could have approached this only by writing a different kind of book, wholly lyrical and tragic in its essence, probably not to be written in prose: certainly not to be written, as I did this one, with the reassuring sense of the confirmatory document at hand, to stabilize my own judgement and to convince the reader that Geddes was not simply an inner projection of mine. But such an inner appraisal was beyond my power: the nearest I came to conveying what was there was in my use of Geddes's own device, the understatement, a form on the whole so foreign to my native way of thought, though I recognize how decisively the book gains in strength by its employment. I had two canons of selection: will this passage mean something to anyone besides Sophy and me? And second: Would Geddes accept this as his own, if he could look over my shoulder? How well these criteria worked I can gauge now from the response of the book's readers: though it has scarcely been noticed and has sold very feebly, the letters that have come to me from "outside" people have revealed the power and the universality of this narrative. You will not perhaps be surprised to know that the most sympathetic of my letters, the most deeply understanding, have been from young men who have seen service, and who find their own grief over the loss of their comrades made articulate and significant in this account of Geddes. This is their book: and in time, I think, it will achieve wide circulation among them. That it has lessons and morals for the parents of the living, I have no doubt; in fact, one of my friends here, who is new Dean of Freshman, finds himself recommending it to the parents he comes in contact with. But it also has perhaps more to say to the parents of those killed than, on first intuition, you realized, if I can judge from some of the responses. Many people who find themselves overwhelmed by their loss do what Alison instinctively did: they retreat from it altogether and lock it up in the most private corner of their heart. They want to express it, but they do not know how; they want to share it, but they do not know with whom. For people like this, Green Memories performs a precious office: it shows them how to uncover their sorrow and look at it, and, by its own confessions, it lessens a little the burden of guilt, which all of us feel in looking back on an incomplete relationship, no matter how dear and warm it has been. The dominant convention in our society is to ignore grief: it must not be heard or seen or symbolized. When I conceived Green Memories I had the alternative of telling the story in a simple sequence, with the moment of grief and desolation sprung at the end; or telling it in such a fashion that the theme of grief and parting would be present at the beginning winding in and out of the other story, of a young life developing, adventuring, growing. I deliberately chose the second method; and for other parents of the dead I believe that gives the book a cathartic quality which would be unbearable if I had told the story in a more natural order. What the book says is that death is with us always, and every moment of life is tragic and irretrievable.

The reception in the public press that the book has received has been both exhilarating and disheartening. Exhilarating because, outside New York, in Philadelphia and St. Paul I have had reviews which express, to a degree utterly unusual in daily journalism, a completeness of understanding and a depth of response comparable to that which you and Jo have shown. To get one such review is almost sufficient recompense for writing a book: it shows one has struck home. On the other hand, the book has been ignored, slighted, treated perfunctorily in quarters where I should have expected just the opposite: particularly in New York, which influences the book market throughout the country. This shelving of the book is not the work of any gang or clique; it is not due to any personal animosity: it has occurred so widely that I must treat it as something organic, something which reveals the bias *toward* the trivial and insignificant and spiritually dead, which characterizes a disintegrating social order, along with a positive bias against work of a higher quality. This bias is entirely impersonal: it resulted, for example, in the Times Book review editor's mercilessly butchering a review of Frost's Masque of Mercy in the same number that had Hillyer's review of Green Memories; and I suspect, from the altogether favorable and heart-warming notice by Hillyer, that his review had been treated in the same fashion, so that two absolutely insignificant pictures should be displayed fulsomely on the same page: indeed, the reviews of Frost and myself were treated as mere *picture-frames.* There is no comeback against that sort of thing. But unfortunately, it dooms my book; and if my works have any regenerative power—as the comments from war-veterans make me think they have—it dooms this power, too: thousands of people who might find their faith renewing itself will not even know of the existence of Green Memories. So at the height of my powers I find my books having less attention paid to them, and being of less effect, than the things I wrote twenty-five years ago; and the result of that is such a feeling of alienation and estrangement as would keep me silent forever were I not, at this moment, supremely healthy—full of caustic Melvillian contempt, but not Melvillian despair—and were I not content to go on writing in my own fashion so long as I have but one reader like yourself, dear Harry, to address myself to.

. . . Your letter, it happened, came yesterday, the very day after I had delivered a lecture to an English class on Melville. You don't know how close you have been to me in your struggles with Pierre: though I had planned to read it through again last summer, I found it unbearable and finally desisted; though I also recognized, more keenly than ever, the greatness of some of its fragments. There is much about Melville I still want to discuss with you; for by now I have caught up with most of what has been written by way of biography and criticism during the last fifteen years. I particularly want to discuss with you the chronology of his "four months" in the Marquesas; for it seems to me that in dealing with Typee Anderson's book, which has so many valuable little details in it in other portions, here commits a monstrous error of scholarship and indeed wantonly libels Melville. I am not convinced by Anderson's demonstration that Melville could not have spent more than four or five weeks with the Typees, though I note that Jean Simon accepted it. Once you accept that, you raise more questions than you settle. You have probably gone into this more deeply than I have but I should like to compare notes with you. As for Anderson's "demonstrations" that Melville was borrowing from books that he denied having seen, they seem to me utterly unconvincing; and they were made without any obligation apparently being evident to Anderson that one should not libel a dead man, nor even cast suspicion on him, unless one can prove one's point with objective evidence. For the question of motive enters into the proof of any crime; and neither Anderson nor Simon have established a reason for Melville's openly and ostentatiously saying that he had spent four months in the Marquesas. (That is quite different from H.M.'s making himself a year younger when he went to sea in Redburn: that involved simple amour propre!)

I hope to be down in New York, dear Harry, between 8 and 12 December. Shall you be there then? If so, we must have a long pow-wow. Among a thousand things we have to talk about, not the least for me is the interesting results of my Rorschach analysis.

A warm embrace

Lewis

P.S. Your offer of the complete Melville overwhelms me by its generosity; but I will not say No. My own collection is spotty; and I spend so much of my life in dual residence that I should like a complete set for Amenia. The lack of the Constable edition and the refusal of the Public Library to buy it for me was a great handicap when I wrote my Melville.

1948–1953

Politics and Criticism

DURING THIS PERIOD of the correspondence, Mumford and Murray were active in political activities in an effort to avert another world war and to oppose the development of nuclear weapons. In essays such as "Time for Positive Morality," Murray promoted the abolition of war through world government, and he became an active supporter of the United World Federalists. In essays such as "Atom Bomb: 'Miracle' or Catastrophe?," Mumford condemned the nuclear option as a matter of political policy and military tactics. Although Murray agreed with Mumford's argument in the article, the style and tone in which it was written provoked some of Murray's harshest criticism of his friend. However, such criticism did not compromise their relationship or lessen Mumford's respect for Murray. Commenting on one of their meetings, Mumford wrote, "I feel in your company . . . that to trade thoughts with a really first-rate mind is one of the solid justifications of existence; and I am mighty lucky to have that pleasure combined with the solid loyalties of friendship" (LM 26 April 1948). Mumford effusively praised Murray's Hendricks House edition of Melville's *Pierre* (1949) as well as his famous essay on Moby-Dick, "In Nomine Diaboli" (1951). In 1951 Mumford published *The Conduct of Life*, the final volume in the Renewal of Life series, and Murray hailed the work with grand praise; the correspondence reveals that Murray read and commented on substantial portions of the book in draft form. However, Murray reiterated his criticism of Mumford's "autocratic temper" by charging that his friend presented several points in the book, positions which they had debated in previous discussions, in the form of "positive statements as if no other alternative were possible" (HAM 14 February 1952).

[handwritten]
125 East 72
[LM] Ans 18 Jan 48

Dear Lewis—

Glad to hear that you are planning to come to New York in the near future. C will be here during February & so that month would be best, if you feel strong enough for 2 birds in one embrace.

In case you have not already seen the publication of the Conference on Science, Philosophy & Religion—'Conflicts of Power in Modern Culture' I am asking that a copy be sent to you in hopes that you will be stimulated to do an article on it.[1]

In regard to H.M. in the South Seas we must accept the fact that a combination of motives persuaded him to deceive the public as to the length of time he spent in Typee valley & the extent of his personal observations. It is *positive* that he deserted from the *Acushnet* within a day or two of July 7, 1842 & *positive* that he was taken on the *Lucy Ann* in early August & *positive* that he arrived in Tahiti in early September. I have forgotten the exact dates, but since Anderson's work, the report of Capt. Venton of the *Lucy Ann* has been unearthed in Sidney, Australia, & it checks closely with *Omoo*. It seems to me that H.M. wanted to tell a dramatic story & he wanted to dramatize himself & the two motives ran together, as with Byron, Trelawney, & others. This made it easier for him to do some of his greatest things in literature, but the self-deception that was involved prevented him from arriving at the truth he was seeking.

Looking forward to seeing you after this long period of privation for me.

Yrs
Harry

[handwritten]
[LM] rec'd 28 Feb 48 Ans 28 Feb 48

Dear Lewis,

I like this piece *immensely* although, in my opinion, it is below your standard of thinking & expression.[2]

You felt a little strange to me—more than usual—on your last visit to New York; & so I am uncommonly restricted, not free to discuss this paper as I might if we were face to face. A few generalities is all I have to offer.

I think you should make more of your *all-important main point*: that the United States must do something to convince the entire world, & Russia *especially* if possible, that its intentions are *not* belligerent but rather to collaborate in the construc-

---

1. *Conflicts of Power in Modern Culture: Seventh Symposium,* ed. Lyman Bryson, Louis Finkelstein, and R. M. McIver (1947).

2. Lewis Mumford, "Atom Bomb: 'Miracle' or Catastrophe?" *Air Affairs,* 2 (July 1948): 326–45; included in Mumford's *In the Name of Sanity* (1954).

tion of a united peaceful world. Here I think it is safe to be dogmatic, because in the mythology of the peoples of this earth the U.S. has become the giant Fafner, the devouring dragon. We *must* do something to dispel this creation before embarking on negotiations for World Government. This is *so* essential that you should pay a great deal of attention to your *manner* of presentation. I am reminded of Lord Chesterfield (of all people!): "The more wit you have, the more good nature you must show, to induce people to pardon your superiority, for that is no easy matter." One of the basic myths in the American mind is that of "Defence & Defeat of the Bully" (first Great Britain, now Russia). This explains, in part, their present attitude towards the Great Bear & explains, in part, their predictable resistance to your autocratic, Mount Sinai mode of dictating policy. In other words I don't think you will succeed in your main objective, if you so arbitrarily assert that *your* way is the only effective way of attaining it. The autocratic temper of your paper is not calculated to convert the prosaic, bantering, give-and-take, middle-of-the road, unrespectful, democratic bulk of Americans. I am strongly in favor of your proposals & hence regret that you have yielded to a spirit which will precipitate their defeat. Politics is the art of the possible. Your proposals—in their present form—are not possible for the American people. But this is merely the opinion of one who has no practical experience in these matters.

If you were here—congenially before me—I would say more, for better or for worse. Anyhow, I am confident that a few strategic changes will be sufficient to give this piece the effectiveness which it now lacks. I wish you the best fortune with it—

Yours
Harry

[typed]
46 College Street
Hanover, New Hampshire
28 February 1948

Dear Harry:

Your main points are very well taken indeed; and I am grateful for your criticism and your help. You need not have handled the matter so gingerly; and if you have more to say of an unfavorable nature, you should come out with it. The abrupt dictatorial method of presentation you dislike was much more a product of haste than of an inflated ego: when one is in a hurry one often forgoes the little ingratiating ceremonials of politeness which smooth the way to cooperation. My intention was to lay down a series of proposals for discussion; and so innocent was this intention that I had no thought, in the act of writing, that the manner in which I did so might seem to betray quite different purposes and attitudes on my own part. Even before your letter came I had, in the re-writing, altered some of the offending passages and confessed what a fool I myself had been in thinking that the bomb would automatically serve as an educator and an awakener. But if the editor decides to use the article at all—I've already sent it away, so that I might get extra time for reconsideration—I shall take great care to put the proposals themselves forward in a more tentative and hypothetical manner. If I were indeed in an "autocratic, Mount Sinai" mood I should, I think, be a little more upset over your calling my attention to it; but on the other hand, I can't altogether dismiss the possibility that you have laid your finger on something in my personal development which may, by reason of its very unconsciousness, be obstructive. When a man's best friend and his most voluble enemies unite in pinning the same vice on him, there must be *something* there to produce that unanimity! Perhaps I have qualities which would do better in a soldier than in a thinker: self-confidence, decisiveness, willingness to take risks; though heaven knows the soldiers who had these qualities even though they produced as many victories as Montgomery, horrified their contemporaries quite as much as I apparently do. (I've been reading de Guingand's Operation Victory and have a very good picture of Montgomery's ability to raise the hackles on everyone around him.)[3] Plainly: it's time for me to fast and pray and examine my sins. Possibly I'm a whited sepulchre and a monument of self-deception. . . . As for the situation the world faces now, I fear we have all done too little and that it is already too late. In view of Russia's present reaction, which I have been expecting all along, it may be a matter of months, rather than of years, before we are involved in large-scale genocide; and then heaven help us all, this sinner included, for having rested on our oars precisely at the moment when the situation demanded that we double and quadruple all our efforts. Actually, though it might have made me an even more unpleasant character, I wish that I had, both in 1938 and in 1945, a little more of the paranoid fanaticism, over-concentration, and delusions of grandeur that would have kept me singlemindedly at the task of carrying through the proposals I originally tossed into the ring on both occasions—and then, except in the most perfunctory way—never followed up. Not that the actual course of history would have been changed, unless a thousand others had done the same thing: I have no delusions about being God. But just a little more willingness to believe in the unconditional importance of what I was saying might, at least, have left me with a clearer conscience than I now have. It is not because I have the notion that I have exclusive possession of the truth, but because I falsely have believed that other people, equally rational, have come independently to the same conclusions and can be relied on to do their job, that I have gone wrong. (This was equally true in the Beard affair; where I imagined that at least a significant minority would understand the issue and make themselves heard. Actually, no single fellow member of the Institute spoke up, even in private correspondence with me.)[4]

3. Francis Wilfred De Guingand, *Operation Victory* (1947).

4. Mumford had criticized the historian Charles A. Beard during the late 1930s for his isolationist views. In 1947 Mumford resigned in protest from the National Institute for Arts and Letters when the or-

But all this leaves us where we started: specifically with my thanks and gratitude for your criticism and with my daring you, masochistically, to make it even harsher, if you have been withholding anything!

Lewis

[handwritten]
[LM] Rec'd—16 Mar 48

Dear Lewis—

This is merely to say that I received your fine letter, the forbearance of which disproved the contents of mine, & that I have been waiting for an hour—which has not yet arrived—in which to answer it. Nothing that I said is in disagreement with your opinion that you should have presented your views more energetically (in the past). The public are largely governed by inertia, & they run along in the old grooves until some tremendous emergency forces them to change their ways. One superb statement—delivered orally or in writing—has practically no effect. It must be repeated over & over again to different groups & in different words. What disturbed me was a too pronounced moral contempt for your audience—an audience composed largely of people who have been taught to resist & defy authority, particularly moral authority, a people whose conception of democracy is "I am as good as you are" (addressed to a superior), not "you are as good as I am" (addressed to an inferior). It is not merely a matter of tact & strategy, but of a profound identification with the *potential* worth of the general run of people. More than this for me is the realization that World Task No. 1 is the harmonization of peoples with opposing ideologies & the attainment of this goal calls for some integration of feeling (fellowship, the disposition to cooperate, etc.) as well as some integration of social philosophies. The former is more fundamental. You can convert a man, or be converted, or arrive at a workable compromise, if the two of you stay together (mutually faithful to the potential virtue & reasonableness of the other) than if you separate & compete as ideological rivals. We are witnessing, I think, the martyrdom of man—martyrized by their own irresistible wills to property, power, & prestige—in the ideological as well as on the material & behavioral levels. If the debacle is to be prevented conversion must occur, & the converters must not themselves exhibit the dispositions & manners which are destroying the rest of us. All this reminds me that I have been writing—in this letter—as if I were on Mt. Olympus, enjoying a superior view, & so you have a good demonstration of the force that is moving us toward war rather than toward fellowship.

Obviously I have been acting contrary to my ideal which is not to preach a value until I have become it—but it is a long pilgrimage (with many slips) to that

---

ganization awarded Beard the gold medal for history; in a November 1947 letter to Van Wyck Brooks, he described Beard as "an intellectual Quisling" (Robert E. Spiller, ed., *The Van Wyck Brooks–Lewis Mumford Letters: The Record of a Literary Friendship, 1921–1963* [New York: E. P. Dutton, 1970], 321).

place, & I have reasons to hope that your charity will be large enough to forgive me this conspicuous backsliding. I have written more than I intended—You can blame my Id.

Best regards—
Harry

I have been waiting for Mr. Brumwell, but he did not appear.[5] I sent you a copy of *Assessment of Men*—just as a token—surely not to read. *Pierre* won't be published until September.

[handwritten]
17 April 48
125 East 72
[LM] Ans in person

Dear Lewis,

I am just back from St. Croix, V.I., considerably refreshed though not exuberant with energy. My letters to you—as you could feel—were written out of a cranky, fault-finding fatigue & were more relevant to my own distempers than to anything exhibited in your article. The truth is that for years—up to about 1937—I did not think that the general temper and achievement of the American people was any business of mine. I assumed that they would come to the necessary reforms of our society in due course. I could contribute more by sticking to my chosen sphere. But as soon as Fascism began to get arrogant I saw that basic philosophic values were at stake & this conflict compelled my attention & thought. During the war, perhaps for the first time wholly & consciously I felt identified with my countrymen & their destiny. More recently, however, I have become more appalled by their commitment to cynical ruthless materialism and by the general degradation of cultural values—by their lack of appreciation of the ways & beliefs & profounder accomplishments of other societies—by their bantering superficiality, irreverence, & adolescent self-assertion, etc.—most particularly, by everything that stands in the way of our immediate commitment to world government, world law & world police force. I have felt that it was essential to resist the alienation which these so repellent & exasperating trends were producing in me & to make my identification deeper & more secure, & also to find the touchstone of their hearts, the way to awaken them & invite them towards the only course that remains open to us if we are to prevent the reign of the Atom & ruination of mankind. Thus when your article came along, its very excellence made me expect the highest efficacy from it, & I was disappointed to find what seemed to me an imperfection—imperfection in relation to the resistance of the American people to anything that flavored of a moralizing Jehovah. Actually it was a perfectly straightforward statement & wholly acceptable to me, but it seemed calculated to antagonize a host of people who are touchy on the

5. J. R. Marcus Brumwell, author of *This Changing World* (1944).

score of their personal sovereignty. Perhaps the strongest force we have to contend against—is just this intolerance of any subordination, personal or political—"What! do you expect that the American people will stand being governed by a lot of damn foreigners!" as one traveling-companion put it. Before admonishing the people I would also like to see whether a dozen intellectuals could get together & hold together & pull together—submerging their personal notions & antagonisms & arriving at a Common Plan with no credit ascribed to individuals. Do you think American intellectuals are capable of that? Questionable.

This then is some of the background & gist of my critical remarks, but you must understand that I would not waste my time being critical if I did not believe that you & your work were our *best* chance of redemption.

When are you coming to New York? I am eager for talk—

Affectionately
Harry

[typed]
125 East 72 Street
New York, N.Y.
April 23, 1948

Dear Zest-giving Lewis,

It was wonderful seeing you the other afternoon. I hope your talk for Mrs. Cranston's group was successful in stirring their enthusiasm and giving direction and substance to their efforts.[6] I very much regret missing this opportunity of watching you bring fire and order to a well-intentioned, though somewhat prosaic and confused, body of men and women.

Let me suggest that you send a copy of your article on the present situation immediately to Einstein in Princeton. He and Shapley are concocting some plan, and your suggestions would be of inestimable value to them.[7]

I am sending you a short review of Murphy's book on *Personality* (please return it some time as it's my only copy), as a means of calling your attention to some of its virtues in case you have not already become acquainted with them.[8] I am also enclosing another piece (which I may have sent you in January) merely to keep you in touch with my recent occupations.[9]

6. Ruth Cranston was a representative of the World Congress of Religion, also known as the World Alliance for International Friendship Through Religion.

7. Albert Einstein (1879–1955), physicist; Harlow Shapley (1885–1972), astronomer.

8. Henry A. Murray, review of Gardner Murphy, *Personality: A Biosocial Approach to Origins and Structure, Survey Graphic* 37 (March 1948): 167.

9. Probably Murray's "Time for a Positive Morality," *Survey Graphic* 36 (1947): 195.

Let us keep in touch this spring—if this fits your present way of life—as life is short, the occasion instant, decision difficult, experiment perilous, but necessary.

Yours,

Harry

P.S.—Just after leaving you Wednesday afternoon I turned into Giller's Bookshop, and, since I was full of your infectious thought mentioned your name, and the good man, a hunchback with a well of sagacity, said, "Oh, he's a great man, he's my favorite American philosopher. A very wise man. Oh, I would like to meet him. I have read all his books. He's a great man, a very great man!" So there, even if the coterie of mean and meager literary critics do not dare to appreciate your writings, there is a multiplicity of other people closer to the realities who do appreciate them—hugely.

[typed]
46 College Street
Hanover, New Hampshire
26 April 1948

Dear Harry:

After our walk and talk together, the rest of my visit to New York was an anticlimax. I didn't bring either fire or order to Mrs. Cranston's group: they are quite decent people, all of them; but the East and West will never meet on the high level of unobjectionable platitudes; or rather, the meeting that can take place at that level is in no sense a solution of any of the tension and hostilities of our day. They were very kind to me, Atkinson in particular; and I am glad that we got together and am willing to go to far greater lengths with them than they will ever be willing to go with me or with those who think like me.[10]

Thank you for your timely suggestion about Einstein: the editor of Air Affairs has just wired me that the proofs will be coming in tomorrow; and I shall ask him to send an extra galley to Einstein. Thanks even more for introducing me to Gardner Murphy's Personality, which in some curious way I had not yet even come upon. I shall order it at once. Such a number of books have come out in the last three or four years that deal, exhaustively and authoritatively, with matters that I had planned to treat in Vol. IV, in a far less systematic fashion, that I am somewhat reconciled to my tardiness, and stimulated by it to somewhat alter the original plan—nearer an intuition than anything so orderly as a plan—of that work. All the better. The idea won't die just because I haven't got around to saying my small part of it.

I gave a talk to a thousand art teachers at Hunter College on Saturday afternoon; and that left my ego pleasantly inflated, though the speech I had so carefully prepared was to my taste a little wooden, and was redeemed only by forty minutes of really exciting discussion. A good many of these people had followed my work

10. Henry A. Atkinson served as general secretary of the World Congress of Religion.

carefully, and would have accepted the chanting of the alphabet by me as holy gospel, if I hadn't managed to say anything better: but that doesn't make your report about your old bookseller less sweetly welcome.

I expect to come to New York by the twentieth of May; and will get hold of you again if you are around. We just scratched the surface of things in our few hours together; but I feel in your company, as I did when I was in Princeton, that to trade thoughts with a really first-rate mind is one of the solid justifications of existence; and I am mighty lucky to have that pleasure combined with the solid loyalties of friendship. Did you see my piece on L.L. Whyte in the current Saturday Review?[11]

> Warmly
> Lewis

[typed]
46 College Street
Hanover, New Hampshire
5 May 1948

. . . One of the things we must discuss when we meet, dear Harry, is the Kinsey Report.[12] I am miles behind everyone in reading it, of course, and on the basis of the over-eager reactions I've got from everyone, I was rather unfavorably set toward it; but I confess that it seems to me, all in all, a magnificent job, though it is not free from faults that seem to me to call for correction, since, after all, only a small fraction of their final 100,000 cases have been examined. I wonder if you've had the same reaction I've had, which I haven't noticed in any of the reviews so far, though I've read a great many; and that is that the equation of "sexual activity" with "orgasm" unconsciously weights the report so that it makes masturbation and nocturnal emissions have the same status as mature sexuality, with its far fuller psychosomatic commitment. But the same token, because women masturbate less frequently and reach orgasms in dreams less easily, it makes their sexual activity seem far more impoverished than man's; although if one could gauge a woman's sexual preoccupations in sex-hours (man-hours!) they might turn out to be much closer to man's level. The unconscious overstress of autoerotic activity comes out even in the questionnaire; for while Kinsey inquires in detail as to the methods used to achieve an orgasm through masturbation, the questions they ask about heterosexual intercourse are relatively limited. Even in pre-coital play they forget to ask about kissing and fondling the body as a whole, or the buttocks; and overlook the role of fingers as substitute sexual end-organs. For men who start out to be thorough and objective, they seem to me to have passed over many obvious points. So

---

11. Lewis Mumford, review of Lancelot Law Whyte, *The Next Development in Man, Saturday Review of Literature*, 24 April 1948, 22–24.

12. Alfred C. Kinsey, *Sexual Behavior in the Human Male* (1948).

again, though they ask about coital positions, they have no further question to ask about coital methods; though surely it is important to know if the initiative is male or female, and if the motion in intercourse is up and down, or circular and screw-wise (by the woman) since in my own experience the latter is a highly important factor in enabling some women to reach an orgasm. Likewise, no question is asked to find out whether the man remains in for a second and third orgasm or whether (pace Toynbee) he practices Withdrawal and Return!

Finally, though Kinsey properly tries to find out whether the partners prefer nudity, and light or darkness, he makes no effort to discover anything about sounds made during coitus: whether the act takes place in silence or with inarticulate groans, whinnies, and ecstasies, or with endearing speech, or with tender obscenities. Since the question of sound has a bearing on many social provisions for sexual intercourse—privacy, soundproof walls, etc.—it is important to know how much vocal abandon exists, and how this is distributed by social classes. I suspect that the poor are grimly silent, and that really good intercourse would more often end in a shout of triumph and glee but for the thought of neighbors across the way, or children in the next room. Finally, some of the questions asked about Homosexuality under 3. Psychic reactions, play a part in heterosexual intercourse, too, and it would be interesting to find the answers in our time: whether people prefer animal musk or perfumed soap, hair or razored skin.

Forgive me for putting all these criticisms before you, rather than Kinsey. But he probably has a correspondence by now as large as a movie star's, if not a crooner's; and there is a better chance, perhaps, of my getting an answer from you. More when we meet.

Lewis

[handwritten]
Grindstone 25 May '48

Dear Lewis,

Your letter has waited a long time for an answer, but I have had a very uneven 3 weeks, full of various distractions. I have been trying to get to the cause of my 9-months headache & have had X-Rays & been on various diets & given up smoking for a while—in fact generally disturbed all the rhythms of 50 odd years of physiological habit! I have been to the Tower, to Cambridge & Boston, to Syracuse (United World Federalists), & for 10 days up here alone in my stone hut on Grindstone Island. I have written the letter to the paper which I mentioned to you in New York, but have not sent it yet.[13] By the way I am very much impressed by the United World Federalists & believe that offers the best channel for our efforts. Individuals

13. Murray wrote a letter supporting the creation of a world federation, *New York Times*, 9 June 1948, 28.

can do a good deal, but when it comes to Congressional action—as it does now—only pressure groups can be effective.

As for the Kinsey Report I must confess that I spent only a few hours on it the day it came out. I met Kinsey & heard him talk 5 years ago, & during my years of practicing psychoanalysis saw (not through a keyhole) so much of the erotic life of the neurotic elements in our society that the Report seemed like an old story. I thought it was a very careful, relatively objective, systematic piece of work—very valuable for our matter-of-fact-minded population. In attempting to be *objective* & *scientific*, Kinsey, as you say, picked on the most tangible fact he could think of, namely, orgasm & based most of his figures on its frequence. This I would say was an instance of misplaced concreteness, only possible in a highly mechanized, eye-minded, superficial culture. For those peripheralists & extraceptors, feelings & emotions must be eliminated—in themselves & from the data they examine. The hidden assumption is that nothing counts except what is photographable. But Nature has not arranged things for the conscience of the matter-of-fact psychologist—the most important things are hardest to get at, hardest to observe. Another index of Kinsey's culture-bound point of view is the emphasis on quantification & statistics. This makes it look scientific—because it bears some resemblance to physics—but it is actually less scientific because it corresponds less to life—where qualitative differences, forms & patterns, are of the very essence. I could go along for pages in this vein, but this is really a criticism of our whole American orientation rather than that of Dr. Kinsey. Kinsey is a zoologist & consequently has not the background which would help him to think of all the questions he should or might ask. I think your questions are more significant than a great many of his & if he had asked them I would have read the book with more eagerness & thoroughness. I am leaving here in a couple of days & going to Boston (37 Brimmer St—a new house for us overlooking the basin) via New York. From now on my address will be Topsfield, Mass. Give my love to the profound Sophy & the incredible Alison, & let me know when you are going to Amenia, & what are the chances for another meeting. I am keen to know *all* the reactions to your paper—anything from Einstein?

Yours

Harry

[typed]
46 College Street
Hanover, New Hampshire
8 June 1948

. . . We have been living for the last ten days, dear Harry—Sophy in fact for a longer time—in the midst of the vast turbulence and upheaval of moving; and in such a state your letter still finds me, though thanks to Sophy's brave efforts a good part of our chattels are now packed and ready for the moving van on Saturday. On Sunday, if all goes well, we quit this place for good: eager to be back in Amenia, and even in the hurly-burly of New York, though not without a few sighs for the handful of good friends we are leaving behind us. For all the length of our stay, and my own many years of visiting, we never quite sank roots here: why, I don't quite know. It is certainly one of the decentest and most civilized parts of the world I know, where the old Puritan mores, mellowed but not obliterated, contribute to a certain up-standingness and inner self respect in all the daily relations. Unfortunately I have been in a shell these last three years; and have seen all too little of the native characters in the hills, people like the old cabinet makers and farmers, who are most worth knowing, though I've had glimpses of them. Now I leave all these unsounded possibilities behind me and turn southward—probably with not a little quiet relief on the part of the faculty, always a little afraid that I might break out in some way distracting or distasteful to them; though, since the Atomic Bomb crusade of 1946, I have kept as quiet as a mouse. It's curious that you should have asked me about that article: when I get down to Amenia I'll send you a copy of it. I ran across it in packing, read it soberly, and decided it was perhaps the most sane as well as the most timely thing I'd ever written; though utterly without effect. My Moral Breakdown address has nothing new in it; I've said all of it better in The Condition of Man; but I think that by now perhaps more people may be ready to listen to the same theme in slightly different words.[14] The Saturday Review will print it in a few weeks. [. . .] I go out to Iowa on 23 June; but after 5 July we'll welcome you at Amenia with wide open arms.

A warm embrace

Lewis

P.S. Professor indeed! No more than you ever will be. . . .

P.S. I was in Amenia ten days: but in N.Y. only the Sunday night I saw Brooks.

[typed]

Lewis Mumford

Amenia, New York

9 July 1948

. . . I am glad, dear Harry, that you reprinted your truncated letter in its full form. When I read it in the Times I was disappointed in it, for your talk about it had let me to expect something more: but I didn't realize the cause of my disappointment till you sent on the crucial omission. I hope you have hauled the Times people over the carpet about this: their attitude toward these matters is infuriating in its irresponsibility and its arrogance. It would be better for them not to publish a letter than to

---

14. Lewis Mumford, "Kindling for Global Gehenna," *Saturday Review of Literature,* 26 June 1948, 7–8.

editorialize it and eviscerate it in the fashion they did with yours. They lack, in their correspondence section, the decency which they show in most other parts of the paper; and they have none of the sense of being a public servant that the London Times has in its correspondence column. By now, when I have something to say, I send it to the Herald Tribune, which I don't, I confess, regularly read. But they treat their correspondence with respect; whereas the Times delays, edits, suppresses, quite at will, without respect to the standing and function of the person whose letter they are so treating.

We have been back here since the 13 June; but are hardly unpacked yet, so busy have we been with the scores of other pleasant chores that a neglected place exacts of one. I went out to Iowa a week after coming here and had a good time after my lecture talking with the Jewish scholar who had been assaulted in the very hotel I stayed in—do you remember the incident the Saturday Review gave publicity to?—but apart from coming home with a pound of bacon from Utopia, the Amana Colony to be more exact, and a rather sizable honorarium, the trip was a great waste of time; in spite of which I have already settled down this week to the writing of my book, which opens with a chapter I am now re-writing for the third time on The Nature of Man.[15] (It doesn't make the immediate task any easier to find myself glancing over my shoulder at the many complex but excellent things I find in Gardner Murphy's Personality, one of the first books of its kind to do justice to symbolism and symbolic conduct.) Sophy and I have both been in an exuberant and altogether relaxed state; but our fingers are secretly crossed since we are conditioned through long experience to regard this as a prelude to sudden catastrophe!

Speaking of editorial mistreatment, the Saturday Review recently printed an article of mine without mentioning that it was an address at a religious conference; and to compound their neglect they attached to it an apocalyptic and irrelevant title that gave the wrong cue to the contents and misstated the whole thing, since my title had been: Moral Breakdown—Symptoms, Causes, Results. I suspect the work of an enemy on the Review, the same who caused my original article against Beard to be pigeonholed. The title "Kindling for Global Gehenna" was exactly the sort of thing such a person would have invented to discredit me.

The days are not long enough for me to write and think in, to garden and relax in, to devour and to enjoy, and I find it much harder to push aside the little claims of life than I used to when I was wholly concentrated on one of my big books: so I will not feel quite safe about the book until it begins to drive me hard and won't let me look to one side of the road or the other. Still, apart from the book, the inner feeling is good: better than I can remember it for years and years. If you plan to be in

15. Elihu S. Cooper, a rabbi and teacher in an Iowa City Jewish school, was attacked by two men in the Jefferson Hotel in Iowa City on 6 May 1947. The men were identified, but Cooper refused to testify against them.

the neighborhood, dear Harry, let us know and stay at least overnight with us. At the moment Sophy is in New York, canvassing the apartment situation; but apart from some unforeseen disaster, I don't expect to leave here before the tenth of September or so; and I probably wouldn't leave then were it not for the fact that I am down to give a paper on The Future of Technics in Western Civilization, at the Washington Centennial meeting of the AAAS. If you have a moment tell me what you are thinking.

Lewis

P.S. My Air Affairs article is out; but I haven't received any reprints yet. You'll get an early one.

N.B. Have you read: Cry, the Beloved Country by A. Paton. The best novel I've read in years. Another book you *must* read is coming out on the 19th: The Home Place by Wright Morris.[16]

[handwritten]
[LM] Recd 15 July 48

Dear Lewis,

I was reinvigorated by reading the enclosed. It is fine. C & I were also particularly impressed by your Sat. Rev. Lit. article. It is a truthful, insightful, forceful, & persuasive piece—movingly written. You are right *all* the time. The difficulty is that the American people are so soft that they can't bear to be told there is anything seriously wrong with them or that Hell is round the corner. Keep on shouting—respectfully—the best men will eventually get on your wagon & ride to salvation—

Affectionately
H

Sailing for England—July 30
Queen Mary

[typed]
Lewis Mumford
153 West 82 Street
New York 24, N.Y.
17 March 1949

Dear Harry:

I was about to write you a note anyway, thinking back to our refreshing evening together, to thank you and Jo for the very happy time I had under your enviable—and herewith envied—roof. But perhaps I wouldn't have gotten around to it so soon if I hadn't noticed your name on the supplementary list of people sponsoring Harlow Shapley's imminent congress of intellectuals. His organization asked me too to sponsor this meeting; and I refused for the same reason that I re-

---

16. Alan Paton, *Cry the Beloved Country* (1948); Wright Morris, *The Home Place* (1948).

fused a similar invitation a year ago, because the whole thing has been rigged, by the communists within his group—with his blind or innocent connivance, I suppose—so that it will serve as a sounding board for Russian communist denunciation of the foreign policy of the United States. The speakers are heavily weighted on the communist side, many of them being open communists; and no opportunity has been given for anyone to discuss any of Russia's sins, misdemeanors and crimes. But there are just enough people like yourself among the sponsors to give the whole affair an air of reputability it does not really possess. You have, perhaps, every personal confidence in Shapley, and I do not deny that he perhaps deserves it: but you should know that the poor man has fallen into a den of communist thieves, who are using him and the people he hooks in for all that they are worth. As you know, I am not an automatic hater of communism, or one who thinks that our foreign policy, these last four years, has been spotless. I told Shapley, in a letter he never had the courtesy to answer, that I would be perfectly happy to sit down with a group of communists and discuss freely, for our common enlightenment, the sins and mistakes of our respective countries; but that I wouldn't be a party to a wholesale whitewashing of Russia and an equally wholesale denigrating of the United States. Actually, this conference will probably do more to promote ill feeling between the two countries and harden lines all ready drawn too tight than a whole barrelful of UnAmerican activities monkeys.

Sophy expects to go to Hanover next week, for a brief vacation: all her disorders, when boiled down, amount to a general psychosomatic derangement, without any one condition demanding medical special treatment.

Affectionately,
Lewis

[typed]
Lewis Mumford
Amenia, New York
29 June 1949

. . . The Melville book came last week, dear Harry; and though I was just about to embark on the final chapter, the chapter that will probably stump me for the rest of my days, even though I call the book finished—for who, faced with the implications of it, can hope to say the final word about his philosophy?—I plunged right into your Introduction and read it through in two sittings.[17] It is the most colossally compact and compactly colossal summation of scholarship and human understanding anyone has brought forth in our generation; and you are entitled to a ten years sabbatical after managing to say so much with such consummate brevity.

---

17. Murray's edition, with introduction and footnotes, of Herman Melville, *Pierre, or the Ambiguities* (New York: Hendricks House, 1949).

Reading it, I had the sense of being present, in a fashion that would be impossible in real life, at an interminable series of psychoanalytic sittings which had somehow, as in a dream, been speeded up sufficiently to avoid the tedium which must accompany such treatments: that is one of those mysteries I've always wanted to be a party to; and here you have made it public, in a fashion that is altogether enthralling. You told me, while you were writing it, that I wouldn't approve of it; and I can't imagine what you were thinking of. I hardly dare to reread my own analysis of Pierre or Melville to find out. Your literary judgements seem to me impeccable; and dispose, forever I hope, of those maudlin scholars who, because they think no one will perhaps bother to find them out, have treated the book as an unqualified masterpiece. If there is any difference between us it would only be in minor matters; or over the fact that, when I wrote my book, I was over-reacting against Weaver, whose judgements I did not respect and whose manner I did not like; so, in interpreting Melville's weaknesses and his illness I was inclined to put the best possible face on every dark incident. (It was partly that and partly the result of my having been free, up to the moment of writing the book, from any of the dismaying experiences and shocks that Melville had suffered: at least, up to that point, I had internal buffers which kept me from being as injured by them as he was.) Even now, my own superficiality has saved a good part of Melville for me; while your autopsy was so thorough-going that even the Last Trumpet would hardly bring the various organs and parts together again. The worst of it is that I must agree with your analysis, as I follow your demonstration, organ by organ; for no one has gotten closer to him than you have. In the very act of penetrating the hidden layers of his being, you followed his own method in apprehending the universe: so that your natural disenchantment with him, finally, springs from the same root as his disenchantment with the world itself. It is only on the surface, perhaps, that any life holds together and can stand up under inspection; if one goes far enough in one's analysis one is left with a hot shower of neutrons disconcertingly unlike a man. The fact is that Melville's inwardness is terrible to behold; and Pierre, which reveals so much of it, is like a living man with his entrails exposed. Perhaps the most necessary element for holding a character together is the skin; once that is penetrated in too many places, once too large a patch of it is burned off, the creature dies. So much in Stubb-like defense of superficiality: for which, like Stubb, I probably deserve a kick in the rump from Ahab! But I'd have to go through your essay, paragraph by paragraph, to dwell properly on all its felicities: you couldn't have written anything more appropriately stimulating to my own thoughts at this particular stage of my own work, when I am dealing with the nature of Man and with what, under heaven, may be done about it. I had already reused, in a different way from Melville, his chapter on Horologicals and Chronologicals for my chapter on ethics; but though I'd escaped his dualism, I overlooked one simple beautiful fact, which your analysis disclosed, namely, that at Greenwich, astronomical time and local time coincide! In actual life, of course, the Astronomer Royal still must carry a watch; and may find that going wrong, just like any citizen in China—etc. What I admire most, I suppose, in the whole performance is the staggering thoroughness of your execution combined with an utter freedom from pedantry and ostentatious learning: compared with which I find my own work, up to the Condition of Man, less thorough and more ostentatious. . . . Some day, I hope, in spite of your present feelings about the subject, you'll go back and finish the book; for your thought has dimensions that are lacking, so far, in any other American biography I've seen.

In another week or ten days I hope to have finished the first draft of Vol. IV, whose every part and section are in a high state of unfinishment. Parts of it are admirable; parts are poor; parts—and some of them the most important—are still nonexistent. But this last six weeks or so have been a fruitful period on the whole; and I see clearer the hard road that I must follow. A week or ten days in the country greatly improved Sophy; but last week, on her coming up from the city in a newly repaired car, the wheel which the mechanics had neglected to tighten on came off; and she brought the car to a stop without suffering a scratch; though the car itself was severely damaged; and the next day, after coming home a little elated over her coolness and good luck, she had a natural letdown; so that it has taken her five days to get back into normal shape again. Otherwise, we have been free from mischief. I wish you'd dropped in for at least an hour when you were over at the Brooks'; but you probably started away in the morning—so I charitably say to myself—and remembered too well my injunction against being interrupted then! Is there any chance that you'll come by again? I shall probably be away for a week or so between drafts; otherwise I shall hold fast to my post here, till frost colors the leaves, and reflects their glow, as I hope, in the final chapter of the book.

Incidentally, did you see Admiral Gallery's article on Atomic Warfare in last week's Saturday Evening Post?[18] The first official sanity on the subject I've read; so I wrote a letter to the Herald Tribune backing him up; and am waiting to see if it will be printed.[19] There is something at once guilty and compulsive about our whole official—it is hard to say whether it is national—attitude toward this subject: part of the unseemly post-war jitters I thought we were going, this time, to avoid.

Ever Yours
Lewis

18. Daniel Vincent Gallery, "Admiral Talks Back to the Armies," *Saturday Evening Post*, 25 June 1949, 25.

19. Lewis Mumford, "Moral Implications of Our Atomic War Policy," *New York Herald Tribune*, 3 July 1949, section 2, 5.

[typed]
[LM] 9 July 1949
64 Plympton Street
Cambridge, Mass.
July 7, 1949

Dear Lewis,

What a man you are! Such praise! A feast to live on for the rest of my life! Enough to reward me for twenty years of labor and to heal every slight, if any, I have received!

The reason I thought you wouldn't like the Introduction is indicated in your letter—because in your eyes my analysis of Pierre would leave Melville in fragments, although in mine he still stands firm, particularly and immensely, of course, as the author of Moby Dick. To analyze Pierre is like analyzing the blood of an athlete as he approaches the finish of a Marathon. To see the book in proper perspective one must know the conditions and also the author's intention—in this case the "utter truth" regardless of consequences. Evidently I failed to bring home the fact that one is dealing with a man who is recklessly attempting the impossible—say, to climb Everest while suffering from cardiac decompensation. Naturally, under these circumstances all his potential frailties become evident, especially when he is compared to those who have remained comfortably unchallenged in the valley below.

In short, I failed to show enough strength in H.M. to outbalance the more conspicuous disease. I suppose—as a doctor—I am accustomed to horrors and can stand a multiplicity of them in myself and in my friends without loss of respect or faith. If a man is born on the back of a hyena it is not easy for him to stay in the saddle for a lifetime, and if he succeeds he deserves special credit. Looking at man with these considerations in mind, then, the more horrible his unconscious impulses, the more admirable he is if he can govern them or transform them into culture-generating works. Hence if I find nothing but a Shetland pony in a man's unconscious I judge that he has had an easy life—psychologically overprivileged. More of this later.

I am thrilled to hear that the first draft is nearing completion. You are at a point where even a few hours with H.A.M. (not H.M.) might throw you off key. But if you dare to open your house to me for a night I could stop on my way to or from the St. Lawrence in July or August—uncertain which.

Now for another matter, which may best be explained by typing out the letter that I am writing MacLeish, Carl Sandberg, and other top-flight poets whom I know much less intimately than I do you, which accounts for its relative formality:

I am about to undertake, with the help of Merrill Moore, a long-range study of the role of the creative writer in the United States (in 1950, say, as compared to 1850), from a psychological and sociological point of view.[20] One of the chief rea-

---

20. Merrill Moore (1903–1957), poet and psychiatrist; as an undergraduate, he was affiliated with the Fugitive group of poets at Vanderbilt University; taught neurology and psychiatry at Harvard Medical School and conducted research with Murray at the Clinic.

sons for this enterprise is the conviction that the partial eclipse of the artist by the scientist (if not by the business man and Babbitts generally) has produced a marked distortion in our whole system of values. For example, most people—educators in particular—have come to identify "thought" (the best kind of thinking) with "scientific thought." (Witness in *The Literary Mind* Max Eastman's implicit acceptance of fact-bound scientific rationality as the standard of excellence.)[21]

The first thing we would like to do is to compare the mental processes of first-rate writers and those of first-rate scientists (and later of successful business men) *under similar conditions.* As procedure, we have devised what might be called a story-telling test. It is not, strictly speaking, an index of creative imagination (which, we assume, is more or less out of reach of the will), but rather an exercise in dramatic improvisation within a limited period of time.

To obtain representative samples of artistic thought (under these uniform conditions) I must somehow engage the interest and cooperation of about twenty of the most creative American writers; and so it is with this aim in mind that I am writing to you, who certainly, by general estimate, belong among the first twenty. Would you be willing, perchance, to sacrifice two hours of your time on the altar of science, that is, to help our enterprise by taking the above mentioned test—Part I (one hour) on one day, and Part II (one hour) on the next? I feel certain that you will find the thing stimulating and enjoyable—not tedious.

Our associate, Mr. Robert Wilson, a mature and sympathetic graduate student in the Department of Social Relations at Harvard, will spend this summer giving the test to poets, novelists, and critics. He has a sound-recording apparatus and a car in which he can reach your home on almost any day you designate, except between the 17th and 29th of August. If you are disposed to help us, will you be good enough to tell me by letter what week this summer will be most agreeable to you?

You can make your own rules as far as anonymity is concerned. According to the present plan only the few whose job it is to analyze the records will know the author of any set of stories and they will be pledged to professional secrecy (as physicians are). Certainly nothing will be published (anonymously or otherwise) without your complete knowledge and consent.

Robert Frost, Robert Lowell, Conrad Aiken, Ezra Pound, Van Wyck Brooks, and of course, Merrill Moore have agreed to take the test. No refusals yet. Naturally, there is no one I would rather have than you, but I don't want to disturb the even tenor of your course this summer, and so I won't press if your first reaction is negative.

The present test, developed out of the TAT, is built on a somewhat different principle and aimed to give the freest scope to the imagination. I think you will enjoy it much more than the Rorschach.* Let me know your decision.

Sophy's performance with the motor fills me with awe. It is tremendous when an introvert surpasses all extroverts in managing a sudden crisis. Embrace her

21. Max Eastman, *The Literary Mind: Its Place in an Age of Science* (1931).

gratefully for me. And again, Lewis, let me thank you for your generous letter, brimming over with Agape.

Yours,
Harry

*N.B. I didn't! LM 29 June 70

[typed]
Lewis Mumford
Amenia, New York
9 July 1949

. . . I was about to write you, dear Harry, when your letter came this morning with its fine words for Sophy, and its interesting invitation for me. (As to Sophy, some offhand amateur psychologist had once called her an *extra*verted sensation type; and those words rankled, despite my assurance that they were entirely incorrect. You lifted that old curse.) What I was going to write you about was something that I have been struggling with by myself for a long time: a matter which I turned to when I finished my draft, though it occurs in the introduction. I want to begin the book with an opening statement on the promises and potentialities of modern life, before I go into our weaknesses and defects; and I have written a fairly convincing summary of the things that seem significant to me. But it is quite likely that I've overlooked many things, obvious or hidden, that someone like yourself has seen quite clearly. So I put the question to you, if you have an hour to wrestle with it. When I get the second draft done I shall call on you for heavy and serious criticism, particularly of the opening and closing chapters; for the whole book of course, if you are in the mood; but at least for these critical chapters on the Nature of Man and on a Discipline for Daily Life. On the latter we can perhaps come to grips when we meet: at least I'll be better able to explain to you then the sort of thing I am after. The introduction you and Kluckhohn did to Personality was extremely helpful; and some of the pieces you've published, which I had not seen before, are good too: although most of my hardest questions begin just at the point where the writers on personality leave off.[22] I think I have something to add on the subject of Drama, the life drama that is; but when you come to examine it you may find it is rubbish, though I think that it puts in more systematic form Kluckhohn's determinants. As to the invitation, I'll be happy to participate in the experiment, if only for the sake of what I shall learn further of your methods—or eventually, about myself. Earlier in August will be better than later; I leave the date to Mr. Wilson, provided he can let me know three days ahead. Only one condition: the experiment must take place in the afternoon: my mornings and my evenings are sacred, while I'm writing the book.

22. Henry A. Murray and Clyde Kluckhohn, eds., *Personality in Nature, Society, and Culture* (1949).

I finished my first draft on Geddes's birthday, just a year from the date when I began it; by one of those "lucky" accidents which, as in William James's demonstration of the heart, one half-consciously assists at. In its present state the book is a vast winding muddy Mississippi sort of creation; but there are two good chapters, one on religion and the other on Sex, Love, and Marriage, chapters that I thought would be the hardest, to encourage me to persevere with the rest; and here and there, like a fish leaping out of the mud, there is a gleam that shows the sun is occasionally shining in the sky above. I have written the book in great tranquility; but the sweat and blood and tears will come, I am sure, presently.

Next week I'm going to make a brief visit to my mother in Hanover; and after that I shall spend the next few days wandering around. Should I be in Boston, I may phone you, to see if you are at hand; but it's all very problematic. I want, desperately, a long drink of the ocean before starting back to this dusty Sahara, where a thin line of hose, once a week, keeps alive our garden. But it may be that if rain comes I'll return here directly, committed as I am to the care of the plants I've started and to a general desire to behold the beauty I've helped bring into the world.

Unless all the beds should be filled, you'll be welcome if you come by here to or from Champlain; if you can tell us in advance, we'll see that a comfortable room is ready for you. When I'm writing, I'm impenetrable and unshakable; so don't fear about disturbing me: there's nothing quite so untouchable as a writer's pregnancy except a real one.

Affectionately
Lewis

Have I yet thanked you properly for Personality? I do now: it's a beautiful job. I missed only one person badly: James Alant.

[typed]
Lewis Mumford
Amenia, New York
20 August 1949

. . . Today I finished page 250 of the second draft, dear Harry, which is about half of the book; and this afternoon we all went walking over the sun-drenched, windswept hills, Sophy, Alison, her cousin, Bob Giroux, Harcourt's editor, and myself: so I write you with the tingle of a glorious day still left in my veins, like good wine. All week we'd kept this thought that you might be dropping in about this time on the way back from Clayton, perhaps because we misunderstood something you'd said; and your letter came as a lean substitute for your presence. Another person who will miss you, if indeed you are not coming, is Alice Sommers; for I think I forgot to tell you, when you were here, that she had just come back from New York after having been operated on for a rather large cancer on the upper part of her breast: something that had been there for ten years and had never been properly di-agnosed, though heaven knows that she had been in the hands of doctors often enough.[23] She took it all very gallantly and feels that, having survived an auto smashup, a complete mental breakdown, and a cancer, she is tough enough to stand anything. If you're in the neighborhood, do plan to see her: Dave will be there, too: a really sound and helpful man in his quiet way. Wilson is a very prom-ising young man indeed; and I was glad to find that we had much in common, though his bookish, etiolated grown-under-glass appearance put me off at first. He came at the worst possible time; for my brother-in-law, who was also a good friend, had died; and this had followed on one of those sudden rifts that happen suddenly, on confronting some painful part of the past, even in a very solid marriage. The re-sult was that I found the test upsetting, in that my responses were feeble, full of blocks, and when I did come up with something it turned out, more often than not, to be so heavily laden with unconscious material, dredged up from the depths, that the very act of giving it forth only increased the inner disruption. I am not sure that I would have had any richer response to the pictures if you had caught me at a high moment instead of a low one; but the whole affair wouldn't, in more normal condi-tions, have left such a bad taste in my mouth. For once I cursed my own curiosity; but since I actually got back to work the following Monday, in my regular stride, it probably argues that my reserves of life-energy are actually as abundant as they have seemed since May, during which time I've written consistently between three and four thousand words a day. If it hadn't been for my friendship with you and for a sense that one feels in such a situation that one must play the game, I probably would have quit cold after the third picture or so. You would probably deduce all this without my help as soon as you read the records; and this will only serve as confirmation.

Today in my mail an unknown English correspondent, who has heard that I'm doing the final volume, beseeches me not to do such a book without reading the works of Wilhelm Reich from beginning to end. Is he really worth serious study? I read his book on the Orgone a few years ago; and found it exaggerated in its claims and slipshod in its thinking. I've also heard, at second hand, about his magical box which generates heat from the body's energies and restores potency or raises it to a higher potential: which seemed to me on about a par with Indian rope-climbing: exciting if anyone had actually seen it firsthand. Should I take him more seriously? And what about Trigant Burrow. He seems to me a man who has talked himself into a semantic knot; and his latest book on The Neurosis of Man is a classic exam-ple of all the mischiefs which his kind of psychology is supposed to overcome. Like Matthias Alexander he has finally ended up his phyloanalysis with a characteristic

---

23. Formerly Alice Decker.

American solution for the world's problems: a physiological form of readjustment, based on a purely physiological diagnostic.[24] It seems nonsense. Or am I wrong?

I pester you with questions. Don't bother to answer them till we meet—if then!

Lewis

P.S. Sophy joins me in warm greetings to you both.

[typed]
Lewis Mumford
153 West 82 Street
New York 24, N.Y.
17 January 1950

Dear Harry:

What a clean, honest, brilliant job you did in all your testimony; and what a good impression your final evidence leaves—I trust on the jurors quite as much as on me.[25] It was an honor to have my name publicly associated with yours, in a case where a man who may be entirely innocent may be blasted by the evidence of a psychopath. Do not give a second thought to the fact that you had, naturally, to mention my name; as a matter of fact, it may be a help rather than a hindrance to have appeared in the public prints in this connection, as preparation for a matter I propose to discuss with you at some later date, when the trial is over.

I know it may be weeks or even months before you are ready to look at this first chapter; but Catherine has just returned it to me, with very pertinent criticisms from the standpoint of a healthy, unconvinced, skeptical extravert: so I send it on to you just so you may pick it up at your convenience.[26] My chief problem, really, is to put my argument in such a fashion that a healthy person can accept it: for it is exactly their health—and the health of three-quarters of our society—that keeps them from recognizing what seems to me the objective state of society. Just as in a person with cancer, the healthy state of most of the organs may too long postpone a visit to the doctor; so that by the time the illness is diagnosed the chance for overcoming it successfully has diminished.

But you need a rest: even from my chatter.

Warmly
Lewis

---

24. Wilhelm Reich, *The Discovery of the Orgone,* 2nd edition (1948); Trigant Burrow, *The Neurosis of Man: An Introduction to the Science of Human Behavior* (1949); Matthias Alexander, *The Use of the Self* (1932), *The Universal Constant in Living* (1941).

25. Murray testified in the Alger Hiss trial, providing a psychological assessment of Whittaker Chambers, Hiss's accuser, on behalf of the defense.

26. Draft portion of *The Conduct of Life* (1951).

[handwritten]
153 W. 82 St. NY 24
12 February 1950

. . . . Your note, dear Harry, came opportunely, at a moment when—partly because of being under the weather for over a month—I was feeling quite low. There is no haste about returning the ms.: but I feel that the first chapter is so inadequate that it is hardly worth any mulling over: while the rest of the book, overgrown and clumsy and tedious, is even worse. Writing it was an almost completely detached act of will: and that explains for me why the results are so disappointing. I am setting the ms. aside for a few months, and I will not go back to it till I feel differently, and can say what I have to say in half the space with twice the force.

I managed to give my lectures at the Naval War College to a fairly lively group of officers: but at luncheon afterward I happened to observe that there was at least a reasonable doubt as to whether Hiss was guilty—and I saw at once that my host (a Vice Admiral) put me down from that moment as a probable communist! That's the state of black, paralyzing, nitwitted suspicion our country is now in: as you of course have been finding out for yourself. The FBI has been building up this state steadily. I was talking to a scientist last night who had seen his FBI dossier (dating back to 1932). He said that whenever the FBI wanted to quote a speech of his & had a choice of clippings between a Times, a Tribune & a Daily Worker quote, they invariably used the Daily Worker. The breaking of the Fuchs case probably postpones indefinitely the investigation of their methods which is so long overdue. Is not "controlled schizophrenia" the disease of our whole civilization, at least our part of it—as perhaps Russia's might be designated as intentional paranoia?

I have to give a talk at MIT on 20 March: and I may run up the weekend just before: so I look forward to seeing you then if not earlier in this city.

Warmly
Lewis

How right you are about Time-Life-Fortune. Chambers was their ideal editor. The motto should be Ex Luce Nox!

[typed]
Lewis Mumford
Amenia
New York
12 June 1950

. . . It's been a long time, dear Harry, since we've seen each other or communicated; though I know, of course, that you tried to get hold of me while I was away in Raleigh—where I spent almost half my time in April and the first part of May. The spring, like the winter, was full of minor physical tribulations, very minor, but enough to upset the rhythm of work; but in spite of that I managed to get the garden planted in April and have been working like a beaver here for the last three weeks or so, while Sophy has come up weekends with Alison. The lateness of the spring has somehow increased its glory; and the place has never looked better, nor I suspect have we—at least during the last ten years. Like Emerson, I find I don't have a thought in my head when I spend too much time digging and hoeing; so very reluctantly I am tearing myself away from this blessed healthy routine and have been limbering myself up for an entirely fresh try at my book. The two years I've spent on it so far are probably not entirely futile; far from it; but I can't find, among the three hundred odd thousand words I wrote during that time, as many as ten thousand that I'd like to salvage. For the sake of clarity of mind and freshness of approach I'll have to put that entire mass of writing clean behind me and begin afresh, with a much more modest contribution in mind. I suspect that I am in the same state that Rousseau confessed, in his preface to the Social Contract, when he referred to a much more pretentious essay, partly written, that he had destroyed; and I shan't regret that result if Volume Four is as well written as the Social Contract was, to say nothing of being as influential. This judgment on what I have done so far is not darkened by my illness, as you may have suspected that my earlier judgment was; on the contrary, the healthier I find myself the worse the manuscript actually seems to me. That is why I haven't paid you a special visit, without waiting for you to come down to New York, to hear what you had to say about that abortive and stuffy first chapter; for it's like nothing I intend to write in the new volume. If I don't succeed in writing the book this summer, on the third try, I shall gracefully toss it aside and turn to something more within the range of my capabilities. . . . Meanwhile I've busied myself with smaller matters. As soon as I get offprints, I'll send you a copy of my most recent article on the Atomic Bomb in Air Affairs, which recapitulates, emphasizing the political rather than the military angle, my talk to the Naval War College In January.[27] You possibly didn't notice the long letter I had in the Times yesterday on our atomic military policy, in reply to one Patterson wrote a few weeks ago.[28] Unfortunately, this is a drastically cut down version of a full-length article I'd written, which the Times felt was too long to print; so the political and moral arguments, which formed the core of the original letter, have been whittled down into nothingness, and in its present form, I regret to see, it seems as if I thought that the answer to our present difficulties was solely a military one, on the right lines. If I hadn't cut the article down hastily and sent it away at once, so surprised that the Times would print it in any form, I'd have seen this and not consented to the bowdlerization. Still, if it awakens argument of any sort, it may well

27. Lewis Mumford, "Alternatives to Catastrophe," *Air Affairs* 3 (Spring 1950): 350–63.

28. Lewis Mumford, "Our Military Policy: Reliance on Atom Warfare Said to Defeat Our Goals," *New York Times*, 11 June 1950, section 4, 8.

do its duty! What is really alarming is that the American people, in regard to the official policy of genocide, have shown themselves morally as irresponsible as the German people about the Nazi extermination camps. I had a phrase about this in my shortened version; and I regret to say that the Times editor took it upon herself to cut this out.

What of yourself? I shall be going down to New York from the fifteenth to the eighteenth; but after that I expect to be here steadily, writing, till the end of July at least, when I may take a few days break at the seashore, as a safeguard against my forcing the pace as stupidly as I did last year. Nothing would give me greater pleasure than for you to turn up and stay here a day or two. Except for my mornings up to 11, I am entirely free; and very eager for a good talk, of which I didn't get too much last winter in New York.

> Ever yours
> Lewis

[handwritten, n.d.]
Mid-River Farm
Clayton, N.Y.
Leaving for 37 Brimmer St.
Boston—Soon

Dear Lewis—

To such statements of principle as: "Physician Cure Thyself" and "Practice What You Preach," I would count myself, if asked, one of the staunchest yea-sayers; but look at me! Dreaming, thinking, & symbol-making about fellowship, & yet leaving your wonderful, soul-satisfying, unexampled letters unanswered for several months. I don't feel quite so shattered about not returning your exciting Chap. 1, as you told me not to. Why? I cannot guess, except that you so far surpassed it in your next version that you could not bear the sight of it. I am returning it nevertheless, so as to give the privilege of attending to its extinction to you, its author. I reread it, today, without even rubbing out more than one or two marginal notes I made in the Spring, & found it better than before. It is expertly planned—starting with summons to renewal, symptoms of disintegration, & following through to your postulates & your apt reference to Maxwell's doctrine of singular points—a scientific justification for an apparently unscientific hope. I agree with *every word* of it, & delight in your inclusion—your eloquent expression—of my greatest aversions and revulsions and tribulations, on the one hand, and my furthest hopes and faith, on the other. Perhaps the extremities of darkness & of light which you picture poignantly and which satisfy me so fully, will not be so deeply appreciated by the average American, who, in recent decades, seems to have been forced—probably by the meaningless succession of stimuli you list so devastatingly—into a state of "affective neutrality," resistant to all emotional exhortations, particularly if they have a moral flavor. The young men I see seem to feel that it is necessary to prove their self-sufficiency, and independence from paternal domination by adapting a negativistic & cynical detachment towards anything that sounds like sermonizing. Since I am always sermonizing, I have found this wall of inertia & resistance very disconcerting & much observation and thought has led me to the conclusion that it has a value which I must understand & take account of whenever I address them. I have not yet discovered the proper method, but I have intimations that I may be on the right track. Certain paragraphs in your Chapter, in which you described how modern man had become bound, like a slave, to a treadmill of routine, mechanized activities, exactly described the conditions that have harassed me since returning to Harvard—which, according to the outworn stereotype, is an Ivory Tower, or cloistered monastery, permitting abstraction, leisurely contemplation, & gentlemanly scholarship. As you know, universities have absorbed the ideology and tempo of the business world, and unless one adopts extreme measures, one's days are an incessant round of prescribed debilitating meetings & appointments. I have gone on half-time—the only professor on half-time at Harvard—and made an iron rule to commit myself to no articles, lectures, or talks that are not already ready (or almost ready), that is, to things that I have written out of upsurging spontaneities, instead out of a sense of duty and obligation. I will not begin to reap the rewards of this rule, however, until next November—after certain tasks to which I committed myself a year ago have been fulfilled. All my headaches & dull depression of the last three years I attribute largely to the same cause—completing a book, out of obligation which I positively detested. The only piece I enjoyed was the Pierre introduction—so you hit the target of my afflictions square in the bull's eye. I find I cannot understand the cause for your own rejection of the first Chapter. It is a little vague and sweeping, but *that* is what it *must* be. You will become more specific & detailed in later chapters. I cannot think of any diseased spot or pus pocket you haven't touched with your lancet, nor any source of strength you haven't listed. It sounds like Social Science written by Ralph Waldo Emerson. I am dribbling at the mouth out of appetite to read the succeeding chapters, particularly to your solution of the problem of machine's dominion over man. Shorter hours with a wholly different kind of community life outside of work, but the assembly-belt remains, as far as I can see. But I have no imagination in that direction—I was *astonished* to hear that you were coming to the end of the entire work. I thought you were allowing yourself *a year more* & that we would find many opportunities to talk out parts of it. Happy for you, but disappointing for me! How rapidly you work! I had my best month ever at the tower in July, but wrote no more than 4 or 5 typewritten pages a day (double-spaced).

You must know how strongly I approve of your letter to the *Times*. It seems to me that we are all being propelled irresistibly towards a horrific wicked suicide—committing every enormity as we go. I am not in favor of trying to contain Russia, chiefly because it is *impossible.* I am inclined to think that, for some countries such as China, Communism is a step towards Democracy, & that if we stopped opposing it, we would take the *steam* out of the movement, & then, eventually, much later, after we had become socialist, arrive at some world government. But this course does not seem possible, because of the temper of the country.

You were an Archangel to advise massage for headaches. By mistake I had run into a lady who could cure me—just as you predicted—in 10 or 15 minutes—marvelous relief—but it returned next morning. If I ever get to New York I shall follow through on your advice & consult Dr. Gurewich—maybe another hand.

Did Emerson say that working with his hands stopped the thoughts in his head? So did Hawthorne 1852 & Melville 1852. Who said it first?

I am sorry that I cannot stop for a night on the way down. Jo & I are attending A.P.A. meeting at Penn State in September & passing through near Amenia about Sept 7th or 8th, but I believe that the 30 minutes that might be taken out of the long drive would be a sort of tantalizing, *painful* Hail & Farewell—So later. My embraces for the "dark, marvelous, and inscrutable" Sophy & the fascinating Alison—

> May Heaven shine upon you & be
> gracious
> Yrs

[typed]
Lewis Mumford
Amenia, New York
18 September 1950

. . . I'm on the last lap of my book, dear Harry, with plenty of wind left in me for the final sprint: altogether this whole summer has been one of the best periods of writing I've had, not perhaps for sheer creativity, but for sustained analytical thinking: which was what my book needed most at this stage. I have interwoven a series of related themes into a well-unified book, unless my critical judgement is at fault. To do this I've had to leave out enough material to make two other books; indeed, in line with my own doctrine of sacrifice (Physician: heal thyself!) I have had to leave out perhaps the most interesting chapter of the earlier draft, that on Sex, Love, and Marriage, including a few fine blistering bibliographic notes on Wilhelm Reich and the good Kinsey, which I can hardly bear to suppress, since that gave me so much pleasure to write. Whether the final chapter, on which I'm now writing, will be quite as good as I want it to be is doubtful: for my desires are set very high; but I think that even there I'll open the path for others, even if I see the promised land only from a distance. At the point I reached this morning, in discussing the need for a modern version of Loyola's Spiritual Exercizes—I made a feeble effort myself for my classes in California, but lacked the creative energy then to see it through—I happened to remember Moreno, as perhaps the only comparable modern parallel, in which the person is made to dramatically enact the experience he would otherwise be only verbally concerned with. This led me to look over his Psychodrama again; and I have come away from that effort with the feeling this his work is a combination of genius, constructive and spontaneous, of a rather high order, reduced in value by this wholesale rejection of everything other people have done, and marred, at times, by sheer drivel.[29] But I realize that I have never discussed Moreno with you; or indeed, for that matter, with anyone; and I have no notion even of what general standing he has among psychologists, though sociologists have (quite rightly) been following his leads.

My own trail crosses Moreno in more than one place; though of course I don't pretend to have discovered any of the things he has discovered. Ages ago, in 1920 in fact, reviewing MacDugall's The Group Mind I pointed out that psychology was still studying disembodied wraiths, either introspective ghosts or laboratory poltergeists; but that its advance depended upon its observing the psyche in the actual physical and social situations in which it was behaving: pure Moreno.[30] Likewise the word psychodrama was in my vocabulary, without any very rich associations, before Moreno had even invented the word for himself: for old Geddes had given a series of London University Extension Lectures on sociology, viewed as a series of dramas, Technodrama, Sociodrama, Biodrama, Psychodrama, etc. The syllabus is a rather bare one; and I don't know how Geddes expanded these concepts: like many more intuitions of his he never gave enough effort to the detailed work of following it up. But in writing my present book I found myself driven by the facts into a dramatic interpretation of civilization itself—already adumbrated in the Condition of Man before I had read any Moreno—and now both my concepts and my functional analysis seems to parallel Moreno in a remarkable way.

Will I lose what few shreds of reputation are left me if I mention his name? Surely he doesn't smell as bad as Reich, does he? If you're just settling down to work, don't bother to answer these questions at once: I shall not be able to send my ms. to the printer till the first of December, probably; so there'll be plenty of time to correct any solecisms. Autumn sounds like a fox in the distance: at the moment, I find a thousand good reasons for being alive.

I hope you do too!

Lewis

29. Jacob L. Moreno, *Psychodrama* (1946).

30. Lewis Mumford, review of William MacDougall, *The Group Mind, Sociological Review* 13 (July 1921): 184–86.

[handwritten]
37 Brimmer Street
Boston 8, Massachusetts
3 Jan '51

Dear Lewis,

I returned to Boston to find your superb piece.[31] In its special way, it is the top creation of your own great powers of interpretation and communication. First it is full of unappreciated truth—rejuvenated truth, lost in the last 50 years, and re-shaped into something New. This truth is an encouragement & ground for fresh faith. Then, second, you have compacted your conceptions into so firm a structure that it stands like Gibraltar in the midst of today's confused flux of thoughts about man's nature. You submerge entirely the mechanical analogy, & restore man to his proper heritage as transformer (I would say). Finally your language—your words & style—is stirring—powerfully exciting—without any of the weakness of texture that so often characterizes enthusiasm in speech.

And so I am immensely expanded and charged and elevated by this work of yours. The fact that it is a much finer expression of what has been growing in my head for several years prejudices me overpoweringly in its favor. But, prejudice aside, I am *positive* that this is Gospel.

What maturity & ripeness of genius!

Embraces to you both—beloved
ones
Harry

[handwritten]
Lewis Mumford
Amenia, New York
19 March 1951

Dear Harry:

I went a few more rungs down the ladder after seeing you: indeed, I got so close to the bottom that I realized that something drastic would have to be done. So I threw off all engagements & duties, after noting that the faintest suggestion of ex-ternal pressure produced unbearable fatigue. Finally, I was just well enough, ten days ago, to risk staying up here alone: and I hadn't been here a few days before— quite magically—I was ready to begin work again. So the nightmare that's been hanging over me is almost lifted—though that was made possible alas! only by throwing overboard, with everything else, my plans for going to Europe. . . . Mean-while, my proofs have been coming in: and even to my coldest critical eye the book looks good: indeed very good. But there are a few passages that I've added at the

---

31. Probably *Man as Interpreter* (1950), an excerpt from Mumford's *The Conduct of Life* (1951) that was specially printed as a 1951 New Year's greeting by his publisher, Harcourt, Brace and Co.

last moment about which I have my doubts. They are not the most original or venturesome in the book, by any means: but I am willing to take my chances of being wrong on matters I've long pondered: last moment inspirations are another matter! One such passage I herewith enclose: *Love and Integration.* If you think it doesn't hold up under examination—of course it occurs in the midst of an elaborate argument—I'll be tempted to leave it out. The frost is out of the ground: but spring firmly refuses to reveal even her ankle.

I leave for Raleigh on Saturday: so write, when you have a chance to 152 W. 82.

In old friendship
Lewis

[handwritten]
37 Brimmer Street
Boston 8, Massachusetts
[LM] Ans 13 June

Dear Lewis,

The *immediacy* of your responses is a repeated source of gratification and wonder—and sometimes, by comparison with my retarded reflexes, of *shame*. Perhaps, in this instance, Sophy or Alison collaborated. Anyhow, the lighter reached my desk several days before I returned from the Tower. C & I decided to create a vegetable garden for the first time in 25 years. The plowing was done with mattock & spade—a plodding method which even our Puritan forefathers of the Bay Colony would have shunned as too laborious. Six tomato plants were levelled by cutworms on the very first night—which is just the beginning of our tribulations I expect.

If you look westward at this hour—8.30 P.M.—you will see Venus between the horns of the moon—beyond the reach of S.T.C.'s poesy. She seems to be prophesying great things for your book. I am certain that *she* will be pleased with it, even though some of the deteriorated book reviewers recoil from the display of so much surplus Vigor & Health.

I wish I had time to talk to you before going to Stockholm, because I am going to propose that the psychologists of the world attempt the investigation (in representative individuals & small groups) of the determinants of the forces specially stressed by the scientists of history (Toynbee, Mumford, Spengler, etc.)—particularly the forces of degeneration & regeneration, destruction and construction, passive acquiescence and creative assertiveness, etc., etc. I find that not a single paper on the program is even indirectly related to the world's plight. Good fortune to you all & again many thanks—

Affly
H

P.S. Perhaps I should apologize for the clouds of gloom that I trailed into your genial room in N.Y. Hope you opened the window & let the sunshine dispel the memory of it after my departure.

[typed]
Lewis Mumford
Amenia, New York
8 August 1951

. . . Welcome home, dear Harry! Your heartening postcards have given us a sense of all the rich stimuli you've encountered on your trip; and I am eager to hear more about it all firsthand. [. . .] As for my book, I won't get the first copies of it, probably, till the beginning of September: all the processes of publishing are now as slow as the proverbial molasses. But I have occasionally sat down over the page proofs, during the last month, with a cold and fishy eye; and though I see much that I could have followed further and brought out more thoroughly, I see nothing that I would change. By valiant effort, I have kept the book to just under three hundred pages: so now one will not have the excuse of saying that it is too long to be readable!

Unfortunately, my publishers have gone back on all the solemn promises they made me over a year ago, about the way the book should be handled; and even when they have fulfilled the bare letter they have deliberately flouted the spirit. This is a serious handicap to the first reception of a book, which depends, to a certain degree, upon the publisher's initial confidence. I am very glad therefore that I have arranged a few cushions to fall back on, one of them being a course on The City I am giving one day a week at the University of Pennsylvania.

The international situation looks more favorable to us at the moment than it has been for years, despite all the threats that remain; but unfortunately there is not one in Washington who knows how to talk peace or to plan for peace: the entire strategy at the State department is one that would have been excellent for dealing with Hitler in 1938.

Have a good rest after your own strenuous winter, dear Harry. Even if we decide to visit the Brookses on the Vineyard we'll probably be back here by the twentieth.

Affectionately
Lewis

[typed]
The Baleen [32]
48 Mt. Auburn Street
Cambridge 38, Massachusetts
September 10, 1951

Dear Lewis:

We sent you a telegram after the first chapter.[33] Since then I have read more chapters and my excitement over its superlative qualities runs on unabated. I have

---

32. "The Baleen" is the name Murray gave to the Harvard Psychological Clinic in 1949.
33. Lewis Mumford, *The Conduct of Life* (1951), fourth volume in The Renewal of Life series.

written Harcourt, Brace briefly, adhering pretty closely to the words of the telegram, which seem to be my total impression. Perhaps the best indication of my whole-hearted approval of your philosophy is the fact that almost every paragraph in my copy is marked with red pencil, supplemented by countless checks and exclamation points, and only a very occasional question mark.

As you know, I have been thinking, and in a small way scribbling, about the same topics for the last year or two, and am gratified to see how closely our courses of thought have run. The fact that you say with exceeding eloquence what I have vaguely believed to be the truth, makes it unnecessary for me to labor any further over certain issues. You have left me many areas to be filed out and expanded, which is probably more than I will have time to do. For these reasons I am most personally grateful for the completion of your thought, so wonderfully ordered and uttered in this crowning volume.

Of course there are scores of points which would make fine topics for future discourses—if there is Time. You expect so much of the New World Citizen that he may not find an hour or two to discuss the riddles of the Universe.

This is merely a note to keep you abreast of my passage through your masterpiece. I shall have more to say after I have digested it as a whole and re-read it. I don't have to have it all under my belt, however, to know that it is absolutely tops, and that you have produced a work of enduring enlightenment. Altogether fine!

I embrace all three of you with warm affections, wonder and congratulations!

Yours,

Harry

Mr. Lewis Mumford

Amenia, New York

[handwritten]

[LM] Oct 6

Reporting an impediment to progress

Dear Lewis,

My passage through your hemispheric, Himalayan book was abruptly checked by a number of events—Jo's arrival in N.Y.C. from Europe (I *almost* had time to stop at Amenia on the way down—but recalled your mention of my hectic hails-and-farewells & decided against it), a flood in our town house, the opening of college, & a number of other things, & so the treasury of vital wisdom is still unfinished on my desk here at my right hand.

It will take me 2 or 3 years to read and inwardly digest and discuss it with you in detail. Every line of every paragraph of every page is both beautifully said and wonderfully true. But there are so many resonations and contrapuntal aspects to everything you say that one must brood over each passage to get all the levels of meaning that are embodied in it. I am not good at writing long letters, and your book calls for a letter much longer than I have ever written, so long that I can't even begin it—not now at least—because I know that after 10 pages I will still be engaged with the early chapters & have to end with many topics hanging in the air in a disquieting way. Your whole conception of the human mind & human personality is way ahead of what any psychologist has written, but you don't acknowledge that a psychologist is constrained by his discipline to write only what he has observed under more or less controlled conditions, and his methods have not been developed to the point where he can study processes which he, as a non-professional, knows to be characteristic of personality. Don't write me until I have written you again after finishing the book slowly at a leisurely pace—I don't have to go any further, however, to tell you that this is the book of our generation & decidedly your Everest. I have seen only one loathsome review (Time), which is a certain sign, though malicious, that your work will endure forever. I expected just this from them. My love and gratitude to you both—& a hug for Sophy & Alison.

More later—
Harry

[handwritten]
Lewis Mumford
Amenia, New York
6 October 1951

. . . Your first letter, dear Harry, was a great act of reassurance and encouragement; and your second, which greeted me at the end of two weary weeks of traveling and lecturing and teaching was a cold beaker of water in a hot desert. There will be plenty of time in future to talk over the book: the main point for me, is that you deem it worth the effort. The book itself is still fermenting in me—if only because, to make it more assimilable, I temporarily cut out some 100,000 words, the core of two other books. Likewise, my belated decision to omit illustrations left certain important matters untouched, because I had intended to put them in more concrete form. No matter: there's plenty left. The book has so disconcerted the reviewers that they have shied away from it. Perhaps a good sign: though a flitting discouragement.

Sophy has been up here with Alison; for the latter has had a severe & persistent throat infection that did not yield to the usual drugs: only now, after three weeks, does she begin to show signs of mastering it. But we shall probably go down to the city at the end of next week—(I teach at the U. of P. every Thursday).

Don't pass by again without stopping in, if only for three minutes!! Among other matters, we would like to consult you on a non-medical problem raised by Alison—the need, not for a psychoanalyst, but for a lay father-confessor!

A warm & grateful embrace

Ever
Lewis

[handwritten]
37 Brimmer
[LM] 10? Oct 51

Solar Lewis,

I was dismayed, distressed, by your letter to C. Having made a correct diagnosis of the degree of American deterioration, you should abide by your estimate, and not expect an *immediate* conversion at the first *sight* of your book. What the deteriorated are looking for is *Catcher in the Rye.* Your book makes them reach for their pulse to see if it is still beating. It will take a year or two or three for your book to get moving—starting with the vital ones and then passing on to others—the young thirsters for wisdom. You can rest secure—placid as one of Whitman's cows—chewing the cud, content that you have done the best work of your generation. Remember that your book is a little insulting to readers, & they can't take it, because they're ashamed of themselves. Pity the book reviewers who have only 48 hours to skim your labors of 30 years' experience and rumination, & get out some kind of comment after a couple of cocktail parties. I am sorry we didn't continue our talks on Purpose, because my mind was not able to meet yours here. Purpose, to me, means some idea, though vague, of a goal. Only a living organism can have an idea (image) of a goal. You might include a creative god, but put him, quite rightly, in the future. A desirable occurrence does not require purpose to explain it, any more than an undesirable occurrence requires purpose. You seem to ascribe "an idea of goal" to carbon atoms or Mother Nature??

Anyhow, everything you have written is startlingly fresh, provocative, stirring. Embraces all round

Harry

Will Alison deign to take a walk with me in Central Park round Sunday, Nov. 18th?

[typed]
Lewis Mumford
Amenia, New York
12 October 1951

. . . I can't remember, dear Harry, what unfortunate phrase or sentence or paragraph may have caused you to interpret my present mood as a much blacker one that it actually has been; but I hasten to write you now that your interpretation reads more into my words than was there. I didn't look for any ovation for the book or any easy acceptance either: in fact, two years ago I wrote a memorandum to Harcourt on the subject, telling that they would have to make an extra effort, be sure that the book went to the reviewers two months ahead of publication instead of the usual month, etc. etc. As early as last April I could tell from the resistance—not quite the same as indifference—that the book was meeting in my publisher's office that my original memorandum was well justified, although it did not do what I had set out to do—overcome the blockage at the source, namely at Harcourt's. Nothing that has followed has surprised me; and certainly nothing that has happened has lessened my confidence in the ultimate fate of the book. (I remember that 900 of the original thousand of *Walden's* first edition came back to Thoreau!) But there is a difference between getting bad reviews or hostile reviews, and getting none at all, or a poor scattering. The latter fate has an immediate effect; and it is with the immediate reception of the book, in terms of space—not the content of the reviews— that has concerned me. That is a practical matter. In the world of ideas I am content to wait, with a more than oriental resignation, never lifting a finger to influence the result, except by continuing the vein of thought I have started. But in the matter of finding an immediate response, sufficient to make possible further work, I have a real stake; since on it both my livelihood and my intellectual usefulness depend. Here, if the publisher had fulfilled his promises, there would have been a different tale to tell in the reviews; and that in turn would have had an effect upon sales. But, as I say, this is a practical matter; and though the failure here is an exacerbation, it is of the same order as missing a train and having to cancel a lecture. (This doesn't affect the lecture itself!) Otherwise, I am quite serene. I have more work at the moment than I can handle, a flatteringly large class on The City at the University of Pennsylvania and a seminar with twice too many people in it, who simply clamored to be let in; and apart from that, everything is serene, now that Alison is over her acute laryngitis. She is quite dizzy over the thought of a walk in the park with you in November; and I gladly release my own time with you to her, provided you and I can get together either before or after, either in New York or in Boston— though Boston will be difficult till this fall semester is over. We have plenty to discuss: on "purpose" and much else. The book is still fermenting in me, as I think I said before; and already I see more clearly many things that were still a little obscure or relatively undeveloped when I was working on the ms.—or at least could now be more explicitly and fully stated. I already came upon a dismaying repetition of a whole paragraph—due to transposing it from one chapter to another without being sure that it was cut out of the original place—and if the book gets into another edition, it will be richer by one further thought! Up to the last moment I had hoped to enrich many of my ideas with actual illustrations; and that, I am sure, would have helped a lot in some places—though not in the definition of purpose! But some day I hope to do an edition with pictures. Lacking them, the text sometimes seems meager to me in its present form.

But if the book is even half as good as your words tell me I'll be well content. Bless you for your insight and sympathy.

Lewis

[typed]
The Baleen
48 Mt. Auburn Street
Cambridge 38, Massachusetts
January 31, 1952

Dear Lewis:

"Toward a Free World" is without doubt the best compressed outline for long-range planning that I have read, and I have read a good many.[34] Some of the things you say we have discussed before, and I still feel you are right in repeating them. Other things are fresh, or at least said in a fresh way, so your point strikes in and sticks.

I think it is so necessary for Dean Acheson to prove to the McCarthys, etc. that he has no Communist leanings that he is not in a position to do what I am sure he would ordinarily be disposed to do, namely advocate and push some of the proposals you have made in your paper.[35]

My *only* petty but persisting quarrel with you, if it could be given such a malodorous term, is your dogmatic way of saying what you have to say. We have discussed this several times and I feel that you are talking in the tradition of Emerson, Thoreau, etcetera, etcetera, back to Ezekiel, if you will, and do not realize well enough that the mental climate has been so changed by science—for better or for worse—that minds with even an average amount of training and discipline begin to bristle the moment one man speaks like an oracle. This is a long story and we must discuss it some more because I am sure it is a crucial one and I am bothered by it myself because I was brought up to talk the way you talk, without making all kinds of qualifications as I went along. But all my observations lead me to believe that only the minds that are both untrained and already on our side will embrace what we have to say in an authoritative manner. Somehow we have to understand how it is that you have said the best things said during these critical years and yet you haven't got a hundred thousand followers.

Charles Morris tells me you are planning to be here in the spring, in which case you will stay with us and we can have Morris round for the evening.[36] Also, we are ready for Sophie and Alison almost any time. A week or two's notice would help as I have a few fixed dates, and other friends are apt to pop up and take the spare room for a night or two. Now that Josephine is in Switzerland we have two spare rooms with three beds; that is ample space for the immortal Mumfords.

Yours,
H.A.M.

34. *Toward a Free World: Long-Range Planning Under Democratic Control* (1952); pamphlet of address presented at the Conference on World Order, Rochester, New York, 13 November 1951.

35. Dean Acheson served as U.S. Secretary of State, 1949–1952.

36. Charles Morris (1901–1979), professor of philosophy at the University of Chicago; visiting lecturer in social relations at Harvard, 1951–1953.

[typed]
153 West 82 Street
New York 24
5 February 1952

Dear Harry:

It was good to see your whalespout again; and in a few weeks after I get through a bout of lecturing at the University of Colorado, I hope to jump into my whaleboat and go after you; that will be the last weekend in February, or rather Saturday the first of March, for I'll be spending Thursday to Saturday afternoon at Brandeis University, engaged in an informal discussion with seniors.[37] On the matter of my written style, you and Van Wyck Brooks have been coming at me from opposite directions and with a different ax to grind; but you both have—properly and usefully—made me conscious of matters that are best left unconscious, unless something is actively going wrong with them, as seems now to be the case. I have no defensive reaction against what you say, unless an explanation can be counted as such. I was brought up in exactly the tradition you beg me to go back to; and some of my earlier work was so hedged about with qualifications and so tentative that it required a little probing to find out what I meant. When I started in on the big series, however, I decided that the time had come to speak in a firmer voice, with less beating around the bush; and I wrote a memorandum to myself, admonishing me to be forthright and deliberately challenging. Since I have a fairly full consciousness of my debts to others and go out of my way to bring in people who have been thinking the same things or even over-acknowledge my debt to them, I had no thought that this manner of writing might seem to others an example of intolerable egoism or self-assurance. But of course that merely means that no one knows his own smell; and on such matters no amount of self-observation can be put alongside the word of a good friend—or even, indeed, an honest enemy. What is to be done about it is another thing; for being old-fashioned and set in my ways, I still admire the Emersons and the Arnolds, to go no further back, and I still despise the mealy-mouthed style when I meet it in others, although I am just as vexed as you are when I come across someone else talking in what seems a high-handed and authoritative way about anything in which I am interested. Such a conflict is hard to resolve. I would take it more seriously, perhaps, if I thought for a moment that the reason my ideas have not gone widely into circulation is because the people of our present age are so imbued with science that they resent such a style and won't listen to it. But observation shows that it is people who offend much worse than I do, like the Communists or the people who are rabid against the Communists, that actually command the most influence outside of a very limited scholarly circle, in which the neutral tone is of course all-important. But there are more substantial reasons than my literary style, I am sure, to account for the failure of my books and essays to find

37. Murray's personal letterhead bears the engraving of a spouting whale.

a wider audience—those reasons being the nature of the ideas themselves, as re-
lated to the audience that is made uncomfortable, nay hostile, by them. For them—
I do not for a moment mean for you—the difficulties presented by my manner are,
I am stubbornly convinced, a mere rationalization.

Sophy and Alison have elected to stay at Cambridge, at a hotel, the one brief
night they expect to be there, on February fifteenth (for they will be arriving late at
night and setting out for an interview, Alison that is, early next morning). They
both hope to see you, if you are available, on that Saturday. But if you have room for
me a night when I come up—that is on the first of March—I'll be delighted to be
with you and Jo. It would be great fun to see Morris too. He has been very generous
toward the Conduct of Life, especially considering my own very gingerly references to his own books; and the other day, at a Unesco Meeting, he singled out the
book in his lecture as an example of the New Trend.

So here's a preliminary embrace, if I survive the damned journey into the wild
and wooly.

Lewis

[typed]
The Baleen
48 Mt. Auburn Street
Cambridge 38 Massachusetts
February 14, 1952

Dear Lewis:

I very much appreciated your swift and cogent answer to my note. The question of how to present one's ideas and convictions has concerned me a good deal
and I am apt to veer, not from one extreme to another, but between two limits somewhere around the middle of the continuum.

I am going to send you a remarkable book, if you have not already read it,
called The Mechanical Bride.[38] It is a thematic analysis of advertising and other
forms of publicity. In a chapter describing the latest type of sex novel the author,
McLuhan, says this: "Is it not strange that amid the unmitigated torrent of sadistic
sex novels, works of reflection are tolerated only if they are gentle, sympathetic and
'warmly human?' The writer who ventures to entertain an idea must abase himself
masochistically before the reader before daring to state it. Sinuous writhings and
self-abasements mark the prose styles of the twentieth century. The reader is to be
habitually soused with sex and violence but at all time protected from the harsh
contact of the critical intellect."

This is a very striking criticism of the method I had been using and a confirmation of your point of view. It seems to me, however, that two unanswered considerations are 1, that people have an allergy today to authoritarian attitude or speech

---

38. Marshall McLuhan, *The Mechanical Bride: Folklore of Industrial Man* (1951).

and they begin to bristle and stop listening to what is said; and 2, that a dogmatic statement is not in truth justified and may make the agreement you are eventually hoping for impossible. For example, here we are, damn good friends and yet on the only four or five specific points that we have discussed and you take up in your book—the question of Purpose, the interpretation of Moby-Dick, Chronometrical, Plinlimmon, and a few others—you make positive statements as if no other alternative were possible. Since we have discussed these questions and you know I hold opposite opinions after a good many years of thought, your certainty seems to obliterate my observations and reflections. If I did the same thing we would have two irreconcilable certainties and no possibility of the unanimity on basic issues that is required for a harmonious world. I brought myself into it just for a concrete illustration. There must be scores of other thinkers who might feel that your method of presentation allows for no flexibility. These remarks are merely to serve as a starting point for discussion when we next see each other.

> [typed]
> Lewis Mumford
> 153 West 82 Street
> New York 24, N.Y.
> 25 February 1952

. . . . I've just come back from a very exhilarating trip to the University of Colorado, dear Harry; but even the prospect of seeing you this coming weekend cannot keep me from saluting your marvellous essay on Melville, written In Nomine Dei, which I read with unbounding admiration and delight last night.[39] It is not merely the very best thing you have written, in its clarity, its penetration, its subtlety, its charity, its depth; but it is the very best thing anyone has written on Melville: volumes have been written without saying half as much. Even after your masterly introduction to Pierre I had been a little worried over the fact that your long researches on Melville hadn't yet come to full fruit in a whole book; but after this essay, which not merely complements and completes what you say in Pierre, but carries the whole interpretation to a final point, I feel no misgivings whatever. Rest easy! It is not by the quantitative results that good thinking and feeling shall be judged. No one can do better than the best. With which Emersonian reflections I turned to my own chapter on Moby-Dick, to see what I had said there: only to find, what I had only half suspected, that my own thought has changed profoundly, not merely on Melville's own intention, but with respect to my own interpretation of evil. I remember how skeptical I was of your interpretation of the White Whale as Christi-

---

39. "In Nomine Diaboli," *New England Quarterly* 24 (1951): 435–52; Murray's famous essay on *Moby-Dick,* several times reprinted.

anity, when you first broached it to me; and though I returned to this symbolism more than once in my own mind, I could not make sense of it, till you laid it out in detail in this essay, which such massive psychological evidence, as the result of your more careful study of the elements of the fable, that it leaves most of my own interpretation lying in pitiable fragments, never to be picked up again. This does not say that your interpretation does not, as the theologians used to say of the evidences of Christianity, present difficulties. It presents, in fact, a very great difficulty in the literary criticism of Moby-Dick: for if you are right, it is not as full and perfect a work of art as I have always felt it to be—and still feel it to be. If the White Whale is the super-ego of puritanic Christianity, then it seems to me a very bad choice of symbols, not merely because it is forced but untrue to the nature of the subject; for Moby-Dick is more primitive than Ahab himself, while the super-ego against which he is struggling and rebelling is not a primitive essence at all, but a monster of human convention: Mrs. Glendinning and the Reverend Mr. Folsgrave incarnate. I can get over this difficulty only by taking a step which you, as a practiced psychologist, must find repugnant: namely by assuming that this symbol has more than one dimension, or at all events, ambivalent references, and that in one moment it is in fact Christianity and at another—this is the only part of my original interpretation I would hold to now—is something more primitive, the chaotic and undirected primordial energies, random motion, accident, all those forces outside of man that so often countervail his efforts and, through his very efforts to understand their irrational nature, *seem* directed against him and his purposes. So in one sense Ahab would be the devil's child, on the side of destruction, tyrannizing over the more rational ego of his mates, and challenging the superego; and on the other side, he is the spirit of man, nay the superego itself, the frail and lonely spirit that nevertheless, while the ship remains afloat, keeps his command; but this superego has been tamed by the very nature of the force it contends against, and by allowing itself to become the image of the thing it hates—as Christianity did by taking on Roman pomp and power, along with Jewish revenge and patriarchal tyranny—becomes in the end its victim. All this may look to your searching eye, dear Harry, like an elaborate attempt on my own part to save my own poor and inadequate interpretation, or at least a few scraps of it; but even if that were the unconscious motive, my greater concern is to save Moby-Dick itself—or at least to explain why it remains intact as a fable, when, if I were to accept your interpretation without reserve, it would have to be counted, for me at least, as great a literary failure as Pierre. More of all this when we meet. Here I will only salute you again for having revealed more of Melville and of Moby-Dick than any other interpreter: with which humble acknowledgement I might better perhaps have held my tongue.

Now a word about your letter. I hadn't, apart from Moby-Dick, the faintest notion that we disagreed in any important way about Chronometricals or Plinlimmon: perhaps my eagerness to widen the area of agreement made me overlook the differences that were vital to you. As to the interpretation of Purpose and Design, I realize that my presentation of these matters has not convinced you; and this is natural, for all that I could do within the compass of The Conduct of Life, is to put, in the most challenging way possible, the opposite set of assumptions to the dominant philosophy, which you accept: in the hope that if the reader had read the people who had influenced me and had had similar experiences and observations to back up such reading, he would find that purpose gave him a clue to many events which causality, however adequate in every retrospective analysis, would not. In a way, as you pointed out when we met last fall, every end process looks purposive, in the sense that the previous events seem inexorably to have led to it; but there is, nevertheless, a difference between such pseudo goals and purpose, as it appears in organisms, connected with their upbuilding processes and their whole life plan in which the future even though invisible and unconscious to the organism, plays a dynamic part in immediate events. Our difficulty, it seems to me, is partly a terminological one: you cannot separate the concept of purpose from a conscious human being or an external agent who appears to operate in the same fashion; whereas I, following Samuel Butler, believe that purpose is manifest in a far lower state of organic evolution, and does not rest on any external agent or conscious organism. But when we discuss such basic matters we are in the realm of postulates; and postulates can hardly be argued about: we must judge them rather by their pragmatic results. A metaphysic without the concept of purpose leaves the world, for me, half-uninterpreted, or radically misinterpreted. But I think you stretch the meaning of authoritarian almost as badly as the Congress has stretched the meaning of subversive when you characterize my attitude, in presenting the case for purpose as authoritarian. I admit that it was too brief to convince those who were not already more than half-convinced; but I did not for a moment assume, even when I rejected your previous criticisms, that the whole matter was beyond argument. You make me feel that perhaps I ought to spend some time writing a philosophic treatise on purpose and design and the nature of the future; so that, instead of merely stating my own position, I should be able to carry the reader over the whole ground and deal with the same difficulties I have faced.

None of this touches on the core of your criticism: the matter of style itself: the actual impression that my words make on the reader: my *smell*. There I have no defense—except the witness of other readers on whom I make just the opposite impression of modesty and reference to the reader's good judgment. "Now who shall arbitrate?"

. . . An unbearingly crowded file of unanswered correspondence is still waiting; so I must bring this to a temporary end. What of next weekend? Shall you be free at any time? I go to Brandeis this Thursday, the 28th; and stay there till some still undefined time on Saturday. Shall you be free any time Saturday, or are you going up to Topsfield? I must be home by Sunday night at latest, for I have much work to do, and apart from that have a sense of being far too long away from

Alison and Sophy. I thank you, before our meeting, for all you did for them two weekends ago.

Affectionately

Lewis

P.S Further thanks for McLuhan's Mechanical Bride. I haven't yet had time to look at it—it is indeed among my still unopened pile of mail!

N.B. I open this to say that I find the *author* has sent me a copy: so don't bother but thanks just the same.

[handwritten, early May 52]
Topsfield.
37 Brimmer St till Thursday,
Hotel Westbury on Friday, 16th,
New York

Dear Lewis,

[. . .]

I have a hunch that if your expectations for the *immediate* acceptance of the Conduct of Man had been lower, this would not have come on now. Instead of feeling, as you should feel, that you have said your say, & that in ten or twenty years the more enlightened ones would take your solutions as the only possible ones, you may have felt that you should give *a still more perfect expression of your ideas.* Economics might have prodded you in this direction. (At which point, let me repeat that I would be honored to furnish the cash necessary for a rest, a vacation, or, if need be, an operation. Don't be proud, but let me know what you want whenever you want it.) Last week a man named Williams visited me to discuss his plan of establishing an information center of all books & articles relating to World Order— which would publish a Newsletter containing reviews & bibliographies, etc. The purpose was to promote the sale of certain crucial books, of which *The Conduct of Man* was foremost in his mind. He believed, as I do, that there is a widespread—& in certain quarters, *calculated*—resistance to the saving truth. There is no question that you have presented the saving truth. The problem now is how to overcome the resistance to it. One key is *not* to press it *directly*, but to insinuate it *indirectly.* You have already delivered yourself of the pattern for the future. Rest. St. Paul, St. Augustine, St. Bernard, & St. Thomas will follow in due course.

[. . .]

I have been very slow in answering your earlier letter, & commenting on what you called my "astringent" (contracting) criticism. It was the kind of criticism that we psychologists exchange everyday, & which I direct at myself everyday, & I offered it merely as a suggestion relative to the question of strategy—the strategy of overcoming the present pathological resistance to what is erroneously regarded as authoritarianism. As I see it, Americans of all ages constitute one great Youth Culture of mediocracy with a profound aversion to moral excellence & authority, & yet with a repressed need for an invulnerable example—or rather incorruptible example—of excellence, a new kind of excellence. I would not have bothered to preoccupy myself with the question of how to touch this repressed need if I were not convinced that your books, especially The Conduct of Man, provide the solution. I visited your house in Amenia (as you may have discovered) in order to discuss this with you, & to reject the word "astringent" as expressive of what was in my mind. I feel that we have (long since) reached the stage when we should work *together* & possibly with a few others. We have to prove to ourselves that we are not merely egocentric, competing thinkers, but are capable—after interludes of solitariness—of mutuality on the philosophic level. We may not be equal to this transformation yet, but, without it, we shall be living outside our own avowed principles. Jo & I are planning to go to Europe (Sicily, Switzerland) in a few days, despite the fact that we have *no* accommodations. We may come to New York next Friday (16th), & go to one pier after the other, in hopes of a last hour cancellation. I shall try to get in touch with you one way or the other—possibly see you in the 19th in N.Y.C. I shall be back in June. In any event I shall be thinking of you daily & praying for the best solution of this miserable condition. Every distress of yours is mine. My embracing love to Sophy, Alison & you—

Harry

[typed]
Lewis Mumford
Amenia, New York
13 May 1952

[. . .]

As for your generous suggestion, dear Harry, I haven't forgotten the earlier one you made during that debilitating and trying spring when The Condition of Man was published; and again I am deeply moved by it, and grateful; and again I hasten to assure you that there is, happily, no need of it on my side. We have more spare cash in the bank at the moment than I think we've ever had: some four thousand dollars saved out of current income this last year; and with a professorship at Pennsylvania waiting for me in the fall, (I shall teach only one term) I expect, so long as my health remains, to be in better shape financially than I've been for many a year; for by October more royalties will have piled up, and there will be two more books, Art and Technics, and a book of readings on American Architecture to swell them. Almost, I am a little afraid of all this wealth: it has usually coincided, in 1929 and in 1938, with a nasty physical blow, Geddes's illness in the first case and Sophy's in Honolulu in the second. A bout of illness for me, at this juncture, looks like nothing else, superstitiously speaking, than justice!

What adventurers you and Jo are to be thinking of such a sudden, unconventional dash to Europe. May you have the success in finding a passage you deserve. If you are in New York, however, next Monday, let's meet. Unless illness drive me back before then I expect to return home late Sunday night. Meanwhile, my very grateful and affectionate embrace.

Lewis

P.S. Your intuitions about my reactions to the reception of The Conduct of Life get to the very heart of the matter, I suspect. I never worked harder on any book than I did on that one; and though I still think it my best, I was not satisfied with it when it left my hands and am still not satisfied with it: for certain ideas in it are still undeveloped and I already have almost twenty extra pages to be added to some future edition. Since that was the case, I depended upon an outside response to what was effectively in the book to compensate my misgivings as to what was lacking. If it had gone well, I would have felt liberated for further effort, and such wounds as the book left in me, in the act of birth, would have been more quickly healed. The joke of the whole matter is that my little book on Art and Technics is being treated by the Columbia University Press with the kind of zeal that I had hoped Harcourt would apply to the Conduct of Life, but didn't; and the further irony is that it will probably—though a small and insignificant job, relatively speaking—get the attention that should have gone to the Conduct of Life, thereby easing the consciences of the people who neglected the more important book.[40] In the long run, it will all come out well, and I am quite serene.

N.B. I won't discuss all the points in your letter now; but one word about astringent. It's almost a laudatory word with me: sharp, challenging, tonic. Russet apples or alcohol on the skin after shaving. If we saw more of each other you'd realize that I can take stiff doses of criticism, without showing abrasions; although I may be slow in the comeback, and may appear to have sloughed off what has been said, instead of taking it in. Good heavens! I even learned something from the academic critics who slew me for the errors I made in my Melville: why, then, shouldn't I patiently learn from you, whose ideas and methods I completely respect.

L

[typed]
Lewis Mumford
Amenia, New York
3 January 1953

. . . It was good to get your Christmas greetings, dear Harry; and we all wish you and Jo all sorts of blessings for the New Year. If you find you have too many blessings to appreciate properly, I will appreciate the loan of one or two; for I seem to be in for a run of ailments, after a life which, in any major way, was for so long unscathed. Possibly you were more right than you knew in your diagnosis of my state last May, when you suggested that I give up any attempt to give out or create. I

---

40. Lewis Mumford, *Art and Technics* (1952).

didn't follow your suggestion any more than my operation compelled me to, but nature seems ready to back you up and it looks as if all my fine plans for retiring here at the end of January and sinking down into the writing or the revision of a book will prove as futile as the other plans I made for last year.[41] You remember my telling you how sleepy and foggy I felt all last fall, from the removal to Philadelphia onward? I attributed this to the operation and having to plunge back to work too quickly. Late in November I reported the symptoms to Dr. Gurewich and he, seeing that I was fifteen pounds overweight, was inclined to think my condition was due to an absence of thyroid. Just the other day the real cause leaked out: a front tooth that had quietly died, and had probably been infecting the system all along. In a sense, I am relieved to know the cause, for I had begun to feel that premature senile decay had set in, particularly because of my foggy state of mind. But I have the immediate problem this next month of trying to keep the wicked tooth in my mouth while I finish up my engagements at the University; and after that there will have to be some further excavations and repairs; so my hoped for spring up here will be a checkered one. This is no sort of mail to begin the New Year with; all the more because you yourself have been going through a bad or frustrating period; but at least, as I told Alice, we can hold hands! Alison looks forward keenly to seeing you again. She has been sweating over term papers all through the Christmas vacation; and has come up with a still disordered, but very suggestive one on Dante, TS Eliot, and herself. Get her to tell you her own theme for a personal Divine Comedy; for in it her deep awareness of her relationship to Geddes, so long suppressed, comes to light in a most curious symbolic balance: the dead coming to life and the living encountering death. (I only wish I could have put it down on the spot as she first told it to us.) She gets tied up into knots over these papers, for both her standards and her ambitions are high; and she is able to see the importance of many problems that she has not enough philosophic background or experience as yet to answer. The inner strain on her is great; and there are moments when I fear for her; for she has none of my or Geddes's offhandedness about academic standing; and her very efforts are often self defeating. If she could be more relaxed and occasionally accept what seemed a second best she would be both happier and more productive, without ruining her sleep and her digestion and even, alas! her final mark!

Despite all our current domestic tribulations—like the egoist I am I have only told you my tale of troubles!—these two weeks up here have bestowed many blessings. This shabby old house is an active mother symbol for all of us, and I almost tremble when I leave it, remembering it is made of brittle and ignitable wood, even as we are made of fragile flesh!

In old friendship
Lewis

---

41. Mumford underwent prostate surgery in August 1952.

[typed]
Lewis Mumford
Amenia, New York
18 March 1953

. . . I have long been meaning, dear Harry, to counteract the morose letter I wrote you a few months ago, when I was still probably suffering from my depressing infection, by another one, in the mood of the last six weeks: weeks of almost pure bliss, watching the gentlest of winters turn into the earliest of springs. Relaxed and rewarding weeks for both of us; and though my anxieties about the state of the world remain pretty much what they were I have stowed them far enough below the surface of my life that I become aware of their existence only when I awake at three in the morning. Best of all, my mental powers which had been blighted by the infection, have returned; and I can once more enjoy the operations of my own mind; that last pleasure of narcissm! But what prompts me to write you now is something quite different. Alison, who has come under all sorts of salutary stimuli and influences this last half year, is now in the midst of a great adolescent anguish over the choice of her life work; and her immediate advisers, I fear, who have awakened her to the keen joys of pure scholarship, are also, too narrow in their outlook to do justice to the abundance of her talents. She desperately would like to talk matters over with you; but she has been hesitant about intruding on your time. In matters like this my counsel is useless; for the kind of work I have done is precisely what her own counsellors have called into question. If you have an hour to spare her some day before vacation begins—or if not then, of course afterwards—that would be a most timely act of friendship.

Warmly
Lewis

P.S. If all goes well—my fingers are still crossed—I sail for England on 6 May, as advance courier to the family.

1954–1963

The Master of the City

WELL INTO HIS SIXTH DECADE, Mumford experienced a renaissance as innovative thinker and prolific writer. While working on *The Transformations of Man* (1956), which he described as "the little discourse on universal history" (20 November 1954), he conceived an original interpretation of human history that inspired him to revise and to expand earlier writings on the city and technological development. Mumford's letters to Murray reveal the crucial importance of *The Transformations of Man* as a foundation for the remainder of his life's work, and Murray astutely recognized his friend's innovations in the book. In 1959, the two friends debated Mumford's use of historical evidence in his *Saturday Evening Post* article, "How War Began"; in 1963 they conducted an extended argument concerning the role of chance versus that of purpose in biological evolution and human development. *The City in History* (1961), for which Mumford was honored with the National Book Award, reaffirmed his status as a contemporary master of urban studies. Murray praised the book as "a gratifying consummation of your long, comprehensive, arduous, dedicated, creative labors" (HAM 2 January 1961). Stimulated by earlier epistolary exchanges with Murray, Mumford mentioned the "little book I am now beginning to write on the origins and the present day outcome of technological development" (LM 4 August 1963). This projected "little book" evolved into the massive *The Myth of the Machine* in two volumes. On personal matters, Mumford offered sensitive consolation upon the death of Murray's wife Jo in January 1962. During this period, the two friends returned to subjects of their correspondence in earlier years—including the mysterious condition of Mrs. Melville's hands and the health of Van Wyck Brooks.

[handwritten]
Lewis Mumford
Amenia, New York
1 Jan 1954

. . . . Happy New Year, dear Harry! My first letter of the New Year goes to you: prompted partly by a guilty conscience over not having written you long before this, partly by having read last night in Perspectives—which waited for me through fall up here—your fine percipient article on Conrad Aiken.[1] That's another topic we haven't ever, in our all-too-brief encounters, discussed. Good heavens, what a lot we have to catch up on, though time gets narrower and space stays as wide as ever as the years pass . . . I've had a good fortnight here, unexpectedly good, because I shall go back to Philadelphia on Sunday with the embryo of my next book well planted and growing in me. "Love and Marriage"—though I find I am charmed by the 50 pages I wrote last spring—will have to wait another season, to add such stray morsels of wisdom as my later years may bring. Alison is in bouncing shape, as a result of her relaxed regime this fall, and Sophy and I are still living like camels on the hump of Europe we brought back with us. With affectionate good wishes from all of us

Lewis

[handwritten]
Lewis Mumford
Amenia, New York
7 August 1954

Dear Harry:

I've long been meaning to write you before this incredibly beautiful summer— I realize I am talking about my inwardness, not just the cool, brilliant days!—comes to an end. What prompts me at the moment is an envelope, addressed to you years ago, I'd judge from the unfamiliar hand: and this guarantees that this letter instead of breaking into your days will be waiting in the shadowing silence of Brimmer Street till you return in September. A week ago I finished, without a wrinkle of fatigue, the first draft of the little book, a sort of discourse on Universal History, I am doing for the World Perspective Series. That makes *two* books since last April, outlined at least—all but the difficult final chapters. Now I shall spend the next six weeks fishing in the waters of my unconscious to see which of many abandoned themes may nibble at my hook. I scarcely dare to confess the utter happiness of the last six months, though it's inconceivable it should last a day longer. Such inner Peace!—as if the world were saved and I had been there, passing the buckets, when the damnable fire was put out. I can't account for the feeling: no visible event has

1. "Conrad Aiken: Poet of Creative Dissolution," *Wake* 11 (1952): 95–106.

caused it. And you? Don't stop to answer if you are busy. But if you should be in the neighborhood before 15 September, drop in: this time to stay at least overnight.

Warmly

Lewis

[handwritten]

[LM] Recd 21 Aug? 25 Aug

Ever-vital Lewis. It was good, very good, to hear that this summer has been "incredibly beautiful" to both your inward & your outward eye. Whether I am played out—though rich as our cob-bursting corn stalks—or just stale, I shall know in due course, but this summer has been dull & wet, with little sun, in the exterior as well as the interior. I have looked forward to this season—leaving Harvard for a while—& had visions of writing as a brook bubbles & bounces down its path, but nothing much has happened. I have a lot in mind that I desperately want to say, but the sentences don't choose to come, so I wait & move about & look around. Since June we have been to Montreal, Oregon, San Francisco, but most of the time I have been at my chief haunt, inventing a revised Pantheon of evolutionary gods. Maybe that's enough for a summer.

I am looking forward to seeing your discourse on Universal History—for its own intrinsic worth as well as for its similarities to & differences from my evolutionary schemes which holds so far as I can see on all levels—

Two unusual characters I met this summer—Alan Watts, head of the Asian Institute of San Francisco (English Buddhist of a sort) & H. Marshall McLuhan (author of "The Mechanical Bride")—both proved to be ardent admirers of your major & minor works.[2] It was very gratifying to revel in praising you with them.

Of course you belong there, passing the buckets that will quench the fires of this world's damnation. No one has done more to bring sanity to bear on the present disastrous current of events. To my eye, however, we Americans are going from bad to worse, & there is no hope of reversing the momentum—so I am working for the post-catastrophic renewal, who knows how many generations hence? In short, I have my eye on the Hereafter—on Earth, as it is in the imagination. If I can see my way to visit you sometime between Sept 3 and 7th I shall drop you a line. In the meantime my devotions to you both—Immortals

Yours

Harry

---

2. Alan Watts (1915–73), Zen Buddhist philosopher.

[handwritten]
Lewis Mumford
Amenia, New York
25 Aug 1954

. . . My long period of bliss came to an end, as I knew it must, almost immediately after I wrote you, dear Harry: the first effect of my stopping work and analyzing with a cold eye what I had written! Not that either of the first drafts is radically bad: just that both of them demand a great deal more work. Meanwhile I've had great fun going through your revised "Personality," getting much help from your first essay and from Erickson: but disappointed because none of the other contributors have tried to answer the questions I want answered.[3] I've just finished Vol. VII of Toynbee and plan to plow through the next three, too: but for all his learning I find the texture of his thought soft and slippery: even worse in cold print than face-to-face.[4] He is great on superficials: indeed he wallows in them, possibly to conceal how little real thinking he has applied to fundamentals. As for my "Discours"—it may turn out to be a pocket-size alternative to Toynbee: and may find favor by reason of its brevity if not its superior insight!

I am sorry that your summer has seemed unproductive: but I don't trust these subjective reactions. Your revised Pantheon probably outshines my six effortful months; and I am very eager to hear about it.[5] Between 3 & 4 September our house should be free of all other intruders & swept and garnished for you: so do come, if it's at all possible. I may have an early copy of "Sanity" to give you then.[6]

Affectionately
Lewis

[handwritten]
The Drake
Spruce Street—West of Fifteenth
Philadelphia 2
3 October 1954

. . . The dislocation of moving down here, and the equatorial heat that has followed, have sunk both of us for the moment, dear Harry: so I write for both of us to

3. Henry A. Murray and Clyde Kluckhohn, *Personality in Nature, Society, and Culture,* 2nd ed. (1953); Henry A. Murray and Clyde Kluckhohn, "Outline of a Conception of Personality," 3–49; Eric Homberg Erickson, "Growth and Crises of the 'Healthy Personality,' " 185–225. Erickson (1902–1994), the celebrated psychoanalyst who studied children, was associated with the Harvard Psychological Clinic, 1933–1935.

4. Lewis Mumford, review of Arnold Toynbee, *A Study of History,* vol. 7–10, *New Republic,* 8 November 1954, 15–18.

5. Published as "The Possible Nature of a 'Mythology' to Come," in *Myth and Mythmaking* (1960).

6. Lewis Mumford, *In the Name of Sanity* (1954).

tell you how touched we were by your letter to Sophy. Though Sophy was the one child (of five) who didn't hate her mother, it was the complicated Dostoyevskyan reactions of her family, rather than grief, that most afflicted Sophy. We packed Alison off to Radcliffe, as far as New Haven, ten days ago; and, at latest reports, she is reasonably happy or at least excited over the fate of the Ottoman Empire, her latest interest. I wish I could give an equally happy report of her father: but the silent treatment that In The Name of Sanity is receiving—alternating with such *personal* hostility as Niebuhr's review in The Times Book Review discloses—leaves me frustrated and discouraged; since, with my last four books, the same pattern is now firmly established.[7] But that will wear off. . . . We are grateful for your suggestion of a visit; but we are studiously keeping out of her way and don't expect to come to Boston, barring accidents, till next spring.

With affectionate greetings
Lewis

[handwritten]
[LM] Oct 1954

Dear Lewis,

Alas, we never met; but you, no doubt, saved yourself from a dreary conversation since I have been so embogged in some kind of dismal Swamp this summer that I would not have helped you to keep afloat at a moment when you wanted to be riding a flood tide. Well, we'll try again.

Our ideas & aims could not be closer, since we have much the same vision of world trends & much the same notions as to what should or might be done to better matters. I have only read parts—all exciting, true, & brilliantly written—of your book, because it arrived when I was in the midst of all kinds of tangles & I did not want to get diverted into another—though parallel—stream of thought. The critics are offish or defensively antagonistic because you have put your finger on the illness from which they too suffer & you are offering solutions which they would have liked to have conceived; but they haven't the energy to work for their redemption, even if they themselves had been profound enough to envisage them. Of course, it's outrageous that a few good critics aren't whole-heartedly calling attention to the resolving power of your ideas—there ought to be a few healthy ones somewhere in this country!—but you have a large following scattered throughout the world & you can forget the New York cliques, etc.

This is no kind of a letter, just a note to thank you for your two last communications, to wish you fortune this fall, to tell you that your writing has never been better, & that I shall give Alison a buzz as soon as I return to Cambridge.

My love to you both—
Harry

---

7. Reinhold Niebuhr, review of *In the Name of Sanity, New York Times,* 26 September 1954, 31.

[handwritten]
The Drake
Philadelphia 2 Penn
20 November 1954

Dear Harry:

I feel guilty at having conveyed to you my first feeling of dismay when I found that In the Name of Sanity was to be treated once more like the three other books that preceded it—smothered in silence, or belittled out of all proportion to its faults. For actually during the last year I have been having a much better time of it than you have had: and it was my turn—at last—to hold your hand, instead of asking for a transfusion from your own seemingly boundless stores of vitality. Part of my re-action—the depression, not the dismay—was brought about by the one kind of at-tack that lays me lower, psychologically, than my real jams and lapses: namely, a bacterial infection, in my teeth. If I were sensible I'd say good-by to these noxious tasks without further ado: for there are enough real palls to hang over one's life without letting a physiological accident poison one's happiness. Is it possible that your own state last summer was the result of some such undermining? The sure sign of it in me is a. depression and b. inability to coordinate ideas, even sufficiently to give a lecture on a familiar subject.

At the moment Sophy is in New York, having a heart-to-heart talk with Alison, who is less in love with Radcliffe than usual but, apparently, more in love with a young man in Washington. We plan to spend the Christmas vacation in Amenia and return there as early in February as possible. I hope to finish the little discourse on universal history I began last August before the buds burst forth in Spring. My classes here are so big that I find my work less rewarding in personal contacts than it was originally; so I am tempted to chuck the job altogether; and would, were it not for the fact that I can no longer look forward to the income from book royalties I enjoyed ten years ago. So I'll probably stick it out for another year or two—with misgivings and resistances.

I have no notion of where or when this will find you: but it carries, in any event, my affectionate greetings.

Lewis

[handwritten]
[LM] Dec 54

Dear Lewis,

O, these long Murray silences, these slow reactions, these interminable latent periods! How unfair to have *all* the spirited currents run from you to me! To have *all* the boundless generosities on your side, & on mine, affections speechless as the desert & expressions dull as dust! The dentist I shall visit soon, but so far as I know I have had nothing but an invasion of viruses to account for my incapacity to order chaos—nothing on the somatic side, that is. I am playing the horse of mental fatigue for the present, & may know whether this is the best diagnosis in the spring when I return from the Mediterranean. Basic to all that I hope to write is a reissued & much more complicated, yet much more coherent & intelligible, classification of human activities, including mental activities, activities, which will account, in part, for evolutions as well as survivals of body forms, social forms, material forms, & representational-symbolic forms. It is the territory you have traversed with such discerning intuitions, sound judgments, & enlightened prophecies. Being duller & trained to the tortoise-ways of anatomy & to hair-splitting distinctions, etc., etc., I must need labor over the principles involved in making, & defining, & inter-relating concepts. Consequently, I am continually in a canebrake with a machete, hacking out paths which only too often lead me back to where I started, baffled as ever. There is no quick cure for me, if I propose to stick to this problem until it is carried at least one step further. One central idea—related to an old discussion of ours about purpose in evolution—is that of on-going transmutations of the germplasma through many successive generations until the full development of the possibilities of some novel mutation has been completed. That is, the various potentialities inherent in a new genetical formation take time (hundreds of generations possibly) to evolve and be manifested in effective forms and functions. But enough of this. I am still lamenting our failure to meet this last September. Strangely enough, none of my colleagues are interested in the field that now concerns me & I have had not one who would listen to and criticize my recent experiments in speculation. Alison, having left Cabot, is harder to hunt down, & unhappily we have failed to capture her when we had, on two occasions, an open evening to which she would have contributed so largely if she had been reachable & so inclined.

So much for the present. Blessings & hopes to you both—

Affectionately
Harry

[handwritten]
Lewis Mumford
Amenia, New York
4 May 1955

Dear Harry:

Sophy has been upstairs in bed for the last few days, with a wickedly infected ear; and, because my days are now a series of interruptions—the sort Virginia Woolf complained of and attributed to the tyranny of men—I have a little time at last to catch up with the offices of friendship. The first two months there were blissfully dedicated to work, and my intellectual pulse has seldom beat faster. But ever since Easter, when our car broke down in New Haven, taking Alison to the train there, I have gone through a series of interruptions and frustrations that have left me ragged: so all my "wisdom" in keeping you at bay till my book was finished has proved vain: the book isn't finished and I am just the poorer for having missed you.

I hoped that by now my spate of work would be over: so that I could at least—and at last!—visit Boston & see both Alison and you. But that hope has gone whistling down the wind; and before I know it, it will be mid-June and I'll be packing off for the Wenner-Gren conference at Princeton. (The old pirate has taken a fancy to me, happily, and presented a copy of In The Name of Sanity to his King and the Prime Minister.)[8] The book I'm working on (The Transformations of Man) has come without effort: a gift from the unconscious, re-assembling in a fresh pattern all I've been thinking for the last twenty years, and stimulating me to fresh explorations: so that I face it, each morning, with an expectant quizzical smile, as a wise man might have consulted the Delphic oracle. But enough of that. What of yourself?

> Affectionately
> Lewis

[handwritten]
The Baleen
48 Mt. Auburn Street
Cambridge 38, Massachusetts
[LM] 14/6/55 3 Aug

Dear Lewis—

I blessed you for your letter—especially as it brought a ray of light, the news that Sophy had turned the corner & was on the path to health, a long way I feared. Van Wyck & Gladys spent the night here and told us that you and Sophy are having Alison with you for the summer. This strikes me as a good deal all round. Alison, the peerless one, has been over-stimulated—as are many other vibrant and imaginative Radcliffe beauties—by men and minds—I would suspect—and a summer of elementary occupations and ruminations should be all to the good. Eh? Maybe she had more colorful and adventurous ideas for her holiday, but it is important to learn the vagaries of Fate before you go too far.

And what of the book? Is it off your solar plexus? & pleasing to the senses and the soul? I guess Yes, despite all the worry & the breaks in continuity.

As for me, my writing has been going very badly as usual, but I enjoy nothing so much—except for the interruptions—the worst in my whole life since May 13 when my great friend Clyde Kluckhohn learnt that his son had accidentally shot a woman at Raleigh, N.C.[9] The trial begins today, & I shall probably go down to be with them when it becomes a horror, as I fear it will. I am let down after Van W B's visit—one evening. He is the most courteous, gentle, gracious fellow I know, but prematurely grey in the brain. Love to you all—

8. Axel Leonard Wenner-Gren (1881–1961), Swedish industrialist who founded the Electrolux Company; supported various foundations for scientific research.

9. Clyde Kluckhohn (1905–1960), anthropologist at Harvard where he helped found the interdisciplinary Department of Social Relations.

Harry

[typed]
Lewis Mumford
Amenia, New York
3 August 1955

. . . Your letter came, dear Harry, while I was at the Princeton Conference—an affair that was both rewarding and a little disappointing, chiefly because many of the participants did not realize the difference between information and discussion—and since coming back from that about six weeks ago I have been devilling at my book. Devilling is the right word: the heat gave the whole process the proper infernal touch; and the worse I worked the more I tried to make up for the lack of spiritual energy by working even harder: something I am never silly enough to do even when I am in my right mind. The idea that had so enchanted me a year ago, and still seemed, six months later, to stand up to my most rigorous criticism, suddenly evaporated: the word that would have made it real, the illustrations that would have made it come alive, were all missing. After weeks of plugging, I wondered if my unconscious, in offering me this free gift, had not diabolically concealed from me its real nature: knowing that I would not look a gift horse in the mouth, it had substituted an old Nag for the Pegasus I thought I was going to ride. What disconcerted me most was not the poor quality of my work—that's remediable, one way or another—but my lack of sure judgment. Even now, I don't dare throw the manuscript into the fire—apart from the fact the very notion of a fire is insupportable—for fear that I might again be showing bad judgment, and that the manuscript, if not as vital and original as I had imagined it to be, is at least better than I now feel. All in all this has been a new experience, and a dusty one. I am now for the moment relieving myself of responsibility by sending the corrected manuscript off to the editor of the series; but in doing so I have none of the blithe sense that the book is finished: rather, I know it will plague me and nag at me till I have Ok'd the final galleys, and may even rise up and reproach me after that. All this inner drought has had accompaniments, as you might guess, in the outside world: the wilting bushes, the shriveled corn, the yellowing cucumbers, the dried river bed, and—yes even this, with psychosomatic classicism, an aching tooth. For the moment, the world is burnt up and I seem burnt out. Yet but a little while ago, before Sophy's illness, I was riding at the top of my powers; and so, looking at it rationally, I am inclined to attribute my defeat to the fact that Sophy's illness exhausted me on the inside more than I realized and that I have been trying to tap sources of creativity that have temporarily gone dry for quite other reasons. As for Sophy, she hasn't looked better for years; and except for a lower level of energy, she shows no signs whatever of her long illness. [. . .] The prospect of going back to Philadelphia again at the end of September is a nightmare to me; so that I have resolved, even if I had to tighten my belt, to give up that particular form of security after 1955: all the easier to do because many attractive offers that I must turn down keep coming my way, and because a number of my books are going back into print. I shall be here straight on, except for business trips to New York; so if there's any chance of your dropping down this way, up to 20 September, please do so and arrange to stay over: my time is free and I hope that my mind will, after a rest, be active and sprightly again. Meanwhile I pray that your own work has been going better, and that all your friendly anxieties about the Kluckhohns were happily resolved.

> Ever
> Lewis

[handwritten]
Clayton, New York
[LM] Ans 5 Sept 55

Dear Lewis,

May the sovereigns of the Milky Way sustain your spirits! Every word you set down went to the marrow of my being, because what you describe as a fall into accidia—temporary & easily to be explained away for you—is my daily, weekly, yearly destiny. I have become so accustomed to it that I am not at all appalled. Perhaps I should say that I have been fortunate—for the most part—in waking each morning with a surplus of zest & when I stop I am not tired & have enjoyed myself—despite the fact that I have been tangled in a score of unsolved problems, & the sentences & images have not poured out in a steady flow & so I have little to show. In July I spent too much time on 2 papers which I had been foolish enough to read at the Religion & Science Conference on Star Island on August 1. (I tried to deal with *Purpose* in evolution, just what we discussed twice without reaching agreement.) As it turned out they were easy to please, & I felt repaid, but the enterprise took me off other rails which are more to my liking. I am sure you will like your book better after a season of relaxation & I am sure I will relish it. But I am confused. Is this the one you were winding up in April? And is the one you mentioned to me last summer—four dominant attitudes of mind, or types of personality & their various permutations, integrations, & conflicts down the centuries? Whatever it is, I for one, am confident of it. Pax Tecum.

I am *so* happy to hear of Sophy's steady recovery & of Alison's achievements in the culinary department, not to speak of others. What does it feel like to sit down to meals everyday with two ravishing Beauties? Love to the three of you & benedictions & prayers

> Yrs
> Harry

P.S. I am writing my last piece on basic theory—foundations—after this—easier & more lively themes—I arrived up here on the St. Lawrence a week ago & am now with Jo & Josephine snug & dry while a tempest of 50 miles per hour tears up the waters and tosses them over dock & bank.

[typed]
Lewis Mumford
Amenia, New York
5 September 1955

. . . By now I should know, dear Harry, that I am not, in the ordinary run of things, a depressible man; and that when I feel as low as I did when I last wrote to you—and evoked your gallant letter—it is always, yes always, due to a bacterial infection. And that proved to be the case again: the result is that, toward the end of August, I had two teeth taken out, and from that time on, despite the run of hot weather that still prevailed, I felt better about the world, about myself, and above all about the book. True: the work that I did on it when the bacteria were beclouding my mind had to be done over again in many spots: but the main idea was still visible, and this week I shall take the finished manuscript into the publishers. At the moment, I should like nothing better than to relax for a month at the sea; but instead, I must go back to Philadelphia after a fortnight, and this means all sorts of preparatory acts, from getting clothes ready to doing some hasty reading for a new course in the humanities that I fathered last spring, only to find myself compelled to play the nursemaid, by being asked to give it, without adequate preparation, during this fall semester. I was probably weak to say Yes: but the course represents a slightly new twist on an old idea and I felt obliged to follow it through, even if at the price of failure. But by now I am determined not to repeat this yearly ordeal in Philadelphia, beyond this coming period: so all in all, my preparation of a new course, always a difficult business, is doubly futile. The course itself? One on religion, using the ancient texts, beginning with the Egyptians, and covering all the classic religions, as a key to the inner life of each civilization. If the University were only, say, New Haven, I wouldn't mind giving it; but it's too far from Amenia to suit my needs—especially since I loathe Philadelphia as a city. I am dreadfully sorry to hear that your own work has been bogged down. The main difficulty, I find with my own writing, is that as one grows old, one's creative powers weaken while one's critical powers become more keen, more demanding. Somehow, one has to suspend one's intellectual faculties and leap back into the deeps of the unconscious, as if one were leaping into a woman's arms. I know that formula isn't unfathomable (a nice Freudian slip: I meant 'infallible'); indeed, as I discovered in writing my last book, one's unconscious sometimes plays malicious tricks and offers one goldbricks instead of ingots. You ask me *what* book I was writing. A good question. The one I spent most of my time on last year I threw aside, as impossible, or at least impossible along the lines I had tried to follow by someone with my preparation. But the book I have just finished is something that I hardly had more than a sketchy anticipation of, before I started to write: it was a pure gift from the nether world. I call it The Transformations of Man; and it is an attempt to give a sort of mythical picture—mythical in that, while it never tries to dispute known facts, it often is bold enough to step beyond them—of the successive stages that transformed man from an inarticulate animal into his present historic self. In a sense the book is an attempt to do in a single, compact volume what Toynbee did not succeed in doing in a dozen long ones. But it approaches the whole subject in a different manner and I hope makes more sense. Its value lies in its succinctness and its simplicity. Whatever errors it reveals will not be hidden under a stuffy bushel basket of scholarship: they will be naked and visible. It should come out in the spring.

Do not confuse this book with another that you will presently be receiving, called Human Prospects: an anthology of my work, done by Harry Moore, the D.H. Lawrence biographer and Karl Deutsch of M.I.T.[10] Rather a good selection, I think, which may surprise many people who think of me as just a clever writer of New Yorker Sky Lines! The present vogue of good paper bound books has had a happy effect upon my opera: one by one, they are all coming back into print; and I now have a decent chance to revise, in something like definitive form, my big series. Indeed, I have already started work on Technics and Civilization. (Sticks and Stones and The Brown Decades have come out, and The Golden Day will follow next year.)

Thank heaven the sear and sweltering summer was ushered out by the flood: a grand spectacle here, without too great a measure of human tragedy in our immediate vicinity. We shall all have something to tell our grandchildren. Did I tell you that I'll be teaching at Brandeis in the spring and must start looking for a house in Cambridge soon? It's a result of Alison's asking: she hates dormitory life.

With affectionate greetings
Lewis

[handwritten]
[LM] Sept 55

Dear Lewis—

Unhappily your letter just missed me on the St. Lawrence & we did not meet for 10 days. But I was delighted to receive it—all your letters are gems!—on my return to Boston. Somehow we seem to be concerned with the same topics, but talking with each other only occasionally across a wide gulf, and our time is getting shorter, if not short. I am pretty well scared away from Amenia, & although I got a *big lift* at the thought of the Mumfords in Cambridge for the spring term, second & third thoughts reminded me that we were both on iron-rails, you a flier, the Shasta Limited, & I on a 50-car freight, stopping & backing, & side tracked most of the time, but yet both pre-occupied.

---

10. *The Human Prospect,* ed. Harry T. Moore and Karl W. Deutsch (1955).

Excuse this writing—the paper is fog-wet.

Kluckhohn and I (a few lectures in the spring) are giving a general education course that should be yours—Natural Man & Ideal Man in the History of Western Thought. We are only going to talk about men & ideas that interest us especially—not attempt a complete coverage. The fall term ends with St. Thomas & is pretty well fixed, but the spring term is open—not settled. What would be your suggestions? Some possibilities—Renaissance Man—Montaigne—Pascal—17–18th Century British philosophers—Rousseau—French Enlightenment—Darwin—Freud—? I am now busy with a "demand" piece—the biography of my supposed "system" of psychology with very exacting specifications.[11] I am happy to hear of the Mumford anthology &, at last, of Mumford in paper books! This is the usual cultural lag & you are fortunate—seeing how far ahead you are—that a few people are catching on to you before the fever of life is over. I dread this fall term for you, because I too detest Philadelphia. Have you seen the editorial in *Life,* asking why there are no sunny American novels? You should answer them. They want a Big Business hero, a Hermes of America, who lives by the Luce periodicals, especially Fortune. I shall be on the River again in October, but after that will try to get hold of the elusive Alison—My best to you three—embraces & wishes—Yours

Harry

[handwritten]
Philadelphia
16 December 1955

. . . . I started the academic year, dear Harry, badly in need of a rest I won't begin to have till I get to Amenia next week, if then; and once more a tooth that had secretly laid me low for more than a month in all sorts of devious ways that made my physician label it a virus infection—by now even good internists, as he himself confessed, tend to overlook the teeth, after having gone wild about them 25 years ago! This at least explains my silence—though all the while I've been meaning to write you to ask for a copy of your summer's address on Religion. My own further delving for my General Ed. course on the subject has fascinated me, because of the fresh historic and social vistas it opens up. I am sure you'll have the same sort of fun with your Natural & Ideal man. I've all sorts of thoughts about that course, too, but you'd probably find them confusing at this late date. Neither Montaigne nor Pascal express, for me, Renaissance vitality, which I find mainly in the artists, Michelangelo, Rubens et al. And doesn't one, in every period, find an Introvert & Extravert ideal: Bacon and Shakespeare: Rousseau and Diderot, each equally representative

---

11. Probably "Preparations for the Scaffold of a Comprehensive System," in *Psychology: A Study of a Science,* ed. Sigmund Koch, vol. 3 (1959): 7–54; reprinted in Shneidman, *Endeavors in Psychology,* 7–51.

of his culture and century. More of all this when we meet. As you know we've settled for an apartment. I am content since Sophy's depleted vitality—despite her surface exuberance—couldn't really have coped with a house. With warm greetings for the coming year

Ever
Lewis

[handwritten]
[LM] Ans 29 Dec 55

Dear Lewis—

What a misery! Another slug from Moby-Dick, your version, from Alpha, in my Pantheon! I am referring, of course, to that tooth or those teeth. If, after attending to this particular urgency, something more radical is suggested, & if you are not certain of the judgment of your own dentist, I would suggest that you wait until you get to Cambridge. We swear by painless Dr. Robinson who keeps in touch via X-Rays with the happenings in our jaws. It sounds as if your Fall term had been no better than you expected. I hope you will like Brandeis better. Its greater challenge might invigorate and exhaust you. Can you find some rest-space before February 1st? Once you have arrived, you will have to fight to keep your time from being eaten up by all those who are hungry for your wisdom. I shall try not to be one of the chief offenders in this regard; but could you not conveniently manage a dinner with us at Brimmer St. early in February? Will you and Sophy pick a night—preferably a Tuesday or a Thursday—& tell me whom you would like to meet—faculty, graduate students, or friends of Alison's? From the glimpse I had of her, Alison is having her best Radcliffe year. Finding that her life-line pointed to Rob has made a difference and her summer with you & Sophy did much to replenish her resources—Anyhow—whatever the confluence of contributing causes—Alison seems to have her destiny in hand—as much in hand as it ever is at her age. We are very much attached to her—enchanted, in fact. Also, I am keen about Rob. Have seen him only 3 times—but feel certain of a large part of him already. Can't we arrange some joint evenings? What is the topic of your lectures this spring? My course in General Education is not concerned with representative figures in Western history, but with representative reflections on the nature of man—hence Montaigne instead of Rubens.

Jo and I were very pleased to receive a copy of the Mumford anthology & to find your celebrations of marriage & family included in the volume. Although you have some immortal pieces here, there are others (that you must be equally proud of) which I would like to add—plenty for another volume.

I trust you all relaxed over the holidays (& your jaw is not a threat for the near future). Solstice salutations

Harry

[handwritten]
Amenia, New York
28 December 1955

. . . . How good it was to hear your voice the other day, dear Harry: doubly good because it was so unexpected. And now your letter: first welcome to Cambridge, which makes all others dispensable. Don't think we'll shrink from the hospitalities and sociabilities of the new scene: quite the contrary. Philadelphia bores us, because we have so little personal intercourse in that scattered city, and I come to Cambridge a free man, with only four hours of classes at Brandeis—nice Freudian slip! avoiding the journey to Waltham!—and with no other heavy task awaiting me except at the beginning, when I must read proof on The Transformations of Man. If ever I was in a mood to relax and talk this is the moment. . . . As for the anthology, like you I would have chosen differently from the editors: but except for calling their attention to some scattered material they'd never come upon I really kept my hands off the selection: so it is an external judgment on my work—interesting to me because the emphasis is in so many cases different from my own. . . . In commenting on your lectures I see that unconsciously I substituted the abortive book I sketched out year-before-last for your own proper theme. Peccavi. The courses I wanted to give at Brandeis unfortunately seemed to infringe on their regular offerings: so I shall have to repeat with variations two of my Pennsylvania courses; on Cities and on American Forms & Values: or 'The Golden Day Revisited.' When I finish this I purpose to close the door finally on teaching for more than six weeks or so in any year.

As usual, Amenia restored me completely within three days: I bask in the beauty of it and the idleness of my hours. This is the vacation I so badly needed in September—and more. Alison and Rob are a delight together: young love has a birdlike charm and tenderness that brings spring right into the house.

A fruitful New Year for you
Lewis

[handwritten]
Cambridge
17 March 1956

Dear Harry:

Your Star Island paper came this morning, and I have just finished devouring it.[12] You shame me by putting a whole book within the compass of a night's talk: but on the other hand, you gladden me because your own analysis, starting from a different basis, substantiates my own and gives The Transformations of Man magnifi-

12. Murray's paper was later published as "Two Versions of Man," in *Science Ponders Religion,* ed. Harlow Shapley (1960); reprinted in Shneidman, *Endeavors in Psychology,* 581–604.

cent support. Your explication of 'creativity' is more explicit, more operational, than mine of 'purpose,' and I take that as a challenge to me either to formulate my own idea more clearly or to drop it in favor of yours, unless I can bring out the residual difference and show that my version goes one point farther. I am not sure that you haven't clung too long to the Darwinian conception of 'combative strength' (p. 13). Is strength more singularly useful than persistence or cunning; and wouldn't 'mutual accommodation' account for survival in more cases than strength? Accommodation even accounts for no small part of what Darwin misread, I think, as the struggle for existence: the capacity to eat other creatures and in turn be eaten by those that have superior claims on their carcass, in a long food chain. Lions do not eat lions but antelopes. One other thing I find lacking in your otherwise compelling picture of the creative process: its tendency to acquire direction and to become cumulative, along certain lines. Sometimes the direction was 'misguided,' as in the overdevelopment of the olfactory lobe in a long line of man's predecessors: but no mere summation of your processes seems to me capable of accounting for it, without having, within 'creativity' itself, some kind of anticipatory, goal-projecting process, however dim & blundering it may have been at the beginning. . . . But there! I am afraid we are back again at the one point where our paths, despite our good will and imaginative sympathy, seem to diverge. . . . Our other points of difference are all very minor: most of them you'll discover for yourself when you read The Transformations of Man. The displacement of woman, for example, I would push back further than the Christian-Hebraic myth, to the beginnings of civilization, after the largely matriarchal, life-centered, sex-appreciative neolithic period, with its domestication of plants, animals & humans. Then, too, I have a different interpretation of the role of early religions, not as agents of repression but as compensations for the life-negating process of compulsive work. But our grounds of agreement and mutual support are so extensive that I hesitate even to mention these residual differences. Many of your formulations have never been put better by anybody: and I kept on saying Amen so steadily in reading this paper that I had to dig up a few contrary arguments just to keep my self-respect. Perhaps, when I go through the paper again I'll find a few more points I'd like to discuss with you: indeed I've already found one on page 24: for I am skeptical about primitive man's creativeness as having been oriented almost entirely to survival; and that technical inventions resulted in more drastic transformations of human behavior than any other kind of variation seems to me even more dubious. What tool or weapon or machine transformed man as much as language?—as indeed in another context you clearly recognize. So, too, Paleolithic art is immensely superior to any skill shown in fabricating tools then. Have we not read back into prehistory our own hierarchy of interests?

See what a flood of thoughts your paper has uncorked!

Ever

Lewis

[handwritten]
[LM] Rec'd 5 July 1956

Dear Lewis,

The Transformations of Man.[13] You can rest on this; your whole future in the minds of men can rest on this, since here you have compacted and set forth in animating prose the essence of Lewis Mumford. All your vast stores of knowledge, brooded over & ordered into new shapes, weighed in the scales of your sensitive spirit, tested and retested, are herein crystallized into the absolutely needed truth for our time. It is a beautiful symphony of ideas and judgments, not a superfluous or wasted sentence, not a single inert thought, nothing irrelevant, nothing trite, all fiery and vital. This is the Elan Vital in words, creative evolution from the anthropoid to modern man with his two options—to keep going as he is now going or to change realizing that the old ways are obsolete. Harper should send this book to every member of the Federal Government. It should be required reading for every Freshman & and then a second time for every Senior.

Your have said almost everything that I have wanted to say and more; but it will do no harm to say it two, three . . . or twenty times again, each time in a slightly different way. Several of the things I have been working on are close parallels, though said in a duller & stoggier fashion without challenging the reader—as you do—to fight for his life. I am somehow still obsessed with the problem of the young American mind of our time—its resistances to straight talk on values, the ways it has of minimizing, denying, shunning, shrugging off, or mocking anything very serious, or dark, or demanding, or prophetic. You, however, will reach the attuned ears and minds, and generate enthusiasm for your message. It's a profound sort of happiness for me to find your embodiment & your fulfillment in this sublime book.

Yours
Harry
Of course—as always—my love goes out to the enchantresses, S & A.

[handwritten]
Lewis Mumford
Amenia, New York
8 July 1956

. . . What can I say in response to your words about The Transformations of Man, dear Harry? Only that, if no other human soul had read or reacted to the book, your own reading of it would, for me, have sufficed and your verdict be a sufficient reward. I always have kept open the possibility that my own evaluation of the book was based in a hallucination: but now that I find you share my judgment, perhaps

13. Lewis Mumford, *The Transformations of Man* (1956).

more fully and appreciatively than the book deserves, I rest easy. Easy at least about its fate in the long run: but Harper's went back on their promises to me even before publication and deserted it; so the book is stillborn and will be buried before it undergoes a resurrection. With your letter before me I can wait: your sympathy, and the sense that we understand each other and are working toward a common end, makes easier the acceptance of this first rejection, by publishers & reviewers.

Your friendship has given me much to be thankful for: and your letter crowns it. I look forward eagerly to your own forthcoming works so that, even if there is less need for it, I shall be able in some way to reciprocate. I have much more to say. This is just a first overflow from the heart—mine & Sophy's.

Lewis

[handwritten]
The Baleen
48 Mt. Auburn Street
Cambridge 38, Massachusetts
8 July, 56

Dear Terrific Mumfords,

My secretary for 22 years (who says, "he's an impossible man but I wouldn't work for anyone else") has always been on the alert for Mumfordiana. You must have a dozen copies of this. Alison, are you there in Amenia? Why didn't you tell me you were planning to invade the subterranean regions of the mind? It was by the pool of Cyane, I believe, in Sicily that Pluto kidnapped Eurydice in the *Fall*. You should not go underground until those days when the birds come back, a very few, a bird or two, to take a backward look—Be sure to look up Josephine (250 E 49. Te. Mu8-4196) who is studying chemistry, presumably on her way to psychiatry.

Have seen no reviews of "Transformations." Have you any extra ones to lend me? But whatever the Critics say *that* book is Immortal. You will be amused to read someday my bad parallels of this book written in 1955 & 56, but without the vision of post-historic man. Of course, *that* is ghastly; but if we escape radio-active particles, my horror is "The Mechanical Bride" (Vanguard).

Who is doing the cooking this summer? I vote for Lewis—your turn. What a winter you have to look forward to! I trust that your health is pleasant to you, Sophy, & that you won't slip on the cobblestones of the Roman road. I was reminded of Lewis the other day when a dentist extracted 4 teeth with a bull-dozer, & found pus running down from the antrum—bottled up there, he said, for 2 years. *Here* is a scape-goat for my bad temper. I am going into hiding for a month to write the scaffold for a theory. No fun this time—

Alien for a while Affectionately
Harry

Lewis Mumford
Amenia, New York
14 July 1956

. . . What a ghastly time you've been having, dear Harry; and how triumphant your letter sounds after emerging from it: like the inner shout of joy one feels upon coming into the sunlight after a long crawl through a choking smoky tunnel. I can sympathize with what you have been through, because ailing teeth have been the chronic ailment of my life; and in each case it was not any pain, but the debilitation and depression caused by the accumulated poisons, that was so ruinous. I am sure that this surgery will be followed by an immense release of your own vital powers: not least by a swift unfolding of the mind, because as you know these infections work more serious damage on one's higher mental functions than on anything else. Only six months or so ago I went through a very disturbing period: heaviness and sleepiness in the mid-day, and inability to concentrate, and perfectly appalling dreams at night. I went to my internist with these symptoms; and he could find nothing on a casual examination that warranted them. Now, though I had told him that the bad dreams and the depression had nothing to do with my emotional life, which was in a beautiful equilibrium, he had not been trained in Vienna for nothing: he smilingly suggested a whole medicine cabinet of sedatives, anxiety relievers, and stimulants, including all the new ones that one uses on bad psychotic cases. A few days later, one of my teeth blew up; and as soon as the decayed pulp was removed all my symptoms disappeared. When I told my doctor about it, he was man enough to write me that he had overlooked my teeth; and the internists generally, who had twenty or thirty years ago blamed the teeth for all otherwise untraceable ills, were now, in reaction over that folly, tending to overlook them—as perhaps your own physician had done, too! At all events, I congratulate you on having at last detected the culprits; and I predict that during the next year all your lifetime's preparation will be effortlessly consummated, in a book or a series of books, beside which my own will be only a shy daisy alongside a brilliant efflorescence of chrysanthemums. [. . .]

I spent a week in Pittsburgh at the end of June, surveying various ventures and possibilities and giving advice to the Mellon Trust; and after doing a thirty page report last week, I've now settled down to the serious business of the summer, going over my voluminous notes on Technics and Cities, and trying to decide whether it is possible to revise the books at all—or whether I should put them behind me and write something entirely fresh within the same fields. What makes revision so difficult—and it may even prove impossible—is that all that I learned in writing The Transformations of Man makes my earlier formulations seem inadequate. So a revision must either be so superficial it doesn't take into account these new insights, or so exhaustive that it would mean, at the end, the rewriting of each book from end to end—a harder thing to contemplate at sixty than the original writing of the big series was at thirty-five. Fortunately, I am under no pressure to make an early decision; and if I give myself enough time the situation may clear up by itself.

I still haven't thanked you half enough for your letter about the Transformations of Man: all I can say is that it transformed one man from a misanthropic wretch, who had the feeling that, intellectually speaking, he had been buried alive and could communicate effectively with no one, into a creature just the opposite, who calmly feels that he has done something that may, in time, prove to be much less casual and conventional than it seems: so that it may help to widen and deepen the whole stream of thought of which it is a part. When I see what a far more modest book, The Golden Day, did in the course of the next generation, I am heartened by the prospects of The Transformations. But when I was thirty people hailed my work with joy: now joy seems to have disappeared generally, and instead of hailing my new book, people wonder why it is that a man who has been around so long still has the effrontery to suggest that people read still another book of his! Before your letter, dear Harry, this made me angry: now, at least, I can smile. Have a good summer and don't think of writing me another line till you have done justice to yourself, in both relaxation and in work.

Lewis

[handwritten]
[LM] Murray 56
The Baleen
48 Mt. Auburn Street
Cambridge 38, Massachusetts

Dear Lewis—

Good to hear from you at last.

My fantasies of a visit to the Mumfords, to bask in their benignity and benevolence—Sophy's bristling beauty, Alison's—having got going with the B's I'd better stay by them to the end—balmy brilliance, and Lewis's blaze of bardic blessings—these fantasies were defeated by a pair of iron railings leading to a date-line on October 1st, now postponed to Dec. 1st. I think I told you of my afflicted state, generated by my agreement to write an impossible treatise according to a set scheme (which I had not examined when I agreed to the idea). It is nothing less than writing a Principia X 100^{10} for psychology in 100 pages. Instead, I seem to be writing a complaint that anyone should be so inflated as to think that psychology is ready for the final organizing formula in which the whole of human nature can be laid down—and buried. I won't bother you with it. If the job has not already defeated my spirit and senilized headpiece, it may turn out to be a blessed bane leading on to resurrection—but so far it is nothing but sheer agony. When I am through with it, I shall go to sleep with Transformations in my arms, hoping to wake in the spring a better man, and a better friend to Sophy, Alison, & Lewis. Damn it all—it doesn't look as if we are going to meet you before you leave in mid-November. Embraces all round—

Harry

P.S. Would like to know exact sailing date. Also Alison's address. I think there is a Radcliffe gal named "Daisy" Margaret Cutler at the Foreign Relations Council.

[handwritten, n.d.]

. . . What a tale of misery, dear Harry! I can match it with a briefer one of my own, for I spent more than a solid month just now writing a talk on the limitations of science & engineering for a short (35 min.) convocation address I gave at Cooper Union last Monday. There were plenty of moments when the only reasonable explanation of my constant failure seemed to be either (a) bacterial infection or (b) senile decrepitude. Actually, I was embarrassed by too many thoughts: so I had to pile the debris of five impossible speeches into one. For your consolation and further encouragement I will add that it turned out, when given, to be all that I wanted it to be, to the demonstrative satisfaction of the audience. But then, I was lucky, for I was preceded by Dr. Mervin Kelly, head of the Bell Telephone Companies, who turned out to be a perfect museum specimen to illustrate the human perils I was talking about. He made no contact at any point with the audience, but dug his head in his paper and read it as rapidly and monotonously as a copy reader, so that no one heard a word. His relation to my thesis was so patent that I had to cut out a passage about "compulsive and driven men." . . . Now I am released, and nothing keeps us from going to Europe except a lingering anxiety about Alison. She's been down with bronchitis for the last few weeks, one of them up here: and the roommate she hopefully embraced has not turned out well. About a month ago I gave up the thought of leaving before the middle of November, and I now have misgivings about that date. It's taken us years to discover that we've been underprotecting Alison in most ways rather than overprotecting her, and we tremble to think what might have happened to her if we had gone off in July as we originally planned. We wish now we'd been more vocally opposed to her psychiatric social work job. Her great trouble at the moment is the failure, or at least underdevelopment, of masculinity in the young men she knows, even when they are not overtly homosexual. Those who are sure of their maleness seem to get married early, and since she didn't get one of these she is baffled. . . . If she has good luck this winter our European trip will confirm her maturity and her self-confidence: but we can't be sure of that good luck: and if the breaks remain against her, we'd be happier to be on call a hundred miles away rather than beyond it three thousand miles away. So our decision about Europe is shaken, after this series of postponements, and it is just possible we may not go till spring. When I said last spring that a winter in Rome at the Academy sounded 'almost too good to be true' I was perhaps speaking more prophetically than I realized! The only happy part about all this is that I may have a chance to see you when your strangulating opus is finished! Sophy, happily, stays well, and physically I'm at top form for one entering—how comic!—his seventh decade.

Warmly

Lewis

P.S. I reply so promptly only because you asked for Alison's address:

Apt. 3D

145 East 21 St.

New York

Tel. Grammercy 5-4649

[typed]

Lewis Mumford

Amenia, New York

4 December 1956

I am pained, dear Harry, not over your silence; but over the cause of it. When you told me last June about your infected teeth, I was sure that this was the main cause of your frustrations; for I know, from repeated experiences of such mischief, how such an infection can paralyze all thinking processes, and cause far worse depressions than any neurosis I've ever been through. I went through such a period for a whole month in September; and was so sure that my teeth were to blame that I was reluctant to leave here before the culprits were detected. I still don't know if that was the trouble then, for the tooth I suspected still aches enough to show that it has some degree of life. Are you perhaps pushing yourself, as I have often done, too, at a moment when you should be relaxing and quietly waiting for something to happen within, without forcing the issue? I know how hard this is: I've just been going through that kind of discipline. But it's better than battering one's head against a solid wall. As for us, we are settling in for the winter, getting all sorts of chores done that our long and repeated absences had left undone for many years. I have no regrets about my decision: nothing but satisfaction, indeed, over the fact that I made it before the crises in Europe, so I have no sense of funking an unpleasant experience, as I would have if I had changed my mind after it became clear that it would be a cold and bleak winter in Europe, with the poorest possible conditions for exploring cities, which, apart from the three months of peace, leisure, and solitude that I hoped to find in Rome, was what the rest of the winter was to mean for me.[14] Peace, the kind that leads to inner productivity, would be very far away from me, I fear, on any part of the planet at the moment; and I do not deceive myself into thinking that they will be on tap in Amenia, either. But at least here I can do all sorts of preparatory tasks, toward writing my next book which I could not have under-

14. "Crises": probably a reference to the Suez Crisis and the Hungarian Revolution.

taken in Rome. If I could, back in July, have imagined the whole course of events, domestic and international, I should have gone over to Europe by myself then and have returned by the end of September. That wouldn't have provided the gay, irresponsible, autumnal honeymoon that Sophy and I had both looked forward to; but once Alison's plans for marriage had been defeated, that dream was largely doomed; for as long as Rob remained even potentially on the scene—and he turned up in the most calamitous fashion in the middle of September—she had need of us, and did not have in herself the resources needed for coping with her bitter realities. By now, she is in much better shape, and we see hardly anything of her; and that is as it should be. Her job is just sufficiently interesting to tide her over the winter; and in making herself fit to carry on, she has had, by an effort of will, to overcome certain gaps in her education, including such laughable ones as the inability to spell; so she is gaining steadily in self-confidence. The one thing that is lacking in her situation is a certain lack of confident masculinity in the young men that she meets: those who are sufficiently sure of themselves are already, alas! married.

As for myself, the one hiatus is that the next three or four months of leisure falls in my lap at a moment when I'm unprepared to make good use of it. I feel under some obligation to write, since months as free of this of economic demands are hard to come by; but I have been all set, for the last half year, to open myself to foreign scenes and foreign people, without any need for productivity; and though I have three or four potential books that I had put aside in my mind till just this kind of time, now that the moment has come, I find no inner response, no spontaneous meeting of the occasion. I keep on making fresh notes for my revisions of Technics and Cities; but, since I don't find myself making notes on these other themes, I feel that they haven't yet got a hold on my unconscious; and if I started work, it would be like hammering cold iron. I daresay that my general mood has not been far from that you've been in, dear Harry, however different the causes in each case. If anything brings you to this neighborhood you'll be very welcome; our guest room can be warmed to sleeping temperature in an hour or two. Otherwise, I'll be passing through Boston, en route for Durham N.H. late in February; and at the end of March, if all goes well, we'll be off for Europe, till the end of July. With affectionate greetings from us both

Lewis

P.S. Sometime, for intellectual instruction, you should leaf through our Wenner-Gren Symposium on Man's Role in Changing the Face of the Earth.[15]

---

15. Mumford's essay "The Natural History of Urbanization" in *Man's Role in Changing the Face of the Earth*, ed. William L. Thomas (1956): 382–98.

[handwritten]
14 Francis Ave
Cambridge 38, Mass
14 Jan. 1958

. . . . The news from the Baleen that you are down with a cold shatters my plans for getting hold of you, dear Harry: what a woeful mess these 'little' illnesses make of the winter! Sophy came down, too, with a 'mild' flu, on New Year's day—for no reason or assignable cause whatever—and has not yet been able to poke her nose outdoors because of the utter exhaustion of it. It's ironic that we've been so near & yet seen so little of each other all this term: just two weeks from tomorrow we start back to Amenia, via Amherst, where I'm to give a lecture. I haven't very much except a pile of notes to show for all the free time my sinecure has given me. But I've had a lot of fun tracing the history of the city back into its buried past, where I find myself confronted with the débris of ancient religions and the divinity of kings; since the city first took shape, as it now seems to me, as the home of a god—at the very moment when the matriarchate was turning into a patriarchate & the gods of the soil were giving way to the gods of the sky. My city planning colleagues won't like this delving: for *their* city is an amorphous mass, neuter, with neither male nor female imprint upon it.

But soon I must turn my back on these devious researches and get to work. And of course Amenia is the place for that.

I've finally written to my friends at Cambridge to tell them that I must give up any thought of a Fulbright professorship if I am to get my books done: so that bridge lies burning behind me. The road before me is clear for at least next year & I have never asked for more security or certainty than that.

Get well soon! And let me drop over for a chat when you are convalescent.

Warmly
Lewis

[typed]
Lewis Mumford
Amenia New York
12 February 1958

. . . We've been back here ten days, dear Harry, and as usual I feel as if I hadn't been away more than that time altogether, but had been living here, really living, all my life; and that what went on outside of these acres was just a dream, sometimes fascinating, sometimes pleasant, but not belonging to the real world. I've spent most of the fortnight—except for a snatch in Washington, helping to outline the nature of a Franklin Roosevelt memorial, sorting my papers; and in a day or two I should be ready at last to begin on my book. What a mouthful I've bitten off! I know twice or three times as much about cities as I did in 1938, when I finished The Culture of Cities;

but I still feel utterly unprepared for the task, since I am aware of the immense gaps that I never will be able to fill, and that won't perhaps be filled during my lifetime by anyone. When I was young, I took such ignorance in my stride: the very absence of data gave me a certain sense of freedom. But not now! I need crutches, and like any cripple, even *value* crutches instead of disdaining them and throwing them away for a leap in the air that, for a moment, gives one the sensation of flight. But for all that I feel very cheerful about the prospect—apart from a tinge of misgiving as to whether, if I am really in the creative state I feel, I should not be doing something more spontaneous and original than this vast revamping of an old theme.

I've mulled over your reproach about our never getting close enough to look into the differences you feel exist between us and need to be reconciled in some fashion; and I am still troubled by it. Partly, it's a defect of my own character, no doubt, which time and habit and a rather solitary life have etched in ever deeper. I didn't begin that way, I am sure; for I can remember endless adolescent arguments and discussions; but for lack of a worthy opponent, later on, I got out of practice and now am rather inept at bringing out a contrary point of view of my own. This weakness is mixed with something that, if not pushed too far, is a virtue: a tendency, when I am with a person, to identify myself with my companion, and 'try on' his ideas, as if they were clothes, to see if they fitted my native form: so that, though I more often than not revert to my former position when we part, for the moment I seem to be in greater accord than I actually am. And when the person concerned is someone I have learned so much from as I have from you, and respect so much that, when I am conscious of a difference, I first suspect my own views rather than yours, the identification is even greater. But I know how infuriating that can be: it is what annoyed me when I met Toynbee and tried to penetrate his armor of smiling sweetness with a few critical shafts, aimed at the very heart of his beliefs. So I share your feelings.

Take the case of the research into myths that you were proposing last autumn. You know far more about the nature of myths, psychologically speaking, than I do: so I am disposed to think that anything you may have to say on the subject would over-ride my skepticism and my objections. Up to a point, I am at one with your diagnosis, I understand it; that the lack of any impelling myth today is the cause for the curious sickness of heart, or existential nausea, as current slang says, of our generation. But, again if I've understood you—perhaps I haven't discussed it sufficiently with you to be sure—you seem to think that, if we put our heads together, we might detect, or even create the myths that would save us. Detect, yes; if the myth were in existence: but since the cause of our meeting is its absence, creation seems to be demanded; and there I have doubts. Do not myths spring out of the uncontrollable and so far undirectable processes of the unconscious? If so, can one do anything about them except wait, and recognize them when they appear? Could the cunningest psychological analysis set a new myth on its conquering way? I doubt it. And so perhaps do you, only—mea-culpa!—we haven't discussed the matter long enough for me to find out. But if you instance Hitler's myth as a contemporary example, I would say it proves my point: *that* myth was in the making for at least three or four hundred years, on my diagnosis, though I do not find it in the medieval German writers; and in so far as Hitler gave it additional force by conscious direction, he only served to wreck it more swiftly on the shores of reality. I would say the same thing for all the minor myth-making our wizards of advertising do. Yet the process is a real one; and one even has a good example of it before one, which I cited when I talked at the Academy the week before I left. Think of the change that has taken place in the attitude toward the family and children since 1940. Perhaps if one went through a thousand psychological histories, during the last twenty years, one would see the symbols of this change, preceding the event: certainly, it was as if there had been an immense campaign to bring about a concern, of the deepest sort, with survival, through eager parenthood. Possibly the impulse and the response were so deeply tied together, so narrowly bound, that it never reached the stage of an explicit myth. But it is on some such change, spontaneous, and in its original phase undirected and undirectable, that I would now put my own hopes for the survival of anything decent and humane in the world, if biological existence should be assured. But I know that the conscious propaganda for bigger families played no part in this change; and I don't think it would have played more if there had been a more colorful and emotionally charged kind of projection.

But here I am, dear Harry, beginning to argue, probably tearing to pieces a self-fabricated straw man, at a moment when you are disentangling yourself from such things for the quick encounters of travel. And what could be more tedious than an inopportune argument about a non-existent difference?

I've forgotten when you are leaving, if I ever exactly knew; but here's a toast to every part of your brief Odyssey. I hope to be working here pretty steadily all through the next eight months; but in May there ought to be a few unhampered weeks for my relaxing and looking back over what I have done, and though you'll be a welcome visitor at any time, you'll be doubly welcome when that moment comes. In the meanwhile, a warm embrace

Ever
Lewis

P.S. Did I tell you that my next two autumns at MIT—and Cambridge—are assured, as well as anything is assurable in this precarious world?

[handwritten on "Italia,"
"Cristoforo Colombo" steamship
stationery]
6 March 58

Dear Lewis,

I had to postpone writing until I came to a break in my round of chores and now I have one on this best of trans-Atlantic ships. Soon we'll be landing in Naples

& going on to Rome for a bit. Then we part for 10 days—Jo to visit friends in Florence, Geneva, & Lausanne & I fly south to Mycenae & Crete, birthplace of Zeus, of a goddess whose nature has not yet been determined, and of European civilization generally. Although I may be more concerned with the ghost of the Cretan goddess, I shall not bypass the Culture of Cities, of which, according to Homer, there were a great many. Knossos, however, will take up most of my eyes' time.

What you call my 'reproach' stems from my own nature. I love to discuss questions, face to face, and thrive on good criticism, which is more helpful to me than anything. Praise merely confirms me in my entrenched errors. Criticism tells me that I have not clarified my ideas, that I have omitted something, that I have made a mistake which requires correction—or that the other fellow has a temperament, set of values, or expertness which is so far from mine that a synthesis is not possible for some time to come. Any one of these outcomes advantages me. Furthermore, I feel that the first requirement for any solution of the world's dilemma is the learned disposition and ability to sit down with one's bitterest opponents and eventually come to some mutual understanding. If the best of friends are incapable of doing this, why sustain hopes that enemies can achieve it? There are, of course, times of isolation and functional segregation when stone walls facilitate the creative processes and make friendships all the more valuable; both of us—particularly yourself—have abundant cherished opportunities for this. What we haven't had are fruitful exchanges at timely seasons. Among many examples of mutual reticence, the most striking possibly, was at the time of your reconsideration of the interpretation of Moby-Dick; because, in this case, we had wrestled with exactly the same problem and had come out with diametrically opposite conclusions, without having the fun of a robust discussion. Perhaps there is a fear lurking in us that a hearty exchange of views would breed ill-feeling, but, if so, this cannot be a sign of health.

As for myth, this is more a matter of temperament. Also, I may be using the term too broadly. For me, myth is the *theme* (plot) of a *story* represented in the *imagination* or in figurative, *pictorial language* which, at the time, is *effective* in shaping values, thought, and conduct. There are hundreds of old, inert myths which—like disproved theories—were once believed to be true or imperative; but the ones which concern me are those which are *basic* to the nature of man or of society & which are *currently* controlling the imaginations of men, or which are just emerging. You instance the new attitude towards marriage as an emergent from the unconscious. Yes, but you wrote a fine piece on the topic several years ago, without waiting for a widespread manifestation of it in conduct. Why couldn't a modern Dante, Goethe, Dostoievski, or whoever represent the major stages—conflicts & solutions of conflicts, etc.—in poetic prose, and thus enchant young people (as 'Thus Spake Zarathustra' enchanted the Germans in another direction) with a vision of the ideal? At the moment the poets are more concerned with the myth of the automatic man, the hollow man, on the one hand, and of the subman or alienated man, on the other. It is a question largely of the language that is used—symbolic & imaginative, or referential & rational—in representing what one has to say or do. Well, here is the end for the time being. Love to you three & good going with culture.

Yours

Harry

[typed]

Lewis Mumford

Amenia, New York

7 April 1958

. . . And now you are back, dear Harry: welcome! Perhaps spring hasn't yet hit you so far north—though probably the sea equalizes our climates and planting seasons—but I hope it finds you feeling as gay as we've been, at the first sight of our spring plantings in three years or more, almost four for Sophy, since she was in the hospital in 1955. You'll probably be having two springs, lucky man, if the season came as early in Greece or Crete as reported. As you must know already, spring came to *me*, in the midst of the heavy frost of February, in the act of writing the successor to the Culture of Cities; and I feel, as I may already have said to Christiana, like an old man who has, for prudence sake, reluctantly made a marriage of convenience, sight unseen, and then discovered that he has fallen upon a young girl and is wildly in love with her. During the last twenty years my interest in cities had grown sluggish; I could barely keep it alive enough to give even a mediocre course on the subject; and I am not happy over the memory of the work I did on the subject in Pennsylvania. But suddenly, almost as soon as I began to write, the subject opened up anew and spread out before me in the most fascinating way, drawing on all that I had absorbed in these last twenty years, and pushing me onto a dozen new trails. So though I'll salvage the equivalent of two or three chapters of The Culture of Cities, which I don't want to alter and can't improve, the work itself, perhaps three-quarters of it, will be fresh; and will bring a great weight of concrete facts to bear in carrying further the insights of The Transformations of Man. I'll be working on it all summer; and since I have been pushed, by my fresh, sometimes daring, but often unsupported intuitions to go into unexplored territory, I'll be lucky if the book is really finished by next January. What I am doing seems to me to throw a light, not just on cities, but on the whole course of human development: if Jung has brought to our attention the persistence of the archetype, I can complement that perception by demonstrating also the "persistence of the container." The one thing I missed when writing the early chapters was just the rough first hand experience of the soil, the contours, the climate of Mesopotamia and the Aegean area: even more necessary for me than the calmer outlines of Egypt. I reproach myself for not having travelled to Greece long ago, for now it is almost too late to catch up, with last moment impressions. Perhaps you'll be able to convey, by some brotherly act of empathy, what you found there, to give just that extra breath of life to my interpretations. (It's not just the classic scene that I want: the ancient theaters at Fiesole and Arles served very well to stir my imagination: it is something more impalpable that I need.) With all this high feeling of writing, at least a book that may eventually seem a classic, and live, if the world lives, as long as Fustel de Coulanges' great work on the Ancient City, I feel pleasantly bewildered and not a little pleased, as you have already detected: but you must allow for this first enthusiasm, and remember that in a few months I will take a more sober view of the whole matter, and see plenty of deficiencies and lapses that now are altogether concealed from me.[16]

As for my pleasant (Freudian for *present*) plans, apart from going on with the book, they all hang on Alison. Six weeks ago she was planning to go to Europe, in order to get sufficiently far away from one of her young men to make sure she didn't want to marry him; but a fortnight ago we got a breathless telephone call from her telling us that she had decided to marry him; and since Sophy had met him for only a brief hour, and I for but twenty minutes, a few days before, she left us rather breathless, too. But this is the real thing: deep, complete, dedicatory, self-yielding love, despite a whole variety of obstacles, of which the worst is the sort of life that a young incipient theatrical director, besieging Broadway but not yet established, can offer her: odd and irregular hours, intense absorption in his work, and an abstemious kind of life, with many little renunciations, possibly only to those who are really in love. But he's twenty-nine, was a marine, a little shorter than she, but with a winning smile: the tough, lean New England kind, by name Chester Morss. We're having a private wedding here, with just the parents, sometime after the middle of May; and they already have an apartment, in the act of being furnished, on Brooklyn Heights, where Sophy and I lived in 1922. (Did you know that I was writing about Roebling and the Brooklyn Bridge, while living over there, exactly at the moment that Hart Crane, unknown to me, was also living there writing his poem on The Bridge? We met and corresponded afterwards.) On the whole, Alison's starting out under more favorable auspices than Sophy and I did; and now that we see what the mere prospect of marriage is doing to Alison, how she is rising to face the obstacles that at first daunted her—she saw the negative side so plainly that we didn't have to add any dusty parental wisdom to restore her balance, rather the opposite—we are deeply happy over the whole situation: Sophy's most nagging thought is the fact that he isn't three inches taller than Alison! By the end of May, this household hopes to be on even keel again, so if you are in the neighborhood, dear Harry, don't think you'll be doing any kindness by whizzing by.

This is not an answer to your letter: that requires time, thought, and even more action. If you don't drop in later, I'll return to it, if only to say something more about the interpretation of Moby-Dick! With affectionate greetings

---

16. Fustel de Coulanges, *The Ancient City: A Study on the Religion and Laws and Institutions of Greece and Rome* (1874).

Ever

Lewis

P.S. Have you read the paper on Babylon & Greece in Cornford's last book? To me it seems decisive, now that Crete seems the stepping stone.

[handwritten]
Amenia, New York
4 June 1958

. . . . How pleasant it was, dear Harry, to have even a brief glimpse of you: but how many things necessarily remained unsaid, to be taken up when we meet again— about my work, about Alison, about my future plans. I am at last back at work on my book, after a six week hiatus; and I expect it will take a week or so before I will be fully saturated with my subject again & bubbling, or appearing to myself to bubble! with fresh ideas. But there are two things I'd like to ask about. 1. Apart from Evans what books have you found helpful on Crete? 2. Is there any good psychological or anthropological interpretation of the religious principle of sacrifice: discussing not the what, of which we know plenty, but the why. It seems to me more enigmatic than guilt, which the dog at least has acquired from us; and it stands at the very portals of history, holding a key, I suspect, to much that followed. The sacrificial victim plagues me; and I'd give a lot to be able to assign a date and a place to the first rite of human sacrifice. I suspect it was rather late: and quite different from the patricide Freud imagined. You see I'm asking for a post-Freudian explanation.

My garden flourishes: so I live vicariously on prospective salads & peas!

Ever

Lewis

P.S. I don't dare begin discussing "J.B." which moved us both when I read it aloud: but disappointed me—grievously.[17]

[handwritten]
3414 Sansom Street
Philadelphia 4
Penn. 21-II-59

. . . . I am writing you this in the study that occupies the middle space in this duplex apartment: quite the nicest study, dear Harry, I've ever had & none the worse, from my perverse standpoint, because its solitary window looks down on an ugly Philadelphia alley, whose massive litter turns one's eyes inward! We had a slightly grim time in Amenia & reached here in a somewhat disrupted state: but time & sleep put us together again, and this week I settled down to the book at long last & think I've finally found the proper opening gambit. Never have I prepared so thor-

17. Archibald MacLeish, *J.B.* (1958), a play.

oughly for a book: so I tremble lest the details of scholarship overballast it and prevent the craft from responding promptly to the rudder. The worst effect of the aging process, as far as I've discovered it, is that one has to work two or three times as hard to achieve the same results that came quickly & easily even twenty years ago. (I only pray that dimming critical faculties don't deceive me as to the final result, once the effort is bravely made!) . . . I had hoped to show you my article on War, for your drastic criticism, before I finally turned it in to the Post.[18] But, after they accepted my second draft, I was so dissatisfied with it that I wrote a third; and by the time that was polished off they would tolerate no further delay. As it stands, it's a little too abbreviated to be convincing to anyone not saturated in the material: so, when my Urban Heritage is done I may expand the war article into a little book. This will, I trust, have the benefit of your unsparing scrutiny of the War essay. But two things still bother me: the meaning of sacrifice, and why anxiety, from an early period onward, seems to increase with prosperity and success. If you have any further light to shed on either subject, dear Harry, I'll be grateful. . . . Our physical quarters, internally, are charming, if austere: but we miss the vivid minds of Cambridge—if there are any here, they are in hiding or blotted out by the general smoke pall. But for the sake of my book perhaps this is just as well. With affectionate greetings from us both

Lewis

P.S. I've not the Baleen's new address. Are you properly ensconced there?

[handwritten]

21 March, '59

Dear Lewis,

Very pleasant to be writing to you—with Sophy also in my mind's eye—at six thirty on a country morning with the sun just emerging from a cloud. The grackles, who spent the winter here, are poking around a decaying apple tree outside, the chickadees are chicking, and the phoebe phoebing.

You are asking yourself why anxiety increases with prosperity and success. How about this?

(1) The succession, or cycle, of *rising* and then *falling* (ascension ➔ precipitation) was *experienced* & *noted* in the environment, millions of times. Whatever rises eventually declines. Also the higher the rise the greater the fall; a short fall is not painful, a long fall may be killing, &, hence, as a child (let us say) climbs higher, he becomes more *anxious*. Fear of heights is very widespread. In the Greek myths, we find the extravagant ambition to ascend (Olympus, the sky, etc.) defined as *hubris*, & punished by the gods with *precipitation*. Pride cometh before a fall. And so, the idea becomes established that the gods (fate) punish an *excess* of vain glorious pride (success, prosperity, etc.), it being the proud gods' disposition to keep men in their

---

18. Lewis Mumford, "How War Began," *Saturday Evening Post* (18 April 1959): 24–25.

places. Hence great prosperity is tempting the gods to *reduce* you, a prospect which arouses *anxiety*.

2. As a person or group becomes more prosperous & successful, rivals (competing persons or groups) become fearful of their own status by comparison, envious, jealous, & hence hostile. Thus, if all men are rivals, the moment one of them becomes more prosperous or successful, he becomes aware of the surrounding envy & hostility, & hence anxious lest he be reduced ignominiously (the first shall end by being last).

Here is the best I can do today with sacrifice:

Sacrifice

1. Sacrifice of a living being (person, animal) to facilitate the timely course of Nature by empathic education. Yesterday (March 20) for example, darkness (enemy of fertility) was about to be surpassed by light (promoter of fertility); the course of the seasons was dependent on this Great Encounter between the opponent of life (the rigid, frigid, aging sterile Old Man Winter) and the bringer of new life (the flexible, warm, ardent, young fertile Son Spring). We side with the young Son-Sun, & hence empathize with him (feeling his feelings), and want to promote his cause, which is to overthrow and kill the useless, aging Old Man (senescent ruler of the universe) & so we kill our aging ruler (father, king, god), the idea being that if we do this, at exactly the right time & in exactly the right way, the new fertilizing Sun will be stimulated (by education on our part) to do the same or assisted in so doing by our additional, participating force. Here the sacrifice is a magical, ritualistic act of killing, in order to free young life and bring renewal to the earth (& thus the survival of society).

2. Sacrifice of a living being in order to please (propitiate, appease, reduce the wrath of, or evoke the help of) the divine ruler or gods of the universe. This is the transition of magic into religion. The deity is conceived of as being more or less above Nature like an aloof Pharaoh who exacts sacrifices (part of the harvest, animal husbandry, and human scapegoats) from his people, particularly if they have displeased him. Sterility of the land, famine, defeat by enemies, etc., is a sign that God is dissatisfied with your behavior. Some payment is required. The theme is that of Crime and Atonement (punishment) which seems to conform to the general rules of a commercial transaction: Prometheus *steals* fire from the gods, & so must *pay* for this by suffering, sacrifice of pleasure, because *this* is what the angry god wants to appease his indignant pride of power.

3. Sacrifice of certain needs & gratifications in order to renew life on a higher level. This might be something that God requires before we are considered fit for admission to spiritual society in the afterlife, or it might be something that occurs in the process of evolution of the self, development, etc.

These are the basic types of sacrifice which jump to mind, and I think I had better stop here, because you are, no doubt, much further along the path of understanding than I am and what I have been saying is stale beer to you. Here is the evolutionary sequence (in summary) so far as I can imagine it.

(1) Social distress in a primitive group (for which the old ruler is blamed—just as we blame Ike); for this the remedy is to kill the old ruler (too feeble to defend himself) & bring in the New. This is not sacrifice yet, merely parricide, regicide, deocide.

(2) This thema is then projected into Nature, & when Nature gets annually old & feeble, the society must facilitate its renewal by killing its king, or a substitute for the king—human, animal, or by a symbolic death & resurrection. Here is sacrifice for the education of a natural process.

(3) Now God has become changeless, infinite, transcendent—undying (cf. the Pharaoh or King refuses to be killed, let us say), but requires a sacrifice as before—a form of propitiation or atonement, & so here we get sacrifice for the atonement of the sins of the world (Christ). So far everything is social.

(4) Now, it is the individual, as a unique person, who must sacrifice something in himself (the Old Adam) in order to achieve renewal (the Kingdom of Heaven in the heart or in the sky). You lose your life (sacrifice your narcism) to gain life in more abundance by devoting it to a higher larger cause. Q.E.D.

Delighted to hear that both of you are pleased with your quarters in Philadelphia. Are you becoming anxious because of the huge salary (prosperity) you are receiving & the huge success of your ideas in recent years—even in the USA? And then, for another idea of sacrifice, the conviction that one must sacrifice one's status in the community (fall in the estimation of one's contemporaries) in order that a new, renewing vision be born to reshape the future. You have been doing this all along (vs. the narrowly proud specialists) by being a generalist in league with a better future.

Writing now about the God (Father) and Satan (Bad Son) thema, I am more aware than ever that I have been too absorbed by the surrounding horrors of our world, & am in process of reformation on the principle that it is 'better to kindle a little light than chide the darkness.'

> Fortune to your lives & works!
> Harry

The new Baleen is no. Seven Divinity Ave.

[handwritten]
3414 Sansom Street
Philadelphia 4, Penn.
5 April 1959

. . . . What a generous overflow of swift thoughts your last letter gave me, dear Harry: I found that they started my own mind moving again in new directions—though what it badly needs, at the moment, is a little stasis; for my thoughts on matters that must remain speculative hardly stay put long enough for me to set them down on paper. But all that you said about Anxiety and sacrifice is helpful—even though some aspects remain mysterious, like all the other impulses that run counter to the life process, yet remain a persistent part of it. . . . My book, the 'final' draft of it, makes good progress: but threatens to become 'unwieldy': so when it's done I'll have to spend the rest of the summer, I fear, cutting out the fatty or indigestible portions of it. I'd hoped to relax by June: but that now seems a dream. But we'll be back in Amenia then, at least, so if any errand brings you near us, please drop in for an overnight visit. Meanwhile, I'd be grateful for a stiff criticism of my war article, which will come out in the 18 April number of the Saturday Evening Post. It had to be brief: so it lacks both supporting data and certain necessary qualifications & reserves. But I am tempted to carry it further in a short book, unless those whose opinion I respect, like you, find the whole thesis too leaky to hold water. With a warm embrace from us both

Lewis

P.S. My fabulous salary here doesn't awaken *too* much anxiety: it enables me to face a pensionless old age a little more gracefully. But the state of the world itself spoils my pleasure in my own fleeting prosperity. I only pray that my forebodings are quite baseless.

[handwritten, LMC]
[LM] Ans 5 May

Dear Lewis,

Regret to report the temporary disappearance of the Sat. Even. Post after I had read only 2 pages of your piece. I am starting an inquiry among my colleagues to lay hold of it once more.

You asked for stiff criticism, but on this point we have always been touchy & in this case I would rather wait until I had finished your essay. I can say, however, that I was disappointed with the beginning. You have enfeebled your position, it seems to me, by being so self-assured about a matter which is still in the obscure past. You speak as if you were present or had received a special revelation—never mentioning in your first part any of the archaeologists & anthropologists whose arduous investigations revealed the few facts that we now possess relevant to your theme. Your proposition that wars were first initiated by a need for sacrificial victims is possible—I remember the Marquesas, for example—but it is difficult to rule out other factors &, if true, the bearing of this origin to the present situation seems highly tenuous. In short, I received the impression that your assurance about a matter of which the authorities are so ignorant, prepares the reader to believe that your later statements—whatever they may be—will be equally unfounded, even though they are actually substantial & wise. I say all this because I feel highly involved in your efforts to reverse America's present foreign policy & hence favor a strong rather than a weak position. I may retract what I have written after I have finished your article, but here, anyhow, is a 'stiff criticism' of your opening paragraphs. You should not have asked for it! My embraces to you both,

Harry

[typed]
3414 Sansom Street
Philadelphia 4, Penn
5 May 1959

. . . I came back from Amenia last night, dear Harry, after a glorious week of spading and planting, which even the rain and the cool weather couldn't mar. Your letter was waiting for me in a dismal pile of other mail, dismal because all the crackpots and unconfined lunatics in America seem to have read my Post article and said to themselves: "This fellow is as nutty as I am; so maybe he'll listen to me." Your criticism was a welcome relief: it at least came from a rational mind and made a rational point, which I would be the first to agree with, though I was amused to find that, as a result of the drastic trimming and cutting that the article underwent, you read self-assurance and cocky overconfidence into an article that I wrote with "fear and trembling," well aware of the weak patches in the argument, knowing that no single strand of the proof was strong enough to hold up my main thesis, though a weaving together of a sufficient number of delicate strands might, in the end, be strong enough to carry a considerable load. You should have seen the first draft of the article: that was full of the kind of judicious qualifications and disclaimers whose absence made you unduly suspicious of the final version. In that version I mentioned the archaeologists and anthropologists who had presented me with the material for my inter-pretation: and if I had been writing a paper for a learned journal you may be sure that they would have been paraded in full force. As it was, I mentioned a handful in the list of books the editors asked for at the end—the missing end you did not read. Do you *really* think I am the sort of person who ignores my sources? If anything I tend to overstate my intellectual obligations and give credit to whoever has been working in the field, even if I have arrived at the same conclu-sions independently. Yesterday, at lunch with my publisher, he reproved me gently for citing too many authorities in the first third of my new book, which he had been reading.

As for my attitude toward the central ideas, I have no sense whatever of having received a special revelation, except in the way that the most modest creature might have if he has stumbled upon a fresh approach that challenges the accepted stereo-types and may, if it proves valid, cause them to be revised. The historical interpre-tation contains not one, but three, fundamental departures: they hang together and yet one of them may be proved erroneous without necessarily upsetting the other two. The first of these is that war is a specific institution of civilization, not to be confused with other forms of rivalry, aggression, or murder that may exist in other societies, earlier or later, more primitive or more advanced. There is no proof what-ever of the existence of war before there was a surplus of food and a surplus of pop-ulation: that is, before neolithic times: or rather, before the neolithic town comes into existence. In surviving primitives, who took over the institution of war, there is a large body of evidence to show that war remained of a symbolic and ritualistic nature for the sake of obtaining sacrificial captives, though this presumably older pattern was displaced, among peoples like the South African natives, by mass slaughter on the later "civilized" pattern. There is no datum to show that mass slaughter was an *original* ingredient of war, since even the most primitive peoples who survived into the nineteenth century had five thousand years or more in which to be affected by the culture of "superior" peoples. The second hypothesis is that war, first as symbolic sacrifice, is associated directly with the institution of kingship and with the identification of the welfare of the community with the life and health of the king. The evidence of this is abundant, but scattered, and of unequal value: in the case of Mesopotamia and Egypt, both war and kingship had reached an advanced stage of development before the written record emerges; so that here we must fill in the blank places by conjecture, reading back from ceremonial sacrifices of animals, children, captives. What makes the interpretation plausible here, is that we have a written record in the case of two parallel civilizations, which had reached by 1500 A.D. a state comparable to that of Ur in 3000 B.C. At present no respectable American anthropologist will admit that there was any possible connection between Mesopotamia and, say, Mayan civilization: all the many close parallels between the two he attributes to their common human traits. Very good: that argument cuts both ways. The Maya and the Aztecs both went to war chiefly to obtain captives for ceremonial sacrifice: twenty-thousand in one year in the case of the Aztecs. If both Aztec and Mayan civilizations have independently reproduced the Pyramid, the cult of kingship, the Solar myth, the division of castes between ruler and ruled, the astronomical calendar, why is it not reasonable to suppose from the many survivals of individual and collective practices of sacrifice, that the Mesopotamian communities originally provoked war for the same reasons as the Aztecs—though by the time history opens those facts have been covered over and rationalized and other circumstances have intensified and widened the capacity for organized aggression. (This was one of the pieces of supporting evidence that I was forced, by lack of space, to leave out.) The third fresh idea came to me rather late in the development of the whole argument, though I had made tentative sallies in its direction in a talk I gave in Rome. This is that a parallel of great significance exists between the early "conquest of nature" (ominous phrase) that marks the beginnings of civilization, on the basis of neolithic domestication, and the present expansion of energy which began, as Henry Adams recognized, in the thirteenth century. These two cases seem to me tied together by many technical and scientific advances of a rational nature; and also—and it is here where I hoped to invoke your vast knowledge and your most severe criticism—by an increase of anxiety and irrationality. In the first case, the anxiety and irrationality became institutionalized in War and the State. (The germ of this whole thought was planted long ago, incidentally, in a book by Rudolph Holsti on War and the Origins of the State, which assembled the anthropological evidence available half a century ago to show that war did not exist in primitive society.)[19] In our time, an even deeper irrationality and anxiety is expressing itself partly by following these well-worn channels of social habit, partly by creating an even more solid mass of totalitarian institutions. In both cases, the transformation has been effected, if I interpret the evidence correctly, by a fusion of temporal and spiritual authorities. While I was developing this part of the thesis I kept on asking myself: What is the relation of anxiety, prosperity, and sacrifice? At no point did I ever feel I had an answer to this question, for me the crucial question. Even after the article was finished, if you will remember, I kept putting this question to you; and I still feel that I have not gotten to the bottom of this subject—and that no one else has gone quite far enough, either. . . . obviously, dear Harry, it would need a whole article to deal with either of the three main ideas I have outlined: even then the final result might not convince you. And you may say, with some justice, that I was imprudent, indeed downright stupid, to use this historic preface as a way to battering down our moral complacency and making us face the madness of our present nuclear and military policies. Perhaps you would be right in this judgment: I weighed the risks and decided otherwise. Even the occasional scholar who will read my article, though he will doubtless share your horror over my appearance of self-assurance and of having a "special revelation," may have a seed of doubt implanted in his mind as to the wisdom of taking for granted as settled the current stereotypes about the nature of collective aggressions, phobias, and war itself. For the fact is that anthropologists no less than the historians have taken war as given: almost a part of man's original nature, too obvious to be subject to clinical description, still more to an inquiry into its origins. It is our stereotypes that don't bear an honest examination. Even if every single point I make proves, on due examination, to be unsound, my opening up of the question itself may be a valid contribution to our thinking. But the writing of the article was an almost impossible task, since one condenses the large body of nebulous evidence, the residue is not sufficiently convincing: as to that your point is well and soundly made. I wince however over your unkind interpretation of my attitude, though your stricture comes partly through applying to a popular article the canons of circumspect statement and scholarly hedging that would be appropriate in a scientific journal, where I was addressing my peers and had to prove, by my very method of doing so, that I was one of him. (I know the rules of that game, too, and played them reasonably well at the Oriental Institute meeting in Chicago, before a highly exacting body of specialists.) As I was writing the article I kept on saying to Sophy: "I can't possibly put this all into an article. Within the limits of five thousand words I cannot even convince myself." One decision I might have made, when I reached this point, was to abandon the article, or reduce it to a single point,

19. Rudolph Holsti, *The Relation of War to the Origin of the State* (1913).

which I could then build up to a satisfactory climax. Instead, I scattered all the ideas broadcast and said to myself: When I get done with my big job I shall put How War Began into a book. Which is what I propose to do, once the cities book, now swollen to gargantuan dimensions, gets born.

We'll be here till the last week in May, probably. Then Amenia for the summer. The book is about 5/8 done: but that means I'll be working at it till September.

> In friendship
> Lewis

[handwritten]
9 June

Dear Lewis,

I trust that Sophy feels much better if not entirely restored by the familiar serenity of your place in Amenia. Your long and generous letter to me was an exciting answer to my first, hurried comment prompted by your previous request for rigorous criticism. Your letter contained the references and arguments which were absent in the article—brilliant intuitions which, in my judgment, should be incorporated in the book or revised edition of your piece. Is it to be a separate volume or part of a larger volume? In any event, the whole matter is so important that the foundations of your thesis should be supported so far as possible by all the evidence you can marshal. Your aim is to change our foreign policy, & since today Americans are addicted to the authority of facts—facts, or approximate facts, are the means of accomplishing your purpose. This runs against my grain—parading & weighing the evidence after I think I have seen how things really stand, and hence most of the things I say fall flat. What you are saying is too important to be allowed to fail on this or another score. Your marvelous letter to me provides the necessary under-pinnings—

I haven't written sooner, because I was asked to give the Phi Beta Kappa oration, & somehow I couldn't eliminate much that I had in mind to say, & condense the remainder into 40 minutes. My head was in a state of chaos until yesterday—'Beyond Yesterday's Idealisms' was received in stony silence by our President, Nate Pusey.[20] Will continue this letter at the next opportunity when I recover from my trance. Embraces to you both—

> Yours
> Harry

20. Henry A. Murray, "Beyond Yesterday's Idealisms," Phi Beta Kappa Oration, Harvard Chapter, 1959, reprinted in Shneidman, *Endeavors in Psychology*, 605–12.

[handwritten]
Address (for next 2 weeks): 7
Divinity Ave
Cambridge 38
[LM] 15 July

Dear Lewis—

One sign of the mental stupor from which I have been suffering all spring is the fact that I have not yet obtained another copy of the Sat. Even. Post. All kinds *of tiny* obstacles were just enough to cause me to postpone mailing the money; but now I have done it, & hope I shall not be frustrated much longer. I am still in doubt as to whether you are planning to expand the article into a small book. (By the way, that was a *superb* photograph of you—really stunning! I didn't know that The Sat Eve Post was equal to anything so good.) I greatly enjoyed your criticism of Mumford in this summer's *Daedalus*.[21] What a really monumental book that was! You should publicize the High School that could give you enough basic knowledge to understand 800 years of technical evolutions. It must have been a very peculiar combination of school & scholar—unique so far as I know. The prophecies—on the hopeful side—are still within the scope of possibility, &, if you decided to be cautious on the question of nuclear fission, take comfort in the fact that Thos. Jefferson (in Paris a few months before the Bastille) had no intimation, & gave no hint of the coming explosion (Vol. XIV, Oct 8, 1788–March 26, 1789).

Have you (to return to the question of nuclear energy) seen 'The Causes of World War Three' by C. Wright Mills? And the pamphlet by Sir Richard Acland on disarmament?[22]

I am leaving for England & Scotland July 28—to Edinburgh for the 1st time with a visit to Geddes's tower (any suggestions for reading or sight-seeing?). Josephine is a sub-intern at the Hospital for Children in Edinburgh. Embraces & best wishes—

Harry

Hope you are both thriving & your thoughts flowing like a clear, deep stream. Delighted to hear of the house you have obtained for the Fall term—nearer to your wants & nearer to the rest of us. Good!

21. "An Appraisal of Lewis Mumford's Technics and Civilization (1934)," *Daedalus* 88 (Summer 1959): 527–36.

22. C. Wright Mills, *The Causes of World War Three* (1958). Richard Acland, *Waging Peace: The Positive Policy We Could Pursue If We Gave Up the Hydrogen Bomb* (1958).

[typed]
Amenia, New York
15 July 1959

. . . It says much about the dreary state both Sophy and I have been in, to get your letter today before I had even gotten around to responding to your letter of early June and to your masterly Phi Beta Kappa oration. I won't go into all our troubles, which have been minor; for they are doubled merely by being told about; but the upshot of it is that the book I had hoped to finish by September won't possibly be done before January. This all came after one of the best winters we've experienced in a long time, so we are not putting ourself forward as Jobian candidates for consolation. But at all events, this explains my silence. You outlined a whole book in your Oration; and I gasped when I realized at the end that you had opened up a whole series of lordly vistas, rear and front, in just twelve pages. You have set out a program for the next hundred years: it won't save us from our impending fate, but if the doom that now seems to me so close proves indeed at the last moment to be a mirage, or a dark cloud, ominously flashing with lightning, that suddenly is scattered to the four corners of the sky—something, incidentally, I've never actually seen in nature!—then you have laid out a banquet to invite our souls and nourish our minds, after all the soiled crumbs of our present life are brushed away. I find myself with less hope in the rational processes making an effective change in the pattern of our lives than I've ever had before: all of us, most of all myself, seem to me like Settembrini in the Magic Mountain, naively thinking that madmen can be brought back to sanity by the liberating forces of reason. If they were open to these forces they would not be mad. Nothing short of a universal Dunkirk will, I think, awaken us; and then of course it may be too late to save all that might have been saved if we had been forethoughted and forehanded, in short alive. You may well not have seen the clipping I'm enclosing: but if I go on writing such things, it is for the mere easing of my conscience, not with any hope of persuading even a few others, for if the facts do not thunder, how should one feeble voice be sufficient to rouse them?[23] Looking back over the last dozen years, which in so many ways have been so kind to me, I realize that a crushing ingot of leaden despair has lain on my chest, enfeebling my energies, sapping my creativity; so that, though I continue to write and seem reasonably productive the effort I must make to do what I actually do is out of all proportion to the result; whereas in better times, I still feel the energies I now give to bare survival might have been lifted to the pitch of creation. The despair has nothing to do with my personal life; I have outlived most of my sins and can cope with my misfortunes: the despair rises out of the situation we all face, and less out of that than out of the loneliness of realizing that those who know what is

---

23. Perhaps Mumford's letter to the editor: "Making Nuclear Decisions," *New York Times,* 6 July 1959, 26.

360 I "In Old Friendship"

the matter and are ready to act on that knowledge, are still after a dozen years only a handful, thee and me, Russell and Schweitzer, and over the whole round planet not enough men and women to make a parade in front of the White House than a policeman would think worthwhile to stop. But I go on writing, as I would keep the hurricane lamp lighted on a sinking ship; there is nothing else to do. Even in the midst of my shrewdest historic analysis of ancient time, I always keep the window open a crack to let in the poisonous blast of air from our own time, in order grimly to temper the reader's enjoyment, if not to overcome the effect of his daily dose of Milltown! . . . As for the thesis on war, I still hope to get it down in proper form in a little book; if I don't get exhausted by finishing this one. But we play with thoughts of a trip to Greece next spring, a trip that would end among the Norse gods of Scandinavia. Today Alison's first joyous page from Athens reached us, full of happiness over the kindness and friendliness and family warmth of the Greeks she met on the boat and even in the streets of Athens. She will be in London for a few days that last week in August, before flying home. . . . What good news about Josephine in Edinburgh, in its famous hospital, which as old Geddes used to say, grew fat on the many diseases generated in its eight and ten story tenements, one room to a family. The only soul I know there now is Arthur Geddes, 'young' Arthur Geddes, now in his sixties, a geographer by trade, but bitter, because he never got a professorship, thanks largely to his father's unconventional experiments in education, thanks partly to lack of talent. He tries to keep alive some last ember of his father's brilliant mannerisms, while clinging to the letter of his father's thought, after fighting with the paternal image all his natural lifetime. As you can gather from this, I don't feel very close to him; but he's really a decent sort; and he might show you parts of Edinburgh that would escape you at first glance: not least his father's Outlook Tower, although that is only a hollow shell now, if I remember right what's happened to it. His address is 70, Cluny Gardens; and we're friendly enough for you to mention my name, if you're disposed to see him. But being only a lecturer, he's as poor as a churchmouse; so don't expect hospitality. The fact that he feels done out of his inheritance by his sister, Lady Mears, has added to his bitterness. Give Josephine a cheery greeting from us. And prepare her for the formidable winter weather of Auld Reekie, so well described by Stevenson. Just as Geddes used to say that Scots whisky lets a man stay sober till he falls dead drunk, so one might say of the climate of Edinburgh, it offers the alternative of staying healthy or dropping dead. Have a good trip, dear Harry: before too long, we hope to see you at our next (and last) Cambridge home: 10 St John's Road, behind the Longfellow house.

> Sophy joins me in affectionate
> greetings
> Lewis

[handwritten, with picture of bust
of Patrick Geddes]
[LM] P.G.! 59?

Dear Brave Lewis

It is just possible that you haven't seen this bust of the man whose memory you have so gloriously honored. How proud he would be of your 30 years' prodigious achievement—even beyond his scarcely-limited dreams. In the long run it may turn out that the postponement of your present book will be somewhat for the best, discouraging though it may be in the heat of August. Contrary to all expectations, we have had seven days of sunshine & warmth to brighten our tour of the Highlands & Lowlands. The Murray motto has been: 'Furth with Fortune & Fill the Fetters,' but in this case, those who filled the fetters became slaves rather than sacrificial offerings.[24]

Embraces all round—
Harry

Amenia, New York
10 September 1959

. . . . Welcome home, dear Harry: I fear this greeting is a little belated: but if I'd written it before this some of the depressed mood of this strange summer might have crept into it: a mood I find I've shared with our weekly char-woman and other neighbors—though I suspect for different reasons. Your benison from Edinburgh touched me. I really wonder what Old Geddes would say to me, if we could meet after these many years. I still remember the final walk we took together down to the Railroad Station in 1925, and the sick feeling of alienation at the pit of my stomach—which I recorded as soon as I got on the train, in a note I still have. If I've exaggerated my 'hands-off' attitude in relation to my students, it is chiefly a reaction against Geddes's way of treating me. And yet, though I no longer live in the mountain's shadow, I still respect its height, when I measure it against the surrounding peaks. Did you stumble across the correspondence about Geddes & D'Arcy Thompson in the Times Literary Supplement last year? Thompson's daughter recalled that after Geddes's death a group of his university colleagues sat around discussing him, & D'Arcy held forth on all his talents & virtues at length. At the end, one of the biologists turned on Thompson and said: 'You've been talking as if he were the greatest of us all!" And D'Arcy retorted: 'Well, wasn't he?' That bronze head does P.G. less than justice: The face is troubled, perhaps from the grief that followed the loss of his favored son and his wife: but the animation, the fire, the fierceness and intensity are not there: absent, too, is the bristling of the beard-tips, the

24. "Furth Fortune and fill the fetters": motto of the Scots Murray clan.

wing-like look of the parted hair, the almost frightening bulge of the brow: all the attributes of a man for whom the fact that the brain is composed of erectile tissue had meaning, for he regarded thoughts as orgasms: a natural attribute of his manhood. He had the same sort of Pan-like joy he had found in Darwin. When he looked into Geddes's microscope and danced with delight over the movements of a common paramecium. . . . How that image and your words, dear Harry, have set me gabbing! Alison came home ten days ago after an adventurous trip, travelling 'hard' like a penurious student, but seeing much, and seeming much stronger for this testing of herself. We've only had a glimpse of her and just a teasing snatch of two of the scenes & people she's been among: but perhaps we'll have more to report when we get to Cambridge. I don't know when I am expected to begin work at M.I.T.: but probably we'll get to 10 St. John's Road (Eliot 4-1880) between the 21st and the 25th. Here's to an early meeting if you are in the neighborhood!

> Affectionately
> Lewis

[handwritten]
Wednesday, 15th Sept
[LM] Ans 19 Sept 59

Fertile Lewis,

Your juicy letter just received, reminding me of your earlier pithy one and your still earlier magnanimous one. A few brief comments before meeting in Cambridge:

1. Yes, I did happen to read the piece on P.G. & D'Arcy Thompson in the London L.S.—a vivid picture, touched possibly by a daughter's devotion.

2. Agree, that bust lacked vitality & lustre. Epstein would have done better.[25]

3. The description of your joy and contentment in the personal sphere, & medley of underlying, dampening emotions in the global political sphere is an almost word-for-word report of my own experience—a little citadel of profound & exuberant happiness surrounded by an Africa of ominous and repellent sights & sounds. I wish I could hold vividly in the forefront of my mind images of other periods in history when humanity manifested even more deplorable dispositions— when civilization seemed to be going straight to hell—& yet there were some healthy islands of creativity & renewal came eventually. Such pictures help me to realize that it's unreasonable & futile to hope that human nature will somehow become far better than it ever has been and that our leaders will be far better than the general run. A week of readings in Scottish history and visiting historic sites recalled the almost perpetual conflicts, wars, murders, treacheries, brutalities, vandalisms, etc., which marked its course. Here were some of my forebears acting like gangsters for hundreds of years up into the 18th century without shame or guilt, & Ah! The murders & destructions committed in the name of Christianity! Today, the

25. Jacob Epstein (1880–1959), American-born modernist sculptor who settled in London.

existence of nuclear energy makes it absolutely necessary that humanity, men & women everywhere—become and remain forever far wiser, more affectionate and self-controlled, than they ever have been in the past, & it seems wholly irrational to expect so much of *all* of us. That's the rub.

4. On my return I found a copy of Sat Even Post, its splendid picture, & some of your telling and persuasive paragraphs—particularly in the later parts.

5. Reading the whole of it has not changed, unhappily, my original opinion, namely:

a) that your thesis about the genesis of war is extremely dubious, the necessary evidence is lacking.

b) that—since the thesis is dubious—your statements are far too dogmatic (proud man—'most ignorant of what he's most assured'), & makes the reader suspicious of what follows when you are standing on a firm ground & need their trust.

c) that—even if your thesis were correct—it is generally accepted that the determinants of the origin of something may be different from the determinants of its perpetuation, & knowing the former does not help much in eliminating the latter.

d) that you condemn Power without defining the ends to which it is committed. Absence of power (impotence) is not admirable: there must be power to influence, persuade, create, heal, comfort, reform, etc. Your own language is very powerful.

e) that—to return to your thesis—you don't make it clear that you understand the nature of the sacrificial rite (to assist the new, young (Spring) God defeat & supersede the old, infertile (Winter) God synchronously to restore the vitality of a society (in conjunction with the restoration of the vitality of Nature) by substituting for its old & waning ruler (Eisenhower of 1956–58) a young & waxing ruler, or the same ruler re-invigorated & reformed by the murder of his old self (ritualistic death-in-life). This, briefly and crudely, is my view. But, in any case, so far as I know, only one substitute for the ruler is required in the death & resurrection ceremony (if the ruler isn't killed himself), & there would be no difficulty in finding a willing or unwilling substitute within the membership of the society itself. Indeed, people were murdered, right & left, without ceremony & in great numbers. Egypt or Babylonia would hardly engage in war to obtain one (or even 20) sacrificial victims from across the borders. But they might do so to capture 10,000 slaves to build their mausoleums, etc. The Murray motto is "Furth with Fortune & Fill the Fetters" (fill them with captives from the neighboring clan to serve as slaves). If sacrificial victims were actually obtained from a subjugated nation (cf. Theseus & others brought to Crete) or from enslaved captives, it doesn't mean that was planned & initiated for *that* special reason.

Well excuse this long harangue, please. Remember you asked for it, because we both want the same thing: to influence the government, directly or indirectly, to change their whole policy, orienting it in a new direction. Parts of your treatise are forthright, eloquent, & irrefutable. Furth with Fortune and Fill the Fetters of your Argument with thousands of Converts!

Keen to embrace you both, soon as possible—

Affectionately

Harry

P.S. Will be in Cambridge-Boston (quite busy) from Sept 21–Oct 1st. From Oct 1st to Nov 10th, I shall be away a good part of the time. After that I'll be available & often bursting in upon you on St. Johns Road.

[handwritten]
Amenia, N.Y.
19 September 1959

. . . . I find to my dismay that my seminar begins this Tuesday: so I'm dashing up to Cambridge Monday, only to dash back to New York on Thursday to seek aid for an ailing tooth & then down to Washington for an 'informal' State Department conference with one of Khrushchev's party. (I don't know if I'd have been invited if the State Dept. had been reading my article in The October Atlantic.)[26] So if we aren't able to meet, dear Harry before you hie off for October this is just to say "Thank you" for your patient criticism. Your warnings & strictures about the Post article are just & helpful. But I think that the seemingly patent weaknesses of my hypothesis were due to the necessary compression and over-simplification: not irremediable: I was foolish, perhaps, not to wait till I had time to put all the pieces together: but I won't be satisfied till I have really marshalled the evidence & made the proof as watertight as possible. The whole interpretation must remain speculative, since it is prehistoric: but it is no more speculative than the notion we so easily take for granted; namely that war has always existed, and that it has a natural *origin* in either (a) a fundamental instinctual pugnacity, or (b) in a demand for territory or slaves or booty, or (c) in the operation of both natural impulse and social demand. What I shall try to show is that war is a typical institution of civilization, for which no earlier evidence exists, & that it originated in the same mythic constellation that made possible civilization, with its over-emphasis of power & its constant restriction & regimentation of other aspects of life. How could you imagine that I overlooked the many beneficent uses of power? It is the cult of power, its removal from the matrix of life, that I look upon as an aberration. But I already have stated much of this in my new cities book, which incidentally is now called 'Power & Form'!, what I haven't been able to put there I shall try to round up in a little book. All that you have said in criticism makes my task easier. About sacrifice, for example, you assume that there was only one kind: that of a single substitute for the king. But there were other forms, growing out of this or widening it: that of a whole court at Ur, for example; or the captives whose blood kept the sun alive among the Aztecs:

---

26. Lewis Mumford, "The Morals of Extermination," *Atlantic Monthly,* October 1959, 38–44.

20,000 of them a year. The widening of sacrifice with the intensification of anxiety, once real (that is justifiable) fears of retaliation supplement irrational anticipations, is one of the most important parts of my thesis: by that time war & civilization have become visible historic facts. The second set of motives have displaced or covered over the original ones—though lingering in the practice of massacring able-bodied prisoners instead of enslaving them.

But enough! This is too long-winded as a way of expressing gratitude—and I spoil it with self-justifications & counter-attacks!

If you're free Wednesday, call me!

> Warmly
> Lewis

[handwritten]
Hotel Royal
Via Partenope, 38
Napoli
5 May 1960

. . . . Good heavens, dear Harry, it's a long time since a word passed between us: the last, in fact, was that said by you one bleak January night, standing by your car and giving us a parting word of advice about Greece. Since this coming Sunday we'll be sailing for Greece in an ancient Italian tub—a converted trireme, probably—it's natural that I should be taking up the conversation again. I can't begin to tell you all that's happened since we started, from an *intra*-marital love affair in Paris to five dark days in Florence, as dark as Dante's smoky hell, when Sophy was battling with an infection that broke out near her nose and was moving inexorably toward her eyes and brain. Fortunately we got hold of an alert young Italian doctor, who applied the newest American antibiotics; and after a while the infection subsided, slowly. But Sophy is now fit for travel again; and with a precautionary parcel of the same antibiotics in reserve we're facing the rest of the trip cheerfully—though we've slowed down the program and have lopt the Scandinavian countries off our schedule. I fear the Swedes will have to think up some reason for giving me the Nobel Prize if they want me to appear in person. Today we 'did' Pompeii—which gave me a far better sense of the classic city than I had expected it to. (Incidentally, the famous bawdy pictures in the lupanar, which ladies are not supposed to see, might be hung in any girls' college dormitory & could be far less obscene than the conversation!) Travelling has the odd effect of prompting fresh thoughts about my book which have no connection with the scene in front of me. But oh! how all the little tensions of travelling drain the energy out of me, from the moment one orders breakfast or has to decide how much to tip the taxi-driver, without being a careless fool on one hand nor an Ugly American gouging poor Europe on the other. . . . I can't guess what you are doing or thinking: but should you be in England between 22 June & 14 July you could reach me C/o Sir Wm Holford, 5 Cambridge Terrace, London NW 1. Affectionate greetings from us both

Lewis

[typed]
3414 Sansom Street
Philadelphia 4, Penn.
3 December 1960

. . . I have thought about you frequently, dear Harry, since I wrote you last spring; and for a time I even harbored the design of attending the Academy's meeting this weekend, with the extra hope of seeing you for a while in mind. But my book caused me to abandon that hope long ago, since it has kept me working to the point of exhaustion, so that I now hold on by the skin of my teeth, in the state that used to be called 'combat fatigue,' which I take it is due more to inner pressures and insistent moment-to-moment demands than to fear or shock.[27] But the combination of seeing the cancelled Academy meeting in my calendar, bumping into Conrad Aiken in New York yesterday, and having a slender hour or two left at the end of a day has at last brought me to the point of writing. I can't hope to tell you all that happened or didn't happen—and there was much that didn't happen, too—since you gave your last bit of advice about Greece on the street by your car in Cambridge, after our walk through the old garden walk you disclosed to us for the first time. The high point of our whole trip was Delphi, though I have managed to put down only a few words of it in my book; and the low point was brought about, almost at the same moment, by the U-2 disclosures, which shocked me by the crude way it disclosed, first, that Eisenhower had no intention whatever of making any serious efforts to arrive at an understanding, and second, that the great minds in the Pentagon were so out of touch with reality that, after four years of successful air invasion, they had never allowed for a failure in either the mechanism itself or the human organism that accompanied it. With that in mind, half the budding hopes I had nourished, hardly visible enough to be called hopes as yet, blackened; and when I came back here I found it almost impossible to rewrite the last chapter of my book—though in a sense the disastrous prognosis confirmed everything I had written about the origin and nature of the city, and the miscarriage, radical from the beginning, of civilization. I wasted six weeks battering my head against this stubborn wall—and then decided, like the Irishman, to leave the last chapter out. But there is a brief coda which perhaps says all that an honest man can say at the moment, both for better and worse. In spite of all this depression the book itself, once set in type, has buoyed me up: the only thing that alarms me a little is the unusually favorable

---

27. Lewis Mumford, *The City in History* (1961).

response, indeed the keen excitement, of my publishers, who are talking about it in the same shamelessly superlative fashion that I talk about it to myself. It is by all odds my solidest work, I am sure, and at the same time my most original: this is not to say that it is without flaws and perhaps serious misinterpretations, but that even in spite of them its virtues heavily outweigh its weaknesses. In that sheer naked-ness of spirit that is possible only between old friends, who have outlived their re-serves, I can say that I know only three other American books I would put on the same shelf with it, for its combination of scholarly exactitude and human richness: James' Psychology, Adams' Mt Saint Michel, and Marsh's Man and Nature.[28] Now that I have said this, I've of course left nothing for anyone else to say; although I could add a few other things that would make this boasting sound even worse to any but the most lenient ears! But it has been a great effort, pursued fairly relent-lessly over three years; and I am tired: literally too tired for words. I must still keep alert for another six months, going back over my own life, rummaging through my ancient accumulations of letters and manuscripts, and generally digging within, not writing a work in obedience to any outside plea. To this end I've even cancelled two short lecture series I had incontinently accepted, when I forgot that this would be an eleven months baby and would need an extra long period of recovery. Drop me a word about yourself: Conrad Aiken hinted that you weren't in your usual good health; and I hope that this was either exaggerated or recorded some passing malaise that time and rest (the old regimen of Salerno!) will cure. At the moment, Sophy is in New York, seeing Alison off on a brief visit to Spain where she will join her husband: otherwise these affectionate solicitudes would come from both of us.

Lewis

[handwritten]
[LM] 2 Jan 61
37 Brimmer Street
Boston 8, Massachusetts

Dear Lewis—

Your second fine letter in 8 months, despite my prolonged and inexplicable si-lence, is another proof—as if I needed any more!—of your tolerant and forbearing spirit. Because of some as-yet-unconquered aversion to letter-writing, my few real friendships have been limited to those who are too generous to yield entirely to re-sentment when they don't hear from me, to those who know somehow that my af-fection is not positively correlated (may sometimes be negatively correlated) with numbers of written communications. Your last letter brings joy to my heart. To have arrived at last at a gratifying consummation of your long, comprehensive, ar-duous, dedicated, creative labors is an experience vouchsafed to but a few rare

---

28. Classic company: William James, *Psychology* (1892); Henry Adams, *Mont St. Michel and Chartes* (1904); George Perkins Marsh, *Man and Nature, or Physical Geography as Modified by Human Action* (1864).

minds whose zest, resilience, continuity and integrity of purpose have overcome a hundred obstacles and come out triumphant. Cheers! Now you will rest—in your incomparable way—at peace with your genius and the universe. The substance of your concern has been so far extended in time and space that I am no longer at all clear as to what will be revealed to me in this huge work; but I am certain of a multiplicity of intellectual excitements and clarifications, and more besides. I didn't expect you to attend the Conference at the Amer. Acad., but we needed you so badly that I could not help lamenting your absence. My own reflections & experiences have brought me to one seemingly-impossible-but-necessary transformation of human nature, if survival and a new era of joy and hope is ever to be achieved. It involves the substitution of something for which I have no fitting word (e.g. synthesism, mutual embracement, on all levels—bodies, psyches, groups, nations, ideologies, religions)—the substitution of this for what has prevailed as highest value down the centuries (e.g. monadism—the glorification of one religion, philosophy, society, ruler, class, or individual, etc.). Somehow we must arrive at a union of diversities without an outside enemy to compel cooperation—

Yours

Harry

P.S. I was glad to see your name as editor of new journal—humanistic psychology.

PSS. Delighted to run across paperback on Architecture edited by you.[29] Am now very much distressed by Harvard's (Sert's, Pusey's) plan to build skyscrapers (Rio Janeiro in Cambridge).

PSSS. Where can I find "Moral Challenge to Democracy"?[30]

My congratulations, salutations, love and best wishes to you both—to the serene, beautiful, unexampled Sophy and to your valiant and victorious Self.

Pax Vobiscum—

Harry

[handwritten]

1 Aug, '61

[LM] 3 Aug

Dear Limitless Lewis,

I am about to step on a plane to London en route to Copenhagen—without having written you, heard from you, or knowing your whereabouts. In my mind's eye I have followed you & Sophy to England, stood in the audience when you received your medal, heard you lecture in various envisaged places such as the seat of your

---

29. Lewis Mumford, ed., *Roots of Contemporary American Architecture* (1959).

30. Lewis Mumford, "The Moral Challenge to Democracy," *Virginia Quarterly Review* 35 (Fall 1959): 560–76.

old exemplar Geddes. By now I have you home in my admiration[31]—knowing in your marrow that people of some intuition & account are beginning to take to heart what you have been saying with eloquence in a variety of modes for three decades. It's good to realize that you have initiated changes of great pith and moment in your own life time & you don't have to rely entirely on faith in coming generations—your resurrection & celebration by posterity. Having made a little progress in your monumental work, I am a little indignant at your speaking of the "shallowness of the reviews." What do you expect when every sentence you write calls for a week of concentrated thought and sensitive interpretations of all that is contained and subtly suggested there? Give me two years & then ask me to write a review that is less shallow. Your book—the richest in pregnant facts, reflections, valid judgments, and potential for creative endeavors in the future that I can name today— has become my favorite present to my most trusted friends. Cheers for you & Delectable Sophy—

Hastily,
Harry

I shall be back in New York for a week—Sept 1–6. When do you leave Amenia? My address (Aug 11–21) will be Hotel D'Angleterre, Copenhagen

P.S. Having given a seminar with Harry Levin on the Devil, this coming Fall the topic is Paradise, Utopias, etc. What you said about Miss Bernesi's book confirmed my own opinion happily. Besides your own first book, I have only found scattered references to Utopias in the "City," although whenever an imaginative plan of a City is drawn up, the structure of a Utopia is implied.

PSS. I don't know how busy you are now, but I am having a copy of my Copenhagen spout sent to Amenia. I fear it will fall flat, but you may be interested in parts of it.

[typed]
Lewis Mumford
Amenia, New York
3 August 1961

. . . . It was a pleasure to have your note coming sailing out of the blue, dear Harry; and even a greater pleasure to discover that there is some chance of your being back and of our meeting again, before we leave for our autumn sojourn in Berkeley. If you find it hard to come up here the week of 1–6 September I'll run down to New York, even if my usual excuse for a visit to the city, a session with the dentist over the few forlorn teeth I still cling to, doesn't materialize!

We had an entrancing five weeks in England, and I would be an ingrate if I

---

31. Mumford's correction: "imagination."

used a less expressive adjective for it. We did more things, went more places, saw more people, ate more food, drank more wine, danced more dances during those festive weeks than we've ever managed to do before in three or four times that number of weeks. Your imagination has probably done justice to most of it; but it was our first jaunt into Wales, which we found almost as exhilarating in its stark beauty and genial primitiveness as Delphi. After that came a night in Manchester, vivid with good talk, as a guest of the university, and almost a week in Edinburgh, with a chain of receptions and student conferences, even a television program. After that London, which I find inexhaustible in both its human and its architectural amplitude.

The presentation of the medal to me was the prelude to an even more exciting week, when we met architects from all over the world who were attending an international conference, magnificently managed—so colorfully and so luxuriously, too—by my British friends.[32] There I met a number of good people from the Iron Curtain countries and found to my surprise that my books had somehow penetrated that barrier. All in all, my ego was fed and cosseted and pampered from one end of the trip to the other; and as a result, all our doubts about this extravagant venture were set at rest, for the stimulus from all these contacts was the last restorative I needed to wipe out the fatigue that hung so heavily over me when the book was finished.

As for the book's reception, I'd be a churl not to be grateful even for the "shallow" reviews: if I used that adjective to you, it was rather out of impatience than an expectation that any reviewer could do more than that in a first go at that long, involved, complex, and often daring interpretation of civilization. As you more than anyone else have reason to know, I finished the book almost in the mood that overtook Melville when the had finished his Moby-Dick: inflated and confident. And I realized then that it might take a few years before the book could even be said to be read and perhaps a generation before it was sufficiently digested to be properly evaluated, with its errors definitely exposed and its originalities and its soundnesses appreciated. It's natural to want to take a peep at posterity's verdict, as Hemingway had the dubious luck of doing when he was first reported dead—though a newspaper obituary, at that, is hardly the verdict of posterity.

But I've reached a point by now when I could calmly await the verdict, if only I was sure that there would be any posterity! Meanwhile I've had a few reassuring reactions from some of the people whose judgment I value highly, not only from a friend or two like yourself, but also from a few scholars of exacting standards whose territory I trespassed upon—like Kramer, the Sumerian translator and interpreter at Pennsylvania and Braidwood, a primitive archeologist at Chicago. I now feel sufficiently released from the whole theme, at least for a time, to go forward with other work. Apart from catching up with little odd jobs of writing, I am devot-

---

32. Mumford was awarded the gold medal for architecture by the Royal Institute of Architects.

ing most of my time now to reviewing my life and work as a whole, to get my directions and bearings, before I plunge into another book.

What a juicy issue of Daedalus was waiting for me in the midden heap of fourth class mail. I haven't tackled it yet, but when I do I shall read it backwards, beginning with your apparently challenging and magistral article. Let's compare notes soon about Utopias: at one moment I almost called my book from Cave to Eutopia; but since I am, at bottom, an anti-utopian, I was afraid that the meaning would be misunderstood, as indeed I was misunderstood when on page three I asked if there was a viable alternative between Necropolis and Utopia—meaning something between those polar opposites. More than one reviewer thought I referred to two open choices, and felt I opted for Necropolis!

There's a woman who lives near Copenhagen who would interest you, and who would profit by knowing you if only you had an hour or two to spare. She's a mycologist who until recently was associated with the Carlsberg Laboratories; and now, at 40, has given up science, because she doesn't like the direction that even the biological sciences are taking. I shall write her about your coming; but will leave it to you to make any advances if you're prompted to. Her address is Lyngbattevej 12, Holte—a village about ten miles from Copenhagen. With affectionate greetings

Ever Yours

Lewis

P.S. Sophy's been rejuvenated by our trip, too: it compensated for all the tensions and disappointments of our 1960 travel.

[handwritten]
Amenia, New York
10 August 1961

. . . . You have done it, dear Harry: superbly, imaginatively, persuasively, dashingly, unevadably—your revelation of the present shortcomings and future potentialities of psychology. The address came yesterday, and unlike the 'Daedalus' number, which I've put off reading until I can confront the whole theme, I began your address at once and finished it, despite interruptions, before sundown.[33] This letter will hardly be an adequate intellectual response to your magnificent conspectus: I must confine it to cheers and congratulations, not merely over the contents of your paper but over the magnificent way you carried it off at every point. If that is the way mescaline really acted we'd all be taking it: but I suspect it was caffeine and salt-air, not the satanic mushroom that gave your words both their crystalline clarity and their power of transmitting & begetting illumination. What you've said

33. *Myth and Mythmaking,* the issue of *Daedalus* 88 (Spring 1959), edited by Murray. "Prospect for Psychology," International Congress of Applied Psychology (Copenhagen 1961); reprinted in *Science* 136 (1962): 483–88.

about psychology applies of course to all the sciences and all the humanities, too, at this dark moment of history: so no matter where else you publish this, I trust it will also be published in 'Nature' or at least in the 'Bulletin of the Atomic Scientists,' & be widely printed elsewhere. You have left nothing further to be said: the rest must come in acts, deeds—and abstentions. I trust this reaction of mine will only be a pallid foretaste of the reception your colleagues at the conference will give to your thoughts. In the midst of my ever-deepening dismay over the callow folly of Kennedy & his fellow-compulsives, your words bring at least a whiff of hope.

With an affectionate & admiring embrace

Ever

Lewis

P.S. In case my first note miscarried, this is the second to Copenhagen.

[handwritten]

[LM] Rec'd 1 Sept 61?

Kungholm

Dear Lewis,

I am doubtful about the arrival of this letter before I have the opportunity of calling you on the telephone from New York after I have discovered the days and hours of my 6 appointments at the meetings of the Amer. Psych. Ass'tion. I have been assured that the strange postage I am using is correct. The letter I received from you on my arrival at Copenhagen was a magnum of Champagne plus benzedrine plus an injection of supernatural encouragement. Nobody else would and could write such intoxicating words. Your letter to C arrived the night before the designated time for my appearance & served as a final re-inforcement. Although this approval from you made me indifferent to approval or disapproval from the audience, I delivered it, I trust, as if this was not the case, & I received a surplus of hyperbolic compliments from a receptive minority, including my Catholic friends (who praised it as a Platonic dialogue!) and my Soviet friends (who invited me to Moscow). But the majority were baffled by the changes of mood and level and by the unfamiliar diction. The newspapers described it as the report of a drug-induced vision! But I think that reading it may clear up some of the confusions experienced while hearing it. Anyhow, thanksgivings to you, great friend, for your large share in my fortitude in facing that medley of minds. I had planned to give a copy of the "City" to each of my special British friends, but was told in every bookstore that it would not appear until September. I heard of you at Bumpus's bookshop. Unhappily the "City" was too heavy to carry abroad & I contented myself with "Erewhon" & "E Revisited," etc. I received a cordial letter from Dr. Roberts's husband but was too busy to accept.

Embraces to you both

Harry

[handwritten]
Santa Fe the Chief Way [letterhead]
En route to Santa Fe
16 January 1962

. . . . The news of Jo's death reached us this morning dear Harry, an hour before we left Berkeley.[34] In all these last years she gave me the feeling of one whose life was fulfilled and inwardly at peace; and I hope that some of that sense comes through and reassuringly pervades your own life (and memories) now. Sophy and I will be close to you as we travel eastward again, to reach Amenia around the end of this month. If you are in the mood for a visit it will be good to see you.

In old friendship
Lewis

[handwritten]
37 Brimmer Streeet
Tuesday, Jan 22

Blessed, dependable Lewis, Your prompt letter from New Mexico brought relief to your old friend (however negligent he may be in practice) in the darkest hour of his life. You and Sophy know this incurable desolation. You have been given few reasons, however, to suspect to what extent the affections and purposes of the three Murrays became, as time went on, inextricably interwoven, with Jo the indispensable warp of the fabric evolving in the loom of time. Josephine and I will have to start again from the ground up and see what we can do with the aid of a thousand images of shared joys and memories of loving expressions of Jo's noble nature, moulded with divine cheerfulness and courage out of disillusionments until it reached the peak of its perfection. Your confirmation of my own (untrustworthy) assurance that Jo had achieved a state of inward peace and genuine serenity constitutes the most consoling, strong support that could be given me for my ascent, if ever, out of the abyss. Bless you, and bless you for your book—tremendous in all ways—which has served as a new New Testament for me, with passages to be read daily from week to week. You have packed your whole self—mind, heart, and taste—into those exciting sane pages.

Gratefully
Harry

P.S. At a marvelous service, 650 people joined in a unanimous tribute to Jo's spirit. You shall hear from me in due course.

34. Josephine Rantoul Murray died on 14 January.

[handwritten]
Lewis Mumford
Amenia, New York
8 February 1962

. . . . Christiana tells me, dear Harry, that you are burdened by the task of answering the hundreds of letters that have been prompted as a natural tribute to both of you, by Jo's death. So I would be silent now, were it not that this needs no answer. If I were your guardian angel now I would say to you: "Remember Loyola's advice: make no important decisions during a period of desolation." Sit quiet and hold fast: change nothing, dispose of nothing, until a year has gone by. The right answer will then come of itself, all the easier if you have not tried, by an act of will, to force a decision prematurely out of your own wounded and weakened soul. For a while even your empty house will be easier to endure than your own emptiness without these vivid reminders of Jo. In time, life will put your world to rights.

Lewis

[typed]
Lewis Mumford
Amenia, New York
14 August 1962

. . . We have been through a dreary round of petty illnesses, dear Harry, too insignificant to be talked about, except for the blight that they have cast on otherwise idyllic days; and I have yet to begin serious work on my book, for this week I shall be interrupted once more by the proofs of the paperback Melville pouring onto my desk. But I am still going though my letter files in a desultory sort of way; and I write you at this moment to pass on a discovery I just made, which shocks me both by what it tells and by my utter forgetfulness of having read this passage in the first place. It occurs in a friendly letter from Frank Mather, in response to my Melville, which had just come out. What he says is this: "A reminiscence to close. When I first saw Elizabeth Melville, a transparent figure, with lace covering her hands, I stupidly offered her mine. She hesitated and I held a hand which had never had fingers. It was a lesson in deportment which I have never forgotten. I tell this because it is one more landmark in Melville's domestic Calvary." How could I have received this without having passed it on to you?[35] How could it be true without having been noted by anyone else—as far, at least, as I know?? Surely, if this were an early injury or birth defect it would account for Elizabeth's clumsiness as a housekeeper—and perhaps many other things, too: the blank space in my memory may be due to the fact that the letter was written in April 1929, just as little Geddes was

---

35. In fact, he had asked Murray about this; see Mumford's letter of 21 April 1929.

coming out of his own illness, and Sophy and I, after the long vigil, were sinking into a deep depression: at that moment Melville was very far away.

Don't bother to answer this, if you are not in a writing mood. You are often in my thoughts, and will remain there even if no words pass between us.

Affectionately
Lewis

[handwritten, n.d.]
22 Francis Avenue
Cambridge 38
Massachusetts

Dear Lewis,

My very-few-now best friends hear from me about twice a year. Why so seldom? Because I have a lot to say to them & feel they deserve & might enjoy a long letter & so I wait for a long morning with nothing on my mind. This fantasied morning never comes & so every 6 mos. in desperation I scribble off a telegraphic note like this one. But I am in transition now, with no distinguishable identity, & there is no telling what kind of character of sub-personalities I shall have when I emerge—one of them may be a letter-writing personality.

For the moment, these are the main items on my agenda.

1. Salvos to you two Immortals for 1963!

2. Hurray for HM in paperback! & many thanks for the gift, the magnanimous inscription, & the accolade in your excellent preface.[36]

3. I am now completely moved &, except for my books & papers, completely settled at the above address, with a room that is yearning to be occupied by you and Sophie. When will you come?

4. Both Eleanor & Harry Metcalf flatly deny the absence of fingers (understandable if HM cut them off in a moment of manic fury).

5. I need a photograph of you (the one that was published in the Sat Eveg Post, say) for my select gallery of those who participated in the shaping of my self—

Embraces for you both—
Harry

Amenia, New York
17 January 1963

. . . . Your letter, your very welcome letter, came this morning, dear Harry: and it finds me at one of those empty moments, between jobs, that may not come again

---

36. Lewis Mumford, *Herman Melville: A Study of His Life and Vision* (1962); revised edition of *Herman Melville* (1929).

for months: so don't be embarrassed if I take advantage of it. Next week I must go to Montreal to find out how successful the Film Board has been in making six short documentary films—'L.M. on the City'; and when I come back I plan, as soon as I'm rested, to plunge once more into the second draft of the autobiography, which has pretty much absorbed me since September. More than half of it is done: and I hope to finish the rest by May—after which I plan to put it aside for a year to see how well it seasons. . . .

As for the purgatorial feelings you now have, in your transitional state, I can easily imagine them. Even the passage from a familiar environment to a strange one every year, with every other relation unchanged, has given us uneasy periods these last twenty years: so much so that we both have specially enjoyed the absence of such pressures this year. But in your case the passage involves a far more radical wrench and readjustment: so that, though I have sometimes been uneasy over your silence, I have not been surprised by it. "Moving from an old house to a new gives one curious things to do." These are not the most poetic lines Babette Deutsch ever wrote: but they are the ones I've found myself repeating most often. Moving from an old self to a new, as you are now doing—and as everyone slowly does in old age or in illness—is a more devastating experience. I have eased the problem a little for myself by reliving my earlier selves in memory: but that of course brings trials of its own, along with obvious rewards and rejuvenations. My book has been teaching me much, if only because it has altered my perspective on much I had taken for granted and uncovered areas that had long been silted over in memory. Fortunately I have copious notes and letters that take me through the most difficult periods and often correct the perversities of memory. I have tried to present my development as honestly and as unsparingly as I might in revealing myself, at last, to a friend I would never see again. I don't know any autobiography that has achieved this yet: so I can't hope I'll fully succeed: but at least I'm making a brave effort to show what the shaping impulses and forces were, as seen from the inside. The volume I'm working on now—a long one—will take me up to 1935: a dividing point in my life. . . .

As to Mather's testimony, I don't think he had the slightest glimpse of the terrible possibility that rose in your mind *as it secretly did in mine.* Was it a hallucination on his part? That seems less likely than it may have been the evidence of a secret that not one in the family could face or even see with their open eyes: evidence that would explain the dire hints and letter-burnings that went on later, and even in a way justify them. Certainly I would not publish Mather's testimony, even to refute it: though I am not sure that Eleanor's evidence, though wholly honest, does refute it. The best reason for dismissing Mather's description is that the maimed hand does not reappear in any of Melville's later fantasies, does it? And could *he* have suppressed it? Surely Ahab's amputated leg preceded any possible date for such an exhibition of manic fury? There I leave it—unresolved, but not dislodged entirely from one's mind.

About Van Wyck. Sophy and I saw him yesterday for three quarters of an hour—the first visit since mid-November. I wrote Christiana briefly about him this morning, before your letter came. You were entirely right about Gladys' homecoming proposal: he is the mere wraith of a man, enfeebled, shattered, dismantled, as if he had just emerged from prolonged torture in a concentration camp. Torture it was: beginning with the "successful" new operation on his carotid artery. That was done in full consciousness under a local—and not entirely effective—anesthetic. When he talked about it last November it was with horror in his voice, and something as near resentment as his mild spirit is capable of expressing. After that worse followed. His failure to hold food on his stomach led, despite the reassuring ex-ray diagnosis of his earlier cancer surgeon, to a 6 hour operation on his intestines, when an advanced cancer was extirpated. For weeks he was fed by tube at the hospital, watched by three nurses: and he might never have been able to return home but for the suggestion made by their Bridgewater maid that he try goat's milk. Fortunately a local supply was at hand: and he lives on goat's milk and honey, holding on to his life by that frail thread. He can now spend an hour or so daily in his study: he told me he was making corrections for a one-volume edition of his autobiography: but apart from his obvious pleasure in seeing us, he was silent, his spirit withdrawing like a wounded animal to the deepest cavern of his being. If he survives the winter it will be a miracle. Until yesterday I was inclined to regard Gladys' unwavering hope and unflagging courage as entirely admirable: but now I wonder, or begin to wonder, whether it may not be mainly self-protective—and whether a more compassionate, indeed a more distressed attitude would not be a kinder reaction to his long bout of suffering, anguish, and humiliation. He is too beaten to cry out: but Gladys' determination to act as if he had no reason now to do so—she is already planning for his convalescence in New York—may only add to his inner sense of helplessness. This technical exhibitionism of modern medicine, in keeping alive the body even though the 'success' is temporary and futile, is one of the grimmest miscarriages of science: it removes the possibility of dying with dignity and reasonable expedition, for no rational purpose whatever. Think what would have happened to Henry James, Sr. if a present-day physician had discovered that he was starving himself to death! He would have been carted off to a hospital, have lived for months, possibly years, by forced feeding: and would have exhausted his estate paying for hospital bills—Van Wyck's hospital expenses alone have been $500 a week—only in the end to die a dog's death. Sophy and I have been so horrified by this spectacle that we have been earnestly canvassing the means of averting it in the case of ourselves: but medical practice & hospital practice is against letting nature take its course even when the situation is hopeless.

Thinking of poor Van Wyck's situation, I am all the more grateful to your wisdom and humanity, dear Harry, in not advising hospitalization for our friend Eva Goldbeck, when she was starving herself to death back in 1935. That proved your human insight and your courage.

Perhaps you already know all the things I have been recapitulating about Van Wyck. But I never get a chance to talk to Gladys, except over the telephone: what I've said is partly what I've gathered from others, especially from his oldest friend now, John Hall Wheelock.[37] Wheelock is afraid that they may be in a tight situation financially: but neither of us can guess what sort of financial back-log they may have, though Gladys gladly accepted a 'loan' from the American Academy of Arts and Letters—of which, quite ironically, I recently became president. (Don't ask what long-suppressed vanity caused me, at this moment of my life, to accept it!)

Now that I've written such a copious letter I might as well cover a few more matters, to clear the table for loftier discourse when we meet. 'The City in History' has done so well that I've been able to turn down four visiting professorships this year: and my publisher, eager for my next few books, has indicated his willingness to stake me further to enable me to devote my next few years exclusively to writing. For a man without a pension this is a huge relief—as close to affluence as I could ever hope to get. When my book is finished Sophy and I might easily be tempted to spend a day or two with you at your new home & on our old familiar street. Though the winter has been a little intimidating we still love it here. . . .

> Affectionately
> Lewis

> [handwritten]
> 22 Francis Avenue
> Cambridge 38
> Massachusetts
> May 19, '63
> [LM] 7 June

Dear Lewis,

I look forward to hearing of your eloquence at the Academy—maybe a little embarrassing before Gladys, who, by the way, seems to be almost settled in her trust as to a continuation of life after death.

Gladys is going to be more or less on her own in Copenhagen for 19 days or more, starting Tuesday, June 11. She knows no Danes. Do you think your friend, mentioned in the Apology, would welcome the opportunity to meet her?[38]

As to Mrs. H. Melville's fingers, I had an opportunity to approach the question stealthily with Agnes Morewood who knew her well, & I got a surprised & completely negative reaction.[39] Moreover I found a picture of her in old age knitting,

---

37. John Hall Wheelock (1886–1978), poet who had been a Harvard classmate of Brooks.

38. Lewis Mumford, "Apology to Henry Adams," *Virginia Quarterly Review* 38 (Spring 1962): 196–217.

39. Agnes Morewood (1879–1966), Herman Melville's grandniece.

but the angle of the camera did not permit a view of more than the beginnings of the fingers on her right hand. Mysterious.

I need a picture of you. Among the many that I have seen and liked, the one that appeared in the Saturday Evg Post struck me as tops. Have you perchance a print of it?

I am still gloating over the Apology.

H. Adams was better at seeing the pathology than he was at designing a remedy—difficult if the majority believe (as Hume suggested) that an inflammation in one's little finger is of greater import than a conflagration of the universe—

Adios
Harry

[handwritten]
22 Francis Avenue
Cambridge 38
Massachusetts

Dear Divinities—

Unrecovered from the dissonance of feeling engendered by the ceremony and lunch at Bridgewater, we were not in the best state to tackle the riddle of the universe at Amenia. But all the same we did hop, skip, and jump over the great issues from parent-child relations to immortality, and you gave your guest a memorable spell of interchange of ideas and of facts (happily without figures), not to speak of other comforts, including an extra pillow stolen from the twin bed. And so, once more, thanksgiving to your souls for resuscitating a flagging spirit.

Reading Apology to Henry Adams was an exciting experience on several counts. First it enlightened me as to the specific prophecies of H.A. and their dates—an impressive record (which one member of the faculty dismissed in the thirties as "the gloomy vision of a dyspeptic old man"). Second, I was impressed by your strategy of using the past—Adams, Geddes, Soddy, Wells—to exemplify the present—the tremendous inertia that must be overcome to inaugurate a shift in outlook. Multiplying technical inventions have produced unparalleled changes in outlook, but in a disastrous line-of-least-resistance toward affectlessness, impersonality, and a state of inflation generated by the potency of modern technics. Those who are on the technocratic band-wagon are convinced that they are pioneers at the forefront of progress, etc., etc., and that those who view this trend with antipathy and suspicion are stick-in-the-mud conservatives, the last leaves on the boughs of the sixteenth century. You are a notable exception in proposing creative rather than destructive modes of advance (instead of trying to obstruct technology as such). Third, the eloquent force of your words is consonant with my own temper, though it may be more stunning than seductive to the minds of academic intellectuals. And finally, fourth, the fine way you had of presenting the case for the wide focus vs. the circumscribed. Here you are especially helpful to me, because I have had to explain my position and my methods for the last 30 years in contrast to the accelerating current towards specialization, quantification, computers, etc. I think we must appreciate that specialization is "a fateful consequence of the very character of science." Without it there would be no science, and hence no valid knowledge for the generalist to use in arriving at his conclusions and predictions. You say that the generalist "keeps every part under equally close and constant observation," but if he can really do this, he must be indebted to hundreds of specialists who have reliably described each part. If the specialist is also a fully-human creature concerned with man's destiny, he should want to be a generalist as well, or, if not that, he should welcome what the generalist has to offer. As I see it, there is only a limited amount of genius in the human species, and a small degree of it can contribute more by specializing than by generalizing. If you speak only of the real geniuses you can make a good case for the generalizer, but consider all the cracked-brain generalizers who have been spouting within recorded history! This is no refutation of anything you have said—merely an acknowledgement of how useful specialists are to us.

Cheers for you! You have said almost everything I want to say (or have said with less knowledge, lucidity, & vigor). I love to read you—Hugs for you both—& thanks—

Harry

[typed]
Amenia, New York
7 June 1963

. . . I've delayed writing you, dear Harry, till I had time to read and digest your essays, all of them stimulating, not least that in Daedalus which I had only half read in 1961, in all the distractions of our homecoming from Europe and our forth-going to Berkeley.[40] And yet I write more promptly than I might have, because the possession of a single copy of anything fills me with anxiety, a feeling that goes back to the time John Gould Fletcher foolishly sent the single copy of a long poem to the American Caravan, and reproached us for losing it, though in fact we had mailed it back. The Personality of Satan, which you thought I would take to least, opens up so many fresh approaches to the mystery of Personality that I shall go back to it more than once, till I am sure that I have assimilated it: I am glad you didn't leave it out of the sheaf.[41] We are so often in agreement in our conclusions, though we start at such different points, that we are under the same disadvantage as to positive poles, be-

---

40. Henry A. Murray, "Unprecedented Evolutions," *Daedalus* 90 (1961): 547–70.
41. Henry A. Murray, "The Personality and Career of Satan," *Journal of Social Issues* 28 (1962): 36–54; reprinted in Shneidman, *Endeavors in Psychology,* 518–34.

tween which there is no flow of current: so the one matter I was most conscious of, as setting us apart, is our fundamental difference about the roles of chance and purpose in the transformations of life. If I were beginning life all over again, I think I'd dedicate myself wholly to biology, for the sake of perhaps being able to re-state the problems of chance, mechanism, causality, and purpose more adequately than anyone has yet done. The more I reflect on the whole process of evolution, the more I find it impossible to accept chance as the key to the whole progressive sequence: even if I follow you in allowing for the abundance of geologic time and an almost infinite multitude of chances, that still does not seem to me to account for the increase of both complexity and directionality. To ascribe all this to time and natural selection seems to me a mere fairy tale: just as audacious, and just as unconvincing, as ascribing it to an equally mysterious being called God. It took mankind thousands of years to arrive at anything like the concept of causality, which gives us the foundations of an orderly and predictable world: and it may take us quite as long, because we have hardly begun seriously yet, in terms of observed phenomena, to arrive at a viable concept of purpose. In a world of pure chance, causality itself would not operate: because the law that was valid one day would not necessarily hold on the next: a minimal amount of order, regularity, and repetitiveness is necessary before we can start making observations; and all this remains as an essential component of a purposeful world. True: organic phenomena are only partly capable of overcoming chance and determinateness, for some of the organic decisions that were made as low down as the order of reptiles still remain an integral part of all later animal evolution. All this I admit: but that still leaves the slow accumulations of purpose and direction, far beyond any conceivable operations of chance, to be accounted for. You fend off this question as most biologists have done in the past, by equating purpose with having a conscious or ultimate goal. That would make any appearance of purpose ridiculous, of course, until we reached man and had a creature capable of holding a conscious purpose in mind. But purposiveness, in my interpretation, must exist on the lowest level, long before there is any detectable appearance of consciousness; and though Leibniz may have been right in attributing some degree of mind to the aboriginal monad, I am quite free to leave that metaphysical question open. It is enough that organic phenomena are directed toward a future fulfillment, and in every species that ultimate fulfillment directs the processes of maturation and selects—whether in the genes or at later stages of growth—those elements that are essential to its growth, and give it, both a characteristic life-pattern, and those variations that will lead to an orderly change. Creativity lies in the variation, not in the post-factum selection. If you look at the phenomenon of life from the bottom, trying to interpret physiological processes in terms of chemical ones, and chemical ones in terms of purely fortuitous combinations of neutral elements, you throw out one of the most important attributes of these elements, even at the sub-atomic level: that these changes and complexities increase the predisposition to organic life, and that the large-scale ecological associations, which Henderson pointed out in The Fitness of the Environment, cannot be described in purely analytical terms. Certainly purpose is not yet visible at the lowest level, even if it is there: if, then, we are to detect purpose in nature, we must begin with the highest phenomena, not merely man, but the most subtle manifestations of mind in art and in science, if we are to get a clue to the way that purpose evolves at a much lower level. Though I don't for a moment think that any combination of accidents will produce purpose, I know by experience that when purpose is present, accidents can be used to great advantage, since they enrich design far beyond the requirements of reason and economy. At this point, I can see a quizzical look in your face: I have talked about purpose without defining it. But you are wrong: I have defined it negatively: it is not conscious, it is not accidental, it can operate without supposing any final goal, though each species seems to reach a new provisional terminal point of its own, only to give way to other species, finally to our own, in which the creative processes that for so many billions of years remained unfocussed in nature, finally begin to cohere and to take on an independent existence in man's consciousness, under his own guidance. As a result, there has been more history, more creativity, more increase of consciousness in a single century of human activity—any human activity, not merely that of our present age of science—than in a billion years before man detached himself from his natural matrix. We have gone over this ground before, dear Harry, as I well remember: if I come back to it again, it is only to re-affirm my conviction in more certain terms than ever: perhaps because even the eyes of biologists are opening to the total inadequacy of their previous mode of explaining cumulative purposive mechanisms in terms of chance; and as René Dubos says in his most recent book, though they reject purpose as a suitable mate to show in public, they resort to her surreptitiously in private because they can't get very far in their investigations, without her assistance.[42]

Now as to more personal matters: and first, Gladys Brooks, who came over for lunch a few days ago, beautifully serene, much refreshed by her visit with you, and on the whole eager for her new adventure though with an undercurrent of trepidations over the jet she is flying off on. We talked about death and immortality and Van Wyck's heroic qualities during his illness; and at the end I learned, to my surprise, almost my dismay, that he had left two thirds of his estate to his sons, instead of keeping their share in trust, at her disposal, till she died. I am afraid a guilty conscience prompted that decision; but from the way that Gladys gaily dropt the news, I think she was a little shocked, too. Life is full of surprises, sometimes unpleasant ones. I suppose she has enough funds, all in all, to keep going nicely: yet perhaps without that extra margin that Sophia and I now find curiously comforting in our old age. I gave her introductions to two very close friends in England; but I didn't dare, somehow, introduce her to my Danish-domiciled biologist; for she, poor woman, now at the menopause, had quite inconveniently directed far more feeling

---

42. René Dubos, *The Torch of Life: Continuity in Living Experience* (1962).

in my direction—though we've never met—than I can, or would ever care to recip-rocate. But I've given Gladys the name of a fine old Danish architect, if she needs help of any kind. The nicest thing that happened in New York was not my Acad-emy meeting, but my first viewing of the six half hour films that Film Board of Canada has been making: Lewis Mumford on the City. Though the director and his associates were extremely intelligent and sympathetic, I had all sorts of misgivings over their ability to interpret this difficult theme successfully—for it is in no sense a travelogue of cities—until the very last moment; and then I was most pleasantly surprised: even the most difficult film, the final one, which had to be done over twice before they whipt together the final version, is much better than I could have hoped. They will appear on television in probably every country but the United States; for I am sure none of the commercial stations would touch them with the proverbial ten foot pole; but it is available for private showing by schools and col-leges, and if I should hear of its being shown around Boston I'll tell you about it.

My final report is on gardening: not merely has your azalea survived magnifi-cently, thanks to the constant irrigation I've had to give, during this long drought, to the entire garden, but there has been such a general floral outburst as to compensate us for the dire winter we went through. But speaking about growing things, we've had Alison here this last week; and we couldn't be happier over the way she is bring-ing up her baby, a most winning little girl, who when she is forcibly awakened from her sleep for feeding at once breaks out into a wide smile. Now I've compassed everything, except that I must add that Sophia is blooming, too; and her bad back seems to be in abeyance, so long as she doesn't overstrain herself physically. As for my autobiography—but that must be read, not talked about, and heaven knows when it will be in shape to read, though the second draft, at least, will only need an-other month's work before I cry: Finis. What a letter! It will take the place of my Academy address, till I get an additional copy.[43] The few I had slipt through my hands.

Warmly

Lewis

P.S. Again about Mrs. Melville's fingers: the mystery has deepened a little. Frank Mather's letter says plainly: "When I first saw Elizabeth Melville, a transpar-ent figure with lace covering her hands, I stupidly offered her mine. She hesitated and I held a hand which never had fingers. It was a lesson in deportment which I have never forgotten." But I came upon his review of my Melville in the Saturday Review of Literature, in going through old clippings; and there he recalled nothing of Mrs. Melville, but said that he had met her daughter, Elizabeth, who at the time of their meeting might well have been living with her mother; but who could only doubtfully be described, one might suppose, as a transparent figure, though she

43. Mumford delivered his inaugural address as President of the American Academy of Arts and Letters at the spring awards ceremony, 22 May 1963.

died a few years later.[44] Since Melville's 'insanity' was a matter of common gossip, there might well have been some other skeleton in the closet that caused the whole-sale burning of his papers. I wouldn't hazard a guess; but one feels uneasy. Either a prenatal misfortune or orthodox surgical amputation, for reasons, might explain Mather's experience. It's hard to believe that he invented this, or that he transferred it from his encounter with someone else.

> [handwritten]
> Amenia, New York
> 11 June 1963

. . . . What a fine tribute the very title of your birthday gift is, dear Harry: and how good it is to find out, before going to Heaven, what an impact your thought and ex-ample have had on your colleagues![45] The introductory eulogy was far from being sufficiently laudatory: for despite all you have done to release them the young still fear that any show of emotion or ostensible devotion will be read as a betrayal of science or an affront to democracy: but on skimming over the pages I see that I have much to catch up with, though I am reassured by finding I shall terminate in the arms of Erikson, a subtle but bold mind to whom I owe much, in the intermittent but deep fashion I owe even more to you. . . . But the occasion for the book is a blow between the eyes—you? Seventy? Quite impossible. This is a joke in the worst pos-sible taste: a joke Life keeps on the shelf till it's quite stale before springing it on us, so that, in our shocked silence, life may have the last laugh. The fact that so much youth is left in one still, so much that is still untried, unfulfilled, forward moving, only increases one's dismay over the calendar's message. Surely this message was meant for someone else? And perhaps, after a deep breath, that's the best way to take it. . . . But this is a very tedious way of saying: Thank you and bless you: for I would have to write a whole book of my own to record my gratitude for all that your work and our friendship has brought me.

> Lewis

> [handwritten]
> 22 Francis Avenue
> Cambridge 38
> Massachusetts

Dear Lewis,

Thanks for the quick return of my only copy of that paper. I scratched off 2 re-actions to your thoughtful argument on two points (each of which I now enclose); but *now* it is apparent that I have done nothing but repeat myself.

---

44. Frank Mather, *Saturday Review of Literature*, 27 April 1929, 945.

45. Robert W. White, ed., *The Study of Lives: Essays on Personality in Honor of Henry A. Murray* (1963).

As an excuse for repeating myself on the subject of evolution I might say that it seemed as if you had misread me; as if you thought I was advocating Accident or Chance, and you were advocating Purpose. I mentioned a number of factors, of which Chance is surely one, but my emphasis was on *Creativity* in nature (& finally in human nature)—the combination of elements (chemicals, genes) to form new entities with unexampled properties. If you said that the *direction* of these chemical & genetical processes is toward greater size and complexity (in the main) etc., etc., and that this *compositional* (anabolic, formative) *direction* of processes has surpassed, in the long run, the *decompositional* (catabolic, disintegrative) *direction* of processes, then we would be in essential agreement. But when you put the term *purposive* in place of *direction*, then confusion results in the minds of others, because according to general usage (the OED for example) some (*human*, or maybe animal) intention is always implied. So my first point would be: better chose a word that is not confusing to others. The second point would be: if you use "purpose" all the way up and down the evolutionary scale (e.g. the purpose of the sun is to exert gravitational force & keep the planets in their orbits), then you have to find another word for human intention (the experience of having a goal in view). The third would be that, in view of man's primitive tendency to project his own psychic experiences into natural objects and into the ether (anthropopsychic spirits and gods, etc.), we should be wary about yielding to this natural (& often completely invalidated) disposition. Three other points are mentioned in the accompanying sheet. The final 7th point is that if one explains everything by some undefined mystical 'purpose' in the universe, then one is not led to conduct specific detailed studies of micro-phenomena, which have often in the past succeeded in revealing the miraculous workings of nature—

Well, well, I ended by repeating myself again for the 3rd time—to no purpose, & hence this way of talking should eventually become extinct—

Hail to you

H

The marvels of genetical micro-chemistry were entirely unsuspected when you studied science.

As for "purpose" in evolution, it is certainly up to you to define what you are designating by this word.

You were arguing with Darwin, *not* with Murray, because I made a *special* point *against* accident or chance as a sufficient explanation. Chance certainly had something to do with your meeting Sophy at the precise time & place, & under the exact prevailing conditions, etc., etc.—but what followed—the mutual affinity and attraction, the procreative conjugation, and the particular, unique genetical resultant, etc., etc., was no accident—but the operation of successive phases of the creative process in nature.

There are reasons to believe that the *majority* of these creative processes resulted in non-viable entities which are not extinct; what remains are organisms with serviceable or life-sustaining processes (& hence purposeful in this sense). It is only man's narcism which leads him to believe that the *purpose* of 2 billion years of evolution was to produce *Him*, & if a genocidal war were to eliminate the species, it would have to be said that death—or a self-annihilating organism—was the *purpose* of the whole process.

A couple of off-the-cuff retorts.

Harry and Eleanor Metcalf & Agnes Morewood assure me with unquavering eyes that there was *nothing* wrong with the hands of Elizabeth Shaw Melville. A fairly good photograph partly confirms this. Elizabeth Metcalf, the daughter, however had crippling arthritis of both hands with fingers tightly drawn into the palms of her hands. She was also extremely thin (more 'transparent,' I would guess, than her mother). Mather mentions the daughter but *not* the wife, & he does not impress one as a reliable witness, because he says "a hand *which never had fingers*"—a statement which nobody could make without a careful anatomical examination. Diagnosis: the irresponsible report of a slightly doddering academic man whose mind was in the habit of outrunning his imprecise perceptions.

QED (until more evidence is forthcoming)

> Lewis Mumford
> Amenia, New York
> 14 June 1963

. . . . Just an interim line, dear Harry, to tell you how relieved I am by your disposition of Mather's tale: the daughter's rheumatic hand explains everything, and disposes of the horrid hypothesis that entered *our* minds, but I'm sure never touched his, for he had lived in an innocent age, and the horrors of our time have tainted even us. What he wrote me about was not a sinister possibility about Melville, but a happy 'lesson in deportment.' Had he thought of it in any biographic sense, he would have passed it on to me when we first compared notes about Melville. Well: that damned spot is out: forgive me for soiling your mind with it. (Even I was innocent in 1929: otherwise I wouldn't have forgotten it so easily!).

I'll go back to more important matters later: our discussion has only begun and I see we'll both need another lifetime to finish it. Also I have something to say, still unsaid, in response to your generalist-specialist reference a month or so ago.

But my whale is now in the final flurry: I am two chapters from the end of Vol. 1. 'midway on the journey of my life.' I begin to weary: half a lifetime is quite enough to go through a second time.

> Lewis

[typed]
Amenia, New York
4 August 1963

. . . How many times during the last month or so, dear Harry, I have wished we were near neighbors, so that I could drop in for a chat, to discuss some of the ideas that have been flitting through my mind, sometimes like butterflies, sometimes like bats, or again like mosquitoes. Jung's autobiography, for example: I should like to have spent a whole evening or two with you on that alone: so full of astonishing revelations, cunning insights, and yet—for me—so bafflingly inconclusive, indeed downright evasive, on the very subjects on which one expected to have some final summation of his life-wisdom.[46] It seems to me a false humility on his part to say that at the end he can say nothing, because he is as much surrounded by the mystery of his private experience as he was at the beginning. This is the right response to the overconfident, who think they have trapt the universe in their little net; but it leaves too much unsaid; and even if one shouldn't expect more from a man as near the grave as he was when he finally communicated his thoughts, I still ask why he didn't think of giving forth more of himself (his deepest, maturest self) at an earlier stage, when his energies were high. The thing that really surprised me in this confession is something I didn't for a moment anticipate; and that is how deeply alike, beneath all their superficial antagonisms, Jung and Freud actually were: each more "mystical" or what in older parlance would be called superstitious, than he would dare publicly to admit: each hiding this trait under the white surgical uniform of science. Whether Jung actually had his phallic dream at four or five may be doubtful: but if Freud insisted theoretically on his pansexual interpretations, Jung's nonsexual theory of the dream only served to disguise the fact that, in actual life, he was a better Freudian than Freud himself, who managed, it would seem, to talk himself out of sex, lest he himself surrender totally to it. Jung's ability to recall in detail a dream he had many years before seemed to me suspicious: for how could so much remain engraved on the mind, and accessible? But as it happened, I stumbled upon the same trait, at the same time, in the very person that Jung mentions as having been a possible ancestor, namely Goethe; for Goethe's Poetry and Truth is replete to the point of tediousness with the same total recall of the events of his youth! . . . All this is not to say that many passages of the book did not make a profound impression on me (especially the building of his house!): for the first time I felt that I had fully come to grips with Jung's interpretation of the unconscious; and that somehow gave me the courage to peer even deeper down the long tunnel of the past, in the little book I am now beginning to write on the origins and the present day outcome of technological development. I began this book very confident, a

46. C. G. Jung, *Memories, Dreams, Reflections* (1961); Mumford's review published in *New Yorker,* 23 May 1964, 155–56.

month ago, that I already had all the data I needed to elaborate the theme I presented at the Fund for the Republic Conference last January, on the two technologies, one empirical, the other magical, one democratic, the other authoritarian; one man-centered, the other system-centered.[47] But I hadn't spent a fortnight on it before I realized that there were further problems, beneath those I thought I had the solution for: so that before I knew it I was floundering around in a speculative swamp, trying to put together a plausible picture of the development of language and ritual, and then finally trying to carry further a thought you implanted in my mind twenty years ago, on the function of repetition in the human psyche, and the disordered manifestation of this trait in a compulsion neurosis. (Is there a classic text on this subject?) I shall never have enough adequate knowledge to solve this problem satisfactorily, and as far as the pre-historic development of technics goes, neither will anyone else. But I think I can at least remove one obstacle to sound thinking; and this is the exaggerated notion people have acquired of the making of tools as the prime attribute that defines the human species. Language was already a highly articulated machine at a time when tools were little more than roughly formed stones. When I put all this together, I shall beg you, dear Harry, to put your searching critical mind to work on it, to bring out all the flaws in the thesis, including those that I won't be able to correct; but until then, if we were neighbors, I would be pestering you with some of the problems that keep on bobbing up, as I bring together the known data in the history of technology.

As for our discussion of purpose, I do not flinch from carrying it further with you, though I shall not do so in this letter: partly because I have been having a very illuminating discussion, not yet exhausted, with a young physician who has been doing a series of papers, attempting to define purpose in sufficiently rigorous terms to achieve scientific acceptance. I would agree heartily that our positions are not very far apart, when we are considering life's actual manifestations; the real block between us is that the word purpose is charged in your mind with meaning that I do not attach to it: first the idea of an ultimate end, implicit from the beginning, toward which all intermediate transformations are directed. This is an ancient theological position; and I respect it altogether: if God meant to create man, he chose a very devious path when he created the dinosaur. The other obstructive notion is that purpose must be conscious, as it so often is in man. This too I reject: if we cannot define purpose without adding consciousness, it obviously cannot be applied to creatures in whom consciousness, if it exists, must be minimal and non-rational. Then is your 'creativeness' sufficient to cover what I mean by 'purpose'? Unfortunately not: for creativeness (spontaneity, exuberance) though an essential part of the process, does not embrace the peculiar attributes of purpose, as I see it: the fact that it is not only directional, but (1) cumulative, becoming more firm in its inten-

47. Lewis Mumford, "Challenge to Democracy in the Next Decade," printed as "Authoritarian and Democratic Technics," *Technology and Culture* 5 (Winter 1964): 1–8.

tions with each successful step toward its partial fulfillment, (2) anticipatory, combining a still unrealized organic change with the past that makes it possible. When the young doctor and I are done with our discussions, I shall send you his scientific papers, alongside my own purely philosophic definitions. But of one thing, dear Harry, I feel pretty sure: that the phobia of rigorous men of science before the very word "purpose" is a suspicious symptom: it may conceal the fundamental weakness in the whole seemingly rational schema in which science since Galileo and Descartes has been operating. When purpose is ruled out of the universe by definition, the only purpose left is that of science itself, which is then at liberty to deal freely with all phenomena, by substituting the question-begging term mechanism (as if machines were not the very paragon of purposeful contrivances) for that of purpose. If the *idea* of purpose cannot be admitted into the scientific vocabulary, then it will never be discovered in the actual world: those purposeful phenomena which cannot be interpreted, by reading backward, as a causal sequence, will drop out of sight altogether. This is the reason I do not shy away from the word purpose itself, even though it is badly enmeshed in false interpretations which go far beyond those anticipatory reactions and goal-seeking activities that point to its existence. Without purpose, creativity would not have a chance, and chance would not so often turn out to be a marvellous instrument of creativity! But I have already said enough: or rather twice too much, since I am still withholding my effort at definition, until I can make it strong enough to stand up before your searching gaze.

This has been a busy, exceptionally sociable summer for us: after the winter's dearth we've now had our fill, and more than our fill, of company. But Sophia, despite the fatigues of hospitality, has been enjoying it; and so for that matter have I. Both the flower and the vegetable gardens have been bountiful; and for once in these many dry years, even the grass has stayed green into August, because we've had "normal" rainfall. We'll be here till the third week in September, when we go off to Wesleyan; and you, dear Harry, will be thrice welcome any time in September you can be tempted, by the call of friendship, to sweep down into these parts.

Please don't look upon these rambling letters of mine as needing any answer, if you are not in a letter writing mood: they are just the overflow of an idle mind. And don't think my failure to send you a photograph till now is due to any coyness: it's just the result of not having at hand any pictures that satisfy my residual vanity and bear some resemblance to the object himself. I am a hard man to photograph and a harder one to please. What is worse, the sort of photo I might choose might be so different from the one you'd care to remember me by that I think the only safe thing to do is to wait till you can take your pick. When I saw myself a few months ago in the Canadian films on the city, I was taken aback: who was this authoritative looking ancient that was speaking to me so deliberately? I didn't recognize him, and of course I didn't like him. How easy it was for me to sympathize with my enemies' feelings about me! While I'm going over this ego-image let me share with you the picture I have imprinted on the minds of three contemporaries: an Italian poet, a few years ago, described me a looking like "an old colonel." An English reporter as a "higher civil servant." (As you know, in England that's supposed to be rather flattering, if also limiting.) And finally Berenson, in his Diaries which are coming out in the Fall found me looking "like a physician." The three definitions of course coincide: a *colonel,* not a general: a *civil servant,* not a prime minister, a *physician,* not a great specialist. In short, an image of authority*; but without the flair that goes with the higher ranks. That composite portrait has the stamp of objectivity! But I look inside and smile. (The general and the prime minister are waiting in the wings.)

With affectionate greetings
from us both
Lewis

*But to none of them do I look like a writer! My vocation has left no outward marks!

PPS: I open this letter because I forgot to thank you for that fine color print of Sophy & me & the flowering of New England bush—likewise for your exegesis of our symbolic roles.

[handwritten]
Sept 7, '63

A Telegram to my Fine Old Friend, LM

1. Have smacked my lips with gusto while reading your scrumptious, generous, copious letters from June to August. What a feast for me!

2. During that period I was harried by the obligation of writing a piece on "Human Nature in relation to its present Plight." This was a topic for *You,* & I often wished you were within reach. It went on for 40 pages before I realized that I was limited to $7\frac{1}{2}$ pages. This meant an intolerable series of amputations, which were uncompleted, & I ended with a botch at the symposium in Philadelphia.

3. Another Occasion in Philadelphia was a dinner of the colleagues & former students who contributed to that 70th birthday Festschrift. I decided to write a poem to each of them (with some plagiarisms from E.A. Robinson & others); but having never written a poem, I discovered that poetry does not start at 70, & fumbled round for words every evening for 3 weeks until I had 20 concoctions which I read at the dinner. Drink obscured the difference between poetry & jingles.

4. Also, I was occupied with a piece on Felix Frankfurter for a Festschrift to be presented to him on his 81st birthday.

5. Now I am engaged with "Dead to the World" (Subtitle: Herman Melville and Latter-Day Ishmaels) to be presented in Los Angeles on Oct 6th.[48] Then I turn to a book with relief.

---

48. Henry A. Murray, "Dead to the World: The Passions of Herman Melville," in *Essays in Self-Destruction,* ed. E. S. Shneidman (1967): 7–29; reprinted in Shneidman, *Endeavors in Psychology,* 498–517.

6. You said—as you always do—some apt & penetrating things—so true & devastating that my nerves tingled—in your Presidential address. Around us we see so much that is radically wrong, that it is hard to put one's finger on the tap-root of it all, & see the interconnections of the roots and branches. You have omitted nothing, but maybe something remains to be done down at the roots of all this internal, frantic, economic racket: outer *vs.* inner; material possessions *vs.* worth of character as goal and basis of prestige; things *vs.* persons; everything money can buy *vs.* what no money can buy; quantity *vs.* quality; Bigness *vs.* Smallness; speed by clock-time *vs.* pace by organic time; superficiality *vs.* depth; perpetual motility and change *vs.* steadfastness; instrumental technics *vs.* humane ends; utility *vs.* beauty; short time perspective *vs.* long time perspective; egotistic greed *vs.* generous sharing—objective facts and acts *vs.* subjective states of feeling—there is no end to these dichotomies. What is at the core of it all and why? Do we come back to Henry Adams: adoration of the productions and dimensions of physical science— the power of things vs. adoration of a personified superpersonal ideal—the power of creative love (the *largest quantity* of outer energy *vs.* the *best quality* of inner energy.*) More later. Salvos to you & Sophy—

Harry

*What was meant to be a clock-time telegram turned into the beginning of an organic-time dissertation. When are you off to Wesleyan? I must come there for a private session.

[handwritten]
35 Home Avenue
Middletown, Conn.
14 Nov 1963

. . . . Your September 'telegram' has long been waiting for an answer, dear Harry: but my dreams of doing so in person, by a dash up to Cambridge, have dissolved under the harsh sunlight of reality: sundry duties, including the damned Academy, in New York, interruptions that include a conference held by the Conservation Foundation, next week, and will keep bobbing up till 6 December when I am scheduled to give a memorial tribute to Van Wyck, at our usual annual meeting, when we pay our respects to the dead—including, of course, Robert Frost. My time here has been too tattered for me to do any serious writing on my book: but to make up for that I've done a great deal of reading in fields I've had to cultivate more thoroughly in order to round out my thesis on the origins of modern technology: This saturation in books not available at Amenia would alone justify the move here, quite apart from my sometimes stimulating contacts with my colleagues, including a physicist, Peterson, who was Bohr's secretary. But in all my excitement of my new flood of ideas and hypotheses—prehistory is alas! doomed to be largely hypothesis, since some of the functions of even the artifacts can only be guessed at—I have pushed myself a little too hard; and as usual my heart has protested by becoming rapid & irregular, leaving me tired and depressed. But a medical checkup the other day, a quite thorough one by a young doctor who applied all sorts of new tricks of diagnosis, showed that I was still organically sound, with a normal cardiogram that broke only at a few skipt beats. The tablets he gave me to slow me down have already begun to work: and I have aided the cure by cancelling nine lectures I was supposed to give next spring. Last night I gave my last lecture—my first public one here—to an audience that endured an hour and a half's effort to condense a whole course (my new book) into one little pellet. A foolish attempt: but they responded kindly. . . . We have two guest rooms here, for you to choose to sleep in, if only you'll drop in. We'll be here till the end of January.

Warmly

Lewis

P.S. When may I read your paper on The Nature of Man?

N.B. I've almost decided to review Jung's memories for The New Yorker: I've just read that tantalizing book for the second time.

1964–1981

Faithful Friends Renewing

DURING THE FINAL DECADE AND A HALF of the correspondence, Mumford completed his last major work, *The Myth of the Machine: I. Technics and Human Development* (1967) and *II. The Pentagon of Power* (1970). As always, Mumford solicited his friend's ideas and advice as he was writing the volumes, and Murray responded to the published works with high praise. As he prepared his autobiography, *Sketches from Life* (1982), Mumford reread many of his letters from earlier years, including those he had written to Murray and Christiana Morgan, which Murray had returned to him. One might view this final stage of the correspondence as something of an epistolary peroration, for both men sought to reaffirm and memorialize their friendship. The two friends discussed the vicissitudes of their relationship, caused by various factors including physical separation, absorption in their work, and temperamental as well as intellectual differences. The letters detail physical deterioration and other challenges of aging. Mumford wrote several sensitive, comforting letters as Murray suffered the grief of Christiana Morgan's death by drowning in 1967. Responding to the first of these, Murray wrote, "In the whole history of human communications, of affectionate friendships, there has never been a letter, I am sure, such as the one you wrote to me" (HAM 26 March 1967). These letters, exchanged in March–April 1967 as well as those of June 1976, eloquently document the enduring strength of the "old friendship." Mumford twice cites the refrain from one of his favorite poems, Richard Edwardes's "Amantium Irae": "The falling out of faithful friends renewing is of love." Mumford also wrote moving letters of sympathy and encouragement as Murray and his second wife Nina (Caroline Fish Murray) coped with Murray's serious stroke in 1978.

[handwritten]
Amenia, New York
28 November 1964

. . . . This week, dear Harry, has past almost too quickly for words: or I should have written before this to tell you how refreshed I was by our talks together, which were in effect merely carried further by the stimulating Daedalus conference. That conference convinced me that the Symposium will be lacking its very keystone unless you contribute a paper emphasizing the positive existential aspect of utopian thought and feeling. (Forgive me for using that nauseating academic slang!) I have already said this to Grabard: and if he has in turn said it to you I trust that you'll heed him! . . . Sophy's low grade infection has been helpt by sulpha nose drops & her sinuses have cleared up, too. So except for four days of boredom she was none the worse for my going. . . . Now I have to finish my damned Encyclopedia article![1]

Affectionate greetings
Lewis

P.S. I marvel how well Christiana has survived the ordeal of this last year, both physically & spiritually. Not a murmur of complaint from her. . . . Strangely, almost while we were talking about her, my Catherine was killed by an accidental fall while on a lonely walk. She was found face down, in the position she always slept in.

[handwritten]
22 Francis Avenue
Cambridge 38
Massachusetts
Feb 23
[LM Mar 22]

Great Lewis, horn of plenty—of generosity & lots of other things. Perhaps Christiana intimated that my life was at a very low ebb—senescent mental paralysis, or pervasive fatigue and staleness, with 10 half-finished books in my files—and this accounts for your extravagant, exhilarating and medicinal letter, with such praise that no one but you can pour forth with tact and eloquence.[2] It is cheering to be told

---

1. Mumford here was perhaps referring to "City: Forms and Functions," *International Encyclopedia of the Social Sciences* (1968): 447–55.

2. Mumford to Christiana Morgan, 31 January 1965: "I've just finished Harry's quite marvellous, indeed magical, exposition of 'Bartleby & I,' which came this morning, and since I might embarrass Harry by my unstinted praise I've chosen to heap it rather on your lap, so that it may reach him, not exactly diluted, but tempered and reduced to body heat by you. As a psychological-literary analysis, it is diabolically penetrating, on a par with his exposition of Pierre: but it has, in addition, a kind of effortless incisiveness, like that of a skilled swordsman, that puts it at the very peak of his own work—and of all Melville literary criticism at the same time. I'm old enough to recognize a masterpiece when I see one, and this is Harry's masterpiece. He no longer dare, as the silent Dean of Melville biographers, to say, 'I

that anything I could put together during this so-dismal year could please you at all, & I am very grateful for the manna I received from you. But that Bartleby piece was inept in several respects, and did not deserve your glowing celebration of it. Never mind, I was nonetheless encouraged and now I must set about a radical re-construction of my way of life and of my expectations in regard to rates of produc-tivity, etc., etc. C and I are about to take flight for a quiet, solitary beach on St. Johns Island via St. Thomas, to return on March 15th. Any chance our seeing you & Sophy before you take off? I have forgotten the details of your plans, exactly when you leave & when you return. When I return to Cambridge all my things from our cozy old workshop will have been moved to the top (15th) floor of the new, hermetically-sealed, air-conditioned William James Building—which will inaugurate an era of more intense & unleavened mechanistic, technocratic Scientism, with Man as the forgotten subject of concern. My disentanglement from all that is timely. Perhaps after March 15 you will give me good news of your writing to cheer me up. In the meanwhile hug Sophy for me & enjoy the sparkling snow—

> Gratefully
> Harry

> [handwritten]
> 22 Francis Avenue
> Cambridge 38
> Massachusetts
> Preparatory greetings to you
> divinities!
> Sept 17

Dear Lewis,

Glad to hear from you, to hear that you are both well, you wrestling with your great work that is going to disprove some worn-out theories about the killer in human nature. ???

I have to be in Washington on Tuesday, Oct 4 for a few days, & may not disturb you until the following week. I would like to propose that you & Sophy take a little constitutional walk, & sample Sarah's cooking, leave early, & sleep soundly, every week—just for a change.

In preparation for the Melville-Hawthorne meeting (great success for most of the 200 people) C and I have been delving into Hawthorne. We can't say that he has an irresistible attraction for us, but by peering into his own heart he made some precocious discoveries about the serpent of egotism and unconscious motivations, etc., etc. He put a thin coating of Christian candy & genteel fastidiousness around

---

prefer not to.' *He's done it!* Melville's life is all there in a nutshell. What a man!—Harry I mean, not Her-man."

the macabre core of most of his stories, which even now convince readers that he has a redeeming message for mankind.

Think no more about my disc; after a little venturesome ramble it decided that every part of a system should accept its appointed station & abide by it. An entire summer of no exercise, however, has left me repulsively sluggish and infirm. In the meanwhile, Mammon continues on its all-infiltrating-and-defiling, ugly and triumphant course. Ah, Beauty, what feud is this—

Hugs to you both—
Harry

[handwritten]
[LM] Ans 4 October 66

WELCOME.

Tried to reach you through Leverett House Secretary & Cambridge Information.[3] The god who establishes exclusive barriers and insures privacy is named *Na* (nay). He is a beneficent force in your life most of the time, but . . . What a fine chapter you have written about the cross purposes in your relationship with Patrick Geddes![4] I have never met an American who was so intent on exploiting the admiration, energies, & genius of a younger man. Freud was propelled by a comparable need for faithful disciples. How well you portrayed it all—Geddes's obliviousness of your own center of creativeness! The paragraph you quoted showing that Geddes was aware of self-centeredness in thinkers like himself was telling. The question is whether *all* thinkers *have* to maintain isolated solar systems of their own and keep intercommunications at a minimum. What would have happened if you had been open and candid with Geddes at the start? Could he have taken it if you had held the mirror of your own center up to his? Maybe we overestimate the narcistic sensitiveness of others and underestimate their capacity for self-criticism and reconstruction. Anyhow that was a subtle, deft, and beautifully written piece of yours. I am off to Washington & will try to reach you at my first opportunity—

Hugs for you both
Harry

3. Leverett House: a residence house at Harvard University that has lodged distinguished guests; the top floors of Leverett Towers offer fine views of Boston.

4. Lewis Mumford, "The Disciple's Rebellion: A Memoir of Patrick Geddes," *Encounter* 27 (September 1966): 11–21.

[handwritten]
F-110 Leverett House
29 December 1966

. . . . Sophia phoned you, dear Harry, the day before we left for Brooklyn, to invite you here for dinner when we came back. Since we returned with a pair of depressing colds, it is just as well that we didn't fix a date. These holiday jaunts, so full of fond expectations, too often turn into a nightmare. But we hope to recover in good time for closing the long gap of silence between our households. By working furiously on the Index for a week, in order to get it done before Christmas—a happy precaution it turned out!—we have finally put the book to bed. What happens hereafter is in the hands of the gods—and the reviewers, from neither of whom do I expect too much. The last three months have simply flown for us; and the next one, I fear, will fly even faster. Then Amenia, and back to work on Vol. II. But thanks to this perfect apartment and its constantly changing vistas of river and sky, we've never enjoyed this city, indeed any city, more. What great luck it was to be invited here!

Christiana tells us of your plan for gathering your papers and essays into two or more books. A happy idea: indeed you should have done it long ago, if only to have made your thought more accessible, and so more widely influential. We both join in affectionate good wishes for your health and work during the coming year. And may the dry branch of our friendship again bear flowers, as of old!

Lewis

[handwritten]
22 Francis Avenue
Cambridge 38
Massachusetts
Jan 2
[LM] 5 Jan 67

Dear Lewis,

Hail to Sophy for her first and last greeting of 1966 which I happily received before the commercial turmoil of Christmas. May 1967 bring you no more colds but much warmth from the god of chance, and gratifying feedbacks, ample and brimming over, from the reviewers as surplus payments for the long months of parental concern you have devoted to the shaping and delivery of your million-year story of man! A long sentence—prophetic, I trust, of the long procession of rewards and honors you will receive after your first and then your second volume is presented to the public.

For the next two weeks—to my misfortune—I am wholly occupied in trying to write something for the Festschrift in honor of an old classmate—something which in my prime might have taken me a month—you know I write at the rate of one page to your ten—but now, with fading energies, I must somehow put together in a fortnight, or a little longer, to meet the deadline. It seems that our cycles of work and rest are not at all in step. I go to Lev. House on Wednesdays only when my disc allows me to walk there without crouching.

Assuming you have a little time on your hands, I may, in the meanwhile, send you a couple of inconsequential bits, one of which is a professional autobiography (not the real thing)—to break my silence.[5]

On your part, since you prefer writing to talking, you might give me your version, if you dare, of why the branch of our friendship is as dry as you say it is.

Cheers

Harry

[handwritten]
F-110 Leverett
5 January 1967

. . . . As it turns out, dear Harry, we are both under 'house arrest.' I spent six whole days in bed with one of those devastating viral infections that still goes by the name of 'cold': actually a longer period than I've ever been confined to bed in *all* my life—or at least since I had measles at aet.6. And now I'm on my feet just in time to look after Sophy, who had vainly been fighting off a similar attack. A grim omen to start the New Year!—all the more because our last year was such a healthy and happy one.

But don't think you are alone in your literary struggles: it takes me twice the usual time and effort to approximate the same results. More than age, in the physical sense, is involved in this: one becomes more self-critical as one grows older, and one also sees more alternative modes of expression and wavers between them: likewise one begins to over-qualify one's thoughts and then becomes disgusted with the muddy results. I almost ruined a chapter I thought I was improving: but awoke just in time to restore the sharp original version.

As to our friendship, I don't think we'll hasten its fresh blossoming by pulling it up to see if a worm has been gnawing at the roots. Love has its seasons, and friendship, though steadier and more equable, may know winter & summer too. No rational analysis, nor mere act of will, even obvious good will, can alter this process. Fortunately we both have a treasure of good memories to sustain us.

Do send me your 'professional autobiography'—or any other papers you've done.

Bedside greetings from both of us

Lewis

---

5. Henry A. Murray, "The Case of Murr," in *A History of Psychology in Autobiography,* vol. 5, ed. E. G. Boring and G. Lindzey (1967): 285–310; reprinted in Shneidman, *Endeavors in Psychology,* 52–78.

[handwritten]
F-110 Leverett House
7 Jan. 1967

. . . . You couldn't have performed a friendlier service, dear Harry, than to send me over your papers so promptly.[6] After six days in bed I was relaxed, released from all concerns about my book; and my mind, if not my head, was clear, and open to fresh thoughts. I began reading before dinner, and an hour after my usual invalid's bed-time Sophia called out, just as I was finishing 'Narcissism Re-Exhibited,' "Do you realize what time it is?" In spite of our long discussions & intimate interchanges during the thirties much of the story of your intellectual life and your family background was new to me—and endlessly fascinating for what it told and what it implied. What a superb foundation for your intellectual development you reveal in the 'Scaffold' paper: and what a comment it is upon the academic mind that these massive qualifications should at first have operated as a handicap. I take with proper skepticism your picture of yourself as a 'poor' student: your swift accumulation of degrees disproves that. But, like Darwin, you weren't an *ordinary* student: and your picture of yourself confirms the doubts I've always had about current grading of a student's capabilities. The failure to take too seriously the academic routines often indicates that the mind was busy elsewhere, with what eventually turns out to be more important matters. The 'Narcissism' paper has other dimensions, equally significant. You've always seemed so completely on top of everything that it was a shock to realize what handicaps you faced and what slights endured: that over-zealous eye operation was an eye-opener. Likewise Conant's hostility, despite your meticulous scientific preparation. Yet your mind mightn't have ranged so widely if you had fallen into the usual professional groove, as surgeon or biochemist or teacher. So all's well that ends well! Your acute review of 'The Sins of the Father'—generous, perceptive, challengingly critical—is a model for such efforts, and it shows, in the face of your subjective anxieties about the aging process, not the slightest diminution of your powers. The beastly thing about senescence is that it prompts one to read into the normal ups and downs of health a sinister sign of a more permanent 'downness': and often—not always of course—that reading is false, though it may in time produce confirmatory symptoms. I wonder if the time hasn't come for you to dessert your scaffolding of synthesis, now almost a self-sustaining structure in its own right, and to perform or rather *embody* your synthesis in a large, free portrait, more than a mere biography, of Melville and Hawthorne: the task for which your whole life has been a preparation. The part of your thought that can't be classified or categorized—perhaps the most

6. The papers Murray sent obviously included his "Preparations for the Scaffold of a Comprehensive System"; "Narcism Re-exhibited," the original title of "The Case of Murr" (in Shneidman, *Endeavors in Psychology,* 52–78); "The Freudian Hawthorne," review of Frederick C. Crews, *The Sins of the Fathers: Hawthorne's Psychological Themes, The American Scholar* 36 (Spring 1967): 308–12.

important part—would come out in this manner. Possibly your inward blockage at present is due to the fact that the tasks you've accepted, apart from these autobiographic accounts, which are precious, have prevented you from approaching this other goal, though in the end this act of free creation may in fact put the capstone of viable reality on your more systematic thought.

These papers will be simmering inside me for a long while yet: this is just the first boiling over of the pot. I speak both as a friend and a 'fellow-traveler,' knowing, even while I whistle cheerfully, that night is falling and no inn is in sight.

> In old friendship
> Lewis
>
> [handwritten]
> 22 Francis Avenue
> Cambridge 38
> Massachusetts
> Sat, Mar 18 '67

Beloved Sophy and Lewis,

I have just returned from the Caribbean, and if I had control of my voice I would be telephoning you, at this my first opportunity, to let you know that at noon on Thursday, my darling, my soul's joy—who loved you both so dearly—was drowned in shallow water on the coral beach of the Denis Bay Plantation, island of St. John. We had three beatific weeks together, despite a few minor bodily frailties, first on remote Anguila island, and then staying, as we have many times before, at a friend's guest house, fifty feet from the sea on the north coast of St. John. Next to our Tower on the tidal river at Newbury, this spot enchanted Christiana (who lived for beauty) more than any in the world. It happened that Monday, March 13, marked a high point in our year: my back was almost well and Christiana, suntanned as a Polynesian, seemed to be at her peak of healthfulness and radiance and both of us were looking forward to being married, for comfort's sake, with the blooming of the flame azaleas in the spring. Next day our host left us in sole possession of the beach, and I—maybe for the first time in my life—lay down for a morning nap. When I arose twenty minutes later, I went out on the beach and was stunned by the ultimately dreaded and appalling sight. Dr. Decker, who has faithfully cared for her since that radical operation on the nerve supplies to her arteries in 1943, believes that she had one of her recurrent fainting attacks, but this time fell under water and was immediately deprived of oxygen & drowned. I lifted her out of only a foot and a half of water, and tried mouth-to-mouth resuscitation for $1\frac{1}{2}$ hours, but not a flicker of consciousness returned. I am telling you all this because she loved you, & you—*both* of you *especially*—will understand my utter desolation, too deep to be reached by words. Maybe later you will let me talk with you.

> Affectionately
> Harry

[handwritten]
Amenia, New York
21 March 1967

. . . . Your letter came this morning beloved and bereft friend; and I am answering it
even before Sophia comes back from a visit to Alison, though only her woman's
arms, embracing you, and her woman's tears, could convey to you what is in my
heart. My first concern is for you: the incredible shock: the effort at resuscitation:
the emptiness and desolation of the days that followed and of the days that are still
to come. There is no way of softening this terrible blow: even at a distance it is difficult to bear, and nothing anyone else can say to you or do for you will lift the burden of your days, you who have lived as a brother with Melville need no reminder
of this. You will need all your immense vitality, all your well-earned knowledge, to
offset this blow; and when you find this lacking, come to us, draw upon us, even
though we share your grief and know that our own energies are fading, too. Just
yesterday, going through an ancient file of letters, about Alice, I came upon a magnificent letter from you in which you made just such an offer to me. And I can only
say, in the same spirit, 'If you need me, I am your man.'

I have said nothing about Christiana, for it is the living, not the dead, who need
consolation. Yet the description you've given of your last weeks together makes me
feel that—apart from the effects of her sudden departure upon you, she might have
felt that this was the perfect ending of the life you shared together—herself in good
health, aglow with the beauty of nature, united not only in the memory of your past
life but in anticipation of the formal acknowledgment of its deep reality. What more
at that moment could life offer her? If she had been given a choice she might with
open eyes have gladly accepted this swift, probably unconscious ending, at the ultimate point in your relationship, rather than the sad slow weakening of vital
power which would have mocked the passionate reality of your old life together. In
this sense, the fates were good to her, though harsh to you. What I say about Christiana, in honesty, does not apply to you: so I minimize nothing. Yet both of us by
now know enough about the oncomings of old age to realize that for most people
Browning's line, "The best is yet to be," is more false than true: even in good health
those words become more and more ironic. Something worse could have happened
to Christiana than her own death: far worse. And that is your death, *whilst* she lingered on. Against that agonizing possibility life protected her; and for her sake, that
should be a consolation to you. Often Sophia has said to me, almost pleadingly: 'I
want to die before you do. Don't leave me alone.' And I find myself, while dreading
the thought of parting for either of us, dreading even more the kind of parting that
takes place by slow degrees, even when living together, when now this organ &
now that fails to function and even the memory of high energies and passionate
embraces, becomes ever fainter—or what is worse, remains as a bitter and ironic reminder of one's present condition. Of all the possible openings for death, my

beloved Harry, it seems to me that your high-spirited Christiana took the best: the one that beautifully expressed her whole style of life and preserved intact the treasure you shared, before the moths and the rust corrupted it.

. . . . And now you must face your loneliness and your grief, unrelieved by the fact that we who loved you both, and love you now more than ever, likewise must face it in our own fashion. As you know, there are no remedies for this state except to go on living, with all the courage and resolution you can summon. You still have much unfinished work to do, and Christiana will still be at your side, now more than ever, while you are doing it. . . . Give me your hand, and let Sophia embrace you!

In old friendship
Lewis

[handwritten]
22 Francis Avenue
Cambridge 38
Massachusetts
[LM] 22 March 67

Dear Old Fellow,

From the days when we reached our peak of joy, beyond what we had ever imagined life could be for a man and woman, we began to think occasionally of death, and more recently of funeral rites, and so forth. We agreed that we wanted our ashes scattered, at a certain spot, with an inconspicuous slate tablet (Here were strewn the ashes of. . . .) to mark the place; and also that we would like to have a few of our favorite passages read, and possibly others—but no minister, no references to the God, etc., of Christianity, greenery, music, and a few kith and kin. We thought of this vaguely as occurring at the Tower—informally, outdoors and indoors. We both thought of you as the chief reader, with possibly two or three others. We have quite a collection from which to choose a variety of appropriate passages, as they stand or revised.

Now, I remember your saying that you might be going abroad this spring, and, if so, you would not be within range between mid-May and mid-June; and also, if you were within reach, you might not be disposed to honor Christiana in this *particular* way. This is the reason for my writing so soon—to fix an approximate date, to correspond to the blooming of the azaleas, dogwood, lilacs, rhododendrons, or mountain laurel. I am thinking of getting a special tree planted that will be blossoming on the appointed day, and much else. I am trying to approach Christiana's vision of the ideal, and you were her first—in fact her only—choice, except me, and my powers of control may not be dependable. Let me know at your convenience. Love to you two greats.

Harry

[handwritten]
Amenia, New York
22 March 1967

. . . . I intended to write you again today, dearest Harry: so your letter only adds another theme. How parallel our ways have gone, for all our differences in background, training, and experience! Sophia and I have been slowly assembling our thoughts about the great transition, sharing with you and Christiana an unwillingness to accept the stereotyped forms, and feeling that some more fitting ritual must somehow be invented . . . yet never quite certain about what that was to consist of, or where it was to be. We learned something about it from the ceremony I improvised for Sophia's father. The family assembled at the spot where he used to sit at the end of the alley, looking out over the hills, and as house-father I read the famous passage from Ecclesiasticus—'Let us now praise famous men,' a passage that happily terminated in praise for those who, though worthy, remained unknown. We had prepared, on the site of the bench he used to sit on, a grave just large enough to receive the metal urn of his ashes; and the ceremony was completed by each member of the family coming forward and throwing a handful of earth upon the spot. The ceremony was brief: but the act of participation moved each member of the family, even the crassest ones; and they walked slowly back through the alley, choked with tears, feeling ennobled and fulfilled.

I tell you about this, dear Harry, not because this is different from what you have planned for Christiana, but for a quite different reason. To my surprise I found that there was something *uncanny* about even handling the 'urn.' The ashes are not ashes, but an almost unbearably living presence, even in their container. And I realized then and there that the actual scattering of Sophia's ashes, as I too had planned, would be impossible for me. These are not the embers from an ordinary fire: too much life is still left in them! This part of the ceremony, if we are alike in this respect, too, you might find even more difficult to carry through than the spoken word. But the traditional rite of throwing earth on the spot, with others following your example, would bind you and Christiana together by something deeper than words. So much for my own experience.

Nothing would mean more to me than joining you on this solemn and beautiful occasion: blessed in prospect by Christiana herself. I could not be sure that my voice would be under better control than yours: Sophia will tell you how often I burst into helpless tears when I read her some passage about human heroism, devotion, or gallantry: and the sense of Christiana's own special devotion and gallantry which I have always carried around with me has been intensified by your picture of those last days you had together: so sunny and exalted. This of course would not keep me (us) from being present in silence, but for one mischievous and I fear irremediable event: during the week of your agony I accepted an invitation to receive a special doctorate from the University of Rome: and we are scheduled to sail on whatever ship will give us accommodations between the end of April and mid-May. To be away from you both at that time will be a real trial: but I fear it will be impossible to back out, since I said 'Yes' and the wheels over there are already in motion. How hard it is to say this, and how many times harder it will to be thousands of miles away from you at that time! May all your good memories carry you through that day, and give you peace—even though it's the peace of resignation. May you become pregnant with the seed she has left in you!

Lewis

[handwritten, LMC]
22 Francis Avenue
Cambridge 38
Massachusetts
Mar 26 67 [LM] 28 Mar 67

Beloved Lewis (Embrace the beloved Sophia with my thankfulness)

In the whole history of human communications, of affectionate friendships, there has never been a letter, I am sure, such as the one you wrote to me: so close to the pith of another's abysmal feeling state, so close to the utterance of the unutterable, so profoundly wise and warm and all-embracing, so right, so perfect. I keep re-reading it, and will re-read it periodically to the end of my days, inevitably with tears, coupled with gratitude for the abundant life that was vouchsafed the two of us, despite everything, and for having had such accepting, nourishing, and noble friends as you and Sophy. To love Christiana for a few years would have provided me with my brimful share of life. But to have been *in love* with her every day for more than forty years within a discipline which we shaped to suit us—*that* amounted to an ever over-brimming goblet of joyous life which was far beyond my just deserts. Before her radical surgery in 1943, C was told that she had 2 more years to live at most; but, as her doctor told me yesterday, she stood up better than any other patients who were subjected to that procedure. And so our thankfulness was immense, though bounded by premonitions, of course—a series of diverse, scarcely discernible, little hints in the last week that (despite the surface glow of health) her energies were running out, to end a year too early maybe, but otherwise exactly as she would have chosen—at the verge of the sea amid all that beauty, with me alone to find and bless her. This is precisely what you said in your wondrously knowledgeable letter which I am taking the liberty to show to Josephine and Counce for their comfort and inspiration.[7] In your second letter you don't mention the date of your return from your triumph at Rome and from this I infer that you would rather not take part in any ceremony at the Tower—in late June, for example,

---

7. Josephine: Murray's daughter; Counce: Councilman Morgan, Christiana's son.

amid the mountain laurel. I can readily understand this. What good you have done me, great man!

Yours forever
Harry

P.S. Darling Sophy, What a love you were to write me separately, with such consoling words! I felt your hand in mine & linked with you in spirit at this dark hour.

Gratefully
Harry

[handwritten]
Amenia, New York
28 March 1967

. . . . Whenever I remember, dear Harry, with bitter self-reproach, how often in a crisis I have failed those I loved & wanted to help I shall turn to your last letter to restore the balance. Such occasions as these are a sort of dress rehearsal for the Last Judgment—and they tempt one to revise the whole plot of one's life, in order to give the last act a different ending. If that has been happening to you this last week it has been happening to me, too, by a sympathetic coincidence, not brought on by your ordeal but intensified by it. With me it means deciding how much of my closely noted personal life can or should be opened to public inspection. The decisions I must make would be easier were it not imperative to consider the effect upon Sophia and Alison; and Thompson's life of Frost doesn't make it easier for me to trust even the most painstaking of biographers.[8] Next winter, I hope, we shall find it possible to discuss the problems: though, as always in tidying up my affairs before a long absence, I must make some of these decisions before we leave.

Now as to our coming back. The only reason I didn't mention this was because the dates you gave were in May or June. Much as I would like to be at your side, dearest Harry, at that moment, I would have to cut short our trip by a whole month; and that would mean leaving many tasks in preparation for Vol. II undone, and many old and dear friends, whom we might never see again if we put off this meeting, unvisited. Sophia and I both reluctantly realize that our horizon has begun to shrink, and that we dare not turn our back to opportunities that may never come again. It was this thought that made us regard the honor in Rome as a providential decision—to end our debate over the European journey, and to redeem the last three months we have wasted in illness and exhaustion.

What a consolation you must find, after the surgeon's dire prediction, in the long reprieve Christiana enjoyed after her operation: the gift of so many extra years

---

8. Lawrance Thompson, *Robert Frost: The Early Years* (1966), a candid, unflattering account of the poet's life.

together. This is no vain consolation, though it does not abate one's grief or repair one's loss.

Forgive me for referring earlier to my own troubled & harried days, dear friend: They bear no comparison to your burden; and in a way I welcome them, for they bring us closer together.

> With affectionate sympathy
> Lewis

P.S. I know how impossible it is to talk: so I refrain from phoning.

> [handwritten]
> 22 Francis Avenue
> Cambridge 38
> Massachusetts
> April 1, '67
> [LM] 26 Apr

Dear Lewis,

Your great creation arrived yesterday with its heart-warming inscription.[9] Your two unparalleled and unforgettable letters to me must have pretty nearly coincided with its birth at the publishers—a fact which increases my wonder at your immense resources and powers.

The book is a handsome object with a sturdy forthright physique—no nonsense about it—with striking titles and sub-titles to keep the reader in line with your thought, and, as usual, stunning illustrations with accompanying expositions which are extraordinarily informative and compact. They bring much to light to an inveterate visualizer. Dipping into the text here and there, re-reading a few previously published passages and a score of others, I was happy to be assured that your zest, vigor, vividness, and eloquence is as remarkable as it ever has been—maybe more remarkable. What an accomplishment on your 22nd volume! (In collecting Christiana's papers, I chanced to open on a page of her diary which was entirely devoted to expressions of admiration of your spirit, confidence, courage, and felicity of style. I did not note what book she was talking about; but she and I agreed that these qualities are excitingly present in all your writings.)

We have so many basic values in common, and we agree—in a general way at least—on so many issues, large and small, that I have never been satisfied with our inability or disinclination to explore our differences. I am eager to resolve our differences, since my respect for your opinions is so high; and if we cannot resolve them, to discover what central dispositions in each of us are acting as impediments. Of course, we can decide that we aren't up to it: our self-love naturally craves agreement, recognition, and praise, and, if we stick to that level, we will avoid the possibility of hurts and wounds, and consequent resentments and coolness. This

---

9. Lewis Mumford, *The Myth of the Machine: I. Technics and Human Development* (1967).

seems to be where we are now and may be the course of wisdom, and I shall reluctantly abide by it. But to repeat what I have often said before: criticism is my meat, because I can grow from it, and if it comes from you it doesn't hurt in the least because I rely on your good-will and my good-will toward you is boundless.

I say all this because I have a premonition—from the little that I have read so far—that we have a totally different conception of myth. I may find as I read your tremendous panorama of human development that you have made your meaning of the word clear, in which case I can compare it to my meaning which I did not quite succeed in defining in "The possible nature of a mythology to come," and translate one into the other.[10] It may turn out that our talking a different language, in this respect, is irrelevant to the main thesis—with which I am wholly at one with you. The megamachine is the Devil's method of destroying man's soul. I wonder whether he realizes what a formidable antagonist he has in you. Also with unabated love,

> gratefully
> Harry

[handwritten]
Amenia, New York
4 April 1967

. . . . Our friendship began, dear Harry, with your generous sharing of your knowledge of the Gansevoort papers & was sealed by your over-generous response to my Melville study. Going through my notes of the last forty years—notes never included in my published work—I am repeatedly reminded of your intellectual companionship and personal understanding, with stimulating ideas and helpful admonitions at the right moments, and repeatedly. That our thoughts haven't fused into a Siamese-twin unity is our good luck, not our misfortune; and, such is the nature of organic individuality, there will always be difference, I suppose, which no amount of earnest discussion will ever completely bridge. As for the conception of 'myth' the major difference between us, perhaps, is that, without violating any of its vague traditional usages, each of us is referring to a different area of experience—though doubtless there are points where our respective boundaries overlap. 'Myth' I use partly in the traditional sense, as in my chapter on Language in relation to Max Müller—'myth is the disease of language'—and partly in Fouilée's sociological sense, as an 'idee-force,' in either case largely spontaneous and unshaped by rational criteria until a very late stage.[11] But we'd better put off

---

10. Henry A. Murray, "The Possible Nature of a 'Mythology' to Come," in Murray, ed., *Myth and Mythmaking* (1960).

11. Friedrich Max Müller, *Lectures on the Science of Thought*, 2 vols. (1862–65); Alfred Fouilée, *Morale des Idées Forces* (1908).

any further talk until you've had time to take in the entire picture. I've tried here to hold fast to conventional usages: but a word like 'myth' with such a long history, is hard to pin down—or get away from!

In getting my papers in order, separating very private from public documents, and sorting through files of old letters, I've been keenly aware of Christiana's friendship, too: vivid & quick, even though distant. It's been a consolation to feel her so near, precisely at this moment. What a generous giver of sympathy & understanding she was—what a gallant soul! . . .

Don't let the reading of my book hang over you, dear Harry, as a 'duty.' Put it aside until it really tempts you to explore it. With a warm embrace

As ever
Lewis

[handwritten]
22 Francis Avenue
Cambridge 38
Massachusetts
Apr 22 '67
[LM] 26 Apr 67

Dear Lewis,

On the eve of your departure, let me wish you and the goddess Sophia a happy, fruitful voyage, free from interferences by invading viruses or any accidents of fortune, and a triumphant celebration in Rome, not as a killer of old, but as a creator whose conquered territory is in the domain of human understanding and whose bound slaves are autonomous disciples in many lands.

Also, I would like to transmit a few off-the-cuff impressions I have gained on my travels through the first 200 pages or so of your momentous book. First of all it is unique in its imaginative reconstructions of pre-history and early history, as if written by an intuitive eye-witness and judge of people's actions in those days (as put in one of the favorite poems of your youth, 'I am a part of all that I have met . . . '). It reads, in many of its most vivid and enlightening passages, like a great allegorical epic, or morality play, of man's evolutionary career down the ages—exciting and dramatic. I go along with you readily, since your enemies—tyrants, megamachines of all sorts—are my enemies, and your friends—the neolithic villages for one—are my friends. Your judgments of the past are illumined and strengthened by your numerous analogues to current conditions—apt and convincing—and I predict that your book will be very influential as time goes on. I would be more inclined to put more emphasis on increasing Bigness, the formation of ever-larger and hence impersonal social units, and the necessity—if the once-rivalrous and combative, component units are to be co-ordinated—of having a much greater centralization of power. How few people in the history of the world have been capable of exercising the necessary power without being corrupted!

What is disheartening to me is the veneration of Power down the ages by the world at large. As Otto has shown the original idea of the Holy is Power, Omnipotence, not goodness—and when it came to the creation of a God to accord with the heart's desire of a disinherited people, we get Jahweh, fashioned in the image of an Oriental despot.[12] Today—when reverence is at its lowest ebb—the USA is fast becoming a breeding ground of young emancipated criminals—freedom *ad absurdum.* You are eloquent in denouncing the preposterous pretensions of the Egyptian-King (eternal life, the power of flight, etc.); but, since only the fantasies of Kings were recorded, we know nothing of the dreams of the proletariat in those days. Two or three thousand years later it was precisely the (repentant) proletariat who were offered eternal life; and it was a carpenter's son who ascended into heaven by flight (as the Egyptian Pharaoh did in his boat along the Milky Way). It was not the famous Daedalus, by the way, who fell to his death but his over-aspiring little son (p 204). I guess I am arguing here that an addiction to grandiose or murderous fantasies were always, as they are now, pretty well distributed throughout the population; but in early times only the fantasies of kings were recorded and only kings of large social units were in a position to put them into practice. In short, only the criminality of leaders is visible in ancient history. Very probably they discovered that the only way to unite the masses was to direct *their* criminality toward an outside enemy.

I very much agree with your emphasis on imagination—fantasy, mythology, etc.—and play, games, and ritual, as precursors in the human race, as they are in childhood, of rationality and technical effectiveness. But maybe in pointing out that the enlargement of the brain with its potentialities for concept-formation and language, etc., preceded tool-making, you are making an unwarranted distinction between brain and hand, as if it were *not* the brain (but the hand) that invented tools & weapons. Once tools and weapons, with their accompanying rationality, were developed, they were more directly serviceable in the struggle for existence, vis-à-vis Nature, animals, and human enemies—than wildly irrational myths and horrendous religious rites. Today I see Greed, the lust for material possessions and success, etc.—sacrosanct business prosperity—as the greatest of enemies. How in this rage can beauty and the good life hold a plea?

Your book is a great inspiration, and a warning of the perils that confront us on all sides. Here I see over-population of people and of automobiles (as you do) at the root of a hundred apparently insoluble dilemmas. I hope 'The Myth of the Machine' will be very widely read by those who are in a position to apply appropriate remedies. I haven't seen any reviews yet, but I expect an enthusiastic chorus because it is a beautifully written, exciting testament—a 'must' for those who have the world's future at heart. Thanksgivings to you! I have still a good many pages to

12. Perhaps a reference to Walter Friedrich Otto, *The Homeric Gods: The Spiritual Significance of Greek Religion* (1954).

look forward to. And so farewell for a few months. You can relax, your book is a monument of wisdom. Love to you both—

Harry

[handwritten]
Amenia, New York
26 April 1967

. . . . We have only a fortnight left, dear Harry, before sailing. And now that your second letter has come before I've had an opportunity to answer your earlier one, I'd better utter a few words of gratitude before we're swamped in last-moment details. I appreciate your just & measured criticism of what you have so far read—all the more, no doubt, because 'Harcourt's' informs me that a quite different judgment will appear in next Sunday's Times Book Review.[13] (Though I told the dear people that I didn't want to look at reviews for six months, they insisted on telling me how scurrilous this one was! I should have timed my exit before publication! . . .) Some of the points you make you'll find answered in the later chapters: on one or two other matters you've overlooked the passages that show I am in agreement with your views. But no matter: there will still be much to discuss when we come together in the fall. What is valid in my thesis may not fully come to light for a whole generation: whereas the errors & slips, like 'Daedalus' for 'Icarus' (thank you!) will be visible & correctible almost at once. Despite all my care over the galleys I've already found half a dozen annoying busts, and more will doubtless come to light.

My time has been extra crowded because of my having spent a whole week preparing a statement for Senator Ribicoff's committee dealing with urban renewal; and I had to testify in person, under the glare of television lights, last Friday.[14] More of that, too, when we finally meet! I emerged with high respect for both Ribicoff & his immediate colleagues. If the rest of the Senate were of the same calibre we might all sleep more easily!

Have you chosen yet a day for the sad farewell rites? We both, even at a distance, would take comfort over being present, at least in our thoughts. May the air be fragrant and the day not too bright, lest the contrast between the outer and the inner scene be too painful.

Again, we both embrace you lovingly

Lewis

13. Edmund Carpenter, "Man, the Mind-Making Animal," review of *Technics and Human Development, New York Times Book Review,* 30 April 1967, 1.

14. On 21 April, Mumford testified before Senator Abraham Ribicoff's Subcommittee on Practical Reorganization in hearings on "Federal Role in Urban Affairs"; Mumford's testimony received national media attention; his formal statement was published as "A Brief History of Urban Frustration" in *The Urban Prospect* (1968).

[handwritten]
F-111 Leverett House
26 November 1967

. . . . The Memorial Leaflet came yesterday, dear Harry, and we are both grateful for it. Every part of it—the typography, the order of the rite, the expressions of Christiana's friends, the verses, and the marvellous final photography, symbolizing life & eternity—honors Christiana and beautifully expresses her spirit. She lives in those pages as she lives in our hearts, bearing witness to her gift for friendship, intimate understanding, and dedicated love. The fact that so much of Christiana remains in these pages is the only possible compensation for all that is gone. May this visible presence console you, dear Harry, as it does us—not by lessening your grief but by restoring her to life.

In old friendship
Lewis

[handwritten]
F-111 Leverett House
31 January 1968

. . . . You have been often in my thoughts this last year, dear Harry: but grief builds a protective wall about one, as I know from my own experience, and even a friend dare not penetrate it. All I want you to know is that you are not alone: if I stand outside, it is to wait for the moment when you will come forth into the daylight once more. The other day, glancing through 'Green Memories' I came upon a letter of Christiana's I had quoted, full of tender insight into the defiant spirit of youth. That brought you both very close again. I hope that many similar expressions of hers will rise up in your memory and console you, keeping you company through these dark February days. With an affectionate embrace

In old friendship
Lewis

[handwritten]
22 Francis Avenue
Sept 4, '68
[LM] 5 September

Dear Lewis, Old Friend,

Hope your head is pumping along as copiously and eloquently as it has for years, or, at least, as you can expect it to be pumping at your age under the miserable wide-world conditions in which we are inexorably involved—with no prospect for us here but two artificial, spuriously-grinning, shallow aspirants to steer our course for the next four years.[15]

I expected that I would be passing your way in the spring; but that plan had to be postponed until fall. When are you moving to Cambridge? Around Oct 1st I shall be leaving for Nohawkers, my solitary claustrum on the St. Lawrence River, for a fortnight. After that I shall be in Cambridge, steadily as I have been all summer, except for a short appearance in San Francisco over Labor Day.

I am sending you a copy of *Psychology Today*, with a report of an interview which shows how dull I have become these days—at least when not aroused by some inviting questions. Despite a score of mistakes and misquotations, it is better than I deserve from the Press.[16]

Your delightful narrative in the *New Yorker* of your European tour was cause of a little furor at the Jung Institute.[17] I haven't yet had a chance to read your book on the urban crisis, but will before I see you.[18] Affectionate hugs for you both—

Harry

[handwritten]
Amenia, New York
12501 5 September 1968

. . . . How wonderful, dear Harry, to get such a swift answer to the unsent letter I've been writing you all summer, and was just about actually to write during the few idle days Providence wisely allotted me this week, disguising that heavenly blessing as a mild attack of bronchitis. (The attack came three hours after I told Sophy: "I walked to the lake, had an exhilarating swim in the cold crystal water, and walked back again, feeling younger than I've felt in years!" But the gods were listening & promptly sent back their admonitory message, via my larynx: "Not so young as you'd like to think, Old Man!") But apart from this, or rather even *with* it, we've

---

15. "Pumping along" was a favorite expression of Murray and Christiana Morgan. Morgan wrote Mumford: "Little Hallee had breakfast with me every morning—an enchanting hour. Like all fond grandparents I have to repeat 'sayings.' One morning—after looking over some art books with her we came upon a picture of the crucifixion—'That's Jesus on the cross, Mum, with the 2 bad men on either side of him.' Pause—'Shame that they had to kill him. If they hadn't he might be pumping along with us here, right now.' Harry and I have incorporated this expression with delight. Harry is at present 'pumping along' with his chapter for a book which is to incorporate the statements by various psychologists on their theory" (2 September 1955).

16. Mary Harrington Hall, "Interview with Henry A. Murray," *Psychology Today* 2 (September 1968): 56–63.

17. Lewis Mumford, "Reflections: European Diary," *New Yorker*, 6 July 1968, 30–43. Mumford describes his lecturing on Jung at Küsnacht, Jung's residence near Zurich. He mentions Jung's "ambivalent attitude toword the Nazi movement . . . and his equally ambivalent attitude toward the Jews"; he also discusses the "unresolved questions" in Jung's relationship with Antonia Wolff (37–38).

18. Lewis Mumford, *The Urban Prospect* (1968), a collection of previously published essays.

had—do I dare provoke the gods again?—an unusually rewarding five months here: a tropical spring, bursting with flowers and lush foliage—nettles seven feet high, blackcap bushes turning into vines fifteen feet long, hollyhocks ten feet high!—and for most of the summer the beauty remained, so satisfactory, now that all our planting has taken shape, that we hardly budged from our home acre, lest we miss this or that lovely change. Even the vegetable garden was better than usual, all but the peas; and as for zucchini, we could feed a whole Italian village. But of course all this personal felicity, including a happy month with our grand-children & Alison, was spoiled, whenever we raised our eyes from our own soil, by the state of the world: that ugly fly—no, that stink bug!—in everyone's ointment, spoiling its perfume. We are all Czecho-Slovaks now, in a planetary concentration camp, and I have to turn to Viktor Franck's account of his experience under such pressures to recover enough courage to go on with my book.[19] I can't recall another period of history when violence and madness assumed such pandemic propor-tions: can you? . . . Still, I've gone on with the re-writing of Vol. II, sometimes at a trot, sometimes at a gallop, and am now within three chapters of the end—though at least six months more of work will be necessary before I dare show the work to my publishers. Already the book is so much richer, fuller, deeper than the original draft that I am glad I didn't publish it as a single, only half-baked volume. What-ever the defects that remain, I've managed at least to pose some fresh problems and to state them clearly, though it may take a century or two to formulate and enact the answers. It is sure to be more scathingly attacked than the Myth of the Machine: yet it may have a more lasting effect than any other book I have written . . . if anything survives these grim days!

We both look forward to reading your interview, sure that if anything about it is dull, the interviewer is to blame, because the questions he asked you were those *he* felt capable of answering. As with lecture audiences, they get what they deserve! When we meet we must compare notes about the Ency. Of Soc. Sciences: I trust fewer editorial errors were made in your article than were foisted on mine.[20] As for our reunion, it looks as if it must wait till we go back to Leverett House: sometime between the 10th & 15th of October, probably. You'll hear from us soon enough thereafter. . . . Your St. Lawrence hideout at last has a name: almost Indian! But for safety I'm sending this to Cambridge.

Don't let The Urban Prospect disturb you: it's like all our other prospects; and I'm rather sorry I published it, for no one, apparently, wanted to listen now to the things I said 40 years ago, when—if they *had* listened—things might have turned out differently. As for the professional urbanists they can't forgive me for offering a correct diagnosis of the conditions they consistently ignored, along with an alter-

---

19. Viktor Frankl, *Man's Search for Meaning* (1962).

20. Henry A. Murray, "Components of an Evolving Personological System," *International Encyclo-pedia of Social Science* 12 (1968): 5–13; Lewis Mumford, "City: Forms and Functions," vol. 2, 447–55.

native program which they superciliously rejected as out of date—only to find it forced on them by events. But enough of that kind of egoism! . . .

What an interminable letter! Proof enough that I was writing it all summer! Rest well at Nohawkers: let no noise of the outside world penetrate your leafy, Thoreauvian retreat: made suddenly vivid to me by the photo. Sophy joins me in an affectionate embrace—

In old friendship

Lewis

P.S. If my books got as much attention as that light-hearted 'European Diary' I'd be a famous author. Yes: I heard from Zurich, too!

[handwritten]
Lewis Mumford
Amenia, New York 12501
9 May 1970

. . . . We've been back here for a whole fortnight, dear Harry: but this is the first moment I have had to write a non-business letter. Meanwhile I trust that you and Nina are both in better shape than when I dropt in.[21] What a ghastly winter it was: one can see the effects of it here both on our bushes and on the bleak faces of our neighbors. Our spring flowers open one day and are gone the next, whilst the weather itself lurches from winter to summer, without giving a tranquil day to spring. . . . I am still sweating over the text for my illustrations: and what with the page proofs and the index Sophia and I will be busy till July. But after that nothing would please us more than a visit from you. . . . Part of our blood, sweat & tears over 'The Pentagon of Power' comes from the fact that Harcourt's suddenly discovered that it is a *timely* book—though I first conceived it fifteen years ago; and in a strange way they are right![22] The young, despite their studious ignorance and bedevilled confusion, are now catching up with me, and this looks as if it might be *their* book—to supplant the Eldridge Cleavers, the McLuhans, and the Marcuses! More of all this when we meet. With affectionate greetings to you both—

Lewis

[handwritten]
Amenia, New York 12501
18 August 1971

. . . . What a pleasure it was to talk with you the other morning, dear Harry: such a cheerful talk, too, without either of us hiding anything, either! Except what we al-

21. Murray married Caroline C. Fish, "Nina," in 1969.
22. Lewis Mumford, *The Myth of the Machine: II. The Pentagon of Power* (1970).

ready know. There were many external causes for our difficult & disappointing so-journ in Britain: from the Queen Elizabeth II—a kind of floating juke-box—to the miserable weather, the wettest June in 69 years. But there was an inner reason, too: for the first time, in our sodden state, we were really confronting Old Age! Oh! There have been plenty of admonitory prods and twinges these last twenty years: but they could be disguised as tension, fatigue, illness. This was the reality of it: The grim implacable face of time itself. The ship was filled with people like ourselves, mostly over fifty, many over seventy: putting on a brave face over their plight, but unable to conceal their weak grip; their uncertain steps; and instead of making conversation with them, as one does with one's peers, I found myself turning away from them and secretly disliking them. And why? One day I discovered the reason: I was looking at myself! And I who had evaded all groups, clubs, coteries was now, willy-nilly, just an elderly person, classified, ready to turn savagely on any one calling me a Senior Citizen. Sophia confesses to having had the same reaction; and this explains more than anything why our succession of minor misadventures was so disconcerting, and in the end so disruptive of our plans. We sought to be rejuvenated: but the youth we wanted was neither in us nor around us, for most of our dear friends were in the same state. So we fled home & found at least in our memories here what we lacked in the nakedness of travel.

Now you know the whole story. Once on our own soil we bloomed again as our sere garden did with a week of rain: so the wet weather that frustrated us in England helped us recover here! Sophia's bad leg still keeps her on a short tether: but otherwise she, too, is once more her old self, or as near to it as the calendar will permit.

We are both keen for a long visit from you & Nina, as soon as you have quieted down from the gay strains of the wedding.

What a pleasant picture of the Grand Old Man you have dug up—even without the youthful gesture that the inventor of the Thematic Apperception Test has invested him with. Much less hateful than what I find in more solitary communion with the mirror! I'll hold it in ransom till you come. With affectionate greetings to you both

Lewis*

*This signature is even more revealing than the TAT photo. You can't guess how many feminine names the L has penetrated!

[handwritten]
22 Francis Avenue
Cambridge 38
Massachusetts
Aug 30, '71
[LM] 21 Sept

Dear Lewis,

Your last letter initiated a score of conversations to be enjoyed with you (in the near future I hope), as have each of a weighty packet of communications just unearthed. They are phenomenal! read like spontaneous products of a fertile field of vegetation, yet without a weed, each an essay, a model of good writing, ready to meet the most fastidious tastes at any high class Stop and Shop. Your reaction to the oldsters on board the Queen Elizabeth proves that by a wise regimen coupled with the beauty and heartiness of Sophia, you have managed to foil the ravages of senescence for at least 10 years: The traditional turning point when one must steal oneself to the designation 'Senior Citizen' is 66, usual age of retirement, and look what you have produced since then! Having given countless (indispensable I was persuaded) hostages to arteriosclerosis in the form of alcohol, I could not delay the Enemy of Senility for more than 4 years, and for the last 2 years my mail has been packed with notices such as the enclosed, the profusion of which may be partly explainable as a devilish reaction to America's denial of death by a cloak of sickening euphemisms: 'The Home for the Incurables,' to which my mother paid monthly ('charitable') visits, became 'The Institute for Living' etc., etc. Anyhow, a respectable minority seems to have become inclined to wrestle with the problems of dying rather than to imprison them, or exile them from consciousness. Personally I am not disposed towards either pole, and most of what I have said here is shallow.

One extract from my collection of received letters might interest you. It came from my mother: "I bought the Mumford Melville just for the preface." What a beautiful tribute, almost worth the spoiling of your own production. May the book carry your name down into the ages to come. See what you did for her before she died in 1940?

Salvos and hugs to you both from
us both
H

[handwritten]
Amenia, New York 12501
30 October 1971

Dear Harry, dear Nina:

We kept on hoping for you both to help usher in the autumn colors here, right till the moment that your letter of 8 October arrived. But oddly enough the autumn never came—we haven't seen a touch of frost yet!—and, less oddly, neither did you. We both know from experience the "summations of little things" that spoil one's plans: our whole visit to Britain was such a teasing and troublesome summation—as if whatever we touched was accompanied by a poltergeist effect that marred our intentions. To add to the mischief, we both found ourselves in the loneliness of our London visit, at last facing the inevitability of the inevitable—otherwise known as old age. What brought it out was the drenching rain, day after day: the rainiest June in 69 years. We had never before in all our travels been so put out by bad weather: we didn't know what to do with ourselves. And suddenly I realized why: when it rained too hard to roam the streets or visit the galleries, there was often an even more attractive alternative: we'd go back to the Hotel & make love! But now even walking back has become a problem for Sophia, and I need hardly tell you about my problem, too. . . . For all that we've both been in good spirits since we came back here, enjoying the spacious days, free of pressures, with no need to cut our pleasure short in order to go back to Cambridge, for we'll be staying on here till February, when we've agreed to spend a few months at the University of Virginia. . . . Last week was our only interlude, a visit to Washington to get the Hodgkins gold medal from the Smithsonian and to take part in a discussion at a meeting of the new American Studies Associations on—guess what?—'Lewis Mumford and the Future of American Studies.' All the professors who had promised to give papers on the subject got cold feet at the last moment—probably because they didn't have time to read me—so I had the platform more or less to myself, with 500 people in the audience to keep me from feeling lonely.

So much for gilded gossip. If you are moved to visit us when you come back from the West Indies our arms will still be outstretched—and we'll promise not to resurrect the poltergeists!

Affectionately

Lewis

P.S. Robinson tells me that he's had a very rewarding summer with you. I hope you feel rewarded too![23]

[handwritten]

As of Amenia, New York 12501

20 Feb. 1972

. . . . How often during the last few months, dear Harry, I have had the impulse to write you and Nina! But always, on the point of writing, I would get a reassuring word, from Cambridge or California, to quiet any anxious inquiries about you. And since my own life was somewhat disturbed by a knock-down fight with my publisher—now happily settled—I kept our own troubles to myself. . . . Recently Sophia and I have been playing with the thought of coming back to Cambridge

---

23. Forrest G. Robinson, Murray's biographer.

again next winter: but when we face that prospect realistically we must admit to ourselves that the Cambridge we'd like to return to is that which existed fifteen years ago, with ourselves precisely that much younger! Though my friends at M.I.T. have offered me an official niche as Institute Lecturer, with only minimal obligations, even that doesn't tempt me as much as it once would have done: especially since my unfinished 'Life & Times' can only be written in the ambience of Amenia—and my voluminous files & notes. So we trust that you'll come for a visit to Amenia later on—summer or fall—when we return there. This letter, as it happens is written in one of Jefferson's domiciles at the University of Virginia: and on his birthday in April the Thomas Jefferson gold medal will be added to my private Nibelungen hoard of invisible gold medals!

> With affectionate greetings to you
> both
> Lewis

> [handwritten]
> 22 Francis Avenue
> Cambridge 38
> Massachusetts
> 24 March
> Vernal Equinox better than usual
> up here

Beloved Lewis & Sophy, or, to neutralize any floating belief that I am nothing but a male chauvinist pig, Beloved Sophy & Lewis

Actually I have not felt that we have drifted apart this winter. Last spring you, L, wrote a kind of farewell note in which you intimated that our last meeting had been memorably generative and joyous for the four of us, having left in its wake a *remanence* capable of energizing our friendship for some time to come. (You didn't use *any* of these words & maybe you implied *no* such enduring hoops of magnetism—I must look up your letter.) Anyhow the feeling that persisted in me made me think of the two friends who sat on each side of the fireplace smoking clay pipes in complete silence for an entire evening. Wasn't Carlyle one of them? Who was the other, and what did he say when he left? In short, my chronic aversion to writing letters was shored up by your letter. Another factor was the frequent exhilarating references to you, L, I encountered in the newspapers and in journals, such as finding that you were as impressed by Marshacks's *Roots of Civilization* as I was, reading about your predictions in connection with the burial and importunate unearthing of Mr. Simon's strong-box, happening on an inviting review in TLS of your correspondence with Osborne, the Englishman, of whom I have never heard you speak, and much else, which served to keep images of you and Sophy coursing happily through my mind (It helps to believe that you are remaining in a familiar & cherished place for a while).[24] Finally, there is the fact that I've been half-sick during this winter with several relapses of this unclassifiable virus that's visiting the East Coast and aside from this, I had a session in the hospital in which a catheter was inserted into my femoral artery (inguinal region), then into iliac artery, aorta, and finally at right angles into renal artery (absorbing to watch the whole process on a fluoroscopic screen). (N.B. Mail leaves in 10 minutes, so I must summarize): i) Examinations did not show Ca but a benign cyst in the kidney, ii) Now I feel almost recovered from the flu, but didn't want to write with only ailments as a topic, iii) The crowning irony is the fact that we are leaving early Tuesday AM, April 3 for West Indies for 2 week recuperation!! Leave as much time for us as possible after our return on April 18th. We'll make up for Fate's frustrations. Will write soon: 19 Salvos & Hugs to you both—

H & N

[handwritten]
Amenia, New York 12501
26 March 1973

. . . . What a pleasure it was, dear Harry,—yes, and what a relief!—to see your firm handwriting once more, though the story it told about your ordeals fully justified my silent anxieties. Thank heaven that your worst miseries came, not from your body, but from the refined diagnostic procedures of modern medicine. And I begin to wonder which is worse: the ailment or the treatment? My own ills this winter were nothing to talk about, but when I found myself seized by a sudden crippling attack of arthritis I kept away from the hospital, whose standard response is ex-rays and a month in bed. Instead I hobbled around and took 2–3 grams of vitamin C daily; and after 3 weeks of this I began to walk again. I had learned about this from a one-time medical missionary I've been in correspondence with; for he has taken a friendly interest in Sophia's arthritic difficulties. He told me he's had miraculous recoveries by this treatment, but (alas!) it doesn't always work. Happily, in my case it did! But there! I'm being as bad as Bernard Berenson, whose diaries are filled with detailed reports of the aging process. When I read that horror story I swore I'd never imitate him: but how hard it is to keep these nagging symptoms to oneself! When one was young one just said: I am ill. After 70 the same difficulties cause one to say: Dammit—this is old age! There is no cure for *that*!

We are both keen about getting back to Cambridge, and we pray that by the time you & Nina get back all four of us will be sufficiently rejuvenated to enjoy

---

24. Alexander Marshack, *The Roots of Civilization: The Cognitive Beginnings of Man's First Art, Symbol, and Notation* (1971); Michael Hughes, ed., *The Letters of Lewis Mumford and Frederic J. Osborn: A Transatlantic Dialogue, 1938–70* (1971).

each other, without even a whimper about our disabilities. (Sophia's natural sto-icism & inner buoyancy can always be counted on to counteract my Melvillian blackness. As for you, one must dig for information before one gets a hint of what's been happening.)

So have a good trip to the fabulous Indies: we'll welcome you both with open arms.

In old friendship
Lewis

[handwritten]
Amenia, New York 12501
9 September 1973

. . . . From time to time, dear Harry, I find myself writing little notes to you in my mind: and if I never transfer them to paper it is because I hopefully have an ear cocked for a phone call that will tell us that you and Nina are about to descend on us. I might still be waiting for that message if I hadn't an hour ago picked up Parker & Haywood's 'Moby-Dick as Doubloon' and this put me so immediately in your presence that I felt bound to resume the long conversation we began in 1928 & will never be finished this side of eternity.[25] We are, I suppose, past the need for words: so that makes this letter easier & shorter, despite the fact that there are endless things to say, if not to 'clear up' about Melville. I never showed you the poem I ad-dressed to Melville, shortly after I met you: but I came upon it the other day & de-cided to keep it in my autobiographic chapter on Catherine where I deal with the great shaking up of my life in 1930 when I recognized how different the inner man was from the outer one. Both Melville & you had a part in that awakening: and so I outlived your well aimed reproach over my 'rationality.'

If I go on, this will turn into the sort of letter you may feel you have a duty to an-swer; so I'll stop & hope again for a phone call. Since coming back from Cambridge we've both been pleasantly but not brilliantly busy, what with the garden and the last few chapters of Vol. I of 'L.M.' If all goes well—how often one has to cross one's fingers after 70!—I hope to go back to M.I.T. next February for three months. Don't tell us that you & Nina will then be in the South Seas!

Affectionate greetings from us both
Lewis

25. Hershel Parker and Harrison Hayford, eds., *Moby-Dick as Doubloon: Essays and Extracts, 1851–1970* (1970).

[handwritten]
Amenia, New York 12501
26 October 1973

Dear Harry, dear Nina:

We still bask in the sunlight of your visit here: you have become an extra fragrance, mingling with the old farm house smell! (That sentence is almost worthy of Harry!) Put in plain English, it means we loved it: or, to paraphrase one of our favorite poems: "The falling *in* of faithful friends renewing is of love."[26] The days pass all too quickly: but the decision about MIT remains in suspense.

With an affectionate embrace

Lewis

P.S. We didn't thank you properly for either the wine or the book: but we have still to sip the one or read the other. A day of just 24 hours is too short!

[handwritten]
22 Francis Avenue
Cambridge 38
Massachusetts
Jan 9 '74
[LM] 14 Jan 74 came and answered

Beloved Mumfords,

Here is hardly more than a brief announcement that the Murrays are still above ground and trust that this is equally true for you two cherished and indispensable friends. To be above ground, we think, is a good deal, considering how much stoicism is required these days to keep up one's American chin during the exposure of such shameless shambles at our nation's seat of government.

I have also to convey my apologies for the long silence that has followed your two letters, Lewis, in celebration of the convivial cerebrations which marked our last reunion at Amenia with the lovely Alison importantly participating. My chronic spasms of silence are attributable to a defect which I deplore, not to a characteristic of deity which I am desirous of emulating ("Silence is the only Voice of our God," said Melville, after heaven proved deaf to his bootless cries.). Thirdly, let us say that we are eagerly looking forward to your advent in the near future, trusting that no deficiency of Energy outside or inside of you will necessitate any alteration of your program. We are *hungry* for your company!

Appendix

Before our reunion a fragment of autobiography, mostly from me, will bring you up to date with us.

As you know I haven't been able to write anything publishable for 10 years; I

---

26. The refrain from Richard Edwardes, "Amantium Irae": "The falling out of faithful friends renewing is of love."

have 10 half-finished books in my files, and time is getting very short. But lately I have become somewhat heartened by evidences that B12 deficiency has had something to do with this disability and have decided to concentrate on 2 closely related books which might be completed, with sufficient Luck, Love, and Logic, before my Nunc Dimmitis, say in a couple of years if Nemesis is forbearing. This brings me back to our old friend, H.M. who said: "From my 25th year (1844 when he started writing) I date my life." Book I, then, will be a biography of Young Melville (the relatively unselfconscious activist). What do you think of some title such as "Melville, From First to Second Birth" or "Past History of Melville"? I wrote a first draft of all these chapters almost 40 years ago; but now I find that only about half of this stuff (segments here and there) can stand as written, my standard having risen—happily—over the years. Book II would consist of essays or chapters, each dealing with a major work (or a related topic, "Melville, as Depth Psychologist," say)—about 70 per cent of which are already in publishable form. As a title, how about *What Melville Had to Say?* By the way, I think you were largely right about *Ethan Brand* (where you came to think you were wrong). The story was lost to the public (and to HM) in the files of a defunct periodical, and I believe that Hawthorne dug it out and had it published when he did to convey a message to Melville (more of this later).

Now (to devote 10% of available space to Nina) let me say that she is pumping along at a superb tempo reading extensively and writing several chapters on her chronicle of the Children's Crusade (1212) and related matters. We think of you two and your works with waves of affection, esteem, and gratefulness—The art, and maybe the science and morality, of autobiography are awaiting our mutual consideration.

Halleluyah & love to you both
H & N

*Hurriedly written & unreread to catch the mail.

P.S. By the way, let's not forget to debate Herman as a vaingloriously deceitful reporter of his experiences.

[typed]
Amenia, New York 12501
14 January 1974

. . . Your letter of the *ninth* came only an hour or so ago, dear Harry: and I am answering it forthwith, for you can't possibly guess how much delight it gave both of us. And reassurance about the state of your health, too, from the very first sentence: for it completely lacked any signs of the tremor I had noticed in your earlier handwriting, as if to confirm the magic powers of Vitamin B-12! Unlike me, whose handwriting varies so widely from day to day that I could almost use it much as a doctor uses a fever chart to give an indication of the state of my health: now firm, now uncertain; now constrained, now free-flowing, now even, now a little wild, with intrusions of alien words with similar sounds to the one I was consciously using if my attention relaxes for a moment and I am at the mercy of some lesion in my reflexes! But your handwriting was always a different matter: firm and imperturbable, no matter what crises you were passing through: a perfect marvel of accurate cerebral organization, in spite of all the ups and downs of the past few years.

What your handwriting told me, first, dear Harry, the actual contents of your letter confirmed: the return of your old creativity in full flood. As I see my own creative powers lessening from year to year, even quantitatively measured, with my need to spend three hours on pages I could once toss off in one, I can appreciate all the more what a godsend this resurgence must be for you—and for your friends, too, who realized how much more you still had to say. This isn't an unusual experience in the creative life, quite apart from vitamin deficiencies! Rainer Maria Rilke waited for a dozen years in utter despair because the poems he had conceived remained as if they had died in the womb, with not even a miscarriage to testify that they had once existed. And then suddenly, without premeditation, in a few swift weeks, he wrote the Dunio Elegies, which he considered his supreme achievement. And now the God has taken possession of you, with Nina holding the door open for him! No one else but you can tell the inner story of Melville's transformation: only those who like you have been twice born—I alas! am not one of them—should attempt it. 'Melville From First to Second Birth' is surely the right title. But in editing this forty-year-old manuscript don't be too harsh, dear Harry, on your early self: possibly some of the things you wrote then are still true to his experience, though no longer to yours; and younger readers might find in those passages—of course I am speaking in the air!—that which they will look in vain for from your maturer self. Still, weeding and pruning are always in order with old manuscripts: how much I would give to be able to eliminate prosy passages and needless adjectives and adverbs from my own printed work! But be on guard about adding fresh passages: they are the voice of another self, possibly incongruous, even when excellent if taken alone.

As for your studies on Melville as Depth Psychologist: this has long been your appointed task, and of course in your studies of Pierre and Bartleby, some of your essential insights are already firmly in print. 'What Melville Had to Say' is a good title, at least a modestly descriptive one: but knowing something of the contents I am tempted to suggest: 'What only Melville Could Say,' although to be truly accurate and comprehensive, a still bolder title occurs to me: 'What only Henry Murray could say about Melville'—though I fear that this title must be left, as a chapter heading, to your biographer. As for your astonishing news about Ethan Brand, it vindicates both of us; but you even more than me. It was you who called my attention to the portrait of Melville in Ethan Brand; and I am still rightly held at fault because I didn't verify the date of that story's publication, partly because of a certain scholarly carelessness, not to say innocence; but partly also because no data were available then in Amenia. Your discovery won't rehabilitate me in the judgment of academic Melville scholars: but it is one more evidence of your marvellous combination of intuitive flashes and scholarly assiduity.

Now a word about us, to match your welcome news about Nina's buoyant activities. We've had a good winter and were all set to return to M.I.T. the first week in February for the whole spring term. But ten days ago two battered wrecks of teeth, which my Sharon dentist urged me to have removed three years ago, became infected; and I now have to undergo the usual extensive repairs and psychological accommodations that must follow. So I've told my MIT sponsors of my plight, and since I can't promise to appear there until the third week in February, and will be lucky to be in shape even by then, I've released them from this commitment and from our claim to the apartment they had assigned us. I am still eager to go up, and Sophia is, if anything even more so, if only for the pleasure of seeing our old friends and in particular embracing you and Nina once more. We have never felt closer to either of you in all these years! In addition, I had looked forward to devoting a whole seminar to rethinking my Transformations of Man: a kind of key book in my intellectual life these last twenty years, though there is much I should like to add and to take away before I take leave of that work. So I hope that some sort of compromise arrangement can be made with M.I.T. Meanwhile, all sorts of other good things have been happening to me—you see I have been taking Vitamin B 12 these last few months, too!—but I postpone touching on them while there is any prospect of our being able to converse face to face.

With an affectionate embrace all round from both of us

In old friendship

Lewis

P.S. If I had read your last letter *before* my taking Vitamin B-12 I would have said that it was your letter that produced the sense of inner vigor I have recently been feeling. It is only my flubbed typing that now reminds me how old I actually am!

[handwritten]
22 Francis Avenue
Cambridge 38
Massachusetts

Great Lewis,

The arrival, 2 days ago, of your *Findings and Keepings*—with its felicitous dedication to the delectable Sophia—gave cause for rejoicing at 22 Francis Ave.[27]

We had seen the Jovanovich clarion announcement, which struck us as more veritably enthusiastic than your account of things had prepared us to expect. In such a situation I am apt to hear HM saying: "not one man in five cycles, who is wise, will expect appreciative recognition from his fellows, or any one of them. Ap-

---

27. Lewis Mumford, *Findings and Keepings: Analects for an Autobiography* (1975).

preciation! Recognition! Is love appreciated? . . . etc." Regarding which I have mixed thoughts and feelings. Not true as a generalization: Melville has just received what he describes as a profoundly satisfying letter of recognition from Hawthorne. And I as well as several others have been rewarded—over rewarded—by utterly understanding, eloquent appreciations by none other than LM.

Telephone interruption.

I see that I have but 5 minutes to reach the postbox before the last mail is seized. So I shall let what I have here stand as a first gesture of thanksgiving—token of our gratitude for your gift from which we shall expect much enlightenment and edification. Much love to you both from us both—in extreme haste

H & N

[handwritten]
Amenia, New York 12501
30 May 1976

. . . What a long time has past, dear Harry & Nina, since your note about Findings & Keepings came. Until March we half planned to spend a month in Cambridge: but instead I lost myself in my still unfinished story of my life & we only left here to talk to that part of Cambridge which came to the April meeting of the American Philosophical Society! We still hope you plan to invade Dutchess County this summer. Meanwhile I have a somewhat embarrassing request to make—or at least humbly beg for. If any of my letters to Harry between 1929 and 1949 still exist—and could be dug out without too much exertion—may I have a loan of them for a month? When I've made my selection I'll submit them to Harry to be sure I've not included anything of his too private for public consumption. . . .

You'll gather from this request that my long battle with HBJ has terminated in their unconditional surrender—not to me but to our common business interests, which Jovanovich had overlooked. So in due time the two volumes will come out in a single book under a new title! For the moment Sophia & I are in a state of sweet serenity: even her arthritis has abated under a newish drug. And our spring garden was never lovelier. I trust you have equally good news about yourselves.

With an affectionate embrace.
Lewis

[handwritten]
22 Francis Avenue
Cambridge 38
Massachusetts
June 1, '76
[LM] 6 June 76

Dear Lewis,

I keep more constantly in touch with you (your phantom self at least) than you imagine, aided, as I am, by sight of your thoughtful visage as I go to and from my desk, say seven times a day. The orange walls of the corridor that leads to the locus of my daily labors are reserved for photographs of the arch-angels to whom I am most indebted for benefits received over the years. This order of the selves portrayed is largely chronological; but that factor is not enough to account for the triangle of Mumford, Freud, and Jung on the same orange panel. On the back of your portrait is a fine declaration of our shared friendship at first sight in 1928. Thinking of the shock of your Zurich article in the New Yorker, I not infrequently chuckle inwardly as I pass.

Three months ago I started on a letter to you in this vein which was prompted by the early arrival of some rather rare birds—for Cambridge—magnolia warbler, cardinal, goldfinch, titmouse—which turned my thoughts toward the Mumfords, with queries as to your plans, the possibility of our meeting in Cambridge, etc., etc.

The thought that maybe you were reliving a portion of your life—in connection with the autobiography—led me to think below the surface about our friendship, its vicissitudes, its recent lag. Finally, I arrived at the conclusion that I could not choose among several possibilities as to the determinants of your cooling toward me; but the reasons for my cooling toward you had been pretty clear in my mind for some time: you seemed unable to deal with criticisms of your ideas or of your ways of expounding them. I was raised to *enjoy* heated discussions without arousals of anger or resentment, and I am tongue-tied if I don't feel free to express my views to a veteran friend without raising a tempest—and so on, etc., etc. I have several times broached this topic in a mild way; with increasing degrees of failure. Is there any enlightened way you can suggest of my dealing with my present nearly hopeless state of mind?

As to the exciting cause of my writing you this letter. Of course, I have all the letters you have ever written me (although many of them are chronologically misplaced), and I can find time to draw out successive batches of them to send for you to keep as long as you want. This is a hurried note which must rely on whatever lenience you can spare. Salvos & hugs to both of you.

N & H

Our garden has also enjoyed its finest hour, this spring.

Amenia, New York 12501
6 June 1976

. . . Your letter has touched me deeply, dear Harry, and I am grateful to you for breaking the ice, which has alas! grown thicker in the winter of our lives. I was aware of this chilling in the forties: so neither of us may console himself with the thought that this is just one of the inevitable lapses of old age. It would take many letters to disentangle the intellectual and emotional reasons for our drifting apart, even when my winter sojourns at Cambridge brought us more frequently than ever within hailing distance: and I don't know whether the longest and most open interchange could at the end have done as much in repairing the breach as your generous letter already has. How monstrous it would be if either of us were to die without gratefully recognizing how much our friendship has meant to each of us & how deep a mark it has left on our lives! More than once during these later years I have found myself repeating Melville's Monody over Hawthorne: all the more aptly because my way of avoiding *oral* discussion of our differences—a habit that has baffled Sophia, too, in our personal life—corresponds to Hawthorne's silences with Melville. . . .

"And then to be estranged in life,
And neither in the wrong."[28]

I won't try to explain or apologize for any part of my remoteness, dear Harry: for I feel far more contrite over the fact that I yielded to you the honor of restoring our friendship by speaking out. Your *action* here has done more to re-unite us than the lengthiest inquest into our lives, our different temperaments, our deepest convictions, could do. This at least is solid ground: we have re-affirmed the reality of our friendship. No matter how far we have been blown apart—or may be driven again!—here is our unmistakable landing field.

As ever
Lewis

[handwritten]
22 Francis Avenue
Cambridge 38
Massachusetts
June 9th, lunchtime
[LM] 3 July 1976?

Dear Lewis,

In Aristotle's judgment wasn't Magnanimity the topmost virtue? If he did not express himself in just those words, my faltering memory tells me that they are consonant with his central plexus of values. Anyhow, regardless of Aristotle and his

---

28. From Herman Melville, "Monody" (1891).

wisdom—*there* at the top of the pyramid you stoutly stand, proved for the nth time by the last letter just received here. Beautiful! was Nina's immediate declaration—beyond the compass of what even the best of this age is capable, was my thought. More later. I'm fully occupied at the moment with a pressing job, wrestling with that which will no longer be snarled by uncertainties regarding the tactless wording of my letter to you. Thanks to you.

The enclosed packet was found in chronological order except for the letters from 1929–31, and those from 1931–1944. The greatest abundance of my collection of these gems comes after 1949, I would say. (The currently missing letters will surface soon.) I am too busy to read these gloriously friendly letters this P.M., but I did glance at one to sample its flavor, and I found you *zealously* urging me to be critical even brutal!

I am unspeakably grateful to you.

> Salvos
> Harry

> [handwritten]
> Amenia, New York 12501
> 3 July 1976

. . . . two messages came to me on the same day, dear Harry: your letter of the ninth of June and an official announcement of my having been awarded the Prix Mondial Cimon del Duca. I was of course deeply moved by the Prix, for the jury was a distinguished one, the pick of French scientists & scholars; and they had given the honor to, among others, my M.I.T. colleague, Weisskopf and to the Russian physicist, Sakharov.[29] But though I was elated by this recognition of my work as a whole, I was even more profoundly grateful, dear Harry, for your letter. As one of my favorite ballads puts it, "The falling out of faithful friends renewing is of love."

Perhaps Sophia said some of this when she phoned. But it bears repeating. As for my trip to Paris, it was from first to last a nightmare: and I'll spare you the gruesome details not only now but when we meet. Happily, I found Sophia fully recovered from the tensions of my swift departure and our garden looks like a second Eden.

> We embrace you both
> Lewis

---

29. Victor F. Weisskopf (1908–2002), distinguished MIT physicist; Andrei Sakharov (1921–1989), Soviet physicist and dissident, awarded the Nobel Peace Price in 1975.

[handwritten]
Amenia, New York 12501
16 August 1976

. . . What a treasure load of my past, dear Harry, you sent on to me with Christiana's letters! Back in the forties our intellectual relations were more stimulating than I had remembered, and Christiana was the most adequate of all our friends in her responses to Geddes's death. What a warm heart & courageous mind she had! Thank you for unearthing these letters. Among them, incidentally, I found two letters to her from Jung, which should be in your authorized hands, not mine. The one three years later is strangely cold & distant, isn't it? Perhaps done by his secretary? I've already found much I'd like to use in my letters to you, & if you ever lay your hands on any more I'll of course be equally grateful.

Lewis

[handwritten]
Amenia, New York
14 November 1976

. . . . Good heavens! Dear Harry, I haven't yet responded to your letter of 19 August, though I hope I promptly thanked you for your packet of my letters to you, which neatly fill a void in my memories of the 1930's. I haven't yet found a new name for my greatly expanded version of Findings & Keepings. But no matter what I finally call it, I fear it will not keep people from asking when the 2 vol. *Autobiography* will be ready. They imagine that this will be the real thing: but they forget that sketches from life, even by great artists, are often far more 'real' than the finished painting. In any event I have no intention of publishing the formal work before 1982—unless I have the grace to die before then!

Christiana's letters have unearthed hidden treasures in my intellectual past: so may I keep my letters to her till I've had time to absorb hers? There's no convenient place hereabouts where I can have them xeroxed.

Sophia & I had hopes of making a brief visit to Cambridge in the fall after you & Nina returned: we even had an apartment at 1010 at our disposal. But the book will keep us busy till next April, when I hope to turn it in to the publisher, on our way to the spring meeting of the American Philos. Soc. . . . What of you and Nina? Alas! That time shrinks and distances lengthen with old age. . . .

An affectionate embrace from us both
Lewis

[handwritten, misdated]
Amenia, New York 12501
1 January 1976

. . . . A New Year's embrace, dear Harry, dear Nina: with all the blessings we can pull down from the skies! Like the rest of the country, we are ice-bound here, with only wood-fires & whiskey to add sufficiently to our warmth. But thank heaven we've both been busy: and I've been able to make good use of the caches of letters you sent me. As a result, my main job on the second, all-embracing volume of 'Findings' is done—though it will be April before the book will be ready for the printer.[30] At intervals, unexpectedly good things have been happening to us this last year: the latest being my series of BBC interviews, which went off far better than I dared hope: for my answers were given impromptu, and quite astonished me by both their facility & their felicity! What is better, this has offset my awareness of the increasing flaws in both my memory and my visual-auditory perceptions—as if the normal weakenings of old age needed such humiliating reminders! Poltergeist phenomena, one should call them, I suppose. In our more rational interpretation of nature we forgot its trickiness, not just accidental irregularities, but quasi-malicious disturbances of order!

We'd both welcome some word of you, since by now there's no early prospect of our visiting Cambridge.

Affectionately
Lewis

[handwritten, LMC]
22 Francis Avenue
Cambridge 38
Massachusetts
Feb '77

Dear Lewis,

What a warm hug you gave the Murrays on January first, on the energy of which we could better stand up to the taxing temperature of the coldest winter I can recall! Naturally we think of the friends who are less comfortable than we are at 65° day and 60° night, indoors. Our preference is for snuggling up to a fire of sturdy logs that Josephine brings up to us from the country; but I haven't been sure how much firewood you can cut on your place (it's $120 a cord up here), and so images of you two enjoying the same luxury are not steadfast. Also I'm uncertain about whether you use artificial or natural gas. In any case you have gotten round to thinking of yourselves as up-country folks, if not pioneers, and therefore liable to be insulted by any insinuation that you can't manage in sub-zero weather. I might

30. Mumford's book was published as *My Works and Days: A Personal Chronicle* (1979).

think of you—living in the outskirts of civilization—as deprived in other ways, say, newspapers and magazines. But somehow you get round to reading more than we do with our 2 to 3 dozen subscriptions. A case in point would be the enclosed extract from the New Yorker which appealed to us enormously. I have had a score of copies xeroxed to send to those pairs of friends who are worthy of it in our eyes. Can you find out, or do you happen to know who wrote it?

I have been very tardy in answering your letter—the chief reason being that several searches have failed to disclose the 2nd packet of letters written to me. At one time I had all your letters, but you asked only for those written from 1927 to about 1950. These you have received as well as *all* your letters to Christiana; but the quarter century series of letters which I carefully put away ready for immediate dispatch have eluded my memory as well as my probing hand and eye. A part of this ineptitude of mine is senescence; but they may show up tomorrow. Have we passed the deadline? Too bad, because there is a quality in *all* your letters which, within my knowledge, has never been equaled. I'll be more explicit one of these days. It's like trying to define spiritual health—a great abundance of it, with limitless resources of language to give it (your health) fresh, admirable, and apt expression. Our constant love to you both. You say we are not going to see each other!? I'm a bit confused between 2nd volume of Findings and Autobiographical Chapters. How are we going to hear BBC interviews? Salvos!

H

[typed]
6 February 1977

. . . I answer your letter in haste, dear Harry, in order to relieve you of any further effort to unearth my later letters to you. (Their disappearance does not mystify me: in this household we call such things 'poltergeist phenomena,' and thank heaven they are not accompanied by explosions!) I've made good use of both Christiana's letters and yours; but I already have far more material than I know what to do with; and I am content to let some other poor devil try to make anything out of the thousands of other letters I have written. My problem, from this point on, is to clean out the sometimes amusing rubbish I've written to old friends: amusing, sometimes, but still rubbish, patiently awaiting the final verdict of a fire.

I am not surprised that you are a little puzzled over what book I am writing now: the proper autobiography I began in 1956, or the improper one which I somewhat too lightheartedly assembled in 1975, leaving the reader to fit the scattered pieces together in his own mind, as he might solve a crosswords puzzle. Never did I make a worse mistake, which I worsened by my prefatory words about the nature of Analects. I forgot that neither reviewers nor readers deign to read Prefaces, even when they are cleverly disguised. As it turned out, 'Findings' was a predestined failure, thanks mainly to Jovanovich, but also, I now realize, to my own willful naiveté. As a sop, the publisher offered to put it in paperback, when I did the second volume, from 1935–1975. But instead I preferred to court a greater failure by turning all my material into a single volume, more studiously edited and more coherently organized. I am not sure that this won't be a greater failure than the first volume: but it will soothe my wounded pride! As you will find it is more 'Improper' than ever, if only because it is far richer in personal letters.

Where does that leave the more conventional autobiography? Within three chapters of being ready for publication, covering the period from birth to 1940. But I am holding this back, in case I should live long enough to write the later part of my story. But I have no strong impulse to handle the later years myself: they are still too near, and involve critical estimates of my life I'd prefer some more objective mind should make. I understand that many people, even old friends, think that the Proper Biography will be the 'real thing' and are impatient over my diversionary tactics. So be it! If I were sure that my mind would recover the élan it had between 1955 and 1970, I'd chuck any further work on the biography at once, now that I have privately settled accounts with myself.

I can't stop without telling you about a slightly eerie experience, in which your New Yorker editorial played a part. The night before it came, Sophia and I had been discussing two books she had been reading—one a boastfully pornographic novel by Francine Gray—and another in which the subjects are trying to 'find themselves' by breaking up all other human relations—as if this were the ultimate triumph.[31] But neither of us had read the New Yorker editorial: so your letter was like a continuance of our conversation. We four have proved that the only way to find our 'real' self is to find each other! Perhaps a little ESP helps! Hurrah!

Lewis

P.S. I don't know a soul on the New Yorker any more except Shawn, the Editor. But of late years the leading editorial has often been first-rate: sharp and courageous.

> [handwritten, LMC]
> 22 Francis Avenue
> Cambridge 38
> Massachusetts
> April 30 [LM] 11 May 77

Dear Lewis,

Your letter arrived at this house in March, one day after we left for Virgin Gorda, B.W.I. (The pure air plus swimming is the best treatment for my creeping emphysema.) And so, unfortunately, your request had to wait till now for an answer. It didn't seem so urgent as some of the more importunate other letters awaiting my return, letters from a few friends bedeviled by nearness to poverty, to lunacy, or to lethality. (I want to return to these later.)

---

31. Francine du Plessix Gray, *Lovers and Tyrants* (1976).

I sensed from your letter that you knew in your guts (limbic region of the brain) that I would never object to anything that was approved by your Monitor. Temperamentally I'm on the diffident side, by my vocations (say, both therapy and biography) and the current Zeitgeist (exposure of everything) have combined to outmatch the reticence, provided the show is not chiefly for the show's sake. Publish whatever you see fit. If in *real* doubt, of course, send the passage up to me.

You're by far the best letter-writer I have ever known and your letters will be published sooner or later. No matter what criteria the editor adopts he-she will want some of the letters I have sent you. In which case it would be a great help if the more telling ones were conspicuously designated (starred) by you. The Aiken letters (without responses I think) will be published by Yale University Press in the Fall. I believe you've read his autobiography—*Ushant.*

We've missed you in Cambridge this Spring, even though our meetings have become very sparse. Next certain opportunity would be August *1st* after a Tanglewood week-end.

I have more things on my mind to say—related to Sophia, to you, and to your work, but I see that the Saturday noon mail goes in 10 minutes.

I'm happy to be able to think of 2 too precious ones liberated from the imprisoning freeze of the last winter & much else.

Salvos and love to you both
H & N

[handwritten]
Amenia, New York 12501
11 May 1977

. . . How wise you & Nina were, dear Harry, to leave this sullen climate in March for the West Indies. Your script tells me that the benefit to your emphysema has been shared by the rest of your body: your hand writing is again as *firm* as it was twenty years ago. (I find, incidentally, that I get from my own handwriting a sharper, earlier picture of the state of my health than any conventional medical diagnosis provides: for it records mental as well as physical pressures.) This winter has been the cruelest one, physically, that we've ever experienced: I spare you the domestic breakdowns we've been through, for I've probably mentioned some of them already. We haven't yet emerged from our long incarceration, for we escaped three weeks ago to attend a meeting of the American Philosophical Society only to succumb to a viral infection we are only beginning to throw off. Naturally, this has been a bad period for polishing off the revised 'Findings & Keepings': so I have still a few months work ahead of me. But by now I've winnowed out most of my letters to you and to Christiana: only a tiny sample of either, without the benefit of your spirited challenges. Someday, perhaps, my collected correspondence, if intelligently selected, will give a more adequate account of our friendship & all that it has meant to me. The enlarged version of 'Findings' will be more systematically organized, with a brief biographic or historic introduction to each section. I'm enclosing my note on Christiana. If it needs revision don't hesitate to tell me. Though I draw on some of my letters to you they don't constitute a separate section.

We've played with plans for spending a few months next winter at Cambridge: but have finally had the sense to realize that the Cambridge we'd like to visit, except for one or two surviving old friends—you & Nina, Carl & Anne Cori—no longer exists; nor, for that matter, are we the same people who, between 1958 and 1972, found Cambridge so exhilarating. The real horror of old age is to watch *oneself* disappear! But if you *do* come to Tanglewood, let us entangle you for a visit here!

> Affectionately
> Lewis

> [handwritten]
> Amenia, N.Y. 12501
> Rte 1—Box 187
> 10 March 1978

. . . Greetings, dear Harry! I'm tempted to write you not just because there's a faint breath of spring in the air but because you entered my consciousness in a quite unexpected way. A few weeks ago I began to clear my bookshelves of dead lumber and picked out a book I'd never seen—and certainly never read—before: Morris Cohen's 'A Dreamer's Journey.'[32] How had I passed it by? For I knew Cohen casually from my City College days (1912–14) and later. I respected him, but felt unattracted by his supercilious, didactic manner. When I casually dipt into the book, its biographic details mostly grim—held me: and when I read further I discovered that his philosophic views were close to my present ones, though by 1914 I had become a 'Pragmatist.' How could I have let this book stay on my shelves unread? When had I bought it? At last I turned to the inscription page for a clue. And what did I find?

> For Lewis
> Pax Vobiscum for 1950
> from Harry

What a priceless gift had lain waiting for me all these years! The gift of Cohen of course: but even more, dear Harry, the gift of your friendship!

> Lewis

P.S. I should not lessen the gift even by adding this postscript. So I spare you any notes about the weather or health. Like the poor they are always with us.

---

32. Morris Cohen, *A Dreamer's Journey: The Autobiography of Morris Raphael Cohen* (1949).

[handwritten, LMC]
Jan 10—79 [LM] 14 Jan 79

My dear Sophie and Lewis,

No cheerful greeting, this sad, sad news. Harry has had a series of strokes, leaving him weak on the left side, with a faulty gag reflex so that he constantly chokes, periods of rage, longer stretches of weeping, and often a mind that rambles back & forth in time & space. Can't read. He can't remember that his leg & arm won't support him, so that in spite of nurses around clock, he has had 3 disastrous falls, one putting him in hospital for a week over Xmas. Last fall probably broke his back, but I am doing all I can to maintain him here—with o.k. from M.D. However M.D. is lowering the boom & insists I'm wearing down & H. must go to nursing home. I *resist*. Will try & delegate more authority, etc., etc. Miserable.

On the Good Side: (Pollyanna rises & smiles before me every day.) Around 11 o'clock, H. surfaces at 22 Francis Ave., is taping his experiences as a stroke patient, does amble a bit, can sit at table, can *talk*—also can write, but nothing so far put down. Sees friends.

I weep watching this great man being peeled away, layer by layer, to a broken, unarticulated skeleton underneath. H. asked me to write you. We love you—

Nina

[handwritten]
Amenia, New York 12501
14 January 1979

. . . The news in your brave letter about Harry pained us, dear Nina, but did not altogether surprise Sophia or me, for we have experienced similar shocks coming, not only from our circle of surviving friends but from our own bodies the last few years. We cannot console you for these erratic tricks of nature or attempt to soften your pain: but at least we are grateful that you have let us share the darkness you are now stumbling about in . . . Brave Harry! Still the dedicated scientist, recording with what is left of his consciousness his actual experience as a stroke patient. How like the man I knew in the thirties, admired, and sometimes quarreled with—as only solid friends dare to quarrel! Please kiss him tenderly for Sophia & me without telling him, even if he is "conscious," where the kiss came from.

Sophia and I have had to face the problem raised by the meaningless survival of the body in her older sister: and so we have been canvassing the very grim alternatives you must now choose from—home, a nursing home, or a hospital. As long as the Pollyanna in you does not go under, too, your impulse to keep him near you is what the mind as well as the heart commands—provided you can give yourself occasional breaks, complete breaks, for a day or two, or even a week, to keep the tension from snapping. But how dare I offer even affectionate advice, dear Nina, since we have yet to face these last stages in our own life?

Sophy joins me in these anxiously loving greetings—

Lewis

P.S. Tell Harry there *must* be a heaven: he and I still have such a lot of things to thresh over.

[typed, LMC]
22 Francis Avenue
Cambridge 38
Massachusetts
16 February 1979
Mr. Lewis Mumford
Amenia
New York 12501

Dear Lewis & Sophy Both Beloved,

Since last communicating with you I have been struck by a stroke that landed in my right hemisphere and incapacitated me largely on the left side of my body (left leg, left arm and hand), but also resulted in a decline of my thought processes, not interfering much with comprehension, but mostly in composing sentences to express what I have to say. For instance, I find it hard to think up a sufficient way of answering questions I am asked.

Although such cognitive processes are diversely affected it looks as if some return toward normal could be expected. Some of the professional experts, anyhow, seem to think I am doing well, getting better and better.

In any case I wanted you to know that from now on, however much I will surely appreciate your letters with their often interesting enclosures, I cannot answer them. I shall not be able to answer them.

Here I am sending you anticipations of my thanksgivings to your bounty. May you have a following wind from here on.

Harry

[handwritten]
Amenia, N.Y. 12501
3 Nov. [crossed out] February* 1979

Dear Harry, dear Nina:

Harry's brave letter, with his characteristic analysis of his present state, touches us to the quick. And I am near enough to Harry in age & experience to recognize at least the premonitory symptoms of his present plight. This doesn't help him, of course, but it tightens all the old bonds of our friendship and brings our households together without need of words.

At present the blows Sophia and I are forced to cope with are mainly external. Two weeks ago, after a bout of 15° below zero nights our water pipes froze solid & we were forced to take refuge in the guest apartment of a nearby neighbor and friend. The only solution was to dig the well that is now almost ready: but a dozen other readjustments must be made & tested before we can go home. For the present we are exiles & refugees in our own village!

This offers no hopeful therapy to you, Nina, or Harry: it merely unites our plight with that of a large portion of mankind, whose chronic woes we had known before only from a distance. What cold comfort, all too realistically, for all of us!! We both pray that the gods are in league with Harry's hopeful physicians! Sophia joins me in an affectionate embrace for each of you.

Lewis

*What a classic Freudian error! November was an incredibly balmy and golden month.

[typed, LMC]
22 Francis Avenue
Cambridge, Mass. 02138
16 May 1979

Great Man,

Hallelujah! Your fine book—I won't call it your final book—is off your hands and at this moment literally in mine. A noble object into whose crystal-clear waters I have had a little time to dip here and there, guided by the topical index. You are the best writer—most fluent, natural, and felicitous—that I have known intimately, and many of your interests have been to a remarkable degree similar or closely related to mine. And so, of course, this book of yours is as the pull of gravity on me. By now I would be deep in its subject-matter were it not for my impaired cortex, which forces me to husband the few hours a day of mental energy that I am vouchsafed.

I love the whole conception and its actualization in this volume, and judging by those parts which I have read, you have equalled here if not excelled some of the most inspired and masterly passages for which you have long been famous.

Fortunately you have retained the necessary health, basic competence, and brilliance to do what you have done here, so far as I can estimate it, that is to re-examine the various records of your life's work and make what alterations seem appropriate. While reading the last version of your development, I can count on the surfacing of abundant memories of you and many of our numerous rich exchanges of views. I will be remembering with thankfulness the scores of benefits I have received from you at various times. I have never been able even to approach your superlative style of letter-writing, so that in expressiveness mine has lagged miserably behind yours, and now what little powers I had of that kind have been massively depleted by the accident last November. What I would like to do, and am now planning to do, is to write you as the spirit moves me during the course of my reading and brooding over your *Works and Days.*

Another Matter

In my will I am leaving enough ducats to start a fund for an archive of American authors, and I had thought that I couldn't do better than to donate the scores of letters I have received from you as an initial contribution to start the thing going. The Houghton Library, as you know, is serving as the depository of the Melville papers, a suitable neighbor for your papers, but I don't want to do anything that will interfere with Sophia's disposing of your papers for a handsome sum. It would be an odd coincidence if my bequest to the library would serve as the magnificent Sophia's remuneration (like life insurance). I have expected—maybe erroneously—that you would return the packets of letters I sent you some time back. You have never told me, however, what you and Sophia are planning to do about your voluminous correspondence and documents of other sorts. Please let me know at your convenience, but I hope you don't expect immediate answers to your letters, as in one day I can scarcely do more than dictate a note such as this one.

Here I will close for the moment, with a very grateful acknowledgement of the gift of your latest book. Its appearance will certainly be welcomed by a great majority of your inveterate readers.

H

Henry A. Murray

P.S. I meant to say earlier that I think that what you wrote about me was very generously imagined and handsomely conveyed.

[handwritten]
Amenia, New York 12501
8 June 1979

. . . . "Whatever the gaps of space & time in our friendship, dear Harry, I've long been acquainted—at least in significant samples!—with most of the disconcerting experiences you've been going through.". . . .

With these words I began a long letter to you, two days after I came back from the Hospital. Thanks to Sophia's heroic efforts, we have at last re-assembled the errant letters, and I have spent two whole days in greedily re-scanning their contents, almost as if for the first time, though they bear notations that date back to 1970! *Peccavi!*

What an honor to our friendships & ultimately to Melville you have conceived, dear Harry! I can think of no fitter repository for this constellation than the Houghton Library & herewith Sophia & I donate the entire collection, in the name of our friendship. All my other personal papers, including 3 filing case drawers not to be examined until a decade after our death, we have in our wills bequeathed to the University of Pennsylvania, (the Van Pelt Library) where my papers will be flanked by a group of contemporary writers, headed by Van Wyck & Waldo Frank. For my many years of association with Penn makes this a happy resting place for my all-too-copious files. We have reserved for private use only our personal family papers—and for private possible *sale* only an odd assemblage of letters from VIP's—otherwise of no value except monetary. Happily, even the inflation does not yet seriously threaten us: our real problems are not financial but psychological & personal; and these of course are tied up with those of our disintegrating civilization.

Don't let my 'Works & Days' sap any of your strength in reading it, dear Harry: but it has plenty of light hearted passages, especially in the letters & private notes which at the right moment may amuse you.

Sophia joins me now in a loving embrace for both you and Nina.

Lewis

P.S. Today—Friday—we are posting to you, first class three weighty packages containing all my and your letters, along with Christiana's. Perhaps Nina will drop us a card when they arrive.

[handwritten]
Lewis Mumford
Amenia, New York 12501
12 June 1979

. . . . Greetings again, dear Harry! Herewith I send back a group of letters I had set aside for further reading—but forgot to include in the packets I sent you. One or two of them I wish I had included in 'My Works & Days.' Meanwhile I trust all the others have reached you.

The hospital is now only a fading memory, for each day—it's now ten days since I came home—shows some definite physical improvement. Far better & quicker—thanks mostly no doubt to my deft and bold surgeon, than I had any reason to expect—or dared to hope for.

Your provision of a home for our letters was nothing less than an ultimate testimony to our friendship—and it still helps my heart to pump more faithfully.

If this keeps on, I may write again soon—without any further reports about the nagging facts of life at our age!

Meanwhile Sophia joins me in an affectionate embrace for Nina and yourself.

Lewis

[handwritten]
Amenia, New York 12501
15 June 1979

. . . If you are surprised to get this final batch of my letters to you and to Christiana, dear Harry, you are no more so than I am. Another lapse of memory on my part! For it is quite by accident that I stumbled on this cache just three days ago. My own notation in red ink shows that I had read these letters in July 1976 and found some of them so interesting that I turned them over to Sophia for copying. Some of them, in fact, I actually used in 'My Works & Days'! But in the pressure of getting my book ready for the printer I clean forgot to send *any* of your letters back to you promptly. And but for my chance discovery the other day these letters, too, might still be hiding! But now I'm pretty sure you have *all* our correspondence for your proposed collection at the Houghton Library.

Samuel Butler once wisely observed that forgetfulness was as essential to thinking as remembering: but by now we'll both agree that old age is too heavily weighted on the forgetful side!

Though Sophia & I still have a long way to go before we overcome the effects of this crippling winter: this last fortnight has done much to restore us. The response to my book & to my television interview with Dick Cavett has done much to restore both of us. Partly as a result, the U.S. Navy inquired the other day whether I'd take part in a July conference in Virginia on Technology & Environment & give the keynote speech at a dinner. Sophia explained why I couldn't: but as an 'Old Navy Man' I swelled with pride! More pleased than I would be by a dozen favorable reviews!!

We trust that your vacation with Nina in Nantucket will wipe out some of the strains you have both been under all winter. Sophia & I will keep you company, affectionately & sympathetically, in our imagination.

In old friendship
Lewis

N.B. Herewith we're sending on the letters in a separate envelope.

[typed, LMC]
22 Francis Avenue
Cambridge 38
Massachusetts
8 August 1979 [LM] 15 Aug
Mr. Lewis Mumford
Leedsville Road
Amenia, N.Y. 12501

Dear Lewis:

What a fine chorus of letters I have received from you—some old, some new—which taken together make a warm, spirited conclusion to a half-century's correspondence, a good deal more than half of which, I should say, was written eloquently by you. I have many gratifying memories of special parts of it (starting with your first mention of me in your preface to your biography of Melville). At the moment I'm a little busy with other correspondence, but am hoping for a space of time in the near future to catch up with you better than I have this summer.

My locomotive system is now in good enough repair to risk a visit to Tanglewood and Amenia on the way home, but other things have an earlier priority, and I am tending toward a decision to go to Virgin Gorda, B.W.I., exactly one year after we were at the San Juan Airport when we were a little shaken out of the even tenor of our lives. That would mean Nov. 2, but Nina doesn't think we shall be in shape that soon for climbing into a little airplane for the last leg of the journey.

We are both eager to see you soon. (I haven't even thanked Sophia for her considerate letter to me when you were shipped off to a hospital. In my P & S school days, the Sharon Hospital was always spoken of with great respect, a famous Dr. Coley being Chief of the Surgical Service.) We hope you survived the record breaking hot weather of recent days and have not beem afflicted by any new horrors. More later

H

Henry A. Murray

I liked Don Miller immensely.[33] I think you can count on a fair deal from him. No soul in my dictated notes.

[typed, 15 August 1979]

Amenia, New York: 12501

. . . Young Miller, dear Harry, wrote me such glowing sentences about the impression you made on him, that I knew a little while before your letter came that you must be in better health; and that relieved a little lurking anxiety before your letter came. I share your satisfaction over the fact that our correspondence is now gathered together and will be reasonably accessible. Your example prompts me to add the letters I received from Patrick Geddes to the collection of my letters in Geddes's file at the National Library of Scotland.

By now both Sophia and I are almost recovered from our shattering winter experiences: so a visit from you and Nina will be welcome, for except for a brief visit from my newly acquired Literary Agent, we have had to keep our friends and relatives at bay, since we needed all our spare energy to get through the day. Naturally, the unanswered letters in my file have become so oppressively numerous that yesterday I took most of the day off to answer the most urgent—or the most attractive!—of them; and still the mass—or more accurately the mess!—has not visibly thinned. By now we're both thirsty for company, if not, like you for travel. But there is a chance that we'll have both the first week or so in November, for out of a clear sky a group of people at the Harvard Law School have asked me up to be the first recipient of an award they are offering to those who have made a contribution to land development; and, though a little uneasily, with my fingers crossed I've consented; and if we are able to go at all, we may be in Cambridge the better part of the week of the fifth of November: so if you don't drop in here, perhaps we'll see you then. . . . unless you are in Virgin Gorda!

---

33. Donald L. Miller, Mumford's biographer.

It would take a whole day of typing to make our now parallel lives come together; and that, I am afraid, is a more likely job for a mathematician than a writer. So we must be resigned to sweet sessions of silent thought!

> With an affectionate embrace for
> you both
> Lewis & Sophia

[typed]
Lewis Mumford
Amenia, New York 12501
10 August 1981

. . . What a happy surprise it was, dear Nina and dear Harry, to read the masterly account in the Times yesterday, of Harry's many-sided and fruitful career.[34] A century from now the story of Harry's development will loom even more marvellously—provided anything is left of our harried and battered civilization.

But it was even more wonderful to find, to our surprise that a young relative of our Hindu friend and neighbor, Santha, had recently spent an hour or so with Harry and had actually had a lively talk with him! At my own advanced age—soon I'll be 86—this seems nothing less than a miracle. Once one is past eighty, one discovers to one's surprise that both Heaven and Hell are real!

With a loving embrace from both Sophia and me.

> In fast friendship
> Lewis and Sophia

---

34. Joseph Adelson, "Against Scientism," review of Edwin S. Shneidman, *Endeavors in Psychology, New York Times Book Review,* 9 August 1981, 10.

Index